COPING
WITH
AUSTERITY

Nora Lustig, *Editor*

COPING WITH AUSTERITY

Poverty and Inequality in Latin America

*A study jointly sponsored
by the Brookings Institution
and the Inter-American Dialogue*

THE BROOKINGS INSTITUTION
Washington, D.C.

Copyright © 1995

THE BROOKINGS INSTITUTION

1775 Massachusetts Avenue, N.W., Washington, D.C. 20036

All rights reserved

Library of Congress Cataloging-in-Publication data

Coping with austerity : poverty and inequality in Latin
America / Nora Lustig, editor.
    p.   cm.
    Includes bibliographical references and index.
    ISBN 0-8157-5318-7—ISBN 0-8157-5317-9 (pbk.)
    1. Poverty—Latin America.   2. Income
distribution—Latin America.   3. Structural adjustment
(Economic policy)—Latin America.   4. Latin
America—Economic conditions—1982–
I. Lustig, Nora.
HC130.P6C67   1995
339.4'6'098—dc20   94-28839
                                        CIP

9 8 7 6 5 4 3 2 1

The paper used in this publication meets the minimum requirements of
American National Standard for Information Sciences—Permanence of Paper
for Printed Library Materials, ANSI Z39.48-1984

Typeset in Times Roman

Composition by Blue Heron, Inc.
Lawrence, Kansas

Printed by R. R. Donnelley and Sons Co.
Harrisonburg, Virginia

Foreword

The countries of Latin America endured severe economic adjustments during the 1980s. This volume addresses one of the central policy concerns in the wake of those austere cuts in government programs: What has happened to the poor? Through case studies and surveys of regional trends, the contributors portray the impact of this so-called lost decade on poverty and inequality. They usually conclude that poverty increased and income inequality widened. But the studies go beyond such general conclusions to address the definition and causes of poverty, the influence of adjustment policies on social welfare, and policy options for ameliorating poverty and inequality.

The book is divided between regional studies and studies of individual countries. The regional chapters concentrate on the relationship between economic performance and poverty and inequality; the educational, occupational, locational, and gender determinants of income level; the effects of macroeconomic and social policies on social welfare; and the success of targeted programs in fighting poverty. The individual studies of Argentina, Brazil, Chile, Mexico, Peru, and Venezuela provide detailed discussions of how governments responded to the crisis. In particular, they examine social spending and the use of safety nets to shield the poor from the effects of adjustment. In the first chapter the editor, Nora Lustig, presents an overview of the main issues and summarizes the papers and conclusions.

The chapters in this volume were originally presented at a conference cosponsored by the Brookings Institution, the Inter-American Dialogue, and the North-South Center. The editor and authors greatly benefited from the comments of Harold Alderman, Jere Behrman, Hans Binswanger, Mario Blejer, Eliana Cardoso, William Cline, Jorge Daly, Jaime de Melo, Gary Fields, Nicolás Flaño, Carol Graham, Darryl McLeod, Phillip Musgrove, Moises Naim, Richard Newfarmer, Per Pinstrup-Andersen, Helena Ribe, Paulo Renato Souza,

Webb, and Richard Weisskoff, as well as the anonymous referees that reviewed the chapters. The chapters also reflect presentations by Gary Burtless, Marcelo Cavarozzi, Homi Kharas, and Richard Webb, and the concluding panel led by Oscar Altimir, Richard Feinberg, and Marcelo Selowsky. Finally, the book has benefited from the constant flow of ideas, guidance, and support provided by Peter Hakim, president of the Inter-American Dialogue and co-organizer of the project.

The editor wishes to thank many staff members at Brookings and the Inter-American Dialogue who contributed to the project. In particular, she wishes to thank Paul Winters for his help in organizing the conference during his stay as an intern at Brookings. The conference would also not have been possible without the aid of Jenifer Ezell and Lisa McGregor from the Inter-American Dialogue and Charlotte Baldwin, Z. Selin Hur, Susanne Lane, Annette Leak, and Arianna Legovini from Brookings. In addition, Maureen Merella and Jeremy Harris provided assistance to the project at Brookings. Milena Alberti, Marcelo Cabrol, Andres Escalante, and Gary Gordon helped to find documentation and prepare the chapters and tables. Jay Smith and Jim Schneider edited the manuscript, Gary Gordon, Abigail Golden-Vasquez, Alexander Ratz, Andrew Solomon, and Christopher Watkins verified its factual accuracy, and Lisa Bevell, Trisha Brandon, Annette Leak, and Louise Skillings prepared it for publication. Ingeborg Lockwood, Carlotta Ribar, and Trish Weisman proofread the galleys, and Vicki Agee compiled the index.

Funding for this project was provided in part by the John D. and Catherine T. MacArthur Foundation and the North-South Center. Their support is gratefully acknowledged.

The views expressed in this study are those of the authors and should not be ascribed to any of the persons or organizations mentioned above, or to the trustees, officers, or other staff members of the Brookings Institution and the Inter-American Dialogue.

BRUCE K. MACLAURY
President

May 1995
Washington, D.C.

Contents

Tables

Figures

Preface

Peter Hakim

Whatever progress has been made in Latin America toward consolidating democratic politics, restoring economic dynamism, and building toward an economically integrated hemisphere has been tarnished and jeopardized by the mass poverty and profound inequalities of income and wealth that plague most nations of the region. It is not only that glaring income disparities and extreme poverty are morally offensive. It is also that their persistence could defeat the region's struggle for sustained economic growth and undermine prospects for stable democracy.

In many countries of Latin America, market-oriented economic policies have become widely identified with unending austerity, and are often considered detrimental to the interests of the poor and even the middle class. Accurate or not, such perceptions can produce pressures to modify or abandon sound policy directions. They can also undercut the credibility of governments trying to carry out the policies. Indeed, under conditions of extreme income inequality, social conflicts can make it difficult to implement coherent economic programs of any kind.

National productivity also inevitably suffers in economies with poorly educated, low-skilled work forces. Unless they are able to raise the skill and educational levels of their populations, Latin American countries will have a hard time competing for capital and export markets in the international economy.

And widespread poverty imposes other burdens on the national economy. It can, for example, lead to large-scale environmental damage when subsistence farmers plant crops on steep, erosion-prone hillsides; when poor families decimate forests to secure wood for charcoal to cook and heat their homes; when thousands of impoverished laborers turn to gold mining and use chemicals that dangerously pollute waterways. Costly epidemics—cholera and tuberculosis, for instance—as well as high crime rates are often linked to poverty.

The political consequences of mass poverty and inequality can be equally devastating. Although guerrilla leaders are usually drawn from the middle class, it is poverty, inequality, and injustice that most often fuel the Shining Path, the Zapatistas, or other insurgent movements. Even those insurgencies that do not challenge national power can provoke security forces to violent repression that degrades and subverts democratic institutions. Internal war is usually economically disruptive, and sometimes can be devastating.

Where poverty and inequality do not spark armed rebellion, they often produce political apathy, disaffection, and hostility. Destructive rioting is sometimes the result. Other consequences are a broad distrust of political leaders and institutions, the heightened appeal of demagogues, and abstention from elections and other political activities. Still another manifestation is popular support for antidemocratic challenges to entrenched leadership, as witnessed in both Peru and Venezuela in recent years.

Large social and economic disparities in a country—particularly where they are reinforced by racial or ethnic differences—can undermine any sense of national cohesion and identification. The sense of belonging to the same society and of being represented by its leaders and institutions is vital for a functioning democracy. It is imperiled wherever class divisions are profound.

When all is said and done, democracy is incompatible with persistent and gross social inequities. Democracy and equality are intertwined concepts. It is hard to build and sustain democratic institutions in a society divided sharply by income and wealth.

All told, confronting poverty and expanding opportunities for the poor are no less crucial for economic progress than investing in industry or controlling inflation. Reducing inequality is no less vital for democratic stability and advance than conducting fair elections or ensuring civilian control over military forces.

In recent years, Latin America has largely turned away from authoritarian rule and made impressive strides toward democratic politics. Most nations of the region have also made important progress toward reforming their economies and improving their economic performance. Sustaining and deepening these advances now requires that Latin America face up to the challenges of mass poverty and inequality. Democracy must be anchored in social justice if it is to endure. A vibrant and growing economy requires that all sectors of the population be productively employed.

CHAPTER ONE

Introduction

Nora Lustig

At the end of the 1980s, although Latin America had proportionally fewer poor than other parts of the developing world, its income distribution was more skewed.[1] Exact poverty estimates vary according to statistical definitions, but a number of studies have shown that in mid-decade Latin America had only about two-thirds the proportion of poor that was average in the developing world.[2] The figures for income distribution create a somewhat differ-

I am very grateful to Marcelo Cabrol and Gary Gordon for research assistance, to Ann Mitchell for her assistance in preparing the tables, and to Trisha Brandon for retyping the many changes made to the introduction. Also, I thank Harold Alderman, Jere Behrman, Susan Benda, Jorge Domínguez, Albert Fishlow, Peter Hakim, John Steinbruner, Richard Webb, and John Williamson, as well as the authors included in this volume for very useful comments on an earlier draft. All the usual disclaimers apply.

1. Poverty here will refer to what in the literature is called "moderate" poverty in contrast to "extreme" poverty, unless specified. Moderate poverty usually refers to a poverty line that is equal to the amount of income or consumption required to cover a minimum food basket (which is equal to the extreme poverty line) and other basic consumption items. In quantitative terms, the moderate poverty line is usually equal to the extreme poverty line multiplied by the reciprocal of the proportion of total consumption allocated to food by those households who are living in extreme poverty.

2. According to the World Bank, the head-count ratio, or proportion of poor people, for Latin America was 19 percent versus 33 percent for all developing countries. The index for extreme poverty, which uses a poverty line of $23 ($1,985 in purchasing power parity) a month, was 12 percent for Latin America, compared with 18 percent for all developing countries; World Bank, *World Development Report 1990* (1990, table 2.1). Ravallion, Datt, and van de Walle

1

ent image. Comparable data for all countries are not available, but one study finds that the average Gini coefficient for Latin America at the end of the 1980s was 0.50 compared with 0.39 for non–Latin American countries.[3] The wealthiest 20 percent of the population in Latin America had an average income 10 times higher than that of the poorest 20 percent compared to 6.7 times in other low- and middle-income countries for which data are available.[4]

On social welfare indicators, Latin America's performance compared favorably with that of other developing regions. By 1990 Latin America had brought its infant mortality rate to 48 per 1,000 live births, compared to a world average of 52, an average of 79 in the Middle East and North Africa, and 93 in South Asia. The average Latin American's daily caloric intake in 1989 was slightly higher than the world average.[5] Primary school enrollment rate estimates for the same year also placed Latin America slightly above the world average, with gross enrollment rates at 107 percent of the eligible age group.[6]

Although Latin America was a region of sharp economic inequality before the debt crisis,[7] in general—as we shall see later—inequality and poverty increased during the 1980s in many countries. In addition to moral considerations, why should one be concerned with the evolution of poverty and inequality? The

(1991, table 2) get similar results using poverty lines of $31 a month and $23 a month. And poverty, as measured by the poverty gap, was less severe for Latin America than it was for the developing world as a whole. Ravallion, Datt, and van de Walle (1991) report a poverty gap index of 6.9 percent for Latin America, as compared with 10.2 percent for the developing world (p. 354). The poverty gap measures the amount of income required to raise all the poor to the poverty line, expressed as a proportion of the poverty line. However, as discussed in the appendix to this chapter, all these estimates must be approached with caution.

3. Psacharopoulos and others (1992, p. 17). Figures for non–Latin American and Caribbean countries are from an earlier period, but the authors contend that the disparity between Latin American and Caribbean countries and other countries is "still quite relevant, and could possibly have increased over time." The Gini coefficient is a common measure of inequality that indicates a greater degree of inequality the closer the coefficient is to unity.

4. World Bank (1994, Tables 8-1, 8-2) and author's calculations based on data in World Bank, *World Development Report 1991* (1991, table 30).

5. World Bank, *World Development Indicators 1992*, database. Average daily intake was 2,721 calories for Latin America, 2,711 for the world, 2,617 for East Asia and the Pacific, and 2,225 for South Asia.

6. World Bank, *World Development Indicators 1992*, database. The world average was 105 percent.

7. In the 1970s, for example, the bottom 40 percent of Latin America's population earned 10.1 percent of total income, compared with 14.8 percent of income in Southeast Asian and Asian countries. The shares of the highest 10 percent were 40.1 percent of income and 34.1 percent, respectively. When compared with any developing region of the world, the share of income of the bottom 20 percent was lowest in Latin America. Latin America's poorest 20 percent received 2.9 percent of total income, compared with 6.2 percent in Sub-Saharan Africa, 5.3 percent in the Middle East and North Africa, 6.2 percent in East Asia and the Pacific, 7 percent in South Asia, and 5 percent in Southern Europe. World Bank (1994, tables 8-1, 8-2).

peasant uprising in the state of Chiapas, Mexico, in 1994 and the urban riots in Santiago del Estero, Argentina, in 1993 and Caracas, Venezuela, in 1989 might be seen as examples of how poverty amidst increasing inequality is a threat to social and political stability. But outbursts of social and political violence cannot be attributed to these factors alone. Social explosions are complex phenomena, and it may well be that harsher economic conditions are as much to blame as the perception that governments are unwilling or unprepared to soften the blow to the poor brought on by economic crisis, or worse, that the government's actions themselves (that is, stabilization and adjustment programs) are to blame.

Even if frustration with growing poverty and inequality and the government's response to them does not often manifest itself in armed uprisings or violent riots, their economic and political consequences are still matters of concern. In contrast to a belief formerly held, recent research shows that income inequality can be detrimental to growth, because it can hinder the accumulation of human and physical capital. A more egalitarian income distribution, for example, may increase aggregate school enrollment and, thus, growth.[8] And the greater sociopolitical instability fueled by inequality creates greater uncertainty that in turn reduces investment and growth.[9]

Policymakers and politicians are increasingly concerned with the effects of poverty and income inequality on political stability and economic prosperity. High and rising levels of poverty and inequality, some argue, could undermine economic reform, bring back the so-called populist policy agenda, intensify environmental degradation, put social and political stability in jeopardy, and reduce long-run economic growth. This view is not ill-founded. The fear that increased poverty and economic inequality may breed a political backlash against fiscal prudence and efficiency-oriented structural reforms is based on the acknowledgement that large groups in the population identify stabilization policies and structural reform, whether accurately or not, as detrimental to the poor and as the cause of greater inequality.

These issues raise important questions that this book attempts to answer. First, was the increase in economic inequality and poverty in Latin America during the 1980s very significant? Did the increase result from economic crisis and its inevitable aftermath? Or was it a result of specific policies adopted by governments to restore economic stability and growth? How did governments in specific countries respond to the imperative of austerity? Were safety nets put in place? Given the constraint imposed by fiscal discipline, market-oriented reforms, and the potential resistance of the wealthy to be taxed more heavily, what policy instruments should be used to reduce inequality and poverty?

8. Bourguignon (1993). See also Birdsall and Sabot (1994); and Rodrik (1994).
9. Alesina and Perotti (1993).

Poverty and Income Distribution

In the 1980s, growing domestic macroeconomic imbalances coupled with adverse world economic conditions resulted in severe balance of payments crises and produced sharp economic downturns in most Latin American countries.[10] For practically every country in the region the accumulated growth rate in per capital GDP was either negative or close to zero between 1982 and 1989. The economic crisis forced most countries to go through drastic adjustments and profound economic restructuring.

How did poverty and income distribution change when countries had to endure stagnant or negative growth, reduce their budget deficits, and introduce far-reaching economic reforms? Unfortunately, this question cannot be answered fully for any country in Latin America. As the appendix to this chapter demonstrates, paired income surveys with the characteristics necessary for a complete and reliable comparison do not exist for any country in the region.[11]

It is, however, possible to identify some trends with the existing information. Of the four countries (Brazil, Costa Rica, Panama, and Venezuela) with data comparable at the national level, poverty increased in three during the 1980s (tables 1-1 and 1-2). For Costa Rica the result is ambiguous: some sources find that poverty and inequality decreased and one concludes that it increased.

For six countries—Argentina, Chile, Colombia, Paraguay, Peru, and Uruguay—the question can be answered for urban sectors only.[12] In Argentina, Chile, and Peru, urban poverty expanded substantially (table 1-1). In Colombia and Paraguay it decreased and in Uruguay the result is ambiguous, but the change was probably very small. Urban inequality increased in Chile and Brazil and grew strongly in Argentina and Peru; it shrank in the other three (table 1-2).

In three other countries there were two countrywide surveys during the 1980s, but the earlier survey was collected after the debt crisis had already

10. Factors include the fall of commodity prices in the early 1980s, the recession in developed countries, higher world interest rates, and the sudden cutback in external financing, especially from private sources.

11. Ideally, there should be two surveys at the national level taken at the end points of the relevant period (about 1980 and again about 1990), which include a complete measure of total income, one that includes nonwage and nonmonetary income and for which underreporting of income and consumption is low.

12. Actually for Colombia there is data at the national level for at least two years: 1978 and 1988. It remains unclear why the studies by Altimir and Psacharopoulos et al did not use this data. The results at the national level, however, are qualitatively the same as those found for urban areas. (Londono de la Cuesta, 1990).

begun to take its toll so that a before-and-after comparison is not possible. Of these three, Guatemala and Mexico show increasing poverty and inequality nationwide (tables 1-3 and 1-4). Poverty and inequality decreased in Chile between 1987 and 1990, however, especially poverty in rural areas. In Bolivia and Honduras, which have data for cities only, poverty and inequality increased (tables 1-3 and 1-4).

Were the poor hurt disproportionately during the 1980s? That is, did their share fall by more (in percentage points, not in proportional terms) than that of other groups? According to the available data, Peru is the only country in which the share of the bottom 20 percent of the population decreased by more than the share of the middle and upper middle ranges.[13] However, the costs of the crisis and subsequent adjustment efforts were borne disproportionately by the middle (Argentina, Brazil, and Panama) and upper-middle (Honduras, Mexico, and Venezuela) segments of the population half the time. These groups are likely to be composed of blue-collar (the former) and white-collar workers (the latter) in the cities. Perhaps the most important result of the economic crisis is that in country after country where the bottom or the middle range's share shrank, the income share of the top 10 percent increased, sometimes substantially.[14]

Social Indicators

Indicators of public health such as infant mortality rates and life expectancy generally continued to improve during the 1980s for the six countries discussed in this book (table 1-5).[15] How should one interpret table 1-5? The first temptation is to say that the crisis and adjustment years had no significant negative effects on such a crucial social indicator such as the infant mortality rate. In a way this is not surprising; the infant mortality rate is determined by factors that are the result of past increases in the number of public hospitals and doctors per inhabitant, improved water and sanitation facilities, higher educational attainment of mothers, and widespread implementation of health practices such as oral rehydration therapy and inoculations.[16]

13. The middle segments are shown as deciles 3 to 6 and the upper middle as 7 to 9.
14. The only exception is Colombia. However, in this country, overall urban inequality actually declined.
15. For a more comprehensive discussion of social indicators in Latin America and the Caribbean see, for example, Psacharopoulos and others (1993, chap. 5).
16. See chapter 7 in this book. Also see Musgrove (1992).

Table 1-1. *Poverty Head Count Ratios for Selected Latin American Countries, before and after the Crisis, Selected Years, 1979–91*[a]

| | | National | | | At least two surveys with national coverage | | | | | |
| | | | | | Urban areas | | | Rural areas | | |
Country	Year	Altimir	Psacharopoulos	Country studies in this book	Altimir	Psacharopoulos	Country studies in this book	Altimir	Psacharopoulos	Country studies in this book
Brazil	1979	39	34.1		30	23.9		62	55.0	
	1981						29.1[b]			
	1989		40.9			33.2	27.9[b]		63.1	
	1990	43			39		28.9[b]	56		
Costa Rica	1981	22	13.4		16	9.9		28	16.7	
	1989		3.4			3.5			3.2	
	1990	24			22			25		
Panama	1979	36	27.9		31	26.0		45	33.0	
	1989	38	31.8		34	26.9		48	36.8	
Venezuela	1981	22	4.0	18	18	2.5		35	9.0	
	1989		12.9	41		10.8	15		23.5	26
	1990	34			33		38	38		60
	1991			35			31			53

At least two surveys for urban areas only

		Urban areas		
Country	Year	Altimir	Psacharopoulos	Country studies in this book
Argentina	1980	5[b]	3.0[b]	7.6[b]
	1986	9[b]		
	1989		6.4[b]	
	1990			28.5[b]
	1991			23.2[b]
Chile	1980			40.3[b]
	1987	37		48.6[b]
	1989		9.9	
	1990	34		
Colombia[c]	1980	36	13.0	
	1986	36		
	1989		8.0	
	1990	35		
Paraguay	1983		13.1[b]	
	1990		7.6[b]	
Peru	1979	35		
	1985/86	45	31.1[b]	
Uruguay	1981	9	6.2	
	1986	14		
	1989	10	5.3	

Sources: Altimir (1993). Estimates are based on household per capita income adjusted for underestimation and country-specific poverty lines representing minimum normative budgets of private consumption based on minimum food baskets that adequately cover nutritional requirements. Psacharopoulos and others (1993); the same poverty line of U.S.$60 a month in purchasing power parity dollars was used for all countries. Poverty book estimates are those presented in the country studies in this book. For all countries, except Chile, poverty estimates were calculated by the author and are therefore comparable across years. The estimates for Chile are from PREALC (1990). Blank cells indicate that data are not available.

a. When estimates of both extreme and moderate poverty were given, the table presents the results for moderate poverty.

b. Based on a household survey for the metropolitan area or areas only.

c. Data exist for the national level, but they were not included either in Altimir (1993) or Psacharopoulos (1993) and others. The estimates of poverty show that it fell from 28.6 percent in 1978 to 24.7 percent in 1988 (Londono de la Cuesta, 1990).

Table 1-2. Gini Coefficients in Selected Latin American Countries, before and after the Crisis, Selected Years, 1979–90

		At least two surveys with national coverage												
Country and source	Income[a]	1979	1980	1981	1982	1983	1984	1985	1986	1987	1988	1989	1990	Percent change[b]
Brazil														
Bonelli and Sedlacek	YHPC	0.57		0.56		0.59		0.60	0.58					0.52
Almeida Reis	YHPC					0.59	0.59	0.60	0.59	0.60	0.61			3.38
Psacharopoulos (1993)	YHPC	0.59										0.63		6.57
Hoffman	YH	0.59								0.60		0.62		5.08
Fiszbein and Psacharopoulos	PYEA	0.574										0.625		8.89
Costa Rica														
Gindling and Berry	YHPC		0.40	0.40	0.42	0.38	0.38	0.37	0.36	0.42	0.42			6.08
Sauma and Trejos	YHPC					0.42			0.42					0.00
Psacharopoulos (1993)	YHPC			0.48								0.46		-3.16
Fiszbein and Psacharopoulos	PYEA			0.451								0.41		-9.09
Panama														
Psacharopoulos (1993)	YHPC	0.49										0.57		15.78
Fiszbein and Psacharopoulos[c]	LYHPC[d]	0.376										0.446		18.62
Venezuela														
IESA	YHPC			0.40						0.44	0.46		0.44	10.00
CEPAL in Altimir	YH			0.39				0.42				0.44		12.82
Psacharopoulos (1993)	YHPC			0.43								0.44		3.04
Fiszbein and Psacharopoulos	LYHPC[d]			0.512								0.498		-2.73

At least two surveys for urban areas only

	Measure[a]											Change[b]
Argentina												
Psacharopoulos (1993)	YHPC		0.41	0.43	0.40	0.40		0.43	0.45	0.48		16.67
Fiszbein (1989)	YHPC		0.41				0.40					11.60
Fiszbein and Psacharopoulos	PYEA		0.389							0.461		
Brazil												
Barros and others (P.B.)	YHPC	0.59	0.58	0.59	0.59	0.59	0.59	0.60	0.61	0.63	0.61	3.39
Chile												
Mujica	YHPC	0.52	0.53	0.54	0.54	0.56	0.54	0.53				2.51
Colombia[e]												
Altimir (1993)	YHPC		0.48				0.47					-2.08
Altimir (1993)	YHPC		0.47				0.45					-4.26
Psacharopoulos (1993)	YHPC		0.59							0.53		-9.06
Fiszbein and Psacharopoulos	PYEA		0.578							0.515		-10.90
Paraguay												
Psacharopoulos (1993)	YHPC				0.45					0.40		-11.75
Peru												
Psacharopoulos (1993)	EHPC					0.43				0.44		2.34
GRADE	YHPC		0.34	0.39			0.40	0.39		0.41		29.41
Uruguay												
Psacharopoulos (1993)	YHPC		0.44							0.42		-2.75
Fiszbein and Psacharopoulos	PYEA		0.452							0.42		-7.08

Sources: Psacharopoulos and others (1993, annex 3); Fiszbein and Psacharopoulos (chapter 3 in this book); and Barros, Mendonca, and Rocha (chapter 6 in this book). All other data are from Morley (chapter 2, table 2-1, in this book). Blank cells indicate that data are not available.

a. YHPC is household income per capita; LYHPC is household labor income per capita; YH is average household income per capita; EHPC is household consumption expenditure per capita; and PYEA is total personal income (from work, rent, transfers) of all individuals 15 years of age or older that were in the labor force and had positive income.

b. Percentage change between earliest and latest year.

c. Based on survey data for employees only (that is, no self-employed or employers).

d. The income measure is defined as income from work; rents and transfers are excluded.

e. Data at the national level exist but were not included in the studies by Altimir (1993) and Psacharopoulos and others (1993).

Table 1-3. *Poverty Head Count Ratios for Selected Latin American Countries, after the Crisis, Selected Years, 1977–89*[a]

At least two surveys with national coverage

Country	Year	National			Urban areas			Rural areas		
		Altimir	*Psachar-opoulos*	*Country studies in this book*	*Altimir*	*Psachar-opoulos*	*Country studies in this book*	*Altimir*	*Psachar-opoulos*	*Country studies in this book*
Chile	1985			45.0						
	1987	38		38.1	37		48.6[b]	45		
	1989		10.0			9.9			10.4	
	1990	35		34.6	34			36		
Guatemala	1986-87		66.4							
	1989		67.0			50.9			76.5	
Mexico	1977	32								
	1984	30	16.6		23			43		
	1989		22.6[c]							

At least two surveys for urban areas only

Country	Year	Urban areas		
		Altimir	*Psachar-opoulos*	*Country studies in this book*
Bolivia	1986		51.1	
	1989		54.0	
Honduras	1986		48.7	
	1989		54.4	

Sources: See table 1-1. Blank cells indicate that data are not available.
a. When estimates of both extreme and moderate poverty were given, the table presents the results for moderate poverty.
b. Based on a household survey for the metropolitan area or areas only.
c. A preliminary estimate because it is based on an unweighted sample that may not reflect actual population composition.

However, except for Chile, where the decrease was more than 5 percent a year, the rate of reduction of infant mortality was slow. And even in Chile most of the reduction occurred between 1980 and 1982; from 1984 to 1988 there was little change (see chapter 8). Most of the countries included in table 1-5 showed a slower pace of improvement in the 1980s compared with the pace in the 1970s, particularly for Argentina (about 1 percentage point a year slower). For Brazil, according to one source, the pace of improvement was faster in the 1980s; according to another it was slower.[17]

It is conceivable, then, that had there been no economic crisis, infant mortality rates would have been dropped more quickly. For example, in chapter 7 Ricardo Barros, Rosane Mendonca, and Sonia Rocha find that, although the evidence is not conclusive, cyclical fluctuations in GDP had some effect on infant mortality in Brazil during the 1980s. In chapter 9 Santiago Friedmann, Nora Lustig, and Arianna Legovini show that infant and preschool mortality caused by nutritional deficiency increased in Mexico in the 1980s, reversing the trend that was observed for the 1970s. In addition, Dagmar Raczynski and Pilar Romaguera argue in chapter 8 that the data on low birthweight infants and undernourished children in Chile show variability that may be associated with changes in economic conditions. For example, a systematic decline in the two indicators in the 1970s was followed by ups and downs in the 1980s, a pattern that reflects the general course of the Chilean economy.

As with infant mortality rates, illiteracy rates fell and average years of schooling increased for the six countries (table 1-6). This, too, should not be surprising because changes in educational indicators in one decade often reflect investments made earlier. But the rate of improvement was slower in the 1980s than in the 1970s. However, although an economic slowdown can lead to a reduction in private and public investment in education, one should not attribute the slower rate of improvement in the 1980s to deteriorating economic conditions until further research is done on the factors that influence these rates. It may simply be that literacy rates, especially when they start at relatively high levels, invariably reach a plateau after a period of improvement.

There may be other indicators of educational performance that are more sensitive to economic downturns. For example, in chapter 11 Gustavo Marquez shows that in Venezuela the literacy rate for people age 15 to 19 actually fell between 1981 and 1990. Friedmann, Lustig, and Legovini find in chapter 9 that in Mexico the proportion of appropriate-aged children entering first

17. Also, infant mortality rates in Latin America show important regional differences within countries. Psacharopoulos and others (1993, table 5.3).

Table 1-4. *Gini Coefficients in Selected Latin American Countries, after the Crisis only, 1980–90*

Country and source	Income[a]	1980	1981	1982	1983	1984	1985	1986	1987	1988	1989	1990	Percent change[b]
At least two surveys with national coverage													
Chile													
Altimir (1992)	YHPC								0.47			0.46	−2.13
Psacharopoulos (1993)	YHPC										0.57		
Guatemala													
W.B. country memo	YHPC		0.48					0.53					10.42
Psacharopoulos (1993)	YHPC									0.58	0.60		2.76
Mexico													
Lustig	YH						0.44						
ENIGH	YH						0.47						
Psacharopoulos (1993)	YHPC						0.51				0.55		8.70
At least two surveys for urban areas only													
								1986	1987	1988	1989	1990	
Bolivia													
Psacharopoulos (1993)	YHPC							0.52				0.53	1.74
Honduras													
Psacharopoulos (1993)	YHPC							0.55				0.59	7.65

Sources: See table 1-3. Blank cells indicate that data are not available.
a. YHPC is household income per capita; YH is average household income per capita; LYHPC is household labor income per capita; EHPC is household consumption expenditure per capita; and PYEA is total personal income (from work, rent, transfers) of all individuals 15 years of age or older that were in the labor force and had positive income.
b. Percentage change between earliest and latest year.

Table 1-5. *Infant Mortality Rates and Life Expectancy, Six Countries, Selected Years 1970–90*

Indicator	1970	1980	1988	1989	1990
Argentina					
Infant mortality rate (IDB)[a]	51.8	38.0		30.4	
Life expectancy (IDB)[b]	66.8	69.3		70.9	
Brazil					
Infant mortality rate[a, c]	114	88			
Infant mortality rate[a, d]		75	48	45	
Infant mortality rate (IDB)[a]	94.6	74.2		59.9	
Life expectancy (IDB)[b]	59.0	62.8		65.6	
Chile					
Infant mortality rate[a]	82	33	19		16
Life expectancy[b, e]					
Men	60.0	63.9	67.8		
Women	66.5	70.6	74.6		
Mexico					
Infant mortality rate[a]		53.1	40.6	39.3	
Life expectancy (IDB)[b]	61.7	66.6		69.4	
Peru					
Infant mortality rate[a, f]		102			82
Life expectancy (IDB)[b]	53.9	57.9		62.1	
Venezuela					
Infant mortality rate[a, g]	49.8	35.2			25.5
Life expectancy (IDB)[b]	65.2	68.5		69.9	

Sources: Data were obtained from country study papers in this volume, except items noted as IDB (Inter-American Development Bank, 1991, p. 15). Blank cells indicate that data are not available.
a. Number of infants per 1,000 live births who die before reaching one year of age.
b. Life expectancy at birth, in years.
c. Estimates based on household surveys.
d. Estimates based on vital statistics corrected for underreporting.
e. 1970 figures are for 1972 and 1980 figures are for 1982.
f. Estimated "by extrapolation." The precise methods used to estimate these figures are unclear.
g. 1970 figure is for 1971 and 1980 figure is for 1981.

grade shrank. They also found that the proportion of students moving to high school after completing junior high, or to university after completing high school, decreased during the 1980s (table 1-7).

Such trends appear to result from a decision by some households to reduce their investment in education rather than from fewer educational services or services of lesser quality. Smaller earnings may have led households to postpone their children's entry into primary school because of the costs of transportation, school materials, and so forth. And smaller household incomes may have forced children and young adults to join the work force instead of continuing their education.

Table 1-6. *Average Years of Schooling and Illiteracy Rates, Six Countries, Selected Years, 1970–90*

Indicator	1970	1980	1989	1990
Argentina				
Average years of schooling[a, b]	6.1	8.64	9.63	
Illiteracy rate (%)—IDB[c, d]	7.4	6.1	4.5	
Brazil				
Illiteracy rate (%)[e]	34	26		19
Average years of schooling[f]	2.50	3.9		4.9
Average years of schooling[a]		4.47	5.8	
Chile				
Illiteracy rate (%)[g]	11			
Average years of schooling[h]	5.76	6.43		
Mexico				
Average years of schooling[i]	3.40	5.4	6.3	6.4
Illiteracy rate (%) (IDB)[c, d]	25.8	17.3	9.7	
Peru				
Illiteracy rate (%)[j]	28	18		12
Average years of schooling[h]	4.28	5.51		
Venezuela				
Illiteracy rate (%)[k]	24.1	14.0		9.3
Average years of schooling[a, b, l]	3.7	6.4	7.6	

Source: Data are from the country study papers in the tables listed by country below except where noted.

a. Average years of schooling of the working population, which consists of all people 15 years of age or older who were in the labor force and had positive income. Figures from Fiszbein and Psacharopoulos in this book. Argentina figures are for Greater Buenos Aires; Brazil and Venezuela figures are national. Brazil 1980 figure is for 1979.

b. 1970 figures from World Bank, TFP Project Data, databank (1994).

c. Proportion of the population 15 years of age and older that cannot, with understanding, read and write a short simple statement on everyday life. International Development Bank (1991, p. 15). Peru and Venezuela figures for 1970 are actually for 1972 and 1971, respectively.

d. 1989 figure is for 1985.

e. Percentage of the population 15 years old or older who cannot read or write a simple message.

f. Average number of years of schooling completed by the population 25 years and older.

g. Percent illiterate of the population 15 years and older.

h. World Bank International Economics Department, TFP Project Data, databank (1994).

i. Average years of schooling of the population 15 years and older.

j. Figures are for the years 1972 and 1981, 1989; estimates are based on census data and the 1989 figure is an extrapolation.

k. Data are literacy rates; figures were converted to illiteracy rates to make them comparable with the numbers from the other chapters.

l. 1980 figure is for 1981.

The Crisis or the Policies: Which is at Fault?

Did poverty and inequality increase with the economic crises when per capita income fell? Samuel Morley in chapter 2 and Ariel Fiszbein and George Psacharopoulos in chapter 3 comment that in most of the countries where per capita income was lower in the 1980s, inequality was greater.[18] Morley finds a similar pattern for the relationship between poverty and economic perfor-

18. Income per capita is actually GDP per capita.

Table 1-7. *Primary, Secondary and Tertiary Enrollment Rates, Six Countries, 1970, 1980, 1989*

Percent of age group

	1970	1980	1989
Argentina			
Primary	105	116	111
Secondary	44	56	74
Tertiary	22	23	41
Brazil			
Primary	82	93	105
Secondary	26	32	39
Tertiary	12	12	11
Chile			
Primary	107	117	100
Secondary	39	55	75
Tertiary	13	12	19
Mexico			
Primary	104	120	114
Secondary	22	37	53
Tertiary	14	15	15
Peru			
Primary	107	112	123
Secondary	31	56	67
Tertiary	19	16	32
Venezuela			
Primary	94	104	105
Secondary	33	39	56
Tertiary	21	21	28

Sources: Figures for 1970 are from World Bank, *World Development Report, 1994*, table 28. Figures for 1980 are from World Bank, *World Development Report, 1983*, table 25. Tertiary enrollment rates are for 1979. Figures for 1989 are from World Bank, *World Development Indicators, 1992*, databank.

mance. Poverty is more prevalent in most countries in which per capita income decreased.[19] However, these results have to be viewed cautiously: for Argentina, Colombia, Paraguay, and Uruguay, the data cover urban areas only. If countrywide surveys are considered, in five countries—Costa Rica, Chile, Mexico, Panama, and Venezuela— out of seven a lower GDP is associated with more inequality.[20]

Although it seems almost self-evident that an economic downturn should

19. Similar results are found by Altimir (1993). Morley also suggests that the elasticity of poverty with respect to the level of income is greater during the short-run cycle than it is in the long run: economic recoveries that follow a downturn or crisis cause a very rapid reduction in poverty. On the other hand, there are some instances in which poverty increased when per capita income increased. For three of eleven periods analyzed by Morley, this is the case. It happened in Brazil in 1981–88 and 1979–89 and Guatemala in 1986–89 (Psacharopoulos and others, 1993, table 4.5).

20. The relationship does not seem to hold for Brazil and Guatemala, and it does not hold for Venezuela if the Theil index is used instead of the Gini coefficient.

result in increased poverty, it is far less clear that it should be accompanied by greater inequality. Why are the poor less able than the wealthy to defend themselves in times of crisis and adjustment? One important effect on income distribution is likely to be produced by inflation, which can alter the distribution in many ways.[21] The less educated and poorer wage earners are likely to have weaker bargaining power, so the indexation of their wages will be less prevalent. Inflation "taxes" the poor more heavily because they hold proportionately more of their money in cash. Also, inflation "subsidizes" those (likely the nonpoor) who have liabilities with fixed-rate mortgages and other nonindexed interest rates.

More importantly, the poor are far less likely to protect their wealth via domestic indexed or foreign- denominated financial instruments.[22] Big gains can be made overnight by the groups (the better-off to begin with) who have better information and easy access to instruments such as dollar-denominated assets during a stepwise devaluation of the domestic currency that increase in value, sometimes at incredibly fast rates. The 1980s were replete with anecdotes of large windfall gains as a result of a devaluation from dollars purchased cheaply at an overvalued exchange rate. The counterpart to these gains were the losses of those with no savings or whose assets were not indexed to the dollar—that is, the vast majority—because of the recession and lower wages caused by the devaluation.

Even if the rise in poverty and inequality was an inevitable consequence of the economic crisis, there is a recurring question in reviewing the 1980s: Did the stabilization and adjustment policies increase inequality and poverty even further? The macroeconomic policies and the structural adjustment programs recommended by the International Monetary Fund and the World Bank and implemented by many of the governments in Latin America were, and continue to be, the target of critics both inside and outside the borrowing countries.[23] There are two main questions that are relevant to this issue. First, did stabilization and structural adjustment policies yield greater poverty and inequality than would have resulted in the absence of such policies? Second, do

21. See Kane and Morisett (1993). Also Cardoso (1992).

22. Sturzenegger (1992).

23. See, for example, Cornia, Jolly, and Stewart (1987). Often the critics fail to acknowledge that the economic crisis itself, absent any deliberate policies, would have increased poverty and inequality. The stabilization and structural adjustment programs did not cause the crisis. The economic crisis that hit most Latin American countries in the early 1980s was the consequence of policy errors that led to overexpansionary and unsustainable economic activity and of slow and inadequate responses to external shocks such as changes in oil prices, the rise in world interest rates, and the drying up of credit sources.

some stabilization and adjustment policies exacerbate or diminish the impact of economic crisis on poverty and economic inequality more than others?[24]

In chapter 4 Elizabeth Sadoulet and Alain de Janvry use a dynamic computable general equilibrium model to try to answer these questions. Although the model captures the economic and social structure of Ecuador, the authors use it as "a policy laboratory with generic Latin American features." Assuming that an economy has been subject to a major external shock (that is, a rise in world interest rates, a fall in the price of the main export commodity, or a sudden stop in capital flows) that also affects fiscal revenues, they set out to compare alternative scenarios. In the first the economy is assumed to adjust without any policy intervention; that is, the exchange rate adjusts (the domestic currency devalues) until macroeconomic equilibrium is restored. The authors correctly assume that the alternative of no policy is not equivalent to the status quo but to a situation in which the real exchange rate (its value in the illegal market if the country has exchange controls) changes until the balance of payments equilibrium is restored. In the presence of explicit policies, the authors introduce fiscal and monetary instruments to restore macroeconomic equilibrium through exchange rate adjustment.

The simulations in chapter 4 demonstrate that the no-policy adjustment has a low cost in economic growth in the very short run but in the medium run leads to a sharp increase in interest rates and inflation, resulting in declining economic growth. If the fiscal deficit is adjusted to the preshock levels with reductions in public current expenditure and investment, the effect in the short term is recessionary, but the long term brings greater economic growth than in the no-policy (exchange rate only) adjustment. Finally, a monetary approach to stabilization—cutting back the annual growth in money supply—results in a less severe short-run recession but at the cost of slower long-run economic growth than with fiscal adjustment only.

In the short run (two to three years) and particularly for the rural population, the incidence of poverty is lower under the no-policy scenario than under monetary or fiscal adjustments, and fiscal adjustment has the greatest short-run cost on growth and poverty.[25] In the long run, however, the opposite is true: fiscal adjustment results in the highest growth rate and the lowest incidence of poverty for the rural population, although this outcome is less clear

24. See the points made by Blejer (1992).
25. As Cline notes, it may be misleading to use preadjustment levels of fiscal spending (on subsidies and social services, for example) as a benchmark if they were unsustainable. Some concept of "sustainable best-policy poverty incidence" fiscal balance is necessary to make the comparisons useful. (Cline, 1992).

for the urban population.[26] This result is important because it may provide an explanation for why governments and people resist the adoption of explicit stabilization and adjustment policies.[27] In addition, if this result is an accurate description of reality, compensatory policies designed to smooth out the income stream are warranted from the standpoint of efficiency (growth is slower under the no-policy adjustment), welfare (poverty will end up higher under the no-policy scenario), and political feasibility.[28]

Aside from the insights provided by economic models, there is prima facie evidence that some policies may have unnecessarily increased poverty and skewed the distribution of income. The subsidies given in 1983 to Chilean banks and financial institutions (which were burdened with substantial dollar-dominated debt) were, according to one author, equivalent to ten times the annual cost of the emergency employment program.[29] An analogous problem occurred in 1982 when Argentina converted the dollar-denominated private sector debt into domestic debt at a very favorable exchange rate. Almost overnight the external debt held by the government, and with it the obligations to service it, increased considerably. Thus the burden of formerly private debt was socialized under rules of the game that were unfair. Those who had savings had a chance to send them safely abroad and subsequently extract high returns (at least as measured in domestic currency); those who did not eventually saw their real incomes decrease sharply.[30]

26. See chapter 4, figures 4-4 and 4-5. See also, *World Development*, vol. 19 (November 1991). This issue of the journal includes several articles that examine the tradeoffs in other regions of the world as well.

27.Unfortunately, de Janvry and Sadoulet's analysis does not include the impact of eliminating general food subsidies and agricultural price supports. Such changes were part of many stabilization and adjustment programs, and it would be useful to assess their consequences, particularly in terms of poverty. Venezuela, where the population responded to the elimination of food and fuel subsidies with bloody street riots in 1989, demonstrates the potential implications of such cutbacks.

28.The authors do not explicitly address the problem of inequality. They divide the poor along urban and rural lines. As a result, the fortunes of one segment of the poor may improve while the rest of the poor become worse off. The author do not consider the overall impact on poverty or income distribution.

29. See Flaño (1992).

30. The other policy that deserves further scrutiny for its effect on the distribution of income and wealth is the privatization of public enterprises. In carrying out the privatization, did the government provide certain groups with inside information or special purchase conditions? Did the regulatory framework put in place after the privatization guarantee the existence of a competitive market, or did it protect new monopolistic interests? These questions, however important, are beyond the scope of this book.

Country Experiences

How did governments in various countries respond to the imperative of austerity? Did they try to protect the poor from the brunt of the crisis and adjustment process? Were the losers from economic reform compensated? These questions are discussed for Argentina, Brazil, Chile, Mexico, Peru, and Venezuela. The general conclusion has to be that the sturdiness of the social safety nets before the crises, the characteristics of the political systems—whether they were democracies or authoritarian regimes—and the extent of the power exercised by unions, the business community, and other groups strongly influenced the distribution of cost sharing during the adjustment process.

Argentina

In the 1980s Argentina's economy performed like a roller coaster. GDP and real wages fell and rose several times. Inflation was high throughout the period, often bordering on hyperinflation, and hyperinflation actually occurred. In the way the story of Argentina during the 1980s is that of a country in which society resisted adjustment and, for a while, was successful in its resistance. In the end, however, adjustment was inevitable, and real national income in 1990 was 20.8 percent less and real wages in the manufacturing sector 14.4 percent lower than they had been in 1980.

Although there is no nationwide information, poverty in Greater Buenos Aires, where more than a third of the country's population lives, rose very sharply. In chapter 6 Luis Beccaria and Ricardo Carciofi estimate that the proportion of households below the poverty line increased from 7.6 percent in 1980 to 28.5 percent in 1990.[31] Others have estimated smaller proportions of households below the poverty line.[32] But all agree that poverty became much worse. One striking feature of poverty in Greater Buenos Aires is that it is very sensitive to growth performance. According to Beccaria and Carciofi, in

31. Poverty due to "unmet basic needs" changed from 15.9 percent of the households in 1980 to 16.1 percent in 1990, a change that is not significant (see chapter 6). A household is classified as poor according to this criterion if it does not meet at least one of the five basic needs.

32. See chapter 6; and Psacharopoulos and others (1993, table 4-1). Among existing estimates, Samuel Morley calculates that the poverty head count ratio rose from 6.3 percent in 1980 to 21.5 percent in 1989, and the World Bank estimated that it rose from 3 percent in 1980 to 6.4 percent. The differences are best explained by the fact that the studies use different poverty lines and that Beccaria and Carciofi did not correct for underreporting.

1991, when real GDP grew by 8.5 percent, the proportion of households below the poverty line fell by more than 5 percentage points.

At first glance, data on public social spending in Argentina for the 1980s might lead one to believe that it should be viewed as a model country. After per capita public spending in the social sectors declined sharply in 1982, it rose almost steadily between 1984 and 1987, and in 1988 was still above the 1980 level (see chapter 6). A superficial interpretation of these figures would be that the Argentine government made a concerted effort to compensate the population for income losses in the market by expanding the provision of publicly delivered goods and services and the introduction of social emergency programs. Unfortunately, this is not what happened.

It is true that the democratic government, which took power in 1983, was probably more committed to protecting social expenditures than was the previous military government. One clear example of this commitment was the launching of the National Food Program in 1984. This program provided a food basket for poor families designed to satisfy 30 percent of the nutritional needs of a family of four and was the first food program in Argentina with national coverage.[33]

At the same time, however, according to Beccaria and Carciofi, Argentina's fiscal accounts during the 1980s reflect the enormous difficulties encountered by the government in cutting the deficit and reforming the public sector. The obstacles included large fluctuations in prices; problems of coordinating the central, provincial, and municipal governments; the presence of an uncooperative opposition in Congress; and the resistance of such powerful unions as the teachers' union within the public sector itself. Because of these factors, public expenditures in the social sectors and public sector spending in general were not subject to the type of downward adjustment seen, for example, in Mexico. And it was not until after the hyperinflationary episode in 1989 that adjustment of the fiscal accounts began. But the apparent protection of social spending probably did not result in protection of the quality of the services.[34] Attempts to decentralize social services (which started under the military regime), particularly education, turned out to be harmful if not disastrous. Decentralization meant that responsibility for carrying out the services was dumped on underfunded and undertrained local governments.

33. World Bank (1990, p. xii); and chapter 6.
34. A series of strikes by the teachers union, for example, sometimes kept teachers' salaries from falling but caused classes to start late or be interrupted on several occasions. These interruptions most likely did not help improve the quality of education.

Brazil

Although Brazil experienced periods of economic expansion and contraction in the 1980s, per capita GDP at the end of the decade was about what it had been at the beginning. The debt crisis did not impose as heavy a blow on Brazil as it did, for example, on Argentina or Mexico. Per capita GDP fell 0.6 percent in the 1980s and wages contracted but total employment continued to grow at a much faster pace than total output. At the same time, income distribution became much more unequal, especially between 1986 and 1989, and poverty increased. Chapter 7, by Ricardo Barros, Rosane Mendonca, and Sonia Rocha shows how sensitive the incidence of poverty is to economic fluctuations and how sensitive the measure of poverty is to the definition of the poverty line and the choice of the base year.

As in the case of Argentina, the onset of democratization in Brazil was accompanied by increased social spending, particularly after 1985. Although data on disaggregated public spending are apparently hard to obtain, available indicators show that public spending on education, public health, food assistance programs, and assistance to unemployed workers rose during the 1980s. In fact, unemployment insurance and some food assistance programs were launched in the mid-1980s. According to Barros and colleagues, however, most of these programs had serious targeting problems and failed to reach the poorest segments of the population. Unfortunately, lack of information does not permit analyses analogous to those of the other countries.

Chile

Chile was a pioneer in pursuing market-oriented structural reforms. The process began soon after the military coup in 1973. Throughout the 1970s the military rulers introduced tax reform, liberalized trade, and deregulated the financial sector. Between 1973 and 1979 collective bargaining and strikes were prohibited; these restrictions were partially lifted in 1979. The reforms did not, however, shield Chile from a crisis similar to those experienced by Brazil and Mexico, which were still under the import-substitution and more statist model.[35]

35. Although Chile had introduced market-oriented reforms, it had not avoided risky macroeconomic policies (such as an overvalued real exchange rate) that resulted in an increasing current account deficit, and external private and public debt. The 1982 crisis highlighted the need for reregulation of financial markets, which was subsequently carried out in 1986. Marfán and Bosworth (1994, p. 192, note).

Of the six countries discussed in this book, Chile is the only one that undertook a major overhaul of its policies, institutions, and financing mechanisms in the social sectors that started before and continued after the debt crisis. Privatization of the delivery of many social services and decentralization were the order of the day. In contrast with Argentina but in ways similar to Mexico, Chile was able to implement adjustment and stabilization programs with little social resistance. Unlike Mexico, Chile had the advantage of having introduced structural change, especially trade liberalization, a few years before it was hit by the debt crisis. This may explain why its recovery was faster and more sustained than Mexico's was after its 1983 program.

It is difficult to know the extent of the increase in poverty in Chile during the 1980s because no comparable nationwide surveys were taken before or after the crisis. But assuming that the study by Altimir in 1970 and the subsequent CEPAL studies are comparable, poverty increased from 17 percent in 1970 to 38.2 percent in 1987, and extreme poverty rose from 6 percent to 13.5 percent. PREALC's study of Greater Santiago indicates that poverty expanded from 28.5 percent in 1969 to 40.3 percent in 1980 to 48.6 percent in 1987. Even if these numbers are not fully accurate, they leave little room for doubt that poverty increased substantially. The reduction of poverty in Chile during recovery appears to be less spectacular than in Argentina: between 1987 and 1990 per capita GDP grew at 4.7 percent a year, and poverty was reduced from 38 percent to 34 percent.

Public social spending began to decrease after the 1973 military coup. The reduction was not continuous, but by 1989 the level of real public social spending was still below the 1970 figure. In fact, the government did not subject all of the components of social spending to the same treatment. Spending for education, health, and housing fell, both in relative and absolute terms; spending for social security and other social spending rose in relative terms. This last category is very small in comparison to the other items, but it includes the public emergency employment program and other safety net programs. Spending for social security increased as a result of a reform introduced in 1980 that had the effect of transferring active workers to the new, privately administered system while the government took care of the passive beneficiaries of the old system, paid "seniority bonds," and guaranteed a minimum pension.

Raczynski and Romaguera find that, as in Mexico, the cuts in education and health care represented a reduction of investment and, above all, a deterioration in the real wages of teachers and physicians and other health care workers in the public sector. In addition to experiencing budget cuts, the public health system was decentralized. Its financing mechanism was changed to support demand rather than supply, and a greater reliance on private sector providers and administrators. The system also replaced universal care with programs targeted on the poor and the mother-child population and implemented cost recovery policies. Education and housing were subject to fundamental changes as well.

According to Raczynski and Romaguera, the impact of these reforms on the welfare of the poor, the level of social security of the population in general, and the quality of the services was mixed. Providing preventive health care services to the poorest people and targeting infants, mother, and pregnant women reduced infant mortality significantly, but other sectors of the population were neglected. The authors claim that the priorities were inappropriate given the changes observed in biomedical indicators: that is, the main causes of death and morbidity became cardiovascular diseases, cancer, cirrhosis, and illness of old age.[36] Social security reform resulted in reduced benefits with no increase in coverage. The reasons for the latter, however, remain unexplained by the authors and this view is not shared by others.[37] Finally, the authors argue that the reforms in the educational system did not necessarily result in a clear improvement in its quality.

Mexico

Mexico was simultaneously hit by the decline in world oil prices and the debt crisis. In fact the Mexican involuntary moratorium in mid-1982 triggered the debt crisis. Unlike the governments of Argentina, Brazil, Peru, and Venezuela, and more like that of Chile, the Mexican leadership introduced a very ambitious program of fiscal adjustment almost immediately.

Santiago Friedmann, Nora Lustig, and Arianna Legovini show in chapter 9 that external shocks delivered a heavy blow to the Mexican population generally and to wage earners in particular. Between 1983 and 1988 real wages declined at an average of 7.7 to 10.5 percent a year (depending on the category). Unfortunately, Mexico is one of the countries for which a before-and-after comparison of the evolution of poverty and income distribution cannot be made. If survey data between 1984 and 1989 are corrected for underreporting, poverty and extreme poverty expanded. The surveys also indicate that income became much more concentrated between 1984 and 1989. The share of the top 10 percent of the people increased by almost 5 percentage points.

36. Castañeda (1992, p. 112).
37. Castañeda (1992, pp. 185–86) arrives at a different conclusion concerning the benefits of educational reform.

According to the authors in chapter 9, social spending fell at a faster pace than the rest of non-debt related expenditures, but most of the decline was caused by cuts in wages and investment. The strategy of protecting public employment at the expense of government wages, and particularly public investment, has met with criticism. However, by protecting employment, the Mexican government "socialized" the cost of austerity among public employees. In a country where there were no unemployment insurance or employment programs in place, this may have been a safer strategy, both from a political and social insurance point of view. In addition, keeping the work force in health care and education more or less intact meant that provision of these services did not have to be reduced (although their quality may have worsened).

In stark contrast to Argentina, for example, the Mexican government enjoyed much greater freedom in managing fiscal retrenchment because it did not have to deal with strong independent unions within its bureaucracy. Also, during the 1980s the government did not attempt to protect spending on social programs that were geared to the very poor. These programs suffered greater budget cuts than the rest of social spending, and they were subject to a decentralization process that according to some analysts seems to have seriously diminished their impact.[38] The government also tried to replace the general price subsidies for food with food subsidies targeted to the poor. But these targeted programs did not really reach the poorest people effectively because of leakages, and general food subsidies were not in the end eliminated. Also, the targeted subsidies were probably insufficient to fully compensate the poor for their decreased income.

Peru

Of the six countries reviewed in this book, Peru stands out as having experienced the most drastic fall in living standards. According to Adolfo Figueroa in chapter 10, in 1991 real GDP per capita was equivalent to 70 percent of its 1981 value. Social spending fell precipitously both in absolute value and relative to GDP. In 1990 social spending was equal to 21 percent of its 1980 value. Wages in the public sector in 1991 were less than 10 percent of their 1981

38. In December 1988, six years after the crisis ended, the new government announced the launching of the Programa Nacional de Solidaridad or PRONASOL, which was supposed to address poverty with demand-driven targeted programs. For a further description see Lustig (1994b).

level. Urban poverty and inequality increased substantially.[39] One study, for example, finds that extreme poverty (defined as the inability to cover the household's basic nutritional requirements) in Lima where 30 percent of the population lives went from 0.5 percent of the population in 1985–86 to 17.3 percent in 1990. The provision of potable water and sewage services in Lima also deteriorated during this period.[40]

In contrast to the other countries, Peru experienced a significant drop in school enrollment, perhaps as a consequence of the private costs associated with sending children to school. The infant mortality rate, however, continued to decline.[41] Figueroa argues that the performance of the infant mortality rate may be a consequence of the continuation of immunization programs.

Figueroa defines the situation in Peru as a "distributive crisis," which in his view occurs when real wages, and living standards in general, fall below a threshold that is socially tolerable. Under a distributive crisis, the falling private investment, increasing social violence, and the impoverishment of the masses are all endogenous variables. Although the concept of a distributive crisis is interesting, it is not clear which factors determine the threshold of intolerance.[42] Indeed, one would expect that this threshold would vary from country to country and would be determined by the overall historical and political conditions.

All in all, Peru is an extreme example of a country where the attempt to avoid the adjustment process worked for a while but planted the seeds of a severe backlash. Adopting an expansionary macroeconomic program, suspending payments on foreign debt, and introducing redistributive policies through heavy government intervention in price settings were policies that caused a severe economic contraction, very high inflation, and a sharp rise in poverty.

Venezuela

Gustavo Marquez describes the Venezuelan situation in the 1980s as one in which successive governments have been prisoners of the same dilemma: the

39. The reader should recall that there is no information to make the comparison for rural areas in Peru.

40. Glewwe and Hall (1992, pp. 48, 49).

41. One should bear in mind that this information is based on extrapolations and not on actual data.

42. A somewhat similar concept underlies the "new political economy" analysis conducted by those such as Alberto Alesina and Perotti (1993); and Alesina and Rodrik (1991, 1992).

desire to sustain the expansion of the public enterprise sector while providing sufficient resources to the traditional social sectors. The competing interests of groups supporting deficit-ridden public enterprises and social service institutions under increasingly tight fiscal budget restrictions, generated first an unsustainable increase in the external debt, later rising inflation, and finally the collapse of 1989. In Venezuela the political conditions resulted in a pattern similar to that observed in Argentina, Brazil, and Peru: the existing coalition made an orderly adjustment impossible.

During the 1980s poverty and inequality increased sharply in Venezuela. Poverty, measured by the head-count ratio, doubled between 1981 and 1989. Marquez analyzes whether this increase can be attributed to behavioral variables such as changes in family size and the rate of participation in the labor force. He finds that because family size decreased and the rate of participation increased, these factors cannot explain the increase in poverty. The basic explanation instead is falling average earnings, especially real wages. As in the case of Mexico, unemployment was not the cause of declining incomes.

Social spending per capita fell during the 1980s, but social spending was not affected disproportionately in comparison with other budget items. However, Marquez believes that the change in the composition of the social sector ministries was detrimental because the share of expenditures allocated to the support, planning, and administration programs increased and the share allocated to operational programs and inputs decreased. In particular and to the detriment of primary education and medical services, pressure groups organized around unions, and the vocal university and medical personnel lobbies ensured that the claims of personnel, universities, and high-level medical facilities on the budget were fulfilled. However, as in the other countries examined here, Marquez finds that neither indicators of health or education show long-term deterioration, despite the cuts in per capita social spending.

One dilemma that Marquez poses is whether fiscal cuts in the social sectors should be implemented by reducing employment in those sectors rather than by lowering the wages of workers. In Mexico the government chose to lower wages. In principle, this strategy seems less likely to result in political conflict in the short run and may protect the quantity of social services delivered to the population. Nonetheless, the strategy may run counter to more fundamental reforms needed in the public sector. This issue clearly deserves greater analysis.

Circumventing the bureaucracies of the social sector ministries after 1989, the government introduced various programs designed to reach the poor. Marquez notes that the switch from indirect to direct subsidies resulted in an improvement in efficiency. But the amounts involved were insufficient to fully compensate the poor for their losses. More important, the failure to reform the traditional social sectors ended up rendering these efforts much less effective than had been hoped.

The Determinants of Inequality and Poverty

To obtain empirical estimates of the contribution of the various factors influencing inequality, Ariel Fiszbein and George Psacharopoulos in chapter 3 decomposed total inequality into four (or three where the data did not permit the use of four) explanatory variables: age, employment category, education, and economic sector. In applying this analysis to a sampling of seven Latin American countries, the authors find that education is the variable with the strongest impact on income inequality and poverty.[43] On average, about one-fourth of total inequality can be explained as inequality between individuals grouped according to their level of schooling.[44] Similarly, the authors find a positive association between education and being out of poverty. Using logit analysis they find that the probability of belonging to the bottom 20 percent of income earners was higher the less educated the individual. For most countries in their sample, an additional year of schooling reduces the probability of being poor for an average individual by 3 to 4 percentage points.

Education and its distribution as an explanation for inequality and poverty is only part of the story: Is Latin American poverty caused more by a person's lack of education or by insufficient opportunity to put that education to work? If lack of opportunity is more, or even equally, important, policies designed to reduce poverty should concentrate not only on improving the skills of the poor but also on increasing demand for the labor of the poor and their newly acquired skills.[45] In addition, education may be associated with other variables—more ability, greater motivation, more sophisticated household envi-

43. Argentina, Brazil, Colombia, Costa Rica, Panama, Uruguay, and Venezuela. Data for Argentina, Colombia, and Uruguay are not for the whole country but for the main metropolitan area or urban areas.

44. Also, in the first version of their chapter, Barros, Mendonca, and Rocha cite their own findings on the relationship between education and inequality. They show that if all wage differentials by education level were eliminated, overall inequality would be reduced by almost 50 percent.

45. Fields (1992).

ronment, and so forth—that might also affect poverty and inequality. Because the analysis apparently does not control for these factors, its emphasis on the importance of education may be overstated.[46]

Fiszbein and Psacharopoulos mention gender and ethnic discrimination as factors in determining who is poor. They find that when all other factors are equal, working women have 34 percent probability of belonging to the bottom 20 percent, as opposed to 14 percent for men. They also note that indigenous people in Bolivia and Guatemala have more than a 20 percent probability of belonging to the bottom quintile, as do mulattos and blacks in Brazil. Discrimination, in particular ethnic discrimination, has usually not been a serious study or matter of significant policy in Latin America. In light of these results, the eradication of discriminatory practices in the labor market should become a primary concern for governments and international lending institutions. Discriminatory practices and market failure in the capital market—although not analyzed in this book—can be another important source of inequality and poverty.

Do the factors that explain the long-run determinants of poverty and inequality also explain their changes during economic crisis and adjustment? Does human capital provide as good a shield from the impact of a crisis as physical or financial capital? The evidence suggests that the answer to the first question is no. Neither education, age, occupation, nor economic sector change rapidly enough to explain the observed changes in inequality and poverty during the 1980s. For example, one cannot attribute the significant deterioration of income distribution that occurred in Brazil between 1981 and 1983 as the result of changes in the distribution of education. The poor do not lose their skills so quickly, nor do the rich acquire them.[47]

Education clearly seems to be an important variable in determining the probability of being poor. But education alone was not a strong enough protection against poverty during the economic downturn of the 1980s. Indeed, Fiszbein and Psacharopoulos find that the probability of being in the bottom 20 percent at the end of the decade increased even for those with a university education in all seven countries except Costa Rica. Sam Morley, too (in chapter 2) shows that the incidence of poverty among the well-educated in Argentina and Venezuela increased during that period. None of the authors asks whether the probability of becoming poor during an economic slowdown is greater the less educated the person. If this question were answered yes, one

46. See Behrman (1990a, 1990b, 1990c).
47. Cardoso (1992).

may conclude that although more education does not protect people from falling into poverty during a crisis, more education might diminish the probability of its happening.[48]

Despite the importance that the characteristics of labor demand may have in explaining long-run inequality and poverty, the contribution of demand to the changes in those variables during the 1980s seems to be weaker. Sam Morley finds that in Argentina and Venezuela poverty was not primarily a problem confined to those who were unemployed or retired. Undoubtedly, there was a dramatic increase in the incidence of poverty in both groups. The percentage of the unemployed or retired who received an income less than the poverty line rose dramatically. However, in 1989 76 percent of the poor in Argentina and Venezuela worked, and the incidence of poverty among the working population also shot up, particularly in the so-called informal sector, but in the formal sector as well.

Because yearly data was available for Brazil, some of the relationships could be examined using econometric analysis. According to the studies cited in chapter 7, changes in the structure of wages and employment or education that could explain the changes in inequality in Brazil between 1960 and 1970 were no longer able to explain these changes during the 1980s. Neither could inequality in levels of education. Based on the results of other studies, Barros, Mendonca, and Rocha argue that the changes in inequality in the 1980s are primarily explained by macroeconomic variables such as inflation and slower economic activity.[49]

Targeting to Reduce Inequality and Poverty

Targeting public resources to specific population groups can be used for three distinct but not mutually exclusive purposes. Targeting can compensate those who lose income as a result of a policy change, protect the most vulnerable groups from the harmful effects of an economic crisis, or make more efficient use of fiscal resources to reduce poverty. For multilateral financial institutions and governments alike, targeting has become a way to introduce

48. The results for Peru in Glewwe and Hall (1992, p. 48) seem to support this. In a different framework, Pessino (1993, p. 31) finds that education seems to work as a protection during periods of high inflation.

49. The authors admit, however, that although the studies are very successful in explaining the increase in inequality up to 1989, they are much less successful in explaining the sharp decrease in inequality from 1989 to 1990.

poverty reduction programs that use fiscal resources more carefully and keep government interventions in specific markets to a minimum.

Margaret Grosh in chapter 5 discusses the way a government should choose among different programs. In theory the best program is that which most increases the present discounted value of social welfare, given all the costs and all the market and nonmarket interactions, behavioral reactions in the economy, and the asset endowments.[50] Nevertheless, Grosh believes that, in general, governments cannot base their decision on a rigorous framework because the information requirements for good cost-effectiveness analysis are formidable (and usually unavailable).

As an alternative she proposes a set of straightforward criteria to select among programs. The proposed criteria are: administrative feasibility, political feasibility, collateral effects on efficiency, ability to target, and tailoring the solution to the problem. Using these criteria, Grosh compares programs such as general food subsidies, food stamp programs, food commodity distribution, school feeding programs, social funds, and microenterprise credit schemes.

The targeted food stamp, commodity distribution, and school feeding programs are (as would be expected) more cost-effective than the general food subsidies. Nonetheless, since there is more dissent as to whether particular targeted options can meet minimum levels of administrative and political feasibility, the details of program design, institutional capacities, and other objectives will determine selection among programs that often fall in the same range of cost-effectiveness with regard to the transfer they provide. This might be the case, for example, when governments have to choose among food stamp programs, food commodity distribution, and school feeding programs. Because food commodity distribution programs always have higher transport and spoilage costs than food stamp programs, if all other things are equal, food stamps are preferable.

The so-called social funds compare unfavorably with food stamps, food commodity programs, or school feeding programs if only direct transfers are calculated. However, a proper assessment would have to incorporate the benefit from the infrastructure created or redistributed and not only on the effect on employment. Although microenterprise projects have the potential advantage of resulting in a permanent boost in earnings capacity, Grosh argues that, at least from those programs observed, microenterprise projects can only reach a limited number of beneficiaries.[51]

50. Behrman (1992).
51. On the discussion of the political benefits associated with different forms of safety nets, see Graham (1994).

Grosh comes to one important conclusion. Her research indicates that the details of program design and context influence the cost-effectiveness of programs more than the type of program. For example, the highs and lows of the administrative costs within a program show larger differences than the means among the program types. The implication is that more importance should be given to identifying adequate institutional arrangements for the targeted programs than has been the case in most studies and analysis. Finally, Grosh's chapter underscores the problem discussed in the appendix, which is the lack of adequate information to make the best program selection and the difficulty of monitoring such programs.[52]

Conclusion

Poverty and inequality increased in Latin America during the 1980s, particularly in countries that had a lower per capita income at the endpoint of the comparison. Although the poor were not disproportionately hurt in every country, in about half of the countries for which there is information, they suffered the brunt of the crisis. In the rest, the middle or upper middle classes suffered relatively more than the poor. In each of the countries analyzed except Colombia, the wealthiest 10 percent of the households improved their relative position. Infant mortality, gross school enrollment rates, and other social indicators continued to improve, albeit more slowly. They could probably have improved at a faster rate were it not for the economic crisis.

One clear reason inequality increases with an economic crisis is that the poor are less able to protect themselves from inflation. They are especially unlikely to protect their wealth with indexed or foreign-denominated financial instruments. Did the stabilization and adjustment policies increase inequality and poverty beyond what a policy of no policy would have done? Available results indicate that for the medium and long run the answer is no. In the end, a failure to act to reduce the fiscal deficit and restrict domestic credit causes more poverty.

The different approaches to adjustment in each of the countries, and particularly the ways governments reacted to the conditions imposed by austerity, suggest several important observations. First, none of the countries (with the possible exception of Chile) was ready to protect the poor from the impact of

---

52. Program evaluation is made particularly difficult by the fact that usually no provisions are made to have adequate counterfactuals.

the crisis and the adjustment programs.[53] A recent study focusing on social investment funds corroborates this impression for other countries in the region as well. In fact, social investment funds were usually implemented several years or even a decade after the crisis had erupted.[54]

Second, the maintenance of social spending at close to precrisis levels during crisis and adjustment is not an indication of a government's desire and ability to protect the poor during the crisis. It is equally possible, indeed more likely, that maintenance of social spending reflects the difficulties governments encountered in reducing the wages paid in the social sectors, where workers were usually protected by powerful unions.

Third, premature efforts to devolve the provision of social services to states and municipalities can seriously damage provision, especially when decentralization is not accompanied by adequate financing and training of the local governments. Finally, the analysis of fiscal adjustment programs indicates the difficulties, for governments that want to make the public sector more efficient and effective, posed by large fluctuations in price levels and the lack of coordination among the various levels of government.

One obvious way to reduce poverty is through economic growth.[55] To the extent that the increase in income inequality in the 1980s was associated with high inflation and the economic crisis, the recovery of sustained economic growth and macroeconomic stability may reduce inequality. Sustained growth requires adequate macroeconomic policies (which do not result in inflation and a balance of payments crisis or unemployment) and a regulatory and legal environment that encourages private investment, competition, and technological change. However, sustained growth also requires mechanisms to shield countries from external shocks. In this sense, governments should implement, and the multilateral institutions should encourage, policies that smooth the impact of external shocks.

At the same time, growth alone may reduce poverty and inequality too slowly. Are there proactive policies that a government can undertake to speed up the process without jeopardizing growth?[56]

The changes in macroeconomic policymaking and the economic reforms undertaken in the 1980s introduced important restrictions (most for the better) on the type of instruments that governments can use to redistribute income. In

53. Chile had a long-standing tradition of progressive social policy and a fairly well developed system of safety nets.
54. World Bank (1994).
55. Birdsall, Ross, and Sabot (1994).
56. See, for example, Bourguignon (1991, p. 315).

the past, redistributive policies almost always implied some form of market intervention and could absorb great fiscal resources. The adoption of fiscal discipline and market-oriented reforms in most of Latin America in the 1980s changed this. For example, general subsidies were largely eliminated. The privatization of public enterprises removed the possibility of subsidizing producers and consumers by providing some goods and services at below market prices. Even if the enterprises were still in government hands, their pricing schemes are increasingly bound by the regulations governing the use of subsidies in international trade. Independent central banks put more constraints on credit policy. Open markets for goods and capital put floors on domestic interest rates and ceilings on tax rates. Trade liberalization implied the elimination of import and export controls and targeted industrial programs, and it forced domestic prices to move closer to international prices. Finally, elimination of exchange and capital controls restricted the use of the exchange rate for redistributive purposes.

There are, however, many policy alternatives still open to governments. Improving the level of people's education and reducing the inequality in its distribution is an important tool. Because of its impact on labor productivity, education has the additional advantage of resulting in higher growth rates.[57] The most progressive approach to public spending on education, given that the poor tend to have more children, is to make primary education a priority. Higher levels of education should also be made accessible to lower-income groups, and upper-income groups should be required to pay for their own university education.

Policies that can transfer current income to the poor are also helpful. In general, these take the form of transfers designed to increase food intake of the poor and improve their nutritional status.[58] In Latin America it is not only important to reduce poverty and income inequality, but also to improve access to social services and social infrastructure: poor people with access to free or inexpensive health care will not only enjoy higher levels of welfare but also increase their earning capacities. The same applies to improving sewerage systems, ensuring potable water, and improving distribution of electricity. Other policies that can help reduce poverty and inequality include the redistribution of resalable assets, such as land, preferential credit programs for low-income housing, and intervention in situations where market failure or social

57. Bourguignon (1993).
58. These include, for example, food stamp programs, food commodity distribution, ration shops, and school feeding programs. Which one is best might change from country to country (see chapter 5).

practice results in limited access to credit or employment or other forms of discrimination against the poor.

Because discriminatory practices may result in lower pay for women and some indigenous peoples, blacks, and mulattos, a reform in the countries' legal systems, including the development, implementation, and enforcement of laws prohibiting such discrimination, may be necessary. A number of initiatives could also help the poor defend themselves. As it is, the poor often do not have regularized property titles, they can be subject to extortionate conditions in the credit market, and they often do not have access to the judiciary system (for example, they often cannot afford to hire a lawyer).

Most of the initiatives require government resources to be put into practice. To avoid inflationary deficit financing, governments will have to make tough decisions in allocating limited revenues, perhaps diminishing one worthy program to promote another. In fact, in addition to a progressive public spending policy, the governments need to make the tax system as progressive as possible, while at the same time not putting growth in jeopardy.

Redistributive initiatives are likely to encounter political resistance, even if the economy is growing. A high concentration in the distribution of income and wealth stands as a significant impediment to more egalitarian policymaking.[59] The wealthy could react very violently to redistributive policies, particularly if they believe the policies are radical. However, coalitions with economic clout have been known to block redistributive policies even when the policies are not at all radical. If the rate of taxation is viewed as excessive, for example, those with savings may deposit them abroad. A landed aristocracy may prevent a progressive and efficient agrarian reform even if the reform includes adequate compensation.[60] The major challenge facing Latin American governments is to introduce reforms and undertake policies to reduce inequality and poverty without succumbing to measures that are either economically or politically unsustainable. Taking stock of past mistakes and practices that have proven successful should facilitate this task.

Experience from other countries indicates that a very important factor contributing to reducing inequality and poverty was the shift in employment from low-productivity to high-productivity sectors. This speaks in favor of policies that encourage the expansion of the latter. Open trade and investment regimes

59. The opposite may also be true, however. Because Latin America has such economic inequality, self-defeating redistributive policies are more frequent as governments try to accommodate the demands of those who are not privileged. See Sachs (1989); and Dornbusch and Edwards (1991).

60. For a discussion on the politics of redistribution, see Ascher (1984).

and competitive exchange rates are probably key elements of such policy.

In addition, policies that avoid wide swings in countries' economic output are very important to protect living standards from falling. Evidence in this book shows that inequality is prone to increase sharply during periods of crisis. These severe downturns—caused more often than not by a combination of external factors *and* policy errors—can quickly reverse reductions in poverty and inequality that might have taken years. The Mexican financial crisis triggered by the devaluation of the peso at the end of 1994 is a clear reminder that countries, even those that have made great progress in overhauling their economies and making economic policy, are not at all immune from facing yet another period of austerity. Institutions and policies—both at the national and the international level—that keep countries better insured against these sharp falls must be conceived as an essential part of the strategy to reduce poverty and inequality.

Appendix: Measuring Poverty and Inequality in Latin America

It is common to hear that accurate measures of poverty and inequality in Latin America and the Caribbean are not important because both are self-evident to even the most casual observer. But how can the size of the effort that needs to be made to reduce poverty be determined if its extent is not known? How can the potential impact on poverty of a specific policy change be assessed without information on household income and its determinants? How can the potential and actual effectiveness of antipoverty policies be evaluated without comparable measures of poverty over time? Countries spend a great deal to measure inflation, the fiscal deficit, output, and the balance of payments accurately. Poverty, income distribution, and social indicators are never measured with equal care.[61]

The most widespread measure of welfare is household income, and the most common sources for data on household income are the household or income-expenditure surveys. Even if one is willing to work with surveys that have a less than complete definition of income or may not be comparable over time, there are only four countries in Latin America (out of close to thirty) for

---

61. For recommendations on a possible way to deal with the problems discussed here see Lustig (1994). Concerning the noncomparability of aggregate economic and social data among countries and over time, see Ahmad (1994); Behrman and Rosenzweig (1994); Chamie (1994); Fields (1994); Heston (1994); and Srinivasan (1994).

which a before-and-after analysis of poverty in the 1980s can be made at the national level. Table 1A-1 summarizes the characteristics of the data for eighteen Latin American and Caribbean countries for which a readily available household survey exists.

—Eleven countries—Brazil, Chile, Costa Rica, the Dominican Republic, Guatemala, Honduras, Jamaica, Mexico, Panama, Peru, and Venezuela—have at least one survey in the 1980s with data at the national level.[62]

—Among these, a before-and-after adjustment comparison can be made only for Brazil, Costa Rica, Panama, and Venezuela.

—There are no surveys, or at least none for the period between 1979 and 1989, for Barbados, Cuba, Grenada, Guyana, Haiti, Nicaragua, Trinidad and Tobago, and Suriname.[63]

—Surveys from Argentina, Bolivia, Colombia, Ecuador, El Salvador, Paraguay, and Uruguay do not include the rural sector.

—Only three countries have at least one survey that recorded total income: Chile, Mexico, and Uruguay.[64] In the rest of the countries, either nonwage income is excluded or there is no estimate of self-production or other forms of nonmonetary or imputed income.

In addition to the gaps in the data, the existing surveys have other important problems and limitations.

—Because of methodological differences, surveys for the same country (let alone across countries) are often not really comparable over time.[65]

—Underreporting is very serious in all surveys. The estimates that correct for underreporting can give results that are several orders of magnitude different and even opposite from uncorrected estimates. For example, in Mexico poverty between 1984 and 1989 decreases before the correction is made and increases afterwards.[66] The coefficients used to "correct" for underreporting are not at all small. For example, in the study by Psacharopoulos and others, the coefficients are often greater than two.[67] This means that a not negligible

62. Other sources indicate that Colombia had at least one survey with national coverage in the 1980s (see Londono de la Cuesta, 1990). It remains unclear why these data were not used in the studies by Altimir (1993) and Psacharopoulos and others (1993).
63. Or if there are, they are not available, at least according to the overview documents by Altimir and Psacharopoulos.
64. See Psacharopoulos and others (1993).
65. For example, Mexico 1977 and 1984.
66. See Lustig and Mitchell (1994); Psacharopoulos and others (1993); and Instituto Nacional de Estadística Geografía e Informática (1993).
67. See Psacharopoulos (1992, tables 9.1 and 9.2). Other studies do not publish those coefficients, but corrections for underreporting are made (for example, in CEPAL's periodic reports on poverty).

Table 1A-1. *Characteristics of Household Survey Data for Eighteen Latin American and Caribbean Countries*

	More than one survey since 1979?	National	Urban only[a]	Total income[b]
		Geographical coverage		
Argentina	Yes	No	Yes	No
Bolivia	Yes	No	Yes	?
Brazil	Yes	Yes	Yes	No
Chile	Yes	Yes	c	Yes
Colombia	Yes	No	Yes	No
Costa Rica	Yes	Yes	c	No
Dominican Republic	No	Yes	c	No
Ecuador	No	No	Yes	No
El Salvador	No	No	Yes	No
Guatemala	Yes	Yes	c	No
Honduras	Yes	Yes	Yes	No
Jamaica	No	Yes	c	?
Mexico	Yes	Yes	c	Yes
Panama	Yes	Yes	c	No
Paraguay	Yes	No	Yes	No
Peru	Yes	Yes	Yes	No
Uruguay	Yes	No	Yes	Yes
Venezuela	Yes	Yes	c	No
Total "yes"	14	11	10	3

Source: World Bank (1993); and Altimir, (1992).

a. In some cases "urban" includes the largest metropolitan areas only, and in other cases it includes all major cities or all cities above a certain population size.

b. A no means that survey data exclude at least one of the following items necessary for estimating total income: monetary nonwage income, monetary income from secondary activities (not the main income source), nonmonetary income, including self-production and the imputed value of owner occupied housing. When total income data are available they may be available for some, but not all, of the existing surveys for that country. A question mark means that from the available description it was not clear whether the survey included all the concepts of total income.

c. Urban data are available from the national survey.

portion of the estimated headcounts available in most studies are the result of postsurvey manipulation of the data. However, the latter is inevitable since the poverty estimates obtained straight from the surveys are in the majority of cases not reasonable. The problem is compounded by the fact that the discrepancy between income (or consumption) data from national accounts and household surveys varies over time for reasons that remain unclear. This lack of constancy in the discrepancy (in proportional terms) lies behind the peculiarity of the results using Mexican data mentioned above.

—Surveys generally have no information on assets or on crop cultivation despite the great bearing of both for determining poverty.

—Surveys usually do not compute or distinguish the value of government transfers as part of a household's income.

—In many instances, because of the difficulties involved in processing data or because governments want to conceal the information from the public eye for political reasons, survey results are not known until years later when the information is no longer current.

Data on social indicators fare no better than data on income distribution and poverty. The primary problem is the variations in information from different sources. For health indicators some of these differences can be seen in table 1-9. Any reader who is interested in seeing more discrepancies in health indicators can compare World Bank (table 8.9), Psacharopoulos and others (1993, table 5.1), and table 1-5. In table 1-5, for example, the infant mortality rate for Brazil is 75 per 1,000 live births in 1980 and 48 per 1,000 in 1988. According to Psacharopoulos and his colleagues, it was 86 in 1986. Both sources cannot be right. Psacharopoulos shows an infant mortality rate for Mexico equal to 56.2 in 1987; in Table 1-5, the rate is 53.1 in 1980 and 40.6 in 1988. Fortunately, data on life expectancy are practically the same regardless of the source. Nonetheless, an accurate and comparable measure of infant mortality is of the essence to monitor the evolution of poverty and the effectiveness of programs designed to reduce it.

The problems with the data for poverty analysis are probably germane to all the developing world. To improve the quality of data, increase the frequency of its availability, and ease the access to data on poverty and social indicators, multilateral bodies will have to coordinate actions and provide the appropriate incentives to national governments. In particular, multilateral financial and nonfinancial institutions in collaboration with governments should explore three courses of action. They should solve methodological problems, encourage production of accurate and timely statistics, and develop an easy-access information system on poverty and social indicators.[68]

References

Ahmad, Sultan. 1994. "Improving Inter-Spatial and Inter-Temporal Comparability of National Accounts." *Journal of Development Economics,* 44 (June), pp. 53–76.

68. In fact the Inter-American Development Bank in collaboration with the World Bank and CEPAL (UN Economic Commission for Latin America) are in the process of launching a project in Latin America and the Caribbean whose objective will be to achieve these three goals.

Alesina, Alberto, and Dani Rodrik. 1991. "Distributive Politics and Economic Growth," NBER working paper 3668. Cambridge, Mass.: National Bureau of Economic Research.

————. 1993. "The Seizure of Economic Power and Economic Growth: A Simple Theory and Some Empirical Evidence." In Alex Cukierman, Zvi Hercowitz, and Leonardo Leiderman, eds., *The Political Economy of Growth and Business Cycles.* MIT Press.

Alesina, Alberto, and Roberto Perotti. 1993. "Income Distribution, Political Instability, and Investment," NBER working paper 4486 (October). Cambridge, Mass.: National Bureau of Economic Research.

Altimir, Oscar. 1993. "Income Distribution and Poverty through Crisis and Adjustment." United Nations working paper 15 (September).

Ascher, William. 1984. *Scheming for the Poor: The Politics of Redistribution in Latin America.* Harvard University Press.

Behrman, Jere R. 1990a. *Human Resource Led Development?* New Delhi: ILO/ ARTEP.

————. 1990b. "The Action of Human Resources and Poverty on One Another: What We Have Yet to Learn," LSM 74. Washington: World Bank Population and Human Resources Department.

————. 1990c. "Women's Schooling and Nonmarket Productivity: A Survey and a Reappraisal." Department of Economics, Williams College (September).

————. 1992. "Comments on Margaret Grosh's Paper, 'Choosing a Poverty Alleviation Program: The Relative Merits of Alternative Interventions.'" Paper presented at the Brookings Institution and Inter-American Dialogue conference, Washington, July 15–17.

Behrman, Jere R., and Mark R. Rosensweig. 1994. *"Caveat Emptor:* Cross-Country Data on Education and the Labor Force." *Journal of Development Economics,* 44 (June), pp. 147–72.

Birdsall, Nancy, and Richard Sabot. 1994. "Virtuous Circles: Human Capital, Growth, and Equity in East Asia," 2d draft. Washington: World Bank,

————. 1994. "Inequality and Growth Reconsidered." Washington: World Bank.

Blejer, Mario. 1992. "Comments on Sam Morley's Paper." Paper presented at the Brookings Institution and Inter-American Dialogue conference, Washington, July 15–17.

Bourguignon, François. 1991. "Optimal Poverty Reduction, Adjustment, and Growth: An Applied Framework." *World Bank Economic Review* (May).

————. 1993. "Growth, Distribution, and Human Resources: A Cross Country Analysis." Document 93-13 (revised). Paris: EHESS and DELTA.

Chamie, Joseph. 1994. 'Population Databases in Development Analysis." *Journal of Development Economics,* 44 (June), pp. 131–46.

Cardoso, Eliana. 1992. "Poverty and Inequality in Brazil: Comments on Barros, Ricardo, et al., 'Welfare, Inequality, Poverty, and Social Conditions in Brazil in the Last Three Decades.'" Paper presented at the Brooking Institution and Inter-American Dialogue conference, Washington, July 15–17.

Castañeda, Tarsicio. 1992. *Combating Poverty: Innovative Social Reforms in Chile during the 1980s.* San Francisco: International Center for Economic Growth.

Cline, William R. 1992. "Comment on Morley's 'Determinants of Poverty.'" Institute for International Economics (June).

Cornia, Giovanni Andrea, Richard Jolly, and Frances Steward, eds. 1987. *Adjustment with a Human Face*. 2 vols. Oxford University Press.

Dornbusch, Rudiger, and Sebastián Edwards, eds. 1991. *The Macroeconomics of Populism in Latin America*. University of Chicago Press.

Fields, Gary S. 1991. "Growth and Income Distribution." In George Psacharopoulos, ed., *Essays on Poverty, Equity, and Growth*, pp. 1–52. Pergamon Press.

———. 1992. "Comments on 'Income and Inequality Trends in Latin America in the Eighties: A Decomposition Analysis,' by Ariel Fiszbein and George Psacharopoulos." Paper presented at the Brookings Institution and Inter-American Dialogue conference, Washington, July 15–17.

———. 1994. "Data for Measuring Poverty and Inequality Changes in the Developing Countries." *Journal of Development Economics*, 44 (June), pp. 87–102.

Flaño, Nicolás. 1992. "Comments on Dagmar Raczynski and Pilar Romaguera's 'Chile: Poverty, Adjustment, and Social Policies in the 1980s.'" Paper presented at the Brookings Institution and Inter-American Dialogue conference, Washington, July 15–17.

Glewwe, Paul, and Gillette Hall. 1992. "Poverty and Inequality during Unorthodox Adjustment: The Case of Peru, 1985–90," LSM 86. Washington: World Bank.

Graham, Carol. 1994. *Safety Nets, Politics, and the Poor: Transitions to Market Economies*. Brookings.

Heston, Alan. 1994. "A Brief Review of Some Problems in Using National Accounts Data in Level of Output Comparisons and Growth Studies." *Journal of Development Economics*, 44 (June), pp. 29–52.

Instituto Nacional de Estadística Geografía e Informática. 1993. *Magnitud y Evolución de la Pobreza en México, 1984–1992*. México City.

Inter-American Development Bank. 1991. *Economic and Social Progress in Latin America: 1991 Report*. Johns Hopkins University Press.

Kane, Cheikh, and Jacques Morisett. 1993. "Who Would Vote for Inflation in Brazil? An Integrated Framework Approach to Inflation and Income Distribution," Policy research working paper, WPS 1183. Washington: World Bank.

Londono de la Cuesta, J.L. 1990. "Income Distribution During the Structure Transformation: Colombia 1938–88." Ph. D. Thesis, Department of Economics, Harvard University.

Lustig, Nora. 1994a. "Measuring Poverty and Inequality in Latin America: The Emperor Has No Clothes." Brookings (July).

Lustig, Nora. 1994b. "Solidarity as a Strategy of Poverty Alleviation." In W. Cornelius, A. Craig, and J. Fox, eds., *Transforming State-Society Relations in Mexico: The National Solidarity Strategy*, pp. 79–98, Center for U.S.-Mexican Studies, University of California, San Diego.

Lustig, Nora, and Ann Mitchell. 1994c. "Poverty in Times of Austerity: Mexico in the 1980s." Paper presented at the XIII Latin American Meetings of the Econometric Society, Caracas, Venezuela, August 2–5, 1994.

Marfán, Manuel, and Barry Bosworth. 1994. "Saving, Investment, and Economic

Growth." In Barry Bosworth, Rudiger Dornbusch, and Raúl Loban, eds., *The Chilean Economy: Policy Lessons and Challenges.* Brookings.

Musgrove, Philip. 1992. "Comments on 'Social Policy and Economic Adjustment in Peru' by Adolfo Figueroa." Paper presented at the Brookings Institution and Inter-American Dialogue conference. Washington, (July 16–17.)

Pessino, Carola. 1993. "From Aggregate Shocks to Labor Market Adjustments: Shifting of Wage Profiles under Hyperinflation in Argentina." Centro de Estudios Macroeconómicos de Argentina 95 (December).

Psacharopoulos, George, and others. 1993. "Poverty and Income Distribution in Latin America: The Story of the 1980s." Latin America and the Caribbean Technical Department Regional Studies Program Report 27. Washington: World Bank.

Ravallion, Martin, Guarav Datt, and Dominique van de Walle. 1991. "Quantifying Absolute Poverty in the Developing World." *Review of Income and Wealth* 37 (December).

Rodrik, Dani. 1994. "King Kong Meets Godzilla: The World Bank and the East Asian Miracle." In Catherine Gwin and Albert Fishlow, eds., *Miracle or Design? Lessons from the East Asian Experience* (pp. 13–54). Washington: Overseas Development Council.

Sachs, Jeffrey. 1989. "Social Conflict and Populist Policies in Latin America." NBER working paper 2897. Cambridge, Mass.: National Bureau of Economic Research.

Srinivasan, T.N., 1994. "Data Base for Development Analysis: An Overview." *Journal of Development Economics,* 44 (June), pp. 3–28.

Sturzenegger, Federico. 1992. "Inflation and Social Welfare in a Model with Endogenous Financial Adaptation," NBER working paper 4103. Cambridge, Mass.: National Bureau of Economic Research.

World Bank. 1990. "Argentina: Reforms for Price Stability and Growth." Washington.

———. 1993. *Latin America and the Caribbean: A Decade After the Debt Crisis.* Washington.

———. 1994. "Poverty Alleviation and Social Investment Funds: The Latin American Experience." LA2HR. Washington (May).

———. Annual. *World Development Report.* Washington.

CHAPTER TWO

Structural Adjustment and Determinants of Poverty in Latin America

Samuel A. Morley

INCOME distribution and poverty have always been the dark side of development in Latin America. According to one 1980 estimate, 35 percent of the population, or 130 million people, were still below the poverty line after thirty unprecedented years of rapid economic growth.[1] The harsh structural adjustments of the 1980s have significantly worsened the poverty problem. Casual evidence from virtually every country confirms the deterioration of living standards and the widening inequality of the past decade.

This chapter first establishes a link among macroconditions, poverty, and inequality, and then, using case study evidence, examines possible explanations for differences among the poverty records of various Latin American countries during the adjustment period. The first section presents all the available evidence on poverty and inequality during the 1980s. The second section includes findings on poverty decompositions and wage differentials from case studies of Argentina, Costa Rica, and Venezuela. The third suggests structural explanations for why Costa Rica, Colombia, and Paraguay were able to reduce

The author thanks William Cline, Martin Ravallion, and Mario Blejer for their useful comments.
1. CEPAL (1990, p. 62).

poverty in spite of slow growth, while countries such as Argentina and Venezuela were not. A final section draws conclusions based on both macroeconomic and case study evidence.

The Distribution of Income

Latin America has always had a relatively unequal distribution of income.[2]
It is thus natural to ask what happened to income distribution during the adjustment process of the 1980s. My answer draws heavily on an analysis of
household surveys in ten countries recently completed by George Psacharopoulos and others, and on other sources for years and countries not available
to this study.[3] Table 2-1 displays the Gini coefficient estimates from these various studies. Wherever possible these coefficients are based on family income
from all sources per family member and on nationwide data.[4] However, data
for Argentina, Bolivia, Colombia, Paraguay, and Uruguay cover only urban or
metropolitan areas.

The study by Psacharopoulos and others includes eight countries with
observations made at the beginning and end of the decade. Of those eight,
Argentina, Brazil, Panama, and Venezuela show an increase; Colombia,
Paraguay, and Uruguay show a reduction. Costa Rica also shows a reduction
in inequality, but this result is controversial.[5] Trends in inequality appear to
have been significantly influenced by trends in per capita income. In three of
the four countries with an increase in inequality during the 1980s, per capita
income decreased during the decade. This was the case in Argentina, Panama,
and Venezuela. Brazil, by contrast, had greater inequality and higher per
capita income by the end of the decade. Countries such as Colombia and

2. Around 1980 the average Gini coefficient of seven Latin countries for which national
household surveys are available was .52, whereas the average Gini for six Asian countries for the
early 1970s was only .36. For Latin America see Psacharopoulos and others (1992, p. 16). The
Asian countries are Sri Lanka, India, Korea, Taiwan, Pakistan, and the Philippines, and the data
for author's calculations come from Fields (1980, pp. 91, 197, 205, 221, 231); and Chenery (1974,
p. 253). This section draws heavily on Morley (1992c).

3. See Psacharopoulos and others (1993).

4. Those not based on income per family member are Hoffman (1991) for Brazil, Lustig
(1990b) for Mexico, and CEPAL (1990) for Venezuela, all of which are based on household
income.

5. For Costa Rica, sources disagree about the direction of change. A CEPAL study found an
increase in income inequality during 1981–88 in urban areas. See Altimir (1992, table 4). A recent
Inter-American Development Bank study concluded that "income is more equitably distributed in
1990 than it was in 1980, although only marginally so." See IDB (1992, p. 205). This seems a reasonable inference.

Table 2-1. *Income Inequality in Selected Latin American Countries, 1979–90*
Gini coefficient[a]

Country and study	1979	1980	1981	1982	1983	1984	1985	1986	1987	1988	1989	1990
Argentina[b]												
Psacharopoulos		0.41									0.48	
Fiszbein		0.40	0.43	0.40	0.40		0.40		0.43	0.45		
Bolivia[c]												
Psacharopoulos								0.52			0.52	
Brazil												
Barros and others	0.59						0.59	0.59	0.60	0.61	0.63	0.61
Psacharopoulos	0.59				0.59	0.59	0.59				0.63	
Hoffman[d]	0.59								0.60		0.62	
Chile												
Mujica and Harrañaga[e]	0.52	0.53	0.52	0.54	0.54	0.56	0.53	0.54	0.53			
Altimir									0.47			0.46
Colombia												
Altimir[f]		0.48						0.47				
Altimir[g]		0.47						0.45				
Psacharopoulos[c]		0.58									0.53	
Costa Rica												
Gindling and Berry		0.40	0.40	0.42	0.38	0.38	0.37	0.36	0.42	0.42		
Sauma and Trejos					0.42			0.42				
Psacharopoulos			0.48								0.46	

Country / Source						
Guatemala						
Psacharopoulos	0.48					0.59
World Bank			0.58	0.53		
Mexico						
Psacharopoulos		0.51				0.55
Lustig[d]		0.44				
Panama						
Psacharopoulos	0.49					0.56
Paraguay[h]						
Psacharopoulos		0.45				0.40
Peru						
Psacharopoulos[i]		0.43				0.44
GRADE[j]	0.34	0.39	0.40	0.39		0.41
Uruguay[c]						
Psacharopoulos	0.44					0.42
Venezuela						
Marquez and others	0.40		0.44	0.46		0.44
CEPAL[d]	0.39		0.42			
Psacharopoulos	0.43					0.44

Source: Psacharopoulos and others (1993, table 2.2).
a. Coefficients represent the distribution of household income per capita except where otherwise indicated.
b. Greater Buenos Aires area.
c. Urban areas.
d. Coefficients represent the distribution of household income.
e. Greater Santiago area.
f. Bogotá area.
g. Urban areas other than Bogotá.
h. Asunción area.
i. 1985 figure based on national expenditure survey, and 1990 figure based on Lima expenditure survey.
j. Lima area.

Paraguay enjoying greater equality in 1989 tended to have a higher per capita income or were in a recovery like Uruguay. Table 2-2 shows GDP per capita in constant 1988 U.S. dollars for the period under discussion.

According to the study by Psacharopoulos and others, in Costa Rica and Uruguay inequality decreased despite constant or declining per capita income, while in Brazil the opposite happened. The difference between these cases is that in 1989 Costa Rica and Uruguay were both in extended recovery phases after severe recessions earlier in the decade. Perhaps they were beginning to enjoy the benefits of the painful adjustments they both made between 1980 and 1985. Brazil, in contrast, was struggling to control its inflation and had essentially zero per capita income growth since 1986. Even so, the boom in Brazil between 1983 and 1986 was so strong that in 1989 per capita income still exceeded its 1979 level.

The link between recession and inequality appears also in Colombia, Argentina, and Panama. Colombia did not have a recession during the 1980s and was growing, albeit slowly, in 1989. Argentina and Panama were both in severe recession. Thus not only the level, but also the rate of change, of per capita income during the survey period has an effect on the level of inequality. Recessions, defined as periods of stagnating or declining per capita income, were inequitable in that the burden of falling incomes was especially heavy for those at the bottom of the income ladder. Recoveries had the opposite effect.

Evidence in table 2-2 from sources other than the study by Psacharopoulos and others permits a better idea of the link between income distribution and the business cycle. The data in table 2-1 and 2-2 strongly confirm the relationship between inequality and per capita income. In most cases with comparable observations, falling per capita income was accompanied by increased inequality, while inequality decreased when per capita income increased. Table 2-3 categorizes each country according to trends in per capita income and inequality, illustrating the inverse relationship. For observations spanning the decade, the table compares the state of the economy in 1989 with what occurred in earlier years, rather than comparing income levels in the end years alone. Thus Uruguay represents a recovery even though its per capita income declined between 1981 and 1989, because its economy hit its trough in 1984 and subsequently grew. Conversely, Brazil is classified as a recession even though per capita income increased between 1979 and 1989, because its economy peaked in 1987 and then entered a period of decline.

Inequality appears to be countercyclical, increasing in recession and decreasing in recovery. This is true for twenty-one of twenty-six cases in table 2-3.

Table 2-2. *GDP per Capita, Selected Latin American Countries, 1979-90*

Constant 1988 U.S. dollars

Country	1979	1980	1981	1982	1983	1984	1985	1986	1987	1988	1989	1990
Argentina	3,608	3,579	3,249	2,999	3,038	3,052	2,869	2,998	3,027	2,897	2,715	2,672
Bolivia	1,197	1,173	1,152	1,069	986	972	945	902	901	902	898	892
Brazil	2,199	2,314	2,193	2,173	2,048	2,108	2,225	2,349	2,377	2,326	2,355	2,216
Chile	2,200	2,329	2,414	2,046	1,961	2,040	2,042	2,120	2,207	2,330	2,520	2,527
Colombia	1,211	1,236	1,236	1,224	1,220	1,240	1,258	1,313	1,355	1,386	1,404	1,425
Costa Rica	1,779	1,747	1,658	1,517	1,513	1,584	1,551	1,590	1,618	1,625	1,668	1,685
Ecuador	1,354	1,378	1,391	1,370	1,276	1,281	1,303	1,303	1,221	1,284	1,262	1,260
Guatemala	1,088	1,097	1,074	1,008	955	933	902	877	883	891	900	901
Honduras	858	855	835	788	754	757	765	748	768	780	785	762
Mexico	2,312	2,436	2,586	2,498	2,325	2,354	2,364	2,215	2,203	2,183	2,212	2,266
Panama	2,053	2,267	2,317	2,374	2,315	2,259	2,317	2,352	2,353	1,960	1,905	1,961
Paraguay	1,435	1,560	1,642	1,572	1,476	1,476	1,489	1,441	1,461	1,511	1,554	1,557
Peru	1,872	1,889	1,933	1,883	1,587	1,621	1,610	1,752	1,891	1,685	1,439	1,350
Uruguay	2,694	2,835	2,867	2,593	2,422	2,373	2,393	2,584	2,774	2,755	2,754	2,760
Venezuela	4,294	4,112	3,969	3,881	3,555	3,343	3,323	3,432	3,491	3,611	3,218	3,295
Latin America	2,188	2,259	2,211	2,138	2,021	2,041	2,066	2,110	2,134	2,101	2,078	2,034

Sources: Inter-American Development Bank, *Economic and Social Progress Report* (1992, table B-2). Figures before 1982 are from Economic Commission for Latin America (1986, 1987).

Table 2-3. *Income Inequality and the Business Cycle in Selected Latin American Countries, Selected Periods, 1979–90*

Income distribution	Recession[a]	Recovery[a]
More equal or same	Argentina 1981–82 (+)[b]	Brazil 1983–86 (–)
	Argentina 1982–85 (+)	Chile 1983–87 (–)
	Brazil 1979–83	Chile 1987–90 (+)
		Colombia 1980–89 (+)
		Costa Rica 1983–86 (+)
		Costa Rica 1981–89 (+)
		Uruguay 1981–89 (–)
		Venezuela 1989–90 (+)
Less equal	Argentina 1980–89 (–)	Chile 1979–87 (–)
	Bolivia 1986–90 (+)	Guatemala 1986–89 (–)
	Brazil 1986–89 (–)	
	Brazil 1979–89 (–)	
	Chile 1980–83 (–)	
	Costa Rica 1980–82 (–)	
	Guatemala 1981–86 (–)	
	Mexico 1984–89 (–)	
	Panama 1979–89	
	Peru 1981–84 (–)	
	Peru 1984–89 (–)	
	Venezuela 1981–85 (+)	
	Venezuela 1981–89 (–)	

Sources: See tables 2-1 and 2-2. Real wage data are from Edwards (1991, table 2); and Inter-American Development Bank (1993, pp. 58, 70, 152, 180).

a. Recession is defined as having a lower per capita income in the end year. Recovery is defined as the opposite. Although some data in table 2-1 is not for the country as a whole, the assumption is that changes in per capita income in urban or metropolitan areas reflect changes in national per capita income.

b. The signs that follow each entry reflect the direction of change in the real minimum wage in each period. No sign means no change

What explains this relationship? My hypothesis is that recession in Latin America created severe downward pressure on wages and employment for those at the bottom of the income pyramid. With insignificant levels of unemployment insurance available, workers in the formal sector faced severe real wage reductions or unemployment unless they sought work in the informal sector. For new labor market entrants, the choices were equally stark. This group accounted for the bulk of rising unemployment. For new entrants who found jobs, the evidence on wages suggests an increase in the age differential in most countries for which such statistics have been calculated.[6]

6. See Morley and Alvarez (1992a, 1992b, 1992c) and Morley (1992b) for evidence from Costa Rica, Colombia, Venezuela, and Argentina on changes in age differentials during the 1980s.

What Is the Poverty Record?

The great difficulty with poverty estimates is achieving comparability across countries or over time. Yet comparability is crucial if one wishes to draw policy conclusions or analyze causal relationships that affect poverty. There is now a large literature on alternative measures of poverty.[7] For simplicity, the measure used here is the poverty head count ratio, which is defined as the proportion of people or households below a certain income level called the poverty line. Defining this line is obviously a key problem in estimating the amount of poverty in a country. The typical procedure is to set the line with reference to the cost of a minimum basket of goods. In Latin America that is generally defined to be twice the cost of the food component of this basket. Household consumption surveys are used to determine the cost of food containing nutritional minimums of calories and protein.[8] Poverty lines in nominal local currency for other years are then obtained by adjusting for increases in the overall cost of living, the price of food, or a special price index for the poor. It is important to note that this procedure is arbitrary and that it has significant implications on the measurement of poverty. In low-income countries a large part of the population is likely to have incomes close to the poverty line. Small variations in the definition of that line thus significantly affect the number who are defined as poor.

To complicate the problem of comparability, the income measures on which poverty indexes are based differ widely across countries. Some countries report only labor earnings, while others report both earned and nonearned income. Virtually none report imputed rent on owner-occupied housing or income in kind, which are surely important in rural areas, where people grow much of their own food.[9] Furthermore, there are serious problems of underreporting of income.[10] With all these difficulties, of what use are comparisons such as those in this chapter? While it is difficult to determine the level of poverty with any certainty, one can use observations at different points in time

7. See Ravallion (1992) and Foster (1984).

8. See CEPAL (1990) for a careful discussion of how poverty lines were constructed for Latin America.

9. See Psacharopoulos and others (1992, pp. 10, 49–50, annex 2, annex 9).

10. Income underreporting can be observed, for example, by comparing the average level of income reported in the survey with the level implied by the national accounts for the comparable earnings category. See CEPAL (1990, pp. 31–35) for a detailed discussion of the correction procedure.

to determine trends in poverty, provided that the measures being compared are constructed with a common methodology and a constant poverty line.

Poverty levels are very sensitive to where one sets the poverty line. This appears to be much less true of changes in poverty, as the case of Costa Rica illustrates. The study by Morley and Alvarez summarized in table 2-4 estimated that 25.4 percent of Costa Rican households were in poverty in 1981. If one were to raise the poverty line by 20 percent, the poverty estimate would increase about 25 percent, illustrating the sensitivity of the measure to the level of the poverty line. However, had the same measurement error been made in both 1981 and 1989, there would have been virtually no change in the estimate of the change in the incidence of poverty, which would have fallen 59 percent rather than 60 percent. Changes in poverty over time are thus relatively less sensitive to where the poverty line is set than they are to the level of poverty at any one point in time. This feature of the poverty indexes is important. It implies that while it probably is difficult to measure poverty accurately at one point in time, trends over time in the same country can be compared, provided the estimates use the same methodology.

Table 2-4 presents internally consistent measures of poverty across a range of countries. Each row in the table shows the part of the population below the poverty line for different years. Because one cannot be sure of the consistency of estimates by different authors with regard to either the poverty line or the treatment of underreporting, each series is displayed separately. For the reasons given earlier, one should not pay too much attention to the variation among series either within the same country or between countries. Rather one should use the data to examine the likely direction of changes in poverty over time within each country.

Of particular interest are the effects of growth and adjustment on the level of poverty. The data in table 2-4 suggest that sustained economic growth, measured by the change in per capita income, is a potent force for poverty reduction. This is true for years before and during the 1980s, especially in Brazil, Colombia, Mexico, and Costa Rica.[11] In all four countries, rapid economic growth substantially reduced poverty. In Costa Rica, for example, per

11. This coincides with the findings of Fields (1991) for a worldwide sample of countries. My conclusions are more optimistic than those of Altimir (1992b), who uses CEPAL data that show a far smaller reduction in poverty during the 1970s than do the studies used here. That is because between 1970 and 1980 CEPAL changed the composition of its minimum food basket, thereby increasing its cost. I have compared the 1970 and 1980 poverty lines used by CEPAL. In most cases the 1980 lines rise by more than twice as much as the CPI, which raises the 1980 poverty estimates and lowers the amount of poverty reduction that took place over the 1970s. See Altimir (n.d.).

capita income grew more than 30 percent between 1961 and 1971, and poverty was cut in half. By 1977 income had grown an additional 22 percent, and the poverty level was cut in half again.[12] Even in Brazil, perhaps the quintessential example of inequitable growth, after a 150 percent rise in per capita income between 1960 and 1980, poverty fell by more than 50 percent.[13]

The inverse relationship between growth and poverty holds in countries that did not grow, such as Chile between 1969 and 1976, or that grew very slowly, such as Argentina between 1970 and 1980. In both cases poverty either remained constant or increased.[14] One conclusion to draw from this is that growth in Latin America was not immiserizing. This is not to say that growth alone is the most rapid, effective, or desirable method of poverty alleviation. But if rapid enough, growth will significantly reduce poverty.

Rapid economic growth, particularly in the urban sector, was Latin America's solution to the potentially explosive issues of poverty and social injustice. Thirty years ago the bulk of the poor were in the countryside, with little land or education. Land reform, in most cases, was not politically feasible, and education was expensive. As a strategy to address social problems, rapid urban growth was politically feasible and offered an escape to the urban sector for the rural poor. It was a solution that neatly stood Turner's hypothesis on its head.[15] Turner argued that the United States avoided social unrest because the urban poor could migrate to the frontier, where they established homesteads. But in Latin America, instead of the frontier's being the safety valve for the urban poor, the urban economy was a safety valve for the landless rural poor.

Rapid urban growth presented three problems. First, the growth was exceedingly inequitable, as the poor benefited far less than did those of higher socioeconomic standing. Second, the solution did not work well in the small agricultural economies of Central America, which were unable to generate strong urban growth, in part due to the absence of a manufacturing export base. Finally, and most important, the rate of growth required to reduce poverty significantly was not sustainable after 1980, when the debt crisis mounted. Thus, while rapid growth may reduce poverty, in the difficult cir-

12. Fields (1980, table 5.7); and Fait and Trejos (1990). Fields's figures are not strictly comparable to those of Fait and Trejos because the authors use different poverty lines. Per capita income figures are from World Bank (1983).

13. World Bank (1990, table 3.2). Per capita income figure is from World Bank (1983, pp. 22–23).

14. CEPAL (1990, p. 62) estimated that poverty in Argentina rose from 8 percent to 9 percent between 1970 and 1980. For Chile there is no national estimate, but PREALC (1990b, p. 5), estimated that poverty in the Santiago area rose from 29 to 57 percent between 1969 and 1976.

15. Turner (1920).

Table 2-4. *Proportion of Individuals or Households with Incomes below the Poverty Line, Selected Latin American Countries, 1977–91*

Percent

Country and study[a]	1977	1978	1979	1980	1981	1982	1983	1984	1985	1986	1987	1988	1989	1990	1991
Argentina[b]															
INDEC				10.1		28.0			20.6		25.2	27.9			
Morley and Alvarez				6.3						10.9			21.5		
CEPAL				6.0						11.0					
Psacharopoulos				3.0									6.4		
Brazil															
Fox and Morley					46.0		52.0								
Psacharopoulos			34.1							31.0			40.0		
Colombia															
CEPAL				42.0						42.0					
Londono		29.0										25.0			
Morley[c]				34.0						33.0			34.0		
Psacharopoulos[c]				13.0									8.0		
Costa Rica															
Ginding and Berry[d]				48.0	62.0	78.0	69.0	58.0	63.0	52.0	45.0				
Morley and Alvarez					25.4					27.0					
CEPAL					24.0							27.0	10.2		
Psacharopoulos					09.9								3.5		
Psacharopoulos[e]					16.7								3.2		
Chile															
PREALC[b, d, f]			36.0	40.3		31.2		48.5	45.4	50.9	48.6				
CEPAL[c]											38.0			35.0	
CEPAL[c]											37.0			34.0	
Guatemala															
CEPAL[c]				47.0						60.0					
CEPAL[e]				84.0						80.0					
Psacharopoulos[c]										48.7			50.9		
Psacharopoulos[e]										71.8			76.5		
Mexico															
CEPAL	40.0							37.0							
Psacharopoulos								16.6					22.6		

Panama					
CEPAL[c]	36.0	36.0			
CEPAL[e]	50.0	52.0			
Psacharopoulos[c]	26.0			25.9	
Psacharopoulos[e]	33.0			36.8	
Paraguay[g]					
Psacharopoulos	13.1				7.6
Peru					
CEPAL	53.0	60.0			
Uruguay					
Altimir[c,f]	9.0	14.0		10.0	
Altimir[e,f]	21.0	23.0		23.0	
Psacharopoulos[c]	6.2			5.3	
Venezuela					
CEPAL[c]	22.0	33.0		48.2	
CEPAL[e]	43.0	42.0		41.3	
CEPAL	25.0	32.0		10.8	
Morley and Alvarez	24.0	29.0		23.5	
Marquez	18.0	28.4	31.8		34.6
Psacharopoulos[c]	2.5				
Psacharopoulos[e]	9.0				
Psacharopoulos	4.0			12.9	

Sources: All references to CEPAL refer to CEPAL (1990). References to Psacharopoulos refer to Psacharopoulos and others (1993). Additional sources for specific countries include: *Argentina,* INDEC (1990); Morley and Alvarez (1992c); *Brazil,* Fox and Morley (1991b); IDB refers to Inter-American Development Bank (1993), p. 233. *Colombia,* Londono (1990). *Chile,* PREALC (1990b); CEPAL (n.d.). *Costa Rica,* Gindling and Berry (forthcoming); Morley and Alvarez (1992a). *Paraguay,* unpublished worksheet calculations by the World Bank based on 1983 and 1990 household surveys. *Uruguay,* Altimir (1992a). *Venezuela,* Morley and Alvarez (1992b); Marquez (n.d.).

a. The Psacharopoulos entries use a uniform poverty line of $60 per month per household member, based on 1985 purchasing power parity dollars. All other poverty lines are country specific, based on the cost of a minimum subsistence basket of food. All estimates are based on income adjusted for underreporting and represent the proportion of individuals in poverty, except where otherwise noted.

b. Metropolitan areas.

c. Urban areas.

d. Not adjusted for underreporting.

e. Rural areas.

f. Proportion of households in poverty.

g. Asunción area.

cumstances following the debt crisis, more than mere trickle-down effects will be required to make further progress in reducing poverty, especially in the long run.

While growth, if rapid enough, reduces the level of poverty, the style of growth also matters. Brazil and Mexico had far less equitable growth than did Costa Rica or Colombia. In Brazil per capita income had to grow 141 percent between 1960 and 1980 to reduce poverty from 50 percent to 21 percent of households. Mexico required 82 percent growth to cut poverty in half between 1963 and 1984. Colombia and Costa Rica achieved almost the same percentage reductions in poverty during the 1970s with far lower rates of growth. Per capita income grew 27 percent in Colombia between 1971 and 1978 and 36 percent in Costa Rica between 1971 and 1977.[16]

Both poverty and inequality are strongly procyclical. Both increased during the adjustment recessions of the 1980s and both decreased, often quite sharply, during periods of recovery. As a check on the validity of this proposition, I have collected all available information for both rural and urban sectors since 1980 in an attempt to define all intervals of recession or recovery.[17] A recession implies at least two years of falling per capita income. With all other observations classified as recoveries, there are fifty-eight periods of recession in all. (In some countries there are multiple observations for the same interval.) In fifty-four of those fifty-eight cases, poverty increased. Since 1980 there have been twenty-eight periods of recovery. In twenty of those intervals poverty decreased, in two cases there was no change, and in the remaining six poverty increased.[18] The evidence thus supports the not very surprising proposition that poverty is sensitive to the level of aggregate per capita income.[19]

---

16. For Mexico, Hernandez-Laos (1990) estimated that extreme poverty fell from 69.5 percent to 26.1 percent between 1963 and 1984. For Costa Rica, the World Bank (1990, pp. 43, 45) calculated the decline in the number of individuals with household income of less than $80 a month in 1985 purchasing power parity dollars. For Colombia, see Londono de la Cuesta (1990, p. 9).

17. For more information, see the previous version of this paper prepared for the conference Confronting the Challenge of Poverty and Inequality in Latin America, Brookings Institution, Washington, July 16–17, 1992 (Morley, 1992d).

18. The six cases were the metropolitan areas of Colombia (1980–86), Argentina (1974–80 and 1985–88), Chile (1984–86), the urban sector of Colombia (1986–89), and Colombia (1984–88).

19. In a previous version of this paper prepared for the conference Confronting the Challenge of Poverty and Inequality in Latin America, Brookings Institution, Washington, July 16–17, 1992, I used a regression model of the head count ratio to confirm the negative relationship between growth and poverty. My estimate of the income elasticity of poverty was a bit larger than –2.0, which implies that poverty rises by 2 percent for each 1 percent decline in the growth rate of income. See Morley (1992c).

The evidence also suggests that the elasticity of the poverty index with respect to the level of income is greater over short-run cycles than long-run cycles. Almost every case where data are available for the relevant time period supports this claim, including recoveries in Costa Rica after 1982, Brazil between 1983 and 1986, and Chile between 1976 and 1982. (See table 2-2 for data on trends in per capita income.)[20] In all three cases recovery caused a very rapid reduction in poverty.

Even more obvious is the impact of recession on the level of poverty. The data are absolutely convincing on this score. Consider Argentina after 1980. In Greater Buenos Aires, poverty more than tripled in response to a 26 percent decline in real per capita income between 1980 and 1989.[21] In Venezuela a decline of 19 percent in per capita income between 1981 and 1989 led to a 100 percent increase in poverty. The same pattern appears in Costa Rica between 1979 and 1982, Brazil between 1981 and 1983, Chile between 1969 and 1976, Chile between 1982 and 1985, and Guatemala between 1980 and 1986.

Many studies have examined the relationship between adjustment policies and the rise in poverty during the 1980s in Latin America. There is strong evidence to support the claim that in the 1980s there was a large increase in poverty and inequality. But one has to be careful in drawing the conclusion that this was the result of adjustment programs. The problem is that there is no legitimate counterfactual with which to compare the postadjustment observations. Certainly data from 1980 do not serve that purpose. Most Latin American economies at that time had severe balance of payments and fiscal deficits. They were then financing these deficits with capital inflows, which could not have continued indefinitely. The relative prosperity of 1980 was in part borrowed from the future. When one says that the adjustment process caused the observed changes in poverty between 1980 and 1989, one implicitly assumes that the conditions of 1980 would have continued had it not been for the adjustment. That assumption is probably not warranted.

Three Case Studies of Adjustment

It is useful to take a more careful look at three case studies of the effects of the adjustment process on the poor. Argentina and Venezuela suffered through

20. For per capita income trends in Chile, see World Bank, *World Tables 1992* (Johns Hopkins University Press, 1992, pp. 180–81).

21. See Morley and Alvarez (1992c, p. 1).

an extended period of adjustment in the 1980s. Per capita income fell by 25 percent in the former and 20 percent in the latter between 1980 and 1990 (see table 2-2). This decline in income has imposed a high cost on the poor. Costa Rica, the third case, is the only country to have gone through both a phase of short-run adjustment (between 1980 and 1982), during which per capita income fell by 13 percent, and a subsequent recovery (between 1983 and 1989), during which per capita income grew by 10 percent. Thus Costa Rica allows comparison of the long-run benefits of adjustment and the short-run costs of recession.

Consider first the effects of the recession that accompanied adjustment in Venezuela between 1981 and 1989 and in Argentina between 1980 and 1989. Table 2-5 documents the dramatic rise in poverty caused by the recession across different groups of the population. For simplicity the poverty measure used here is the head count ratio, which essentially represents the proportion of individuals or households that are poor. The head count ratio has two advantages: it is the most widely used measure of poverty, and it can be decomposed to show both who the poor are and which subgroups contributed most to changes in poverty over time.[22] The poverty lines in table 2-5 were directly drawn from the CEPAL poverty study, with an adjustment for changes in the cost of living. The base year index for each country also parallels those found in the CEPAL study.[23]

Other columns in table 2-5 show the percentage of the poor coming from different groups. These fractions indicate who the poor are and quantify the contributions of different groups to the poverty population. In Argentina, for example, 33.6 percent of illiterates were below the poverty line in 1980, and illiterates comprised 36.5 percent of the population living in poverty. By 1989 the incidence of poverty in this group had risen to 51.4 percent, but that group comprised only 10.8 percent of the poor. This shift implies that more populous subgroups in the labor force, such as grade school graduates, became poor during the recession. The larger groups swamped the increase in poverty incidence among the illiterate. In Venezuela also the share of illiterates in the poverty population fell sharply between 1981 and 1989, even though the incidence of poverty within that group almost doubled. Illiterates were concen-

22. The deficiencies in the head count ratio, in particular its insensitivity to transfers among the poor, are well known. See Ravallion (1992) and Foster (1984) for surveys of alternative measures. In their country study, Psacharopoulos and others (1993) used measures for Venezuela, Argentina, and Costa Rica that put more weight on the very poor. However, these alternatives produce roughly the same conclusions as the head count ratio about the composition of and changes in poverty. For a description of the decomposition methodology, see Morley and Alvarez (1992c).
23. CEPAL (1990).

Table 2-5. *Poverty in Argentina and Venezuela, by Group, Selected Years, 1980–89*

Percent

	Argentina				Venezuela			
	Poverty head count ratio[a]		Proportion of all poor in group		Poverty head count ratio[a]		Proportion of all poor in group	
Category	1980	1989	1980	1989	1981	1989	1981	1989
Level of educational achievement								
Illiterate	33.6	51.4	36.5	10.8	43.6	70.3	31.1	18.6
Grade school	5.3	27.0	50.8	69.7	24.3	55.1	53.8	55.0
High school	3.0	13.3	10.9	16.9	9.6	35.5	7.7	19.8
University	1.2	4.3	1.8	2.2	2.1	11.7	5.0	2.1
Total[b]	...	...	100.0	100.0	...	...	100.0	100.0
Gender								
Male	6.6	21.9	91.9	86.6	22.7	47.1	79.7	82.0
Female	4.0	19.1	8.1	13.4	30.3	53.0	20.8	18.0
Urban labor market segment								
Formal	8.3	20.1	66.6	43.9	15.3	36.4	37.4	42.7
Informal	4.3	23.5	18.1	32.7	18.4	48.5	36.5	33.7
Unemployed	6.8	47.5	0.7	5.4	56.7	76.6	4.8	5.6
Inactive	4.1	18.8	14.5	18.0	28.6	56.0	21.2	18.0
Economic sector								
Agriculture	...	58.9	...	0.3	48.0	68.3	27.7	19.2
Industry	4.6	20.3	17.8	19.5	18.3	41.1	10.0	10.8
Construction	10.1	31.4	16.5	12.1	19.0	48.9	7.4	7.5
Commerce	2.8	18.8	5.4	11.5	17.7	44.1	11.5	15.2
Services	3.7	21.8	7.4	17.5	20.5	40.2	16.5	16.0
Transportation	4.1	18.3	4.1	7.6	12.8	41.0	4.6	6.5
Other	39.4	63.2	32.6	6.0	14.8	63.4	...	0.1
Unemployed	6.8	47.5	0.7	5.4	...	...	...	...
Total[b]	...	...	100.0	100.0	...	...	100.0	100.0
Entire population	6.3	21.5	...	...	24.0	48.2	...	...

Sources: Morley and Alvarez (1992b and 1992c).
a. Proportion of group with income below the poverty line.
b. Totals may not add to 100 percent because of rounding.

trated in the rural sector. Their share of total poverty fell because of dramatic increases in poverty among better educated, urban workers.

In terms of the effect of recession, table 2-5 shows dramatic increases in poverty in both countries. Adjustment clearly imposed a very heavy short-run cost on those at the bottom of the income pyramid. Poverty was not a problem confined to those who were either unemployed or retired. In both countries the incidence of poverty increased dramatically in both groups, but table 2-5 clearly shows that most of the poor worked. In 1989 workers comprised about 76 percent of the poor in Argentina and in Venezuela, and not all worked in the informal sector. Almost half of the urban poor in Argentina worked in the formal sector in 1989, and only a slightly smaller fraction did the same in Venezuela. The evidence thus suggests that the recessions were severe enough to squeeze all parts of the labor market and to prevent formal sector firms from paying an adequate wage to many employees. It is also clear that the effects of recession were not confined to the bottom of the education pyramid in the urban sector. In Argentina, where the data are exclusively from Buenos Aires (excluding the federal capital), the incidence of poverty rose so fast among graduates of grade school and high school that it swamped the increase in poverty among illiterates.

The economic crisis also affected wage differentials and the distribution of household earnings. Evidence on these issues appears in table 2-6, which includes data from Argentina in 1986 because of differences in the adjustment process between the first and second halves of the decade. The data refer to earnings per worker, not household income per capita. First, table 2-6 shows a significant rise in earnings inequality in Argentina and Venezuela, since the decline in real wages (relative to the base year) is far greater in lower than in higher income deciles.

Table 2-6 also shows an increase in the age differential of earnings. Recessions generally impose heavy costs on new entrants to the labor force because of the scarcity of entry-level jobs in a contracting economy. Argentina and Venezuela followed this pattern, as new entrants were forced to take low-paying jobs or to endure unemployment. The widening in the age differential was more pronounced in Argentina than in Venezuela. There is a curious and somewhat unexpected difference between the two countries with respect to changes in the education or skill differential. It widened slightly in Argentina: between 1980 and 1989 the real wage fell by 51 percent for illiterates and by 49 percent for university graduates. In Venezuela this differential narrowed, as the wage for illiterates fell by only 53 percent, compared to 59 percent for college graduates.

In developing countries one might expect this differential to be procyclical, given a very elastic supply of low-skill labor available at a subsistence minimum wage. Under those conditions, a rise in demand increases the wages of skilled labor and the employment of unskilled labor. This logic leads one to expect a narrowing of the differential during recessions. In developed countries, by contrast, the supply of unskilled labor is less elastic than that of skilled labor, at least in the short run. These conditions tend to make the differ-

Table 2-6. *Real Earnings in Selected Countries, by Group, 1986, 1989*
Index[a]

Category	Argentina (metropolitan)		Venezuela (1989)		Costa Rica (1989)	
	1986	1989	Urban	Total	Urban	Total
Income Deciles						
1st	.93	.28	.05	.09	1.65	1.96
2d	.97	.35	.27	.27	1.38	1.66
3d	.96	.35	.35	.36	1.30	1.51
4th	.97	.33	.36	.36	1.28	1.42
5th	.94	.32	.37	.38	1.30	1.40
6th	.91	.31	.39	.39	1.30	1.39
7th	.92	.31	.40	.40	1.28	1.42
8th	.93	.33	.41	.41	1.27	1.41
9th	.85	.33	.41	.42	1.30	1.36
10th	.88	.41	.47	.46	1.39	1.43
Age						
Younger than 16	.89	.33	.44	.45	2.82	3.23
16–20	.87	.44	.51	.50	1.98	2.23
21–25	.92	.46	.46	.46	1.27	1.37
26–30	.91	.51	.44	.45	1.17	1.21
31–35	.95	.51	.42	.43	1.27	1.33
36–40	1.09	.54	.44	.45	1.33	1.40
41–45	.92	.51	.46	.47	1.42	1.41
46–50	.86	.55	.48	.48	1.10	1.26
51–55	.77	.45	.50	.50	1.52	1.50
56–60	.83	.48	.47	.48	1.37	1.42
61–65	.73	.52	.49	.50	.84	1.11
66 and older	.78	.46	.51	.51	.85	1.06
Level of educational achievement						
Illiterate	1.01	.49	.47	.47	n.a.	1.32
Grade school	.93	.47	.44	.44	n.a.	1.49
High school	.89	.48	.46	.46	n.a.	1.34
University	.85	.51	.41	.41	n.a.	1.28

Sources: Morley and Alvarez (1992a, tables 7a, 7b, 7c; 1992b, tables 7a, 7b, 7c; 1992c, tables 7a, 7b, 7d, 7e, 7g); and author's calculations.
n.a. Not available.
a. For Argentina and Venezuela 1980 = 100; for Costa Rica 1981 = 100.

ential countercyclical, likely to contract in booms and widen in recessions. Whatever the reason, the skill differential seems to be countercyclical in Argentina and procyclical in Venezuela.

Recession clearly increased poverty and earnings inequality in both countries. In Argentina that pattern held across deciles of income distribution, age groups, and levels of education. In Venezuela the same thing happened across the first two categories, but not the third, level of education. Table 2-6 shows that in Venezuela, while earnings inequality increased, the education differential narrowed. This shift implies a significant amount of downward mobility, high unemployment, or very poor entry-level wages for the educated. Whatever the cause, this finding supports the claim that the costs of adjustment were not confined to the bottom of the education pyramid, particularly in Venezuela.

For Argentina and Venezuela it is important to remember that the data come from the middle of the recession that accompanied the adjustment program. For Costa Rica, by contrast, the data offer a chance to observe the effects of adjustment and recovery. Between 1980 and 1982 Costa Rica had a severe foreign exchange adjustment, during which per capita income fell by 13 percent and real wages by 29 percent.[24] After 1982 the economy recovered, as per capita income grew by 10 percent by 1989 and real wages recovered most of the ground they lost during the recession. The first observation is for 1981, in the midst of the adjustment process. The second is for 1989, when the economy had recovered from the recession and returned to its long-run growth trajectory. Unfortunately, there are no data from the late 1970s, before the whole process started, which prevents accurate comparisons of poverty before and after adjustment. But the data do allow assessments of the effect of recovery on poverty and the labor market.

The incidence and decomposition of poverty for Costa Rica appear in table 2-7. Recovery was highly beneficial to the poor between 1981 and 1989, with significant reductions of poverty in every segment of the labor market. The impact of recovery was particularly pronounced in rural areas, where the incidence of poverty fell by almost two-thirds, while the shares of the agricultural sector and rural families also shrank. This pattern helps explain why the share of illiterates and grade school graduates in the poverty population also fell sharply, since both are highly concentrated in the countryside. Recovery not only reduced poverty in Costa Rica, it was also strongly progressive. Table 2-6 shows that real earnings gains were greatest at the bottom of each distribution, whether defined by income, age, or education.

The Role of Economic Structure

The preceding comparative evidence raises a number of questions.[25] What is it about Costa Rica that permitted significant reductions in poverty in spite of slow or even negative income growth? Why did Argentina and Venezuela

24. For the real wage data, see Edwards (1991).
25. This section of the paper draws heavily on Morley (1992c).

Table 2-7. *Poverty in Costa Rica, by Group, 1981, 1989*
Percent

	Poverty head count ratio[a]		Proportion of all poor in group	
Category	1981	1989	1981	1989
Level of educational achievement				
Illiterate	49.1	18.4	20.0	18.4
Grade school	29.3	11.5	74.5	67.9
High school	7.2	5.7	4.6	11.1
University	3.4	2.8	0.9	2.5
Gender				
Male	22.6	9.0	79.6	75.3
Female	48.8	17.7	20.4	24.7
Urban labor market segment				
Unemployed	59.5	46.9	6.7	4.7
Inactive	46.3	17.6	37.8	24.7
Formal				
Private	11.5	5.5	17.0	18.1
Public	7.2	2.4	8.2	5.9
Informal	20.9	13.5	30.4	46.6
Economic sector				
Agriculture	30.7	13.9	37.7	36.3
Industry	11.0	7.0	5.1	9.3
Construction	9.6	1.5	3.2	1.0
Commerce	12.0	8.1	5.3	10.0
Services	9.4	6.0	4.7	10.3
Transportation	4.1	4.1	4.1	1.9
Geographical area				
Metropolitan	19.5	10.0	16.7	21.8
Urban	20.4	8.8	18.6	23.2
Rural	29.8	11.0	64.7	55.0
Entire population	25.4	10.2	...	...

Source: Morley and Alvarez (1992a, tables 3a, 3b, 3c, 3e, 3g, 5a, 5b, 5c, 5e, 5g).
a. Proportion of group with income below the poverty line.

have such rapid increases in poverty? What effect do differences in policy or economic structure have on the relationship between poverty and growth?

To explain sharp differences in performance during and after economic crisis, the key variables include the size and role of the traded goods sector and the relationship of the poor to that sector. Economic theory suggests that devaluation of the real exchange rate, which is a key element in structural adjustment to a balance of payments deficit, helps the traded goods sector and hurts the nontraded goods sector by raising the relative price of all traded goods. Producers of traded goods are thus helped by real devaluation, while consumers of traded goods are hurt. The size of the traded goods sector helps determine how large the real devaluation must be. Generally, the bigger the traded goods sector, the easier the adjustment and the smaller the necessary real devaluation. From the point of view of poverty, the most favorable situation for adjustment is in countries where the poor are producers but not consumers of traded goods. The least favorable situation is one in which the poor consume but do not produce traded goods. Clearly no country is a perfect example of either polar case, but it appears that Costa Rica has a relatively favorable structure compared to Venezuela and Argentina.

In Costa Rica the agricultural sector mainly produces traded goods and employs more than two-thirds of the poor (table 2-3). Real devaluation after 1980 had a powerful positive impact on agricultural production, exports, and wages. For example, Gindling and Berry estimate that real wages in the exportable sector, which is primarily agricultural, rose 10 percent relative to wages in the nontradables sector between 1980 and 1989.[26] In a household survey, the urban-rural average income differential fell from 1.94 in 1981 to 1.81 in 1989.[27] Costa Rica was thus fortunate to have a relatively large traded goods sector that was able to push up wages and incomes for the rural poor during the recovery. The impact on rural poverty during the adjustment was dramatic. According to table 2-4, the rural head count ratio fell from 16.7 percent to 3.2 percent between 1981 and 1989.[28]

Argentina and Venezuela are in a completely different situation. In Argentina the main traded goods are all products of agriculture, such as wheat, beef, hides, soybeans, and sunflower oil.[29] But clearly these are also important wage goods. Because real devaluation drives up the price of these commodities, it can be expected to hurt the poor as consumers, particularly those in the urban sector. But does it help them as producers? The answer appears to be not much. Argentina has a substantial manufacturing sector, but it is highly protected.[30] This means that while Argentina produces tradable goods, those goods are not traded. More important, the sector as a whole is hurt more than it is helped by real devaluation because prices are determined internally, not by the real exchange rate. For Argentine manufacturing, real devaluation

26. Gindling and Berry (1992, table 3).

27. Author's calculations based on data in Morley and Alvarez (1992a, table 7).

28. Paraguay and Colombia are two other Latin American countries that have managed to reduce poverty and income inequality during the 1980s (see tables 2-1 and 2-3). However, in these countries GDP per capita had increased by the end year.

29. See Economic Commission for Latin America (ECLA) (1991).

30. In a study of effective protection in six developing countries, Balassa (1982, table 2.3) found that on average Argentine manufacturing had an effective protection rate of 112 percent in 1969, the highest of any country in the sample.

drives up the price of essential imported intermediates and capital more than it raises the prices of its own output. Hence, real devaluation is likely to hurt the urban poor, both as producers and as consumers. Furthermore, the urban traded goods sector appears to be relatively small in Argentina.[31] That reduces the flexibility of the economy to respond to changes in the real exchange rate, implying that structural adjustments are likely to be long and difficult.

Venezuela has a different problem. It is the quintessential mineral economy. The dominant traded good is oil. Unfortunately, real devaluation does not have much of an impact on the production of oil, because oil production is controlled by quotas on world markets. The rest of the potential traded goods sector in manufacturing and agriculture is abnormally small.[32] Therefore, devaluation did not help the poor much in Venezuela as producers. But it hurt them as consumers, because some food is imported, and its price rose with the exchange rate. In addition, the elimination of food subsidies, an important part of the adjustment program, further increased the price of food. Thus, like Argentina, Venezuela is an economy in which devaluation seems to hurt the poor as consumers but not help them as producers. Under these unfortunate structural conditions, adjustments to balance of payments deficits are likely to be long, to require extended periods of recession, and to generate bitter disputes over real wage reductions.

Minimum Wages and the Poor

If countries are forced to accept a period of recessionary adjustment, are there any complementary policies that might mitigate the impact of adjustment on the poor? Among the many candidates, this section focuses on one, the minimum wage, in light of extensive cross-country time series evidence. Those interested in equity have long contended that maintaining or raising the minimum wage is progressive, since it improves the distribution of income and alleviates poverty. That argument rests on two questionable assumptions. First, the poor must be working in minimum wage jobs. Second, the number of such jobs must be insensitive to the level of the minimum wage in real terms. Neither of these conditions appears to hold in Latin America, except

31. Production in manufacturing responded very little to real devaluation after 1980. The real exchange rate tripled between 1980 and 1989, but manufacturing output fell by 20 percent. For the real exchange rate, see IDB, *Economic and Social Progress Report* (various years); for manufacturing output, see ECLA (1991, table 130).

32. Agriculture and manufacturing together accounted for only 21 percent of GDP in 1981 according to ECLA (1990).

during recession. Many people work in the urban informal sector or in agriculture at wages well below the minimum wage. Such people could be helped, not hurt, if a decline in the minimum wage expands formal sector job opportunities. However, if the decline in the minimum wage takes place during a recession, when the number of formal sector jobs is itself declining, the cost of the policy to workers in the formal sector will not be offset by gains to the newly employed. Furthermore, by affecting the distribution of income, the minimum wage may also affect the demand for formal sector output. Lowering the real minimum wage may decrease demand for goods intended for the mass market, thus amplifying the reduction in labor income and worsening the recession.

These questions cannot be resolved by economic theory. They require an appeal to experience, and Latin America offers a rich laboratory of alternative patterns of real wages, adjustment, and poverty. The record may suggest policy lessons.

The record includes several types of evidence, none of which is definitive, but all of which are suggestive. The first type is data on changes in income distribution during business cycles in the 1980s, displayed in table 2-3. That table also indicates what happened to the real value of the minimum wage in each episode. Under the combination of recession and less equal income distribution, the real minimum wage fell in nine cases, held constant in three, and increased slightly in the case of Venezuela.[33] With that single exception, in every case in which the real minimum wage increased, the distribution of income improved. The majority of those cases, not surprisingly, involved periods of recovery. The three cases that defy this pattern are Brazil, Uruguay, and Chile, where income distribution improved during recovery despite a decline in the real minimum wage. In all three cases, the recovery was accompanied by a substantial increase in employment and by a rise in the average wage relative to the minimum wage.[34]

The next type of evidence is a cross-tabulation of the fifty-eight recession and twenty-eight recovery observations that have comparable poverty statistics. Table 2-8 classifies them by the change in poverty, the state of the econ-

33. This calculation relies on the real minimum wage indexes reported in Edwards (1991, table 2). The real wage for Venezuela in 1991 was not available.

34. In Chile unemployment fell from 22 percent to 12 percent between 1983 and 1987, while in Brazil employment rose by 25 percent and in Uruguay unemployment fell almost by half between 1983 and 1989. Furthermore, in contrast to the minimum wage, the average real wage rose in Brazil and Uruguay and held constant in Chile. See Edwards (1991, table 1) for average real wage data; ECLA (1991) for unemployment rates; and IDB (1993, p. 244) for employment figures in Brazil.

Table 2-8. *Poverty, the Business Cycle, and the Minimum Wage*
Number of periods[a]

Level of poverty	Periods of recession	Periods of recovery
Increases	Minimum wage rises = 11 Minimum wage falls = 44 Total = 55	Minimum wage rises = 1 Minimum wage falls = 5 Total = 6
Remains unchanged		Minimum wage rises = 1 Minimum wage falls = 1 Total = 2
Decreases	Minimum wage rises = 2 Minimum wage falls = 1 Total = 3	Minimum wage rises = 16 Minimum wage falls = 4 Total = 20

Sources: See appendix; and author's calculations.
a. This table excludes three CEPAL observations for 1981–88. CEPAL claims that poverty increased over the period. Work by the author and the World Bank, based on surveys from 1981 and 1989, shows a substantial decrease in poverty. Because there is no indication of a dramatic change in conditions between 1988 and 1989, the CEPAL observations seem unnecessary.

omy, and the change in the real value of the minimum wage. One expects poverty to rise in recession and to fall in recovery, and that is what one generally observes in table 2-8 because most observations are in the upper-left or lower-right quadrants. Table 2-8 also indicates a fairly high correlation between the minimum wage and the state of the economy. Most cases in which the minimum wage rose were recoveries and most cases in which it declined were recessions. Of more interest are the unexpected cases in which poverty falls during recession or rises in recovery (the upper-right and lower-left quadrants). There are nine such cases, and they suggest the importance of the minimum wage. In two of the three cases of recession and decreased poverty, the minimum wage rose. In five of the six cases of recovery and increased poverty, the minimum wage fell. Thus in the majority of cases in which poverty did not respond to the economic cycle as one might expect (rising in recovery or falling in recession), changes in the minimum wage help explain the anomaly.

Conclusion

Macroeconomic conditions are a major determinant of poverty. In the long run in all countries, even those where it was relatively inequitable, growth was a potent force for poverty reduction. In the short run both poverty and inequality are procyclical, meaning they rise in recession and fall in recovery. Poverty in particular is highly sensitive to the performance of the economy, partly because there are many people close to the poverty line and partly because the distribution of income itself is affected by the state of the economy. In every case studied in detail, income differentials increased in recession, implying that the poor were less able than the rich to defend themselves during economic downturns. The relationship found in a few cases of recession between increased minimum wages and decreased poverty rates deserves further analysis.

These relationships give rise to two conclusions. The first is that during recessions the poor will pay a heavy price. Governments and multilateral lending institutions should design their policies so that recessions are as mild and as short as possible. In some cases there is no choice but to accept a recession, with all the costs it imposes on the poor. But in others recessions have been prolonged unnecessarily, particularly by the desire to wring inflation out of the economy. The poor pay a very heavy price for such polices, given the sensitivity of poverty to the level of economic activity.

A second conclusion is that adjustment need not always be accompanied by sharp reductions in the minimum wage. There is evidence that under some conditions the minimum wage is not a barrier to real devaluation. Since other evidence suggests the minimum wage is a significant determinant of the level of poverty in the short run, governments should ensure that conditions require such a move before forcing down the minimum real wage.[35]

The distinction between traded and nontraded goods was useful for comparing performance across countries. Growth was positively correlated with the ability to expand exports. Countries with small traded goods sectors, such as Venezuela and Argentina, were unable to increase production in response to real exchange rate devaluation. They tended to have long periods of adjustment, because the expansion in traded goods was not large enough to offset the reduction in absorption. Where the traded goods sector was large and a major employer of the poor, as in Costa Rica, Paraguay, and Colombia, devaluation was progressive, with a short adjustment period and a decline in poverty.[36]

As a whole, the 1980s were a development disaster for Latin America. Only two countries, Chile and Colombia, managed to increase per capita income. Rising poverty and inequality were quite widespread. At the conclusion

35. I recently examined the relationship between the minimum wage and the real exchange rate and found that while both tended to decline during the 1980s, in three cases of fifteen the real minimum wage increased and there was a real devaluation. Significantly, those cases include Colombia, Costa Rica, and Paraguay, the three countries where poverty declined over the decade. See Morley (1992c).

36. See Morley (1992b) for an analysis of Colombia.

of this difficult adjustment, however, there were encouraging signs. Chile, Argentina, Venezuela, and Mexico, four of the countries hardest hit earlier in the decade, were all undergoing recovery by 1991.[37] There are not yet any data on trends in poverty and inequality, but if the past is any guide, both will decrease. At present, poverty is highly localized in Brazil, Peru, and Bolivia, which have not yet found a sustainable growth path.[38]

If adjustments in Latin America were long and difficult, it was not because the patients did not take their prescribed medicine. There were substantial real devaluations, cuts in the minimum wage, and export increases in most countries.[39] If it took a long time to reap the benefits of adjustment policies, it was mainly because of the large shifts in demand and supply that were required. Also a difficulty was that at the outset of the decade the traded goods sector in most countries was too small or unprepared to offset the contraction caused by currency devaluation. As a result, poverty increased rapidly while Latin American economies adjusted their production structures, reduced the size of their public sectors, and expanded their exports. Finally, at present, the positive results of these efforts are beginning to appear in part of the region.

37. In 1991 real per capita income in these four countries grew by an average of 5.4 percent. See IDB, *Economic and Social Progress Report* (1992, table B-2).

38. Between 1989 and 1991 these three countries suffered an average reduction of 3 percent in real per capita income. See IDB (1992).

39. For exports and the real exchange rate see IDB, *Economic and Social Progress Report* (1992, table B-2). For the real wage see Edwards (1991).

68 MORLEY

References

Almeida Reis, Jose G., Jose S. Rodriguez, and Ricardo Paes de Barros. 1991. " A desigualdade de renda no Brasil." In *A Questão Social no Brasil*, edited by João Pavlo Velloso. São Paulo: Nobel.

Altimir, Oscar. 1992a. "Cambios en las desigualdades de ingreso y en la pobreza en América Latina."

———. 1992b. "Crecimento, distribucion del ingreso y pobreza en America Latina: algunos hechos estilizados." Santiago: CEPAL.

———. 1992c. "Income Distribution and Poverty through Crisis Adjustment." Santiago: CEPAL.

———. n.d. "Latin American Poverty in the Last Two Decades." Santiago: CEPAL.

Balassa, Bela, and others. 1982. *Development Strategies in Semi-Industrial Economies*. Johns Hopkins University Press.

Barros, Ricardo Paes de, and others. 1993. "Welfare, Inequality, Social Indicators, and Social Programs in Brazil in the 1980s." Rio de Janeiro: IPEA.

Bergsman, Joel. 1980. "Income Distribution and Poverty in Mexico." Working Paper 395. Washington: World Bank.

Bonelli, Regis, and Guillerme Sedlacek. 1989. "Distribuicao de renda: evolucao no ultimo quarto do seculo." In *Mercado de Trabalho e Distribuicao de Renda: uma coletanea*, edited by Guillerme Sedlacek and Ricardo Barros. IPEC Monograph 35.

CEPAL. 1990. "Magnitud de la pobreza en América Latina en los años ochenta." Santiago (May).

———. n.d. "La pobreza en Chile en 1990." Santiago.

Chenery, Hollis, and others. 1974. *Redistribution with Growth*. Oxford University Press.

Economic Commission for Latin America (ECLA). 1990. *Statistical Yearbook for Latin America and the Caribbean*. New York: United Nations.

Edwards, Alejandra Cox. 1991. "Wage Trends in Latin America." LATHR Report 18. World Bank.

Fait, Pablo Sauma, and J. D. Trejos. 1990. "Evolución reciente de la distribución del ingreso en Costa Rica: 1977–86." Working Paper 132. San José: University of Costa Rica.

Fields, Gary S. 1980. *Poverty, Inequality, and Development*. Cambridge University Press.

———. 1990. "Poverty and Inequality in Latin America: Some New Evidence." Cornell University (October).

———. 1991. "Growth and Income Distribution." In *Essays on Poverty, Equity and Growth*, edited by George Psacharopoulos, 1–52. Oxford: Pergamon Press.

Fiszbein, Ariel. 1989. "An Analysis of the Size Distribution of Income in Argentina, 1974–88." Ph.D. dissertation, University of California at Berkeley.

Foster, James, 1984. "On Economic Poverty: A Survey of Aggregate Measures." *Advances in Econometrics* 3: 215–51.

Foster, James, Joel Greer, and Erik Thorbecke. 1984. "Notes and Comments: A Class of Decomposable Poverty Measures." *Econometrica* 52 (May): 761–65.

Foster, James, and A. F. Shorrocks. 1988. "Poverty Orderings." *Econometrica* 56 (nos. 1–3): 173–77.

Fox, M. Louise. 1990. "Poverty Alleviation in Brazil, 1970–87." Washington: World Bank.

Fox, M. Louise, and Samuel A. Morley. 1991a. "Who Carried the Burden of Brazilian Adjustment in the Eighties?" Washington: World Bank.

———. 1991b. "Who Paid the Bill? Adjustment and Poverty in Brazil, 1980-95." Working Paper 648. Washington: World Bank.

Gindling, T. H., and Albert Berry. 1994. "The Performance of the Labor Market during Recession and Structural Adjustment: Costa Rica in the 1980s." *World Development* 20 (no. 11): 1599–1616.

Glewwe, Paul, and Dennis de Tray. 1989. "The Poor in Latin America during Adjustment: A Case Study of Peru." LSMS 56. Washington: World Bank.

GRADE. 1992. "Gestión pública y distribución de ingresos: tres estudias de casa para la economia peruana."

Hernandez-Laos, E. 1990. "Medición de la intensidad de la pobreza y de la pobreza extrema en México (1963–88)." *Investigacíon Económica* 191 (January–March): 265–98.

Hoffman, Rudolfo. 1991. "Economic Crisis and Poverty in Brazil during the 1980s."

Inter-American Development Bank (IDB). 1992. *Socioeconomic Report: Costa Rica.* DES Report 13 (October). Washington.

———. 1993. *Socioeconomic Report: Brazil.* GN Report 1801. Washington.

———. Various years. *Economic and Social Progress Report on Latin America.*

INDEC (Instituto Nacional de Estádistica y Censos). 1990. *La Pobreza Urbana en Argentina.* Buenos Aires.

International Monetary Fund. 1990. *International Financial Statistics Yearbook.* Washington.

Kanbur, Ravi. 1987. "Measurement and Alleviation of Poverty." *IMF Staff Paper* 34 (March): 60–85.

———. n.d. "Malnutrition and Poverty in Latin America." Washington: World Bank.

Levy, Santiago. 1991. "Poverty Alleviation in Mexico." Working Paper 679. Washington: World Bank.

Londono de la Cuesta, Juan Luis. 1990. "Income Distribution during the Structural Transformation: Colombia 1938–88." Ph.D. dissertation, Harvard University.

Lustig, Nora. 1990a. "Economic Crisis, Adjustment and Living Standards in Mexico 1982-85." *World Development* 18 (no. 10): 1325–42.

———. 1990b. "The Incidence of Poverty in Mexico, 1984: An Empirical Analysis." Washington: World Bank.

Marquez, Gustavo. 1992. "Poverty and Social Policies in Venezuela." Caracas: IESA.

Marquez, Gustavo, and others. 1993 "Fiscal Policy and Income Distribution in Venezuela." In *Government Spending and Income Distribution in Latin America,* edited by Ricardo Hausmann and Roberto Rigabon. Washington: Inter-American Development Bank.

Morley, Samuel A., 1992a. "Macroconditions and Poverty in Latin America." Washington: Inter-American Development Bank.

————. 1992b. "Policy, Structure and the Reduction of Poverty in Colombia: 1980–89." Working Paper 126. Washington: Inter-American Development Bank.

————. 1992c. "Poverty and Distribution during Latin American Adjustment in the 1980s." Washington: World Bank.

————. 1992d. "Structural Adjustment and the Determinants of Poverty in Latin America." Washington: Inter-American Development Bank.

Morley, Samuel A., and Carola Alvarez. 1992a. "Poverty and Adjustment in Costa Rica." Working Paper 123 (July). Washington: Inter-American Development Bank.

————. 1992b. "Poverty and Adjustment in Venezuela." Working Paper 124 (July). Washington: Inter-American Development Bank.

————. 1992c. "Recession and the Growth of Poverty in Argentina." Working Paper 125 (July). Washington: Inter-American Development Bank.

Mujica, Patricio, and Osvaldo Larranaga. 1993. "Social Policies and Income Distribution in Chile." In *Government Spending and Income Distribution in Latin America,* edited by Ricardo Hausmann and Roberto Rigabon. Washington: Inter-American Development Bank.

Pollack, Molly. 1985. "Household Behavior and Economic Crisis: Costa Rica, 1979–82." Working Paper 270. Geneva: Programa Regional del Empleo para America Latina y el Caribe.

————. 1990. "Poverty and the Labour Market in Costa Rica." In *Poverty and the Labour Market: Access to Jobs and Incomes in Asian and Latin American Cities,* edited by G. Rodgers. Geneva: International Labour Office.

PREALC. 1990a. *Colombia: la Deuda Social en los 80.* Geneva.

————. 1990b. "Pobreza y empleo: un análisis del periodo 1969–87 en el gran Santiago." Working Paper 348 (July). Geneva.

Psacharopoulos, George, and others. 1993. "Poverty and Income Distribution in Latin America: The Story of the 1980s." Human Resources Division Report 27 (December). Washington: World Bank.

Ravallion, Martin. 1992. "Poverty Comparisons: A Guide to Concepts and Methods." Working Paper 88. Washington: World Bank.

Ravallion, Martin, and Monika Huppi. 1991. "Measuring Changes in Poverty: A Methodological Case Study of Indonesia during an Adjustment Period." *World Bank Economic Review* 5 (January): 57–84.

Tolosa, H. C. 1991. "Pobreza no Brasil: Uma avaliação dos anos 80." In *A Questão Social no Brasil,* edited by João Paulo dos Reis Velloso. São Paulo: Nobel.

Turner, Frederick Jackson. 1920. *The Frontier in American History.* Henry Holt.

World Bank. 1990. *World Development Report 1990.* Oxford University Press.

————. 1991. "Guatemala: Country Economic Memorandum." Report 9378-GU. Washington.

CHAPTER THREE

Income Inequality Trends in Latin America in the 1980s

Ariel Fiszbein and George Psacharopoulos

LATIN AMERICA is a region with well-documented historical inequalities, often greater than those of any other region of the world.[1] Most of the available evidence on income distribution is dated, ending with the 1970s for some countries. This chapter examines what happened to income inequality during the 1980s, a period of economic crisis and adjustment for most Latin American countries. Our intention is to identify the main factors associated with income inequality in this region and to provide a functional description of the people who make up the bottom 20 percent of the income distribution.[2]

In the past few years there has been increased interest in these issues, as recent analyses of income distribution and poverty data attest. However, it is usually very difficult to compare findings for different countries or for different periods, because analysts use various data sources and methodologies.[3]

We are indebted to Francisca Castro for her efficient research assistance, and to Haeduck Lee and Hongyu Yang for their computer assistance. We would also like to thank Gary Fields for his useful comments. The views expressed here are those of the authors and are not necessarily shared by the World Bank.

1. For international comparisons see Fields (1988); LeCaillon and others (1984); Van Ginneken and Park (1984); and World Bank (1991).
2. This chapter concentrates on this measure of relative poverty rather than on measures of absolute poverty. Subsequent reports will deal with the distribution of total per capita household income derived from labor and nonlabor sources.
3. For comparability problems see Van der Walle (1991); and Altimir (1987).

This study attempts to solve the problem of noncomparability by using similar concepts in defining the database to which we apply a consistent methodology for each country. The goal is to obtain a perspective on the structure and pattern of change in inequality for the whole region. Despite this objective, the heterogeneous characteristics of data in some countries still present obstacles to direct comparability.

The Data

This discussion uses household surveys from seven countries—Argentina, Brazil, Colombia, Costa Rica, Panama, Uruguay, and Venezuela—taken at two points in time. The early data come from a survey taken during the late 1970s and early 1980s; the later come from the late 1980s. By using data from two points, the chapter provides a historical perspective on changes in income inequality during the decade.

Data availability determined the selection of countries. Appendix table 3A-1 provides details on the nature and coverage of the surveys. It should be noted that coverage differs between countries—in some cases it is national, in others only urban. This variation limits the comparability of results across countries.

The survey samples include all individuals fifteen years of age or older who were in the labor force and had positive income. Because these factors identify personal (rather than household) characteristics, it seemed appropriate to relate them to personal (as opposed to household) income. We chose the most inclusive measure of income available in each survey, although none included imputed rents or auto consumption. In five of the seven countries this measure is income from all sources, including work, rental income, and transfers. In Panama and Venezuela, the income measure corresponds solely to income from work and excludes rents and transfers. Within each country, however, the same definition of income is used for both periods, which allows comparisons over time. The surveys from Panama are special in that they cover only employees, excluding employers and the self-employed.

The Distribution of Income

What happened to income inequality during the 1980s? This section presents evidence on changes in the distribution of income in seven Latin American countries.

Table 3-1. *Income Inequality Measures, Seven Countries, 1979–81, 1989*

Country	Gini coefficient 1979–81[b]	1989	Standardized Theil index[a] 1979–81	1989	Change in standardized Theil index (percent)
Argentina	0.389	0.461	3.25	5.02	1.77
Brazil	0.574	0.625	5.86	7.27	1.41
Colombia	0.578	0.515	7.20	5.16	–2.04
Costa Rica	0.451	0.410	3.76	3.49	–0.27
Panama	0.376	0.446	2.98	4.09	1.11
Uruguay	0.452	0.420	4.22	3.51	–0.71
Venezuela	0.512	0.498	3.95	4.08	0.13

Sources: See tables 3A-2 through 3A-8.
a. For a definition of this standardized index, see equation 3-2. For definitions of the Theil and Gini indexes, see Kakwani (1980, chap. 5).
b. See table 3A-1 for exact survey dates, geographical coverage, and definition of income.

The appendix presents the income distribution by deciles, as well as the mean incomes by deciles, for all fourteen surveys (tables 3A-2 through 3A-8). Table 3-1 summarizes the results, and figure 3-1 provides a graphical overview. Although this chapter uses the Theil index of inequality for the purpose of decomposition analysis, table 3-1 also reports the Gini coefficient, a more widely used measure.[4]

The Theil index indicates that income inequality increased in four of the seven countries: Argentina, Brazil, Panama, and Venezuela. The largest increases were in Argentina, Brazil, and Panama. In the case of Venezuela, the change in the overall distribution was such that there is a discrepancy between the Theil index and the Gini coefficients. In fact, when the distribution by deciles is considered, the share of total income accruing to those in the first to sixth deciles increased at the expense of those in the seventh to ninth (table 3A-8).

The other three countries in the sample show a significant reduction in income inequality. The reduction is particularly impressive in the case of Colombia, where the equivalent of 5.5 percentage points was transferred from the top two deciles (particularly the highest) to the lower eight. Somewhat less dramatic, but still very significant, were the reductions that took place in Costa Rica and Uruguay.

Despite the differences in coverage across countries, the results in table 3-1

4. For the definition of the Theil index, see equation 3-1. The choice of the Theil index was based on its decomposability, discussed by Bourguignon (1979) and Shorrocks (1980), and on the availability of a previous study by Altimir and Piñera (1979) that used a similar methodology, enabling comparison.

Figure 3-1. *Income Inequality, Seven Countries, 1979–81, 1989*[a]

Standardized Theil index[b]

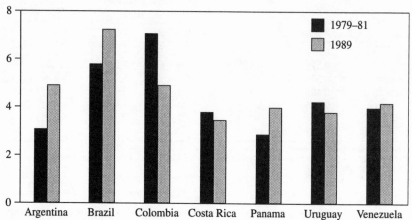

Source: Psacharopolous and others (1992, p. 33).
a. See table 3A-1 for exact survey dates, geographical coverage, and definition of income.
b. For a definition see equation 3-2.

also allow comparative analysis. Thanks to its large reduction in income inequality during the 1980s, Colombia no longer has the least equal distribution
in the sample. Brazil has replaced it at the top of the list. There have also been
some changes near the bottom. In the late 1970s and early 1980s, Argentina
and Panama had the lowest levels of income inequality among the seven countries. But by 1989 income inequality was moderately high in Argentina and
had worsened in Panama as well. Costa Rica and Uruguay, which in the early
1980s already had exhibited relatively low income inequality, ranked lowest
by the end of the decade.

Figure 3-2 plots the changes in income inequality and per capita income for
the seven countries. With two exceptions, the evidence suggests a negative
correlation between changes in income and changes in inequality. The two exceptions are Brazil, where inequality increased at the same time as per capita
income, and Uruguay, where inequality and income were both in decline.[5] The
different performance of the seven countries on income distribution suggests a
role for overall economic performance. However, the diverse patterns found
within this sample clearly rule out the existence of a simple relationship between changes in average per capita income and changes in inequality.

5. Chapter 2 in this volume argues that Brazil was in a recession, despite the fact that per
capita income was higher in the end year and that inequality increased during the recession.

Figure 3-2. *Income Inequality and per Capita Income for Workers, Seven Countries, Selected Years, 1979–89*

Standardized Theil index

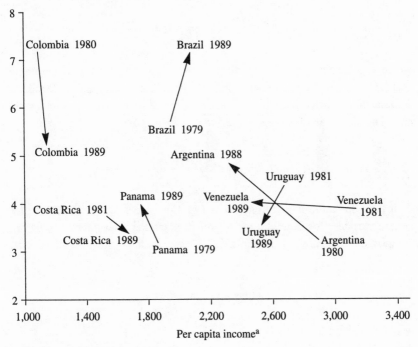

Per capita income[a]

Source: Psacharopolous and others (1992, p. 35).
a. Constant 1987 U.S. dollars.

Decomposing Levels of Income Inequality

Our first goal was to assess the relative influence of several variables in explaining the level of income inequality at a given time. To achieve this we performed a decomposition of the Theil index of inequality.

Altimir and Piñera performed a similar analysis for nine Latin American countries using information from around 1970.[6] While three of the countries in the Altimir and Piñera paper—Chile, Mexico, and Peru—are not included in this analysis, their study did not include Uruguay. Although the two studies are not strictly comparable because they use different classifications, it is nonetheless interesting to determine the extent to which they offer results that are consistent over the span of two decades.

6. Altimir and Piñera (1979).

Method

The Theil index of inequality (T) can be defined as follows:

$$(3\text{-}1) \qquad T = \sum_{i}^{N} y_i \ln \frac{y_i}{1/N} \quad \varepsilon[o,1nN],$$

where y_i is the share of the i th individual in total income, and N is the sample size.[7] This index fluctuates between zero (perfect equality) and ln N (all income accrues to one individual), so that its value increases with the sample size. The index can thus be standardized (T^*) as

$$(3\text{-}2) \qquad T^* = \frac{T}{1nN} \quad \varepsilon[o,1].$$

If the population is partitioned into J groups according to the values of a certain variable (for example, $j = 1,2$ for gender), the Theil index can be decomposed into a between (B) and a within component (W), with each defined

$$(3\text{-}3) \qquad B = \sum_{q=1}^{Q} y_q \ln \frac{y_q}{\frac{N_q}{N}}$$

and

$$(3\text{-}4) \qquad W = \sum_{q=1}^{Q} y_q T_q,$$

where N_q is the number of individuals in group q; y_q is the source of income of group q as a proportion of total income; and T_q is the Theil index for group q. Thus, for example, if the population is grouped according to gender, total inequality (T) could be decomposed into inequality between males and females (B) and a weighted average of the inequality among males and females (W). It is then conventional to treat the between component as the inequality "explained" by the variable (in this case gender) and the within component as the "unexplained" inequality.

We define the gross contribution of variable j (G_j) as the inequality between the groups defined for the characteristic j. If j is gender, q equals two (male

7. See Theil (1967).

and female), and G_j measures the inequality between males and females. It is equal to B in equation 3-3. Similarly, the joint contribution of variables j and k (G_{jk}) is defined as the inequality between the categories defined for those two variables. In the previous example, if one further separates males and females according to height, with categories for short and tall, the joint contribution of gender and height would be the inequality between the four groups. Finally, the marginal contribution of variable k given variable j (M_{kj}) is the difference between the joint contribution and j's gross contribution:

$$(3\text{-}5) \qquad M_{kj} = G_{jk} - G_j.$$

In the previous example, the marginal contribution of the variable for height would be the difference between the inequality between the four groups and the inequality between males and females. When the decomposition includes more than two variables, marginal contributions of several orders can be defined.[8] Our analysis presents only the marginal contribution of last order, which can be interpreted as the increase in explained inequality obtained by adding a variable to a decomposition that already includes all the other variables. For three variables, this marginal contribution, M_{lkj}, is $G_{jkl} - G_{jk}$.

Variables in the Theil Decomposition

Our decomposition analysis uses four variables: age, education, employment, and economic sector. All four have been categorized in a discrete fashion, with the same criteria for all countries. Although every system of classification is arbitrary to some extent, the fact that the same criteria are used consistently in all cases implies that differences in explanatory power across countries and time are not caused by the method of variable selection.[9]

The age variable is categorized in four groups: 15–25 years, 26–40 years, 41–55 years, and 56 years or older. Similarly, education is categorized according to length of enrollment, with 0–5 years, 6–8 years, 9–12 years, and 13 or more years. No sensitivity analysis was done with respect to changes in these categories. It should be noted that the original (noncategorized) variables for education and age were used in the logit analysis presented below.

Economic sector is categorized in eight groups: agriculture, mining, manu-

---

8. More generally, when z variables are included it is possible to calculate the marginal contributions from order 1 to order $z-1$.

9. The variables in this study are categorized following criteria different from those used by Altimir and Piñera (1979), making comparisons difficult.

Table 3-2. *Characteristics of the Working Population, Seven Countries,*
1979–81, 1989
Percent

Country	Characteristic[a]	1979–81[b]	1989[b]
Argentina	Postsecondary education	15	20
Brazil	No primary education	72	58
Colombia	Postsecondary education	12	17
Costa Rica	Self-employed	16	21
Panama	Postsecondary education	15	24
Uruguay	Self-employed	17	20
Venezuela	No primary education	34	23

Source: Authors' calculations based on surveys described in table 3A-1.
a. Characteristics that changed most during the period under consideration.
b. For exact survey dates see table 3A-1.

facturing, transportation-communication-utilities, construction, commerce, financial services, and nonfinancial services. Because of limited survey coverage, some countries have no entries for the agriculture and mining sectors.

Finally, employment is broken down into employees, self-employed, and
employers for Argentina, Brazil, and Costa Rica. For Colombia, Uruguay, and
Venezuela, employees are further divided into those working in the public sector and those in the private sector. Because the Panama survey has only a single category for all employees, the employment variable is excluded from the
analysis. Table 3-2 summarizes the characteristics of the working population
that changed most during the 1980s.

Results

Tables 3-3 and 3-4 show the main results of the decomposition. Table 3-3
presents the gross and marginal contributions of each variable. For example,
in Venezuela in 1981 inequality between the four age groups amounts to 6.3
percent of total inequality. The marginal contributions are calculated using the
models with the highest joint contributions, which appear in table 3-4. With
two exceptions, these models have three variables. For Brazil and Venezuela,
the large sample size allows the use of all four variables in the decomposition
exercise. The marginal contributions identify the most important variables in
terms of their quantitative contributions to explain inequality. For example,
for Venezuela in 1981, the marginal contribution of age indicates that when
the groups defined by the other three variables are subdivided according to
age, the share of total inequality explained increases by 7.2 percentage points.

The joint models shown in table 3-4 explain approximately 45 percent of

Table 3-3. Decomposition of Theil Indexes: Contributions of Individual Variables to Inequality, Seven Countries, Selected Years, 1979–89[a]

Percent

Country and year	Gross contribution (g_j)				Marginal contribution (M_{lkj})			
	Age	Employment	Education	Economic sector	Age	Employment	Education	Economic sector
Argentina								
1980	8.6	7.7	18.2	3.6	12.7	5.7	23.7	n.a.
1989	6.9	6.2	20.2	4.7	11.3	4.2	23.3	n.a.
Brazil								
1979	8.3	13.1	28.8	7.7	9.1	8.9	25.6	6.7
1989	7.1	14.1	26.5	5.9	6.9	10.7	23.7	5.9
Colombia								
1980	10.1	16.4	35.1	5.4	7.0	8.6	31.1	n.a.
1989	10.6	15.2	30.2	3.9	6.6	7.1	27.8	n.a.
Costa Rica								
1981	12.4	1.6	26.4	12.8	13.6	n.a.	20.3	4.3
1989	7.7	3.0	23.6	11.1	8.0	n.a.	18.3	5.7
Panama								
1979	7.5	n.a.	35.8	10.2	11.0	n.a.	34.4	7.2
1989	13.3	n.a.	28.8	10.0	14.9	n.a.	26.9	6.6
Uruguay								
1981	8.1	13.1	13.4	5.0	9.9	10.4	17.2	n.a.
1989	8.1	11.8	10.1	5.8	10.1	10.8	14.2	n.a.
Venezuela								
1981	6.3	11.9	26.3	6.7	7.2	8.8	21.5	4.2
1989	8.3	19.6	23.1	4.9	6.0	15.7	20.9	4.4

Source: Authors' calculations based on country surveys.
n.a. Not available.
a. For explanation of numbers for gross and marginal contributions, see text accompanying equations 3-3 and 3-5.

Table 3-4. *Decomposition of Theil Indexes: Joint Contributions of*
Variables to Inequality, Seven Countries, Selected Years, 1979–90
Percent

Country	Year	Explanatory variables	Joint contribution $(G_{jkl})^a$
Argentina	1980	Age + employment + education	38.1
	1989	Age + employment + education	35.8
Brazil	1979	Age + employment + education + economic sector	55.5
	1989	Age + employment + education + economic sector	50.6
Colombia	1980	Age + employment + education	53.4
	1989	Age + employment + education	48.5
Costa Rica	1981	Age + education + economic sector	44.9
	1989	Age + education + economic sector	36.6
Panama	1979	Age + education + economic sector	52.2
	1989	Age + education + economic sector	50.4
Uruguay	1981	Age + employment + education	36.0
	1989	Age + employment + education	32.6
Venezuela	1981	Age + employment + education + economic sector	46.9
	1989	Age + employment + education + economic sector	53.0

Source: Authors' calculations based on country surveys.
a. For explanation of joint contributions, see text following equation 3-4.

total inequality. The average joint contribution for the two periods together is
44.7 percent. In every case except Costa Rica the variables for education and
employment are part of the model with the highest joint contribution.

With the sole exception of Venezuela, the decompositions show that the between component is larger in the earlier periods than in 1989. The average
joint contribution was 46.7 percent in the earlier period and 43.9 percent in
1989, which means that the unexplained inequality (the within component) increased. This evidence suggests that in 1989 other factors became more important in explaining income inequality. However, a more comprehensive explanation of the changes would require the use of a so-called dynamic
decomposition analysis, which considers the effects of changes in relative incomes, relative size of the groups, and inequality within the groups.[10]

The most striking finding of the decompositions is the overwhelming preeminence of education as a contributing factor (figure 3-3). In thirteen of the
fourteen cases—the exception being Uruguay in 1989—education had the
highest gross contribution of all the variables, on average 25 percent. In other
words, one-fourth of total inequality can be explained as inequality between
individuals with different levels of schooling. In all fourteen cases education

10. See Ramos (1990); and Fiszbein (1991).

Figure 3-3. *Marginal Contributions of Individual Variables to Inequality, Seven-Country Averages*

Percent

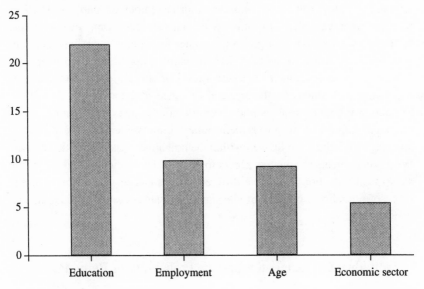

Source: Authors' calculations based on table 3-3.

also had the highest marginal contribution to total inequality, which implies that education's contribution is rather robust.

This finding appears to be consistent with the results of Altimir and Piñera.[11] The only other variable with a similar contribution to inequality was occupation, which our analysis does not include.

Employment is the second most important variable in the decomposition. Its average gross contribution is approximately 11 percent—less than half that of education, but larger than that found by Altimir and Piñera. The contribution of employment in Costa Rica is unusually low. This may be related to two factors. First, compared with the other countries in the sample, the share of employees in the labor force is very high in Costa Rica. Second, their income is extremely close to the overall mean income—it equaled mean income in 1981 and was 97 percent of mean income in 1989.

The contribution of age is on average somewhat smaller than that of employment. With very few exceptions, economic sector contributes least to in-

11. Altimir and Piñera (1979, table 3).

come inequality among the four variables in this study. Once again, these two findings seem consistent with those of Altimir and Piñera.

The preeminence of education as a source of income inequality compared with age, employment, and economic sector has important implications. Unlike the other variables, education is a relatively permanent characteristic. People move from one age group to another throughout their lives and, depending on the degree of mobility in each country, may change jobs from one economic sector to another. A person's level of education, by contrast, does not change very much once he or she has reached adulthood.

Among the four variables under consideration, however, education is the one most influenced by government policy. Improvements in the provision and quality of education lie well within the domain of feasible public policies. Were governments to equalize access to and the distribution of education, the subsequent reduction in income differentials associated with higher average levels of schooling would contribute significantly to reductions in income disparities.[12]

Individual Characteristics and the Probability of Being Poor

The preceding decomposition of the Theil index, though informative, is based on just a few of the many independent variables that help explain income inequality. This section examines essentially the same problem, but takes a more detailed approach and analyzes additional independent variables.

Tables 3A-9 through 3A-15 present the results of a multivariate model that standardizes the many factors that simultaneously affect the probability of someone's belonging to the bottom 20 percent of the income distribution. Each country is analyzed separately. Given the emphasis on distribution, the focus is on measures of relative, not absolute, poverty. Because this dependent variable is limited, we have fitted a logit model.[13] The model expresses the probability (P) of someone's being at the bottom of the distribution as a function of various personal characteristics (X), such as age, gender, years of schooling, and sector of employment, where

12. However, it should be noted that static decomposition analysis is not the most appropriate method of analyzing the dynamic effects on income inequality of changes in the distribution of education among individuals. The key matter in such an analysis is the expected change in income returns to education associated with an increase in the average level and dispersion of schooling.

13. See Cramer (1991).

$$(3\text{-}6) \qquad\qquad P = \frac{1}{1 + e^{-\Sigma \beta_i X_i}}.$$

The reported coefficients are partial derivatives indicating the change in the probability of belonging to the bottom 20 percent relative to a unit change in one of the independent variables, such that

$$(3\text{-}7) \qquad\qquad \frac{\delta P}{\delta X_i} = \beta_i \, P \, (1 - P),$$

where P refers to the dependent variable (the probability of the event), ß is the logit coefficient, and X is the string of independent variables used in the regression. The value of this partial derivative corresponds to the marginal effects column in the tables.

For example, table 3A-10 indicates that in Brazil in 1989, each additional year of schooling could be expected to decrease the probability of a worker's belonging to the bottom 20 percent of the income distribution by 4.2 percentage points—a sizable effect—controlling for the other factors in the regression.[14]

Tables 3A-16 through 3A-22 show the results of simulations that keep all other variables at their mean and assign different values to the target characteristic. These simulations have several notable features. In every country, there is remarkable stability in the probabilities between the first and second surveys. No group, among those considered, significantly changed its position in the income distribution during the 1980s. But it is worth noting that women in Brazil improved their chance of not being in the bottom 20 percent by about 4 percentage points. The uneducated in Colombia and Costa Rica were more likely to be in the lowest two deciles in 1989 than in 1980 (see tables 3A-18 and 3A-19). And in all countries but Costa Rica, where there was no change, those with a university education were more likely to be in the bottom 20 percent at the end of the decade than at the beginning. This shift may reflect civil

14. Given the nonlinearity of the logit model, the value of the partial derivative depends on the value of all explanatory variables. For example, the extent to which an additional year of schooling reduces the probability of an individual's being in the bottom 20 percent of the distribution depends on the individual's level of schooling. The partial derivatives, or marginal effects, we report were evaluated at the means of the explanatory variables. The changing marginal effects are implicit in the simulations reported in tables 3A-16 through 3A-22.

Table 3-5. *Probability of Belonging to the Bottom 20 Percent of the Income Distribution, by Education and Gender, Seven Countries, 1989*
Percent

Country	None	Primary	Secondary[a]	University	Male	Female
		Level of education				
Argentina	69	36	13	6	13	37
Brazil	54	19	5	2	14	37
Colombia	67	32	9	4	16	27
Costa Rica	55	25	8	4	16	34
Panama	83	45	12	4	13	34
Uruguay	65	31	10	4	13	34
Venezuela	50	25	10	5	15	38
Average	63	30	10	4	14	34

Sources: See tables 3A-16 through 3A-22. Probabilities are rounded to the nearest full percentage point.
a. Corresponds to twelve years of schooling.

service pay cuts and downward pressure on salaries caused by an increased supply of graduates.[15]

Among the various sample characteristics considered, education again has the widest range of probabilities. In 1989 the chance of being at the bottom of the income distribution ranges on average from 63 percent for those with no education to 4 percent for those with a university education (table 3-5).[16] An additional year of schooling reduces the probability of being poor—for an average individual—by 3 to 4 percentage points, an approximate average of the marginal effect in each country, with the effect strongest in Panama and Brazil. This finding suggests that additional years of formal education may have a relatively strong impact in terms of alleviating poverty.

Gender also has a strong relationship with poverty. Women have a 34 percent probability of being in the bottom two deciles, versus 14 percent for men (table 3-5). The most striking aspect of these results is their consistency across countries, which can be taken as evidence of gender discrimination.[17] Not surprisingly, the probability of being at the bottom of the income distribution diminishes with age and hours worked in all countries. The magnitude of those effects, however, varies among countries.

A separate study has shown that indigenous people in Bolivia and Guatemala are 20 percent more likely to be in the bottom quintile than are mu-

15. See Psacharopoulos and Ying (1994).
16. These probabilities are based on a worker with the average individual characteristics in the sample and the specific level of schooling being considered.
17. See Psacharopoulos and Tzannatos (1992).

lattoes and blacks in Brazil.[18] Finally, workers in the public sector are consistently less likely to have low incomes than are those in the private sector. Where such information is available, people in urban areas have a similar advantage over those in rural areas. Both results are consistent with traditional views of widespread poverty in rural areas and little poverty among public sector employees.

Conclusion

We have examined household survey data from seven Latin American countries for two time periods during the 1980s. The results show that income inequality, measured in terms of the Theil and Gini indexes, increased in Argentina, Brazil, and Panama and decreased in Colombia, Costa Rica, and Uruguay (table 3-1). In the case of Venezuela the Theil index increased, while the Gini coefficient decreased. Also, the evidence suggests an inverse relationship between per capita income and inequality in five of the seven countries (figure 3-2).

In both the decomposition and the probability analyses, education is the variable with the strongest impact on income inequality and poverty. On average, one-fourth of total inequality can be explained by level of education (table 3-3). The probability analyses show that in all seven countries the chance of being in the bottom 20 percent of the income distribution diminishes monotonically with education (tables 3A-9 through 3A-15).

Another finding from both the decomposition and probability analyses is great stability in the results between the beginning and the end of the decade. This consistency suggests that the determinants of income inequality and poverty remained unchanged during the 1980s.

We conclude that education is one of the most powerful weapons for combating poverty and income inequality. By equalizing the distribution of education and reducing education-based income differentials through higher average levels of schooling, Latin American governments would reduce income disparities between salaried and nonsalaried workers.[19]

18. The link between ethnicity and poverty is noted in Psacharopoulos and others (1992, p. 44). For a more extensive analysis of the income position and living conditions of indigenous people in Latin America, see Psacharopoulos (1993); and Patrinos and Psacharopoulos (forthcoming).

19. For supporting evidence from a number of Latin American countries, see Psacharopoulos (1989); and Gomez-Castellanos and Psacharopoulos (1990, figure 2).

These results highlight the importance of the choice of educational strategies. In general, strategies that emphasize literacy and primary education reduce income inequality because they equalize the distribution of education. They also reduce poverty by increasing the productivity of the poor, improving their chances of obtaining higher-wage employment, and generating a mechanism of upward social mobility for the economically disadvantaged, particularly children born in poor households.

References

Altimir, O. 1987. "Income Distribution Statistics in Latin America and their Reliability." *Review of Income and Wealth* 33(2): 111–55.
Altimir, O., and S. Piñera. 1979. "Análisis de descomposiciones de las desigualdades de ingresos en América Latina." In *La Distribución del Ingreso en América Latina*, edited by O. Muñoz Goma. Buenos Aires: El Cid Editores.
Bourguignon, François. 1979. "Decomposable Income Inequality Measures." *Econometrica* 47 (July): 901–20.
Cramer, J. S. 1991. *The LOGIT Model: An Introduction for Economists*. London: E. Arnold.
Fields, Gary S. 1988. "Income Distribution and Economic Growth." In *The State of Development Economics: Progress and Perspectives*, edited by G. Ranis and T. P. Schultz. Basil Blackwell.
Fiszbein, Ariel. 1991. "Essays on Labor Markets and Income Inequality in Less-Developed Countries." Ph.D. dissertation, University of California, Berkeley.
Gomez-Castellanos, L., and George Psacharopoulos. 1990. "Earnings and Education in Ecuador: Evidence from the 1987 Household Survey." *Economics of Education Review* 9(3): 219–27.
Kakwani, Nanak C. 1980. *Income Inequality and Poverty: Methods of Estimation and Policy Applications*. Oxford University Press.
LeCaillon, Jacques, and others. 1984. *Income Distribution and Economic Development: An Analytical Survey*. Geneva: International Labor Organization.
Patrinos, Harry, and George Psacharopoulos. Forthcoming. "Socioeconomic and Ethnic Determinants of Age-Grade Distortion in Bolivian and Guatemalan Primary Schools." *International Journal of Educational Development*. Washington: World Bank.
Psacharopoulos, George. 1989. "Time Trends of the Returns to Education: Cross-National Evidence." *Economics of Education Review* 8(3): 225–31.
———. 1993. "Ethnicity, Education, and Earnings in Bolivia and Guatemala." *Comparative Education Review* (February).
Psacharopoulos, George, and Ying Chu Ng. 1994. "Earnings and Education in Latin America." *Education Economics* 2 (2):187–207.
Psacharopoulos, George, and Zafiris Tzannatos. 1992. *Case Studies on Women's Employment and Pay in Latin America*. Washington: World Bank.

Psacharopoulos, George, and others. 1992. *Poverty and Income Distribution in Latin America: The Story of the 1980s*. Latin America and the Caribbean Technical Department Report 27. Washington: World Bank.

Ramos, Lauro. 1990. "The Distribution of Earnings in Brazil: 1976–85." Ph.D. dissertation, University of California, Berkeley.

Shorrocks, A. F. 1980. "The Class of Additively Decomposable Inequality Measures." *Econometrica* 48 (April): 613–25.

Theil, H. 1967. *Economics and Information Theory*. Amsterdam: North Holland.

Van der Walle, Dominique. 1991. "Poverty and Inequality in Latin America and the Caribbean during the 70s and 80s: An Overview of the Evidence." LATHR 22. Washington: World Bank.

Van Ginneken, W., and Park Jong-goo, eds. 1984. *Generating Internationally Comparable Income Distribution Estimates*. Geneva: International Labor Organization; and Washington: World Bank.

World Bank. 1991. *World Development Report*. Oxford University.

Table 3A-1. *Income Survey Data Descriptions, Seven Countries*

Country and date	Survey name	Executing agency	Geographical coverage	Number of observations	Income concept
Argentina					
October 1980	Encuesta Permanente de Hogares (EPH)	Instituto Nacional de Estadística y Censos	Buenos Aires metropolitan area	3,440	Income from all sources
May 1989	Encuesta Permanente de Hogares (EPH)	Instituto Nacional de Estadística y Censos	Buenos Aires metropolitan area	5,358	Income from all sources
Brazil					
November 1979	Pesquisa Nacional por Amostra de Domicilios	Fundaçao Instituto Brazileiro de Geografía y Estadística (PNAD)	National	134,017	Income from all sources
Fourth quarter 1989	Pesquisa Nacional por Amostra de Domicilios	Fundaçao Instituto Brazileiro de Geografía y Estadística (PNAD)	National	109,497	Income from all sources
Colombia					
September 1980	Encuesta Nacional de Hogares - Fuerza de Trabajo (ENH)	Departamento Administrativo Nacional de Estadística	Barranquilla, Bogotá, Bucaramanga, Cali, Manizales, Medellín y Pasto	11,502	Income from all sources
September 1989	Encuesta Nacional de Hogares - Fuerza de Trabajo (ENH)	Departamento Administrativo Nacional de Estadística	Barranquilla, Bogotá, Bucaramanga, Cali, Cartagena, Manizales, Medellín y Pasto	26,533	Income from all sources

	Survey	Institution	Coverage	Sample	Income concept
Costa Rica					
July 1981	Encuesta Nacional de Hogares - Empleo y Desempleo (ENH)	Dirección General de Estadística y Censos	National	8,219	Income from all sources
July 1989	Encuesta de Hogares de Propósitos Múltiples (EHPM)	Dirección General de Estadística y Censos	National	8.965	Income from all sources
Panama					
September 19–October 28, 1979	Encuesta de Hogares, Mano de Obra (EMO)	Dirección de Estadística y Censo	National	7,431	Labor income
August 1989	Encuesta de Hogares, Mano de Obra (EMO)	Dirección de Estadística y Censo	National	6,734	Labor income
Uruguay					
Second half 1981	Encuesta Nacional de Hogares (ENH)	Dirección General de Estadística y Censos	Urban	11,461	Income from all sources
Second half 1989	Encuesta Nacional de Hogares (ENH)	Dirección General de Estadística y Censos	Urban	11,911	Income from all sources
Venezuela					
Second half 1981	Encuesta de Hogares por Muestra (EHM)	Oficina Central de Estadística e Informática	National	62,843	Labor income
Second half 1989	Encuesta de Hogares por Muestra (EHM)	Oficina Central de Estadística e Informática	National	62,247	Labor income

Table 3A-2. *Income by Decile and Income Inequality, Argentina,*
1980, 1989

	1980		1989	
Decile	Mean income[a]	Income share (percent)	Mean income[b]	Income share (percent)
1	371	2.6	1,413	1.6
2	569	3.95	2,762	3.2
3	716	5.0	3,691	4.3
4	837	5.8	4,407	5.1
5	988	6.9	5,283	6.1
6	1,151	8.0	6,343	7.4
7	1,420	9.85	7,652	8.9
8	1,737	12.0	9,700	11.3
9	2,267	15.75	13,550	15.7
10	4,355	30.3	31,360	36.4
Mean	1,441	. . .	8,616	. . .

Summary statistic

Gini	0.389		0.461
Theil	0.264		0.431
T^* (percent)[c]	3.25		5.02
$T_d^{\;d}$	0.245		0.355
Number	3,440		5,358

Source: Authors' calculations based on country surveys.
a. Thousands of current pesos.
b. Current australes.
c. $T^* = T/(\ln N)$ is the standardized Theil index.
d. T_d is the Theil index of inequality between deciles.

Table 3A-3. *Income by Decile and Income Inequality, Brazil, 1979, 1989*

	1979		1989	
Decile	Mean income[a]	Income share (percent)	Mean income[b]	Income share (percent)
1	6,829	1.0	84	0.8
2	14,595	2.2	196	1.8
3	20,282	3.0	253	2.3
4	24,742	3.7	319	2.9
5	30,504	4.5	425	3.8
6	38,393	5.7	552	5.0
7	49,667	7.4	747	6.7
8	68,147	10.1	1,071	9.6
9	105,473	15.6	1,769	15.9
10	316,330	46.9	5,715	51.3
Mean	67,496	. . .	1,113	. . .

Summary statistic

Gini	0.574		0.625
Theil	0.691		0.843
T^* (percent)[c]	5.86		7.27
$T_d^{\;d}$	0.575		0.692
Number	134,017		109,497

Source: Authors' calculations based on country surveys.
a. Current cruzeiros.
b. Current cruzados novos.
c. $T^* = T/(\ln N)$ is the standardized Theil index.
d. T_d is the Theil index of inequality between deciles.

Table 3A-4. *Income by Decile and Income Inequality, Colombia, 1980, 1989*

	1980		1989	
Decile	Mean income[a]	Income share (percent)	Mean income[b]	Income share (percent)
1	510	0.5	6,726	1.1
2	1,669	1.7	15,461	2.5
3	2,761	2.8	22,781	3.7
4	4,281	4.4	31,353	5.0
5	4,666	4.8	34,819	5.6
6	5,651	5.8	40,118	6.4
7	7,326	7.5	49,923	8.0
8	9,740	9.9	66,361	10.7
9	15,577	15.9	96,148	15.4
10	45,668	46.7	259,290	41.6
Mean	9,785	...	62,298	...

Summary statistic				
Gini	0.578		0.515	
Theil	0.673		0.526	
T^* (percent)[b]	7.20		5.16	
T_d[c]	0.586		0.459	
Number	11,502		26,533	

Source: Authors' calculations based on country surveys.
a. Current pesos.
b. $T^* = T/(\ln N)$ is the standardized Theil index.
c. T_d is the Theil index of inequality between deciles.

Table 3A-5. *Income by Decile and Income Inequality, Costa Rica, 1981, 1989*

	1981		1989	
Decile	Mean income[a]	Income share (percent)	Mean income[b]	Income share (percent)
1	194	1.0	2,823	1.6
2	379	1.9	6,061	3.4
3	642	3.2	8,813	4.9
4	1,043	5.2	10,866	6.1
5	1,397	7.0	12,741	7.1
6	1,820	9.1	14,760	8.3
7	2,203	11.0	17,425	9.8
8	2,799	14.0	21,119	11.8
9	3,585	18.0	28,112	15.8
10	5,891	29.5	55,741	31.3
Mean	1,994	...	17,846	...

Summary statistic				
Gini	0.451		0.410	
Theil	0.339		0.317	
T^* (percent)[b]	3.76		3.49	
T_d[c]	0.326		0.274	
Number	8,219		8,965	

Source: Authors' calculations based on country surveys.
a. Current colones.
b. $T^* = T/(\ln N)$ is the standardized Theil index.
c. T_d is the Theil index of inequality between deciles.

Table 3A-6. *Income by Decile and Income Inequality, Panama, 1979, 1989*

Decile	1979 Mean income[a]	1979 Income share (percent)	1989 Mean income[a]	1989 Income share (percent)
1	52	2.3	53	1.5
2	96	4.2	103	3.0
3	119	5.2	144	4.2
4	146	6.4	186	5.4
5	169	7.4	226	6.6
6	194	8.5	279	8.1
7	222	9.7	329	9.6
8	265	11.6	410	11.9
9	340	14.9	546	15.9
10	683	30.0	1,155	33.7
Mean	228	...	343	...

Summary statistic

Gini	0.376	0.446
Theil	0.266	0.361
T^* (percent)[b]	2.98	4.09
T_d[c]	0.233	0.321
Number	7,431	6,734

Source: Authors' calculations based on country surveys.
a. Current balboas.
b. $T^* = T/(\ln N)$ is the standardized Theil index.
c. T_d is the Theil index of inequality between deciles.

Table 3A-7. *Income by Decile and Income Inequality, Uruguay, 1981, 1989*

Decile	1981 Mean income[a]	1981 Income share (percent)	1989 Mean income[a]	1989 Income share (percent)
1	710	1.5	28,000	1.6
2	1,496	3.1	60,000	3.4
3	2,025	4.2	82,000	4.7
4	2,564	5.4	101,000	5.8
5	3,047	6.4	122,000	6.9
6	3,667	7.7	145,000	8.2
7	4,387	9.2	172,000	9.8
8	5,477	11.5	211,000	12.0
9	7,445	15.6	278,000	15.8
10	16,723	35.2	560,000	31.9
Mean	4,754	...	176,000	...

Summary statistic

Gini	0.452	0.420
Theil	0.394	0.329
T^* (percent)[b]	4.22	3.51
T_d[c]	0.339	0.286
Number	11,461	11,911

Source: Authors' calculations based on country surveys.
a. Current pesos.
b. $T^* = T/(\ln N)$ is the standardized Theil index.
c. T_d is the Theil index of inequality between deciles.

Table 3A-8. *Income by Decile and Income Inequality, Venezuela, 1981, 1989*

Decile	1981 Mean income[a]	Income share (percent)	1989 Mean income[a]	Income share (percent)
1	169	1.1	535	1.1
2	291	1.8	980	1.9
3	391	2.4	1,312	2.6
4	553	3.4	1,912	3.8
5	843	5.3	3,367	6.6
6	1,218	7.6	4,357	8.6
7	1,719	10.7	5,335	10.5
8	2,265	14.1	6,432	12.7
9	3,200	19.9	8,626	17.0
10	5,406	33.7	17,860	35.2
Mean	1,606	...	5,072	...

Summary statistic

Gini	0.512		0.498	
Theil	0.436		0.451	
T^* (percent)[b]	3.95		4.08	
T_d^c	0.422		0.402	
Number	62,843		62,247	

Source: Authors' calculations based on country surveys.
a. Current bolívares.
b. $T^* = T/(\ln N)$ is the standardized Theil index.
c. T_d is the Theil index of inequality between deciles.

Table 3A-9. *Probability of Belonging to the Bottom 20 Percent of the Income Distribution, Argentina, 1980, 1989*

Independent variable	Logit coefficient	Variable mean	Marginal effect
1980			
Age	−.035*	37.21	−.56
Schooling	−.234*	8.64	−3.74
Male	−1.368*	.67	−21.89
Salaried[a]	−.049	.73	−.78
Hours worked	−.038*	44.77	−.61
Summary statistic			
Constant	4.211	1.00	
Chi square	642		
Number	3,440		
1989			
Age	−.039*	38.21	−.62
Schooling	−.225*	9.63	−3.6
Male	−1.345*	.62	−21.52
Salaried[a]	−.668*	.73	−10.69
Hours worked	−0.31*	40.72	−.50
Summary statistic			
Constant	4.381	1.0	
Chi square	1,050		
Number	5,279		

Source: Authors' calculations based on country surveys.
* statistically significant at the .001 level or better.
a. Reference category is all nonsalaried workers, that is, self-employed and employers.

Table 3A-10. *Probability of Belonging to the Bottom 20 Percent of the Income Distribution, Brazil, 1979, 1989*

Independent variable	Logit coefficient	Variable mean	Marginal effect
1979			
Age	-.045*	34.39	-.72
Schooling	-.317*	4.47	-5.07
Male	-1.404*	.71	-22.46
Hours worked	-.036*	47.94	-.58
Self-employed[a]	-.389*	.31	6.22
Summary statistic			
Constant	3.631	1.00	
Chi square	5,790		
Number	26,911		
1989			
Age	-.039*	34.87	-.62
Schooling	-.263*	5.80	-4.21
Male	-1.263*	.66	-20.21
Rural	.999*	.22	16.00
Hours worked	-.037*	44.56	-.59
Mulatto	.661*	.36	10.58
Black	.537*	.06	8.59
Self-employed[a]	.411*	.24	6.58
Summary statistic			
Constant	2.759	1.00	
Chi square	5,568		
Number	21,899		

Source: Authors' calculations based on country surveys. Model fitted to 20 percent random subsample.
* statistically significant at the .001 level or better.
a. Reference category is those in dependent employment.

Table 3A-11. *Probability of Belonging to the Bottom 20 Percent of the Income Distribution, Colombia, 1980, 1989*

Independent variable	Logit coefficient	Variable mean	Marginal effect
1980			
Age	-.020*	33.65	-.32
Schooling	-.246*	7.35	-3.94
Male	-.401*	.61	-6.42
Hours worked	-.016*	48.10	-.26
Public sector	-2.064*	.11	-33.02
Employer[a]	-3.101*	.04	-49.62
Self-employed[a]	-.871*	.24	-13.94
Summary statistics			
Constant	2.122	1.0	
Chi square	1,931		
Number	11,052		
1989			
Age	-.040*	34.47	-.64
Schooling	-.249*	8.49	-3.98
Male	-.673*	.61	-10.77
Hours worked	-.012*	49.02	-.19
Public sector	-1.491*	.11	-23.86
Employer[a]	-2.616*	.05	-41.86
Self-employed[a]	-.848*	.23	-13.57
Summary statistic			
Constant	3.033	1.0	
Chi square	5,207		
Number	26,532		

Source: Authors' calculations based on country surveys.
* statistically significant at the .001 level or better.
a. Reference category is employees.

Table 3A-12. *Probability of Belonging to the Bottom 20 Percent of the Income Distribution, Costa Rica, 1981, 1989*

Independent variable	Logit coefficient	Variable mean	Marginal effect
1981			
Age	-.092*	33.80	-1.47
Schooling	-.207*	6.80	-3.31
Male	-.451*	.74	-7.22
Rural	-.293*	.49	4.69
Salaried[a]	-.135*	.81	-2.16
Hours worked	-.044*	46.04	-0.70
Summary statistic			
Constant	4.917	1.0	
Chi square	1,661		
Number	8,219		
1989			
Age	-.019*	34.42	-.30
Schooling	-.219*	7.31	-3.50
Male	-1.003*	.70	-16.05
Rural	.819*	.48	13.10
Salaried[a]	-.446*	.76	-7.14
Hours worked	-.065*	48.87	-1.04
Summary statistic			
Constant	3.914	1.0	
Chi square	2,213		
Number	8,965		

Source: Authors' calculations based on country surveys.
* statistically significant at the .001 level or better.
a. Reference category is self-employed workers and employers.

Table 3A-13. *Probability of Belonging to the Bottom 20 Percent of the Income Distribution, Panama, 1979, 1989*

Independent variable	Logit coefficient	Variable mean	Marginal effect
1979			
Age	-.046*	33.42	-.74
Schooling	-.378*	8.66	-6.05
Male	-2.070*	.61	-33.12
Public sector[a]	-.298*	.40	-4.77
Hours worked	-.044*	42.64	-.70
Summary statistic			
Constant	6.014	1.00	
Chi square	1,972		
Number	7,431		
1989			
Age	-.059*	35.16	-.94
Schooling	-.299*	9.96	-4.78
Male	-1.22*	.60	-19.52
Public sector[a]	-2.153*	.37	-34.45
Hours worked	-.054*	43.02	-.86
Summary statistic			
Constant	6.572	1.00	
Chi square	2,182		
Number	6,734		

Source: Authors' calculations based on country surveys.
* statistically significant at the .001 level or better.
a. Reference category is private sector employees.

Table 3A-14. *Probability of Belonging to the Bottom 20 Percent of the Income Distribution, Uruguay, 1981, 1989*

Independent variable	Logit coefficient	Variable mean	Marginal effect
1981			
Age	−.053*	38.05	−.85
Schooling	−.247*	7.83	−3.95
Male	−1.316*	.63	−21.06
Public sector[a]	−1.638*	.25	−26.21
Private sector[a]	−.331*	.54	−5.30
Hours worked	−.039*	44.61	−.62
Summary statistic			
Constant	5.057	1.00	
Chi square	2,286		
Number	11,461		
1989			
Age	−.054*	39.56	−.86
Schooling	−.238*	8.48	−3.81
Male	−1.199*	.60	−19.18
Public sector[a]	−2.434*	.23	−38.94
Private sector[a]	−.847*	.52	−13.55
Hours worked	−.045*	44.04	−.72
Summary statistic			
Constant	5.768	1.00	
Chi square	3,294		
Number	11,911		

Source: Authors' calculations based on country surveys.
* statistically significant at the .001 level or better.
a. Reference category is the self-employed.

Table 3A-15. *Probability of Belonging to the Bottom 20 Percent of the Income Distribution, Venezuela, 1981, 1989*

Independent variable	Logit coefficient	Variable mean	Marginal effect
1981			
Age	−.038*	34.76	−.61
Schooling	−.232*	6.37	−3.71
Male	−1.632*	.73	−26.11
Rural	.927*	.22	14.83
Weekly paid	4.506*	.44	72.10
Hours worked	−0.43*	43.25	−.69
Public sector[a]	−.885*	.23	−14.16
Employer[a]	−3.286*	.06	−52.58
Self-employed[a]	−.466*	.22	−7.46
Summary statistic			
Constant	.812	1.00	
Chi square	5,843		
Number	12,769		
1989			
Age	−.033*	35.69	−.53
Schooling	−.180*	7.6	−2.88
Male	−1.289*	.71	−20.62
Rural	1.021*	.14	16.34
Weekly paid	3.837*	.32	61.39
Hours worked	−.046*	42.39	−.74
Public sector[a]	−.849*	.18	−13.58
Employer[a]	−1.923	.07	−30.77
Self-employed[a]	.605*	.23	−9.68
Summary statistic			
Constant	1.498	1.00	
Chi square	5,532		
Number	12,360		

Source: Authors' calculations based on country surveys. Model fitted to 20 percent random subsample.
* statistically significant at the .001 level or better.
a. Reference category is private sector employees.

Table 3A-16. *Probability of Belonging to the Bottom 20 Percent of the Income Distribution, by Selected Sample Characteristics, Argentina, 1980, 1989*

Percent

	Probability	
Characteristic	*1980*	*1989*
Years of education		
0	65.4	68.6
6	31.7	36.1
9	18.7	22.4
12	10.2	12.8
16	5.3	5.6
Male	13.7	13.0
Female	38.5	36.5
Salaried	19.8	17.3
Nonsalaried	20.6	28.9
Overall probability	20.0	20.0

Source: Authors' calculations based on country surveys.

Table 3A-17. *Probability of Belonging to the Bottom 20 Percent of the Income Distribution, by Selected Sample Characteristics, Brazil, 1979, 1989*

Percent

	Probability	
Characteristic	*1979*	*1989*
Years of education		
0	50.8	53.5
6	13.0	19.2
9	5.6	9.7
12	2.2	4.7
16	0.6	1.7
Male	14.2	14.0
Female	40.4	36.5
Self-employed	24.6	25.5
Rural	n.a.	35.3
Mulatto	n.a.	27.6
Black	n.a.	29.3
Overall probability	20.0	20.0

Source: Authors' calculations based on country surveys.
n.a. Not available.

Table 3A-18. *Probability of Belonging to the Bottom 20 Percent of the Income Distribution, by Selected Sample Characteristics, Colombia, 1980, 1989*
Percent

Characteristic	Probability	
	1980	1989
Years of education		
0	60.4	67.4
6	25.8	31.7
9	14.3	18.0
12	7.4	9.4
16	2.9	3.7
Male	17.6	16.1
Female	24.2	27.4
Public sector employee	3.8	6.2
Employer	1.3	2.0
Self-employed	11.4	11.5
Overall probability	20.0	20.0

Source: Authors' calculations based on country surveys.

Table 3A-19. *Probability of Belonging to the Bottom 20 Percent of the Income Distribution, by Selected Sample Characteristics, Costa Rica, 1981, 1989*
Percent

Characteristic	Probability	
	1981	1989
Years of education		
0	50.5	55.3
6	22.8	25.0
9	13.7	14.7
12	7.9	8.2
16	3.6	3.6
Male	18.2	15.6
Female	25.9	33.5
Salaried	19.6	18.3
Nonsalaried	21.8	26.0
Rural	22.5	27.7
Urban	17.8	14.4
Overall probability	20.0	20.0

Source: Authors' calculations based on country surveys.

Table 3A-20. *Probability of Belonging to the Bottom 20 Percent of the Income Distribution, by Selected Sample Characteristics, Panama, 1979, 1989*
Percent

| Characteristic | Probability | |
	1979	*1989*
Years of education		
0	86.8	83.1
6	40.6	45.0
9	18.0	25.0
12	6.6	12.0
16	1.5	3.9
Male	10.0	13.3
Female	46.9	34.2
Public sector employee	17.3	6.5
Overall probability	20.0	20.0

Source: Authors' calculations based on country surveys.

Table 3A-21. *Probability of Belonging to the Bottom 20 Percent of the Income Distribution, by Selected Sample Characteristics, Uruguay, 1981, 1989*
Percent

| Characteristic | Probability | |
	1981	*1989*
Years of education		
0	63.4	65.3
6	28.2	31.1
9	15.8	18.1
12	8.2	9.8
16	3.2	4.0
Male	13.3	13.4
Female	36.4	33.9
Public sector employee	6.8	3.7
Private sector employee	17.7	14.3
Overall probability	20.0	20.0

Source: Authors' calculations based on country surveys.

Table 3A-22. *Probability of Belonging to the Bottom 20 Percent of the Income Distribution, by Selected Sample Characteristics, Venezuela, 1981, 1989*

Percent

Characteristic	Probability	
	1981	*1989*
Years of education		
0	52.3	49.5
6	21.4	25.0
9	12.0	16.3
12	6.3	10.2
16	2.6	5.2
Male	13.9	14.7
Female	45.1	38.4
Public sector employee	11.2	11.1
Employer	11.3	4.0
Self-employed	14.8	28.5
Rural	34.0	37.6
Overall probability	20.0	20.0

Source: Authors' calculations based on country surveys.

CHAPTER FOUR

Poverty Alleviation, Income Redistribution, and Growth during Adjustment

Elisabeth Sadoulet and Alain de Janvry

ACHIEVING stabilization in response to the international financial and commodity market shocks of the 1980s has not been easy for Latin America. Most countries went through a series of policy reforms before successfully controlling inflation, and others have not achieved stabilization despite a decade of renewed initiatives.[1] The shocks exposed the existence of serious disequilibria and economic mismanagement during the previous decade of favorable commodity prices and rapid debt accumulation, and they also exacerbated the region's extensive poverty. Stabilization and adjustment policies thus needed not only to overcome external shocks, but also to correct unsustainable disequilibria and cope with the pressures of poverty. In addition, the sharp redistributive effects of the shocks and the policy measures unleashed political battles that made policy sustainability a major determinant of success. Because

We are indebted to Jaime de Melo and Darryl McLeod for useful suggestions.

1. With an inflation rate of 30 percent as the dividing line, El Salvador, Bolivia, Chile, Mexico, Paraguay, Costa Rica, Colombia, Honduras, Venezuela, and Guatemala had achieved stabilization by 1991, while Ecuador, Jamaica, the Dominican Republic, Uruguay, Argentina, Peru, and Brazil remained above this inflation threshold. See Inter-American Development Bank (1992).

there is a spectrum of instruments that governments can use for stabilization, policies have taken a variety of forms, with diverse consequences for economic growth, the welfare of the poor, and the political mobilization of civil society. This chapter analyzes these policy alternatives and the trade-offs among them.

We use a dynamic computable general equilibrium (CGE) model to analyze jointly the economic, welfare, and political implications of alternative policy packages. This permits us to assess complex trade-offs among these three dimensions, both at one point in time and over time. Such analysis is necessary for the design of economically effective and politically sustainable stabilization policies that minimize welfare costs. The model in this chapter captures the economic and social structure of Ecuador. We have chosen to use Ecuador as a policy laboratory because it has many features that are generic to Latin America. Because inflation, capital flight, and interest rates play key roles in stabilization and adjustment, the model incorporates not only the real side of Ecuador's economy, but also its financial sector. We consider the impact of different stabilization and adjustment policies one at a time, and then simulate a policy package similar to that implemented in Ecuador. Finally, the model links stabilization policies to other measures designed to protect the poor.

The key question in this chapter is whether the policy instruments available for stabilization and adjustment involve trade-offs among the goals of political feasibility, economic effectiveness, and poverty alleviation. The general conclusion is that there are very sharp trade-offs, which suggests the difficulty of achieving adjustment. The optimum policy package for a particular country must take account of its economic, social, and political structure, as well as the magnitude of its initial disequilibria and external shocks. Unanticipated additional shocks, imperfect information, and divisions among policymakers have made defining a feasible and effective policy package even more difficult. In many countries, the road to adjustment has been protracted. In Ecuador, as of 1991, stabilization was still incomplete, as inflation remained at 49 percent.[2]

More specifically, our conclusion is that policies most effective at restoring economic growth are also most effective at reducing poverty in the long run. Growth is thus the best long-run solution to poverty, but adjustment policies are very hard to implement because in the short run they increase absolute poverty and arouse political opposition among urban groups. As a result, if of-

2. International Monetary Fund (1994).

ficials want to use policies that effectively restore economic growth, explicit political management is necessary to make them politically feasible and sustainable, and safety nets must be introduced to shelter the poor during the transition. We find that in a recessionary economy, when political support for taxes and subsidies is very difficult to organize, foreign transfers need to fund domestic safety nets. But if the adjustment process proceeds without setbacks, and the foreign resources are effectively targeted and managed, the necessary transfers are both small and brief. The implication is that resources for political and welfare management should be an integral component of structural adjustment loans.

The Socioeconomic Structure of Ecuador

Tables 4-1 through 4-4 characterize the economic and social structure of Ecuador in 1980, before the outbreak of the debt crisis. That year provides a baseline in our construction of a social accounting matrix and serves as the reference point in our analysis of the subsequent impact of the debt crisis and stabilization.

Structure of the Economy

The sectoral structure of Ecuador's economy in 1980 reflected a low level of industrialization (table 4-1). The share of GDP originating in manufacturing was only 17.5 percent, compared to an average of 25 percent in Latin America.[3] The industry that previously emerged under import substitution and an overvalued real exchange rate was of necessity very intensive in capital and in import content. The share of labor employed in industry was consequently low, as it absorbed only 10 percent of the economically active population (EAP).[4] High import dependency, of course, made this infant industry particularly vulnerable to the foreign shocks that occurred in the early 1980s. The oil sector, with a very small share of total employment, accounted for 11.5 percent of GDP.[5] The agricultural sector in 1980 accounted for only 13 percent of GDP, even though it absorbed 40 percent of the EAP. The economy was heavily dominated by utilities, construction, transportation, trade, services, and government, which together represented 58 percent of GDP and absorbed

3. Inter-American Development Bank (1988, p. 62).
4. Population Census (1982).
5. Central Bank of Ecuador (1982).

Table 4-1. *Structural Characteristics of the Economy, Ecuador, 1980*
Percent unless otherwise specified

Macroeconomic characteristics

GDP per capita	U.S.$1,406	Balance of trade deficit/exports value	1.0
Population	7.65 million	Balance of payments deficit/exports value	19.5
Imports/domestic demand	15.6	Balance of payments deficit/GDP	5.4
Exports/GDP	27.4	Fiscal deficit/GDP	3.7

Sectoral characteristics

	Agriculture	Oil	Industry	Utilities, construction, services	Admininistration
Share in GDP	13.0	11.5	17.5	48.1	9.9
Share in exports	9.6	54.7	23.0	12.7	0
Share in imports	3.3	7.8	74.1	14.8	0

Government budget

Shares in total government revenues		Shares in total government expenditures	
Income taxes and transfers	28.2	Current expenditures	52.4
Indirect taxes and import tariffs	34.8	Transfers to rest of world	
Oil revenues	37.0	(including debt service)	9.9
Deficit	17.6	Miscellaneous current	
Total	117.6	account transfers	9.9
		Investment	22.9
		Miscellaneous capital	
		account transfers	4.8
		Total	99.9

Financing the deficit	
Foreign borrowing	143
Domestic borrowing	-32
Credit from Central Bank	-11

Sources: Banco Central del Ecuador, *Cuentas Nacionales del Ecuador,* various issues, annex table.

45 percent of the EAP. The dominance of the nontradable sectors was characteristic of an economy that had grown very rapidly on the basis of a primary sector boom that encouraged sharp appreciation of the real exchange rate and rapid growth in nontradables.

In 1980 Ecuador's economy was fairly open to international trade, with imports representing 15.6 percent of domestic consumption and exports 27.4 percent of GDP (table 4-1). The structure of trade, however, was not very diversified on the import or export sides. Imports were dominated by production requirements: the production goods sector accounted for 69 percent of total imports, while consumer goods (agriculture, food processing, and cloth-

Table 4-2. Economy of Ecuador, by Sector, 1980
Percent unless otherwise specified

Item	Agriculture exports	Other agriculture	Oil	Industrial construction	Production	Utilities, construction, transportation	Trade	Services	Government services	Total Millions of sucres	Total Percent
Share in sectoral expenditures											
Intermediate input	15.7	16.2	14.9	61.4	64.0	42.8	37.0	34.3	38.3	187,061	41.0
Labor	19.6	47.5	4.8	12.1	17.5	37.1	29.4	49.5	61.7	143,814	31.5
Profits	64.7	36.3	80.3	26.4	18.5	20.0	33.7	16.2	0	125,135	27.4
Domestic supply[a]	14,193	27,638	36,431	79,129	46,084	81,294	57,940	70,221	43,080	456,010	...
Share in total supply											
Domestic supply	70.9	74.1	74.8	78.9	32.7	95.3	90.0	95.7	100.0	456,010	74.4
Trade margins	27.7	20.4	3.5	12.6	21.8	0	0	0	0	58,182	9.5
Taxes and tariffs	1.3	-1.1	9.8	4.7	8.9	1.0	0.4	2.0	0	24,388	4.0
Imports	0	6.7	11.9	3.8	36.5	3.7	9.6	2.3	0	74,527	12.2
Total supply[a]	20,014	37,308	48,687	100,239	140,784	85,267	64,387	73,341	43,080	613,107	...
Share in total demand											
Intermediate demand	53.9	55.9	12.1	21.4	52.0	27.3	14.8	41.7	0	187,061	33.7
Private consumption	10.7	40.5	2.9	62.2	22.3	21.3	25.7	57.4	1.2	174,875	31.5
Government consumption	0	0	0	0	0	0	0	0	98.8	42,562	7.7
Exports	33.7	0.9	82.8	15.1	1.3	6.0	59.5	0.8	0	73,797	13.3
Investment	1.7	2.8	2.1	1.3	24.3	45.3	0	0	0	76,630	13.8
Total demand[a]	20,014	37,308	48,687	100,239	140,784	85,267	6,205	73,341	43,080	554,925	...
Sectoral Shares											
Value added	4.4	8.6	11.5	11.3	6.2	17.3	13.6	17.2	9.9	...	100.0
Domestic supply	3.1	6.1	8.0	17.4	10.1	17.8	12.7	15.4	9.4	...	100.0
Imports	0	3.3	7.8	5.1	69.0	4.2	8.3	2.3	0	...	100.0
Exports	9.1	0.4	54.7	20.5	2.5	6.9	5.0	0.8	0	...	100.0

Source: Input-output table in Central Bank of Ecuador, National Accounts, 1988.
a. Thousands of sucres.

Table 4-3. *Structure of Household Incomes, by Type of Household and Source of Income, Ecuador, 1980*
Percent unless otherwise specified

Type of household	Class income (sucres)	Sources of income								Benefits from government current expense (percent of income)
		Labor			Unincorporate capital				Transfers from government	
		Agriculture	Unskilled non-agricultural	Skilled non-agricultural	Agriculture	Industry	Other non-agricultural	Other		
Small farms	33,966	22.5	39.8	3.8	9.3	7.1	11.8	4.3	1.3	4.5
Medium farms	11,326	30.2	16.3	2.6	34.0	3.8	10.5	2.4	0.2	3.0
Large farms	13,093	22.5	9.0	4.0	46.2	2.3	13.5	2.1	0.4	3.0
Rural nonagricultural	19,253	3.2	39.7	9.7	9.1	8.7	24.8	4.1	0.6	10.6
Urban low education	70,911	1.4	44.5	8.8	2.7	11.7	19.8	7.3	3.8	9.6
Urban medium education	55,499	0.5	32.8	29.8	0.7	6.4	14.9	9.6	5.3	9.1
Urban high education	37,893	0.3	4.8	64.7	0.8	0.8	11.3	12.3	4.9	2.3
Rural	77,638	18.8	31.2	5.1	19.1	6.2	15.1	3.6	0.8	5.5
Urban	164,303	0.8	31.4	28.8	1.6	7.4	16.2	9.2	4.5	7.7
Total	241,941	6.6	31.3	21.2	7.2	7.0	15.9	7.4	3.3	7.0

Source: For income, see table 4A-1. For government benefits, authors' calculations based on data in Kouwenaar (1988).

Table 4-4. Income per Capita and Incidence of Poverty, Ecuador, 1980

Type of household	Population share	Income per capita[a]		Utility per capita[a]		Poverty by income class[b]		Total poverty	
		Dollars	Relative to average	Dollars	Relative to average	H[c]	P[d]	H[c]	P[d]
Small farms	30.3	586	0.5	612.5	0.5	57.9	14.0	49.0	59.8
Medium farms	8.1	731	0.6	753.1	0.6	48.1	10.5	10.9	12.0
Large farms	5.0	1,369	1.1	1,410.3	1.0	21.7	3.4	3.0	2.4
Rural nonagricultural	7.4	1,360	1.1	1,504.6	1.1	20.0	3.1	4.1	3.2
Urban low education	32.5	1,141	0.9	1,250.4	0.9	32.7	4.6	29.7	21.1
Urban medium education	12.5	2,322	1.8	2,532.8	1.9	8.6	0.8	3.0	1.4
Urban high education	4.2	4,718	3.7	4,826.0	3.6	1.7	0.1	0.2	0.1
Rural	50.8	799	0.6	843	0.6	47.3	10.9	67.2	78.1
Urban	49.2	1,746	1.4	1,881	1.4	23.8	3.2	32.7	22.2
Total	7.65	1,265	1.0	1,354	1.0	35.8	7.1	100.0	100.0

Source: Table A4-1.
a. Utility is the sum of net income including transfers plus the cost of imputed benefits from government social expenditures.
b. Poverty lines are $530 for rural households and $748 for urban households. H is the head count ratio and P is the Foster-Greer-Thorbecke index.
c. Share of population below poverty line.
d. Poverty index.

ing) represented only 8.4 percent of all imports (table 4-2). For the production goods sector, these imports represented a very large share (67.2 percent) of total supply, reflecting industry's high level of technological dependency.

Exports were similarly concentrated in a few sectors. Oil and oil products accounted for 54.7 percent of all exports; agricultural products for 9.5 percent; and consumer goods, mainly processed foods, for 20.5 percent (table 4-2). Exports of other goods, industrial products in particular, were negligible. Thanks to high oil prices in 1980, the balance of trade in that year was almost in equilibrium. The balance of payments, however, showed a deficit that amounted to 19.5 percent of export revenues, or 5.4 percent of GDP (table 4-1). Half of these foreign transfers were debt service payments (table 4A-1).

Foreign borrowing in 1980 exceeded the balance of payments deficit by 43 percent. This borrowing covered the accumulation of foreign assets by households and allowed for an increase in the foreign reserves of the central bank. The government accounted for 74 percent of foreign borrowing; private firms, the remaining 26 percent (table 4A-1). The debt crisis in 1982 brought this large flow of public foreign borrowing to a halt, making stabilization necessary.

As in many countries that have grown rapidly through a primary sector boom, the government in Ecuador played a large role in the economy. In 1980 the public budget amounted to 32 percent of GDP (table 4A-1). Of particular importance in Ecuador's budget were earnings from mineral exports, as 37 percent of government revenues came from oil (table 4-1). The rest came from income taxes and miscellaneous transfers (28 percent) and from commodity taxes (35 percent), distributed equally between taxes on domestic products and import tariffs. Tariffs were very uneven across sectors. While manufacturing imports were taxed at 22 and 39 percent, the net subsidy on agricultural imports was 24 percent (table 4A-1). In general, income taxes were very weak, with only 8 percent of the EAP paying income tax. Export taxes were also insignificant, particularly on agriculture.[6] The direct link between oil exports and government revenues created a high degree of risk for public expenditures, in that a drop in the world price of oil could dramatically restrict government resources at once, well before any corresponding recession further diminished other revenue sources. But this link also meant that a devaluation of the exchange rate, which increases export revenues in the domestic currency, could alleviate the government's budget deficit. Current expenditures on public services and public investment represented 52 percent and 23 per-

6. Vos (1988).

cent of the government's budget, respectively, the rest (10 percent) being transfers to the rest of the world for debt service and miscellaneous other purposes (table 4-1). Revenues covered only 85 percent of expenditures. Foreign borrowing, however, was sufficiently large in 1980 to enable the government to inject money into the domestic credit market rather than borrow from it, and to reimburse the central bank rather than call on it for money creation.

Oil revenues and foreign credit helped the government sustain an ambitious program of public investment. Yet the strategy of oil- and debt-led growth was seriously flawed in terms of efficiency and sustainability. About half the oil revenues financed consumer subsidies, in particular through very low domestic oil prices.[7] Holding the nominal exchange rate constant despite rising domestic inflation caused the real exchange rate to appreciate sharply.[8] The result was a decline in the domestic value of foreign borrowing, much of which financed consumption or inefficient investment projects.

In sum, the structure of the Ecuadorean economy in 1980 was such that the country—its public sector in particular—was highly exposed to fluctuations in oil export revenues and in the availability and price of foreign loans.

Income and Poverty

Though there had been remarkable progress in the levels of health, education, and per capita income during the previous decade of oil and debt booms, by 1980 Ecuador still had a surprisingly high level of poverty, particularly in rural areas, and inequality was also very high (table 4-4).[9]

Table 4-3 reports the total income of each class in 1980 and decomposes it by source. Small farmers had per capita incomes that were less than half those of large farmers. In rural areas, access to land is the key factor explaining the levels of income. In the urban sector, the level of absolute poverty is far lower, but highly educated households earn four times more than do illiterates (table 4-4). As a study by PREALC and the Hague has shown, the main determinants of poverty in the urban sector are large household size and low educational levels.[10]

The poor in Ecuador have remarkably diversified sources of income, thanks in part to the country's well-developed infrastructure network and decentralized urban pattern, which is unusual among Latin American countries. Small

7. See the input-output table in Central Bank of Ecuador (1982).
8. Keeler, Greene, and Scobie (1988).
9. For inequality data see Barreiros (1988).
10. See Barreiros (1988).

farmers earn 66 percent of their income from labor services (including labor
on their own farm), two-thirds of which originates in nonagricultural activities. All farm sizes obtain about 15 percent of their income from profits in
nonagricultural activities (table 4-3). The urban poor also have diversified
sources of income, with 34 percent from profits in informal sector activities.
This structural feature is important, because it implies that the urban poor are
able to protect themselves rather well from wage repression policies. By contrast, middle-income and rich households in urban areas derive large shares of
their income from market wages for skilled nonagricultural labor. Profits
earned by unincorporated capital and distributed from firms account for
13 percent of the upper-class income. Table 4-4 shows that the bulk of absolute poverty is in the rural sector among small- and medium-sized farms.
These two groups, which account for 38 percent of the total population, in
1980 had an average per capita income of $616, compared to a national aver-
age of $1,265. The extent of rural poverty in Ecuador is surprisingly large and
persistent for a country at that level of per capita income.

Table 4-3 evaluates government expenditures in health and education programs at their cost and attributes them to each class according to their rate of
participation. These have been derived from Kouwenaar's detailed analysis of
the distribution of government benefits across social groups.[11] We define *utility* as the sum of net income, including transfers, and imputed benefits from
government social programs. Looking closely at the distribution of social benefits, we see that urban groups—particularly low- and medium-education
households—and rural nonagricultural groups capture the bulk of benefits, indicating the strong urban and upper-middle-class biases of public services.
These three groups, respectively, derive 9.6 percent, 8.8 percent, and 8.3 percent of their total utility from government benefits. This helps explain why
stabilization programs that impose fiscal austerity on current expenditures
strongly affect these groups. The incidence of benefits is nevertheless progressive in the urban sector, though regressive in rural areas.

To calculate poverty indexes, we must both define an absolute poverty
level and characterize the distribution of income or utility within each class.
The poverty line (B) represents the cost of a basic needs consumption basket.
Different patterns of consumption and prices in rural and urban areas lead to
different poverty lines, which we estimate at $530 and $748, respectively.
Lognormal frequency distributions are assumed within each class. Their parameters are computed on the basis of independent estimations of the percentage

11. Kouwenaar (1988, p. 229).

of poor and the average income for each class in 1975.[12] Poverty is measured by the share of the population below the poverty line (H) and by a poverty index (P) that reflects social aversion to extreme levels of poverty. Following Foster, Greer, and Thorbecke, we define the loss function as the square of the distance to the poverty line and the index as the sum of these squares over the poor population. If B is the poverty line for that group, the poverty index P, measured relative to the square of the average poverty income level, is:

$$P = \int_0^B (\frac{B-y}{B})^2 \, f(y) \, dy,$$

where $f(y)$ is the frequency distribution of income. For estimated values of the parameters of the lognormal for each social class, we can thus characterize the welfare effect of each policy alternative by the changes it causes in H and P. A desirable property of these indexes is that the total population index is the weighted sum of the group indexes, where the weights are the groups' population shares.

The head count ratio H shows a high incidence of poverty in rural areas, where an average of 47.3 percent of the population is in absolute poverty, including more than 58 percent of numerous small farmers (table 4-4). In urban areas, by contrast, poverty is less extensive and mostly observed in the low-education group largely because the urban population benefited most from the period of sustained growth that accompanied the oil boom between 1974 and 1980. The poverty index P shows that poverty was three times more severe in rural areas than in urban areas.

Combining the level of poverty in each group with its share of the total population gives the relative weight of each group in overall poverty. According to both indexes, the rural poor contribute to more than half of overall poverty. Their share increases from the H index to the P index, indicating that extreme levels of poverty are found in rural areas. Landless and small farmers, who represent 30.3 percent of the total population, account for 49.0 percent of the poor, and as much as 57.9 percent of them are below the poverty line (table 4-4). Only 32.7 percent of those with low education in urban areas are below the poverty line, indicating a clear rural bias in the incidence of poverty. Figures 4-4 and 4-5 report urban and rural contributions to poverty in the form of an indicator that equals $N \times P$, where N is the group's population share from table 4-4. The base values for the rural and urban populations respectively are 5.5 and 1.6, which sum to the total poverty index of 7.1.

12. Kouwenaar (1988, p. 89).

The 1980 Social Accounting Matrix

Table 4A-1 summarizes the structure of Ecuador's economy in a consistent and convenient manner by presenting a Social Accounting Matrix (SAM). The economic disaggregation includes nine sectors: two agricultural sectors, one for exports and one for other goods, which are mainly nontradable foods; the oil sector; two industrial sectors, one for consumer goods (including food processing, textiles, and leather), the other for producer and capital goods; and four mostly nontradable sectors, with trade, services, the government, and a combination of utilities, construction, and transportation. The social disaggregation includes three labor categories—skilled, unskilled, and agricultural labor—and seven household classes: small farmers, medium farmers, large farmers, and nonagricultural households for rural areas; and households with low, medium, and high levels of education for urban areas.

The most novel part of this SAM is its record of transactions on financial assets. All entries report transactions that occurred during 1980. The capital accounts report the assets of households, firms, government, and the central bank. The different assets include real assets (stocks, housing, household capital, government capital, and shares) and financial assets (money, domestic bonds, and foreign assets).

The aggregate asset structure of households shows that capital stocks dominate their total wealth. Holdings of unincorporated capital and housing represents 72 percent of all household assets. Holdings of firm shares, which represent another 9 percent of total assets, should also be considered capital stock, rather than financial savings, because there is no market for shares in Ecuador. The counterpart to large holdings of productive assets is low participation in financial savings, as only 11 percent of household assets are in domestic currency, 13 percent in time deposits, and 14 percent in foreign currency. The structure of asset ownership according to socioeconomic class shows distinctive patterns. Foreign currency is held mostly by the urban rich and, to a lesser extent, by urban middle-income households. Time deposits and shares are more equally distributed among the three urban income groups. As for unincorporated capital, it is widely spread across household classes, with 28 percent in the hands of the low-income urban group and 10 to 15 percent in those of each of the other groups.

The structure of asset portfolios, however, varies greatly across urban households, with the rich saving mostly in foreign currency and deposits; the middle-income group in housing, foreign currency, deposits, and shares in almost equal proportions; and the poor largely in housing. The savings of all rural groups are mainly in the form of productive assets.

The structure of firm portfolios varies across sectors. The share of the informal sector (identified with household capital) in nonagricultural activities varies from 23 percent in production goods to 46 percent in trade. The need for working capital is very high in construction and transportation, trade, and services, where holdings average 7 to 8 percent of the value of production. Stock holdings are relatively low, except in production goods and trade, where they reach 9 and 11 percent of annual production respectively. The structure of debt shows the agricultural sector to borrow mostly from domestic sources, while the production goods sector has nearly half its debt from foreign sources.

The capital accounts show the government's foreign borrowing to have exceeded its financial needs for 1980 and indicate that it both accumulated deposits at the central bank and supplied private credit markets with capital. The government was responsible for 74 percent of total foreign borrowing in 1980. Capital transfers to the rest of the world were high, equal to almost half of foreign borrowing, with household transfers as important as debt repayment by the central bank. Public investment represented 27 percent of domestic investment.

The Computable General Equilibrium Model

We now briefly describe the computable general equilibrium (CGE) model we constructed to analyze how alternative policy packages fare in terms of adjustment to an external shock. A detailed presentation of the model and its calibration can be found in de Janvry, Sadoulet, and Fargeix.[13]

Real Side of the CGE

The real side of our CGE follows the standard neoclassical specification of CGE models. The standard framework, however, was extended to capture two features of importance for the analysis of stabilization policies: the role of current government expenditures in creating utility, and the role of public and private investment in creating productivity gains.

The short-term impact of decreasing government expenditures is twofold. Its first effect is Keynesian, as a decrease in current expenditures reduces the

13. See de Janvry, Fargeix, and Sadoulet (1991a). For a similar model see Bourguignon, de Melo, and Suwa (1991).

level of activity of the public sector, and a decrease in investment reduces the demand for construction and services. These reductions decrease employment through multiplier effects induced by corresponding decline in household income. The second effect of decreasing government expenditures is a reduction in the provision of public goods. Because public goods are provided free of charge to households, they do not count as part of real household income and are not considered at all in standard CGE models. Our model, by contrast, computes household utility, including both real income and imputed benefits from the use of public goods, holding constant the share of current government expenditures on social services that generate utility (health and education) and the distribution of these benefits across household groups.

Investment has almost no impact on production in the short term, except through demand effects generated by demand for investment goods. It is worth noting, in this respect, that private investment includes a large amount of machinery and equipment with high import components, while public investment consists mostly of public works, which create demand in the construction and service sectors. A shift in the balance between public and private investment, therefore, is not neutral in its effect on the economy in general or on the equilibrium exchange rate in particular, even in the short term. The main impact of investment takes place over the long term through capital accumulation. The principal effect of private capital accumulation, however, is not in the mere increase in the capital stock, but in the technological changes and productivity gains associated with investment. The principal role for public investment is to enhance the productivity and profitability of private investment. The model captures this effect by making total factor productivity in each sector a function of both private and public investment.

Financial Side of the CGE

Introducing a financial sector allows us to endogenize the determination of two key monetary variables—the interest rate and the inflation rate. Corresponding to these two new endogenous variables are two markets, the market for loanable funds and the money market.

The households savings rate responds to the average real return on all household assets. Household savings are held in the form of money—whether domestic currency, domestic bonds, or foreign assets—or invested in productive physical assets and housing. Money demand is given by a traditional function that depends on real income, the price level, and the average return on all other assets. Residual savings are then allocated on the basis of the relative expected real returns of the competing assets. In addition, expected inflation directly induces an increase in foreign asset holdings over physical assets and domestic bonds, since the risk of investing in domestic assets increases with inflation. The savings of firms come from after-tax profits. Their money holdings for working capital are proportional to the value of production. Private investment demand by sector depends on the rate of return to capital in that sector relative to the cost of domestic borrowing and on inflation, which at high levels deters investment by creating unpredictability and risk. Financial needs are then covered by domestic and foreign borrowing, with shares depending on their relative costs. Government savings equal revenues less current expenditures. Public investment is a policy variable, financed by three sources: direct central bank credit, domestic borrowing, and foreign borrowing. Their respective shares are also considered policy variables.

Equilibrium on the loanable funds market implies that total commercial bank deposits less reserve requirements equal borrowing by firms and the government. In equilibrium on the money market, demand for money by households and firms equals the money supply, as determined by the central bank. This money supply is proportional to the monetary base, which is the sum of central bank credit to the government and the local currency value of the bank's foreign reserves. These equilibria determine the domestic interest rate and the overall price level in the economy.

Since domestic bonds, foreign assets, and domestic currency compete in the asset portfolios, there are direct spillover effects from one market to the others. In particular, increasing inflation or decreasing domestic real interest rates trigger capital flight, which precipitates devaluation. Conversely, devaluation directly induces inflation and indirectly drives the interest rate up by increasing money demand and decreasing deposits.

The formation of expectations is important in both portfolio and investment decisions. For financial assets, only the nominal rate of return is known at the time when a decision is made. The expected real return is computed by discounting it by the expected rate of inflation. For physical assets, the expected rate of return is approximated by the rate of return on capital in the current year. Expectations of inflation are formed adaptively as a weighted average of inflation rates in the past period and the current period. As for expectations of devaluation, we assume agents do not expect any real devaluation or revaluation, so expected devaluation is equal to expected inflation.

The flexibility of the real economy in responding to price changes depends heavily on adjustments in the labor market. We specify a mechanism of partial adjustment in the real wages. The nominal wage of each labor category is determined first by updating last period's nominal wage to past inflation, and then by adjusting this new level for any change in inflation. Finally, the wage undergoes a Phillips curve-type adjustment based on the unemployment rate in the past period.

The instruments controlled by government are in three categories: trade, fiscal, and monetary policies. Trade policies are defined by the tariff structure. Fiscal policies include control of the budget deficit and control of allocation between current expenditures on public services and public investment. We analyze the growth, welfare, and political effects of distributing the burden of fiscal austerity in different ways between current expenditures and public investment. Monetary policies include financing the deficit through some combination of domestic borrowing, foreign borrowing, and central bank credit, and fixing the reserve ratio, which determines the multiplier between the monetary base and money supply. These two instruments of monetary policy, however, are perfect substitutes for each other. The use of either instrument depends on the institutional constraints in the economy regarding the government's ability to obtain credit from the central bank and to operate directly on the domestic credit market. The target of any monetary policy changes is the money supply, which we use as the indicator of monetary policy.

An expansionary fiscal policy, with no changes in the money supply and no increase in foreign borrowing, increases the burden of government borrowing on the domestic credit market. The immediate result is upward pressure on the interest rate. But there is no immediate effect on inflation. An expansionary monetary policy, by contrast, increases the supply of credit, which lowers the interest rate, stimulates investment and consumption, and brings inflationary pressure.

The impact of monetary policy on the real economy depends on the flexibility of supply, which is particularly sensitive to adjustments in the labor market. The role of monetary policy in decreasing the money supply is to hold inflation in check; its impact on the real economy is thus directly related to the real impact of inflation. In this model, higher inflation directly decreases private investment, which over time decreases capital stock growth and, more important, productivity gains. Higher inflation also decreases expected returns on domestic assets, which induces a shift in asset holdings toward foreign assets (capital flight) and a decrease in household savings rates. An increase in inflation causes a relative decline in labor costs, as wages do not adjust fully to higher prices, and real wages fall. Conversely, a drop in inflation causes higher labor costs and lower growth. Monetary policies, therefore, are more effective when the financial sector is more flexible, with relatively high elasticities of substitution among assets, and when inflation is more influential in investment decisions.

Restrictive fiscal policies curtail the budget deficit by cutting some combination of current expenditures and public investment. These cuts, by reducing the pressure government borrowing puts on the domestic financial market, decrease the interest rate and protect private investment. Sound fiscal policies thus encourage long-run growth, and their impact is enhanced by productivity gains from investment and by the response of private investment to interest rates. The negative effects of restrictive fiscal policies stem from their Keynesian impact, as government expenditures have a much larger domestic component than does private investment. In terms of distributional effects, cuts in current expenditures injure the groups and sectors that benefit from the corresponding public services, including government employees, a skilled labor group that is politically important. Cuts in public investment injure the construction and service sectors, which use unskilled labor intensively. Their short-term welfare costs are lower, but they involve losses in terms of long-run growth. Fiscal policies are likely to be more difficult to implement politically than are monetary policies, particularly when directed at current expenditures in the short run. Monetary policies, by affecting broad macroeconomic variables, have more neutral distributional effects and are thus less likely to be resisted politically.

Elasticities and Base Run Calibration

Parameters for the real side of the model are derived mostly from econometric estimates. Parameters for the financial side have not been estimated due to a lack of data. To limit the number of arbitrary parameter choices, all nonestimated elasticity parameters are constant across households and across firms. Econometric estimations were done at the aggregate level and compared with estimates in existing studies. Our final choices reflect both econometric analysis and information from other sources.

The model is calibrated to reproduce a steady-state economy when no foreign shocks occur, with trends as close as possible to those observed before the crisis in Ecuador, when the annual growth rate for GDP was 3.4 percent; for government expenditures, 1.5 percent; and for the money supply, 28 percent.[14] These growth rates imply a rate of inflation of 25 percent. These rates are used in the base run reported in table 4-5.

14. Central Bank of Ecuador (1982, 1988).

Table 4-5. *Terms of Trade and Debt Crisis under Alternative Adjustment Assumptions, Ecuador*

Percent deviation from year 1 unless otherwise specified

Characteristic of economy	Base values year 1	Base run: no shock				Terms of trade and debt crisis							
						Exchange rate adjustment				Stabilization and liberalization			
		Year 2	Year 3	Year 7	Last year growth	Year 2	Year 3	Year 7	Last year growth	Year 2	Year 3	Year 7	Last year growth
GDP													
Real GDP growth[a]	3.4	3.4	3.1	2.6	n.a.	-0.1	-2.1	0.4	n.a.	-0.8	-1.0	0.8	n.a.
Real GDP	293,341	3.4	6.6	18.9	2.6	-0.1	-2.2	-1.8	0.4	-0.8	-1.8	1.2	0.8
Government deficit / GDP	0	-3.5	-5.3	-1.3	n.a.	76.6	113.0	160.9	n.a.	-0.7	-2.0	0.4	n.a.
Money													
Monetary base[a]	20.1	21.5	23.9	36.7	n.a.	111.9	95.8	53.4	n.a.	121.1	81.9	41.9	n.a.
Money supply[a]	28.0	30.0	30.0	30.0	n.a.	40.0	40.0	40.0	n.a.	30.0	30.0	30.0	n.a.
Inflation[a]	25.0	26.2	26.5	27.2	n.a.	46.7	46.1	40.3	n.a.	34.8	32.6	29.6	n.a.
Expected real interest rate[b]	0	-0.3	0	3.8	n.a.	22.5	29.8	43.0	n.a.	31.6	36.3	44.2	n.a.
Private investment (dollars)	41,949	2.8	5.2	13.2	n.a.	-39.3	-47.3	-48.5	n.a.	-35.5	-39.3	-38.2	n.a.
Balance of payments													
Exchange rate[a]	25.0	25.0	25.1	25.3	n.a.	75.3	42.4	39.8	n.a.	-37.9	-69.8	-70.9	n.a.
Exports (dollars)	73,797	4.2	8.4	24.1	n.a.	10.8	10.2	12.8	n.a.	9.6	9.9	15.7	n.a.
Imports (dollars)	74,526	3.6	7.0	20.9	n.a.	-14.8	-16.8	-15.9	n.a.	-14.7	-15.4	-12.4	n.a.
Current account deficit / GDP	0	-6.4	-12.3	-28.7	n.a.	-33.6	-39.0	-38.7	n.a.	-25.0	-28.1	-34.0	n.a.
Capital flight	4,900	8.9	16.0	35.0	n.a.	-27.5	-27.2	-45.6	n.a.	-47.3	-49.7	-57.6	n.a.

Employment													
Employment	1,593	0.3	0.4	0.7	n.a.	2.5	-4.7	-4.7	n.a.	-0.1	-4.7	-3.2	n.a.
Average real wage	90	4.4	8.9	26.7	n.a.	-6.7	1.1	1.1	n.a.	-2.5	2.5	4.0	n.a.
Welfare													
Income													
Rural small farmers	33,968	3.8	7.4	20.8	2.7	0.2	-1.6	-2.5	0	1.6	0.9	2.9	0.6
Rural medium farmerrs	11,325	3.7	7.0	18.7	2.3	2.4	0.8	-3.0	-0.6	4.4	4.1	4.0	0
Rural large farmers	13,094	3.4	6.5	16.9	2.1	2.8	0.8	-3.7	-0.7	4.9	4.3	3.5	-0.1
Rural nonagricultural activities	19,251	3.6	7.0	19.9	2.7	-0.4	-3.3	-3.4	0.3	0.6	-1.1	1.4	0.7
Urban low education	70,912	3.7	7.3	21.2	2.9	-1.6	-3.7	-2.0	0.6	-0.8	-2.0	1.8	1.1
Urban medium education	55,501	4.0	7.9	23.4	3.2	-2.9	-4.2	-2.1	0.6	-1.9	-2.5	1.5	1.1
Urban high education	37,893	4.6	9.1	27.0	3.7	-3.7	-4.0	-2.0	0.5	-2.5	-2.5	1.3	1.0
Utility													
Rural small farmers	35,483	3.7	7.2	20.3	2.7	0.3	-1.4	-2.0	0.1	1.5	0.9	3.1	0.6
Rural medium farmers	11,665	3.6	6.9	18.4	2.3	2.3	0.8	-2.7	-0.6	4.3	4.0	4.1	0.1
Rural large farmers	13,486	3.3	6.4	16.7	2.1	2.8	0.9	-3.3	-0.6	4.7	4.1	3.6	0
Rural nonagricultural activities	21,294	3.4	6.6	18.9	2.6	-0.2	-2.7	-2.2	0.4	0.4	-1.0	1.8	0.8
Urban low education	77,705	3.5	6.9	20.1	2.8	-1.3	-3.1	-1.1	0.7	-0.8	-1.8	2.2	1.1
Urban medium education	60,557	3.8	7.5	22.3	3.1	-2.5	-3.6	-1.2	0.7	-1.9	-2.3	1.9	1.1
Urban high education	38,778	4.5	8.9	26.6	3.6	-3.6	-3.8	-1.8	0.5	-2.5	-2.4	1.4	1.0

Source: Authors' calculations using CGE model.
n.a. Not available.
a. Growth rate.
b. Value.

Growth and Income Effects of Alternative
Adjustment Instruments

The foreign shock simulated by the model involves a 40 percent reduction in the government's foreign borrowing and a 30 percent fall in the price of oil, Ecuador's primary export. We first analyze a minimum response to the shock, through exchange rate adjustment, which requires no direct government action. Second, we assess the different instruments for adjustment—fiscal, monetary, and liberalization policies—one at a time. Finally, we analyze an adjustment package that closely resembles the policy mix in Ecuador during the 1980s. Fiscal, monetary, and liberalization policies are always complemented by whatever level of devaluation remains necessary to stabilize the foreign exchange market. Tables 4-5 and 4-6 report the preshock values in year one, the effects of the shock in years two and three, and the values reached in the last year simulated, year seven. The tables also report GDP and per capita income or utility growth rates in year seven, which are important in assessing future growth. The political feasibility of a policy is assessed by its impact on the utility of medium- and high-education urban groups, which are taken to be politically dominant.

Exchange Rate Adjustment

In the minimum adjustment scenario, presented in table 4-5, the foreign exchange market is allowed to adjust for itself through the exchange rate, with no active government intervention to facilitate the adjustment. In this case, current government expenditures and public investment continue to grow, as in the base run before the shock, at an annual rate of 1.5 percent. Because the exchange rate is flexible, the currency depreciates to save the foreign exchange required by the foreign shock. Depreciation implies imported inflation. The money supply is thus allowed to increase by an exogenous 40 percent annually, compared to 27 percent annual growth in the base run, to accommodate the rising demand for money.

Relying on exchange rate adjustment, in lieu of fiscal and monetary policies, has two consequences that are common in real CGE analysis. The loss of foreign exchange leads both to a sharp depreciation of the exchange rate (75 percent in nominal terms by year two) and to a fall in absorption. Both effects have a contractionary impact on GDP (figure 4-1).

The financial CGE captures three other phenomena. First, the rising price of tradables, induced by exchange rate depreciation, creates inflation. Because wages are only partially indexed to inflation, real wages fall by 6.7 percent in year two. The quantity of labor supplied in some of the more tradable sectors thus increases and employment increases temporarily. Overall, the short-run recession is minimal, with a –0.1 percent change in GDP relative to its pre-shock level.[15] In year three, however, the inflation rate starts to decline and real wages overshoot, as the crisis hits full force. Employment falls by 4.7 percent and GDP by 2.2 percent. The partial wage adjustment, therefore, delays the recession, but the full negative effect of the crisis materializes within two years.

Second, the drop in foreign borrowing, when not matched by a reduction in expenditures, increases the government budget deficit by 76.6 percent. As the government borrows on the domestic market, interest rates rise sharply and private investment is crowded out, falling by 47.3 percent in year three. This rise in interest rates eventually forces the government to implement new fiscal policies.

Finally, inflation has a direct detrimental effect on investment, by increasing unpredictability and risk. It may also have a negative effect on investment indirectly, by increasing capital flight and decreasing investable funds. In this case of exchange rate adjustment, there are no indirect effects, as the sharp rise in interest rates counteracts capital flight.

The lack of active policy adjustment to the crisis thus has a low cost on economic growth in the short run because of the lag in wage adjustment. In the medium run, however, it leads to a sharp increase in interest rates and inflation, which causes a decline in economic growth. It is to counteract these interest rate and inflation effects that fiscal and monetary policies are eventually introduced in most cases.

In terms of welfare, table 4-5 shows that real exchange rate depreciation produces terms of trade effects that benefit agricultural households and hurt urban households. In the short run, the main winners are the large farmers. Over time, the gradual restoration of growth and decline in inflation lead to an appreciation of the real exchange rate, eroding the large farmers' real income gains, which become negative. In the short run, the main losers are medium- and high-education urban households. Real wages fall in year two, then employment falls in year three when wages recuperate, producing in all years a decline in their wage bill. Low-education urban households, sheltered by the

---

15. Unless otherwise noted, all effects are measured as percentage changes relative to preshock levels.

Table 4-6. Alternative Stabilization and Liberalization Policies in Response to a Terms of Trade and Debt Crisis, Ecuador

Percent deviation from year 1 unless otherwise specified

	Base values year 1	Terms of trade and debt crisis																
		Fiscal adjustment				Fiscal adjustment, cut current				Monetary adjustment				Trade liberalization			
Characteristic of economy		Year 2	Year 3	Year 7	Last year growth	Year 2	Year 3	Year 7	Last year growth	Year 2	Year 3	Year 7	Last year growth	Year 2	Year 3	Year 7	Last year growth
GDP																	
Real GDP growth[a]	3.4	-3.0	-0.6	1.3	n.a.	-3.3	-0.2	1.8	n.a.	-2.3	-0.5	0.9	n.a.	1.2	-3.1	0.6	n.a.
Real GDP	293,341	-3.0	-3.6	2.8	1.3	-3.3	-3.5	4.8	1.8	-2.3	-2.8	1.5	0.9	1.2	-1.9	-1.6	0.6
Government deficit / GDP	0	-16.9	0	-5.0	n.a.	0.3	-0.1	8.7	n.a.	107.6	130.6	140.5	n.a.	104.0	142.3	190.9	n.a.
Money																	
Money supply[a]	28.0	40.0	40.0	40.0	n.a.	40.0	40.0	40.0	n.a.	25.0	25.0	25.0	n.a.	40.0	40.0	40.0	n.a.
Inflation[a]	25.0	48.3	41.7	38.8	n.a.	47.9	41.1	38.1	n.a.	32.4	26.3	24.5	n.a.	44.3	48.2	40.1	n.a.
Expected real interest rate[b]	0	-0.1	3.7	7.7	n.a.	1.1	3.7	4.0	n.a.	34.4	40.5	46.0	n.a.	0	0	0	n.a.
Private investment	41,949	-28.7	-33.2	-27.2	n.a.	-28.8	-32.0	-21.9	n.a.	-39.2	-40.6	-37.5	n.a.	-37.6	-47.5	-48.0	n.a.
Balance of payments																	
Exchange rate[a]	25.0	81.1	38.5	38.0	n.a.	-20.1	-61.5	-62.5	n.a.	54.3	24.0	24.0	n.a.	-24.1	-55.8	-60.2	n.a.
Exports (dollars)	73,797	12.0	12.6	21.8	n.a.	11.9	13.0	24.8	n.a.	8.4	8.8	15.9	n.a.	11.2	10.0	12.6	n.a.
Imports (dollars)	74,526	-16.2	-16.5	-10.1	n.a.	-15.9	-15.8	-7.7	n.a.	-15.8	-15.9	-11.8	n.a.	-13.7	-16.8	-15.9	n.a.
Current account deficit / GDP	0	-48.1	-49.3	-53.0	n.a.	-45.4	-47.4	-54.7	n.a.	-25.6	-25.6	-32.6	n.a.	-28.9	-36.8	-36.7	n.a.
Capital flight	4,900	5.2	0.2	-8.4	n.a.	1.5	-2.0	-3.1	n.a.	-50.5	-57.6	-63.0	n.a.	-36.2	-31.9	-50.2	n.a.

Employment																
Employment	1,593	0	-5.5	-1.6	n.a.	-0.8	-5.7	-1.0	n.a.	-4.0	-7.0	-2.8	n.a.	4.7	-5.3	-4.9	n.a.
Average real wage	90	-8.9	-3.3	-1.1	n.a.	-8.9	-3.3	-1.1	n.a.	0	4.4	3.3	n.a.	-6.0	2.8	3.2	n.a.
Welfare																
Income																
Rural small farmers	33,968	-1.9	-2.0	3.8	1.2	-1.7	-1.5	6.2	1.7	-1.6	-2.0	1.3	0.7	3.4	0.8	-0.5	0.1
Rural medium farmes	11,325	1.3	2.1	6.9	0.9	1.1	2.2	9.4	1.5	0	-0.9	0.6	0.3	6.3	5.0	0	-0.7
Rural lage farmers	13,094	1.8	2.4	6.6	0.7	1.6	2.5	9.2	1.3	0	-1.2	-0.2	0.2	7.0	5.4	-0.5	-0.8
Rural nonagricultural activities	19,251	-3.1	-4.6	1.0	1.2	-3.0	-4.1	3.4	1.7	-2.6	-3.4	0.5	0.8	2.8	-1.8	-1.8	0.5
Urban low education	70,912	-4.7	-5.9	0.6	1.5	-4.4	-5.3	2.8	1.9	-3.2	-3.3	1.7	1.1	1.1	-3.0	-0.9	0.8
Urban medium education	55,501	-7.2	-7.8	-1.6	1.5	-7.8	-8.1	-0.7	1.9	-3.8	-3.4	1.5	1.1	-0.3	-3.3	-0.9	0.8
Urban high educatin	37,893	-10.1	-10.1	-4.6	1.5	-11.8	-11.9	-5.6	1.9	-3.7	-2.9	1.5	1.1	-1.3	-2.9	-0.7	0.6
Utility																
Rural small farmers	35,483	-2.5	-2.6	3.2	1.2	-2.7	-2.5	5.2	1.7	-1.5	-1.8	1.6	0.7	3.3	0.9	-0.1	0.1
Rural medium farmers	11,665	0.8	1.6	6.4	0.9	0.4	1.5	8.6	1.5	0	-0.7	0.8	0.3	6.1	4.9	0.2	-0.6
Rural large farmres	13,486	1.3	1.9	6.1	0.7	0.8	1.7	8.4	1.3	0	-1.0	0.1	0.2	6.8	5.3	-0.3	-0.7
Rural nonagricultural activities	21,294	-4.4	-5.6	-0.1	1.2	-5.1	-5.9	1.3	1.7	-2.3	-2.8	1.3	0.9	2.7	-1.3	-0.7	0.6
Urban low education	77,705	-5.7	-6.7	-0.3	1.5	-6.2	-6.8	0.9	1.9	-2.8	-2.8	2.3	1.1	1.2	-2.5	0	0.9
Urban medium education	60,557	-8.0	-8.4	-2.3	1.5	-9.2	-9.4	-2.2	1.9	-3.4	-2.9	2.1	1.2	-0.2	-2.7	-0.1	0.8
Urban high education	38,778	-10.2	-10.2	-4.8	1.6	-12.1	-12.1	-5.9	1.9	-3.6	-2.8	1.6	1.1	-1.3	-2.8	-0.5	0.6

Source: Authors' calculations using CGE model.
n.a. Not available.
a. Growth rate.
b. Value.

Figure 4-1. *Real GDP under Alternative Adjustment Policies*

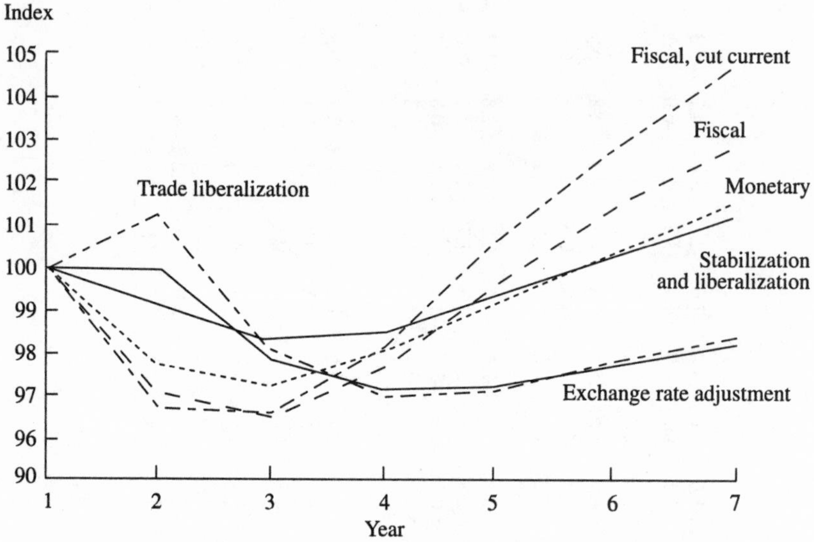

Index

Sources: Tables 4-5, 4-6.

informal sector, suffer a smaller decrease in real income. In the long run, however, income levels by class tend to return to their initial levels, and relative losses in per capita income are due only to differential population growth rates in urban and rural areas. These per capita effects appear in figures 4-2 and 4-3. While all poor households lose from exchange rate adjustment, the loss is greater in urban than in rural areas, in both the short and the long run, as migration depresses urban per capita incomes.

Fiscal Adjustment

Under the fiscal adjustment scenario, the government cuts public expenditures in the shock year to maintain the deficit at the preshock level (see table 4-6). In the first simulation, the spending cut reduces both current expenditures and public investment by 18 percent relative to what they would have been without adjustment in year two. In a second scenario, the government cuts only current expenditures in an attempt to preserve public investment. In either event, government expenditures in subsequent years grow at an annual rate of 1.5 percent, as in the base run. The money supply continues to grow by 40 percent annually.

Figure 4-2. *Rural Poor per Capita Income and Utility under Alternative Adjustment Policies, Ecuador*

Index

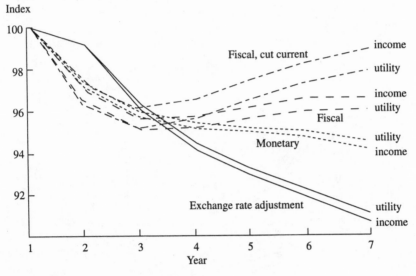

Sources: Tables 4-5, 4-6.

With a reduction in current expenditures and public investment, the budget deficit and government borrowing decline, easing pressure on the interest rate, which falls sharply relative to the case of exchange rate adjustment. With fiscal policy adjustment, private investment and long-term growth are both higher. The long-term benefits of fiscal policies are even larger when the productivity effect of private investment dwarfs that of public investment.

This long-term positive effect of fiscal policy is compromised by two negative short-term effects. First, fiscal austerity changes the composition of aggregate demand. Government spending is largely directed at labor-intensive nontradables (public services and construction), while private investment has high shares of capital-intensive commodities and imported capital goods. Spending cuts, through negative Keynesian multiplier effects, thus reduce economic growth in the short run.

The second negative effect is monetary in origin. Falling interest rates encourage households to reduce their savings deposits and to hold higher levels of currency. This cash hoarding reduces demand and lowers economic growth. One dollar of public expenditures is thus replaced by less than one dollar of private expenditures, strengthening the short-run Keynesian effect and deepening the recession.

Figure 4-3. *Urban Poor per Capita Income and Utility under Alternative Adjustment Policies, Ecuador*

Index

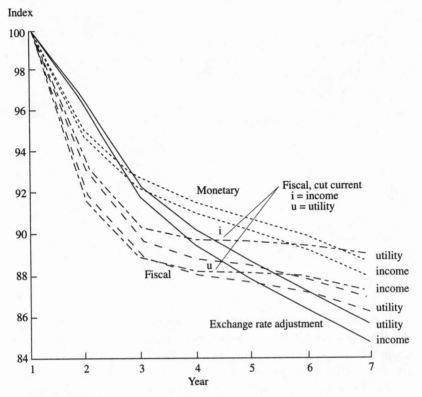

Sources: Tables 4-5, 4-6.

In terms of social welfare, all households suffer from the short-run recession induced by fiscal policy, compared to the case of exchange rate adjustment (figures 4-2 and 4-3). The main losers by far are the urban medium- and high-education households, as fiscal austerity causes many to lose jobs in the public sector. Low-education urban and rural nonagricultural households lose utility primarily from reduced access to government benefits. Politically, the short-run cost of fiscal adjustment is likely to be high, which provides an interesting contrast with exchange rate and monetary adjustment. With fiscal adjustment, utility losses always exceed income losses. The opposite occurs with exchange rate and monetary adjustment, during which the government maintains its provision of public goods. In the long run, however, fiscal adjustment increases economic growth and reduces poverty, particularly in the rural sector.

While fiscal policies are usually necessary to protect private investment and long-term growth, they may fail if public investment plays an important role in productivity growth. This suggests that spending cuts should perhaps concentrate on current expenditures. We thus compare the original program of proportional cuts in both current and capital expenditures with an alternative scenario in which current expenditures alone bear the burden of adjustment.

The simulation results show little difference in terms of short-run economic efficiency. Public investment has a slightly smaller Keynesian multiplier effect than current expenditures, but this difference is of a secondary order of magnitude. In the long run, however, the efficiency gains of protecting public investment are large (figure 4-1). Therefore, placing the burden of adjustment exclusively on current expenditures is economically superior to sharing it with capital expenditures. This policy, however, is perceived very differently by the different social groups. Capital expenditures generate demand principally for construction projects, which employ unskilled labor among the urban and rural poor. Current expenditures mostly benefit skilled labor in public services, increasing the income of urban medium- and high-education households. If a stabilization package is applied, the politically dominant groups prefer to cut investment and current expenditures proportionally, instead of cutting current expenditures alone. Only in the long run does the increase in growth obtained by protecting investment reverse this policy ranking.

Monetary Adjustment

Under the monetary adjustment scenario, the government limits annual money supply growth to 25 percent in all periods to fight the inflation that is fueled by depreciation and the government's domestic borrowing (see table 4-6). Government expenditures continue to grow at 1.5 percent a year, as in the case of exchange rate adjustment.

Monetary stabilization produces a smaller short-run recession, but a lower level of long-run economic growth. In the short run, reductions in the money supply increase interest rates and sharply decrease private investment, which falls by about 40 percent, as it did under exchange rate adjustment (tables 4-5 and 4-6). The decline in GDP produced by monetary adjustment is smaller than that produced by fiscal adjustment, because government expenditures continue to increase, avoiding the negative short-run Keynesian effect of fiscal cuts. In the short run, the decline in private investment has little effect on productivity growth.

By controlling inflation, monetary adjustment has long-term beneficial effects on investment. Reduced inflation directly boosts investment by increasing the clarity of price signals and reducing risk. In addition, reduced inflation contains capital flight to about 40 percent of the precrisis level, while fiscal adjustment has no impact on capital flight. Reduced capital flight increases the availability of loanable funds and puts downward pressure on interest rates, encouraging investment.

In terms of social welfare, monetary adjustment alters the distribution of income less than does fiscal adjustment. The smaller currency depreciation benefits large farmers less and hurts urban consumers less. Reduced inflation raises real wages, which benefits both the rural poor and the urban classes. Finally, employment in public works projects and government services does not fall, which is of greatest benefit to medium- and high-education urban households.

Trade Liberalization

Under the trade liberalization scenario, the government replaces its uneven tariff structure with a uniform tariff of 10 percent across all sectors. This shift brings tariffs down from the previous average of 20 percent, penalizes formerly subsidized food imports, and encourages imports of industrial consumer products that were previously taxed at 38.9 percent.

Trade liberalization has strong positive growth effects in the short run, with improved terms of trade for the large food sector, reduced inflation, and real exchange rate depreciation that benefits all tradables. Nevertheless, significant recession follows in year three, though growth resumes by year five.

In terms of social welfare, the main winners are clearly the rural groups, particularly the large farmers. Their gains, however, erode during the recession, and by year seven their real incomes are only 1 to 3 percent higher than in the case of exchange rate adjustment (table 4-6).

In conclusion, the short-run cost of the crisis on economic growth is smallest with exchange rate adjustment and smaller with monetary than with fiscal adjustment. The decline in growth, however, can be more than compensated by the positive effects of trade liberalization. Failure to adjust, though tempting in the short run, has high opportunity costs in the long run. Fiscal adjustment hurts growth much more in the short run than does monetary adjustment. In the long run, however, fiscal is superior to monetary adjustment in terms of economic growth. In terms of welfare, these policies produce sharply contrasting results. Trade liberalization and exchange rate adjustment favor the agricultural sector. Fiscal adjustment, in particular any cut in current expenditures, hurts urban groups. Monetary adjustment tends to be more neutral in its impact on different socioeconomic groups.

A Stabilization and Liberalization Package

The last simulation, reported in table 4-5, is a policy package similar to the one Ecuador implemented. Implementation in Ecuador was far from smooth, as the government repeatedly backtracked in part from a succession of policy reforms. The problems were due in part to a very unstable environment, with recurrent internal and external shocks, and in part to domestic political constraints. However, on average between 1982 and 1988, current government expenditures declined by 1.5 percent a year, public investment declined by 5 percent a year, annual monetary growth was 30 percent, and tariffs fell both on average (to 10 percent) and in spread.[16] The stabilization and liberalization column in table 4-5 simulates these policies. Complementarity among the components of this policy package explains its achievements. The government avoided a short-term recession by liberalizing trade, and growth resumed with monetary and fiscal adjustments. While long-run growth fell short of what a stronger fiscal policy could have achieved (figure 4-1), the government maintained the package's political feasibility—defined as positive utility for medium- and high-education urban households—relative to the counterfactual of exchange rate adjustment. A stricter fiscal policy was not politically feasible when compared to exchange rate adjustment. The negative short-run effect on urban poverty was also less than that of nonintervention or any other policy instruments. This result stresses the importance of realizing short-run efficiency gains by removing existing distortions to compensate for the recessionary short-run impact of fiscal and monetary adjustment.

Sectoral Differentiation of Poverty

The poor in Ecuador constitute a very heterogeneous group, including mostly small and landless farmers and the urban low-education group, but also some medium and a few large farmers. The composition of income by source differs sharply across these groups (table 4-3). It is thus not surprising that in the process of crisis, adjustment, and structural change, with resources reallocated across sectors and wage and profit shares changing, these different

16. Central Bank of Ecuador (1982, 1988).

Figure 4-4. *Rural Poverty under Alternative Adjustment Policies*[a]

Poverty Index

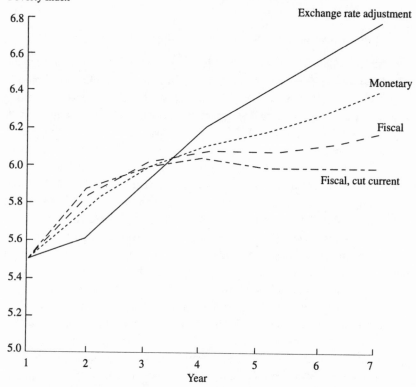

Source: de Janvry, Sadoulet, Fargeix (1991).
a. Rural and urban poverty are measured by $F_r w_r$ and $F_u w_u$, respectively, where F represents the Foster-Greer-Thorbecke index and w the shares of rural and urban population in total population. Hence total poverty, F, is equal to the sum of rural and urban poverty: $F = F_r w_r + F_u w_u$.

socioeconomic groups fared quite differently. The result is important structural change in the composition of urban and rural poverty that justifies separate analysis of its evolution over time.

The rural and urban poverty indexes reported in figures 4-4 and 4-5 include two distinct components, the impact of the crisis, which is exchange rate adjustment, and the impact of the alternative adjustment policies: monetary, fiscal with proportional cuts, and fiscal with cuts in current expenditures.

The shock imposed on the economy does not itself have any particular sectoral bias. But exchange rate adjustment, which relies exclusively on currency realignment to balance the external account, has a very asymmetric impact. It favors tradable over nontradable sectors. Because agriculture is more tradable

Figure 4-5. *Urban Poverty under Alternative Adjustment Policies*[a]

Poverty Index

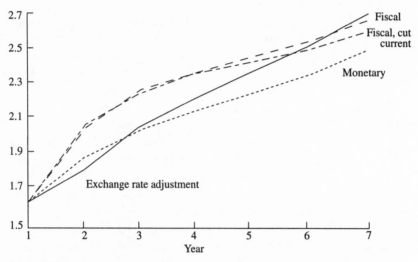

Source: See figure 4-4.
a. Rural and urban poverty are measured by $F_r w_r$ and $F_u w_u$, respectively, where F represents the Foster-Greer-Thorbecke index and w the shares of rural and urban population in total population. Hence total poverty, F, is equal to the sum of rural and urban poverty: $F = F_r w_r + F_u w_u$.

than most labor-intensive urban sectors, the rural population benefits more than its urban counterparts, as the evolution of real incomes in table 4-5 illustrates. Monetary policies do not directly affect any specific group, but they reduce the required amount of exchange rate adjustment by controlling capital flight and the foreign deficit. Thus, while rural areas are still less adversely affected than urban areas, monetary adjustment does not favor rural areas as much as exchange rate adjustment. Fiscal policies that curtail government expenditures to protect private investment have a very transparent and direct effect on urban populations, reducing employment at both ends of the labor spectrum (from high-salary civil servants to low-income construction workers) and limiting public goods benefits.

The main implications of these differential poverty effects are clear in figures 4-4 and 4-5. First, there is no alleviation of poverty within seven years of the shock. On the contrary, overall poverty increases in every case, particularly during the first few years. This is no surprise in a period of crisis and at best slow recovery, with aggregate growth rates still far below the population growth rate.

Second, the rise in rural poverty slows but does not stop when growth resumes after the implementation of monetary and fiscal policies. Only when fiscal adjustment involves current expenditures alone are growth rates high enough to stabilize rural poverty.

The situation is quite different for the urban population. The direct negative effects of fiscal policies overwhelm their indirect positive effects, so that fiscal adjustment aggravates poverty more than does exchange rate adjustment. Only the faster recovery produced by fiscal policies that maintain public investment reduces poverty deterioration.

The differences lead to an insoluble conflict of interest among the poor. The fate of the rural poor is attached to aggregate recovery, for which fiscal policies always fare better. The fate of the urban poor, by contrast, is similar to that of rich urban groups, who always suffer from fiscal austerity. Beyond exchange rate adjustment in the very short run, they favor monetary adjustment. The aggregate poverty level follows the evolution of rural poverty at the beginning, until the growing urban poor impose the weight of urban poverty in the aggregate. The optimum policy for poverty alleviation therefore depends on the discount rate. The real trade-off is a matter of the relative weights attached to two distinct groups, urban and rural.

In conclusion, the politics of stabilization implies a clash between the welfare of the rural and urban poor, with the interests of the former tied to the state and to the promotion of economic growth and the interests of the latter tied to those of the politically dominant urban coalition. With political considerations dictating the choice of instruments, both economic growth and rural poverty may be sacrificed to the interests of the dominant coalition, which happen to coincide with those of the urban poor.

Compensation Policies

Because the only way to alleviate poverty in the long run is to promote growth with fiscal cuts in current expenditures, the question arises as to how to protect the poor during the adjustment period. We analyze income transfer policies and the trade-offs they imply among growth, welfare, and political feasibility. The income transfer targets three groups that contain a majority of the poor: small farmers, medium farmers, and urban low-education households. The objective of the transfer is to maintain real incomes at the levels they would have obtained in the absence of active adjustment, with exchange rate adjustment. The idea is to compensate for the adjustment policy, not for the external shock.

As table 4-7 shows, the transfer required to compensate the poor through year seven equals 3.5 percent of the base year (1980) GDP, a total that does not incorporate the effects of its implementation. This amount is not large, and it highlights the fact that sheltering the poor from stabilization is a matter of political will, not lack of resources. Half of this transfer (1.7 percent of 1980 GDP) is incurred in the first year, and the transfers need to be sustained over no more than four years, after which growth reestablishes the real income of the poor at the level they would have secured under exchange rate adjustment.

The actual effects of these transfers, however, depend on the way they are financed. Alternative sources of finance are money creation, cuts in government consumption, cuts in government investment, progressive income taxes, and foreign aid. Table 4-7 explores these alternatives. The results show that the first four schemes are all inadequate, either for the economic costs they involve or for the negative political responses they produce.

While money creation is attractive in the short run, it is very inflationary and has high costs on long-term growth. It also requires transfers over the entire seven-year period, with the total equal to 5.9 percent of 1980 GDP. Money creation is politically feasible only in the short run, as it significantly reduces the utility of medium- and high-education urban groups. Cuts in government consumption and investment have negative growth consequences: the former in the short run through Keynesian multiplier effects, the latter in the short run (for the same reason) and in the long run through forgone productivity gains. These two approaches are politically infeasible, because their short-run effect on growth creates large utility losses for medium- and high-education urban groups. Income taxes have the smallest negative effect on growth, but require a very large tax on the nonpoor, which sparks a strong negative political response. Compensating the poor through foreign aid thus appears to be the only option with no negative effect on growth. It also requires the smallest total transfer (2.6 percent of 1980 GDP) because of the growth it creates, and is clearly feasible politically. Interestingly, the duration of the necessary transfers is brief (four years), and half the total is incurred in the first year. The total is equal to 36 percent of annual foreign borrowing in the precrisis year, an amount approximately equal to the annual cut in foreign borrowing caused by the debt crisis (recall that the shock was defined as a 40 percent reduction in foreign borrowing). This finding suggests that structural adjustment loans could contain provisions that compensate the poor for the hardships of stabilization without jeopardizing the political feasibility of the most effective policy approach.

Table 4-7. *Targeted Income Transfers to the Poor, Ecuador*
Percent deviation from base policy unless otherwise specified

			Source of transfer finance			
Item	Base policy fiscal policy[a]	Money creation	Cut in government consumption	Cut in government investment	Income tax	Foreign aid
GDP						
Year 2	-3.3	1.7	-1.5	-0.6	0.1	1.2
Last year	4.8	-5.8	0.6	-1.4	-0.1	-0.1
Accumulated inflation in last year	...	112.0	4.1	6.2	4.9	4.9
Transfer (percent of 1980 GDP)		...	2.9	...	...	...
Year 2	1.7	1.1	2.6	2.1	2.9	1.2
Year 3	1.1	1.7	1.5	1.6	1.9	0.7
Year 4	0.5	1.6	0.7	0.9	0.7	0.4
Year 5	0.1	1.5	0.1	0.5	0.2	0.1
Year 6	0	1.3	0	0.1	0	0
Year 7	0	1.1	0	0	0	0
Total	3.5	5.9	4.8	5.2	5.6	2.6
Percent of 1980 source budget[b]	...	...	33.8	85.3	...	36.4
Per capita utility						
Year 2						
Small farmers	-3.8	3.1	3.1	3.1	3.1	3.1
Medium farmers	-0.8	1.9	1.9	1.9	1.9	1.9
Large farmers	-0.3	2.1	-0.5	0.5	-4.0	-0.5
Urban low education	-8.5	4.8	4.8	4.8	4.8	4.8
Urban medium education	-11.3	0.8	-3.7	-0.9	-3.7	1.3
Urban higher education	-14.2	0.4	-4.6	-0.4	-3.7	1.6
Year 7						
Small farmers	-1.9	-1.5	0.7	-1.3	-0.1	0
Medium farmers	1.4	-6.3	1.0	-1.3	-0.1	0
Large farmers	1.2	-6.2	1.0	-1.3	-0.1	-7.5
Urban low education	-12.8	-1.7	0.4	-0.9	-0.1	-0.1
Urban medium education	-15.4	-4.9	0.3	-1.1	-0.1	0
Urban higher education	-18.7	-4.9	0.2	-1.1	-0.1	0.1

Source: Authors' calculations.
a. Percent change over the precrisis base year level.
b. The total cost of transfer is evaluated as a percentage of government consumption, public investment, and foreign borrowing in the precrisis year, respectively.

Conclusion

Before recommending stabilization and adjustment policies that have the smallest negative effect on poverty, we need to place several caveats on the types of recommendations that can be derived from this study's CGE approach. Such an approach, by construction, focuses on macroeconomic and sectoral phenomena, privileging equilibrium and market processes. By operating at a high level of aggregation, it focuses on processes that tend to affect the economy and society as a whole. It is thus particularly appropriate for analysis of foreign shocks and alternative approaches to stabilization and adjustment, especially with the introduction of a financial sector. In terms of poverty, it stresses indirect approaches to poverty reduction, namely, processes that tend to occur through growth, such as employment creation, increased wages, and increased value added in economic sectors where the poor are important producers. The CGE approach enables some analysis of direct approaches to poverty reduction, such as targeted income transfers to broad social groups. Yet it does not allow analysis of direct approaches that are finely tuned because it operates at a level of aggregation that is too high for effective program design.[17]

The model's results show that none of the policy interventions is politically feasible if the public judges their effects against precrisis utility levels. Political feasibility is attainable only with a package of stabilization and liberalization policies that is judged against the counterfactual of no intervention (exchange rate adjustment). This requires political management, to inform the public and gain its acceptance. For more stringent fiscal approaches to be politically feasible, the government must be politically sophisticated in its use of foreign aid transfers, or build a social pact that lowers discount rates and increases the acceptance of social goals, namely, economic growth, over individual utility gains.

The model also indicates conflict between the goals of efficiency (econom-

17. In addition, in our CGE model cuts in current expenditures, which affect education and health among other social services, have utility but not productivity effects. This seems reasonable over the seven-year time horizon. If, however, stabilization is protracted due to recurrent shocks or policy mistakes, productivity losses should be associated not only with cuts in public investment (which includes construction and infrastructure associated with education and health), but also with cuts in current expenditures on social services. Similarly, the model assesses the benefits of safety nets in terms of utility, but does not include incentives effects and productivity gains at the level of individual behavior. These effects cannot be introduced in CGE models until there is serious empirical analysis measuring their magnitude and lags.

ically optimum stabilization) and welfare (adjustment with a human face). In the short run (or with a very high discount rate), economic and welfare criteria both dictate an exchange rate approach over all others. In the longer run (or with medium and low discount rates), however, there is conflict between two coalitions. The state (with its postulated economic efficiency objective) and the rural population, including the rural poor (the labor-intensive tradable sector), prefer a strongly growth-oriented approach, while the urban coalition, which cuts across all classes (the nontradable and service sectors, the bureaucracy, and the military), prefers either the exchange rate approach or stabilization programs that preserve government current expenditures.[18] Sheltering the poor during stabilization requires the introduction of safety nets. To be politically feasible, they need to be financed through foreign transfers.

The rural poor benefit from growth-promoting policies because these policies increase their employment opportunities in three sectors. The first is agriculture, which becomes the most dynamic growth sector after real exchange rate appreciation. The second is public works programs, which are preserved by fiscal policies that maintain public investment. The third is nontradables, particularly construction and services, where the income effects of economic growth increase demand.

The urban poor prefer another approach to stabilization. In both the short and the long run, they should oppose restrictive fiscal and monetary policies, preferring adjustment through the exchange rate only. If a restrictive policy is to be implemented, they prefer monetary over fiscal instruments. One reason why the urban poor prefer the same policy package as the urban middle-income and rich is that, in terms of total utility, they benefit most from current public expenditures. Thus, while in terms of income they would prefer fiscal austerity through cuts in current expenditures, in terms of utility they prefer policies that preserve current expenditures. Among policies for long-run growth, they favor monetary instruments that protect benefits while allowing for more growth than does exchange rate adjustment. Among fiscal policies, which all reduce benefits (though cuts in current expenditures reduce them marginally more), the urban poor favor cutting current expenditures, because it generates more growth than do proportional cuts, and growth benefits them

18. This conflict emerges in Ecuador because there is separation between gains from adjustment associated with sectoral tradability (here mainly agriculture) and political dominance (here urban). other cases, such as the Asian newly industrializing countries, the labor-intensive industrial sector is tradable, which allows governments to reconcile political feasibility and poverty alleviation. It is thus no wonder that those Asian countries have found it easier politically to stabilize the economy, with interventions that are more efficient for both growth and welfare. For analysis of the role of a tradable industrial sector in stabilization, see Faini and de Melo (1990).

both through unskilled employment creation and through expansion of the informal sector.

We have shown that effective and equitable adjustment requires both political management and social safety nets. For these purposes, an active and credible state is essential. State contraction through fiscal austerity, therefore, must not occur at the cost of reducing the state's ability to perform (or to supervise the performance of) these functions.

References

Barreiros, Lidia. 1988. "Ecuador's Development Profile and Basic Needs Performance." In *Theory and Policy Design for Basic Needs Planning*, edited by R. Teekens. Brookfield, Vermont: Gower Publishing.

Bourguignon, François, Jaime de Melo, and Akiko Suwa. 1991. "Modeling the Effects of Adjustment Programs on Income Distribution." *World Development* 19 (11): 1527-44.

Central Bank of Ecuador. 1982. *Cuentas Nacionales*. Quito.

———. 1988. *Boletin Anuario*. Quito.

de Janvry, Alain, André Fargeix, and Elisabeth Sadoulet. 1991a. *Adjustment and Equity in Ecuador*. Paris: OECD Development Centre.

———. 1991b. "Politically Feasible and Equitable Adjustment: Some Alternatives for Ecuador." *World Development* 19 (11): 1577-94.

Faini, Ricardo, and Jaime de Melo. 1990. "Adjustment, Investment, and the Real Exchange Rate in Developing Countries." *Economic Policy* 11: 492-519.

Foster, Janos, Joel Greer, and Erik Thorbecke. 1984. "A Class of Decomposable Poverty Measures." *Econometrica* 52 (3): 761-66.

Inter-American Development Bank. 1988. *Economic and Social Progress in Latin America*. Washington.

International Monetary Fund. 1994. *International Financial Statistics*, electronic edition. Washington.

Keeler, Andrew, Duty Greene, and Grant Scobie. 1988. "Exchange Rates and Foreign Trade Policies in Ecuador: 1960-85." Raleigh, North Carolina: Sigma One Corporation.

Kouwenaar, Arend. 1988. *A Basic Needs Policy Model: A General Equilibrium Analysis with Special Reference to Ecuador*. Amsterdam: North Holland.

———. 1986. *Poverty in Latin America: The Impact of Depression*. Washington: World Bank.

Pfefferman, Guy. 1987. "Public Expenditures in Latin America: Effects on Poverty." Discussion Paper 5. Washington: World Bank.

Vos, Rob. 1988. "Rural Development, Industrialization, and Employment." In *Theory and Policy Design for Basic Needs Planning*, edited by R. Teekens. Brookfield, Vermont: Gower Publishing.

Appendix

Table 4A-1. *Social Accounting Matrix, Ecuador, 1980*
Millions of sucres

Current Accounts	Ag. Exports 1	Other Ag. 2	Oil 3	Ind. Consom. 4	Product. Goods 5	Util.Cnstr Trnsp. 6	Trade 7
1 AgExports	18	0	26	8174	2292	80	0
2 Other Ag.	0	758	0	18247	139	0	0
3 Oil	177	52	176	307	1322	3410	33
4 Ind. Consom.	128	1336	48	15206	636	55	31
5 Product. good	1392	1846	2825	4552	23022	21245	4761
6 Util. Cnstr. Tr	152	245	1725	1355	1443	2943	9978
7 Trade	−4	131	−182	−314	11	458	0
8 Services	363	109	808	1096	642	6620	6626
9 Govt Services	0	0	0	0	0	0	0
Total commodities	2226	4477	5426	48623	29507	34811	21429
Skilled	95	259	1295	1934	2067	6448	3720
Unskilled	124	197	443	7429	5829	23711	13059
Ag. Labor	2559	12670	6	214	146	27	231
Total labor	2778	13126	1744	9577	8042	30185	17010
Capital	453	1316	29261	7086	5384	4382	5298
Trade Margins	5545	7612	1682	12624	30719	0	0
Urb. Low Edu	1478	423	0	7204	1070	5585	5315
Urb. Med. Edu	148	269	0	2493	1074	2224	2959
Urb. High Edu	214	101	0	157	164	658	460
Rural NonAg.	1718	40	0	1405	278	1319	2232
Small Farms	1675	1494	0	1980	437	1287	1863
Medium Farms	1337	2508	0	363	72	289	566
Large Farms	2166	3884	0	241	56	554	808
Total household	8736	8719	0	13843	3151	11916	14203
AgExports	0	0	0	0	0	0	0
Other Ag.	0	0	0	0	0	0	0
Ind. Consom.	0	0	0	0	0	0	0
Product. Good	0	0	0	0	0	0	0
Util. Cnstr.Tr	0	0	0	0	0	0	0
Trade	0	0	0	0	0	0	0
Services	0	0	0	0	0	0	0
Private Oil	0	0	0	0	0	0	0
Public Oil	0	0	0	0	0	0	0
Total Firms	0	0	0	0	0	0	0
Financ. Insti	0	0	0	0	0	0	0
Indirect Tax	263	179	4681	3215	1501	845	242
Import Tariff	3	−606	88	1477	11062	0	0
Rest of World	10	2485	5805	3794	51418	3128	6205
Total	20014	37308	48687	100239	140784	85267	64387

Service 8	Govt service 9	Total Comm.	Skilled 10	Unskill 11	Ag. Labor 12	Total Labor	Capital 13	Trade Margins 14
148	46	10784	0	0	0	0	0	0
1278	416	20838	0	0	0	0	0	0
116	322	5915	0	0	0	0	0	0
3051	933	21424	0	0	0	0	0	0
4099	9519	73261	0	0	0	0	0	0
2147	3315	23303	0	0	0	0	0	0
−100	918	918	0	0	0	0	0	58182
13333	1021	30618	0	0	0	0	0	0
0	0	0	0	0	0	0	0	0
24072	16490	187061	0	0	0	0	0	58182
14880	21343	52041	0	0	0	0	0	0
19814	5149	75754	0	0	0	0	0	0
68	98	16019	0	0	0	0	0	0
34762	26590	143814	0	0	0	0	0	0
−877	0	52303	0	0	0	0	0	0
0	0	58182	0	0	0	0	0	0
3175	0	24250	6275	31578	968	38821	0	0
3085	0	12252	16537	18188	291	35017	0	0
3164	0	4918	24511	1802	130	26442	0	0
1229	0	8221	1870	7641	612	10122	0	0
872	0	9608	1294	13522	7652	22468	0	0
335	0	5470	297	1848	3417	5562	0	0
404	0	8113	519	1175	2950	4644	0	0
12264	0	72832	51303	75754	16019	143076	0	0
0	0	0	0	0	0	0	453	0
0	0	0	0	0	0	0	1316	0
0	0	0	0	0	0	0	7086	0
0	0	0	0	0	0	0	5384	0
0	0	0	0	0	0	0	4382	0
0	0	0	0	0	0	0	5298	0
0	0	0	0	0	0	0	2207	0
0	0	0	0	0	0	0	8845	0
0	0	0	0	0	0	0	20416	0
0	0	0	0	0	0	0	55387	0
0	0	0	0	0	0	0	−3084	0
1438	0	12364	0	0	0	0	0	0
0	0	12024	0	0	0	0	0	0
1682	0	74527	738	0	0	738	0	0
73341	43080	613107	52041	75754	16019	143814	52303	58182

Table 4A-1. (continued)

Current Accounts	Urban Low Ed. 15	Urban Med. Ed 16	Urban High Ed 17	Rural NonAg. 18	Small Farms 19	Medium Farms 20	Large Farms 21	Total Hholds
1 AgExports	812	433	203	159	307	110	119	2143
2 Other Ag.	4570	2404	1153	1007	3736	1153	1075	15096
3 Oil	529	295	165	123	195	51	49	1406
4 Ind. Consom.	20413	12282	6323	4895	11584	3639	3253	62390
5 Product. Good	8957	6943	4490	3074	4780	1487	1678	31408
6 Util.Cnstr.Tr	5358	4190	3019	1708	2405	591	925	18196
7 Trade	493	331	194	129	279	83	84	1592
8 Services	12608	10361	6812	3641	5668	1472	1563	42126
9 Govt Services	141	129	101	37	62	19	30	518
Total commoditi	53880	37366	22460	14774	29015	8605	8775	174875
Urb. Low Educ	1041	1151	918	6	12	4	9	3141
Urb. Med. Edu	986	1099	920	5	8	3	5	3026
Urb. High Edu	774	921	736	1	1	0	1	2435
Rural NonAg.	0	0	0	148	246	79	156	630
Small Farms	0	0	0	333	554	182	349	1418
Medium Farms	0	0	0	60	102	32	63	258
Large Farms	0	0	0	39	64	21	40	164
Total household	2801	3171	2575	594	987	321	623	11071
AgExports	0	0	0	0	0	0	0	0
Other Ag.	1	1	2	0	0	0	0	4
Ind. Consom.	19	17	10	0	1	0	0	47
Product. Good	90	162	105	2	2	1	0	362
Util.Cnstr.Tr	128	176	110	12	6	1	3	436
Trade	98	133	99	3	2	1	0	335
Services	8	22	126	0	0	0	0	157
Total non oil f	344	511	452	17	11	4	4	1342
Financ. Insti	1217	1277	1367	406	549	323	494	5632
Income tax	2389	4041	4213	444	372	42	29	11530
Government	0	0	0	0	0	0	0	0
Rest of World	0	0	38	0	0	0	0	38
Capital Accounts								
37–43 Household	10280	9133	6789	3020	3033	2030	3169	37453
44–52 Firms	0	0	0	0	0	0	0	0
Total	70911	55499	37893	19253	33966	11326	13093	241941

Ag. Exports 22	Other Ag. 23	Ind. Consom. 24	Product Goods 25	Util. Cnstr Trnsp. 26	Trade 27	Service 28	Private Oil 29	Public Oil 30
0	0	0	0	0	0	0	0	0
0	0	0	0	0	0	0	0	0
0	0	0	0	0	0	0	0	0
0	0	0	0	0	0	0	0	0
0	0	0	0	0	0	0	0	0
0	0	0	0	0	0	0	0	0
0	0	0	0	0	0	0	0	0
0	0	0	0	0	0	0	0	0
0	0	0	0	0	0	0	0	0
0	0	0	0	0	0	0	0	0
11	10	417	69	119	231	9	37	3
15	14	360	208	123	272	20	36	2
40	35	108	220	116	274	141	33	1
0	0	30	5	28	29	1	0	0
2	2	4	2	4	5	0	0	0
3	3	1	0	0	1	0	0	0
12	16	3	0	12	6	0	0	0
82	81	924	504	403	818	171	106	6
0	0	0	0	0	0	0	0	0
0	0	0	0	0	0	0	0	0
0	0	2	2	3	3	1	0	0
1	1	16	18	23	21	6	0	0
2	2	20	23	29	26	8	5	0
1	1	15	17	21	19	6	0	0
1	1	7	8	10	9	3	0	0
5	5	61	68	86	77	23	5	0
109	564	2055	2200	647	1350	926	20	40
50	49	752	436	175	797	159	0	0
55	103	176	70	1044	168	34	8264	17235
70	288	2082	1626	1322	1247	759	499	0
0	0	0	0	0	0	0	0	0
82	236	1139	1262	2022	1579	486	191	3135
453	1326	7188	6168	5700	6036	2558	9085	20416

Table 4A-1. (continued)

Current Accounts	Income Tax 32	Indir. Tax 33	Import Tariff 34	Governt 35	Rest of World 36	Urban Low Ed. 37	Urban Med. Ed 38	Urban High Ed 39
1 AgExports	0	0	0	0	6737	0	0	0
2 Other Ag.	0	0	0	0	329	0	0	0
3 Oil	0	0	0	0	40333	0	0	0
4 Ind. Consom.	0	0	0	0	15131	0	0	0
5 Product. Good	0	0	0	0	1859	0	0	0
6 Util.Cnstr.Tr	0	0	0	0	5116	0	0	0
7 Trade	0	0	0	0	3695	0	0	0
8 Services	0	0	0	0	597	0	0	0
9 Govt Services	0	0	0	42562	0	0	0	0
Total commoditi	0	0	0	42562	73797	0	0	0
Urb. Low Edu	0	0	0	2666	33	0	0	0
Urb. Med. Edu	0	0	0	2920	22	0	0	0
Urb. High Edu	0	0	0	1875	10	0	0	0
Rural NonAg.	0	0	0	125	0	0	0	0
Small Farms	0	0	0	437	0	0	0	0
Medium Farms	0	0	0	18	0	0	0	0
Large Farms	0	0	0	58	0	0	0	0
Total household	0	0	0	8099	65	0	0	0
Financ. Insti	0	0	0	26	2088	0	0	0
Government	16859	12364	12024	0	931	0	0	0
Rest of World	0	0	0	8026	0	0	0	0
Capital Accounts								
Government	0	0	0	10614	0	1157	1011	696
Rest of World	0	0	0	0	14423	0	0	0
Stocks	0	0	0	0	0	0	0	0
Housing	0	0	0	0	0	3808	2103	632
Household cap	0	0	0	0	0	1652	760	169
Firms capital	0	0	0	0	0	0	0	0
Banks capital	0	0	0	0	0	0	0	0
Govt capital	0	0	0	0	0	0	0	0
Shares	0	0	0	0	0	848	1161	1019
Money	0	0	0	0	0	1211	988	482
Reserve	0	0	0	0	0	0	0	0
DCGovt	0	0	0	0	0	0	0	0
Dom. borrowing	0	0	0	0	0	0	0	0
Time deposits	0	0	0	0	0	1209	1572	1529
Foreign borro	0	0	0	0	0	0	0	0
Foreign curre	0	0	0	0	0	395	1538	2262
Total	16859	12364	12024	69327	91304	10280	9133	6789

Rural NonAg. 40	Small Farms 41	Medium Farms 42	Large Farms 43	Total Hholds	Ag. Exports 44	Other Ag. 45	Ind. Consom. 46	Product. Goods 47
0	0	0	0	0	0	0	0	0
0	0	0	0	0	0	0	0	0
0	0	0	0	0	0	0	0	0
0	0	0	0	0	0	0	0	0
0	0	0	0	0	0	0	0	0
0	0	0	0	0	0	0	0	0
0	0	0	0	0	0	0	0	0
0	0	0	0	0	0	0	0	0
0	0	0	0	0	0	0	0	0
0	0	0	0	0	0	0	0	0
0	0	0	0	0	0	0	0	0
0	0	0	0	0	0	0	0	0
0	0	0	0	0	0	0	0	0
0	0	0	0	0	0	0	0	0
0	0	0	0	0	0	0	0	0
0	0	0	0	0	0	0	0	0
0	0	0	0	0	0	0	0	0
0	0	0	0	0	0	0	0	0
0	0	0	0	0	0	0	0	0
0	0	0	0	0	0	0	0	0
0	0	0	0	0	0	0	0	0
225	432	68	36	3626	0	0	0	0
0	0	0	0	0	0	0	0	0
0	0	0	0	0	70	199	1004	1070
486	502	525	674	8730	0	0	0	0
1447	1249	1084	1346	7707	-528	-1594	-826	-307
0	0	0	0	0	1129	4781	6276	6828
0	0	0	0	0	0	0	0	0
0	0	0	0	0	0	0	0	0
211	20	18	146	3423	-50	-378	-646	-846
345	810	263	242	4342	52	205	469	411
0	0	0	0	0	0	0	0	0
0	0	0	0	0	0	0	0	0
0	0	0	0	0	-554	-2453	-4050	-4432
155	20	21	219	4725	0	0	0	0
0	0	0	0	0	-44	-401	-927	-1282
150	0	50	505	4900	0	0	0	0
3020	3033	2030	3169	37453	75	359	1298	1441

Table 4A-1. (*continued*)

Current Accounts	Util. Trnsp. 48	Cnstr Trade 49	Service 50	Private Oil 51	Public Oil 52	Total Firms	Governt 53
1 AgExports	0	0	0	0	0	0	0
2 Other Ag.	0	0	0	0	0	0	0
3 Oil	0	0	0	0	0	0	0
4 Ind. Consom.	0	0	0	0	0	0	0
5 Product. Good	0	0	0	0	0	0	0
6 Util.Cnstr.Tr	0	0	0	0	0	0	0
7 Trade	0	0	0	0	0	0	0
8 Services	0	0	0	0	0	0	0
9 Govt Services	0	0	0	0	0	0	0
Total commoditi	0	0	0	0	0	0	0
Capital Accounts							
AgExports	0	0	0	0	0	0	-13
Other Ag.	0	0	0	0	0	0	108
Ind. Consom.	0	0	0	0	0	0	120
Product. Good	0	0	0	0	0	0	134
Util.Cnstr.Tr	0	0	0	0	0	0	4129
Trade	0	0	0	0	0	0	289
Services	0	0	0	0	0	0	142
Private Oil	0	0	0	0	0	0	0
Public Oil	0	0	0	0	0	0	-719
Total firms	0	0	0	0	0	0	4190
Government	0	0	0	0	0	0	0
Comm. Banks	0	0	0	0	0	0	0
Rest of World	0	0	0	0	0	0	0
Stocks	757	1769	218	51	140	5277	712
Housing	0	0	0	0	0	0	0
Household cap	-1422	-1934	-1096	0	0	-7707	0
Firms capital	10458	3916	4455	221	2241	40306	0
Banks capital	0	0	0	0	0	0	0
Govt capital	0	0	0	0	0	0	18646
Shares	-1276	-228	-331	-75	0	-3830	2564
Money	1334	1702	1174	69	35	5450	0
Reserve	0	0	0	0	0	0	0
DCGovt	0	0	0	0	0	0	1320
Dom. borrowin	-1900	-2482	-2964	-75	0	-18911	3858
Time deposits	0	0	0	0	0	0	0
Foreign borro	-1669	-818	-810	0	0	-5952	-17050
Foreign curre	0	0	0	0	0	0	0
Total	6282	1925	645	191	2416	14632	14240

Central Bank 54	Commer. Banks 55	Rest of World 56	Stocks 57	Housing 58	Firms Capital 59	Banks Capital 60	Govt Capital 61	Total 62
0	0	0	350	0	0	0	0	20014
0	0	0	391	113	520	21	0	37308
0	0	0	1033	0	0	0	0	48687
0	0	0	1294	0	0	0	0	100239
0	0	0	2517	4965	22924	935	2915	140784
0	0	0	1719	3652	16862	688	15731	85267
0	0	0	0	0	0	0	0	64387
0	0	0	0	0	0	0	0	73341
0	0	0	0	0	0	0	0	43080
0	0	0	7304	8730	40306	1644	18646	613107
0	5	0	0	0	0	0	0	75
0	14	0	0	0	0	0	0	359
0	41	0	0	0	0	0	0	1299
0	45	0	0	0	0	0	0	1441
0	131	0	0	0	0	0	0	6282
0	57	0	0	0	0	0	0	1925
0	18	0	0	0	0	0	0	646
0	0	0	0	0	0	0	0	191
0	0	0	0	0	0	0	0	2416
0	311	0	0	0	0	0	0	14633
0	0	0	0	0	0	0	0	14240
0	0	0	0	0	0	0	0	4008
0	0	0	0	0	0	0	0	14423
0	1315	0	0	0	0	0	0	7304
0	0	0	0	0	0	0	0	8730
0	0	0	0	0	0	0	0	0
0	0	0	0	0	0	0	0	40306
0	1644	0	0	0	0	0	0	1644
0	0	0	0	0	0	0	0	18646
0	-3540	1383	0	0	0	0	0	-0
-3254	-6538	0	0	0	0	0	0	-0
-1409	1409	0	0	0	0	0	0	0
-1320	0	0	0	0	0	0	0	0
922	14132	0	0	0	0	0	0	0
0	-4725	0	0	0	0	0	0	0
0	0	23001	0	0	0	0	0	0
5061	0	-9961	0	0	0	0	0	0
0	4008	14423	7304	8730	40306	1644	18646	

CHAPTER FIVE

Five Criteria for Choosing among Poverty Programs

Margaret E. Grosh

THIS CHAPTER addresses how to choose among discrete poverty interventions such as food stamps programs, public works, and small-enterprise credit schemes. Its aim is not to advance the science of policy modeling, but to improve the art of program selection when little policy modeling is done before decisions are made. Without a clear framework for discussion, such as rigorous cost-effectiveness or cost-benefit analysis, debates about program choice often become endless, mired in a morass of conflicting goals, criteria, and ideology. A lack of data often forces analysts to rely on impressionistic and conflicting information about predicted or real program outcomes, which further confuses their discussions. This chapter proposes a set of criteria that can help analysts think through program choices in an organized way. It then reviews the available evidence from Latin America on several common types of poverty alleviation programs. The proposed criteria cover the main dimensions of cost-effectiveness analysis, although the absence of quantitative information may render the considerations qualitative and subjective.

The chapter arises from my having been present when policymakers, faced with economic depressions and macroeconomic adjustment programs of the

The findings, interpretations, and conclusions expressed here are entirely those of the author and should not be attributed in any manner to the World Bank, its affiliate organizations, its executive directors, or the countries they represent. The author would like to thank Jere Behrman, Nora Lustig, and Erik Thorbecke for their useful comments.

last few years, have asked, "What new welfare program do we need?" In my experience in observing and analyzing these decisions, policymakers rarely do full-fledged cost-effectiveness analysis of alternative poverty interventions before making program choices. They often make such choices after exploring options for only a few weeks, using scarce data and rudimentary analysis. In the absence of a well-specified analytical framework, the need for new ways to order our thoughts is great.

In contrast to the resources that are available, the requirements for good cost-effectiveness analysis are formidable. Some of the costs, such as direct program benefits and administration, can be fairly easily estimated from program budgets. But determining the gross distribution of benefits between the poor and the nonpoor requires household welfare data. To estimate the net distribution of benefits (discounting for, inter alia, costs to recipients of program participation, changes in labor supply, and changes in private interhousehold transfers stemming from the introduction of the program) requires both household data and analytic sophistication.[1] While these issues are usually handled in a partial equilibrium framework, others—such as the effect of labor supply on the product markets from which labor might be withdrawn as a result of the postulated program, or the effects of the financing mechanism on the markets and on incomes—require general equilibrium analysis, which is even more demanding.[2]

In addition to the strictly economic aspects of cost-effectiveness analysis, issues of administrative and political feasibility must be assessed. Because feasibility is influenced by program design and reflected in program costs, it is in part addressed by cost-effectiveness analysis. For example, providing adequate resources for salaries, equipment, supplies, transport, and communications can improve the administrative feasibility of even large or complex programs. Political feasibility can be improved through direct expenditures for public relations or through program designs that allow leakage to the nonpoor or that provide markets for the products of influential groups.[3] Other aspects

1. See van der Walle (1992); and Gill, Jimenez, and Shalizi (1990, pp. 10, 24–28).

2. Three examples illustrate the partial equilibrium approach: Newman, Jorgensen, and Pradhan (1992) estimate the forgone earnings of participants in Bolivia's Emergency Social Fund. A review of the labor supply effects in the United States of Aid to Families with Dependent Children is in Moffitt (1992). Cox and Jimenez (1992) calculate the magnitude of changes in private interhousehold transfers resulting from the Peruvian social security system. For examples of general equilibrium analysis, Binswanger and Quinon (1988, p. 85) model the effect of choices about where to obtain subsidized commodities and how to finance food subsidy programs. Cavallo and Mundlak (1982) investigate how alternate subsidy policies affect agricultural investment and growth. The fiscal and foreign trade effects of alternate food subsidy schemes are modeled in Lustig and Taylor (1990).

3. For examples, Bolivia's Emergency Social Fund conducted a public awareness campaign when it found its beneficiaries unfamiliar with its program. See Grosh (1994, p. 32). Chile's Pro-

148

of administrative and political feasibility are not easy to capture in this way. The intangibles of work culture, stigma, and power relations are hard to convert into a monetary measure.

This chapter focuses narrowly on how to choose among programs often suggested as part of the safety net. It takes as given that a complete poverty reduction strategy entails much more: a thorough, permanent structuring of policies and investments in ways that allow the poor and their children to earn higher wages throughout their productive lives. The 1990 *World Development Report*, for example, concludes that a complete poverty reduction strategy requires two lines of attack to reduce poverty in the long run, while a third complementary line of action may be taken to support the poor who remain.

> (i) Promote efficient, labor-intensive growth. This will result in employment and earnings opportunities based on labor, which is the poor's most abundant asset. Tax, trade, exchange rate, monetary and labor policies will be important points of intervention. Investment in basic infrastructure and social and political institutions will also be required.
>
> (ii) Provide basic social services to the poor. Primary health care, family planning, nutrition, and primary education should be provided to the poor. These basic social services are human capital investments that help the poor to become productive workers. They are also humanitarian actions that provide a minimum standard of welfare even for those with low money incomes.
>
> (iii) Targeted transfers and social safety nets. Even where the two-part strategy for long-run poverty alleviation has been fully implemented, some poverty will remain. The sick, the old, and those in the poorest regions are unlikely to be able to take advantage of adequate earnings opportunities. Others will suffer from temporary setbacks owing to seasonal variations in income, loss of the family breadwinner or famine, or macroeconomic shocks. And while the long-run measures take effect, some shorter term relief may be deemed desirable.[4]

The chapter first sets out the criteria for choosing among transfer or safety net programs. It then evaluates several of the most common program alternatives in terms of the criteria, using recent examples of programs in Latin America. Finally, it applies the criteria to the situations faced in Bolivia in 1986 and Jamaica in 1988 to illustrate how they accommodate country-specific details and to see whether they support the (generally successful) strategies chosen in each case.

---

grama Nacional de Alimentacion Complementaria gives rations to all children who use public health centers, with larger rations going to those who are considered to be at high risk of malnutrition. Half the products distributed go to the 17 percent of the children at risk. Thus the program is in part targeted, but maintains the political support of a universal program. See Grosh (1994, pp. 124–25). Finally, Ballenger and Harold (1991, p. 2) illustrate the origin of the Temporary Emergency Food Assistance Program in U.S. farm commodity surpluses.

4. World Bank (1990d, p. 3).

Criteria for Program Choice

A minimum set of criteria on which to judge the relative merits of poverty programs should include administrative feasibility, political feasibility, collateral effects, targeting, and tailoring the solution to the problem. It is assumed that each program would operate in a reasonably efficient manner. The choice is not between a good school lunch program and a bad one (which is easy) but between, for example, a good school lunch program and a good social fund. It is also assumed that the program is required to have a noticeable impact on the poor within a government's term of office, which is from one to five years. If this constraint were relaxed, the list might include a sixth criterion: the time profile of benefits. I briefly consider each of the five criteria in turn.

A program must possess some minimum level of administrative feasibility before it can be viable. Having achieved that minimum, policymakers can choose among degrees of feasibility based on the level of imperfection that is tolerable and the resources that are available to bolster administrative capacity. The issue of administrative feasibility affects both the choice among different kinds of programs and the detailed design of the program selected. A program must also possess a minimum level of political feasibility to be viable. Beyond that threshold there are degrees of feasibility that depend on program design and issues particular to the country, such as the relative power of beneficiaries, suppliers, and administrators; how the program is promoted to the public; and how coalitions of supporters or opponents are formed.

A program must also possess a minimum level of political feasibility if it is to be viable. Beyond that threshold there are degrees of feasibility that depend on program design and issues particular to the country, such as the relative power of beneficiaries, suppliers, and administrators; how the program is promoted to the public; and how coalitions of supporters or opponents are formed.

In adopting a safety net program, policymakers should consider the program's possible collateral effects, such as changes in the participants' labor supply, participation in other programs, or receipt of private interhousehold transfers, as well as the effects of these changes on markets and government finances. These collateral effects may be positive, negative, or neutral with respect to the overall poverty reduction strategy.

Targeting is critical if poverty programs are to reach the poor. Leakage of benefits to the nonpoor reduces program effectiveness, because funds are used on those who are not in need. Furthermore, programs must be able to reach significant numbers of the poor to avoid the problem of undercoverage. If it is incapable of doing so, the program will be ineffective.

Program choice should be tailored to the problems faced in the particular country and time. For example, where the poor have suffered a loss of real wages rather than a loss of jobs, transfers to the working poor may be more relevant than job creation. While this criterion seems almost too obvious to include, initial proposals of what to do about poverty programs often ignore it.

If analysts had quantitative information about program results on these criteria, they could do full cost-effectiveness simulations. They would start from a fixed program budget and a known distribution of welfare. From the budget they would deduct administrative costs and any monetary costs necessary to gain political feasibility, and they would exclude from the choice set those programs for which reasonable expenditures could not provide minimal administrative or political feasibility. They might also introduce a constraint function on political feasibility, as de Janvry, Fargeix, and Sadoulet did in their study of alternate macroeconomic adjustment packages.[5] They would then simulate a new welfare distribution, taking into account the level of program benefits available in the remaining budget, the targeting outcomes achieved, and the direction and magnitude of the collateral effects. The extent or depth of poverty could be measured by an index of poverty, such as those in the Foster-Greer-Thorbecke family of measures.[6] The best program option would be that which produced the lowest poverty measure for a given budget.

In the absence of enough quantitative information to carry out the full program simulation, it is possible to use the proposed criteria to analyze the available evidence in an organized fashion. However, without the simulation—which would implicitly provide weights for the different criteria—there is no firm way to order preferences. I therefore suggest that program options must first clear a rough pass/fail test on each criterion, which will eliminate those that are unlikely, whatever their other advantages, to pass muster in the end. For example, some programs might be infeasible on political or administrative grounds, even if considerable ingenuity and expense went into their design. This test would eliminate them. Programs with very large negative collateral effects might be excluded on the grounds that they would require very large offsetting advantages or complicated compensatory arrangements that are unlikely to materialize. Very poorly targeted programs that reach large numbers of the nonpoor or fail badly to reach the poor might also be omitted, as might programs that do not rather directly address the problems at hand. To choose among programs that pass these first feasibility tests, I can only suggest reliance on professional judgment of qualitative tradeoffs among options.

5. de Janvry, Fargeix, and Sadoulet (1989).
6. Foster, Greer, and Thorbecke, (1988, pp. 173–77).

Program Experience

When it is not possible to do full cost-effectiveness evaluations before making program recommendations, a review of recent program experience in Latin America helps show how different program options might fare. Of course, prudent adjustments must be made for how programs or contexts differ across countries.

This review of program experience sets aside several issues that generally affect the impact of transfer programs: offsetting declines in private transfers, the effects of taxes that support the program, and the secondary effects of income transfers. The effect of each of these issues is sketched briefly before the review, which evaluates several different types of programs.

First, the net benefits of public transfer schemes are influenced by how private transfers (for example, from family members) change in response to them. Cox and Jimenez, for example, simulate the effect of social security on private transfers in Peru. Average social security payments were about 30 intis, and the average amount by which social security was estimated to reduce private transfers was 10 intis, so that the net benefits of the social security payments were about one-third lower than gross benefits.[7] If this result is widely applicable to other countries and programs, then any estimate of the cost-effectiveness of a government transfer program that does not allow for changes in private interhousehold transfers will overestimate its impact.

There is still no evidence as to whether the response of private transfers differs depending on the form in which the government transfer is received, be it in cash, in kind, or in reduced prices for commodities or services. Indeed, there is no evidence on how any of the specific programs reviewed in this section influenced interhousehold transfers. In the absence of empirical evidence, I assume that behavioral responses do not vary with the form of transfer. This assumption allows me to set aside the issue of how large offsetting declines in private transfers might be (which addresses whether governments should provide transfers) and proceed with the choice among programs (which addresses how government should provide transfers).

The net benefits of public transfer schemes are also influenced by how they are financed. Binswanger and Quizon, for example, model the effect of financing schemes on several food policy options in India. When assuming the hypothetical programs are financed through foreign aid, the real per capita in-

7. Cox and Jimenez, (1992, pp. 161, 167).

come of the poorest rural quartile improves 0.86 percent for urban ration shops, 5.2 percent for untargeted subsidies, and 17.6 percent for food stamps. Assuming the same programs are financed through a domestic excise tax, incomes improve 0.3 percent, 4.3 percent, and 16 percent, respectively.[8] The financing mechanism thus reduces benefits to these groups from two-thirds to one-tenth of the level predicted when tax effects are not considered.

In this review I generally ignore the issue of how programs are financed. The implicit assumption is that the question is not whether or how to raise revenue and spend it for a poverty program. That a certain amount of existing revenue will be spent on a poverty program is taken as given. The question, then, is which kind of poverty program it should be. I concentrate not on whether to have a program, but on how.

A third indirect effect of transfer programs lies in the fact that the recipients of transfers spend them, which may in turn improve the welfare of those who supply the products they purchase. This effect accounts for the increase (albeit small) in the welfare of the rural poor when Binswanger and Quizon modeled the effect of urban ration shops that directly benefit only urban residents. A second example comes from an evaluation of the employment effects of Bolivia's Emergency Social Fund (ESF). A general equilibrium model estimated that of the total employment effect of ESF expenditures, 53 percent was due to indirect effects and only 47 percent to direct effects, implying a multiplier effect of 1.1.[9] I exclude these secondary effects of program transfers in the review, again to focus on direct program effects.

Finally, I should clarify that although several of the programs reviewed use food as a transfer mechanism, this chapter examines the implicit income transfer, not the extent to which that income improves nutrition. Although transfers are often intended to improve nutrition, the empirical evidence on their success is mixed.[10] Because my performance measure is the pre- and post-transfer income-based poverty index, it is the income effect of the transfers that matter, whether embodied in food or in some other vehicle. With that preface, I move to the review. Table 5-1 summarizes the review.

General Food Price Subsidies

Many countries have used general food price subsidies over the years. The subsidies most studied are those in Mexico, Brazil, and Argentina, with less

8. Binswanger and Quizon, (1988, pp. 306–09).
9. Unidad de Análisis de Políticas Económicas (1988, p. 13).
10. For a review, see Behrman (1990, pp. 80–86).

Table 5-1. *Assessments of Six Types of Poverty Reduction Program*

Criterion	General food price subsidies	Food stamps	Food commodities through clinics	School feeding	Social funds	Microenterprise credit
Administrative feasibility	Usually good	Medium to high requirements depending on design	Medium to high requirements depending on design	Medium requirements	Agility may require exceptions to procurement and civil service standards	Demanding, usually successful only on very small scale
Political feasibility	Excellent	Controversy over dependency, effect on work ethic	Usually good, occasional objections to paternalism	Excellent	Popular with people; may have opponents in bureaucracy	Good
Collateral effects	Distorts economy; deleterious to growth	Depending on design, may encourage use of primary health care or schools	Increases use of preventive health care	Encourages school attendance and learning	Can provide basic infrastructure and social services	Complements growth
Targeting	Poor	Good	Good	Variable—from neutral to good	Not well measured yet; job benefits well targeted, infrastructure and service benefits may be less so	Excellent
Tailoring solution to problem	Lowers food cost to net purchasers	Reaches working poor and vulnerable groups	Provides pregnant or lactating women and young children synergy of health care, health education, and income transfer	Lowers implicit cost of schooling	Provides temporary full-time work to young male heads of households	Improves lot of the informal sector, which grows during hard times

widely circulated studies of others such as Jamaica and Venezuela.[11] In most cases, the bulk of the subsidy value has gone to staple items that are a larger share of the food basket for the poor than for the nonpoor. In Latin America their contribution to the poor's welfare has sometimes been small. In Jamaica in 1988 the value of the subsidies on the most important subsidized commodi-

11. For Mexico, see Lustig, (1988, 1986). For Brazil, see Calegar and Schuh (1988). For Argentina, see Mundlak, Cavallo, and Domenech (1989); and Cavallo and Mundlak (1982). For Jamaica, see Planning Institute of Jamaica (1987); and Statistical Institute of Jamaica (STATIN) and World Bank (1988). For Venezuela, see World Bank (1988d).

ties was less than 5 percent of the poorest quintile's food expenditures.[12] For the nation as a whole, food expenditures were about half of total expenditures.[13] The value of the subsidies in the poorest quintile's total expenditure was probably 2.5 to 3.0 percent. In Belo Horizonte, Brazil, the value of subsidies on wheat and rice in 1974 was about 6 percent of the poorest quintile's total expenditure.[14]

ADMINISTRATIVE FEASIBILITY. General food price subsidies can be administered in a variety of forms.[15] Governments can import the items through monopoly trading agents at one price and sell to the distribution chain at a lower price, as in Jamaica.[16] If the good is locally produced, the price can be regulated, leaving the cost to be borne as an implicit tax on the producers. Alternatively, governments can purchase locally grown crops through a state commodity board and sell at a lower price, as in Mexico.[17] The common use of food subsidies indicates that their administrative feasibility is generally good.[18]

POLITICAL FEASIBILITY. Low food prices can be very popular politically. Net consumers are always happy to receive their benefits. The beneficiaries can range from the lion's share of the urban population to the lion's share of the whole population, depending on which commodities are subsidized. The benefits can thus be very widespread. They usually include the politically vocal urban and middle-class groups.

COLLATERAL EFFECTS. General food price subsidies may distort the free market and work against measures aimed at improving long-term economic growth, especially in agriculture.[19] Implicit consumer food subsidies maintained through artificially low producer prices can reduce farm production and incomes. Reducing consumer prices increases demand, which is often met through imports that require scarce foreign exchange. If a large portion of the price subsidy is provided implicitly through an overvalued exchange rate, incentives throughout the economy are distorted. The severity of these draw-

12. STATIN and World Bank (1988, p. 62); and Lustig (1986, p. 6).
13. STATIN and World Bank (1988, p. 18).
14. Calculation based on Calegar and Schuh (1988, pp. 37, 39, 53).
15. See discussions in Bale (1985, p. 62); and Valdes (1988, p. 85).
16. Planning Institute of Jamaica (1987, pp. 23–24).
17. Lustig, (1988, p. 278).
18. Bale (1985, p. 13).
19. See Pinstrup-Andersen (1988); Scobie (1988); and Bale (1985).

backs depends on the size of the subsides, the way they are financed, and the effects of a series of macroeconomic and agricultural policies. In their analysis of Brazilian wheat price subsidies, Calegar and Schuh estimate that the economic inefficiencies (deadweight losses) induced by the program equaled about 15 percent of its cost.[20]

TARGETING. General food price subsidies tend to benefit the rich more than the poor in absolute terms, but not in relative terms.[21] In the case of Jamaica's general food subsidies (which have been eliminated), the subsidized foods were well chosen, in that the subsidized staples constituted a larger share of the food budgets of the poor (3.7 percent) than of the rich (1.1 percent).[22] The rich, however, spent much more in absolute terms than the poor, so that only 14 percent of the transfer benefits accrued to the poorest quintile of the population, while 26 percent went to the richest (see table 5-2). This same pattern can be observed in the other countries for which incidence information is available.

The incidence of food price subsidies is determined by the income and price elasticities of the commodity that is subsidized. If programs subsidize commodities with negative income elasticities or high own- and cross-price elasticities for the poor and low elasticities for the rich, the incidence of the overall subsidy is progressive.[23] But there are apparently few examples of food commodities with these characteristics that are also important in the food basket and have production patterns that facilitate the administration of subsidies. Governments typically subsidize commodities with low but positive income elasticities, which has led to the incidence patterns observed above.

20. Calegar and Schuh (1988, p. 10).
21. Whether this effect is classified as progressive or regressive depends on their definitions. If a progressive action is one that equalizes the welfare distribution (ignoring financing issues), general food price subsidies are progressive. A more demanding definition of progressivity requires that the absolute benefit be larger for the poor than the rich. By this definition, such subsidies are regressive.
22. STATIN and World Bank (1988, p. 62).
23. A negative income elasticity means that if household income goes up, the amount spent on the commodity goes down, which is rare. For most staples, the share of the total budget spent on the item will decline, but the absolute amount spent will rise with income. As Thornbecke has commented, it is also possible for the subsidization of commodities with high own- and cross-price elasticities for the poor but low own- and cross-price elasticities for the rich to result in progressive incidence. Many staples show high own-price elasticities for the poor but low own-price elasticities for the rich, and there is some evidence of similar patterns in cross-price elasticities. Of course, the commodity must still be important in the poor's food basket and have a suitable production pattern. For a simple primer on these issues, see Foster (1992, pp. 113–36). For a more detailed treatment, see Alderman (1986).

Table 5-2. *Incidence of General Food Subsidies, Three Countries, 1974, 1988*
Percent

Country	Commodity	Year	Quintile				
			Poorest	*2*	*3*	*4*	*Richest*
Brazil (Metro	Rice	1974	19[a]	⊢——— 66[b] ——⊣			15[c]
area of Belo	Wheat		15[a]	⊢——— 62[b] ——⊣			23[c]
Horizonte)							
Jamaica	Powdered milk, wheat, cornmeal	1988	14	20	20	21	26
Mexico	Corn, sorghum, beans, wheat, rice	1988	20[d] ——⊣		⊢——80[e] ——⊣		

Sources: Brazil: Calegar and Schuh (1988, tables 11, 13, 28); Jamaica: Statistical Institute of Jamaica and World Bank (1988, p. 62); and Mexico: World Bank (1990d, p. 7) and Torche (1991, p. 24).
a. Incomes less than Cr$11,299 (18.4 percent of population).
b. Incomes greater than Cr$11,299 and less than Cr$45,200 (62.6 percent of population).
c. Incomes greater than Cr$45,200 (19.0 percent of population).
d. Incomes less than 1.5 minimum salaries (33.7 percent of population).
e. Incomes greater than 1.5 minimum salaries (66.3 percent of population).

TAILORING SOLUTION TO PROBLEM. Food typically comprises the largest share of the consumption basket, accounting for over half that of the poor in most cases.[24] Food price subsidies, therefore, may be an attractive way to keep total living costs down.

Food Stamp Programs

Currently Jamaica, Venezuela, Honduras, and Mexico are operating food stamp programs.[25] In the first three cases, the coupons are denominated in currency and are redeemable in many participating commercial outlets, with few attempts made to ensure they are used for any particular items. In Mexico the Tortivales program distributes a specified weight of tortillas, available in only that form.

In the programs with which I am familiar, the income transfer has generally provided recipients a small percentage of their consumption bundles on an ongoing basis. The scale of programs has varied, but the largest programs proba-

24. World Bank (1990d, p. 36).
25. All these programs are briefly described in Grosh (1994). For more detailed information on Jamaica's program, see Grosh (1992b). For Venezuela, see Garcia and Levy (1992). For Honduras, see Grosh (1991); and World Bank (1992h). For Mexico, see Baker (1992c).

bly reach one-third to a half of poor households. Collateral benefits sometimes include an increase in the use of preventive health services or school enrollment, which foster human capital formation and labor productivity in households previously without those services.

ADMINISTRATIVE FEASIBILITY. Administering food stamp programs requires three principal tasks. The first is the selection of beneficiaries. It may be relatively complicated, when means tests are used in each household, as in the case in the Mexican Tortivales program, the Honduran Bono Madre Jefe de Familia program, and the family plan part of Jamaica's food stamp scheme. Or it can be much simpler, with benefits going to all users of a designated social service, as in the Honduran Bono Materno-Infantil program, the Venezuelan Beca Alimentaria program, and the maternal-child categories of the Jamaican food stamp program.[26] The means tests require more sophisticated administrative capacity, although the administrative burden placed on schools or clinics by food stamp paperwork and clients in even simple programs should not be underestimated.

The second major task is distributing the food stamps. The logistical requirements of regularly handing out stamps to tens or hundreds of thousands of beneficiaries are not inconsiderable. Performance has generally been acceptable, but there is apparently room for improvement. The Mexican Tortivales program has avoided the need for monthly distribution of food stamps by providing members with reusable plastic cards that certify them as eligible for one kilo of tortillas daily from designated tortilla shops.[27]

Unlike many otherwise similar food supplement programs, food stamps do not require the public sector to haul and store food commodities. The savings in transport costs and food wastage can be considerable. In Colombia the administrative costs of the food coupon program were estimated to be 25 percent of total costs, whereas for a parallel food commodity distribution program they were 70 percent.[28]

Finally, food stamp programs require a reclamation process. Commercial stores must be recruited to receive food stamps in payment for purchases, and instructed as to how to convert the food stamps into cash. In all the countries that use food stamps, this process has gone smoothly and is regarded as a much smaller logistical problem than the selection of beneficiaries or the distribution of stamps.

26. Grosh (1994, pp. 61, 68–69, 125–27).
27. Baker (1992c).
28. See Uribe (1980, p. 22).

POLITICAL FEASIBILITY. More concerns seem to be expressed about the political feasibility of food stamp programs than about the viability of many other poverty programs. There are two principal objections. First, many government officials contend that Latin Americans often brand food stamps as *asistencialista*. Food stamps are seen as creating the dependence of recipients on the state rather than as empowering recipients to do without state support. Because this criticism equally applies to many other safety net programs, why food stamps in particular receive so much criticism in this vein is somewhat unclear.

A second concern, usually voiced by international agency staff, is that well-targeted food stamp programs may have too small a political constituency to maintain their share of the budget. The Colombian and Sri Lankan food stamp schemes are cited as examples.[29] This analysis is somewhat simplistic, for it fails to take into account the opportunities that governments have to build supporting coalitions through program design and publicity.[30] At any rate, that fine targeting limits budgetary support is as true of other equally well-targeted programs with different benefits as of food stamps.

COLLATERAL EFFECTS. Food stamp programs can have significant collateral benefits by increasing the coverage of basic social services. The extent of the collateral benefits depends on the initial coverage levels and the design of the programs. The contrast in the design of the Honduran, Jamaican, and Mexican programs and their results is illustrative.

In Honduras the Bono Materno-Infantil program provides food coupons worth U.S.$3.70 monthly to pregnant and lactating women and children under age five who use preventive care in participating public primary health centers.[31] The participants register for the program and receive food stamps at the health clinics. To maintain eligibility they must show they are using a minimum of preventive health services: growth monitoring and immunization for the children, and pre- and postnatal care for the women.[32] During the program's pilot phase, the number of such visits to the participating health centers increased markedly over previous years (see table 5-3).

In Jamaica the maternal-child portion of the food stamp program is supposed to work in a broadly similar way. There have, however, been problems in implementation.[33] The health care workers have not provided the main

29. World Bank (1990d, p. 92); and Alderman (1991).
30. For a fuller discussion of why it is simplistic, see Grosh (1994, pp. 11–14).
31. World Bank (1992h, p. 4).
32. Grosh (1994, p. 126)
33. Grosh (1994 , pp. 127–28).

Table 5-3. *Increases in Maternal and Child Health Activities in Pilot Health Centers, Honduran Bono Materno Infantil, 1990–91*
Percent

Activity	Urban centers	Rural centers	Total
Well child checkup	132	171	155
Growth monitoring	137	230	186
Prenatal first visit	108	11	46
Prenatal follow-up	99	60	79
Postnatal	56	6	34
Total infant/maternal	119	140	131

Source: World Bank (1992h, p. 6).

labor inputs in the clinics. Instead, officers from the Ministry of Labour, Welfare, and Sport have visited clinics on a rotating basis for a few days each month to carry out registrations. The delivery of food stamps sometimes takes place in the clinic but frequently does not, and in many cases it occurs when the clinic's health services are closed. The participants thus fail to get both food stamps and health care from a single investment in travel and waiting time, and there is little increase in the use of preventive care. Indeed, the pattern of health care use changed little after the introduction of the food stamp program in 1984.[34] This outcome may be acceptable, because preventive services in Jamaica had excellent coverage before the food stamp program was introduced. To wit, 90 percent of the population lived within ten miles of a health center that provided free preventive care by well-trained nurses.[35] Malnutrition rates were measured at only 7.4 percent for children under the age of three in a 1985 household nutrition survey. Vaccination rates in that survey were 73 percent for oral polio and 71 percent for diphtheria-pertussis-tetanus among children nine to fifty-nine months of age. Those rates compare favorably with those of other developing countries.[36]

In Mexico the Tortivales program has not been linked with health care in any way, nor has the family plan part of Jamaica's programs.

TARGETING. The targeting of food stamp programs can be quite good, depending on the exact criteria employed. In a review of thirty targeted social pro-

34. Grosh, Fox, and Jackson (1991, table 5) show little change in health care use from 1984 to 1985 or 1986, as measured by the percentage of children under six months making their first visit to public clinics and children under three participating in growth monitoring.

35. Grosh, Fox, and Jackson (1991).

36. For the survey, see Ashley and Fox (1985, tables 30 and 51). They use grades two and three on the Gomez scale as the definition of malnutrition. For cross-country comparisons, see United Nations Development Program (1990, pp. 146–47).

grams in Latin America, the Jamaican food stamp program (the only one with incidence that is well quantified) rated in the top half of programs for the share of benefits accruing to the poorest 40 percent of households.[37]

TAILORING SOLUTION TO PROBLEM. Food stamps can increase the purchasing power of the poor. Eligibility may be contingent upon a low income, which allows the working poor to benefit. Or it may be contingent upon the use of preventive health care by vulnerable groups, so that the health intervention and income transfer together protect them from the risk of malnutrition.

Food Commodity Distribution

Food commodity distribution has long been one of the most popular options for combatting poverty. Chile's Programa Nacional de Alimentacion Complementaria (PNAC), for example, dates to 1924. Many of these programs operate through health clinics, giving food packets to all pregnant or lactating women and young children, as in the Chilean PNAC and the Venezuelan Programa Alimentario Materno-Infantil (PAMI); to those meeting certain risk criteria, as in the Dominican Republic's Programa Materno-Infantil (PROMI) and Peru's Programa de Alimentacion y Nutricion para Familias de Alto Riesgo (PANFAR); or to malnourished children only, as in Jamaica's Supplemental Feeding Program.[38]

Many of the logistical and targeting considerations in food commodity distribution programs are similar to those in food stamp programs operated through the health system. The income transfer amounts to a few percentage points of the family's food basket over an extended period. Collateral health benefits may accrue, given the same design features discussed under the food stamp programs.

ADMINISTRATIVE FEASIBILITY. Identifying beneficiaries is usually manageable. Since these programs are geared to pregnant and lactating women and to young children who come to clinics (either to all or to those with obvious biomedical risk factors), it is easy to identify and screen beneficiaries. These programs usually do not attempt the means tests that at times prove complicated

37. Grosh (1994, table 4.2).
38. For information on the Chilean PNAC, see Vial, Camhi, and Infante (1992b). For the Venezuelan PAMI, see Garcia and Levy (1992). For the Dominican Republic's PROMI, see Baker (1992a). For Peru's PANFAR, see Yamada (1992); and for Jamaica's Supplemental Feeding Program, see World Bank (1992g).

in food stamp programs. The transportation and storage of the food commodities, however, can present large and expensive logistical problems. Delays and lost deliveries are common.[39] These problems are worst in remote areas or where terrain is difficult. Perhaps the sharpest illustration of the impact of storage and transport costs is that cited above for Colombia: otherwise similar programs showed administrative costs (as a proportion of total costs) to be 70 percent for food commodity distribution, compared to 25 percent for food stamp distribution.[40] Musgrove's study of many food commodity distribution programs shows that food costs as a share of total costs range from 10 to 100 percent, with the median at 71 percent. The remainder consists of administrative costs, transportation costs, and, in some cases, nonfood benefits of the programs.[41]

POLITICAL FEASIBILITY. Food commodity distribution programs seem to be more politically acceptable than food stamp programs. This advantage may be due to their more uniform link to the health care system, to their focus on mothers and children, or to the belief that food rations are more likely than cash to be used in a worthwhile manner.[42]

COLLATERAL EFFECTS. Food distribution programs operating through health clinics can increase the use of health care where it has previously been low, depending on the same factors discussed above for food stamp programs. In Venezuela, for example, there are anecdotal reports of increases in clinic utilization similar to those reported for the Honduran Bono Maternal Infantil program.[43]

TARGETING. The incidence of benefits in food commodity programs falls in the same range as benefits in other types of targeted programs, with 60 to 80 percent accruing to the poorest 40 percent of households.[44] Leakage is higher

39. Musgrove (1991, pp. 84–86).
40. Uribe (1980, p. 22).
41. This derivation is based on Musgrove (1991, table A-14).
42. This paragraph is based on numerous conversations through the years with government officials from many countries. Economists, of course, contend that whether received in food itself, in food stamps, or in cash, the transfer's effect on overall food purchases will be identical, as long as the value of the transfer is less than would have been spent on food. If the household is given a kilo of powdered milk or tortillas, it implicitly saves the price of those commodities that it would otherwise have purchased. Thus the money saved can be used as flexibly as a cash transfer. It may in part be spent on extra food, but some will also be spent on raising the level of nonfood consumption.
43. Garcia, conversation with author, Alajuela, Costa Rica, April 23, 1993.
44. Grosh (1994, figure 4.7).

when all who come to claim benefits are eligible, lower when only those meeting some risk criteria are eligible, and lowest when only the malnourished qualify. Coverage is determined by the extent of coverage in the public health system and by the eligibility criteria. Where the public health system does not cover large segments of the poor, the food commodity programs will not be able to reach them either. The lure of food grants can increase the use of health services where they are physically accessible, but where there are no such services, there can be no food supplement program.

TAILORING SOLUTION TO PROBLEM. Food commodity programs are tailored to situations where the combination of poverty, low use of preventive health services, and ignorance of good health practices causes malnutrition and illness among those who are biologically most vulnerable. The food commodity supplements income, and the link with preventive health services and health education achieves the synergy of benefits needed to reduce malnutrition effectively.

School Feeding

School feeding programs, like food supplement programs, have long been very popular. Most countries with a population of more than 1 million in Latin America and the Caribbean have such a program, though not always on a large scale.[45] One reason they do not frequently appear as a safety net option may be that they are already so prevalent. Of course there is ample scope for expanding their coverage or increasing the amount of food rations delivered. Typically, school feeding provides a small indirect income transfer. The form of the transfer is such that it may improve the school attendance and learning of children in the neediest families.

ADMINISTRATIVE FEASIBILITY. Because so many school systems of such widely divergent degrees of sophistication have school feeding programs, they are broadly feasible, without a doubt.

POLITICAL FEASIBILITY. The political feasibility of school feeding programs is excellent. Politicians, the community at large, and beneficiary households all think that school feeding is a good initiative.

45. See Musgrove (1991, table A-14).

COLLATERAL EFFECTS. School feeding programs have at least the potential to produce collateral education benefits, as they can help improve attendance. They do so by lowering the real costs of schooling or providing an in-kind income transfer.[46] School feeding programs can also help improve learning, since hungry children are less attentive. Feeding children before or early in the school shift (which may mean a breakfast or snack rather than lunch) can help increase their attention and learning.[47] School feeding programs are not likely to have a large impact on child nutrition. School children are past the age when they are most vulnerable; the amount of calories and number of days per year of feeding are small; and children are likely to receive less food at home if fed at school.[48]

TARGETING. School lunch programs in some countries, such as Costa Rica, include all students, rather than focusing only on the needy. Others, such as those in Jamaica, target schools in poor areas. In Chile both poor schools and the poorest students in the schools are targeted.[49] In Costa Rica, 62 percent of the lunches are served to children from the poorest households, while in Jamaica the figure is 72 percent and in Chile, 79 percent. In countries with less than full enrollment, school lunches are not a good vehicle for reaching the very poorest, as they are the children least likely to be in school.[50]

TAILORING SOLUTION TO PROBLEM. School feeding programs provide in-kind income transfers and can be targeted to schools in poor areas. Also, because one possible survival strategy for poor households is to take children out of school and increase their labor activities—which is apparently happening in Peru—new or expanded school feeding programs may help counter that incentive and keep children in school.[51]

46. Levinger (1984).
47. Lockheed and Verspoor (1991, p. 75).
48. Jamison and Leslie (1990, p. 26); Austin (1980, pp. 14–15); Von Braun (1992, p. 24).
49. For Costa Rica see Trejos (1992). Almost all schools participate in the program, and it is only since 1990 that there has been an attempt to differentiate subsidy levels so that poor schools receive higher per lunch subsidies. For Jamaica, see Baker (1992b). And for Chile, see Vial, Camhi, and Infante (1992a).
50. Grosh (1994, tables 4.2 and 8.5).
51. Enrollment rates among children ages eleven to twenty in the poorest three deciles of Lima's population fell from 81 to 76 percent between June/July and November of 1990, apparently in part as a result of households trying to cope with the adjustment program imposed in August of that year. No similar decline appeared for middle-income youth. See Instituto Cuanto (1991, table 43).

Social Funds

Social funds have become quite popular in Latin America since Bolivia first developed the Emergency Social Fund (ESF) in 1986. By a social fund, I mean a demand-driven institution set up to finance many small development projects.[52] The projects are proposed, carried out, and supervised by other agencies, which are usually a mix of nongovernmental organizations, municipalities, and the local offices of national or regional government agencies. To be financed, a project must use labor-intensive methods for any construction activities. The mix of projects to be funded usually includes a large share of construction or basic infrastructure rehabilitation (clinics, schools, small-scale water and sanitation, roads) and a smaller share of social service provision (personnel and resources for clinics, day-care centers, school feeding programs, adult education). Microenterprise projects are sometimes sponsored, as in Bolivia and Honduras. Sometimes employment is an explicit goal—as in Bolivia's ESF, Haiti, Honduras, and Nicaragua—and sometimes the benefits of the infrastructure or services provided are the main goal, as in Bolivia's Social Investment Fund (SIF), Guatemala, and Guyana.

Very large numbers of people can benefit from the services or infrastructure produced by a social fund. The benefit per household can be very large, as when water or sewerage services are provided to a relatively small number of households. In other cases, larger numbers of households benefit less directly, such as those who use roads that are being maintained better than before. The workers who receive wage benefits usually constitute a very small fraction of the openly unemployed, their jobs are very short-lived, and their forgone earnings may be a large share of actual earnings.

ADMINISTRATIVE FEASIBILITY. Social funds require excellent administration, which is usually accomplished by waiving the civil service pay scales, interinstitutional consultation, planning procedures, and procurement policies that are assumed to bog down public administration. The great virtue of social funds is that they can operate in an environment where the surrounding public agencies are less than agile. Indeed, that is one of the main reasons for their existence. When agencies that might implement large-scale poverty programs are incapable of doing so, social funds provide a way to circumvent the problem of low administrative capacity.

52. This section is drawn from the following World Bank project documents, as well as from the specifically cited references: World Bank (1988a, 1988c, 1990a, 1990b, 1992a, 1992b, 1992c, 1992d, 1992e, and 1992i).

POLITICAL FEASIBILITY. Social Funds can be quite popular with their beneficiaries and with the people they employ. Established agencies may have cause either to welcome social funds or to oppose them.

The popularity of social funds with beneficiaries of their projects stems largely from their demand-driven nature and their relatively streamlined bureaucratic procedures. Rarely have local groups received funding for their project requests so promptly. Their popularity is greatest when fund portfolios are large enough to reach numerous communities, and when they include a wide range of project activities.

In Bolivia workers employed by the ESF generally reacted positively. They were grateful for their employment when jobs were scarce, although some complained of the low pay, lack of job security, and lack of training.[53]

The first factor that affects the reaction of established agencies to social funds is whether they perceive the budget of the funds as a supplement to or substitute for their budget. Central ministries in particular may believe they have lost out as a result of the creation of a social fund. By contrast, municipalities or individual school and health districts may see the social fund as a new and unexpected source of financing.

A second factor is whether the fund's project selection criteria agree with those of the established agencies or were chosen in concert with them. Clearly, where the criteria differ, there is room for conflict. Consulting the line agencies when establishing project selection criteria and allowing them a short review of each project during the appraisal process can help dampen their opposition.

COLLATERAL EFFECTS. Social funds can claim to address all three prongs of the overall poverty reduction strategy to some extent. If carefully selected, infrastructure projects should encourage economic growth. The rural road rehabilitation activities, for example, should improve market access and the returns to agricultural activities in remote regions. The rehabilitation of schools and clinics and the social service projects should improve the provision of social services to the poor. The provision of work and labor income to the unemployed is the main safety net contribution, although some nutrition projects also contribute through the income transfer element of food distribution.

However, social funds may produce fewer collateral benefits than equal amounts of money directly invested in infrastructure or service provision. For example, the project selection criteria of social funds may be less rigorous

53. Molino Rivera and others (1988, pp. 18–23).

than those of the ministries or may include objectives (such as labor content or poverty targeting) that run counter to the goal of the highest investment return. Social funds that operate with an emergency mandate and attempt to maximize the quantity rather than the quality of investment are especially likely to have this problem.

The extent to which projects improve infrastructure and service provision is difficult to assess. Individual projects are very small, and because they are driven by demand, they often look like a patchwork rather than a coherent infrastructure development plan. Nonetheless, in some countries the overall scope of investment is significant. In Bolivia the total investment channeled through the ESF in 1989 equaled about one-third of traditional public investment.[54] In Honduras the scale has been smaller, but the FHIS has funded projects in every *municipio*. It has repaired about 10 percent of health posts nationwide and is estimated to be able to build about five times as many classrooms each year as the Ministry of Education.[55]

TARGETING. Wage benefits to workers in social funds are self-targeted, in that unskilled, physically demanding work is offered at the market wage, which tends to be low. Only the poor are expected to be willing to accept such work. Some social funds use poverty maps to help target projects. For example, in Honduras and Guatemala the size of each *municipio*'s allotment of funds depends upon its poverty index.[56] In most social fund projects, the project type is another means of targeting. The menu of sponsored activities helps avoid leakage to the nonpoor. For example, community water taps and latrines are unlikely to appeal to well-off communities that have indoor plumbing in each household.

A full evaluation of the targeting of social funds should include the targeting of both wage benefits to workers and project benefits. To date, little evidence exists on either point, except for a study of workers in urban projects of the Bolivian ESF, a very small survey of project beneficiaries of the Honduran FHIS, and studies of the geographic targeting of each program.

In Bolivia analysts simulated the likely earnings of workers on urban ESF projects in the labor market and compared them to what they made while working for the ESF. These simulations showed that 76 percent of ESF workers would have belonged to the poorest 40 percent of the economically active

54. Grosh (1992a, p. 47).
55. See World Bank (1992d, pp. 7–8); World Bank (1992c, p. 11). A *municipio* roughly corresponds to a county in U.S. nomenclature.
56. World Bank (1992d, p. 12; and 1992a, annex 5).

urban population without their ESF jobs. With the jobs, only 15 percent fell in this range.[57]

There is one piece of evidence from the Honduran FHIS regarding the income levels of beneficiaries of completed infrastructure projects. A small survey of ninety-two households served by eighteen social infrastructure projects showed that every household that benefited from the projects had income levels below the poverty line used by the Inter-American Development Bank.[58] While this survey is too small to be conclusive, this first piece of evidence suggests that targeting by project type may indeed work.

Targeting by geographic area seems to have been less successful in both Bolivia and Honduras.[59] In Bolivia richer areas received markedly more funding than poorer areas. In Honduras the funding pattern is less clear. Both assessments are inexact, however, because they cannot assess to what extent the projects in richer cities actually benefit only the poorer households.

TAILORING SOLUTION TO PROBLEM. The employment provided by the social fund projects is largely full time and temporary.[60] Individual projects last for only a few months. Much of the work is done on even shorter daily or weekly contracts. The construction contracts are awarded to private sector contractors who are accountable for the quality and cost of the infrastructure investment, but who have complete liberty to hire whomever they choose as workers. The workers are, therefore, presumably chosen on the basis of their output and reliability. The result is that many have come from the construction trades and are, in general, young male heads of households.

How well social funds meet the needs of the right individuals depends in part on the country and in part on the way program goals are expressed. In general, social funds are not able to reach specifically defined groups such as those laid off from public enterprises or those hurt most by structural adjustment policies. Instead they tend to help a subset of the chronically poor and underemployed.

Microenterprise Credit

The "best practice" microenterprise credit programs have several common characteristics. They offer small initial amounts of credit, with subsequent

57. Newman, Jorgensen, and Pradhan (1992, p. 61).
58. Vargas-Olea (1992, table 2, p. 4).
59. See Grosh (1992a, table 3.4); and World Bank (1992d, table 2).
60. Newman, Jorgensen, and Pradhan (1992, p. 62).

loans being contingent on a good repayment record. They charge market interest rates. They use group lending with community guarantees rather than formal collateral. They have flexible repayment schedules and excellent repayment rates. They start on a very small scale and grow gradually, which allows for some learning by doing on the part of the agency and the community. It also ensures that supervision and training activities can keep pace with the lending activities.[61]

Microenterprise credit organizations in nine Latin American countries are affiliates of ACCION, a nonprofit organization that encourages the creation of solidarity group microenterprise credit schemes.[62] A number of other countries have different credit schemes, many of which are tiny. In a review of seventeen programs in operation in the mid-1980s, the largest had about 150,000 beneficiaries and most had fewer than 10,000. The loans they offered were also very small, with the largest loans ranging from U.S.$140 to U.S.$10,000.[63]

ADMINISTRATIVE FEASIBILITY. ACCION affiliate programs that had been operating for at least two years were able to cover at least half of their operating costs (excluding start-up capital), and some programs did even better.[64] How far and fast these programs can expand is unclear. In general, the scope seems very limited, although Bolivia's PRODEM lent more than U.S.$9 million in its first three and a half years of renewed activity after the economic crisis; its repayment rate never fell below 99 percent during that time. Bangladesh's Grameen Bank with 800,000 beneficiaries and Indonesia's Badan Kredit Kecamatan (BKK) with 2.7 million beneficiaries indicate that larger scale operations ought to be possible.[65]

POLITICAL FEASIBILITY. Microenterprise credit is generally very popular in Latin America. It is easy to sell on the grounds that it "provides fishhooks to fishermen," thereby achieving permanent increases in the well-being and independence of the participants. Issues of dependency or reliance on charity are seldom raised.

COLLATERAL EFFECTS. Microenterprise credit schemes support the growth component of the overall poverty strategy. A series of very small studies (usu-

---

61. Ribe and Holt (1991); and Otero (1989).
62. Otero (1989, p. 84).
63. Lycette and White (1989, table 2.2).
64. Otero (1989, p. 94).
65. Ribe and Holt (1991, table 5).

ally of fewer than one hundred participants) has shown that microenterprise credit schemes helped raise participants' incomes from 5 to 75 percent. However, they were less effective in increasing the number of jobs available in each enterprise.[66]

TARGETING. In the "best practice" microenterprise credit schemes, the targeting can be excellent. A survey of eight solidarity group programs in Colombia shows that program beneficiaries came from the poorest quintile of the economically active population in urban areas.[67]

TAILORING SOLUTION TO PROBLEM. These projects are well suited to meeting the problems that prevail in most Latin American economies. The informal sector, where the clients of these schemes are concentrated, contains many of the poor in the first place. But it is also where those who have lost jobs in the formal economy may first turn to look for opportunities.

Applications

I now examine the program choices made by two countries: Bolivia in 1986, and Jamaica in 1988.[68] By applying the proposed program choice criteria to the decisionmaking process of each of these countries, I hope to provide an example of how to take into account specific country circumstances in weighing program options and to assess the validity of these criteria in practice. Of course, this test of the criteria will only work if the programs chosen were good ones. Both the Bolivian and Jamaican programs have been featured in numerous World Bank forums as good examples of poverty reduction programs,[69] and both programs were continued by governments of the opposition party. The assessment that they are good programs is widely shared. As it

66. Otero (1989, pp. 96–97).
67. Otero (1989, p. 89).
68. I was part of the social sectors team that helped to formulate and supervise the World Bank loans made in support of these programs (loans BO-1829, BO-1332, and BO-2127 in support of Bolivia's social funds and loan JM-3111 in support of Jamaica's Human Resource Development Program). This section is based on my recollections and interpretations of extensive contact with government officials and the World Bank team from September 1986 through May 1991 in the case of Bolivia and from January 1988 to the present in the case of Jamaica. Because of the interpretive nature of the "stories" I tell, it is difficult to supply references in the same degree of detail here as in the objective review sections of the paper. Of course, references are provided wherever possible.
69. See, for example, World Bank (1992f, boxes 6.7, A7.30).

turns out, my proposed criteria point toward the choices made. The choices are summarized in table 5-4.

Bolivia's Choices in 1986

In the mid-1980s, Bolivia was just emerging from a prolonged and drastic economic crisis. Hyperinflation was running at about 24,000 percent, GDP per capita had fallen by over 20 percent since 1980, the public sector deficit was about one-quarter of GDP, and the economy was breaking down.[70] In 1985 draconian stabilization and adjustment measures were put in place. Inflation was quickly brought to a near standstill, but growth was slow to resume. Bolivia had always been one of the poorer countries in the hemisphere, but the deterioration of the economy and of the public sector's ability to deliver social services left the poor even worse off than they had been previously.[71] The gross primary school enrollment rate was 87 percent, infant mortality was 111 per thousand live births, and only about a quarter of children one year old were fully immunized for polio and diphtheria-pertussis-tetanus.[72]

In 1986 the Bolivian government had tamed inflation, and it began to look at the next set of problems.[73] In particular, it wanted to do something about poverty for reasons of both real humanitarianism and pragmatic politics. The poor had suffered from the years of economic decline, and there was limited social tolerance in terms of waiting for sectoral reforms to bear fruit. The government wanted an antipoverty program that would be effective and visible and that would have an immediate impact.[74] The government proceeded to investigate a number of different programs, analyzing their suitability to the circumstances and problems Bolivia then faced. Let us now see how relevant my criteria were in this process of evaluating each program.

First, the elimination of general food price subsidies was among the sweeping adjustment reforms that aimed to eliminate distortions in the economy.[75] Food price subsidy cuts were not part of the poverty alleviation scheme; but, having been implemented, they helped prompt the government to establish a new and different antipoverty program.

The government considered a food commodity distribution scheme but, in

70. Schacter, Grosh, and Jorgensen, (1992, p. 3).
71. World Bank (1989, pp. 5, 8–13).
72. UNICEF (1989, tables 1, 3, 4).
73. World Bank (1989, p.i.).
74. Marshall (1992, p. 25).
75. World Bank (1989, p. 7); and Marshall (1992, p. 29).

Table 5-4. *Characteristics of Poverty Reduction Programs, Bolivia, 1986, and Jamaica, 1988*

Characteristic	General food price subsidies	Food stamps	Food commodities through clinics	School lunches	Social funds	Microenterprise credit
Bolivia, 1986						
Administrative feasibility of national program	Assured	No	No	No	Yes	No
Political feasibility	Good	Poor	Poor	Poor	Good	Fair
Collateral effects	Preclusive costs	Undetermined	Mixed	Mixed	Positive	Positive
Targeting	Very poor	Dubious	Dubious	Dubious	Acceptable	Excellent
Tailoring problem to solution	Good	Acceptable	Acceptable	Acceptable	Good	Good
Jamaica, 1988						
Administrative feasibility of national program	Assured	Assured	Dubious	Likely	Dubious	No
Political feasibility	Excellent	Good	Good	Excellent	Good	Good
Collateral effects	Preclusive costs	Neutral	Positive	Slightly positive	Positive	Positive
Targeting	Poor	Good	Good	Good	Acceptable	Good
Tailoring problem to solution	Excellent	Very good	Good	Acceptable	Poor	Acceptable

the end, rejected the idea.[76] In the first place, the scheme would have depended on international food donations, which were deemed to discourage local production. Thus, rather than collateral benefits, the scheme was thought to have collateral costs. The government also decided that there was insufficient administrative capacity to carry out food commodity distribution programs uniformly throughout the country, although several nongovernmental organizations had programs that were important in some regions. It also viewed food distribution as politically undesirable, since the hand-out approach seemed paternalistic and counter to the spirit of the adjustment program. Finally, there was some discomfort with the targeting of existing food

76. Jorgensen (1992, p. 112).

commodity distribution programs. While the criteria were sensible, there were reports of very poor implementation.[77]

The government did not consider introducing a food stamp program, probably because at that time very few existed in the developing world. The same concerns expressed in the case of commodity distribution, regarding inadequate administrative capacity and paternalism, would have applied to food stamps. Furthermore, in a country just emerging from hyperinflation, the notion of a nominally denominated stamp would have been unattractive to recipients, while one denominated in quantities would have been unattractive to merchants due to the difficulties of setting a reimbursement formula during high inflation.

A school lunch program would have been subject to most of the objections raised against a food commodity distribution program. While it might have had some collateral benefits for education, it would have relied on food aid, which was deemed a disincentive to local production. The transport and management logistics would have been as complex administratively as those for food commodity distribution. It would also have had the same paternalistic touch the government sought to avoid. Finally, the targeting would probably have been at best mediocre. The poorest families were the least likely to have children in school, and the poorest communities were the least likely to have the administrative capacity to implement such a program.

Some attention was given to the possibility of introducing a microenterprise credit scheme. The collateral effects would have been attractive, as successful microenterprise credit can help foster income and sometimes employment growth in the poor segments of society. It also seemed an appropriate solution to Bolivia's particular poverty problem. Few of the poor had been able to protect their financial assets from the drastic inflation, and small enterprises had thus been decapitalized.[78] However, widespread public suspicion about the idea threatened its political sustainability. This suspicion was due to Bolivia's history of large-scale, government-subsidized credit schemes with very poor repayment records, which had left the state with large uncollectible debts from loans that had mostly benefited the rich and well connected.[79] But the main reason why the government finally decided against a microenterprise

77. Grosh (1988, pp. 17–18).
78. World Bank (1989, p. 27).
79. For example, 64 percent of loans from Bolivia's agriculture development bank were delinquent in 1986, with delinquency concentrated among large loans often made under political influences. Similar problems are reported for BANEST, the other large public bank. See World Bank (1988b, pp. 41–42, 46; and 1989, p. 27).

credit scheme was that it would not be administratively feasible on the extensive scale that would be required for both visibility and impact (although the social fund that was chosen devoted 4 percent of its funds to cooperatives and small credit projects).

Eventually, the Bolivian government chose a social fund (the ESF) to be the centerpiece of its poverty programs. As a complementary strategy, the budget of the Ministry of Health was increased to approximately its precrisis level, while at the same time the government used international financing to initiate major projects first in health and later in education.[80]

The idea of a social fund fit all of my proposed project selection criteria fairly well. Its administrative feasibility was much enhanced when the government granted it crucial exceptions to civil service pay, planning, and procurement rules. As a result, its record shone especially brightly in contrast to broken down public agencies with mandates in the same sectors.

The political feasibility of a fund that provided financing for locally inspired projects was good. It pleased recipient communities and workers, and fostered support for the coalition government, since many of the executing agencies were local governments of the opposition party. Although there was initial resistance from other institutions, the concerted efforts of ESF managers helped overcome it.

In terms of targeting, the ESF set itself easily achievable standards for reaching the poor, but was not concerned with confining itself to reaching only the poorest of the poor. One of the common refrains of the time was that poverty was so widespread in Bolivia that the ESF was "playing with an infinite dartboard. Wherever it threw a dart [in other words, financed a project] it came up with a winner [in other words, served the poor]." It had clear collateral benefits in that it rehabilitated or expanded the country's insufficient infrastructure and social services.

The ESF was tailored to Bolivia's specific problems in that it provided jobs that helped ameliorate unemployment and seemed a suitable short-term employment alternative for politically powerful miners who were laid off *en masse* as part of the adjustment measures. However, it subsequently turned out that miners comprised a small part of the workers hired and that only a small proportion of miners worked for the ESF.[81]

A further advantage of the ESF was that because it funded small projects in

---

80. See Grosh, (1990, table A.IV.1). The World Bank's credit to support health (BO-8001) was approved in December 1989. Its credit to support education was identified in 1990 and was scheduled for appraisal in 1993.

81. Newman, Jorgensen, and Pradhan (1992, p. 57).

a very diverse portfolio, it could finance other poverty programs on a smaller, more manageable scale. Indeed, it funded food commodity distribution, school lunches, and basic infrastructure rehabilitation in health and education, in addition to playing a major role in recapitalizing the most successful nongovernmental microenterprise credit projects.

Jamaica's Choices in 1988

In 1988 Jamaica faced a situation similar to, if less acute than, that in Bolivia two years earlier. GDP per capita had declined by 20 percent between 1972 and 1987.[82] The social sectors had suffered funding cutbacks over several years with real current expenditures in health and education 32 percent lower in 1985-86 than in 1982-83. The situation, however, was less drastic than it had been in Bolivia. Inflation had peaked at 28 percent in 1984,[83] and before the funding cutbacks, Jamaica had achieved excellent coverage and good quality in most of its social services. The gross primary enrollment rate was 107 percent, infant mortality was eighteen per thousand live births, and over 80 percent of children one year old were fully immunized against polio and diphtheria-pertussis-tetanus.[84]

The Jamaican government went through a similar process of choosing among various antipoverty program options, giving consideration to food stamps, clinic-based food commodity distribution, school feeding, and employment programs.[85] Once again, my criteria in retrospect prove relevant to the decisionmaking process.

Before adjustment, Jamaica subsidized a handful of imported staple foods. Explicit subsidies were relatively small, accounting for only about 4 percent of the food basket consumed by the poorest quintile in 1988, though the somewhat overvalued exchange rate enlarged the implicit subsidy on a broader range of goods.[86] Jamaica's adjustment policies eliminated explicit subsidies and liberalized the exchange rate. As in the case of Bolivia, general food subsidies were thus not among the poverty programs reviewed.

Jamaica had already introduced a large food stamp program in 1984, after it eliminated general food subsidies during adjustment (they were reinstated in 1986). The food stamp program reached about 400,000 beneficiaries with a

82. World Bank (1988e, tables 1, 2).
83. Planning Institute of Jamaica (1989, table 4.2).
84. UNICEF (1989, tables 1, 3, 4).
85. Government of Jamaica (1988).
86. See STATIN and World Bank (1988, p. 62); and Bale (1985, p. 24).

transfer then worth U.S.$1.80 a month.[87] Half of the program granted benefits to poor households identified by a means test or by the registration lists of Jamaica's poor relief and public assistance programs. The other half of the program was for pregnant and lactating women and children under five who registered and received food stamps at public primary health clinics. This part of the program was self-targeted in that the stamps were distributed through public health clinics (which the rich tend not to use), and standing in line to register and pick up stamps cost time, which was a disincentive for the nonpoor.

The administrative feasibility of the food stamp program had already been proven. Although it had its share of imperfections, the program was operational. The food stamp program was politically attractive in that it allowed the government to announce that while food subsidies were being cut, the value of food stamps for the purchase of the same commodities were being increased to compensate. However, food stamps do not reach as many people as food subsidies, with the vocal, politically active middle classes most likely to lose out. Although linking food stamp distribution to public health clinics may provide significant collateral benefits in encouraging the use of primary health care, no such benefit has been observed in Jamaica. The targeting of food stamps was quite good. Also, food stamps were a good way to tackle one of the key causes of poverty in Jamaica, namely the rise in food prices, especially of commodities that had previously been subsidized. There were thus several good reasons for the government to consider expanding its food stamp program.

Jamaica also had in place a small food commodity distribution program that gave food packages to families whose children were identified through the public health system as moderately or severely malnourished.[88] The program was already operating in the clinics nationwide, so in that sense, it had expanded as far as it could. Nevertheless, it might have been possible to relax the criteria for the supplemental feeding program to include mildly malnourished or all children as an alternative to increasing the value of food stamps.

Although the small food distribution program was administratively feasible, a dramatic expansion probably would not have been. The health service in general was understaffed and stretched to the limit. Furthermore, the most problematic part of the existing program was getting the food commodities through customs and into the clinics. The donor agencies had already agreed to the monetization of food aid in the food stamp program; the appeal of expanding the supplemental food program, and thereby multiplying the food handling problems, was thus scarce.

87. For a comprehensive description, see Grosh (1992b).
88. For a comprehensive description, see World Bank (1992g, annex IV).

Because the supplemental feeding program was effectively tied to health care use, it might have produced more collateral benefits than food stamps. However, preventive health care coverage was already satisfactory for the most part, so there was little room for gain. Furthermore, the effectiveness of the link between supplemental feeding and health care depended heavily on the small scale of the program; if the number of beneficiaries had expanded by tenfold or more, that effectiveness might have been compromised.

The targeting of the supplemental feeding program, with eligibility restricted to malnourished children, seemed excellent. If the criteria were less restrictive, it would have been similar in targeting to the food stamp program. Finally, given Jamaica's poverty problems, expanding the supplemental feeding program would have been as appropriate as the maternal-child part of the food stamp program, but supplemental feeding would not have been able to reach as many working poor as the means-tested part of the food stamp program.

School lunches were considered as part of the safety net.[89] Administratively, it seemed feasible to expand the existing programs. Their political feasibility was excellent, as school lunches are noncontroversial and highly valued. The targeting of the lunch programs was not well quantified at the time the government was choosing its antipoverty program, but in fact is as good as that of the food stamp program.[90] Moreover, school lunches are thought to have had a positive effect on education in Jamaica. Finally, they addressed poverty only generally, by providing an indirect income transfer, but were appropriate in that they could reach the working poor.

The government considered implementing an employment program, though not of the social fund variety.[91] The intention was for it to operate through the Ministries of Agriculture and Public Works to implement programs using short-term workers. The projects would be selected by the ministries, not proposed by local groups. The labor-intensive activities envisaged for this program were in areas that, if each project was carefully designed, could have had collateral benefits, such as reforestation, watershed management, rural road rehabilitation, drainage, and flood control.

The administrative feasibility of the program was less than certain. The proposed program was quite large and would have relied on the line agencies for selecting and implementing projects. At the time, the agencies had been

89. See Baker (1992b).
90. STATIN and World Bank (1988, pp. 56, 67).
91. See World Bank (1988e, pp. 28–29).

suffering from several years of cutbacks, which caused some loss of institutional capacity, and they were unlikely to have been able to manage a large program as fast as initially proposed.

The political feasibility of the program would probably have been quite good. Employment provision carries less stigma than food stamp transfers, and the communities likely to benefit from the works would presumably have supported them. Furthermore, elections were approaching, and laborers could have been expected to vote for the party that provided them with jobs.

The rate of return on the projects will never be known. In theory they could have been acceptable with adequate selection criteria and administration, but since these were uncertain, so were the rates of return. Similarly, how well the program would have targeted the poor will never be known. However, it is likely that the level of wages and the kind of work would have caused the program to reach the moderately poor. But since most of them were not openly unemployed, they would have forgone income that may have rivaled their earnings from the program.

How appropriate an employment program would have been to the problems faced in Jamaica was also in doubt. During the years of structural adjustment the unemployment rate had fallen markedly. Thus, rather than being hurt by unemployment, the poor were hurt by falling real wages.[92] An employment program that provided part-time work to large numbers of employed heads of household or secondary workers would thus be more appropriate than one that provided fewer full-time jobs. Preliminary indications of this fact were already available in 1988.[93]

In the end, Jamaica chose a coordinated package of initiatives that came to be called the Human Resources Development Program (HRDP).[94] The largest expenditures were for the expansion of the food stamp and school feeding programs. The government left a slot open for employment programs, but these did not materialize on a large scale, partly because international aid agencies declined to help finance them. In addition, the government took a number of measures to improve the quality of basic health and education services. These included an increase in the share of government financing going to the social sectors, an increase in the share of social sector expenditure going to primary education and health, and the creation of some cost recovery and efficiency in-

92. Witter and Anderson (1991).
93. World Bank (1988e, table 12).
94. Early proposals were analyzed in World Bank (1988e). The most comprehensive description of the policies adopted is found in World Bank (1988g, annex 5).

centives. Schools and clinics were repaired, pharmaceutical stocks were refurbished, training for teachers and nurses was expanded, and textbooks were provided.

Discussion

The review of program experience in general and of program choices in two specific settings leads to three broad conclusions. First, and perhaps most obvious, there is very little evidence on many facets of program impact, particularly on the magnitude of externalities and behavioral responses to program participation.[95] Second, there is a great deal of overlap in the general results of different types of programs. Third, overall cost-effectiveness is very sensitive to details of design and context.

To illustrate these issues, I have assembled information on just two dimensions regarding three kinds of programs. The share of administrative costs and the incidence of food stamp, food commodity, and school feeding programs appear in table 5-5. The number of empty cells is readily apparent (and would be much greater if the table included the other criteria and program types). Where information is available, there are larger differences between the highs and lows of different program types than among their means. For example, the share of administrative costs in the food commodity programs ranges from 3 to 22 percent of the total program budgets. In contrast, the mean share of administrative costs is about 9 percent for food stamps, about 11 percent for food commodities, and about 6 percent for school lunches. There is less diversity in the incidence, with all programs delivering from 62 to 80 percent of their benefits to households in the poorest two quintiles of the population. But again, there is no clear ranking among programs.

The effect of the less well measured factors is just as difficult to rank *a priori*. The review showed that collateral benefits in these programs can range from zero to significant levels. The degree of political acceptability also dif-

95. I have confined the review here to program analysis in Latin American countries. This case selection is perhaps somewhat artificial, but in keeping with the focus of the conference and with my comparative advantage. A broader review of worldwide evidence would probably not alter my conclusions. Even if it did, one could argue that the Latin American examples cited are most likely to be relevant to program design in other Latin American countries to the extent that commonalities of history, culture, institutions, development models, and the like influence program outcomes. Looking beyond this paper, this argument stresses the importance of good program evaluations as part of both program design and the research agenda of those concerned with poverty in Latin America.

Table 5-5. *Administrative Costs and Distribution of Benefits in Food Stamp, School Lunch, and Food Commodity Distribution Programs, by Country*

Program	Administrative costs as share of total budget	Percent of benefits accruing to poorest 40 percent of households
Food stamps		
Jamaica: Food Stamp program	10	75
Honduras: BMJF	12	n.a.
BMI	6	n.a.
Mexico: Tortivales	12	n.a.
Venezuela: Beca Alimentaria	4	n.a.
School lunch		
Chile	5	79
Costa Rica	n.a.	62
Jamaica	7	72
Food commodity		
Chile: PNAC	6	69
Dominican Republic: PROMI	12	80
Jamaica: Supplemental Feeding	22	n.a.
	n.a.	n.a.
Peru: PANFAR	22	n.a.
Venezuela: PAMI	3	n.a.

Source: Grosh (1992a, table 4-2).
n.a. Not available.

fers with context. There was concern that school feeding was paternalistic in Bolivia in 1986, but not in Jamaica in 1988. Food stamps seem somewhat less politically acceptable than the other programs, but the factor is intangible and highly variable across countries. And of course the suitability to the need varies according to the country and the circumstances it faces at the moment of choice.

Comparing social funds to these three program types is complicated by the multidimensional nature of social fund benefits. To compare wage benefits from social fund projects with transfers from food stamp, food commodity, or school feeding programs is tempting, but misguided. The targeting criterion could favor either program, depending on the country-specific details. The direct transfer programs, however, have much higher (more favorable) transfer-to-total cost ratios than a social fund. The social fund has basic administrative costs in the same range as the other programs, but has additional nontransfer costs in the form of equipment, materials, and skilled labor for the employment projects. Furthermore, social funds have much higher participation costs (including the income forgone by social fund laborers) than the food stamp or commodity programs. After discounting for these, social funds compare very badly if the comparison is based only on the distribution of wages. But to evaluate social fund projects only on their wage distribution is to ignore the benefit stream from the infrastructure created or rehabilitated—which is always an important, and sometimes the predominant, goal of the programs. Unfortunately, there is still no good information on the distribution or even the magnitude of benefits from the infrastructure of social funds. Even if the data were available, calculating how that might affect the incomes of those who have access to the infrastructure would be tricky.

In trying to compare microenterprise credit programs to the others there are two problems: scale, and the singular nature of the benefit. The microenterprise credit projects reviewed were only a fraction of the size of the other kinds of programs. Moreover, they provide what is intended to be a permanent boost in earnings capacity, not a temporary transfer of income. Metaphorically stated, the problem is whether it is better to feed a hundred people for one day or to give one of them a fishhook. Adequate economic evaluation of that problem requires a dynamic framework with a long time horizon.

Comparing general food price subsidies with targeted food stamp, food commodity, and school feeding programs is rather more straightforward. With targeting and administrative costs in the ranges observed, the targeted options may perform somewhat better in simulations of how a given level of expenditure reduces poverty.[96] These comparisons become more complicated when the various collateral effects are calculated, but perhaps more dissent is generated by the subjective issues of whether particular targeted options can meet minimum levels of administrative and political feasibility.

The paucity of information on outcomes, the diversity of outcomes within program type according to details of design and context, and the similarity of outcomes across program types together preclude the development of a fully generalizable set of simulated cost-effectiveness calculations or a ranking of programs. It is possible, however, to develop the following general hypotheses or rules of thumb, which can be used to review program options in specific country contexts: Where administratively and politically viable, targeted transfer programs are likely to be more cost-effective than general food price subsidies. Well-managed microenterprise credit schemes are usually able to reach only a very limited number of beneficiaries. Social funds must produce

96. Baker and Grosh (1994, pp. 15–16) provide such a comparison based on administrative costs, targeting outcomes, and transfers for beneficiaries. They do not consider collateral effects.

a significant flow of benefits through infrastructure or social services to be competitive options. As mechanisms to transfer income in the form of wage benefits, they are less cost-effective than transfers imbedded in food stamp, food commodity, or school lunch programs. Food commodity distribution programs always have higher transport and spoilage costs than food stamp programs, but the two have many other characteristics in common, so there is a small advantage in distributing food stamps rather than food commodities. Where income transfer is the goal, among food stamp, food commodity, and school feeding programs, the details of program design, institutional capacities, and secondary objectives should determine the choice, because these programs often fall in the same general range of cost-effectiveness with regard to the transfers they provide. Any of these expectations, of course, may be proved false in particular circumstances, depending on the details of program design and country context.

This chapter has proposed five criteria for choosing among programs designed to ameliorate poverty in the short run: administrative feasibility, political feasibility, collateral effects, targeting, and the tailoring of the solution to the problem. It has marshaled the available evidence on how general food price subsidies, food stamp programs, food commodity distribution programs, school feeding, social funds, and microenterprise credit schemes in Latin America have performed according to these criteria. When applied to program choices made in Bolivia in 1986 and in Jamaica in 1988, the five criteria did point to the choices that were made in each country, choices that were widely deemed to be successful and appropriate. I thus conclude that the program choice criteria proposed here are sensible. In the short term they can help organize debates about program choice when full cost-effectiveness analysis of various options is impossible. In the medium term our knowledge of the magnitude of the various program effects will hopefully be more extensive, so that we can have more complete and robust rules of thumb. In the long term we will hopefully be able to do rigorous cost-effectiveness analysis often, leaving aside these rule-of-thumb inferences.

References

Alderman, Harold. 1986. *The Effects of Food Price and Income Changes on the Acquisition of Food by Low-Income Households*. Washington: International Food Policy Research Institute.

———. 1991. "Food Subsidies and the Poor." In *Essays on Poverty, Equity, and Growth*, edited by George Psacharopoulos. Oxford: Pergamon Press.

Ashley, D., and K. Fox. 1985. "Child Nutrition Survey." Ministry of Health (December). Kingston, Jamaica.

Austin, James E. 1980. *Confronting Urban Malnutrition: The Design of Nutrition Programs.* Washington: World Bank.

Baker, Judy L. 1992a. "Dominican Republic: Targeting Maternal-Child Health Care through PROMI." In "From Platitudes to Practice: Targeting Social Programs in Latin America," vol. II, edited by Margaret E. Grosh. Washington: World Bank.

———. 1992b. "Jamaica: The Nutrition and School Milk Feeding Program." In "From Platitudes to Practice: Targeting Social Programs in Latin America," vol. II, edited by Margaret E. Grosh. Washington: World Bank.

———. 1992c. "The Tortivales Program in Mexico." In "From Platitudes to Practice: Targeting Social Programs in Latin America," vol. II, edited by Margaret E. Grosh. Washington: World Bank.

Baker, Judy, and Margaret Grosh. 1994. "Measuring the Effects of Geographic Targeting on Poverty Reduction." Living Standard Measurement Study Working Paper Series 99. Washington: World Bank.

Bale, Malcolm. 1985. "Agricultural Trade and Food Policy: The Experience of Five Developing Countries." World Bank Staff Working Paper 724. Washington: World Bank.

Ballenger, Nicole, and Courtney Harold. 1991. "Revisiting Surplus Food Programs after Surpluses: The Temporary Emergency Food Assistance Program and Its Role in the District of Columbia." Discussion Paper FAP91-01. Washington: National Center for Food and Agricultural Policy Resources for the Future.

Behrman, Jere R. 1990. "The Action of Human Resources and Poverty on One Another: What We Have Yet to Learn." Living Standard Measurement Study Working Paper 74. Washington: World Bank.

Binswanger, Hans P., and Jaime B. Quizon. 1988. "Distributional Consequences of Alternative Food Policies in India." In *Food Subsidies in Developing Countries*, pp. 301–18, edited by Per Pinstrup-Andersen. Johns Hopkins Press.

Calegar, Geraldo M., and G. Edward Schuh. 1988. "The Brazilian Wheat Policy: Its Costs, Benefits and Effects on Food Consumption." Research Report 66 (May). Washington: International Food Policy Research Institute.

Cavallo, Domingo, and Yair Mundlak. 1982. "Agriculture and Economic Growth in an Open Economy: The Case of Argentina." Research Report 36 (December). Washington: International Food Policy Research Institute.

Cox, Donald, and Emmanuel Jimenez. 1992. "Social Security and Private Transfers in Developing Countries: The Case of Peru." *World Bank Economic Review* 6 (January): 155–70.

de Janvry, Alain, Andre Fargeix, and Elisabeth Sadoulet. 1989. "Economic, Welfare, and Political Consequences of Stabilization Policies: A General Equilibrium Approach." Department of Agricultural and Resource Economics, University of California at Berkeley.

Foster, James, Joel Greer, and Erik Thorbecke. 1988. "A Class of Decomposable Poverty Measures," cited in James E. Foster and Anthony F. Shorrocks, "Poverty Orderings." *Econometrica* 56: 173–77.

Foster, Philips. 1992. *The World Food Problem: Tackling the Causes of Undernutrition in the Third World.* Boulder, Colo.: Lynne Rienner.

Garcia, Haydee, and Alberto Levy. 1992. "Venezuela: Beca Alimentaria." In "From Platitudes to Practice: Targeting Social Programs in Latin America," vol. II, edited by Margaret E. Grosh. Washington: World Bank.

Gill, Indermit, Emmanuel Jimenez, and Zamarak Shalizi. 1990. *Targeting Consumer Subsidies for Poverty Alleviation: A Survey and a Primer of Basic Theory.* Washington: World Bank.

Government of Jamaica. 1988. "The Programme of Social Adjustment: Jamaica" (March). Kingston: Office of the Prime Minister.

Grosh, Margaret E. 1988. "Nutrition Interventions in Bolivia." LATHR Division. Washington: World Bank.

———. 1990. "Social Spending in Latin America: The Story of the 1980s." Discussion Paper 106. Washington: World Bank.

———. 1991. "Analysis and Recommendations for the Honduran Bono Materno-Infantil and Bono Madre Jefe de Familia." World Bank office memo, 1988. Washington: World Bank.

———. 1992a. "How Well Did the ESF Work: A Review of Its Evaluations." In *Bolivia's Answer to Poverty, Economic Crisis and Adjustment: The Emergency Social Fund,* edited by Steen Jorgensen, Margaret Grosh, and Mark Schacter. Washington: World Bank.

———. 1992b. "The Jamaican Food Stamps Programme: A Case Study in Targeting." *Food Policy 17* (February): 23–40.

———. 1992c. *Republic of Honduras: Review of the PRAF Food Coupon Programs.* Report 10488. Washington: World Bank.

———. 1992d. "From Platitudes to Practice: Targeting Social Programs in Latin America," vol. II.

———. 1994. *Administering Targeted Social Programs in Latin America: From Platitudes to Practice.* Washington: World Bank.

Grosh, Margaret E., Kristin Fox, and Maria Jackson. 1991. "An Observation on the Bias in Clinic-Based Estimates of Malnutrition Rates." Working Paper 649. Washington: World Bank.

Instituto Cuanto. 1991. *Ajuste y Economia Familiar 1985-1990.* Lima.

Jamison, Dean T., and Joanne Leslie. 1990. "Health and Nutrition Considerations in Educational Planning." UNESCO and the United Nations Administrative Committee on Coordination, Subcommittee on Nutrition (February).

Jorgensen, Steen. 1992. "Who Needs an ESF?" In *Bolivia's Answer to Poverty, Economic Crisis and Adjustment: The Emergency Social Fund,* edited by Steen Jorgensen, Margaret Grosh, and Mark Schacter. Washington: World Bank.

Levinger, Beryl. 1984. "School Feeding Programmes: Myth and Potential." *Prospects* 14 (3): 369–72.

Lockheed, Marlaine E., Adrian Verspoor, and Associates. 1991. *Improving Primary Education in Developing Countries.* Oxford University Press for the World Bank.

Lustig, Nora. 1986. "Food Subsidy Programs in Mexico." Working Paper 3 (January). Washington: International Food Policy Research Institute.

———. 1988. "Fiscal Cost and Welfare Effects of the Maize Subsidy in Mexico." In *Food Subsidies in Developing Countries,* edited by Per Pinstrup-Andersen. Johns Hopkins Press.

Lustig, Nora, and Lance Taylor. 1990. "Mexican Food Consumption Policies in a Structuralist CGE Model." In *Socially Relevant Policy Analysis: Structuralist Computable General Equilibrium Models for the Developing World*, edited by Lance Taylor. MIT Press.

Lycette, Margaret, and Karen White. 1989. "Improving Women's Access to Credit in Latin America and the Caribbean: Policy and Project Recommendations." In *Women's Ventures: Assistance to the Informal Sector in Latin America*, edited by Marguerite Berger and Mayra Buvinic. West Hartford, Conn.: Kumarian.

Marshall, Katherine. 1992. "The Genesis and Early Debates." In *Bolivia's Answer to Poverty, Economic Crisis and Adjustment: The Emergency Social Fund*, edited by Steen Jorgensen, Margaret Grosh, and Mark Schacter. Washington: World Bank.

Moffitt, Robert. 1992. "Incentive Effects of the U.S. Welfare System: A Review." *Journal of Economic Literature* 20 (March).

Molino Rivera, Ramiro, and others. 1988. *Proyecto de Promocion e Investigacion del Fondo Social de Emergencia: Reporte Final*. La Paz, Bolivia: Emergency Social Fund.

Mundlak, Yair, Domingo Cavallo, and Roberto Domenech. 1989. "Agriculture and Economic Growth in Argentina, 1913-84." Research Report 76 (November). Washington: International Food Policy Research Institute.

Musgrove, Philip. 1991. "Feeding Latin America's Children: An Analytical Survey of Food Programs." Latin America and Caribbean Technical Department Regional Studies Program Report 11. Washington: World Bank.

Newman, John, Steen Jorgensen, and Menno Pradhan. 1992. "How Did Workers Benefit?" In *Bolivia's Answer to Poverty, Economic Crisis, and Adjustment: The Emergency Social Fund*, edited by Steen Jorgensen, Margaret Grosh and Mark Schacter. Washington: World Bank.

Otero, Maria. 1989. "Solidarity Group Programs: A Working Methodology for Enhancing the Economic Activities of Women in the Informal Sector." In *Women's Ventures: Assistance to the Informal Sector in Latin America*, edited by Marguerite Berger and Mayra Buvinic. West Hartford, Conn.: Kumarian.

Pinstrup-Andersen, Per. 1988. "The Social and Economic Effects of Consumer-Oriented Food Subsidies: A Summary of Current Evidence." In *Food Subsidies in Developing Countries: Costs, Benefits, and Policy Options*, edited by Per Pinstrup-Andersen. Johns Hopkins Press.

Planning Institute of Jamaica. 1987. "Food Stamps, Food Subsidies and Alternative Mechanisms for Coping with Poverty in the Jamaican Environment." Kingston, Jamaica.

Ribe, Helena, and Sharon L. Holt. 1991. "Developing Financial Institutions for the Poor and Reducing Barriers to Access for Women." Discussion Paper 117. Washington: World Bank.

Schacter, Mark, Margaret Grosh, and Steen Jorgensen. 1992. "What? Why? How? A Primer on the ESF." In *Bolivia's Answer to Poverty, Economic Crisis, and Adjustment: The Emergency Social Fund*, edited by Steen Jorgensen, Margaret Grosh and Mark Schacter. Washington: World Bank.

Scobie, Grant M. 1988. "Macroeconomic and Trade Implications of Consumer-

Oriented Food Subsidies." In *Food Subsidies in Developing Countries,* edited by Per Pinstrup-Andersen. Johns Hopkins Press.

Statistical Institute of Jamaica (STATIN) and World Bank. 1988. "Preliminary Report: Living Conditions Survey, Jamaica." Kingston, Jamaica.

Torche, Aristides. 1991. "Food Policy and Nutritional Programs in Mexico." Central American Human Resources Division (February). Washington: World Bank.

Trejos, Juan Diego. 1992. "Costa Rica: Los Comedores Escolares." In "From Platitudes to Practice: Targeting Social Programs in Latin America," vol. II, edited by Margaret E. Grosh. Washington: World Bank.

UNICEF. 1989. *The State of the World's Children 1989.* Oxford University Press.

Unidad de Analisis de Politicas Economicas. 1988. "Modelo para Medir el Impacto Macroeconomico de los Proyectos del Fondo Social de Emergencia." La Paz, Bolivia: Bolivian Emergency Social Fund.

United Nations Development Program. 1990. *Human Development Report 1990.* Oxford University Press.

Uribe, Tomas. 1980. "Food Coupons in Colombia: Origins, Current Situation, Replicability and Prospects." Health and Nutrition Division (October). Washington: World Bank.

Valdes, Alberto. 1988. "Explicit versus Implicit Food Subsidies: Distribution of Costs." In *Food Subsidies in Developing Countries,* edited by Per Pinstrup-Andersen. Johns Hopkins Press.

van der Walle, Dominique. 1992. "Whether to Target—and How." *Outreach* 6 (December). Country Economics Department. Washington: World Bank.

Varas-Olea, Sergio. 1992. "Evaluación Ex-Post de Proyectos Financiados por el Fondo Hondureño de Inversion Social." Washington: Inter-American Development Bank.

Vial, Isabel, Rosa Camhi, and Antonio Infante. 1992a. "Chile: Experiencias y Dilemas en la Focalizacion del Programa de Alimentacion Escolar (PAE)." In "From Platitudes to Practice: Targeting Social Programs in Latin America," vol. II, edited by Margaret E. Grosh. Washington: World Bank.

————. 1992b. "Chile: El Programa de Alimentacion Complementaria (PNAC): Evolucion y Mecanismos de Focalizacion." In "From Platitudes to Practice: Targeting Social Programs in Latin America," vol. II, edited by Margaret E. Grosh. Washington: World Bank.

Von Braun, Joachim. 1992. *Food Security of the Poor: Concept, Policy, and Programs.* Washington: International Food Policy Research Institute.

Witter, Michael, and Patricia Anderson. 1991. "The Distribution of the Social Cost of Jamaica's Structural Adjustment 1977–1989." University of the West Indies, Consortium Graduate School and Institute for Social and Economic Research (May).

World Bank. 1988a. "Bolivia: Emergency Social Fund Project." President's Memorandum Report P4594-BO (February). Washington.

————. 1988b. "Bolivia Banking Sector Report." Report 6765-BO (November). Washington.

————. 1988c. "Bolivia: Second Emergency Social Fund Project." Staff Appraisal Report 7066 BO (February). Washington.

————. 1988d. *Country Economic Report on Venezuela: Policy Choices and Economic Growth.* Report 6771-VE (March). Washington.

————. 1988e. "Jamaica: Summary Review of the Social Well-Being Program." Report 7227-JM (May). Washington.

————. 1988f. "Preliminary Report: Living Conditions Survey, Jamaica." (October). Kingston, Jamaica.

————. 1988g. "Staff Appraisal Report: Jamaica Social Sectors Development Project." Document 7573-JM (June). Washington.

————. 1989. *Bolivia Country Economic Memorandum.* Report 7645-BO (September). Washington.

————. 1990a. "Bolivia: Social Investment Fund Project." Staff Appraisal Report 8248-BO (March). Washington.

————. 1990b. "Haiti: Economic and Social Fund Project." Staff Appraisal Report 9058-HA (December). Washington.

————. 1990c. "Mexico: Nutrition Sector Memorandum." Report 8929-ME (July). Washington.

————. 1990d. *World Development Report 1990.* Washington.

————. 1992a. "Guatemala: Social Investment Fund Project." Staff Appraisal Report 11060-GU (October). Washington.

————. 1992b. "Guyana: SIMPAP/Health, Nutrition, and Water and Sanitation Project." Staff Appraisal Report 10146-GUA (April). Washington.

————. 1992c. "Honduras: Second Social Investment Fund Project." Staff Appraisal Report 10451-HO (May). Washington.

————. 1992d. "Honduras Social Investment Fund Project Midterm Review." Report 10281-HO. Washington.

————. 1992e. "Nicaragua: Social Investment Fund Project." Staff Appraisal Report 11108-NI (October). Washington.

————. 1992f. Poverty Reduction Handbook Washington.

————. 1992g. "Protecting Poor Jamaicans from Currency Devaluation: Safety Net Options." Aide Memoire (January 31). Kingston, Jamaica.

————. 1992h. "Review of Two Pilot Food Coupon Programs in Honduras: The Bono Mujer de Familia and Bono Materno Infantil." Report 10488-HO. Washington.

————. 1992i. "Honduras: Social Investment Fund Project." Staff Appraisal Report 10451-HO (February). Washington.

————. n.d. *Bolivia: Country Economic Memorandum.* Washington.

Yamada, Gustavo. 1992. "Peru: The Feeding and Nutrition Program for High-Risk Families (PANAFAR)." In "From Platitudes to Practice: Targeting Social Programs in Latin America," vol. II, edited by Margaret E. Grosh. Washington: World Bank.

CHAPTER SIX

Argentina: Social Policy and Adjustment during the 1980s

Luis Beccaria and Ricardo Carciofi

LIKE many other countries in Latin America, Argentina faced deep and persistent macroeconomic disequilibria during the 1980s. The common expression "lost decade" does not seem to exaggerate the situation in Argentina: gross domestic product decreased by 9.4 percent between 1980 and 1990; gross national income declined even more, by 12.6 percent; investment as a share of GDP reached minimum levels; and the number of transactions in the economy's financial and real markets contracted due to high and variable inflation.[1] The quest for stabilization was a permanent challenge, as the range of policy packages launched during this period suggests.[2] As shown below, the economic crisis was mirrored in worsening social conditions.

While it would be interesting to perform a comprehensive analysis of how

This is a revised version of the paper prepared for a conference held by the Brookings Institution and the Inter-American Dialogue. We are grateful to Nora Lustig for detailed comments and suggestions on the draft version. Richard Newfarmer and Richard Weiskoff made comments on the paper at the conference, some of which we have included in this version. Ann Mitchell made editorial comments. The views and errors are ours.

1. Gross capital formation accounted for 23.7 percent of GDP in 1980. It then followed a downward trend; the investment ratio averaged 8.1 percent of GDP in 1990. Comisión Económica para America Latina y el Caribe (CEPAL) (1992b, tables 1 and 7).

2. For detailed analysis of the macroeconomic policies of the period, see Damill and Frenkel (1990); for fiscal aspects, see Carciofi (1990, pp. 41–67). For a quantitative summary of selected macroeconomic variables, see the tables in the statistical annex.

economic variables influenced standards of living, all the necessary information is not available. This chapter therefore addresses two issues. First, it
traces the evolution of poverty for the area of greater Buenos Aires alone, because there is no nationwide data for the 1980s. Second, it analyzes the evolution of the government's social expenditures and policies during that decade.
In doing so, on the one hand, this chapter summarizes the factual evidence
concerning budgetary allocations to social sectors and problems confronting
sectoral policies. On the other hand, by concentrating on some major aspects
of public delivery and provision of social services, it allows an indirect assessment of the broader question of the social impact of Argentina's economic crisis during the 1980s.

As the following sections show, the available evidence indicates that despite the fiscal crunch public expenditures in the social sectors in the 1980s
did not fall in comparison with the 1970s. We argue, however, that despite the
increase in spending, the quality and coverage of social services deteriorated.
Furthermore, macroeconomic and fiscal instability imposed additional burdens on a welfare state that suffered from longstanding deficiencies.

Argentina's Economic Performance

External account imbalances dominated Argentina's economy during the
early 1980s.[3] As a balance-of-payments crisis erupted in 1981,[4] attempts to
devalue the domestic currency accelerated inflation and plunged the economy
into recession. As later events confirmed, the problem was not transitory, and
it became extremely difficult to match internal and external flows. The rise in
real international interest rates and the end of foreign commercial bank lending in the early 1980s provoked a financial crisis. With no recourse to foreign
lending, the public sector had to finance the public deficit through the domestic financial system, and eventually through money creation.[5]

The macroeconomic imbalances of the 1980s were largely rooted in economic, political, and social transformations that began in the mid-1970s. In a
climate of social unrest, growing inflation, and wage claims, a military coup in

3. The deficit in the current account of the balance of payments averaged U.S.$4.7 billion
during 1980–81; see CEPAL (1992b, table 20); and CEPAL (1986, pp. 131–42).

4. In 1981 foreign reserves of the Central Bank fell by U.S.$3.5 billion. CEPAL (1992b,
table 20).

5. See World Bank (1990, p. 53). For a detailed analysis of monetary policy between 1985
and 1988, see Machinea (1989).

Table 6-1. *Public Finances by Sector, Argentina, Selected Years, 1980–91*

Percent of GDP

Revenues and expenditures	Nonfinancial public sector (accrual basis)[a]								National government (cash basis)[b]			
	1980	1981	1982	1983	1984	1985	1986	1987	1988	1989	1990	1991
Revenues	36.4	35.8	33.1	34.6	33.5	41.5	39.4	36.6	19.8	13.7	19.1	23.1
Current												
Taxes	23.3	20.4	18.7	18.4	18.2	22.1	22.3	21.1	16.3	14.7	16.0	19.7
Other	12.3	14.3	13.5	15.7	14.8	18.5	15.9	14.8				
Capital	0.3	0.3	0.5	0.2	0.2	0.3	0.2	0.2				
Other	0.6	0.9	0.3	0.3	0.3	0.7	0.9	0.4	3.5	4.0	3.1	3.5
Expenditures	43.9	49.0	48.2	49.7	45.4	47.5	44.1	44.5	24.5	24.7	21.2	23.0
Current	34.4	39.4	39.6	40.1	37.6	40.5	36.6	36.1	21.0	21.9	19.2	21.5
Wages and salaries	13.4	12.5	9.9	12.8	13.8	12.8	12.4	13.3	3.6	3.3	2.9	3.5
Interest	3.4	7.4	10.4	6.0	5.0	5.5	3.9	3.7	3.7	6.1	4.2	2.3
Other	17.6	19.5	19.4	21.4	18.8	22.3	20.4	19.2	13.8	12.6	12.1	15.8
Capital	9.5	9.7	8.6	9.7	7.8	7.1	7.5	8.4	3.5	2.8	2.0	1.4
Primary balance[c]	-4.0	-5.9	-4.7	-9.2	-7.0	-0.6	-0.9	-4.2	-1.0	0.1	2.2	2.4
Total balance	-7.5	-13.3	-14.5	-15.2	-11.9	-6.0	-4.7	-7.9	-4.7	-6.0	-2.1	0.2

Sources: Secretariat of Finance, (1988); and Ministry of Economy and Public Works (1992).

a. National and provincial governments. Budget execution data.

b. National government is composed of central, decentralized agencies, special budget accounts, pension fund system, and public enterprises. Data for public enterprises cover operational results, interest payments, and capital expenditures.

c. Excludes interest payments on domestic and external debt.

March 1976 overthrew the Peronist government that had been elected in 1973. The new government sought to replace import-substitution strategies followed since the mid-1940s by promoting Argentina's integration into world markets through trade and financial reform.[6] The government, however, did not introduce changes in public finances. Although short-term fiscal policy managed to reduce the public sector deficit from 15.1 percent of GDP in 1975 to 7.5 percent in 1980 (table 6-1), the government launched a massive investment program, and consolidated expenditures grew by almost 4 percent of GDP between 1975 and 1980.[7] From the mid-1970s onward, the combined effect of recurrent fiscal imbalances, mounting wage pressures, and the distributive conflicts that arise in an economy fairly closed to foreign competition led to inflationary disequilibria. In fact, between 1975 and 1990 annual inflation dropped below 100 percent in only two years: 1980 and 1986.[8]

The fiscal imbalance was further strained by the debt crisis and the consequent increase in debt service payments. The overall public sector deficit rose sharply from 7.5 percent of GDP in 1980 to 15.2 percent in 1983 (table 6-1). Although cuts in noninterest expenditures implied that consolidated expenditures grew by less (4 percentage points of GDP) than interest payments (7 percentage points of GDP) between 1980 and 1982, the overall deficit was increasing rapidly due to declining tax revenues, which fell by 4.6 percentage points of GDP. The primary balance—the overall deficit excluding interest payments—averaged 6 percent of GDP during 1980–84. Although during 1985–86 the fiscal primary balance improved markedly as a result of the Austral Plan stabilization program launched in June 1985, public finances worsened thereafter and did not show a surplus until 1989–90.

Macroeconomic instability and measures to reduce the fiscal deficit had a negative effect on public provision of social services in several ways. First, given recurrent inflation and the changing pattern of relative prices, real tax revenues fell sharply during the first half of the 1980s. As table 6-1 indicates, between 1980 and 1984 tax revenues as a share of GDP declined 28 percent.

6. See Sourrouille (1983, pp. 30–37).

7. The public deficit excludes the quasi-fiscal deficit of the Central Bank. The quasi-fiscal deficit is defined as the operating loss of the Central Bank due to intermediation operations, plus any adjustments necessary to take into account the fact that some rediscounts issued to the financial system will never be recovered. See World Bank (1990, p. 55). An important difference between Argentina and Chile that exacerbated the former's debt crisis was that Chile—despite large fiscal deficits in the mid-1970s—pursued public policies that enabled it to attain a fiscal surplus by 1978. See Larrañaga (1990, pp. 13–18); and Carciofi (1990, table II.1).

8. On the conditions that lead to high and persistent inflation, see CEPAL (1986, pp. 131–42); and Frenkel (1989). On inflation in Argentina, see Damill and Frenkel (1990, p. 7).

More generally, the tax system was unable to develop a solid structure despite several tax reforms.[9] It was not only the steady reduction in tax revenues, but also uncertainty about tax receipts that hindered the development of a well-defined expenditure policy. Revenue uncertainty came from fluctuations in output and prices, as well as from increased use of temporary tax collection measures introduced as part of stabilization packages.

Second, inflation, relative price changes, and revenue uncertainty hindered efficient budgetary programming. The allocative function of the budget lost its meaning, as budget credits had to be allocated to sectoral ministries to keep pace with inflation and to avoid an interruption in services. In this situation, it became increasingly difficult for treasury officials to use policy to determine the appropriate allocation of resources among competing ends. Although public sector enterprises and the social security system collect their own revenues, both requested federal assistance to cover operational deficits.[10]

Finally, the conflicting nature of financial relations between the federal government and the provinces led to greater uncertainty, further strained fiscal resources, and ultimately contributed to the deterioration in the quality of social services. This point is important because the provinces provide and administer most social services.[11] The conflict was rooted in the federal tax-sharing scheme that regulates the distribution of tax revenues to the provinces. The distribution mechanisms are intrinsically complex in a stable context, but they performed even worse as a result of changes in tax levels and in the tax structure. Furthermore, the legal framework that supported federal tax sharing ended in December 1984 and thus had to be renewed. Since congressional negotiations failed to produce a new agreement, the distribution of tax resources between the national treasury and the provinces had to be conducted on a purely ad hoc basis between January 1985 and January 1988, when a new tax-sharing scheme was finally approved.[12]

Weaknesses in these areas—tax collection, budgetary programming, and

9. Carciofi (1990, pp. 68–72).

10. See Schulthess (1990). During the period of growing external indebtedness (1980–81), the central government forced public enterprises to get foreign credit even to cover current account deficits. Public managers had widely believed that debt-service payments need not be counted as a cost and that the federal treasury had to pay for them. Carciofi (1990, pp. 37–38).

11. These tensions were in part caused by political factors: several provinces were governed by the opposition, the Peronist Party. After the provincial elections of 1987, the Radical Party retained control over two provinces. See Mustapic and Goretti (1992, pp. 251–53).

12. See Carciofi (1990, pp. 25–29). The so-called "secondary sharing" scheme, in which resources were distributed among the twenty-two provinces and the municipality of Buenos Aires, was also an important ingredient of the global negotiation on tax sharing. See Secretaría de Hacienda (1989, pp. 96–115).

Table 6-2. *Macroeconomic Indicators, Argentina, 1980–91*

Indicator	1980	1981	1982	1983	1984	1985	1986	1987	1988	1989	1990	1991
	(Annual percent change)											
Real GDP	1.5	-6.5	-5.0	3.0	2.7	-4.4	5.8	2.2	-2.6	-4.6	0.4	8.5
Retail price index[a]	87.6	131.3	209.7	433.7	688.0	385.4	81.9	174.8	387.7	4923.3	1343.9	84.0
	(Percent of GDP)											
M2/GDP	28.4	28.2	2.0	13.6	12.8	12.4	17.2	18.2	15.4	13.2	5.5	8.5
M1/GDP	7.5	6.3	4.9	3.8	3.8	3.6	5.7	5.2	3.3	2.8	2.5	4.4
	(Index, 1980=100)											
Real exchange rate[b]	100.0	157.7	342.4	399.3	363.1	364.4	294.8	338.0	337.9	495.3	242.3	155.2
Real wage[c]	100.0	96.3	84.2	98.8	125.9	114.2	109.9	100.7	99.8	91.0	86.5	82.0
	(U.S.$ million)											
Trade balance	-2520	-287	2287	3331	3523	4582	2129	541	3820	5371	8275	3983
Current account	-4767	-4714	-2358	-2402	-2391	-953	-2858	-4237	-1962	-1308	1764	-2375
	(U.S.$ billion)											
Total external debt	27.2	35.7	43.6	45.1	46.2	49.3	51.4	58.3	58.3	65.5	63.0	65.2

Sources: CEPAL (1992b); and World Bank (1992).
a. Consumer price index (annual rates, December).
b. Unregulated market, adjusted by the evolution of U.S. and domestic CPI indexes.
c. Average wages, private sector (industry, banking, and commerce).

federal-provincial arrangements—worsened during the hyperinflationary episodes of 1989 and 1990 (table 6-2) and almost interrupted the provision of social services. The difficulty of raising government revenue, coupled with strikes and demands for wage increases by state employees, made daily operations difficult. The Law of Convertibility, a stabilization program introduced in April 1991, finally succeeded both in bringing down the inflation rate and in promoting the recovery of domestic activity.[13] Under this policy package, the nominal exchange rate was fixed to the dollar, and full convertibility of the currency was guaranteed by foreign reserves of the Central Bank.[14] A large-scale privatization program and successive reforms of the tax system have provided a solid base for improvement in public finances.[15] The macroeconomic and fiscal achievements of the program have provided a new and more favorable context for public sector provision of social and other state services.

The Labor Market, Income Distribution, and Poverty

As the main nexus between the macroeconomy and social variables, the labor market had an important impact on employment, income distribution, and poverty during the adjustment process of the 1980s. Beginning in 1980, employment in the formal sector decreased sharply, producing a rise in open unemployment and employment in the informal economy, as table 6-3 shows. The aggregate level of underutilization of the work force, which had been relatively low in Argentina by developing country standards, rose to unprecedented levels.[16] In greater Buenos Aires, for example, the visible underemployment rate rose from 5.2 percent in 1980 to 9 percent in 1990.

Though the evolution of employment was important, the principal force driving the decline in living conditions was the behavior of real wages. As table 6-3 indicates, real wages in the formal sector fluctuated along a downward trend from 1974 onward that is mirrored in the evolution of nonwage and pension income. In terms of macroeconomic instability, specific factors in

13. See World Bank (1992, p. 20). Annual GDP growth in 1991 was 8.5 percent (table 6-1). The seasonally adjusted industrial production index by July 1992 was 16.6 percent higher than the year before. During the first three quarters of 1992, monthly inflation in the consumer price index averaged 1.6 percent. CEPAL (1992b, tables 5 and 12).

14. CEPAL (1992c).

15. National tax revenues collected in the first three quarters of 1992 had increased by 27 percent in real terms compared to the same period in 1990. See CEPAL (1992b, table 25).

16. During the 1970s some authors noted that the Argentine labor market seemed to display a limited supply, at least for unskilled occupations. See, for example, Llach (1978).

Table 6-3. *Indicators of Employment, Wages, and Income Distribution, Argentina and Greater Buenos Aires, Selected Years, 1970–91[a]*

	Index of real incomes (1980=100)				Greater Buenos Aires				
Year	Wages in formal sector (manufacturing)	Wage earners	Employed nonwage earners	Retired persons	Unemployment rate	Visible under-employment rate	Share of wage earners in total employment (percent)	Share of poorest 30 percent households in total income[b] (percent)	Share of wages and salaries in national income (percent)
1970	108.7	n.a.	n.a.	n.a.	n.a.	n.a.	n.a.	n.a.	43
1973	114.2	n.a.	n.a.	n.a.	n.a.	n.a.	n.a.	n.a.	44
1974	127.4	118.5	105.8	120.0	4.2	5.0	74.9	12.4	45
1980	100.0	100.0	100.0	100.0	2.6	5.2	70.3	11.1	39
1985	109.7	86.7	81.8	76.3	6.1	7.3	70.8	10.4	38
1987	97.4	84	79.1	68.5	5.9	8.4	71.1	8.7	37
1990	85.6	62.4	57.2	49.9	7.4	9.0	69.2	9.0	32
1991	91.0	69.6	68.3	57.8	5.8	9.0	70.2	n.a.	n.a.

Notes: Wages for the formal sector are hourly average wages for industrial workers estimated in INDEC, *Boletín Mensual* (various issues). Income of wage earners, other employed persons, and pensioners are authors' calculations on data from INDEC's permanent household survey (PHS) for Greater Buenos Aires. Open unemployment and visible underemployment rates are simple averages of the two observations for each year. Visible underemployed means those people working less than 35 hours in the reference week who desire to work more hours. These rates are calculated by INDEC from the PHS and are published in *Boletín Mensual* and press releases. Data on share of poorer households in total income are authors' estimates from permanent household survey microdata. Functional income distribution series is taken from Beccaria (1991).

n.a. Not available.

a. Most data are for September each year.

b. The ranking of the poorest 30 percent of households assumes uniform household size, thereby eliminating the effect of household size.

the labor market—in particular the reduction in labor demand, declining average productivity, and changes in the institutional setting—led to a decline in wages and income between the mid-1970s and 1990.[17] As a consequence of the sharp decline in inflation and the restoration of growth that followed the April 1991 stabilization program, unemployment fell and wages increased during that year (table 6-3).

There is some evidence of an increase in income inequality during the period of adjustment. Income data from greater Buenos Aires indicate that the share of total income going to the poorest 30 percent of households fell from 12.4 percent in 1974 to 8.7 percent in 1987 (table 6-3).[18] While low-income families probably suffered the largest reductions in income, Argentina's sizable middle class did not escape losses in purchasing power.[19]

As a result of both the reduction in average income and the increase in inequality, there was a sharp increase in the proportion of households with incomes below the poverty line. Table 6-4 shows that this proportion, one measure of poverty, grew from 7.6 to 28.5 percent during the 1980s in greater Buenos Aires. During the same period, the percentage of households among the "structural poor," a separate measure, remained almost constant.[20] However, the increase in the share of the structural poor with incomes below the poverty line and the rise in the intensity indicator suggest that their living conditions worsened during the 1980s. In 1991, due to the improvements in real wages, poverty measured by income diminished.

Differences between these two poverty headcount ratios—one based on in-

17. Total employment grew at an annual rate of 1 percent between 1981 and 1990, while the annual change in GDP was –0.9 percent; see Ministerio de Trabajo (1993, table 15). For a description of changes in the institutional setting, see Beccaria (1991, pp. 320–21).

18. Greater Buenos Aries is the largest metropolitan area in Argentina, with a population of 11.3 million according to the 1991 census. Unfortunately, it is not possible to present data on income distribution and related variables for other areas. INDEC's permanent household survey—the only source available—covers twenty-six other major urban centers, but the basic data has not been edited yet. See INDEC (1992, pp. 13, 17).

19. See Beccaria (1991, pp. 331–34).

20. The structural poor are also known as those with "unmet basic needs." Households that do not meet at least one of five basic needs fall into this category. These poverty figures were calculated from INDEC's permanent household survey. See the appendix for information on sources, definitions, and methods. There are other poverty estimates for this same area. For example, CEPAL estimated the proportion of poor households to be 5 percent in 1980 and 9 percent in 1986; see CEPAL (1991, p. 50). Differences are not due to sources, since all use INDEC's survey data, but to the procedures for drawing poverty lines. CEPAL also adjusts the income data for underreporting. We do not regard this type of underreporting correction as adequate; for further discussion, see Beccaria and Minujin (1991, pp. 20, 25–33).

Table 6-4. *Poverty in Greater Buenos Aires, September, 1980, 1990, 1991*

	Structural poor			Nonstructural poor with income below poverty line	Total poor with income below poverty line	Total poor	Nonpoor	Total
Year	*Income above poverty line*	*Income below poverty line*	*Total*					
1980								
Households (percent)	12.2	3.7	15.9	3.9	7.6	19.8	80.2	100.0
Intensity index[a]	0.5	1.3	0.6	1.3	1.3	0.71	0.4	0.3
1990								
Households (percent)	5.8	10.3	16.1	18.5	28.5	34.6	65.4	100.0
Intensity index[a]	0.6	1.6	1.2	1.4	1.4	1.2	0.4	0.5
1991								
Households (percent)	7.6	8.1	15.7	15.1	23.2	30.8	69.1	100
Intensity index[a]	0.5	1.5	1.0	1.3	1.3	1.1	0.3	0.4

Sources: Authors' calculations. See appendix for methods, sources, and definitions.
a. The intensity index is defined as the average over the households of each group of the ratios between the value of the poverty line and the household income.

come, the other on basic needs—reflect their respective concepts of poverty.[21] The reduction in average real incomes, together with the increase in income inequality, had two effects. On the one hand, it pushed many households among the structural poor below the poverty line: the proportion of the structural poor that were also considered poor by income standards rose from 23 percent in 1980 to 64 percent during the 1980s (Table 6-4). On the other hand, it also contributed to the impoverishment of the middle and lower-middle classes. However, because this process of impoverishment did not seem to imply a reduction in the assets of these households, they were not pushed into structural poverty. Problems in the pension fund system led to a fall in the real value of pension benefits even larger than that in wage and salary income (table 6-3). As a result, the share of retired persons among heads of households below the poverty line increased from 14 percent in 1980 to 21 percent in 1990.[22]

Even households with relatively well educated members were pushed into poverty during the 1980s. Among heads of households regarded as poor according to the income criterion but not the basic needs criterion, the share that had attended at least secondary school grew from 19 to 36 percent between 1980 and 1990.[23] This shift suggests that many of those working in skilled and semiskilled positions experienced a fall in income so drastic that it pushed them below the poverty line.

Public Social Spending and Policies

Tables 6-5 and 6-6 present the evolution of major categories of public expenditure in the social sectors as a percentage of GDP and in real terms. The data are a consolidation of figures for the federal and provincial governments, but also include items that reflect state activities in social sectors, which are not subject to specific budget approval.[24] In Argentina state activities include components of the social security system, such as pension funds, health orga-

21. One should consider the limitations of these poverty measures. Both measures fail to take into account the consumption of goods and services freely provided by the state. The structural poverty measure is based on a basic needs indicator that includes only a short range of variables, the selection of which was basically determined by data availability.

22. Authors' estimates based on INDEC's household survey for greater Buenos Aires.

23. These figures correspond to greater Buenos Aires and were estimated by the authors based on data from INDEC's permanent household survey.

24. These figures include the municipality of Buenos Aires—the Federal District—but exclude the expenses of other municipal authorities.

Table 6-5. Public Expenditures as Percent of GDP, by Category, Argentina, 1970–90

| | | Health | | Social Sectors | | | | | Other | | | | Total |
| | | Public | Public | | Social | Pension | Family | | Functioning | Economic | Public[b] | | |
Year	Education	health	health funds[a]	Housing	welfare	fund	allowances	Total	of state	sectors	debt	Total	Total
1970	3.5	1.6	2.0	0.4	0.4	6.0	2.1	16.0	n.a.	n.a.	n.a.	22.0	37.9
1971	3.4	1.6	2.1	0.5	0.5	6.0	1.7	15.8	n.a.	n.a.	n.a.	21.0	36.7
1972	3.3	1.5	1.9	0.3	0.6	4.9	1.6	14.1	n.a.	n.a.	n.a.	21.3	35.3
1973	4.0	1.7	2.3	0.6	0.6	5.4	1.3	15.9	n.a.	n.a.	n.a.	22.0	37.9
1974	4.5	1.8	2.7	1.0	1.0	6.7	1.6	19.3	n.a.	n.a.	n.a.	23.1	42.3
1975	4.3	1.8	2.4	1.3	1.1	5.1	1.3	17.3	n.a.	n.a.	n.a.	24.2	41.5
1976	2.7	1.6	2.1	1.0	0.7	5.3	1.0	14.4	n.a.	n.a.	n.a.	26.2	40.7
1977	2.6	1.5	2.0	0.5	0.8	5.2	1.2	13.8	n.a.	n.a.	n.a.	25.1	39.0
1978	3.6	1.9	2.5	0.7	1.0	6.0	1.4	17.1	n.a.	n.a.	n.a.	27.3	44.3
1979	3.5	1.6	2.7	0.6	0.7	6.2	1.2	16.5	n.a.	n.a.	n.a.	24.4	41.0

Year													
1980	4.0	1.8	3.3	1.2	0.6	7.8	1.4	20.1	8.5	10.3	3.4	22.2	42.3
1981	4.1	2.1	4.7	0.7	0.7	8.4	1.2	21.9	8.8	10.2	7.4	26.3	48.2
1982	3.3	1.7	4.0	0.8	0.5	6.2	0.8	17.3	7.9	11.4	10.4	29.6	46.9
1983	4.0	1.9	4.0	1.2	0.6	6.3	1.0	19.0	8.2	12.5	6.0	26.6	45.6
1984	4.6	2.1	3.6	1.0	0.8	6.6	0.8	19.5	6.6	10.9	5.0	22.5	42.0
1985	4.2	1.9	3.8	0.9	1.0	7.4	0.8	20.0	6.6	9.7	5.5	21.8	41.8
1986	4.6	2.1	3.9	1.0	1.0	7.4	1.2	21.2	7.3	8.6	3.9	19.7	40.9
1987	5.1	2.0	4.0	1.1	1.0	8.0	1.1	22.3	7.5	9.6	3.7	20.8	43.1
1988	4.7	1.5	4.1	0.9	0.9	7.1	0.6	19.8	7.3	10.0	3.1	20.4	40.2
1989	3.9	1.6	3.4	0.7	1.0	5.0	0.6	16.2	6.3	7.6	3.8	17.6	33.8
1990	4.0	1.7	3.9	0.9	0.6	7.3	0.6	19.0	6.0	5.4	2.0	13.4	32.4

Sources: Data for the 1980–90 are from the Secretary of Economic Programming (SEP), Ministry of Economics. They have not been yet fully published but some appeared in Ministry of Economy and Public Works (1992, pp. 75–98). Data exclude municipal expenditures and those made by Sanitary Works, a public enterprise that provides water and sanitation services. This was done in order to make figures compatible with those for the 1970s. For 1970–79, data are basically taken from PRONATASS (1990, tables 4.3, 4.9, 4.11) Sanitary Works expenditures were excluded because they were recorded in a way different from that followed by SEP. Expenditures of Obras Sociales were included; data were taken from FIEL (1990). Expenditures on family allowances were included (unpublished data from SEP). FIEL data on provincial pension funds expenditures were used instead of the original PRONATASS estimates to maintain definitions employed by SEP for the 1980–90 series. Data on nonsocial expenditures and on total public expenditures are not compatible with those for 1980–89.

n.a. Not available.

a. Includes interest owed even if it was not paid.

b. Known as Obras Sociales.

Table 6-6. Index of Real Social Public Expenditures, by Category, Argentina, 1970–90
1980 = 100

| | Expenditures | | | | | | | | Per capita expenditures | | | | | | | |
| | | Health | | | | | | | | Health | | | | | | |
Year	Education	Public health	Social security	Housing	Social welfare	Pension fund	Family allowances	Total	Education	Public health	Social security	Housing	Social welfare	Pension fund	Family allowances	Total
1970	70.9	72.0	49.1	27.0	54.0	61.2	121.5	64.0	82.7	84.0	57.3	31.5	63.0	71.4	141.7	74.6
1971	72.2	75.5	54.0	35.4	70.8	64.5	103.1	66.4	82.9	86.7	62.0	40.6	81.3	74.0	118.3	76.2
1972	73.2	73.9	51.1	22.2	88.7	55.4	101.4	62.1	82.7	83.5	57.7	25.1	100.2	62.6	114.5	70.1
1973	94.7	89.5	66.0	47.4	94.7	64.9	88.0	74.7	105.3	99.5	73.4	52.7	105.3	72.1	97.8	83.0
1974	117.9	104.8	85.7	87.3	174.6	88.7	119.7	100.0	129.0	114.7	93.8	95.5	191.1	97.1	131.0	109.4
1975	116.9	108.8	79.1	117.8	199.4	70.1	101.0	93.1	126.0	117.2	85.2	126.9	214.9	75.5	108.8	100.3
1976	71.5	94.2	67.4	88.3	123.6	71.7	75.7	75.8	75.9	100.0	71.5	93.7	131.2	76.1	80.3	80.5
1977	68.8	88.2	64.2	44.1	141.2	69.9	90.7	72.4	71.9	92.2	67.1	46.1	147.6	73.1	94.8	75.7
1978	86.5	101.5	72.8	56.1	160.2	73.1	96.1	81.4	89.1	104.6	75.0	57.8	165.0	75.3	99.0	83.9
1979	88.3	89.7	82.6	50.5	117.8	79.9	86.5	82.7	89.6	91.0	83.8	51.3	119.6	81.1	87.8	83.9
1980	100.0	100.0	100.0	100.0	100.0	100.0	100.0	100.0	100.0	100.0	100.0	100.0	100.0	100.0	100.0	100.0
1981	97.1	110.5	134.9	55.2	110.5	102.0	81.2	103.2	95.6	108.7	132.8	54.3	108.7	100.4	79.9	101.6
1982	79.5	91.0	116.8	64.2	80.3	76.6	55.0	82.9	77.0	88.1	113.1	62.2	77.8	74.2	53.3	80.3
1983	100.4	106.0	121.7	100.4	100.4	81.1	71.7	94.9	95.7	101.0	116.0	95.7	95.7	77.3	68.3	90.4
1984	122.9	124.7	116.6	89.1	142.5	90.4	61.1	103.7	115.3	117.0	109.4	83.6	133.7	84.8	57.3	97.3
1985	108.9	109.5	119.5	77.8	172.9	98.4	59.3	103.2	100.6	101.2	110.4	71.9	159.7	90.9	54.8	95.3
1986	117.8	119.5	121.1	85.4	170.7	97.2	87.8	108.1	107.2	108.7	110.2	77.7	155.3	88.5	79.9	98.4
1987	131.6	114.6	125.1	94.6	172.0	105.8	81.1	114.5	118.0	102.7	112.2	84.8	154.2	94.8	72.7	102.6
1988	124.1	88.0	131.2	79.2	158.4	96.1	45.3	104.0	109.6	77.7	115.9	70.0	139.9	84.9	40.0	91.9
1989	105.5	96.2	111.5	63.1	180.4	69.4	46.4	87.2	91.8	83.7	97.0	54.9	157.0	60.4	40.4	75.9
1990	90.4	85.4	106.8	67.8	90.4	84.6	38.7	85.4	77.5	73.2	91.6	58.1	77.5	72.5	33.2	73.2

Sources: Table 6-5. Following the original PRONATASS procedure, expenditures were deflated by the consumer price index of Greater Buenos Aires.

nizations, and family allowances, all three of which are financed out of payroll taxes.[25]

Total public social spending averaged about 20 percent of GDP during the period 1980–90 (table 6-5). Despite difficulties in comparing these figures across countries, the amount of resources the Argentine government devotes to the social sectors is among the largest in Latin America.[26]

Total public social spending measured in constant prices was almost 30 percent higher on average during the 1980s than during the 1970s (table 6-6).[27] During the 1980s it decreased sharply in 1982 with the rise in public debt-service payments (table 6-5), increased gradually through 1987, and then fell again in 1988 and 1989. The steep drop in 1989 reflected the harsh economic conditions, including hyperinflation, during that year.

As a proportion of total public expenditures, social spending fell from 41 percent in 1980 to 37 percent in 1982, but then rose until 1986 and reached its highest rate, 58.6 percent, in 1990 (table 6-7). The large amount of government resources needed to service the public debt did not lead—except in 1982—to a reduction in social expenditures. Furthermore, the reduction in real social spending during 1989–90 (table 6-6) was accompanied by a significant rise in its relative share. All public expenditures fell more or less proportionately. In fact, social spending as a share of total public expenditures fell by only 3 percent in 1989 and rose by 22 percent in 1990 (table 6-7). Although cuts in the social sectors were relatively smaller than in some other areas of public expenditure, they led to interruptions and problems in service delivery.

The allocation of public social expenditures across sectors, while fluctuating considerably from year to year, in general has not changed significantly since 1970. The only exceptions are the increase in the share of expenditures allocated to public health funds, which rose from an average of 14.2 percent during the 1970s to 19.8 percent during the 1980s, and the comparable reduc-

25. Health organizations are privately administered funds called Obras Sociales. The pension funds have a rather hybrid nature: a summary version of annual projected expenditures is included in the federal budget, though pension fund authorities are not subject to the same budget regulations and procedures that apply to the national administration. Housing expenses borne by the National Housing Fund (FONAVI) used to be financed also through wage taxes. It should be noted that compulsory contributions apply to health organizations and family allowances even when these institutions are privately administered.

26. See, for example, Hicks (1992).

27. The figures for the 1970s are not directly comparable with those for the 1980s. Unfortunately, it was not possible to reconstruct a series of nonsocial, and thus total, public expenditures for the 1970s comparable to those for the 1980s. As noted in table 6-5, it was possible to produce social expenditure data for the 1970s with the same coverage and sources as those for the 1980s. However, not enough details were available to redefine nonsocial expenditures.

Table 6-7. *Share of Social Expenditures in Total Public Expenditures, Argentina, 1970–90*

Year	Percent	Year	Percent
1970	42.2	1980	41.4
1971	43.1	1981	45.4
1972	40.0	1982	36.9
1973	42.0	1983	41.7
1974	45.6	1984	46.5
1975	41.7	1985	47.9
1976	35.4	1986	51.8
1977	35.4	1987	51.7
1978	38.6	1988	49.3
1979	40.3	1989	47.9
		1990	58.6

Source: Table 6-5.

tion in the share allocated to family allowances, which fell from 9 to 4.8 percent. The rise in social security expenditures was partially due to a rise in the number of beneficiaries.[28] Growth in pension fund expenditures was limited by resource availability, given its dependence on earmarked payroll tax revenues, which fell due to the decline in employment and real wages. The fact that the pension system is subjected to a high degree of control by the federal government also limits its growth.

In per capita terms, real public social expenditures for the period 1980–90 were 8 percent higher on average than during the previous decade (table 6-6). Real per capita social spending fell by about 21 percent in 1982, but by 1987 had regained its 1980 level. A sharp decline occurred again in 1988–89, when real per capita spending fell below its level at the beginning of the decade. There is some evidence that the number of beneficiaries of certain social services and transfers increased at a faster rate than the total population from the mid-1970s to the end of the 1980s. This is the case for education and the pension system, where the fall in expenditures per beneficiary was larger than that reflected in the per capita expenditure series.[29]

28. The number of pensioners grew at an annual rate of 5.3 percent during the 1970s and 3.5 percent between 1980 and 1985. See Carciofi (1990, table I.7). Population was growing at an annual rate of about 1.6 percent. See World Bank (1993, table 10.1).

29. Total enrollment in the educational system grew about 4 percent annually between 1980 and 1991 (table 6-10). The number of pensioners grew at an annual rate of 5.3 percent during the 1970s and 3.5 percent between 1980 and 1985; see Carciofi (1990, table I.7). Population was growing at an annual rate of about 1.6 percent.

The average level of public employment during 1980–87 was 17 percent higher than during the 1970s.[30] Unfortunately, no information exists on its sectoral distribution. The drop in real wages earned by public employees mirrored that experienced by private sector wage earners.

In sum, public social spending in real per capita terms rose steadily between 1983 and 1987 after the sharp reduction in 1982. Although still below their 1980 level (except for 1987), social expenditures were much higher than they had been in the second half of the 1970s. This outcome, however, cannot be considered the result of decisions aimed at protecting social sector expenditures for two reasons. First, these expenditures are planned and executed by a large number of institutions at three different levels of government—federal, provincial, and municipal—among which there is a lack of coordination.[31] Second, high and changing inflation, government wage guidelines for the public sector, and delays in budget execution led to random fluctuations in both the level and the structure of public expenses. Rather than being the result of a coordinated protection effort, the fact that social expenditures did not fall—and in fact rose—was the result of general operational difficulties encountered by the public sector.

Education

Given the overriding importance of the public sector in the total supply of education, it is not surprising that the economic instability of the 1980s greatly affected this sector's performance.[32] However, the problems faced by Argentina's education system in that decade reflected both restrictive financial conditions and longstanding shortcomings in the system.

The government's policy of providing free and public schooling started almost a century ago, soon after the institutional organization of the country. Driven by the need to integrate the immigrant population, Argentina very early adopted compulsory primary education, devoting human and financial resources to the expansion of the educational system. These long-term efforts to provide basic education contributed significantly to overall educational de-

30. This figure corresponds to positions in the federal and provincial governments; see Carciofi (1990, table IV.5).

31. Between 1987 and 1990 the relative shares of social spending are as follows: federal government, 61.4 percent; provincial governments, 32.5 percent; and municipalities, 6.1 percent. Ministry of Economics and Public Works (1992).

32. The shares of public schools in total school enrollment in 1980 were: 81.2 percent at the primary level; 69.3 percent at the secondary level; and 81.7 percent at the university level. See Fundación de Investigaciones Económicas Latinoamericanas (1987, pp. 146, 152, 157).

204

BECCARIA AND CARCIOFI

Table 6-8. *Attendance at School, by Age, and Enrollment Ratios, by Level of Education, Argentina, Selected Years, 1960–80*

Item	1960	1970	1980
Attendance[a]			
7–13 years old	86.7	88.9	94.3
14–19 years old	64.6	70.6	80.8
20–24 years old	7.1	12.2	15.1
25–29 years old	2.5	4.8	6.9
Educational attainment[b]			
No schooling	n.a.	6.9	5.1
Incomplete primary	n.a.	39	29.9
Primary	n.a.	30.2	31.5
Incomplete secondary	n.a.	12.2	16.4
Secondary	n.a.	7.4	9.8
Incomplete higher	n.a.	2.5	4
Complete higher	n.a.	1.8	3.3
Net enrollment ratios[c]			
Primary (6–12 years old)	86	n.a.	91
Secondary (13–17 years old)	24[d]	n.a.	42
Higher (20–24 years old)	n.a.	n.a.	10

Source: FIEL (1990, tables 2 and 3); and World Bank (1988a, table 1.3).
n.a. Not available.
a. Percent of population cohort.
b. Population age 14 and older.
c. Cohort enrollment per level as percentage of total population cohort.
d. 13–19 year age group.

velopment in recent decades, as Argentina has achieved almost universal primary education, with steady growth in enrollment at the secondary and higher levels as well (tables 6-8 and 6-9). In fact, only 5 percent of the adult population has not attended some level of the educational system. Furthermore, ranked according to gross enrollment ratios, Argentina's educational system compares favorably with other countries in the region (table 6-10).

Despite these favorable trends, at the end of the 1970s the quality of Argentina's primary education was rather poor, with high dropout and repetition rates. For example, the gross completion ratio for the 1974–80 population cohort averaged only 53.7 percent nationally.[33] This evidence of poor primary school performance parallels the results of a comprehensive assessment of primary school achievement undertaken during 1984–85 by the municipality of

33. Although the completion ratios show steady improvement for the period where data are available (table 6-11), the national average for the 1974–80 cohort indicates regional differences, with 62.5 percent in urban centers and 30 percent in rural areas. See World Bank (1988a, table 2.2, p. 8).

Table 6-9. *Enrollment, by Level of Education, Argentina, Selected Years, 1966–91*

	Primary		Secondary		Higher[a]	
Year	Thousands	Annual growth rate	Thousands	Annual growth rate	Thousands	Annual growth rate
1966	3,473	1.1	828	4.2	251	1.02
1970	3,632	0.9	975	5.0	275	16.77
1975	3,805	1.6	1,243	1.3	597	–3.79
1980	4,111	3.2	1,327	4.9	492	11.45
1985	4,812	4.9	1,684	7.5	846	6.70
1986	5,050	3.0	1,810	3.6	903	3.59
1991	5,866	n.a.	2,160	n.a.	1,077	n.a.

Sources: World Bank (1988a, table 1.2); and (for 1991) unpublished Ministry of Education enrollment data.
n.a. Not available.
a. Annual growth rates include nonuniversity education.

Table 6-10. *Gross School Enrollment Ratios, Seven Latin American Countries, 1992[a]*

Country	Year	Primary	Secondary	Higher
Argentina	1987	110	74	41
Brazil	1988	104	38	11
Colombia	1986	114	56	14
Costa Rica	1988	100	41	24
Chile	1989	100	75	18
Uruguay	1987	110	68	47
Venezuela	1986	107	54	26

Source: CEPAL and UNESCO (1992, table II.2, p. 42).
a. Total enrollment per level in relation to population cohort.

Buenos Aires. It showed that only 46.4 percent of seventh-grade students had been able to pass language tests, while passage rates were even lower in other areas: 41.7 percent in math and 40.9 percent in the natural sciences.[34]

While pupil performance is closely related to socioeconomic factors, low completion ratios are also indicative of the relatively poor quality of education, which is the result of deficiencies in teacher training, instructional materials, and curricular organization. Low quality does not seem to be associated with an inadequate supply of teaching staff, but rather with poor management of educational resources. In 1988, for the country as a whole, the average pupil-teacher ratio was nineteen, a low level by international standards. How-

34. The municipality of Buenos Aires has the highest per capita income of any federal district, no rural population, and a primary school completion ratio of 74 percent. See World Bank (1988a, table 2.2, p. 8).

ever, the average class size was about thirty students, which is within normal patterns. So the apparently low pupil-teacher ratio can be attributed to the disproportionately large numbers of substitute and special teachers. The system in general employs a large number of teachers, at low wages, with very short working days (averaging only about three hours per day). The low workload per teacher and the small amount of time spent in the classroom are among the principal causes of the low quality of basic education.[35]

In 1978 responsibility for primary school management was transferred to the provincial governments. Decentralization was prompted by fiscal goals; the idea was to match greater tax sharing by the provinces with more involvement in expenditure provision.[36] The transfer scheme, however, did not make any provisions, such as earmarked resources or payroll financing, for bridging potential gaps in local finance. Nor was there a specific set of policy guidelines established to equalize quality standards across the provinces. In fact, at the beginning of the 1980s, quality indicators showed stark regional differences. Expenditure per pupil and cohort completion ratios were positively associated with provincial per capita income.[37]

Secondary education suffered from many of the same problems as primary education, although the institutional arrangements between the central and provincial governments differed. In 1985, 45 percent of secondary enrollment was in national schools, 26 percent in provincial schools, and 29 percent in private schools.[38] Because the federal government has played a leading role in the administration of secondary education, the problems of decentralization and coordination between the central government and the provinces have been minor relative to those at the primary level.[39] In relation to quality, completion

35. World Bank (1988a, pp. 10–11).

36. The transfer of primary education to the provinces occurred in June 1978 under the military government (Laws 21.809 and 21.810); see PNUD (1987, p. 26). Paradoxically, the federalization of primary schools took place at a time when provincial governors were nominated by the military junta and there existed a de facto interruption of constitutional rules and federal institutions.

37. See World Bank (1988a, p. 10).

38. The provincial school system enrolls 73 percent of primary pupils, while 20 percent attend private institutions. See Fundación de Investigaciones Económicas Latinoamericanas (1987, pp. 146, 152).

39. Problems of decentralization and coordination in primary education were threefold. First, the central government took unilateral decisions without consulting the population, as there were no elected governors. Second, the provinces felt the national government was attempting to decrease its budget via expenditure transfers to the provinces, with no contingency measures for educational financing. Third, the transfer procedure muddled the discussion on tax sharing, as provinces were able to argue that they needed to be compensated with larger shares of national taxes.

Table 6-11. *Primary and Secondary Education Completion Rate, Argentina, 1980s*

Primary		Secondary	
Cohort	Percent	Cohort	Percent
1965–71	46.2	1966–70	59.8
1966–72	46.4	1967–71	59.4
1967–73	48.1	1968–72	60.4
1968–74	48.7	1969–73	64.7
1969–75	49.8	1970–74	66.5
1970–76	50.6	1971–75	65.8
1971–77	52.2	1972–76	66.6
1972–78	52.4	1973–77	64.9
1973–79	53.4	1974–78	60.5
1974–80	53.7	1975–79	60.0

Source: World Bank (1988a, tables 4, 9).

ratios for 1975–79 were slightly higher at the secondary level than at the primary level, although regional differences were wider (table 6-11). By 1986 only 5 percent of total teaching positions were full time, while more than half were part-time positions of twelve hours or less a week.[40]

Although a shortage of data precludes comprehensive analysis of secondary school achievement, experts stress the lack of adequate curricula as a major deficiency. In particular, the content and organization of curricula in vocational institutions have become increasingly outdated.[41] The relationship between training at school and labor market requirements has thus been questioned. This linkage is weak in most educational systems in the region, since changes in labor demand have run ahead of curricular changes. Other shortcomings of the Argentine system include obsolete teacher training and the lack of a systematic monitoring system to assess quality. These weaknesses are particularly severe in the technical schools, which had grown at a very fast rate and had offered high-quality training for technicians during the period of import substitution in the 1950s and 1960s.[42] All of these factors help explain why recent estimates of rates of return by level of education found the sec-

40. See World Bank (1988a, annexes 10, 11).

41. Almost 60 percent of total secondary school enrollment is in vocational schools, with the remainder in schools oriented toward higher education. See World Bank (1988a, p. 12).

42. For a general discussion on this point see Tedesco (1977, pp. 15–22). Stagnating employment opportunities in the industrial sector and the economic crisis of the 1980s, of course, have made the situation even worse for vocational secondary schools; see Beccaria (1992, table 1, p. 66).

208   BECCARIA AND CARCIOFI

ondary level to be the poorest in the system, including both private and public
institutions.[43]

During the mid-1970s the university system, which is mostly financed by
federal funds, confronted an explosive growth in enrollment that was not
matched by a parallel change in the organizational structure or the method of
financing.[44] Between 1970 and 1975, as a result of policies that lifted all requirements for entrance examinations, total enrollment grew at an average annual rate of almost 17 percent and more than doubled, thereby increasing the
need for additional financing (table 6-9). In 1976 the military government attempted to control this expansion by limiting access, but made no effort to review the organization, structure, and financing of the university system. In
1984 the new government inherited a higher education system weakened by
previous policies and asymmetrical trends in enrollment and budgetary allocations (tables 6-10 and 6-13). On the one hand, student unions and part of the
academic community raised strong demands for freeing access to university
education. Controls, entrance examinations, and even simple screening methods for testing student abilities were perceived as authoritarian policies of the
past. On the other hand, the system faced a critical financial situation. Between 1975 and 1984 expenditures per student-year at the university level had
dropped 20 percent, whereas expenditures at the secondary level fell by only
10 percent (table 6-13).

In sum, by the early 1980s it became clear that the education sector required comprehensive reforms to tackle its most pressing problems: the quality of primary and secondary education, and the organization and financing of
university education. The system required not only additional budgetary resources, but also improvements in financial administration, institutional management, and coordination between central and provincial governments, particularly at the primary level. Decentralization implied the need for greater
coordination on curriculum design, quality assessment, training, and monitoring. Wage policy also demanded action, since the teachers' unions strongly
opposed wage differentials among provinces, even though the fiscal situation
of each province was not the same.

The fiscal crisis that followed during the 1980s only compounded existing
weaknesses in the education system. Tables 6-12 through 6-14 summarize

43. See National Program for Technical Assistance to the Social Sectors (1990, vol. 3,
pp. 74–78).

44. In 1985 twenty-nine national universities enrolled 88 percent of all university students;
private institutions enrolled 11.4 percent. See Fundación de Investigaciones Económicas Latinoamericanas (1987, p. 157).

Table 6-12. *Expenditure on Education, by Level of Government,*
Argentina, 1980–88
Percent of GDP

Level	1980	1981	1982	1983	1984	1985	1986	1987	1988
Primary	1.86	1.67	1.32	1.79	1.98	2.20	2.54	2.25	2.06
Central government	0.11	0.07	0.05	0.07	0.07	0.06	0.08	0.09	0.08
Provinces	1.75	1.60	1.27	1.72	1.91	2.13	2.46	2.16	1.98
Secondary	1.21	1.27	1.00	1.13	1.40	1.13	0.85	1.14	1.09
Central government	0.96	0.93	0.73	0.93	0.96	0.80	0.73	0.75	0.73
Provinces	0.26	0.34	0.26	0.20	0.44	0.33	0.12	0.39	0.36
Higher	0.63	0.69	0.54	0.60	0.59	0.58	0.56	0.71	0.72
Central government	0.60	0.60	0.48	0.58	0.57	0.55	0.55	0.69	0.70
Provinces	0.03	0.09	0.07	0.01	0.02	0.02	0.01	0.02	0.02
Total[a]	4.02	4.09	3.26	4.00	5.05	4.85	4.62	5.05	4.75

Sources: PRONATASS (1990, vol. 3A, p. 6).
a. Includes other expenditures (see table 6-5).

public education expenditures during that decade. The macroeconomic and fiscal context of the 1980s precluded the adoption of policies to reverse the negative trends in education performance. The Argentine public sector was unable to implement a system of primary school testing at the national level or any other comprehensive measure aimed at improving teaching quality. Without reliable data on academic performance, it is impossible to analyze national trends in achievement, to identify their main causes, and to assess the extent of regional differences in performance. The government took no actions to target poorer groups, even though it knew that dropout rates are associated with socioeconomic factors outside of school.[45] Programs such as school meals and free provision of teaching materials, which are generally believed to help keep children in school when properly designed, thus did not receive particular attention at the national level. Similarly, the government adopted no reforms in either human resource management or institutional setting at the secondary level. Finally, although the government took a relatively more active role at the university level, its elimination of entrance exams in 1984 in response to demands by the academic community further aggravated the budgetary restrictions.

The failure to produce major policy changes cannot be attributed to any

45. World Bank (1988a, pp. 23–25). In the same vein, the school meal program was badly targeted.

Table 6-13. *Public Education Expenditure per Student, Argentina,*
1975–88[a]

Constant 1986 australes

	Primary[b]		Secondary		Higher	
Year	Amount	Index	Amount	Index	Amount	Index
1975	480	100	1,100	100	1,070	100
1976	300	63	690	63	580	54
1977	280	58	680	62	680	64
1978	280	58	800	73	970	91
1979	320	67	860	78	1,060	99
1980	360	75	960	87	1,170	109
1981	300	63	910	83	1,180	110
1982	230	48	700	64	880	82
1983	310	65	800	73	990	93
1984	360	75	990	90	860	80
1985	380	79	720	65	610	57
1986	370	77	640	58	540	50
1987	360	75	650	59	650	61
1988	340	71	n.a.	n.a.	n.a.	n.a.

Source: PRONATASS (1990, vol. 3A, pp. 19, 21, 22).
n.a. Not available.
a. Includes all government levels.
b. Provincial governments and municipality of Buenos Aires.

Table 6-14. *Index of Real Wages for Teachers, Argentina, 1976–88*

Years	Primary[a]	Secondary[b]	Higher[c]
1976	100	100	100
1977	86	118	111
1978	125	173	120
1979	126	175	177
1980	113	209	204
1981	138	192	187
1982	62	131	128
1983	96	123	122
1984	149	182	171
1985	144	146	125
1986	121	107	87
1987	108	115	78
1988	95	123	104

Source: PRONATASS (1990, vol. 3A, pp. 15–16).
a. Full-time, 15 years experience.
b. Part-time, 15 years experience.
c. Part-time, 15 years experience.

lack of vision or knowledge on the part of the authorities about the nature of the problems faced by each level of the educational system. What then explains their extremely passive stance? There are two factors that shed some light on the issue. First, both the education authorities and pressure groups—particularly the strong teachers' unions—were trapped within the narrow limits of wage discussions, despite the fact that their resolution was beyond the scope of sectoral policy and linked instead to the fiscal and macroeconomic situation. In fact, recurrent confrontations over wage levels precluded the development of a long-term, comprehensive policy agenda for educational reform. Second, given the central government's mixed function as regulator at the primary level and direct provider at the secondary level, national authorities were unable to detach themselves from wage negotiations and to focus on the enforcement of national priority targets for the system as a whole.

Fiscal constraints further aggravated the situation, as conflicts over tax sharing pervaded financial relations between the central and provincial governments, particularly after 1984 when the federal tax-sharing scheme ended. For example, in the spring of 1988, ten years after the decentralization of primary schools, the Federal Teachers' Union conducted a national strike. The strike put heavy pressure on the national government, though it was unclear to the population that the government did not have direct instruments to cope with the conflict. The central government believed that most provincial governors, by claiming they had no resources to match wage claims, implicitly agreed with union demands, requiring the intervention of the central government. The dispute lasted more than a month; it ended when the Congress passed a tax law that increased several excise duties and earmarked the receipts for education. The approval of earmarked resources, however, provided only a temporary solution to wage demands, since fiscal accounts worsened in 1989 and 1990.

At the university level, the government's failure to introduce needed policy changes resulted from its overriding concern with budgetary financing. The lifting of entrance requirements for the higher education system caused an enrollment boom that, given budget restrictions, led to a further deterioration in quality.[46] Initially, the academic community pressed for more financial resources for both wages and infrastructure, but rejected attempts to apply partial cost-covering fees. As of about 1990 the climate regarding user fees was rather more favorable.

46. For a discussion of access to university education, see Sigal (1993, pp. 268–75).

Health

In Argentina, three groups are responsible for the provision of health care: the public sector, the private sector, and the public health funds (Obras Sociales). The public funds finance health care for wage earners and cover about 60 percent of the total population, including workers' dependents.[47] The fund system encompasses over three hundred different institutions, which are organized by sector and administered by each sector's trade union. These institutions are financed by a 9 percent earmarked tax on wages and salaries that is divided between employees and employers in a ratio of one to two. Some institutions also receive income that is linked to the revenues of firms.[48] A federal agency, the National Administration of Health Insurance (ANSSAL), is empowered to oversee the functioning of these organizations and to collect 10 percent of the wage funds and 50 percent of their other revenues and redistribute them to institutions with lower per member revenues.[49] The Obras Sociales have developed their own infrastructure for delivering health services, but most of their services are contracted to private suppliers—doctors, laboratories, and clinics—and to public hospitals. The private sector covers privately insured persons, comprising about 8 percent of the total population, but the largest share of its output is sold to the Obras Sociales. Finally, various levels of the public sector—federal, provincial, and municipal governments—directly administer public hospitals and primary health care centers, where some social security affiliates and the uninsured population, who are basically the very poorest, receive care. It is estimated that about 30 percent of the population consumes health services in public facilities.[50]

Total resources, both private and public, devoted to health care comprised about 7 percent of GDP in 1989, a relatively large proportion by international standards.[51] However, despite this spending, the quality of services is severely deficient. The efficiency and equity of the Argentine health system was al-

47. This figure is taken from National Program for Assistance to the Social Sectors (1990, vol. 4, pp. 34–39). The original data source is a household survey carried out by INDEC in nine urban centers in 1989. The number of social security affiliates implied by this estimate is lower than that included in the files of the social security system, which implies a coverage level of 75 percent.
48. For example, the Obra Social for insurance companies' workers receives a percentage of the value of premiums issued during the year. See Centrángolo and others (1992, p. 47).
49. See World Bank (1992, pp. 71–85).
50. Approximately 5 percent of the population belonging to the highest income group buys health services from the private sector without being insured. See National Program for Assistance to the Social Sectors (1990, vol. 4, p. 35).
51. It is similar to those of Australia, Belgium, Italy, Ireland, and New Zealand, and only just below that of Canada or Germany. See Centrángolo and others (1992, table 2, p. 42).

ready low at the end of the 1970s, and it only worsened during the 1980s.

Many studies of Argentina's health sector emphasize its institutional fragmentation.[52] Due to its particular historical development—with the unplanned juxtaposition of provider and financing schemes—the health care system lacks coordination among its providers. As a result, investments and expenditures are duplicated in some areas and specialties, while shortages occur in others. For example, different levels of government, especially provincial and municipal governments, sometimes set up health care facilities in the same neighborhood without integrating their activities. In addition, costly equipment is not fully utilized due to a lack of integration both among Obras Sociales and—in particular—between them and the public sector.[53]

The institution created to control and coordinate the Obras Sociales has been unable to perform its regulatory role, largely due to the politically sensitive nature of its function. The management of the Obras Sociales has traditionally been a major source of power for trade union leaders.[54] Various governments have thus tried to ameliorate potential conflicts by loosening controls. Within the public sector federal, provincial, and municipal authorities often do not coordinate their actions. The transfer of public hospitals and national health programs (such as child-maternal and immunization programs) to the provinces, which occurred during the 1970s and 1980s, was an attempt to address this problem.[55] However, because the federal health authority does not conduct adequate audits, the effectiveness of this transfer is in doubt.

Weaknesses in the health care system result not only from its institutional setting but also from the management of operations by individual health care providers. For example, while the usual ratio between the aggregate number of nurses and doctors is about three to one, in Argentina this ratio is about one to three.[56] As a result, doctors provide services typically provided by nurses, with a correspondingly greater cost. Furthermore, there is evidence that some private clinics perform more complex practices than necessary: a study by the federal agency that controls Obras Sociales indicated that 35 percent of the deliveries they paid for in private clinics were performed by caesarean section; the usual proportion is about 7 percent.[57]

52. See, for example, Isuani and Mercer (1986); and World Bank (1987, pp. 13–14).

53. See World Bank (1987, p. 51).

54. It must be taken into account that there are Obras Sociales with more than 1 million affiliates (commerce, rural workers, metallic workers), some with expenses total of more than U.S.$200 million a year. See Centrángolo and others (1992, tables 8 and 11, pp. 54, 61).

55. World Bank (1988b, pp. 16, 30).

56. See World Bank (1987, p. 38).

57. See World Bank (1987, p. 30).

It is widely known that the lack of control in Obras Sociales gives rise to inadequate compliance with contracts on the part of private providers.[58] Doctors or clinics generally are paid according to the quantity and type of services provided to fund members. In this situation, there is an incentive and a tendency for providers to overbill. In other cases, payments are based on the number of affiliates "registered" with the provider. This system tends to cause doctors, and especially clinics, to provide inadequate levels of service to their clients, a problem that is exacerbated by the fact that affiliates cannot always change providers. Both underservicing and overbilling, among other problems, are caused by low fees. The oversupply of doctors and other professionals, along with financial problems faced by Obras Sociales during the 1980s due to the drop in real wages, tended to keep fees low.[59] Another important feature of the Obras Sociales is their unfortunate reluctance to cover preventive care.[60]

Public sector hospitals and health centers are also highly deficient. They are inadequately managed,[61] their infrastructure has not been upgraded for many years, and low wages have affected the quality of services provided. In particular, low wages have contributed to high rates of absenteeism and to the diminishing chances of hiring experienced professionals on a full-time basis. Regarding public hospital infrastructure, in 1987 an estimated 25 percent of capacity for short-term patient care was dilapidated beyond repair, and another 25 percent required extensive upgrading. Long-term care hospitals are even older, and in 1987 an estimated 50 percent of their capacity was totally obsolete.[62] The management of hospitals that were transferred to the provinces is further hampered by the fact that key decisions are still made by the national ministry. Moreover, the network of public primary health centers devotes an insufficient share of resources to preventive care.[63] The transfer of provincial institutions to municipalities—in progress by 1992 in some jurisdictions—may perhaps help solve some of these problems.[64]

58. Outright connivance on the part of fund managers may also occur. See World Bank (1988b, p. 19).

59. The income of Obras Sociales tended to fall as a result of lower wages and higher interest rates (table 6-3). See Cetrángolo and others (1992, pp. 49–50). Provider fees are negotiated with the participation of professional associations. For a general discussion of the distribution of income in the health sector and its effects, see Katz and Muñoz (1988).

60. World Bank (1988b, p. 15).

61. As stated in a World Bank review, "Public hospitals are administered rather than managed." World Bank (1987, p. 30).

62. World Bank (1988b, p. 16; and 1993, p. 9); also Ministerio de Salud y Acción Social (1992, pp. 2–4).

63. World Bank (1988b, pp. 15–16; and 1993, p. 11).

64. World Bank (1993, pp. 69–70).

Table 6-15. *Monthly Expenditures in Public Health Funds, by Occupation of Affiliate, Argentina, 1985*
March 1992 pesos

Affiliate	Amount
Bank worker	69.5
Insurance company worker	44.1
Teacher and educational worker	20.2
Metal worker	11.1
Construction worker	8.0

Source: Centrángolo and others (1992, table 11).

Most observers agree that public health expenditures in Argentina are progressive. An estimated 44 percent of expenditures on public hospitals went to the "poor" quintile of the household income distribution in 1986.[65] During the adjustment period of the 1980s there was a rise in the number of patients from lower-middle class households using public hospitals. This increase consisted of individuals leaving wage-earning positions and members of Obras Sociales that either offered a narrow range of services or required copayments.[66] Therefore, although public health expenditures are progressive overall, there are a variety of problems affecting the quality of public health care, including delays, lack of inputs, irregular presence of professionals, outdated equipment, and aging infrastructure.

Public health fund expenditures are also progressive, since all members of a given Obra Social receive the same care without regard to position or to wage. However, the redistributive impact is lower than in the centralized public health care systems of many Latin American countries because cross-subsidies arising from differences in average wages (and risks) across sectors are lost. Due to this loss, to the special access some funds have to alternative sources of finance, and to disparities in management efficiency, there are significant differences in expenditures per affiliate among Obras Sociales (table 6-15).

Financial problems have led many public health funds to establish or to increase the size of copayments.[67] In many cases, copayments are required de facto by private providers who receive reduced fees from the Obras Sociales.[68] Although there is no firm evidence on the way copayments are deter-

65. National Program for Technical Assistance to the Social Sectors (1990, vols. 1 and 2, table 7.11, p. 204).
66. See World Bank (1987, p. 50).
67. Nirenberg and Perrone (1992).
68. See Katz and Muñoz (1988, p. 57); and World Bank (1987, p. 47).

mined and charged, they are probably regressive, since their size is generally independent of affiliate income. Copayments therefore can be a significant burden, particularly to low-income households.

In sum, given all this evidence, the most plausible conclusion is that the relative progressivity of the health system—with public health expenditures and the Obras Sociales—did not improve during the 1980s. It probably worsened due to several concomitant factors: the increase in the use of public facilities by middle-class households previously covered by Obras Sociales; the rise in copayments required by Obras Sociales; the decrease in public expenditures by the end of the decade; and the increase in informal workers who are not covered by public health funds.[69]

Despite weaknesses in the overall health care system, recent governments have not taken action to implement comprehensive reforms. In 1987 the government considered a proposal for a system that would integrate resources from the public health funds and the public sector to increase efficiency and to cover more effectively individuals not employed in the formal sector. The proposal failed in part because it faced strong opposition from trade unions that would have lost considerable control over public health fund revenues.

Some provincial governments have also attempted to enlarge the primary health care network.[70] Their emphasis was primarily on the construction of new centers. But because the infrastructure expansion was poorly planned, it led to an unnecessary rise in total health costs in provincial budgets. Although special projects were able to operate while extra funds were available, the reform attempt was on the whole short-lived. In the end, financing was curtailed, causing services to deteriorate.

Housing

The two main mechanisms for state intervention in the housing sector are the National Mortgage Bank (BHN) and the National Housing Fund (FONAVI).[71] From the mid-1940s until the early 1970s, the primary policy tool for housing support was in the form of concessional loans provided by the

69. As indicated in table 6-3, the share of wage earners in total employment remained fairly stable during the 1980s for the greater Buenos Aires area. However, among employees, the proportion of nonregistered or "black" workers not covered by Obras Sociales increased in greater Buenos Aires from 18.7 percent in 1980 to 29.9 percent in 1988. See Beccaria and Orsatti (1990, table 10, p. 274).

70. Ministerio de Salud y Acción Social (n.d.[b], p. 10).

71. Lumi (1989, pp. 53–54).

BHN, primarily to the middle class. Debtors benefited not only from below-market interest rates, but also from the fact that the principal was not indexed to inflation. Rising inflation in the late 1970s and early 1980s implied even greater implicit subsidies to mortgage holders, but left the BHN unable to pay for funds in financial markets. In the absence of alternative funding sources, the Central Bank was called upon to provide financing to the BHN through "rediscount" credits. This system was one of the major sources of monetary expansion that undermined the Austral Plan.[72]

FONAVI, created in 1972, provides subsidized housing finance for the poorest 40 percent of households.[73] It operates as a revolving fund that is financed by a special payroll tax; it also receives other minor contributions, including a share of the social security contributions of self-employed workers. These resources are channeled to provincial housing agencies that arrange contracts for the construction of new houses, which are then sold to low-income families.

The establishment of FONAVI implied an increase in public expenditures on housing construction. The share of public expenditures in total housing construction expenditures grew from an average of 16 percent during 1971–75 to 37 percent during 1976–85. This expansion, however, was matched by a reduction in private housing construction.[74] Despite the growth in public housing expenditures, the number of homes built with FONAVI resources were insufficient to meet demand; the number of houses constructed during 1980–86 represented between 10 and 22 percent of unsafe and overcrowded housing calculated for 1980.[75]

Over its twenty years of activity, FONAVI has faced three major problems. First, because the fund finances only new houses, many poorer families are not eligible even when loans are highly subsidized and have long repayment periods. The government now recognizes that other solutions—such as requiring beneficiaries to participate in construction, improving existing buildings, or financing small buildings that could later be enlarged—would imply lower unit costs. Second, there is evidence that FONAVI's unit construction costs are higher than those of similar privately financed houses.[76] Long construction

72. See Machinea (1989, p. 41).
73. Lumi (1989, p. 53).
74. Lumi (1989, p. 53).
75. The first figure incorporates the number of houses that are inadequate (according to their building materials) or overcrowded, while the second takes into account units that are both inadequate and overcrowded. See National Program for Technical Assistance to the Social Sectors (1990, vol. 6, table 6.2, p. 53).
76. See World Bank (1980b, p. 25–26).

Table 6-16. *Housing Conditions in Major Cities, Argentina, 1978, 1988*
Percent

Condition	1978	1988
Inadequate houses[a]	23	26
Households without toilet	19	16
Households with houses not connected to the sewage system	49	46

Sources: Unpublished 1978 and 1988 INDEC surveys of housing conditions. Data are averages for eighteen major cities.

a. Houses with a lower value of a composite quality index based on factors such as building materials used and access to services.

periods, inadequate building sites, and the use of outdated technology and building methods have been cited as major reasons for these higher costs.[77] Third, FONAVI has a poor record of cost recovery on its loans, which implies that its loans were almost fully subsidized.[78] One cause may be that provincial administrations responsible for collecting payments have little incentive to do so because they are not the direct beneficiaries; they simply transfer collected funds to FONAVI.

These problems have led to a lower housing supply than might have otherwise been possible. The World Bank estimated that housing construction by FONAVI in 1987 totaled about 20,000 units, only one-fourth of FONAVI's potential supply. Targeting has also been inadequate, not only because those areas and households most in need were not always selected, but also because the cost of houses constructed remained too high for many low-income families.[79]

Performance has been even worse in the provision of water and sewage systems. As suggested by figures from INDEC's survey of housing conditions in tables 6-16 and 6-17, provision of bathroom facilities and access to sewerage systems increased only slightly during the 1980s. Moreover, the improvement in the proportion of houses with bathroom facilities that did occur primarily reflects the initiatives of individual households. Unfortunately such initiatives are often inadequate and can be potentially dangerous to the sanitary health of the population. For example, many households install inappropriate septic chambers that can contaminate the water supply.

77. See Lumi (1989, pp. 66–78; and 1990, pp. 200–01).
78. Regarding poor cost recovery, see World Bank (1988b, pp. 25–26); and Lumi (1989, pp. 61–62).
79. World Bank (1988b, pp. 25–26).

Table 6-17. *Coverage of Water and Sewage Systems, Argentina,*
1980, 1985
Percent

Condition	1980	1985
Houses not connected to a piped water system	43	47
Houses not connected to a sewage system	70	73

Sources: Administrative records included in Lumi (1990, p. 214).

Nutrition and Food Programs

With a few short-lived exceptions, nutrition and food programs in Argentina have been delivered through the health and education systems to support program performance and coverage. The provision of meals in primary public schools has been one of the more important nutrition programs.[80] In addition to supplementing children's diets, school meals help reduce dropout rates and absenteeism. Although the goal of the program is to cover primarily children of low-income families, no targeting procedures are in place. The program is run by provincial governments, but receives financial support from the federal level. The federal government covered the cost of school meals for about 1.2 million children in 1991, and with additional funding from provincial governments the scope of coverage was about two million children. As table 6-9 indicates, total primary enrollment in that year was about 5.9 million.[81] A weakness of the program has been that there are no precise national guidelines for provision, targeting, or nutritional content, and schools do not always comply with the guidelines that do exist. The national government does not properly monitor and evaluate program progress or results, and therefore no specific information exists on total program coverage.[82] An external assessment of the program by PAHO and the Interamerican Center for Social Development in 1985 and 1986 showed that the diet provided was of low quality. Program weaknesses were shown to stem from financial constraints and unclear targeting methods. Management problems at the local level were found to have led to a squandering of available resources. The program proved to be effective at keeping children in school only when the quantity of calories supplied was above a minimum critical standard, an amount provided to only 17 percent of beneficiaries in 1986.[83] During the 1980s irregularities in the

80. OEA and OPS (1986–87, pp. 1–3, 2n, note 1).
81. See Britos (1993, pp. 9–13).
82. OEA-OPS (1986–87, pp. 2, 12–15).
83. Britos (1993).

transfer of funds from the federal government to the provinces reduced the quality of diets in some jurisdictions.[84]

Since 1938 the Ministry of Health has run a free milk distribution program. The program is administered by the provincial governments, using transfers of funds or milk from the federal government. The target population—pregnant women and children under two in low-income families—receives the milk through health centers. A central aim of the program is not only to supplement diets, but also to attract pregnant women and mothers to health centers for regular checkups.[85] One deficiency of the child-maternal program, however, has been inadequate promotion. Health centers make no special efforts to attract potential beneficiaries; individuals receive benefits only through their own initiative. As a result, targeting is also weak. In addition, managerial and financial problems during the 1980s often interrupted services.

There is also a national program aimed at supplementing the diets of preprimary age children (between two and five years old) through the provision of meals in kindergartens and community centers. Under this program, federal funds match expenditures by provincial and municipal governments. The program, however, is not well defined and suffers from poor organization. During the 1980s, financial difficulties interrupted services on several occasions.

In 1984 the federal government launched a major National Food Program (PAN) with the explicit goal of offsetting the social consequences of adjustment. The program lasted until 1989. PAN was the first food program in Argentina with national coverage. In fact, unlike other countries in the region, Argentina had never provided food subsidies.[86] PAN gave poor households each month a food basket designed to provide 25 percent of the nutritional needs of a family of four. The program covered 1.5 million households in 1988, and its annual budget amounted to 0.15 percent of GDP (about U.S.$150 million).[87] Geographical areas with high rates of structural poverty were first selected. Within each, households were chosen based on selection criteria, such as the employment status of the head of household and the presence of pregnant women or children under six. Program costs were low and targeting was adequate, but some organizational problems surfaced as a result

---

84. OEA-OPS (1987, p. 23).

85. See Ministerio de Salud y Acción Social (1988, pp. 8–11).

86. To some extent, export taxes on agricultural products transfer income from the rural sector to food consumers. See National Program for Technical Assistance to the Social Sectors (1990, vol. 1–2, pp. 21, 35).

87. Aguirre (1993, pp. 1, 3, 10, 12).

of the highly centralized delivery system.[88] After running the program for two years at acceptable levels, budgetary restrictions reduced the nutritional content of the food basket, and inefficiencies appeared.[89] Despite the importance of the program, the government did not assess the PAN. In 1990 the new government discontinued the program and replaced it with food stamps distributed by provincial and local authorities. By screening applicants through means tests, the program was to reduce the number of beneficiaries. Problems in screening and lack of expertise, however, caused the program to fail; the government abandoned it after only three months amid much criticism.

The Pension System

Almost 90 percent of workers in Argentina obtain pension insurance through the National Pension System (NPS), which maintains three separate funds, with one each for federal government and public enterprise employees, private sector wage earners, and independent workers.[90] The coverage of the system is national, membership is compulsory, and administration is centralized in the Secretariat of Social Security within the Ministry of Labor and Social Security. The NPS operates on a pay-as-you-go basis, which means that the contributions of the employed finance the pension benefits of the retired population. The payroll tax on employees and employers has fluctuated around 20 percent during the past fifteen years (table 6-18).[91] Pension benefits are legally linked to wages earned during working life.[92] Pension expenditures

88. Regional targeting was based upon data from INDEC (1984). For program evaluation, see INDEC (1990, p. 257), which shows that 18 percent of households that received NFP baskets in greater Buenos Aires were nonpoor. This survey showed an even lower incidence of incorrect targeting (between 1 and 12 percent) in four other cities. There has been no assessment of leakage to nonpoor in the rest of the country. Among the organizational problems, it was calculated that prices paid were 50 percent of retail levels. Aguirre (1993, p. 7).

89. Aguirre (1993, pp. 2, 7, 8).

90. See World Bank (1992, pp. 148–49). Members of the security forces and provincial and municipal employees are insured through separate public institutions. About 1 percent of workers obtain insurance from private institutions. There are also pension funds for public sector employees of the provinces that benefit almost 1 percent of the total population, spending almost 1.5 percent of GDP (see sources for table 6-5). In 1987 insurance regulations were changed to allow insurance companies and banks to offer voluntary pension schemes.

91. World Bank (1992, p. 149). From 1980 to 1984 employers did not have to contribute to the social security system, and the payroll tax contribution fell to 11 percent in 1980.

92. Minimum retirement ages are sixty for men and fifty-five for women. Pensionable earnings are based on a three-year average of the highest real monthly wages earned by an individual during the last ten working years. The system thus biases pension levels toward the top segment of life earnings. Pension scales range between 70 and 82 percent of pensionable earnings, depending on retirement age. World Bank (1992, p. 150).

Table 6-18. *Pension System Revenue Variables, Argentina, 1975–90*

Year	Index of real hourly wages (1980=100)[a]	Index of formal sector employment[b] (1980=100)	Ratio of pension system payroll tax to pension system total expenditure	Payroll tax rate[c]
1975	129.4	135.8	0.79	24.0
1976	92.8	131.4	1.10	26.0
1977	81.9	123.1	0.98	26.0
1978	77.5	111.2	0.91	26.0
1979	89.6	109.2	0.94	26.0
1980	100.0	100.0	0.85	11.0
1981	93.8	87.4	0.38	11.0
1982	81.5	82.8	0.40	11.0
1983	101.1	85.5	0.33	11.0
1984	128.5	88.0	0.45	18.5
1985	112.8	84.8	0.68	21.5
1986	106.4	81.3	0.75	21.5
1987	98.3	80.5	0.81	23.5
1988	94.3	81.3	0.70	21.0
1989	81.5	74.5	n.a.	21.0
1990	79.6	71.0	n.a.	n.a.

Sources: CEPAL (1992a, tables 16, 8); Schultess (1990, p. 16); and Ministerio de Trabajo (1991, p. 10).
n.a. Not available.
a. Normal hourly wage (excludes overtime).
b. Industrial employment, survey of 1,500 firms.
c. End of year.

Table 6-19. *Indicators of the Pension System, Argentina, 1977–88*

Year	Total expenditures as percent EDP	Index of pension (1980=100) Wage earners and employees pension fund	Independent workers pension fund	Pension-wage ratio
1977	3.3	79.2	86.9	0.67
1978	4.6	88.3	96.0	0.73
1979	4.9	97.0	95.8	0.87
1980	5.9	100.0	100.0	0.66
1981	6.1	102.0	105.8	0.71
1982	4.8	75.4	88.8	0.62
1983	5.1	91.0	112.2	0.62
1984	5.0	86.0	108.4	0.49
1985	5.6	71.9	90.9	0.67
1986	5.5	66.7	87.4	0.45
1987	5.1	64.5	63.1	0.48
1988	5.2	64.1	61.1	0.51

Sources: Schultess (1990, pp. 3, 26, 39, 42).

averaged 5.4 percent of GDP during 1980–88 (table 6-19), and an estimated 10 percent of the total population received either pension or other benefits from the system.[93]

The erosion of resources in the pension fund during the 1980s was not a new development. It began many years before the debt crisis when the government expanded benefits without commensurate increases in contributions. By the late 1960s, a minor deficit in the fund emerged, suggesting the need for altering the system's basic design to improve its long-term financial viability. These warning signals, however, passed unnoticed; the government made only marginal adjustments in the existing structure. Beginning in 1979, with the system close to a breakdown, the government took ad hoc measures to protect it, substantially reducing pension payments below legal targets, earmarking specific taxes for the NPS, and authorizing transfers from the Central Bank to cover the remaining deficit.[94]

Table 6-19 summarizes selected indicators on the pension system during the late 1970s and 1980s. The real value of average pension payments declined by about 37 percent between 1977–83 and 1987–88. The pension-wage ratio dropped from an average of 70 percent during 1977–83 to an average of only 50 percent during 1987–88, well below the legal standards of 70 to 82 percent.[95] Pensions were increasingly determined on the basis of resource availability rather than institutional rules. In response to low pension levels and the system's legal flaws, lawsuits against the pension system grew dramatically in 1984–85.[96] By the mid-1980s, the system had lost several cases in the courts, inducing more individuals to take legal action to obtain their benefits.

There are two main reasons for the deterioration in the pension system during the 1980s. First, long-term factors such as the aging population (table 6-20) and the rise in unregistered wage employment critically reduced contributions to the system. Access to the system also widened during the 1970s, implying an increase in the rate of benefit growth.[97] In a pension system financed by taxing the working population, the age structure of the population

93. Schulthess and Demarco (1993, p. 33).

94. Carciofi (1990, table I.5, pp. 10–11).

95. World Bank (1992, p. 150).

96. Carciofi (1990, pp. 74–75).

97. This was particularly so in the fund that covers the self-employed: annual benefits grew at an average annual rate of 14 percent between 1975 and 1980. Expanding access was to generate short-term financial improvement, as the government would pay in benefits only a small fraction of total contributions accrued during the working life of an individual. Carciofi (1990, table I.7, pp. 10–11).

Table 6-20. *Ratio of Active to Retired Population, by Sex, Argentina, Selected Years, 1950–2000*[a]

Year	Female	Male	Total
1950	4.9	7.2	5.9
1960	3.7	6.0	4.6
1970	2.9	5.0	3.7
1980	2.5	4.6	3.3
1990	2.3	4.2	3.0
2000	2.3	4.3	3.1

Source: Schultess (1990, p. 66).
a. Ratio of persons 20 to 60 years old to persons 55 or older (female) and 60 (male) years old.

plays a critical role in determining the support ratio: the ratio of the active to the retired population. A proxy is the ratio of the number of working-age individuals (between twenty and sixty) to the number of retirement-age individuals (over sixty). In Argentina this ratio has exhibited a downward trend, declining from 5.9 in 1950 to 3.0 in 1990 (table 6-20).[98] The statistic determining the system's financial viability is the ratio of the number of effective tax contributors to the size of the retired population. This ratio also declined, from 11.2 in 1950 to 2.0 in 1983.[99] In the same vein, rising life expectancy has increased the system's costs. Because tax rates and other administrative costs imply that the ideal support ratio is about four, these estimates indicate an increasing structural imbalance over time.[100]

The second cause of the system's poor performance was the macroeconomic instability of the decade. Increasing inflation, falling real wages, and declining employment in the formal sector all eroded revenues (table 6-18). Fiscal policy also altered the tax base of the system, undermining financial flows even more. In addition, some evidence suggests that adverse economic conditions increased tax evasion.[101] Even though the government increased social security revenues by reinstating employers' contribution at pre-1980 levels, it could not meet its legal pension obligations.

Although there is no reliable data on tax evasion, indirect evidence suggests that evasion of pension contributions may be as high as 70 percent in the independent workers fund and 42 percent in the private sector employees

98. See Schulthess (1990, chapter 5).
99. See Carciofi (1990, table I.6). This figure is not a precise indicator because pension system data include only the total amount of benefits, not the number of beneficiaries.
100. Schulthess (1990, p. 65).
101. Schulthess (1990, pp. 63–64).

fund.[102] The most important tax policy reform occurred in 1980 when general tax revenues were substituted for employer contributions. Growing fiscal restrictions, however, prompted the government to reinstate the payroll tax system four years later, in September 1984, although at lower fixed rates (table 6-18).[103]

As a result of these changes, the pension system was financed by a range of sources, including budgetary transfers and family allowance funds.[104] Despite attempts to transfer more resources to the system, its financial weakness increased during the 1980s. Central Bank credits were increasingly used to balance the pension system's revenues and expenditures, making its financial disequilibrium a significant variable for fiscal and monetary programming.[105]

Falling pensions, large gaps between actual and legally prescribed benefits, massive coverage of 10 percent of the voting population,[106] and financial problems that affected macroeconomic policy targets all help explain how the pension system's crisis became a major political issue during the 1980s. As legal disputes over benefit levels intensified public pressure, the government in 1986 decreed a "state of emergency of the national pension system."[107] With this declaration, the government avoided an open congressional debate over structural reform of the system. In a sense, its strategy reduced short-term political costs, but it squandered the opportunity to introduce deep changes in the system. Beneficiaries were invited to sign individual contracts, which implied that debt accrued during the previous two years would be discounted. In turn, the pension system proposed both a medium-term debt payment plan and a schedule for gradual increases in benefits. This decision prompted criticism

102. See Barbeito and Lo Vuolo (1992, p. 6).

103. The reform was mainly a response to macroeconomic policy objectives and did not provide a solution for the pension system. Moreover, it produced conflict with the provinces by reducing the extent of tax sharing with them. See Carciofi (1990, p. 27), and Schulthess (1990, p. 13).

104. After 1985, for example, 3 percent of wage taxes earmarked for the family allowance funds were transferred to the pension system. Ministerio de Trabajo (1991, table 1, p. 10).

105. Schulthess (1990, p. 19). Pensions are paid through the banking network. If the system does not have enough funds in its bank accounts, there is a direct monetary impact, since banks are allowed to offset pension overdrafts by depleting their reserve deposits at the Central Bank.

106. According to Carciofi (1990, table I.7), the total number of pension benefits was 2.8 million in 1985. The total number of votes cast in 1985 was 15.3 million; see Cabrera (1993, p. 291). That the social security system covers 10 percent of the voters is a rough estimate based on two grounds. First, not all pensioners are affected by low benefit levels. Second, the precise number of beneficiaries is not known—2.8 million is the figure for the number of benefits, but some individuals earn more than one benefit. In any case, 10 percent is a conservative estimate.

107. Carciofi (1990, p. 74).

from opposition parties, which argued that the financial crisis of the pension system was due to insufficient budget support. Eventually, the government managed to obtain congressional confirmation of the state of emergency it declared eighteen months earlier. In 1988, however, the government already had problems meeting the payment schedule, and the Congress decided to increase revenues through new earmarked taxes.[108]

As the overall economic climate worsened in 1989 and 1990, the financial performance of the pension system further deteriorated. Neither the debt-redemption program nor current benefits could be honored, and by 1990 total outstanding debt to the pensioned population was estimated to be U.S.$3.4 billion.[109] This situation led to a consolidation of pension debt in 1991 and a new proposal for comprehensive reform.

Social Sector Reforms

It is instructive to consider the future role of social policies and state intervention within the framework of the trends and problems already discussed. However, before addressing these issues, we first review the guidelines and reform initiatives put forward by the new government since it took power in 1989.

Favored by the macroeconomic improvement that followed the April 1991 Law of Convertibility, the government took some initiatives regarding social policy. It gave a major boost to education. In 1992 the Congress decentralized secondary education, completing the process started in the 1970s at the primary level. In addition, a proposal to allow universities to charge students tuition was submitted to Congress in 1993.

In the public health sector as well, decentralization has been a government objective. The transfer of the national hospital network to the provinces was almost completed in 1992. A proposal that would introduce major changes in the Obras Sociales is being negotiated with unions and the private sector. The blueprint aims to establish a health insurance system with compulsory membership, free choice among pension funds, and differentiated packages within each fund. Payroll taxes would remain at the same level, but beneficiaries would be able to buy health packages in accordance with the absolute amount of their contributions. The new mechanism departs from the previous princi-

108. The taxes included higher surcharges on several public utilities (electricity, telephones, and gasoline). Schulthess (1990, p. 17); and World Bank (1990, p. 37).

109. Schulthess (1990, p. 19); and Brodersohn and Pelufto (1991, table 6-15, p. 33).

ple of cross-subsidization for workers within the same institution, which had been a common trait of the Argentine system. The only redistributive element in the proposal, which resembles a private insurance system, is a minimum level of health coverage for low-income workers. In January 1993 the president decreed the broad guidelines of the reform, but by December 1993 it had not been enacted, nor had the details of the system been defined.

In addition, the government is trying to achieve a comprehensive reform of the pension fund system. As a first step, Congress passed a law that earmarked 11 percent of value-added tax (VAT) revenues for the social security system in the 1992 budget.[110] This measure provides resources that can be devoted to increase both current pension levels and the pace of bond redemption on liabilities held by pensioners. The second stage of the reform, approved in 1993, significantly redefines benefits and funding within the pension system.[111] The new system consists of a two-tiered scheme. At one level, compulsory employee contributions are directed to private insurance companies, with total net savings and interest accrued during one's working life available at retirement age.[112] At the other level, the public sector runs a separate pay-as-you-go fund financed by a 10 percent employer payroll tax and earmarked VAT revenues. The pension rate for each individual is the ratio of total revenues to the number of retired persons. The public system aims to provide a minimum level of income for all pensioners, but serves a redistributive purpose as well. Participating workers will eventually receive two pensions, one from each of the two schemes, private and public. During the transition period, the public system will cover the pensions of those who have contributed to the old system.

It is too early to assess this range of new social policy initiatives. In some cases, aspects of implementation have yet to be resolved, and in others the reforms remain in the planning stages, with discussions and negotiations having just begun. For example, the transfer of secondary schools to the provinces is under way, but the system is still controlled by the central government.[113] Moreover, the entire decentralization process—both in education and in health—has not been led by the sectoral ministries, which have also failed to assume their new roles in policy coordination, regulation, and the setting of

110. World Bank (1993, p. 49).

111. A first draft proposing a somewhat different design for the system was submitted in June 1992, but later withdrawn in favor of the current version.

112. It is estimated that pension funds will deduct 3 percent—out of 11 percent—to cover administrative and insurance costs and life insurance premiums included in the pension package. The proposal also increases retirement ages by five years.

113. Provinces must sign an agreement with the Ministry of Education specifying the details of the transfer. *Trawite Parliamentario* 95 (September 13, 1991): pp. 2831–32.

national standards. Decentralization appears to be primarily an attempt to meet financial objectives. Regarding university fees, the proposed reforms—still awaiting approval in December 1993—would pave the way for private financing, but would require universities to decide on fee levels, the allocation of funds, and rules for grant allotments.

It is also too early to predict the consequences of the recently approved reform of the pension system. A major question concerns the system's medium- and long-term financial solvency. Because the public sector will lose some revenues, it is not clear that the existing level of contributions will cover the range of benefits. The outcome will depend in part on individuals' choices between the public and the private systems. In any event, the principal challenge is to finance the pay-as-you-go system, as revenues are likely to diminish while the retired population grows over the next ten to fifteen years.[114]

Conclusion

In summary, social policy reforms have just begun, and the operational details of the new system remain unclear. In future years, subject to improvements in data coverage and collection, it will be possible to assess the impact of changes in the education, health, and pension systems. At this stage, however, it is more useful to discuss the overall direction of the reforms, comparing new policies with past experience.

Even though this chapter focuses on public expenditures in the social sectors during the 1980s, it is useful to place that discussion in a medium-term perspective. There have been two major trends in the development of Argentina's welfare state during the second half of the century. On the one hand, the government attempted to maintain and improve access to services with mass coverage—universal and free provision were the rule. Demand for private consumption of state services increased, and supply was rationed on the basis of budgetary capacity. Education policy provides the clearest example, given its long tradition and the vast amount of state resources devoted to it. Another example is the public health network, which never applied means tests or user fees. On the other hand, in response to industrialization, the expansion of wage employment, and the unionization of the labor force, the government became involved in establishing a social security network. Pension funds and the system of Obras Sociales, both financed by payroll taxes, are

114. For an analysis of the financial solvency during the transition period, see Cetrángolo and Machinea (1993).

leading examples of this second path. In these areas the public sector was more of a regulator than a direct provider.[115]

By the mid-1970s the social services network faced two major shortcomings. First, individual social sectors had accumulated deeply rooted inefficiencies, and imbalances developed between the system's statutory obligations and actual performance. In some cases, such as the pension system, these inefficiencies led to financial disequilibrium. In other areas, such as education and health, they led to low-quality services, mismanaged resources, and financial constraints. In turn, inefficiency had an impact on equity: access was neither universal nor equal (in terms of quality) for different groups in the population. Second, public policies in the social sectors did not include specific programs coordinated to reduce structural poverty. Programs targeted toward the lowest income groups were mainly uncoordinated initiatives advanced at the sectoral level.

Despite their overwhelming importance, neither of these two shortcomings was a top priority in the social agenda of the mid-1970s. To some extent the economic growth of previous decades had masked these problems. During the 1970s, in a climate of social and political unrest, welfare policy was disregarded because complaints about income distribution focused narrowly on wage policy, precluding a thorough analysis of broader social policy. Therefore, the government made no major attempts to redraw the lines of the welfare state. There are two revealing examples. Although a tax reform in the late 1970s channeled more resources to the pension system, no actions were taken to alter benefit schemes. Similarly, the government decentralized primary education in 1978 without enforcing common guidelines aimed at equalizing quality standards or school access across regions.

It was not until 1989–90 that the macroeconomic instability and fiscal crises of the 1980s led to a significant reduction in public expenditures in the social sectors. During that decade poor economic performance triggered a reduction in household incomes that is reflected in the poverty index. Other social indicators do not show deterioration. For example, the infant mortality rate dropped from 33.2 to 25.6 per thousand between 1980 and 1990.[116] However, the public sector failed to develop comprehensive policies to improve services in individual social sectors. Poverty relief initiatives attracted some

115. The historical development of the pension system reveals a trend of growing state intervention. In the early stages, pension funds were established through private agreements between workers and employers in different trades and industrial activities as insurance schemes for work-related risks. Financial integration and state administration occurred in the late 1960s.

116. See Ministerio de Salud y Acción Social (1990, p. 33).

attention, but lacked a comprehensive approach. In the health sector, trade unions strongly opposed government proposals to integrate the Obras Sociales and the public health system. In education, the dominant issue was always wage bargaining, which inhibited the development of a wider and more comprehensive policy agenda. Although its financial nonviability was evident in the early 1980s, actions to reform the basic framework of the pension system were delayed. Finally, with the exception of the national food program, other social sectors, including education, health, water and sanitation, and housing, did not target specific actions toward the poor. On balance, despite the harsh economic situation of the 1980s, the social sectors did not undergo comprehensive reforms to offset the impact of the crisis. Instead, inertia prevailed over attempts at reform. The severe crisis of the late 1980s, however, did alter the public's perception of the need for reforms. A decade ago social service provision was not an issue, but after the experience of the 1980s there was a broader acceptance that the model had to be reviewed.

Regarding the social policy agenda for the 1990s, it seems that current reforms reflect a two-tiered strategy: decentralization (education, health) and private provision (pensions, health, water and sanitation). In this sense, the Argentine experience is not unique. Other countries in Latin America have been moving toward a similar framework.

Argentina's social policy reforms have been prompted mainly by financial and budgetary concerns. Undoubtedly, fiscal matters are of overriding importance, especially given the country's severe fiscal imbalance during the two preceding decades. Nevertheless, public policy reforms in the social sectors demand an adequate balance between increasing efficiency and equity in the provision of services and meeting budgetary goals. This chapter's analysis reveals the need for improved efficiency and more equitable delivery of services in the social sectors. Several factors—including ineffective policies, interest group pressures, and conflicts between central and provincial governments— have thwarted reform attempts in the past. A new budgetary arrangement cannot by itself solve the social sector's major operational flaws. The challenge, therefore, is to reconcile financial limitations with gains in efficiency and equity, particularly in those areas where provision remains public. Decentralization and privatization can be useful tools, but where these options have been used, the proposed reforms have yet to establish adequate regulatory and organizational frameworks to ensure the efficient operation of the system. Furthermore, where social services will remain public, such as education and health, planning and management capacity at the central and local levels need to be reinforced. After the social and economic crises of the 1980s, Argentina faces a new poverty map that should be addressed through both coordinated poverty alleviation programs and targeted actions by the different social sectors.

It is likely and desirable that macroeconomic stability, fiscal discipline, and the resumption of growth will provide a more favorable climate in which to deal with the questions discussed in this chapter. However, spillover effects will not suffice to ensure equity or to eradicate poverty. Effective social public policies are necessary, and reforms should seek both financial stability and the removal of factors that have produced inefficiencies and inequitable access. The task will require both substantial resource mobilization and coordination among the different levels of government.

Appendix

This appendix briefly discusses the methods we employed to estimate the size of poverty for greater Buenos Aires in table 6-4. Estimates of poverty by income headcount ratios appear in several studies. Altimir and CEPAL performed estimates for Argentina in the context of regional studies that included other Latin American countries using data from INDEC's permanent household surveys.[117] In 1984 INDEC estimated the extent of poverty according to the criterion of unmet basic needs.[118] Between 1987 and 1989 INDEC conducted a special study, including a household survey, that produced estimates of both income and structural poverty for four urban areas in 1988.[119] Several other papers also contain poverty measurements derived from INDEC's permanent household survey data.[120] Our poverty estimates differ from these other studies mainly because we use a different poverty line and make adjustments for income underreporting.

Our estimates in table 6-4 were based on microlevel data from the permanent household survey INDEC carries out twice a year (April and September) in greater Buenos Aires and twenty-six other urban centers. We used only data from the September survey in greater Buenos Aires.

We defined a household to be "structurally poor," or to have unmet basic needs, if it did not meet any of the following five criteria: the ratio of the number of household members to the number of rooms is three or less; the dwelling is classified as a "house," an "apartment," or a "dwelling in work-

117. Altimir (1979); and Comisión Económica para America Latina y el Caribe (1991).
118. INDEC (1984).
119. The main results of this research were published in INDEC (1990).
120. For example, see Minujin (1992); and Beccaria and Vinocur (1991).

place";[121] the dwelling has a flush toilet; all children between six and twelve years of age attend primary school; and the ratio between the total number of household members and the number of employed members is less than four, or—if higher—the head of household attended more than two years of primary school. This classification for structural poverty follows the methodology established by INDEC in 1984 based on the 1980 population census.[122] We defined a household to be "poor by income" if its total money income (the sum of its members' incomes from all sources) was lower than the poverty line. In the calculations presented in table 6-4, we made no corrections for income underreporting.[123]

To calculate the poverty line, we used the basic food approach:

$$\text{Poverty line} = \alpha * \text{basic food basket},$$

where the basic food basket is the value of the food bundle needed to meet the minimum caloric requirement. INDEC calculated this amount by valuing the basket of goods defined in an earlier poverty study, using prices collected for the consumer price index of greater Buenos Aires.[124] The value of α is the ratio of total expenditures to food expenditures for the average household in the second quintile of the per capita income distribution. The survey includes nonpoor (they reach the minimum nutritional standard), low-income households. The data are from the expenditure and income survey INDEC carried out between July 1985 and June 1986.

Caloric requirements depend on sex and age.[125] Therefore, given the sex and age of each household member, we were able to calculate the value of the basic food basket specific to each household. Then, assuming α is constant across all households, we estimated the poverty line for each household.[126]

---

121. The other categories are: "dwelling in shanty town"; "dwelling not for housing"; "hotel"; and "*inquilinato.*"

122. See INDEC (1984).

123. Our estimates include only those households with income data for all income-earning members. However, income nonresponse is high in greater Buenos Aires: about 25 percent. A recent attempt to assign values to the majority of those who did not answer the income question (based on regression analysis and incorporating personal and occupational attributes) indicates that the incidence of poverty is reduced by approximately 1 percentage point. The study reporting these results has not yet been completed.

124. INDEC's series of basic food basket prices remains unpublished. For its earlier poverty study, see Morales (1988).

125. Caloric requirements also depend on the type of activities in which individuals engage. In this case, we always assumed it to be "moderate" activity.

126. In fact, α implicitly reflects the food expenditure ratio of a particular household; one with the average composition of the reference population. This assumption has implications for

Because α also reflects relative prices between food and nonfood goods and services at the time of its calculation (June 1985 to July 1986), we adjusted for subsequent changes in relative prices. For this adjustment we used the index of the basic food basket price, calculated monthly by INDEC,[127] and the average of the eight nonfood groups in the consumer price index.

To give an example of our results, the monthly poverty line for a household with four members (a male head of household and his wife, both forty years old, one daughter age fifteen, and a son age twelve) was U.S.$550 at September 1991 prices and exchange rate.[128]

References

Aguirre, Patricia. 1993. "Aprendiendo de Nuestros Errores. Una Evaluación del Programa Alimentario Nacional, Argentina, 1984–89." Paper prepared for International Seminar on "Programas Governamentais de Assistencia Direta: Um Intercambio de Experincias com a distribucao de alimentos em paises do Cone Sul." Guaruyá, Brasil: Konrad Adenauer Stiftung-FAO, July.

Altimir, Oscar. 1979. *La dimensión de la pobreza en América Latina.* Santiago, Chile: CEPAL.

Barbeito, Alberto C., and Ruben M. Lo Vuolo. 1992. "La Reforma del Sistema Previsional Argentino: El Mercado de Trabajo y la Distribución del Ingreso." Paper prepared for First National Congress on Labor Studies. Buenos Aires: May 26–29.

Beccaria, Luis A. 1991. "Distribución del ingreso en la Argentina: Explorando lo sucedido desde mediados de los setenta." *Desarrollo Económica* 31 (October–December): 320–21.

_____. 1992. "Reestructuración, empleo y salarios en la Argentina." *Estudios del Trabajo* 3 (primer semestre).

Beccaria, Luis A., and Alberto Minujin. 1991. "Sobre la Medición de la Pobreza: Enseñanzas a Partir de la Experiencia Argentine." Working Paper 8. Buenos Aires: UNICEF.

Beccaria, Luis A., and Alvaro Orsatti. 1990. "Precarización laboral y estructura productiva en la Argentina: 1974–88." In *La precarización del empleo en la Argentina,* edited by Pedro Galin and Marta Novick. Buenos Aires: Centro Editor de América Latina.

Beccaria, L., and P. Vinocur. 1991. "La pobreza del ajuste o el ajuste de la pobreza." Paper prepared for the Sixteenth Meeting of the Latin American Studies Association. Washington.

---

estimates of the poverty line, but researchers can do little to sort out this problem with the type of information usually available. For a discussion, see Beccaria and Minujin (1991, pp. 12–16).

127. Because INDEC did not estimate the value of the basic food basket before 1985, we used the food price index of the consumer price index for the years between 1980 and 1986.

128. The poverty line applies to households who pay rent.

234   BECCARIA AND CARCIOFI

Britos, Sergio. 1993. "Comedores Escolares: Frente a la Descentralización." *Boletin Censi* 6 (April): 9–13.

Brodersohn, M., and D. Pelufto. 1991. *La Crisis del Sistema Jubilatorio y las Propuestas de Reforma.* Serie Estudios 3. Buenos Aires: CECE.

Cabrera, Ernesto. 1993. "Magnitud de distrito y fórmula electoral en la representación proporcional." *Desarrollo Económico* 33 (July–September).

Carciofi, Ricardo. 1990. "La Desarticulación del Pacto Fiscal: Una Interpretación sobre la Evolución del Sector Público Argentino en las Dos Últimas Décadas." Documento de Trabajo 36. Buenos Aires: CEPAL.

Centrángolo, Oscar, and others. 1992. "Desregulación y Salud: Un análisis de la reforma del sisteme de Obras Sociales." Working Paper 2. Buenos Aires: Instituto Para el Desarrollo Industrial.

Centrángolo, Oscar D., and José L. Machinea. 1993. "El Sistema Previsional Argentino: Crisis, Reforma y Transición." Documento de Trabajo 6 (January). Buenos Aires: Instituto para el Dessarrollo Industrial.

Comisión Económica para América Latina y el Caribe (CEPAL) 1986.*Tres Ensayos Sobre Inflacion y Politicas de Estabilizacion.* Estudios e Informes 64. Santiago, Chile.

———. 1991. *Magnitud de la pobreza en América Latina en los años ochenta.* Estudios e Informes de la CEPAL 81. Santiago, Chile.

———. 1992a. "Indicadores Macroeconómicos de la Argentina" (March). Buenos Aires.

———. 1992b. "Indicadores Macroeconómicos de la Argentina" (October). Buenos Aires.

———. 1992c. "Nota Sobre la Evolución de la Economía Argentina en 1991 (July). Buenos Aires.

CEPAL and UNESCO. 1992. *Educación y Conocimiento: Eje de la Transformación Productiva con Equidad.* Santiago, Chile.

Damill, Mario, and Roberto Frenkel. 1990. *Malos Tiempos: La Economía Argentina en la Década de los Ochenta.* Documento CEDES 46. Buenos Aires.

Frenkel, Roberto. 1989. *El Régimen de Alta Inflación y el Nivel de Actividad.* Documento CEDES 26. Buenos Aires.

Fundación de Investigaciones Económicas Latinoamericanas (FIEL). 1987. *El Fracaso del Estatismo: Una propuesta para la reforma del sector público argentino.* Buenos Aires: Editorial Sudamericana/Planeta.

———. 1990. *El Gasto Público en la Argentina, 1960–88.* Buenos Aires.

Heymann, Daniel. 1986. "El Plan Austral: Una Experiencia de Estabilización de Shock." In *Tres Ensayos sobre Inflación y Políticas de Estabilización.* Buenos Aires: CEPAL.

Hicks, N. 1992. "Trends in Government Expenditures and Revenues in Latin America." World Bank Internal Discussion Paper. Washington.

INDEC (National Institute of Statistics and Censuses). Various issues. *Boletin Mensual.* Buenos Aires.

———. 1984. "La pobreza en Argentina." Buenos Aires.

———. 1990. "La pobreza urbana en la Argentina." Buenos Aires.

———. 1991. "Censo Nacional de Población y Vivienda." Buenos Aires.

————. 1992. "Censo Nacional de Población y Vivienda por Localidad Buenos Aires." Buenos Aires.

Isuani, Ernesto, and Hugo Mercer. 1986. "La fragmentación institucional del sector salud en Argentina: ¿pluralismo o irracionalidad?" *Boletín Informativo Technit* 224 (September–December): 9–40.

Katz, Jorge, and Alberto Muñoz. 1988. *Organización del Sector Salud: Puja Distributiva y Equidad.* Buenos Aires: CEPAL and Centro Editor de América Latina.

Larrañaga, Osvaldo. 1990. *El Deficit del Sector Publico y la Política Fiscal en Chile, 1978–87.* Serie Política Fiscal 4, Proyecto Regional de Política Fiscal. Santiago, Chile: CEPAL/PNUD.

Llach, Juan José. 1978. "Estructura ocupacional y dinámica del empleo en la Argentina: Sus peculiaridades, 1947–70." *Desarrollo Económico* 17 (January–March): 539–91.

Lumi, Susana. 1989. "Hacia una Política Habitacional." In *Estado Democrático y Política Social,* edited by Ernesto Isuani and others. Buenos Aires: Eudeba.

————. 1990. "Restricciones y posibilidades de la politica habitacional argentina." In *Mucho, poquito y nada,* edited by E. Bustelo and E. Isuani. Buenos Aires: UNICEF-CIEPP-Siglo XXI.

Machinea, Jose L. 1989. "Stabilization under Alfonsin's Government: A Frustrated Attempt." (September) Buenos Aires.

Ministerio de Salud y Acción Social. 1988. *Complementación Alimentaria del Programa Nacional de Maternidad e Infancia con Enfasis en la Rehabilitación Nutricional en atención Primaria,* 2d ed. Buenos Aires.

————. 1990. *Programa Nacional de Estadísticas de Salud,* 2d ed. serie 5, no. 34. Buenos Aires.

Ministerio de Trabajo y Seguridad Social. 1991. *La Recaudación por Impuestos al Trabajo, 1950–1990.* Proyecto Giobierno Argentino, Informe 16. UNDP/ILO Project (February). Buenos Aires.

————. 1993. "Información Estadística Basica Para la Politica Laboral y de Empleo." Buenos Aires.

Ministry of Economy and Public Works. 1992. *Resultados de las Cuentas Del Sector Público No Financiero, Base Caja, 1987–91.* Informe Económico 3. Buenos Aires.

Minujin, Alberto. 1992. "En la rodada." In *Cuesta Abajo. Los nuevos pobres: effectos de la crises en la socíedad argentina.* Buenos Aires: UNICEF-LOSADA.

Morales, Elana B. A. de. 1988. "Canasta básica de alimentos: Gran Buenos Aires." Working Paper 3. Buenos Aires: INDEC.

Mustapic, Ana M., and Matteo Goretti. "Gobierno y Oposición en el Congreso: La Prática de la Cohabitación durante la Presidencia de Alfonsín (1983–89)." *Desarrollo Económico Revista de Ciencias Sociales* 32 (July–September): 251–53.

Nirenberg, Olga, and Néstor Perrone. 1992. *Diagnóstico y Propuestas para el Sector Salud Argentina.* Serie cuadernos de ceadel 21. Buenos Aires: Centro de Apoyo al Desarollo Local.

OEA and OPS. 1986–87. *Evaluación de los Impactos Nutricionales y Educacionales y Análisis Costo: Efectividad del Programa de Promoción Social Nutricional.* Argentina.

PNUD. 1987. *Descentralización, Federalización y Financiamiento del Sistema Educativo.* Buenos Aires.

PRONATASS (National Program for Technical Assistance to the Social Sectors). 1990. *El Gasto Público Social,* vol. 3: *Sector Education*; vol. 4: *Sector Salud*; vol. 6: *Sector Vivienda.* Buenos Aires.

Schulthess, Walter. 1990. *Sistema Nacional de Previsión Social: Su evolución y situación a fines de la década del ochenta.* Buenos Aires: PRONATASS.

Secretaría de Hacienda. 1989. "Política para el Cambio Estructural en el Sector Público." In *Mensaje de los Proyectos de Leyes de Presupuesto, 1986–89.* Pp. 96–115. Buenos Aires: Ministerió de Economía.

Secretariat of Finance. 1988. *Sector Público: Esquema de Ahoffo-Inversión Financiamiento: 1961-1986.* Buenos Aires: Ministry of Economics.

Sigal, Victor. 1993. "El acceso a la educación superior: El ingreso irrestricto—¿Una falacia?" *Desarrollo Económico* 130 (July–September): 268–75.

Sourrouille, Juan V. 1983. "Política Económica y Procesos de Desarrollo: La Experiencia Argentina entre 1976 y 1981." *Estudios e Informes 27.* Santiago, Chile: CEPAL.

Tedesco, Juan C. 1977. *Industrialización y educación en la Argentina.* Project Desarrollo y Educación en América Latina y el Caribe. Santiago, Chile: UNESCO.

———. 1980. "Educación y Empleo Industrial: Un Análisis a partir de datos censales 1960–70. "In *Educación y Sociedad en América Latina.* Santiago, Chile: UNICEF.

———. 1987. *El Desafío Educativo: Calidad y Democracia.* Buenos Aires: Grupo Editor de América Latina.

World Bank. 1987. *Argentina: Population, Health and Nutrition Sector Review.* Report 6555-AR. Washington.

———. 1988a. *Argentina: Reallocating Resources for the Improvement of Education.* Washington.

———. 1988b. *Argentina: Social Sectors in Crisis.*Washington.

———. 1990. *Argentina: Reforms for Price Stability and Growth.* Washington.

———. 1992. *Argentina: Public Finance Review—From Insolvency to Growth.* Report 10827-AR. Washington.

———. 1993. *Argentina: Maternal and Child Health and Nutrition Project.* Staff Appraisal Report 11790-AR. Washington.

CHAPTER SEVEN

Brazil: Welfare, Inequality, Poverty, Social Indicators, and Social Programs in the 1980s

Ricardo Paes de Barros, Rosane Mendonça,
and Sonia Rocha

THE INTERRUPTION in the flow of foreign capital to Brazil in the 1980s demanded a process of structural adjustment that Brazil was unable to implement.[1] The result was a dramatic slowdown in economic growth and an increase in internal monetary and fiscal imbalances. The GDP growth rate
declined from an annual average of 9 percent for the period 1968–80 to 1.5
percent in the 1980s. The inflation rate increased from an average of 1.6 percent a month in 1980 to 27.0 percent a month in 1989, while the government's

The authors would like to thank Eliana Cardoso and Paulo Renato de Souza for their useful
comments.
    1. Over the last two decades, Brazil also suffered from other external shocks, such as the two
oil shocks and the increase in international interest rates, which negatively affected Brazil's terms
of trade, creating large deficits in the current account. However, the economy was able to adjust
more quickly and fully to these terms of trade shocks than to the interruption in the flow of foreign
capital. For example, despite the second oil shock and the increase in international interest rates in
the beginning of the 1980s, by 1984 exports had increased enough to eliminate the deficit in the
current account. The evidence suggests, therefore, that the lack of foreign capital had a considerably greater impact on growth in Brazil in the 1980s than the two oil shocks and the increase in
the international interest rate did in earlier years.

operational deficit increased from 2.0 percent of GDP in 1980 to 6.5 percent in 1989.[2]

At the beginning of the 1990s, Brazil still faced the challenge of regaining a path of sustainable growth, as the economy entered a deep recession, and as both inflation and the public deficit remained uncontrolled. Today, as Brazil rethinks its development strategy and designs and implements structural reforms, it is important to identify the main lessons learned from the failures of the 1980s. In this paper, we draw lessons from the economic slowdown of that decade by evaluating the nature, magnitude and incidence of its costs.[3]

We evaluate the costs of Brazil's economic slowdown in four ways: by measuring the aggregate cost based on the average levels of income and unemployment; by identifying the distribution of costs based on income distribution, income inequality, and the level of poverty; by investigating education and health indicators; and by analyzing the role of compensatory programs in alleviating the consequences of the weak economic performance on the poor. For each of these four aspects, we analyze Brazil's performance in the 1980s, comparing it to previous decades.

The next section, of the paper investigates the evolution in the 1980s of average per capita income and the quantity (employment and unemployment) and quality (wage levels and sectoral composition) of jobs created during this period. We then analyze the evolution of the distribution of income, in relative and absolute terms. Based on these estimates we determine whether or not poverty increased in the 1980s, after first specifying a poverty line. We investigate in great detail the evolution of poverty in metropolitan Brazil, because that is the only area for which it is possible to construct poverty lines based on minimum consumption requirements. We then analyze changes during the 1980s in key education and health indicators, (comparing the 1980s to preceding decades). The final section investigates the role of compensatory programs—unemployment insurance program and food programs—in alleviating the costs of the Brazilian economic slowdown on the poor.

Income, Unemployment, and Sectoral Employment

Table 7-1 shows the evolution of per capita GDP, average per capita family income, and average family income since 1960, with special attention to the

2. See Amadeo and others (1993, tables 2.2 and 2.3).
3. See Silva and Hasenbalg (1992) for a study with similar objectives.

Table 7-1. *Family Income and Wages, Brazil, Selected Years, 1960–90*
1980 = 100

Year	Per capita GDP	Per capita family income	Family income	Manufacturing wages (Sao Paulo)	EAP[a] average wages
1960	42	n.a.	37	n.a.	46
1970	56	49	53	n.a.	57
1979	94	n.a.	97	92	91
1980	100	100	100	100	100
1981	93	88	87	105	88
1982	92	101	97	107	n.a.
1983	87	70	67	94	75
1984	89	76	71	97	75
1985	94	91	85	120	87
1986	100	134	125	151	121
1987	101	100	91	143	93
1988	99	93	84	152	92
1989	100	106	94	166	109
1990	94	97	81	142	89

Sources: Column 1: IBGE (1990); and Amadeo and others (1993, table 2.1). Column 2: Lluch (1981); Hoffmann and Kageyama (1986, p. 44); and IBGE (1944). Column 3: CEPAL (1986, p. 24); Hoffmann (1992, p. 7); and IBGE (1994). Column 4: *Conjuntura Economica*, December 31, 1991, p. 66. Column 5: Langoni (1973, p. 62); and Hoffmann (1992, pp. 2, 17).
n.a. Not available.
a. Economically active population.

1980s.[4] Until 1980, and particularly in the 1970s, income levels grew rapidly. Per capita GDP grew on average by 3.1 percent a year in the 1960s and 6.0 percent a year in the 1970s.[5] This high growth rate in the 1970s was particularly impressive given that Brazil's terms of trade declined considerably after the first oil shock in 1973–74.[6] During the 1980s, by contrast, both per capita GDP and average per capita family income exhibited zero net growth, while average family income declined.

Although the level of income was approximately the same at the beginning and the end of the decade, all the indicators in table 7-1 fluctuated considerably during the 1980s. Overall, income tended to fall at the beginning of the decade, then grew from 1984 to 1986, and declined again between 1987 and

4. These two averages correspond, respectively, to the mean of the distribution of individuals according to per capita family income and the mean of the distribution of families according to total family income.

5. IBGE (1990).

6. From 1973 to 1974, Brazil's terms of trade declined 20 percent. See Amadeo and others (1993, table 2:2).

1990, with the exception of a moderate recovery in 1989.[7] The years of significant growth were 1985 and 1986.

It is interesting to note that these sharp income fluctuations were more closely related to internal macroeconomic instability than external shocks. In fact, most of the oscillations in income levels were associated with a variety of unsuccessful macroeconomic stabilization programs, such as the Cruzado Plan in 1986 and the Collor Plan in 1990.[8]

Wages and Labor Income

Table 7-1 also shows the average income of the economically active population and manufacturing wages. The average income of the economically active population followed the same pattern as per capita family income: rapid growth in the 1960s and 1970s, and zero net growth in the 1980s, with considerable fluctuation during the decade. In 1981, 1983, and 1990 average income declined considerably, whereas in 1985 and 1986 it increased considerably.

Manufacturing wages in Sao Paulo, however, followed a completely different trend. In fact, over the 1980s, despite the stagnation in per capita GDP, manufacturing workers in Sao Paulo obtained wage gains that averaged more than 4 percent a year. The increasing strength of the labor movement during the 1980s, especially in the second half of the decade, may explain the increase in wage levels in the better organized segment of the labor force, since the wage gap between formal and informal workers actually declined in the 1980s.[9]

Employment and Unemployment

Despite the lack of growth in per capita GDP in the 1980s, job creation was never a critical problem. As table 7-2 indicates, employment grew continuously over the decade, at an annual rate (3.5 percent) higher than that of population growth (2.1 percent).[10] In absolute terms, the economically active popu-

7. The stark differences in temporal fluctuations of the different indicators are either the result of methodological differences or an indication that the functional distribution of income changed greatly in the 1980s. Methodological differences would result from the fact that information on per capita family income and total family income is self-reported monthly income obtained from household surveys collected between August and November of each year, whereas the data on per capita GDP refer to the entire year and are derived from the national accounts, which are based on a variety of sources.

8. See Plano de Estabilização Econômica (1986); and Plano Collor (1990).

9. See Amadeo and others (1993).

10. IBGE (1992a, p. 206).

Table 7-2. *Labor Force Participation Rate and Unemployment Rate,*
Economically Active Population, Brazil, 1979–90
Percent

Year	Economically active population (millions)	Participation rate	Unemployment rate
1979	43.9	53.6	n.a.
1981	47.5	53.4	4.3
1982	49.9	54.9	3.9
1983	50.9	54.8	4.9
1984	52.4	54.8	4.3
1985	55.5	56.0	3.4
1986	56.8	55.8	2.4
1987	59.5	57.1	3.6
1988	61.0	56.8	3.8
1989	62.5	56.7	3.0
1990	64.5	56.7	3.7

Source: Amadeo and others (1993, table 3.1).
n.a. Not available.

lation increased from 47.5 million in 1981 to 64.5 million in 1990, implying
that more than 16 million new jobs were created during the decade.[11]

The labor force participation rate increased almost continuously from 1979
to 1987 and was 3.5 percent higher in 1987 than in 1979. Since 1987 the labor
force participation rate has remained approximately constant.

The unemployment rate fluctuated over the decade, increasing during recessions and declining with growth, but it never reached 5 percent (see table
7-2). At the end of the 1981–83 recession, the unemployment rate reached 4.9
percent of the labor force, but then declined quickly to 2.4 percent in 1986.
After 1986 the unemployment rate rose again and remained between 3.5 and 4
percent for the rest of the decade.[12] Compared to the fluctuations in GDP, the
rate of unemployment remained very low and stable during the 1980s.

In summary, despite the lack of growth in per capita GDP during the 1980s,
employment increased at an average rate of 3.5 percent a year, the unemployment rate remained below 5 percent, and the labor force participation rate increased steadily over the decade. Hence, the economic hardships and sharp

11. In 1981 employment was 47.5 (1–.043) = 45.5 million, since the economically active population was 47.5 million and the unemployment rate was 4.3 percent. By the same token, in 1990
employment equalled 64.5 (1–.037) = 62.1 million. Therefore, from 1981 to 1990, the level of employment increased by 16.6 million.

12. Again 1989 is an exception. Growth in that year reduced the unemployment rate to 3.0
percent.

Table 7-3. *Employment among Economically Active Population Fifteen Years Old and Older, by Sector, Brazil, 1981–89*
Percent

Year	1981	1982	1983	1984	1985	1986	1987	1988	1989
Construction	8.4	7.5	9.7	6.1	6.1	6.7	6.9	6.6	6.5
Trade	10.9	10.8	11.1	11.2	11.5	11.9	12.1	12.1	12.8
Transportation	3.9	3.8	3.6	3.6	3.6	3.6	3.7	3.8	3.8
Credit and insurance	2.2	2.2	2.4	2.4	2.6	2.2	2.2	2.2	2.2
Services	26.0	26.9	27.1	27.6	27.9	28.1	29.1	29.9	30.0
Public administration and defense	4.3	4.5	4.4	4.5	4.6	4.9	4.9	5.1	5.0
Agriculture and mining	27.9	28.2	26.3	28.9	27.2	25.0	23.7	23.5	22.4
Manufacturing	15.4	15.2	14.4	14.6	15.2	16.5	16.1	15.6	16.2

Source: Barros and Ramos (1991). Columns may not add to 100 because of rounding.

fluctuations of the 1980s do not seem to have had any significant effect on job creation during the period.

Structure of Employment

The lack of any considerable variation in unemployment or in labor force participation, despite very slow and unstable GDP growth, indicates that the employment problem in Brazil in the 1980s might have been related to the quality instead of the quantity of jobs offered. To investigate this hypothesis, we examine changes in the sectoral composition of employment and in the informality of labor relations during the period.

Changes in the distribution of workers by economic sector presented in table 7-3 indicate that from 1981 to 1989 the proportion of employment in the services and trade sectors increased 6 percentage points, while that in the agriculture and mining sector declined by approximately the same amount. In absolute terms, the services and trade sectors thus generated more than 9 million new jobs, representing an increase in employment in these two sectors of more than 50 percent between 1981 and 1989. Employment in trade and services increased from 16.8 million to 26.1 million. In the same period, employment in agriculture increased by only 6 percent.

The share of employment in manufacturing remained almost constant over the 1980s, implying a 30 percent increase in the level of employment in that sector. The fact that the share of employment in manufacturing remained con-

Table 7-4. *Employment among Economically Active Population Fifteen Years Old and Older, by Working Relation, Brazil, 1981–89*
Percent

Working Relation	1981	1982	1983	1984	1985	1986	1987	1988	1989
Self-employed	26.6	27.3	26.2	27.0	26.4	26.7	26.3	26.8	26.6
Formal[a]	32.9	31.9	30.2	30.5	31.9	33.0	33.2	33.2	34.0
Public servants	10.3	10.4	10.5	10.7	10.9	11.3	11.3	11.9	11.7
Informal[b]	21.6	21.6	24.9	23.3	22.3	21.9	21.7	21.1	20.5
Noon-paid	7.5	7.7	7.1	7.4	7.3	5.9	6.1	5.8	6.0
Others	1.1	1.0	1.0	1.1	1.2	1.1	1.4	1.2	1.1

Source: Barros and Ramos (1991).
a. Employees with formal labor contracts.
b. Employees without formal labor contracts.

stant in the 1980s contrasts sharply with the 1960s and 1970s, when the proportion of employment in manufacturing increased substantially.[13]

The share of employment in public administration and defense increased 0.7 percentage points from 1981 to 1989, with most of the increase concentrated in the 1984–88 period. In absolute terms, this increase corresponded to the creation of 1.1 million new government jobs, or a 53 percent increase in government employment from 1981 to 1989.

In summary, the generation of almost 17 million new jobs in the 1980s despite any growth in per capita GDP was made possible by a sharp increase in employment in the tertiary sector, in particular in trade, services, and government. This fact contrasts sharply with Brazil's experience in the two previous decades, when a substantial fraction of job creation took place in manufacturing.

Informalization of Labor Relations

Table 7-4 presents the evolution in the 1980s of the distribution of the labor force by type of working relation: self-employed, public servants, employees with formal labor contracts, employees without formal labor contracts, and unpaid family members. It reveals that this distribution was relatively stable throughout the 1980s. The proportion of the labor force that was self-employed remained constant at approximately 27 percent. There was, however, a small reduction of about 1 percentage point in the shares of employees without formal labor contracts and unpaid family members, with a concomi-

13. IBGE (1990, p. 73).

tant increase in the shares of employees with formal contracts and public servants. In summary, table 7-4 indicates that working relations in Brazil became slightly more formalized during the 1980s.

These patterns, however, were clearly determined by the reduction in the share of employment in agriculture, since agricultural workers are likely to be unpaid family members or employees without formal contracts. As a matter of fact, when we restrict the analysis to urban areas, we obtain the opposite result, finding a considerable informalization of the labor force. As Cacciamali has shown, the proportion of the urban labor force with formal labor contracts declined by more than 1 percentage point over the 1980s.[14]

Overall, we conclude that Brazil's failure to pursue the necessary adjustment process led to a substantial reduction in the rate of GDP growth in the 1980s. This slowdown in economic growth, however, had little impact on the creation of jobs, as almost 17 million new jobs were created during the period. The main consequence of stagnation during the 1980s seems to have been a deterioration in job quality in urban areas, reflected in an increase in the share of employment in services and informal activities.

Inequality

In this section we analyze the distributive effects of the economic slowdown by investigating changes in income inequality in Brazil during the 1980s. In particular, we compare the magnitude and nature of changes in inequality in the 1980s with those in the previous two decades. In addition, we examine possible explanations for the behavior of inequality in the 1980s. We begin, however, by discussing a few measurement and conceptual issues.

Choice of the Distribution and Inequality Indexes

There is no unique measure of income inequality, but a multitude of measures, which vary primarily on four dimensions: the unit of analysis, the universe, the concept of income, and the inequality index. The unit of analysis can be the individual, the family, or the household. The universe can be all units or, for example, just the economically active population. The concept of income can be total personal income, labor income, or per capita family income, among others. Finally, inequality can be measured using the entire

14. Cacciamali (1992, table 12).

Table 7-5. *Income Inequality, Brazil, Selected Years, 1960–90*

	Economically active by personal population income				Individuals, by per capita income			
Year	Theil index	Gini coefficient	Distribution ratio^a	Distribution ratio^b	Theil index	Gini coefficient	Distribution ratio^a	Distribution ratio^b
1960	.47	.50	3.4	34	n.a.	n.a.	n.a.	n.a.
1970	.64	.57	4.6	40	.58	.63	7.4	n.a.
1979	.71	.58	5.1	54	.72	.59	5.6	51
1980	.76	.59	5.1	47	.70	.58	5.1	51
1981	.66	.57	4.9	51	.68	.58	5.2	59
1982	.68	.58	5.0	55	.70	.59	5.6	54
1983	.72	.59	5.4	52	.71	.59	5.7	55
1984	.70	.59	5.3	57	.68	.59	5.4	49
1985	.73	.60	5.7	66	.72	.59	5.7	55
1986	.74	.59	5.3	50	.71	.59	5.4	52
1987	.73	.60	5.6	61	.73	.60	6.0	62
1988	.79	.62	6.5	80	.77	.61	6.6	72
1989	.91	.64	7.2	82	.89	.63	9.1	80
1990	.76	.61	6.7	60	.77	.61	6.6	72

Sources: Langoni (1973, pp. 21, 64, 67); Denslow and Tyler (1983, p. 877); Lluch (1981); 1980 Demographic Census; and IBGE (1994).
n.a. Not available.
a. Ratio of the income share of the top 10 percent of the distribution to that of the bottom 40 percent.
b. Ratio of the income share of the top 10 percent of the distribution to that of the bottom 10 percent.

Lorenz curve, the Theil index, or the Gini coefficient, among many other indexes.

Table 7-5 presents the evolution of two types of distribution: the distribution of members of the economically active population with positive personal income, and the distribution of all individuals according to their per capita family income. For each of these two distributions, table 7-5 presents estimates of the Theil index (T), the Gini coefficient (G), the ratio of the income share of the top 10 percent to that of the bottom 40 percent of the distribution and the ratio of the top 10 percent to the bottom 10 percent. Table 7-6 and figures 7-1 and 7-2 present estimates of the Lorenz curve for selected years for each of the distributions.

Long-Term Trends in Inequality

Table 7-6 and figures 7-1 and 7-2 reveal that the long-term trend in income inequality depends on the choice of distribution. The distribution of the economically active populations personal income became increasingly unequal

Table 7-6. *Distribution of Income, by Decile, Brazil, 1960, 1970, 1980, 1990*

Decile	Economically active population, by individual income				Individuals, by per capita income			
	1960	1970	1980	1990	1960	1970	1980	1990
1st	1.2	1.1	1.2	0.8	n.a.	0.4	0.9	0.7
2d	3.5	3.2	3.2	2.6	n.a.	1.8	2.7	2.1
3d	6.9	6.1	6.2	4.8	n.a.	4.0	5.4	4.4
4th	11.6	10.0	9.7	7.9	n.a.	6.9	8.9	7.4
5th	17.7	14.9	14.1	11.9	n.a.	10.8	13.5	11.5
6th	25.4	20.8	19.7	17.4	n.a.	15.9	19.4	17.0
7th	34.8	28.2	26.9	24.7	n.a.	22.8	27.2	24.4
8th	45.6	32.8	36.8	35.0	n.a.	32.8	37.8	34.8
9th	60.3	52.5	52.1	51.3	n.a.	49.3	54.0	51.4
10th	100.0	100.0	100.0	100.0	n.a.	100.0	100.0	100.0

Sources: Langoni (1973, pp. 21, 64); Denslow and Tyler (1983, p. 877); Lluch (1981); *Censo Demografico* (1980); and IBGE (1994).
n.a. Not available.

Figure 7-1. *Distribution of the Economically Active Population by Personal Income, Brazil, 1960, 1970, 1980, 1990*

Income share

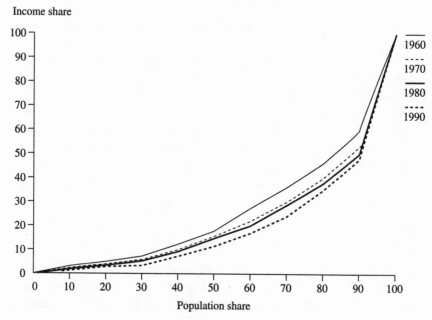

Figure 7-2. *Distribution of Individuals According to per Capita Household Income, Brazil, 1970, 1980, 1990*

Income share

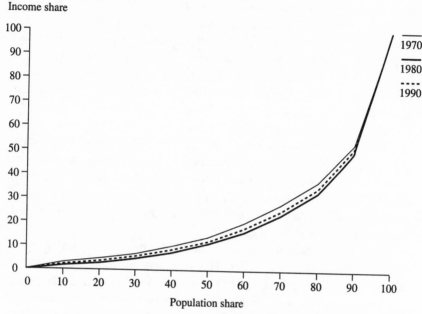

Population share

over the last three decades (figure 7-1). The magnitude of the increase in inequality was, however, considerably smaller in the 1970s than in both the 1960s and the 1980s, when the degree of income inequality increased substantially.

However, the nature of the increase in inequality differed between the 1960s and the 1980s. In the 1960s the group that suffered the greatest relative reduction in income was the middle class (the 4th, 5th, 6th, and 7th tenths), while in the 1980s the group at the very bottom of the distribution suffered most.[15] Therefore, if the level of income were held constant, the increase in inequality in the 1980s would lead to a greater increase in poverty than would the increase in inequality in the 1960s.

This distinction is illustrated by a comparison of the temporal evolution of two different measures of inequality: the Gini coefficient, which gives greater weight to changes at the center of the distribution, and the ratio between the income shares of the top and bottom tenths of the distribution, which, by construction, gives greater weight to changes at the extremes of the distribution. As table 7-5 reveals, while the Gini coefficient changed slightly more in the 1960s than in the 1980s, the income share ratio changed more in the 1980s

15. Barros and Mendonça (1992b, p. 10).

than in the 1960s. This fact confirms that changes at the middle of the distribution were more important in the 1960s, while changes at the bottom and top of the distribution were more important in the 1980s.[16]

In Brazil, the distribution of the economically active population according to their personal income has been investigated far more than the distribution of individuals according to their family per capita income. Nevertheless, the latter is much more important for understanding the connection between inequality and poverty, since poverty is usually defined in terms of inadequate levels of per capita household income or expenditure.

As figure 7-2 reveals, inequality in the distribution of individuals according to their per capita family income declined in the 1970s, but increased in the 1980s. Hence, in the 1970s, the degree of inequality in the distribution of the economically active population according to personal income and the distribution of individuals according to their family per capita income moved in opposite directions. This fact is the result of a significant increase in the number of earners per household during the period.[17]

In summary, in both the 1960s and the 1980s the degree of inequality increased considerably, while in the 1970s inequality remained almost constant (at least when the beginning and end of the decade are compared). Nevertheless, the nature of the increase in the 1960s was very different from that in the 1980s. In the 1980s the increase in inequality was particularly perverse, hurting the poorest segments of the population the most, while in the 1960s the increase in inequality hurt the middle class more than the poor.

Fluctuations in Income Inequality during the 1980s

All the measures of income inequality presented in table 7-5, exhibited similar fluctuations during the 1980s. Inequality remained relatively stable up to 1986, increased steadily until 1989, and then declined sharply from 1989 to 1990.

What factors explain these fluctuations? Several recent studies have tried to relate the temporal pattern of income inequality to changes in the structure of employment and wages.[18] Although earlier studies found that a considerable portion of the increase in inequality in the 1960s was due to changes in the

16. See Barros and Mendonça (1992b) for a detailed account of differences in the nature of the increase in inequality between the 1980s and the 1960s.

17. This issue is further investigated by Hoffmann and Kageyama (1986). See also Barros and Mendonça (1992c); and Pastore, Zylberstajn, and Pagotto (1983).

18. See Almeida Reis and Barros (1989); Ramos (1990); Bonelli and Ramos (1992); and Barros and Mendonça (1992a).

Table 7-7. *Distribution of Individuals According to per Capita Household Income, Brazil, 1970, 1980, 1990*

Average income in 1980 = 100

Tenth	1970	1980	1990
1st	1.8	9.0	6.6
2d	7.0	18.3	14.2
3d	10.6	26.4	21.4
4th	14.4	35.2	29.6
5th	19.0	45.8	40.0
6th	25.1	59.6	53.0
7th	33.8	77.6	71.6
8th	49.0	105.7	101.3
9th	80.8	162.0	161.1
10th	248.6	460.1	471.3

Source: Tables 7-1 and 7-6.

structure of wages and employment,[19] these recent studies have shown that such changes cannot explain the fluctuations in income inequality during the 1980s.

Thanks to the accumulation of data on income inequality, scholars have related the temporal evolution of inequality to macroeconomic variables such as the level of economic activity and inflation. Barros, Cardoso, and Urani, using monthly data on inequality in labor income for Brazil's six largest metropolitan areas, have shown that the level of unemployment and the inflation rate are positively correlated with the level of income inequality. However, although these studies are very successful in explaining the increase in inequality up to 1989, they are much less successful in explaining the sharp decline in inequality from 1989 to 1990.[20]

Welfare and Poverty

Changes in social welfare and poverty depend on changes in both per capita income and the degree of income inequality. In this section, we therefore combine the results from the previous two sections to investigate the evolution of social welfare and poverty in Brazil. We focus mainly on the 1980s, but also consider the 1970s.

Table 7-7 presents average per capita income by tenth for 1970, 1980, and

19. See Langoni (1973, chaps. 4 and 5).
20. See Barros, Cardoso, and Urani (1993). Similar studies have been done using annual data; see Ramos (1990); Bonelli and Ramos (1992); and Hoffman (1992).

1990.[21] Following the poverty ordering approach developed by Shorrocks and Foster, these estimates can be used to determine whether welfare improved and poverty declined in the 1970s and the 1980s.[22]

The 1980s

Between 1980 and 1990 the average income of each tenth in the distribution of individuals according to per capita family income declined, except for a very small increase in the average income of the top tenth (see figure 7-3). Therefore, based on results in Shorrocks, it can be established that the level of welfare unambiguously declined in the 1980s, if one assumes that the society has a preference for equity.[23] Furthermore, the decline in the average income of every tenth (except the top tenth) implies an unambiguous increase in poverty, as long as the poverty line is lower than the level of income in the ninth tenth.[24] These results are consistent with several other studies of the evolution of poverty in Brazil in the 1980s. For example, both Hoffman and Psacharopoulos and others found that poverty increased in Brazil during the 1980s.[25] Moreover, table 7-7 and figure 7-3 also reveal that the decline in average income in the 1980s was greater at the bottom than at the middle and top of the distribution. Thus, the observed trend in income distribution implied that poverty increased by a tremendous amount for the given decline in per capita income.

During the 1970s, by contrast, the overall average income level increased, and the degree of income inequality declined. Moreover, table 7-7 reveals that the average income of every decile in the distribution increased. As a result, welfare improved and poverty declined during the 1970s, independent of where one draws the poverty line.

Hence, performance in the 1970s dominates performance in the 1980s in all respects. The average income level and the level of social welfare both in-

21. The average income of each tenth can be calculated by multiplying ten times the product of the overall average income (table 7-1) and the income share of each tenth, which can be obtained by taking first differences of the Lorenz curve in table 7-6.

22. See Shorrocks (1983); and Foster and Shorrocks (1988).

23. The problem with using decile averages is that we have no information about the trend in poverty within deciles. Other studies with more disaggregated information find that there are "crossings" within the first tenth; See Lustig and Mitchell (1994).

24. See Foster and Shorrocks (1988). Note that because the average income of all tenths, except the top one, declined in the 1980s, the distribution for 1970 dominates the distribution for 1980 by the second-order stochastic dominance criteria.

25. Hoffman (1992); and Psacharopoulos and others (1992).

Figure 7-3. *Distribution of Individuals According to per Capita Household Income, Brazil, 1970, 1980, 1990*

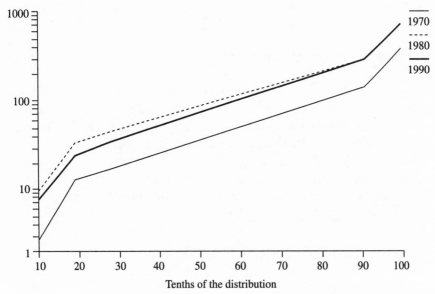

creased in the 1970s but decreased in the 1980s, while income inequality and poverty both decreased in the 1970s but increased in the 1980s.

What were the net changes in welfare and poverty between 1970 and 1990? On one hand, table 7-1 indicates that there was a net gain in per capita income from 1970 to 1990, since the increase in average income in the 1970s was greater than the decline in average income in the 1980s. On the other hand, table 7-6 indicates that the decline in inequality in the 1970s was less than the increase in inequality in the 1980s. As a result, both average income and per capita income inequality were greater in 1990 than in 1970. Since these two factors have opposite effects on the income of the poor, they alone are not sufficient to establish whether there was a net reduction in poverty or gain in welfare.

Table 7-7 and figure 7-3, however, show that the positive contribution of economic growth in the 1970s was large enough to offset the increase in inequality in the 1980s, ensuring that all tenths of the distribution gained when the two decades are taken altogether. As a result, from 1970 to 1990 welfare improved and poverty declined, again independent of the poverty line.

In summary, from 1970 to 1990 average per capita income, income inequality, and welfare increased, while poverty declined. Of course, poverty declined by less than it would have if the degree of inequality had remained constant.

Poverty in Metropolitan Areas

Although the previous sections indicate that poverty increased in the 1980s, they do not specify the level or the marginal change in poverty. To evaluate the magnitude of poverty and its temporal variations, we define a poverty line based on minimum food requirements and other basic goods and services necessary for a person to function in society. We briefly describe the methodology used to construct a set of time- and region-specific Fava-Rocha poverty lines.[26] We then use these poverty lines to estimate the evolution of poverty in metropolitan Brazil during the 1980s.

The Fava-Rocha Poverty Line

Many studies take the official minimum wage or a multiple of it as the poverty line.[27] There are two main problems with using that procedure in the Brazilian case. First, the real value of the minimum wage has fluctuated widely over time. Second, the cost of living in Brazil differs markedly among regions, as well as between urban and rural areas.[28]

An alternative methodology, the Fava-Rocha poverty line, respects regional differences in prices and preferences.[29] According to the Fava-Rocha methodology, poverty lines are based on estimates of the effective cost of fulfilling basic needs, taking into account local consumer preferences and prices. The objective is to allow for significant spatial differences in the cost of living that result from disparities in both price levels and consumption patterns. There is sufficient empirical evidence to support the claim that a single national poverty line, although easier to compute, is analytically inadequate for the analysis of poverty in Brazil. Construction of Fava-Rocha poverty lines requires three steps, the first two of which use information on household prefer-

26. See the appendix and Rocha (1989) for a more complete description of the methodology.
27. See Fishlow (1972); Lodder (1976); Pfefferman (1978); Pastore, Zylberstajn, and Pagotto (1983); Hoffman (1984); and Tolosa (1991).
28. See Thomas (1982).
29. See Thomas (1982); Fava (1984); and Rocha (1988).

Table 7-8. *Poverty Lines as Percent of Highest Average Annual Minimum Wage, Metropolitan Areas, Brazil, Selected Years, 1981–90*

Metropolitan area	1981	1983	1985	1986	1987	1988	1989	1990
Belén	0.63	0.73	0.72	0.81	0.98	0.91	0.85	1.22
Fortaleza	0.59	0.56	0.52	0.49	0.59	0.55	0.51	0.72
Recife	0.60	0.60	0.62	0.54	0.68	0.65	0.62	0.93
Salvador	0.63	0.63	0.64	0.66	0.81	0.74	0.74	1.02
Belo Horizonte	0.52	0.61	0.63	0.58	0.70	0.67	0.65	0.96
Rio de Janeiro	0.58	0.68	0.74	0.62	0.77	0.76	0.75	1.11
Sao Paulo	0.68	0.83	0.79	0.77	0.99	0.94	0.90	1.29
Curitiba	0.43	0.54	0.53	0.48	0.59	0.57	0.57	0.77
Porto Alegre	0.59	0.69	0.71	0.64	0.79	0.75	0.73	1.03

Source: Rocha (1992, p. 11); and Rocha (1991).

ences from the 1974–75 National Household Expenditure Survey (ENDEF). The methodology, proposed by Fava, is described in the appendix.

Poverty lines generated by the Fava-Rocha methodology are available for all years from 1981 to 1990, except for 1982 and 1984. The set of poverty lines is limited to metropolitan areas, because in Brazil time series data on prices is available only for these areas. Nevertheless, metropolitan areas are of foremost importance in poverty studies for at least two reasons. First, 31.8 percent of the Brazilian population in 1989 lived in these areas, representing almost 46 million individuals.[30] Second, these areas have specific poverty-related problems such as high population density and high transportation and housing costs.

Table 7-8 presents the region- and time-specific poverty lines, expressed as a percentage of the highest legal minimum wage. The results suggest there is no correlation between the value of the poverty line and urban population size. With 17.2 million inhabitants, Sao Paulo has relatively high poverty lines, consistent with the rising transportation and housing costs that accompany urbanization. Yet similar values were estimated for Belém, a metropolitan area with only 1.2 million inhabitants.[31] The high value for Belém is the result of its geographical isolation, which leads to high transportation and other commercial costs. Nor does variation in poverty lines follow a definite regional pattern. High poverty lines occur in both northeastern cities, such as Salvador, and southern cities, such as São Paulo. This fact makes it difficult to defend the regionally differentiated minimum wages Brazil maintained until 1984.[32]

30. See IBGE (1994).
31. See IBGE (1994).
32. See Saboia (1984).

The Magnitude of Poverty

Table 7-9 presents estimates of the proportion of persons in metropolitan Brazil living in families with per capita incomes below the poverty line for selected years in the 1980s. These estimates were obtained by comparing the per capita family income of each individual, based on National Household Survey (PNAD) data, with the corresponding time- and region-specific Fava-Rocha poverty line.

As table 7-9 shows, the proportion of the population below the poverty line in 1990 varied considerably among metropolitan areas, ranging from approximately 20 percent in the south (Curitiba and Porto Alegre) to more than 38 percent in the northeast (Fortaleza, Recife, and Salvador). Overall, 28.9 percent of the population in metropolitan Brazil was below the poverty line in 1990. This estimate is quite similar to that obtained by Psacharopoulos and others, despite large differences in methodology. That study estimated that 33 percent of the urban population in Brazil was below the poverty line in 1989.[33]

In 1981 the overall proportion of the population in metropolitan Brazil below the poverty line was 29.1 percent, indicating no change in poverty between the beginning and end of the 1980s. During the decade, however, regional differences in poverty were significantly reduced. Poverty increased in the south (Curitiba and Porto Alegre), the region with the lowest initial level of poverty, and decreased considerably in the northeast (Fortaleza, Recife, and Salvador). In São Paulo, the largest metropolitan area, 22 percent of the population was below the poverty line in both 1981 and 1990.

The finding that the share of the population below the poverty line did not change between 1981 and 1990 for metropolitan Brazil as a whole differs from the conclusions of the previous section, as well as with those of the Psacharopoulos study. The previous section showed that overall poverty in Brazil increased from 1980 to 1990 for any single national poverty line. Psacharopoulos and others, also using a national poverty line, found that poverty increased in both urban and rural areas of Brazil.[34] There are three important methodological differences that could explain the disparity in results. First, there are differences in the population group being considered—metropolitan areas versus Brazil as a whole or urban Brazil. Second, both the Psacharopoulos study and the previous section use 1980 as the baseline year, whereas this section uses 1981 as the baseline. Since it is likely that there was

33. Psacharopoulos and others (1992, table A13.1).
34. Psacharopoulos and others (1992).

Table 7-9. *Persons in Families with per Capita Incomes below the Poverty Line, Metropolitan Areas, Brazil, Selected Years, 1981–90*

Metropolitan area	1981	1983	1985	1986	1987	1988	1989	1990
Belén	50.9	57.6	43.8	45.9	45.1	46.6	39.6	43.4
Fortaleza	54.0	56.2	36.6	30.1	37.8	35.8	40.7	41.5
Recife	55.6	56.6	47.5	39.9	42.8	43.9	47.2	48.5
Salvador	43.1	43.8	39.5	37.5	39.4	33.9	39.0	39.2
Belo Horizonte	31.3	44.1	36.1	26.4	27.7	28.9	27.2	30.3
Rio de Janeiro	27.2	34.7	36.8	23.2	25.9	25.1	32.5	32.7
São Paulo	22.0	34.4	26.9	16.9	20.0	17.5	20.9	22.2
Curitiba	17.4	29.6	24.3	10.5	10.9	10.7	13.5	12.3
Porto Alegre	17.9	29.7	23.3	16.5	18.7	21.2	21.0	21.2
All metropolitan areas	29.1	38.2	n.a.	22.8	25.5	24.4	27.9	28.9

Source: Rocha (1992, p. 4); and Rocha (1991).
n.a. Not available.

an increase in poverty from 1980 to 1981, part of the disparity could be explained by the difference in the baseline year.[35] Third, the Fava-Rocha poverty lines are region-specific, while the previous section and the Psacharopoulos study use a national poverty line that ignores large regional differences in prices and tastes.

Regarding short-term fluctuations, changes in the level of poverty over the decade closely followed fluctuations in per capita income. Poverty increased sharply (9 percentage points) from 1981 to 1983 and declined even more sharply (15 percentage points) from 1983 to 1986. From 1986 to 1990 the level of poverty increased steadily, reaching levels similar to those in 1981 at the end of the decade. In summary, like per capita income, the level of poverty was higher at the beginning and end of the decade and lower at the middle.

Educational Attainment

In this section we evaluate the performance of education in Brazil during the 1980s, compare it with performance in preceding decades. We are particularly interested in identifying any direct or indirect link in the 1980s between educational performance and economic cycles.

35. Comparable data on poverty for 1980 and 1981 do not seem to exist. However, since per capita income declined by 6.5 percent between the two years, and there is no evidence that inequality decreased substantially in the period, we could safely assume that poverty increased.

Table 7-10. *School Attendance, Illiteracy, and School Years Completed,
Brazil, Selected Years, 1950–90*
Percent

Year	School attendance rate[a]	Illiteracy rate[b]	School years completed[c]
1950	n.a.	51	n.a.
1960	53	40	2.1
1970	68	34	2.5
1981	76	26	3.9
1990	85	19	4.9

Sources: Column 1: IBGE (1992, p. 105); and 1960 and 1970 Demographic Census. Column 2: CEPAL (1984); and MEC (1990, p. 20). Column 3: *Censo Demografico* (1960, 1970); and IBGE (1981, 1990).
n.a. Not available.
a. Percentage of children 7 to 14 years old currently attending school.
b. Percentage of the population 15 years old and older who cannot read or write a simple message.
c. Average number of school years completed by the population 25 years and older.

Long-Term Trends

Table 7-10 traces the evolution over time of three educational indicators: the school attendance rate of children seven to fourteen years old, the illiteracy rate for the population fifteen years old and older, and the average number of years of schooling of the population twenty-five years old and older. It reveals that all three indicators improved steadily over the last four decades: the attendance rate increased an average of 10 percentage points each decade; the illiteracy rate declined by approximately 8 percentage points each decade; and the average number of years of schooling increased by almost one year each decade.

Since all indicators of educational attainment have an upper and a lower bound, it would be natural to observe a slowdown in their growth as they approach the upper bound. The fact that table 7-10 does not reveal any reduction in the growth of these indicators in the 1980s suggests that the amount of investment in education did not decline that decade. Thus, despite the economic difficulties of the 1980s, progress in education appears to have been sustained at its historical pace.

However, the correlation between indicators of educational attainment and current levels of investment in education is far from perfect. In most cases, changes in an indicator in one decade actually reflect investments made several decades earlier. This lag certainly applies to the average years of schooling among adults. The adult literacy rate occupies an intermediary position. Although it can be substantially affected in the short run by literacy programs for adults, it is also affected by improvements in the educational system in previous decades, as new cohorts enter the adult population. The lag applies

Table 7-11. *Share of Elementary School Students Who Repeat Grades or Evade School, Brazil, Selected Years, 1980–90*
Percent

Year	School attendance[a]	First grade repeaters	Fourth grade repeaters	Primary school evaders[b]
1980	n.a.	29	12	n.a.
1981	76	29	12	10
1982	74	28	13	8
1983	80	n.a.	n.a.	12
1984	n.a.	23	11	13
1985	82	24	13	11
1986	83	24	13	13
1987	83	24	14	n.a.
1988	84	n.a.	n.a.	n.a.
1989	84	n.a.	n.a.	n.a.
1990	85	n.a.	n.a.	n.a.
1981–83	77	28	12	10
1985–87	84	24	13	12
1988–90	84	n.a.	n.a.	n.a.

Sources: Column 1: IBGE (1985, 1992, p. 105); and PNADs 1983–89. Columns 2–4: MEC (1990, pp. 39–40).
n.a. Not available.
a. Percentage of children 7 to 14 years old currently attending school.
b. Percentage of initial enrollment at the primary level (first to eighth grade) who evade school before the end of the year.

least to the attendance rate, which is the most reliable indicator of current investment in education. Therefore, the fact that the attendance rate increased in the 1980s at least as much as in previous decades suggests that progress in education was sustained at its historical level despite economic difficulties.

To reinforce this finding, table 7-11 presents the evolution of several other indicators of educational performance that should be very sensitive to current levels of investment in human capital. These indicators, which focus on the school-age populations, reveal two facts. First, most of the progress in education during the 1980s took place in the first half of the decade. In that period both the percentage of children seven to fourteen years old not attending school and the repetition rate in the first grade declined by about 5 percentage points. Second, although the proportion of children attending school increased, their probabilities of progression to higher grades, measured by repetition and evasion rates, did not improve much during the 1980s, except for the decline in the first grade repetition rate from 1981 to 1985. In summary, the evidence on educational performance suggests that although access to primary education in Brazil in the 1980s did expand, the efficiency and quality of the education provided did not improve, as repetition and evasion rates remained high.

The Level of Educational Attainment

Despite the progress in education since 1950, the level of educational attainment Brazil remains very low. Almost 20 percent of the population over fourteen years of age is illiterate, approximately 15 percent of children seven to fourteen years old are currently not attending school, 24 percent of students in the first grade are repeaters, and 70 percent of students in the first grade are older than experts recommend for that grade.[36] In addition, Brazilians over twenty-four years of age have completed an average of only five years of schooling.[37]

Brazil's long-term performance in education is weak in comparison to both official education goals and performance in other countries. For example, although the Brazilian Constitution requires compulsory education for all children seven to fourteen years old, 13 percent of children in this age range are currently not attending school. Furthermore, all educational indicators for Brazil are far inferior to those of most other upper middle-income countries.[38] For example, one study by Amadeo and others demonstrated that several educational indicators are considerably worse in Brazil than in Latin America's seven other high-income countries. Compared to the average in those seven countries, the illiteracy rate for the population ages fifteen and older in Brazil is approximately ten percent lower; the attendance rate for children six to eleven years old is 15 percentage points lower; and the proportion of repeaters in the first grade is 10 percentage points higher.[39] In another cross-national study, Behrman found that the expected number of years of schooling in Brazil in 1980 was 2.9 years below the international norm, given Brazil's level of per capita income.[40]

36. MEC (1990, p. 20, 34, 40–41).

37. According to the UNDP (1922, p. 127) the average level of schooling for Brazilians over twenty-four years of age is 3.9 years. This UNDP estimate, however, is not in line with all other available estimates.

38. This group includes countries with 1990 per capita GDP between U.S. $2,466 and U.S. $7,619. See World Bank (1992, p. 221).

39. This group includes Argentina, Chile, Colombia, Costa Rica, Mexico, Uruguay, and Venezuela. See Amadeo and others (1993, figures 5.1.1 and 5.1.2, table 5.6).

40. In principle, such low levels of educational attainment should have severe consequences on labor force productivity, poverty and the ability of the economy to grow. It is, thus surprising that Brazil, with one of the weakest educational records in Latin America, has one of the best growth records, and is not among the countries with the highest levels of poverty. See World Bank

Economic Growth and Educational Performance

An economic slowdown may reduce investment in education through two channels. First, it may decrease private investment to the extent that the level of investment in the education of children increases with per capita family income. Second, it may cause a decline in the share of the national product allocated to public expenditures in education, negatively affecting the public provision of educational services.

Despite the clear theoretical connection between economic growth and investment in education,[41] the evidence for Brazil suggests that there was no connection during the last four decades. In fact, Brazil's educational performance in the 1970s was very close to the average for the entire 1950–90 period despite substantially higher growth in that decade. Even comparing the 1970s and 1980s, two decades with wide differences in economic growth, there is no evidence that Brazil's educational performance was worse in the 1980s than in the 1970s. This evidence contradicts the view that high (low) rates of economic growth necessarily lead to high (low) rates of progress in education.[42]

One possible explanation for Brazil's consistent educational performance in the 1980s in the face of stagnating per capita income is an increase in its propensity to spend on public educational services. Public expenditures in education increased from an average of 1.8 percent of GDP between 1960 and 1965 to 2.6 percent in the 1970s and 4.5 percent in 1986-88. In fact, during the 1980s public expenditures in education increased by more than 50 percent, with most of this increase between 1984 and 1986.[43] Since the school-age population increased on average by 2.3 percent a year in the 1980s,[44] public expenditure in education per school-age individual increased by more than 25 percent during the period. The greater propensity of the Brazilian government

(1991, pp. 204–05). Actually, very few non-oil-exporting countries with levels of education similar to Brazil's are capable of achieving similar levels of per capita income and growth. Turkey, Malaysia, and South Africa are a few exceptions. It remains to be determined, however, to what extent the lower educational level of the Brazilian labor force will become an important constraint on future growth.

41. See Knight and Sabot (1990).

42. The relationship between educational expansion and economic growth in Brazil during the 1970s seems unusual when compared to other countries. For instance, Behrman (1987) estimated that, given the Brazilian growth rate in the 1970s, international norms suggest the average number of years of schooling should have increased by an additional 2.2 years.

43. See Amadeo and others (1993, table 5.2); IBGE (1992, p. 91); and Mussi, Ohama and Guedes (1992, table VIII-b).

44. MEC (1990, p. 34).

to spend on education in the 1980s therefore may in part explain why educational performance did not mirror economic performance in the 1980s. It should be noted, however, that this explanation demands further investigation, because the relationship between education expenditures and educational performance is not supported by the timing of expenditure growth. Most of the progress in education seems to have occurred in the first half of the decade, while the substantial increase in public education expenditures did not occur until later.

In addition, Brazil's strong educational performance in the 1980s could be the result of increased efficiency in the use of the resources devoted to public education. Brazil's public educational system has traditionally been very inefficient, both because it allocates too many resources to post-secondary education and because the regional allocation of resources is extremely perverse, with very few resources reaching the poorest regions.[45] However, we were unable to find any evidence that the level of these inefficiencies declined in the 1980s.

The link between income inequality and educational performance also appears to be weak, despite the fact that educational performance—especially at the primary school level—is more closely related to the income of the poor than to average income. During the 1980s there was a considerable increase in income inequality and no growth in per capita income, yet educational performance was comparable to that of the 1970s. This finding indicates a weak connection between reductions in income inequality and educational expansion.

Because the indicators in table 7-11 are very sensitive to the economic and social environment, they should indicate whether short-term economic fluctuations have identifiable impacts on educational outcomes. Although these indicators fluctuated slightly in the 1980s, these shifts were unrelated to fluctuations in economic activity. For instance, there is no evidence that the education indicators were worse in the 1981–84 period than in the 1985–87 period, despite the fact that per capita income was considerably higher in the later period.

Infant Mortality

In this section we analyze changes in infant mortality in Brazil over the 1980s. We are particularly interested in identifying the effect on infant mortality of the slowdown in economic growth, the cyclical fluctuations in GDP, and the increase in inequality. To pursue this goal we investigate the fluctuations in

45. See Amadeo and others (1993).

Table 7-12. *Infant Mortality Rate (IMR) Estimates, Brazil, Selected Years, 1940–89*

Numbers per million

Based on household surveys		Based on vital statistics	
Year	IMR	Year	IMR
1940	163	1980	75
1950	146	1981	68
1960	121	1982	65
1970	114	1983	67
1980	88	1984	66
1984	68	1985	58
1986	67	1986	53
		1987	51
		1988	48
		1989	45

Sources: For household survey estimates, Simões and Ortiz (1988, table 6); and Simões (1989, table 3). For estimates based on vital statistics, IBGE (1992, table 4).

the infant mortality rate (IMR) in the 1980s and compare the country's overall performance during the period with its performance in previous decades.[46]

The IMR is considered to be not only the single most important health indicator but also the most revealing measure of how well basic social needs are being fulfilled.[47] Moreover, the IMR tends to be highly correlated with other health indicators. Perhaps for these reasons, the IMR is the health indicator for which there is the greatest amount of reliable information.

Measuring Infant Mortality

Table 7-12 shows the temporal evolution of the IMR from 1940 to 1989. The estimates are presented separately to emphasize the methodological differences. The estimates in the first two columns were derived from household surveys using indirect techniques.[48] One advantage is that they can be related to other socioeconomic and demographic information available in the surveys. However, they have the disadvantage of never being very current. They are based on retrospective questions that refer to occurrences two or three years before the date of the survey.

46. The IMR is defined as the number of infants who die before reaching one year of age, per thousand live births.

47. Newland (1985).

48. The data come from Simões and Ortiz (1988) and Simões (1989). See Merrick (1985); McCraken (1990); and Beltrao and Sawyer (1991) for other studies of this type using Brazilian data.

The estimates in the second two columns of table 7-12 were based on vital statistics corrected for under-reporting.[49] These estimates have two advantages: they can be computed for very recent years; and they capture fluctuations in the IMR with greater accuracy. These two characteristics make them particularly useful for investigating fluctuations of the IMR during the 1980s. One disadvantage is that they cannot be used to estimate the relationship between the IMR and socioeconomic or other demographic characteristics.

As tables 7-12 indicates, Brazil experienced a notable decline in the IMR over the last fifty years: in absolute terms, it decreased by more than one hundred deaths per thousand live births. By the late 1980s, the IMR was close to one-third of its 1940 level. However, despite this sharp decline, the IMR in Brazil is still higher than that in almost every other Latin American country.[50]

The sharp decline in the IMR did not occur evenly over the decades. Table 7-12 suggests that the rate of decline accelerated over time, with the clear exception of the 1960s. The decline in the IMR during the 1960s was only one-fourth of the average per decade decline during the entire period. Almost one-third of the total decline occurred in the 1980s, when the IMR fell by thirty deaths per thousand live births, an amount greater than that of any other decade.

Explanations for the Decline in Infant Mortality

A variety of factors, in general, may explain the decline in infant mortality. The list of potential explanations includes economic growth; reduced income inequality; educational advances; improved sanitation; greater access to health services; and progress in health technology.[51] We evaluate each of these possible causes in turn.

ECONOMIC PERFORMANCE. To evaluate the importance of economic growth in reducing infant mortality, we compare patterns of economic growth with changes in the IMR during the last fifty years. If economic performance were crucial, the decline in mortality would have been greater in the 1970s than in the 1980s, since per capita income increased, on average, by 6 percent a year

49. The methodology is described in Simões (1989).
50. See Simões and Ortiz (1988, p. 251); and CEPAL (1991, p. 49).
51. See McCraken (1990, chaps. 5 and 6) for a comprehensive study of the connection between sociodemographic characteristics and infant mortality in Brazil. For the connection between education and infant mortality in Brazil, see Henriques and others (1989); Barros and Sawyer (1992); Beltrão and Sawyer (1991); and McCraken (1990, chapter 7).

in the 1970s, while there was zero net growth in the 1980s. This conjecture is clearly rejected by the evidence in table 7-12. The 1980s had the greatest decline in infant mortality, but the worst growth record. Moreover, although per capita income growth in the 1960s was substantial (3 percent a year), the decline in the infant mortality rate was very small.

It could be argued that the income of the poor is much more relevant to IMR reduction than average income. As noted, the poor suffered more in the 1980s than in the previous two decades. Only in the 1980s did the real income of the bottom 20 percent of the population actually decline. Despite this fact, the IMR declined by more in the 1980s than in any other decade, revealing little connection between economic performance and infant mortality.

EDUCATION. A comparison of the IMR with indicators of educational achievement among adults (illiteracy rates and the average years of schooling) reveals some association. Decades with small educational advances in the adult population, such as the 1940s and 1960s, also had small reductions in the IMR. Hence, at least part of the IMR reduction in the 1980s may be attributed to that decade's large improvement in the educational level of adults.

SANITATION, HEALTH TECHNOLOGY AND HEALTH SERVICES. The failure of changes in economic growth and inequality to explain infant mortality reductions suggests that, in addition to educational advances, progress in health services and sanitation might have been especially in the 1980s. In fact, much of the decline in infant mortality during the 1970s and 1980s has been attributed to a very ambitious sanitation plan (PLANASA) launched in 1971 by the federal government.[52] Two pieces of evidence, however, indicate that the contribution of PLANASA may be limited. First, after investigating the impact of PLANASA on infant mortality, Merrick concluded that "increased access to piped water (played) a secondary role."[53] Second, as the following text table shows, the absolute decline in the IMR during the 1970s was only slightly greater in urban areas than in rural areas. Since the PLANASA aimed to provide adequate sanitation and piped water to urban households only, it cannot explain the decline in infant mortality in rural areas. Therefore, although the PLANASA probably had some positive impact, it was not the major cause of the IMR decline during the 1970s and 1980s.

52. See Fullet (1988).
53. Merrick (1985, p. 19).

Area	1970	1980
Urban	111	86
Rural	115	94
All	114	88

Source: Simões and Ortiz (1988, table 7).

One can evaluate the importance of progress in health technology and improved access to health services by considering the decline in the IMR by cause of death. In 1988, 52 percent of all infant deaths were due to causes that could have been easily avoided.[54] Diarrhea was the leading cause, accounting for 30 percent of easily preventable infant deaths and 15.6 percent of all infant deaths. These numbers, however, represent a considerable decline from the levels prevailing ten years earlier. In 1979, for instance, 65 percent of all infant deaths were due to easily preventable causes, with diarrhea causing 40 percent of these deaths.[55] To a large extent, the subsequent decline in diarrhea-related deaths is attributed to the intensive use of inexpensive oral rehydration therapy.

The importance of improvements in access to health services in explaining the decline in infant mortality during the 1980s is debatable. Whereas indicators of medical personnel (number of doctors and medical assistants) and public health expenditures improved continuously during the 1980s, indicators of medical facilities (hospital beds per capita) deteriorated considerably.[56] In summary, despite weak economic performance and an increase in inequality, Brazil in the 1980s experienced a sharp decline in infant mortality. This leads us to infer that the cause of the decline is likely to be related to advances in education, developments in health technology, continuous investment in water supply and sanitation, and better access to health services. This evidence is contrary to the view that reductions in infant mortality in Brazil since the mid-1960s required improvements in economic performance.[57]

Fluctuations in the 1980s

If progress in health technology dominates the long-term evolution of infant mortality, one might expect a weak correlation between economic growth and the IMR over long periods of time. But if instead the level of income is truly important, short-run fluctuations in income should lead to short-run vari-

54. IBGE (1992a, p. 146, table 6).
55. IBGE (1992a, p. 146, table 6).
56. IBGE (1992a, p. 91); CEPAL (1991, pp. 48–52).
57. See McCraken (1990); and Flegg (1982).

ations in the IMR. Because per capita income fluctuated considerably during the 1980s, being considerably lower at the beginning and end of the decade than in the middle, that period is particularly useful for analysis of this type.

As table 7-12 reveals, the decline in the IMR was not uniform during the 1980s. There was very little progress in infant mortality from 1981 to 1984. Because this period coincides with the severe economic recession of 1981–83, there is some evidence of the sensitivity of the IMR to short-run fluctuations in per capita income. Note, however, that the recession at the end of the decade does not seem to have yet had any significant effect on the declining trend of the IMR.

Social Safety Nets

In this section we investigate the role of programs designed to mitigate the adverse impact of economic adjustment on the poor in Brazil during the 1980s. Our focus is on two programs, unemployment insurance and food assistance.

Unemployment Insurance

Brazil's unemployment insurance program was created in February 1986 as part of the economic reforms of the Cruzado Plan.[58] This program, initially very small and limited in resources, was expanded and reformulated in 1990. The government lowered the eligibility requirements, leading to a sharp increase in the proportion of the labor force covered by the program. In addition, the 1990 reform guaranteed the long-term financing of the program, based on the creation of a fund—the *Fundo de Amparo ao Trabalhador*—financed through corporate income taxes.

To become eligible for unemployment insurance a worker has to meet several criteria. The worker must have been dismissed without just cause; must have had a formal labor contract during the last six months, or have been legally self-employed for at least fifteen months; must have been unemployed for at least seven days; must not be receiving any other pension or insurance; and must have no other source of income sufficient to guarantee the subsistence of his or her family.

The unemployment insurance program offers partial coverage for up to four months of unemployment. The value of the benefit cannot be lower than

58. This section is based on joint work with Edward Amadeo, José Camargo, Valeria Pero and Andre Urani. See Amadeo and others (1993, section VI.E.2).

the value of the minimum wage. Benefits are adjusted monthly for inflation and are based on the average wage received during the last three months of the previous job.

The average value of the benefits, measured in multiples of the minimum wage, declined from the beginning of the program, through 1988 and then rose to 1.81 times the minimum wage by 1991. The program's coverage increased steadily after its inception in 1986, most notably in 1990 when eligibility requirements were relaxed. The number of workers receiving unemployment insurance increased from almost 300,000 in 1988 to 1.4 million in 1989 and then to 2.9 million in 1991. Furthermore, the coverage rate increased from 5 percent of dismissed workers in 1986 to 19 percent in 1989, and 37 percent in 1990, then fell slightly to 31 percent in 1991.[59] Of the total number of workers that applied for the insurance, the number that received benefits increased from 66 percent in 1986 to 94 percent in 1991. This sharp increase in the program's coverage was the natural consequence of the increasing awareness of workers about the program, as well as the relaxation of its eligibility requirements.

In summary, the second half of the 1980s witnessed the creation and growth of a solid unemployment insurance program in Brazil. Given that nearly universal coverage has already been achieved, the current debate focuses on whether the duration and generosity of the benefits should be increased. In the 1990s this program will certainly be an important tool for reducing the distributive consequences of the adjustment process. It must be emphasized, however, that by its very nature this program can only help workers currently in the formal sector of the labor market. Workers in the informal sector and new entrants need alternative assistance programs.

Food Assistance

The aggregate level of food production in Brazil is substantially above the minimum required for meeting the nutritional needs of the entire population. In fact, the production of grains alone (rice, beans, wheat, and corn) generates 3,280 calories and 87 grams of proteins per capita each day, while international recommendations are 2,242 calories and 53 grams of proteins a day.[60] Therefore, the fact that severe malnutrition still afflicts 7 percent of Brazilian children under seven years of age can only be explained by the excessively

59. See Azeredo and Chahad (1992).
60. Peliano (1993, p. 6)

unequal distribution of income and wealth prevailing in the country.[61]
This contradiction—between a large aggregate food surplus and millions of malnourished children—has increasingly demanded government intervention. As a result, government expenditures on the provision of free and subsidized food increased substantially in the 1980s. From 1980 to 1987 the level of government expenditures on food assistance programs increased fivefold, with most of the increase occurring since 1985. Moreover, the number of children zero to six years old assisted in these programs increased by 18 percent between 1986 and 1989. Unfortunately, since 1990 the volume of public resources devoted to these programs has declined substantially. But even at its peak in 1989, the volume of resources available was significantly below what would be necessary to satisfy the needs of the population. In fact, of the 2 million children under four years old affected by severe malnutrition in 1989, only 36 percent were being assisted by at least one government food program.[62]

During the 1980s a variety of new food programs began. These programs were the responsibility of numerous government organizations, which often had overlapping responsibilities. Until 1993 there was no central organization responsible for coordinating government food assistance programs. In 1993, however, a council—the Conselho Nacional de Segurança Alimentar—was created to coordinate national food assistance policy.

Food programs in Brazil can be classified in three groups: those that assist pre-school children, infants, and pregnant women; those that assist children enrolled in primary school; and those that assist workers.

Among all food assistance programs, those targeting pregnant women, pre-school children, and infants are probably the most important, because they target the most vulnerable segment of the population. Although several different programs have been implemented, some of which remain in operation, no firm tradition of assisting this segment of the population was established during the 1980s. Programs in this area have been hard to target and difficult to administrate.[63]

By far the most popular program in this area was the National Milk for Children Program (*Programa Nacional do Leite para Crianças Carentes*), created in 1986. In 1989, 60 percent of the children under seven years of age receiving some type of food assistance were enrolled in that program. The

---

61. Monteiro and others (1992, p. 47).
62. For these statistics, see Peliano (1988; 1992a, pp. 115, 126; and 1992b, p. 25); and Monteiro and others (1992, p. 55).
63. Peliano (1992, pp. 12–13).

government, however, abolished the program in 1991. Peliano and Campino have both argued that the program was inefficient, in that it was considerably more expensive to meet the nutritional needs of the population with the Milk Program than with more traditional programs based on the distribution of baskets of basic food items.[64]

Food assistance programs for school children are well established in Brazil, having been operating for many years. The current goal is to provide free daily meals at school for 30 million children enrolled in public primary schools throughout the country.[65] One of the main problems with this program, however, is poor targeting. About 15 percent of children seven to fourteen years old are not currently attending school. This group is predominantly comprised of children from poor families who are more likely than other children to be malnourished. The most vulnerable segment of the school-age population, therefore, remains uncovered by the program. However, as the proportion of children attending school continues to grow, this problem is increasingly easy to resolve.

Food programs for workers typically provide them with subsidized meals. In the current program, known as the *Programa de Alimentação do Trabalhador*, workers pay only 20 percent of the costs of each meal. The meals are served in the restaurants of the firm, or the workers receive coupons that can be used in most restaurants. Firms are not required to provide these subsidized meals, but if they choose to participate in the program they can deduct the costs of the program from their tax liabilities, up to a set amount. The main problem with this program, again, is poor targeting. Only 10 percent of the labor force (7 million workers) currently receives this benefit, and these workers are typically employed in large corporations in the formal sector. Workers in small- and medium-size firms and in the informal sector have greater needs, but are not covered by the program.

In summary, in the 1980s, and especially the second half of the decade, the resources devoted to food assistance programs increased substantially. A series of new programs was introduced, and the number of persons being assisted rose significantly. Nevertheless, the volume of resources available is still insufficient to satisfy the needs of the population or even the government's goals. According to one author, a threefold increase in food program expenditures is necessary to meet the government's goals.[66] Of the remaining problems, efforts in two main areas are critical. First, a solid program to assist

64. Peliano (1988); Campino (1989).
65. Peliano (1993, p. 8).
66. Peliano (1992b, p. 33).

the most vulnerable segment of the population (children under four years old and pregnant women) is urgently needed. Second, the targeting of the two most effective and well-established programs—the school lunch and worker subsidy programs—need to be improved.

Conclusions

The interruption in the flow of foreign capital to Brazil in the 1980s demanded a process of structural adjustment that for a number of reasons Brazil was unable to implement. The result was a substantial reduction in the rate of annual per capita GDP growth from an average of 6.0 percent in the 1970s to –0.6 percent in the 1980s. The slowdown in economic growth, however, had little impact on the creation of jobs, as more than 17 million new jobs were created in Brazil in the 1980s. Although GDP grew by 22 percent between 1981 and 1990, employment increased by 36 percent. The main consequence of the stagnation of the 1980s seems to have been a deterioration in the quality of jobs created in urban areas, with an increasing proportion of employment in services and the informal sector.

The economic slowdown in the 1980s was not neutral in distributional terms. The degree of income inequality increased substantially, especially from 1986 to 1989. In addition, the nature of the increase in inequality in the 1980s was particularly perverse, affecting the poorest segments of the population the most. In the 1960s, by contrast, inequality also increased substantially, but negatively affected mainly the middle class, not the very bottom of the distribution. Studies of the causes of the increase in inequality in the 1980s have pointed to the increase in inflation as the leading factor, especially between 1986 and 1989.

The decline in per capita GDP in the 1980s, coupled with the increase in income inequality, led to a decline in social welfare and an increase in poverty. In 1990 approximately 30 percent of the Brazilian population in metropolitan areas had per capita income below the poverty line. In northeastern metropolitan areas the proportion of the population below the poverty line in 1990 was greater than 40 percent. As per capita income fluctuated over the 1980s, so did the level of poverty. For example, the proportion of the population below the poverty line in metropolitan Brazil increased from 29 percent in 1981 to 38 percent in 1983, as per capita GDP declined by 7 percent over the same period.

Despite the slowdown in economic growth and the increase in inequality in the 1980s, educational performance improved at its historical rate and infant mortality declined sharply. The strong performance in education was due to the maturation of investments made in previous decades and to the increasing share of GDP currently invested in public education. The decline in infant mortality was due to a variety of factors, including advances in health technology, better access to health services, improvement in adult education, and investment in water supply and sanitation. Cyclical fluctuations in per capita GDP had some effect on infant mortality but no identifiable impact on educational indicators such as attendance, repetition, and evasion rates. All of this evidence is contrary to the view that improvements in education and infant mortality in Brazil must have been accompanied by improved economic performance.

To alleviate the costs of economic stagnation on the poor segments of society in the 1980s, the Brazilian government implemented a series of compensatory programs, mainly after 1985. In 1986 it created an unemployment insurance program. The program subsequently grew in coverage so that by 1991 it assisted 3 million workers. Reforms in 1990 made eligibility requirements for the program minimal. As a result, the main policy debate today centers on whether to enhance the program's benefits, which currently range from one to four times the minimum wage and last for four months. However, this program benefits formal sector workers only.

Since 1985 the government has implemented several food assistance programs, and overall public expenditures on food assistance have increased. The most popular of these programs, the National Milk for Children Program, began in 1986. In the same period, the government initiated a program to provide subsidized food for workers. The free school lunch program is scheduled to assist 30 million children enrolled in public primary schools in 1993.

Overall, the Brazilian democratization process, which accelerated after 1985, brought an increase in government expenditures on social programs. The proportion of GDP spent on public education, public health, food assistance programs, and the assistance of unemployed workers all increased substantially. Most of the social programs implemented in the period, however, have serious targeting problems, and as a result they never reach the poorest and most vulnerable segments of the society. The fact that inequality increased sharply from 1986 to 1989, exactly when the government was giving great emphasis to social programs, is a very important finding that must be investigated in great detail.

Appendix

In the first step, food preferences are determined based on food basket of the second poorest decile of the distribution (in terms of current expenditures). After reducing the number of items in this food basket to improve empirical tractability, the size of basket is adjusted to achieve the ideal daily requirement of 2,400 calories per person.

In the second step, the lowest decile of the distribution that meets the caloric requirements is identified. Next, expenditures on nonfood items are incorporated, using the ratio between food and total expenditures (Engel's coefficient) that prevails in this decile.

In the third step, the region-specific consumption patterns obtained in the first two steps are assumed to be time-invariant over the entire period under study. The value of the poverty line for a given region and time period is then obtained using the average prices (for that period and region) of food items that make up the region-specific consumption basket.

Time- and region-specific poverty lines constructed in this way can be used to compare the incidence of poverty over time and across regions, because they encompass the same basic nutritional norm: a daily intake of 2,400 calories per person.

References

Almeida Reis, José and Ricardo Barros. 1989. "Educação e Desigualdade de Salários." In *Perspectivas da Economia Brasileira: 1989*. Rio de Janeiro: IPEA/INPES.

Amadeo, Edward and others. 1993. "Human Resources in the Adjustment Process." Working Paper 137. Washington: Inter-American Development Bank (June).

Azeredo, B. and José Chahad. 1992. "O Programa Brasileiro de Seguro Desemprego: Diagnósticos e Sugestões para o seu Aperfeiçoamento." Série Seminários 1/92. Rio de Janeiro: IPEA/DIPES (January).

Barros, Ricardo, and Eliana Cardoso, and André Urani. 1993. "Inflation and Unemployment as Determinants of Inequality in Brazil: The 1980s." Texto para Discussas 298. Rio de Janeiro: IPEA (April).

Barros, Ricardo, and Rosane Mendonça. 1992a. "Desigualdade Salarial." Rio de Janeiro: IPEA (August).

———. 1992b. "A Evolução do Bem-Estar e da Desigualdade no Brasil desde 1960." Texto para Discussão 286. Rio de Janeiro: IPEA.

———. 1992c. "A Research Note on Family and Income Distribution: The Equalizing Impact of Married Women's Earnings in Metropolitan Brazil." *Sociological Inquiry* 62 (2).

Barros Ricardo, and Lauro Ramos. 1991. "Employment Structure in Brazil and its Sensitivity to the Current Economic Policy." Texto para Discussão 228. Rio de Janeiro: IPEA.

Barros, Ricardo, and Diana Sawyer. 1992. "Unequal Opportunity to Survive, Education and Regional Disparities in Brazil." Paper prepared for Conference on Women's Human Capital and Development. Bellagio, Italy (April).

Behrman, Jere. 1987. "Schooling in Development Countries: Which Countries Are Over- and Underachievers and What Is the Schooling Impact?" *Economic of Education Review* 6(2): 111–27.

Beltrão, Kaizo, and Diana Sawyer. 1990. "Medidas de Mortalidade: Um Estudo sobre os Efeitos das Mudanças da Escolaridade da Mãee da Estrutura de Fecundidade em Quatro Areas Brasileiras." Relatórios Técnicos 04/90. Rio de Janeiro: ENCE.

Bonelli, Regis, and Lauro Ramos. 1992. "Income Distribution in Brazil: Longer Term Trends and Changes in Inequality since the mid-1970s." Série Seminários 17. Rio de Janeiro: IPEA.

Cacciamali, Maria. 1992. "Mudanças Estruturais e a Regulação do Mercado de Trabalho no Brasil nos Anos 80." Paper prepared for Seminário de Desenvolvimento Econômico, Investimento, Mercado de Trabalho e Distribuição de Renda. Rio de Janeiro: BNDES.

Campino, Antonio. 1989. "Lições do Programa do Leite Fluido." São Paulo: IESP.

Cardoso, Eliana, Ricardo Barros, and André Urani. 1993. "Inflation and Unemployment as Determinants of Inequality in Brazil: The 1980s." Texto para Discussão 298. Rio de Janeiro: IPEA.

Censo Demografico. 1960. IBGE: Rio de Janeiro.

———. 1970. IBGE: Rio de Janeiro.

———. 1980. IBGE: Rio de Janeiro.

CEPAL (U.N. Economic Commission for Latin America and the Caribbean). 1986. *Antecedentes Estadísticos de la Distribución del Ingreso: Brasil 1960–83*. Serie Distribución del Ingreso 2. Santiago, Chile: United Nations.

———. 1984. *Statistical Yearbook for Latin America: 1983*. Santigo, Chile: United Nations.

———. 1991. *Statistical Yearbook for Latin America: 1990*. Santiago, Chile: United Nations.

Conjuntura Econômica. 1979. FGV 33, (12). Rio de Janeiro.

Denslow, David, and William Tyler. 1983. "Perspectivas sobre pobreza e desigualdade de renda no Brasil." *Pesguisa e Planejamento Econômico*. 13 (December): 863–904.

Fava, Vera. 1984. *Urbanização, custo de vida e pobreza no Brasil*. São Paulo: IPE/USP.

Fishlow, Albert. 1972. "Brazilian Size Distribution of Income," *American Economic Review*, (May) 391–408.

Flegg, A. 1982. "Inequality of Income, Illiteracy and Medical Care as Determinants of Infant Mortality in Underdeveloped Countries." *Population Studies* 36 (3): 441–58.

Foster, J., and Anthony Shorrocks. 1988. "Poverty orderings and poverty dominance." *Social Choice and Welfare* 5: 179–98.

Fullet, Ricardo. 1988. "A Crise Econômica e os Investimentos Federais em Desenvolvimento Urbano." In *Crise e Infância no Brasil: O Impacto das Politicas de Ajustamento Econômico.* São Paulo: UNICEF/IPE - USP.

Henriques, Maria, John Strauss, and Duncan Thomas. 1989. "Mortalidade Infantil, Estado Nutricional e Características do Domicilio: A Evidência Brasileira." *Pesquisa e Planejamento Econômico* 19 (December): 427–82.

Hoffman, Rodolfo. 1984. "Pobreza no Brasil." Série Estudos e Pesquisas 43. Piracicaba: ESALQ.

———. 1992. "Desigualdade e Pobreza no Brasil no Periodo 1979–90."

Hoffman, Rodolfo, and Angela Kageyama. 1986. "Distribuição de Renda no Brasil, entre famílias e entre pessoas, em 1970 e 1980." *Estudos Econômicos* 16 (January): 25–51.

IBGE. 1974. *Estudo Nacional de Despesa Familiar* (ENDEF). Rio de Janeiro.

———. 1985. *Indicadores Sociais: Tabelas Selecionadas. 1984*, vol. 2, Rio de Janeiro.

———. 1990. *Estatísticas Históricas do Brasil: Séries Econômicas, Demográficas e Sociais de 1550 a 1988*, 2d ed. Rio de Janeiro.

———. 1992a. *Anuário Estatístico do Brasil*. Rio de Janeiro.

———. 1992b. *Crianças e Adolescentes: Indicadores Sociais*, vol. 4. Rio de Janeiro.

———. 1981, 1990, 1994 (annual). (PNAD) *Pesquisa Nacional por Amostra de Domicilios, 1983–1993.* Rio de Janeiro.

Langoni, Carlos. 1973. *Distribuição de Renda e Desenvolvimento Econômico no Brasil*. Rio de Janeiro: Editora Expressão e Cultura.

Lluch, Constantino. 1981. "Pobreza e concentração de renda no Brasil." *Pesquisa e Planejamento Econômico* 11 (December): 757–82.

Lodder, Celsius. 1976. *Distribuição de Renda nas Áreas Metropolitanas.* Relatório de Pesquisa 31. Rio de Janeiro: IPEA/INPES.

McCraken, Stephen. 1990. "A Multi-Level Socio-Demographic Analysis of Early Childhood Mortality in Brazil." Ph.D. dissertation, University of Texas at Austin.

MEC. 1990. *A Educação no Brasil na Década de 80.* Ministério da Educação.

Merrick, Thomas. 1985. "The Effect of Piped Water on Early Childhood Mortality in Urban Brazil, 1970 to 1976." *Demography* 22: 1–23.

Monteiro, Carlos, and others. 1992. "O Estado Nutricional das Crianças Brasileiras: A Trajetória de 1975 a 1989." In *Perfil Estatístico de Crianças e Mães no Brasil: Aspectos de Saúde e Nutrição de Crianças no Brasil, 1989.* Rio de Janeiro: IBGE/UNICEF/INAN.

Mussi, Carlos, Eduardo Ohama, and José Guedes. 1992. "Análise da Estrutura Funcional do Gasto Público no Brasil 1985–90." Texto para Discussão 249. Rio de Janeiro: IPEA.

Newland, Kathleen. 1985. "Infant Mortality and the Health of Societies." Worldwatch Paper 47, Washington: Worldwatch Institute.

Pastore, José, Helio Zylberstajn, and Carmen Pagotto. 1983. *Mudança Social e Pobreza no Brasil: 1970–1980.* São Paulo: FIPE/Fronteira.

Peliano, Anna. 1988. "Os Programas Alimentares e Nutricionais no Contexto da Recessão Econômica: 1980–84," In *Crise e Infância no Brasil: O Impacto das Políticas de Ajustamento Econômico.* São Paulo: UNICEF/IPE - USP.

———. 1992a. "Os Programas de Alimentação para Mães e Crianças no Brasil," In *Perfil Estatístico de Crianças e Mães no Brasil: Aspectos de Saúde e Nutrição de Crianças no Brasil, 1989.* Rio de Janeiro: IBGE/UNICEF/INAN.

————. 1992b. "Propostas de Política Social." Documento de Política 12. Brasília: IPEA.

————. 1993. "O Mapa da Fome: Subsídios à Formulação de uma Política de Segurança Alimentar." Documento de Política 14, IPEA, March 1993, Brasília.

Pfefferman, Guy. 1978. "Income Distribution and Poverty in Brazil." World Bank Reprint Series 254 (June).

Plano Collor. 1990. In Revista de Economia Política, 10, July–September): 114–48.

Plano de Estabilização Econômica. 1986. In Revista de Economia Politica 6 (July–September):109–151.

Psacharopoulos, George, and others. 1992. "Poverty and Income Distribution in Latin America: The Story of the 1980s." Latin American and Caribbean Technical Department Report 27. World Bank.

Ramos, Lauro. 1990. "The Distribution of Earnings in Brazil: 1976–85." Ph.D. dissertation, University of California, Berkeley.

Rocha, Sonia. 1988. "Linhas de Pobreza para as Regiões Metropolitanas Primeira Metade da Déca da de 80." Belo Horizonte, Anais da Anpec.

————. 1991. "Pobreza Metropolitana: Balanço de uma Década." In Perspectivas da Economia Brasileira - 1991. Brasilia: IPEA.

————. (1992). "Poor and Non-Poor in the Brazilian Labor Market." Texto Para Discussão 278. Rio de Janeiro: IPEA.

Saboia, Joao L. M.. 1984. "Evolução Histórica do Salário Mínimo no Brasil: Fixação, Valor real e Diferenciação Regional." Programa Nacional de Pesquisa Econômica Séries 15.

Shorrocks, Anthony. 1983. "Ranking Income Distributions." Economica 50: 3–17.

Silva, Nelson, and Carlos Hasenbalg. 1992. "Pobreza e Desigualdade no Brasil nos Anos 80." paper prepared for the conference Estintisms Libernio de Refundacao: Dilemas Contempornneos de Des. Rio de Janeiro: IUPERJ.

Simões, Celso. 1989. "Novas Estimativas da Mortalidade Infantil, 1980–87." In Perfil Estatístico de Crianças e Mães no Brasil: Mortalidade Infantil e Saúde na Década de 80. Rio de Janeiro: IBGE/UNICEF.

Simões, Celso, and L. Ortiz. 1988. "A Mortalidade Infantil no Brasil dos anos 80." In Crise e Infância no Brasil: O Impacto das Políticas de Ajustamento Econômico. São Paulo: UNICEF/IPE - USP.

Thomas, Vinod. 1982. "Differences in Income, Nutrition, and Poverty within Brazil," World Bank Staff Working Paper 505.

Tolosa, H. 1991. "Pobreza no Brasil: Uma Avaliação dos Anos 80" In A Questão Social no Brasil. São Paulo: Nobel.

UNDP (United Nations Development Program). 1992. Human Development Report. Oxford University Press.

World Bank. 1991. World Development Report: The Challenge of Development. Oxford University Press.

————. 1992. World Development Report: Development and the Environment. Oxford University Press.

CHAPTER EIGHT

Chile: Poverty, Adjustment, and Social Policies in the 1980s

Dagmar Raczynski and Pilar Romaguera

As is well known, poverty and inequality are long-term structural problems that depend not only on current income, employment, and access to social services, but also on enduring features of socioeconomic structure, including the rural-urban distribution, the relative importance of traditional and modern activities, and inequality in the distribution of assets and opportunities. The Latin American experience, in the wake of the debt crisis, has also shown that poverty and inequality can change dramatically in the short term.

The Chilean experience, in particular, illustrates how poverty and inequality, and the population's welfare in general, have been affected by macroeconomic policies and conditions; labor market conditions; and the nature and magnitude of public social expenditures and policies.

After analyzing Chile's adjustment and social policies during the 1980s, this chapter examines its challenges for the 1990s: to sustain economic growth, to reinforce its export-oriented strategy, and to foster its international eco-

This chapter has made extensive use of material prepared at CIEPLAN in research programs supported by the International Development Research Center (IDRC), the Ford Foundation, CEDEAL Foundation, and the Helen Kellogg Institute of International Relations, University of Notre Dame. The authors would like to thank Nicolas Flaño and Helena Ribe for their useful comments.

nomic competitiveness, while at the same time reversing trends toward income inequality and wealth concentration, strengthening poverty alleviation programs, and dealing with new social problems that necessarily emerge during the development process. These challenges, of course, fall to the newly elected democratic government, which has partly reoriented social programs.[1]

Chile is an interesting but complex case to analyze because of the many changes in the economy, the political system, and the institutional sphere that have taken place in the last twenty years. To understand what happened in the 1980s, it is important to refer to the past, so while the chapter's focus is the 1980s, frequent references link this period to the preceding decade.

Crisis, Adjustment, and Social Effects

During the 1980s Chile experienced profound economic, social, and political changes and transformations. First, the government deepened the process of structural reform that began in the 1970s and instituted new reforms in social policy. Second, the economy underwent a cycle of boom, bust, and recovery, prompting a broad package of adjustment policies after the 1982 crisis. The third important event occurred at the end of the decade, after sixteen years of authoritarian rule, with the election of a democratic government and the new challenges this raised.

In this section we focus on how changes in the economic sphere, including both structural reforms and macroeconomic conditions, affected the labor situation and the population's standard of living. This section thus establishes the economic context in which social policies—the subject of the following section—developed and evolved.

Economic Policy, Performance, and Reform

The reforms initiated after the military coup of 1973 were to transform the Chilean economy from one of the most regulated into one of the most deregulated economies in Latin America. These reforms aimed at decontrolling the price system, privatizing public enterprises, reducing the role of the state, and liberalizing international trade and financial markets.[2] Table 8-1 presents the

---

1. This chapter was written in 1992. The "newly elected" government has since been replaced by a new president.

2. For details on the reforms see Corbo (1985); de la Cuadra and Hachette (1988); Edwards and Edwards (1987); French-Davis (1982); and Foxley (1983).

Table 8-1. *Major Structural Reforms in Chile, 1970s*

Situation 1972–73	Post-1973
	Privatization
More than 500 commercial firms and banks controlled by the state.	By 1980 only 25 firms (including one bank) remaining in public sector.
	Prices and exchange rates
Price controls.	Market-determined prices except wages (official adjustments) and exchange rate.
	Trade and exchange rates
Multiple exchange rate system. Prohibitions and quotas on imports. High tariff (average 94 percent, maximum 200 percent). Prior deposits for imports.	Homogeneous, unified exchange rate. Flat import tariff of 10 percent (excluding automobiles). Absence of other trade barriers.
	Fiscal regime
"Cascade" sales tax. Large public payroll. Large fiscal deficits.	Value-added tax of 20 percent. Public employment reduced. Fiscal surpluses in 1979–81.
	Domestic financial markets
Controlled interest rates. State ownership of banks. Control of credit.	Market-determined interest rates. Reprivatization of banks. Liberalization of capital markets.
	Capital mobility
Total control of capital movements. Government the main external borrower.	Gradual liberalization of capital account. Private sector the main external borrower.
	Labor regime
Unions play large role and have considerable bargaining power. Worker dismissals prohibited. Mandatory wage increases. High and increasing nonwage labor costs (40 percent of wages).	No unions and no collective bargaining power (until 1979). Relaxation of prohibition on dismissals. Severe cuts in real wages. Reduction of nonwage labor costs (to 30 percent of wages).

Source: Meller (1990, p. 55).

main structural reforms of the 1970s. During the 1980s the process continued, as the government tried both to correct errors in financial regulation after the crisis of 1982-83 and to strengthen the market economy through a new privatization process and social policy reforms.[3]

Along with reducing the size of the state, the military government enforced a policy of fiscal balance through both a decrease in spending and an increase in revenue. To achieve the latter objective, it implemented several tax reforms

3. For more details, see Meller and Romaguera (1992); and Meller (1992).

that simplified the tax system, increased the importance of indirect taxes, and modified the administrative system. The reforms sought to increase the system's economic efficiency, giving only secondary importance to the objective of equity.[4]

Trade liberalization, which included reductions in import tariffs and the elimination of nontariff barriers, was complete by 1979 when the government established a flat 10 percent tariff on all imports except automobiles. These policies led to changes in the composition of production, reducing the relative importance of the industrial sector while increasing that of the financial, service, and natural resource export sectors.[5]

Liberalization of the financial system was another central element in the new economic model. The reforms allowed the creation of nonbank financial institutions; the privatization of state banks; market determination of interest rates; and the elimination of quantitative credit controls. The next step, taken a few years later, was the elimination of restrictions on foreign debt, which started to decrease noticeably in 1978. In 1980 all restrictions were lifted except for those on short-term credit, which were eliminated by the end of 1981.[6] These reforms prompted a spectacular increase in both financial activity and private sector indebtedness, which later was one of the triggers of the 1982 financial crisis.

Conditions in the labor market also changed under the military government. During 1973–79 it prohibited union activity, collective bargaining, and strikes. It also modified wages according to official decrees that often included only partial indexation for past inflation. In 1979 a labor plan allowed for collective bargaining and the right to strike under restricted conditions and introduced wage indexation for workers who bargained collectively. These indexing measures drew heavy criticism when the economy went into recession, and the government finally eliminated them in 1982.[7]

Chile's economy over the past decades was marked not only by profound structural reforms but also by great instability in its principal macroeconomic indicators. Figure 8-1 traces the level of GDP from 1970 to 1990, illustrating the cyclical behavior of boom and bust. There have been two serious recessions—in 1975 and 1982—and significant growth followed both. The pattern of unstable growth produced instability in employment and wages, favored income concentration, and had a high social cost. The structural reforms out-

4. See Yañez (1992); and Marfán (1988).
5. See Gatica and Pollack (1986).
6. See Butelmann (1992).
7. See Mizala and Romaguera (1991).

Figure 8-1. *GDP Growth, Chile, 1970–90*
Billions of 1977 pesos

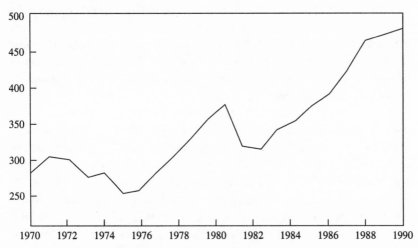

Sources: Banco Central de Chile (1989, p. 17). Figures for 1989–90 are from Banco Central de Chile (1992, p. 1920).

lined above also encouraged the process of capital concentration.[8]

At the beginning of the 1980s there was great optimism among economic authorities about Chile's future. The principal structural reforms were complete, and growth since 1977 was much higher than the historic rate. Nevertheless, some indicators revealed latent problems; the most visible ones were persistent unemployment, very high interest rates, and high (but stable) inflation.[9] At the beginning of the 1980s the economy showed the first symptoms of what would later be a crisis of excessive demand, stimulated by strong liquidity, overly optimistic expectations, and high internal and external debt.

In 1982 Chile faced its worst crisis since the recession of the 1930s, and its

8. Data for 1978–81 showed a significant concentration of wealth, with two economic groups well ahead of the rest. At the end of 1978 the two main economic groups controlled enterprises representing around 50 percent of the wealth of all corporations registered on the Chilean stock exchanges. Among other factors, the privatization process and financial liberalization encouraged this concentration by giving these groups preferential access to foreign loans. See French-Davis and Raczynski (1990, pp. 31–32). For a detailed account of the process of asset concentration see Dahse (1979).

9. The average short-term interest rate was 30.9 percent annually during 1976–80 and 38.8 percent in 1981. The inflation rate was 30.3 percent in 1978, 38.9 percent in 1979, and 31.2 percent in 1980; only in 1981 did it decrease to 9.5 percent. The average unemployment rate for 1976-79 was 17.8 percent (including emergency employment programs), whereas the historical average fluctuated around 6–7 percent.

second serious crisis since the military government came to power. GDP fell
14.1 percent, and the insolvency of the financial system led the government to
intervene in the country's most important banks. Like other economies in the
region, Chile confronted a triple external shock in 1982: high interest rates,
deteriorating terms of trade, and the closing of international financial markets.
However, the international situation seemed to be the catalyst for a latent internal crisis that resulted from problems in economic policy and in the implementation of some structural reforms.

The first symptoms of the crisis appeared at the beginning of 1981 with the
financial system's solvency problems and the growing trade deficit. Also, at
the end of 1981 the capital inflows that had made it possible to finance the current account deficit started to decrease abruptly. This reduction in external
credit at first reflected the international banking community's concern with the
increase in Chilean payment risk due to the evolution of its external accounts.
Later, after the Mexican debt crisis, it also reflected the general decrease in
credit for all Latin American countries. The drop in the inflow of external capital produced an unsustainable reduction in international reserves.

The government's initial response was a policy of "automatic adjustment"
that did not work. Internal prices never adjusted downward to compensate for
the loss in value of the domestic currency. It became impossible to maintain
the fixed exchange rate because of the continuous loss of reserves. In response
to the crisis the government then tried several policies, including peso devaluations, the elimination of wage indexing, and greater financial regulation.
Later it modified exchange rate policy several times; restricted foreign currency transactions; purchased overdue, risky portfolios from private banks;
and fixed a preferential dollar rate for debtors in dollars. In the middle of the
financial crisis (January 1983), the government intervened in the operation of
five banks, liquidating two banks and placing under state supervision a private
investment bank and two other banks.[10]

The government also negotiated payments on private international loans. In
April 1983 it concluded its first agreement with international banks. The deal
included the reprogramming of payments on foreign loans and fresh money to
cover in part interest payments on loans from multilateral organizations. The
government also promised to guarantee private sector foreign loans.

At the beginning of 1985, after changes in economic authority, the government reinitiated a process of internal spending adjustment. The priority during
this period was to strengthen the external sector through policies of real deval-

10. For an analysis of the regulatory problems of the financial reform and the system's "endogenous" crisis, see Held (1990).

Table 8-2. *Macroeconomic Indicators, Chile, 1980–90*

Year	GDP growth (percent)	Inflation rate (percent)	Balance of payments (millions of dollars)	Terms of trade (1980=100)	Labor rate[a]
1980	7.8	31.2	1.244	100.0	14.2
1981	5.5	9.5	67	87.4	16.7
1982	-14.1	20.7	-1.165	75.3	13.4
1983	-0.7	23.1	-541	82.1	9.9
1984	6.3	23.0	17	76.4	11.2
1985	2.4	26.4	-99	71.1	8.6
1986	5.6	17.4	-228	77.2	6.8
1987	6.6	21.5	45	80.9	7.3
1988	7.4	12.7	732	98.9	8.1
1989	9.9	21.4	437	97.1	9.3
1990	3.3	27.3	2.368	n.d.	8.3

Sources: Meller and Romaguera (1992, pp. 53–54); Banco Central de Chile (1994a, 1994b).
a. At 180 days. Data are from Banco Central de Chile (1989; 1992, p. 1858).

uation, tariff reduction, export promotion, loans from multilateral organizations, as well as internal austerity.

As of 1986 the economy began a process of sustained recovery, and GDP grew during 1986–89 at an average annual rate of 7.4 percent. This expansion coincided with an increase in state regulation. New legislation in the financial sector discriminated among banks according to their risk portfolios, strengthened their capital situation, and permitted a sustained decrease in domestic interest rates in the context of reduced international rates.

The recovery in the terms of trade, the decrease in interest rates, the reorganization of the financial system, and the increase in international credit, plus a macroeconomic policy that showed greater concern for domestic and foreign balances, all had a favorable impact on economic growth (see table 8-2).

Social and Distributive Effects

The economic reforms of the 1970s and 1980s, the economic cycles, and the adjustment policies that followed the crisis of 1982 all had significant social and distributive effects. Privatization programs increased the concentration of property. Tax reforms, which increased the importance of indirect taxes and eliminated other taxes, also seem to have contributed to income concentration. The rescue of the financial system and the initiation of subsidies to debtors committed important fiscal resources to high-income sectors. Further, the decrease in public spending naturally affected some sectors more than others. Changes in relative prices also had distributive effects.[11] Finally, Chile's economic recessions caused increases in unemployment and decreases in real wages.

PUBLIC EXPENDITURES AND FISCAL ADJUSTMENT. The macroeconomic conditions and debt problems of 1982 led to an important fiscal adjustment that directly influenced employment and wages in the public sector, as well as social expenditures. Before the foreign debt shock, the public sector maintained a balance and even a surplus in its fiscal accounts.[12] Fiscal deficits began to appear in 1982 as a result of the decrease in tax revenues associated with the recession, the decline in the world price of copper, and the significant increase in debt-service payments caused by the transfer of debt from the private to the public sector. The deficit emerged despite the spending cuts that accompanied the adjustment process.

Although the fiscal deficit fluctuated within a moderate range—especially the net deficit, which excludes debt-service payments—the fiscal adjustment was more severe than these figures indicate, because during that period public spending increased in several other areas. Among these additional expenditures were emergency employment programs, whose cost fluctuated between 1 and 1.5 percent of GDP; the 1981 reform of the social security system, which generated a sustained annual operating deficit that fluctuated between 3 and 4 percent of GDP; the quasi-fiscal subsidies provided by the Central Bank to resolve the financial crisis, which surpassed 4 percent of GDP for several years; and foreign debt-service payments, which rose from 0.5 percent to almost 3 percent of public expenditures after 1981.[13]

Several public sector variables presented in table 8-3 demonstrate that these additional expenditures were possible because of the decrease in employment and real wages in the public sector, the reduction in social expenditures, and the drop in the real value of pensions. The reduction in salaries and public employment affected a large group of medium- and low-income workers. The reduction in social expenditures affected the middle and lower social strata, although it did not necessarily affect the extremely poor.

---

11. The real devaluation in the 1980s disproportionately affected consumption by lower-income families, whose consumer basket is skewed toward tradable goods. See Meller (1992, pp. 75–76).

12. The surplus was 1.7, 3.0, and 1.7 percent of GDP in 1979, 1980, and 1981, respectively.

13. See Meller and Romaguera (1992, pp. 44–46).

Table 8-3. *Fiscal Deficit, Public Employment and Wages, and Social Expenditures, Chile, 1980–90*

Year	Fiscal gross (percent of GDP)	Deficit net[a] (percent of GDP)	Public employment (thousands)	Index of public sector wages[b]	Social expenditures (billions of 1986 pesos)
1980	3.0	4.2	335.9	93.8	564.8
1981	1.7	2.5	313.2	102.2	621.2
1982	-2.3	-1.3	305.2	109.0	676.4
1983	-3.8	-2.5	300.3	93.8	616.5
1984	-4.4	-2.4	300.7	94.4	628.4
1985	-6.9	-1.8	306.0	89.0	613.6
1986	-3.3	0.0	n.a.	85.9	599.1
1987	-0.5	2.9	n.a.	83.2	583.8
1988	-2.0	4.4	n.a.	90.5	603.9
1989	-1.3	5.5	n.a.	92.0	597.4
1990	1.3	3.1	n.a.	88.1	592.1

Sources: Fiscal deficit: Romaguera (1991, pp. 58–59). Wages: authors' calculations based on data in Banco Central de Chile (1991, pp. 1666–71); figures are deflated using Banco Central de Chile (1992, pp. 1968–69). Employment: Velásquez Pinto (1988). Social expenditures: Cabezas (1988, p. 24). From 1987 onward Cabezas's figures are updated using data from Ministry of Finance reproduced in Crispi and Marcel (1993).

a. Net of debt amortization. Negative figures represent a deficit, positive figures a surplus.

b. December 1982 = 100.

UNEMPLOYMENT AND WAGES. At the beginning of the 1980s the Chilean economy faced a serious unemployment problem, despite the strong growth of the 1977-79 period. The unemployment rate reached a historic peak after the 1975 recession and remained stubbornly high, at about 17 percent, including workers in government emergency employment programs (see table 8-4). Therefore, when evaluating the social cost of adjustment, it is necessary to consider that when the 1982 crisis occurred, unemployment levels were already high compared with historic patterns. That recession further increased unemployment, which reached a rate of 30 percent in 1983.

Emergency employment programs were first implemented in 1975 (the Programa de Empleo Mínimo, or PEM) and later extended to other segments of the population (the Programa Ocupacional para Jefes de Hogar, or POJH). These programs absorbed a significant percentage of unemployed workers. Despite the minimal income they provided,[14] they nevertheless played an

14. See Carol Graham (1991); and table 8-5. PEM was initially directed toward unemployed workers in general, giving priority in the selection process to heads of household. POJH specifically targeted unemployed heads of household. After the creation of the POJH program at the end of 1982, the PEM program assisted women and youths. The monthly income per beneficiary was higher in POJH than in the PEM program.

Table 8-4. *Unemployment and Wage Indicators, Chile,*
Selected Years, 1970–90

Year	Unemployment rate: open[a] (percent)	Unemployment rate: plus PEM and POJH[b] (percent)	Index of real wages[c]	Minimum income (April 1989 pesos per month)[d]
1970	5.7	n.a.	109.1	n.a.
1974	9.2	n.a.	64.1	15,407
1975	14.9	17.3	62.3	14,669
1976	12.7	18.1	78.6	16,259
1977	11.8	17.7	79.6	16,968
1978	14.2	18.4	84.7	20,031
1979	13.6	17.5	91.7	19,404
1980	10.4	15.7	99.6	19,437
1981	10.8	15.6	108.5	22,524
1982	19.6	28.0	108.2	22,663
1983	16.8	30.3	96.7	18,254
1984	15.4	24.4	96.8	15,601
1985	13.0	21.4	92.7	14,797
1986	10.8	16.0	94.6	14,301
1987	9.3	12.2	94.4	13,424
1988	8.3	9.0	100.6	14,386
1989	6.3	n.a.	102.5	15,999
1990	6.0	n.a.	104.4	17,090

Sources: Unemployment rate: authors' calculations based on data from INE; 1970 and 1974 figures are from Ministerio de Hacienda (1989, p. 67).

Real wages: authors' calculations based on Banco Central de Chile (1991, pp. 1666–71). Figures are deflated using Cortazar and Marshall (1980, pp. 199–200); and Banco Central de Chile (1992, pp. 1968–69).

Minimum income: authors' calculations based on Banco Central de Chile, *Indicadores* (1960–88). Figures for 1975 and 1976 are from Banco Central de Chile, *Indicadores* (1960–82, p. 164). Figures for 1988–90 are from Banco Central de Chile (1992, p. 269). Figures are deflated using same sources as above.

n.a. Not available.

a. Unemployment data correspond to the following periods: 1970–74, ODEPLAN yearly estimation; 1975, May–December; 1976–80 and 1982: October–December; 1981, April–June and October–December; 1983, May–December; 1984–90, January–December.

b. PEM and POJH are goverment employment emergency programs.

c. December 1982 = 100.

d. Owing to the effects of the provisions of social security reform, starting in March 1981 the minimum wage was increased by 20 percent.

important role in the survival strategies of the poor (see table 8-5).[15]

Chile has a very limited unemployment insurance system, both in coverage and the amount of the subsidy. Programs like the PEM and the POJH, in practice, thus replaced unemployment insurance for those in the less-skilled sectors. This fact raises questions regarding the population's survival strategies during long periods without income, and it also explains the growth in the informal sector observed in the 1980s. Estimates of the size of the informal sector indicate that it fluctuated between 30 to 35 percent of the labor force be-

15. On survival strategies, see Raczynski and Serrano (1985).

Table 8-5. *Employment Emergency Programs, Chile, 1975–88*

| | Labor force emergency programs beneficiaries | | | Real value of the subsidy (1988 pesos per month) | |
Year	PEM (thousands)	POJH (thousands)	Total as percent of labor force	PEM	POJH
1975	72.7	n.a.	2.3	12,920	n.a.
1976	172.0	n.a.	5.4	11,746	n.a.
1977	187.7	n.a.	5.9	8,397	n.a.
1978	145.8	n.a.	4.2	6,333	n.a.
1979	133.9	n.a.	3.9	5,775	n.a.
1980	190.7	n.a.	5.2	5,494	n.a.
1981	175.6	n.a.	4.8	4,680	n.a.
1982	226.8	81.2	8.4	5,403	13,099
1983	341.6	161.2	13.5	5,147	10,293
1984	167.6	168.7	9.0	4,294	8,588
1985	134.3	190.0	8.4	4,928	8,213
1986	81.0	140.4	5.2	4,125	6,874
1987	35.7	88.4	2.9	3,441	5,734
1988	9.0	24.9	0.8	3,000	5,000

Sources: PEM and POJH participation data are from Banco Central de Chile, *Indicadores* (1960–88) (1989, pp. 301–06). Value of subsidy calculated using Banco Central de Chile (1989, p. 2522); and Banco Central de Chile, *Indicadores* 1960–85 (1986, p. 229). Deflators are from Cortazar and Marshall (1980); and Banco Central de Chile (1992).

tween 1980 and 1985. And when hiring in emergency employment programs slowed, employment in the informal sector increased. Unemployment was concentrated among young people between 15 and 24 years of age; adults who had not completed high school; and in certain communities.[16]

The main policy designed to stimulate employment sought to reduce labor costs. This policy initially involved subsidies for employers that hired new workers and a decrease in employers' social security payments. After 1982 the government also eliminated indexation and the wage floor for collective bargaining and decreased both the real minimum wage and public wages.[17]

The growth of the economy, which began in 1984, led to continuous drops in the unemployment rate. Among the factors that contributed to the recovery of employment were slower growth in labor supply, relative expansion of labor-intensive sectors, and increased flexibility in the labor market.[18]

16. See Romaguera (1989); and Sanfuentes (1988). It is interesting to note that among youths fifteen to twenty-four years old the unemployed are not necessarily less educated.

17. Although until 1982 the public sector played a leading role in determining wages in the private sector, these policy measures eliminated that role. Empirical estimates indicate that the public sector lost its leadership role in setting salaries in 1982, becoming a follower of private sector wages. See Mizala and Romaguera (1991).

18. Another hypothesis is that during a sectoral shock, such as trade liberalization, the increase in unemployment is more persistent than during an aggregate shock such as the debt crisis.

Figure 8-2. *Real Wage Indexes, Chile, 1970–90*
December 1982 = 100

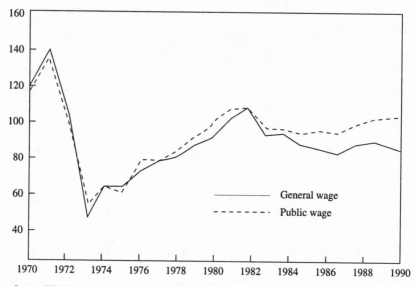

Sources: INE; Cortázar and Marshall (1980); and Schmidt-Hebbel and Marshall (1981).

The evolution of salaries, like the evolution of unemployment, was strongly procyclical, but it also showed the strong impact of inflation on the deterioration in real wages. Figure 8-2 shows the evolution of the general and the public sector wage indexes between 1970 and 1990. In 1974 real wages (before the first recession) were very low, as the hyperinflation of 1972–73 had caused reductions of almost 50 percent. Between 1976 and 1981 wages showed a sustained recovery, but then dropped after the 1982 recession. The economic expansion that began in 1984 was accompanied by a slow recovery in real wages and by an especially severe drop in public-sector wages.

INCOME DISTRIBUTION AND POVERTY. The persistence of high levels of unemployment for long periods of time and the severe drop and slow recovery of real wages led to a deterioration in workers' standards of living. One of the most illustrative indicators of the population's standard of living is per capita consumption. The evolution of the per capita consumption index over the past fifteen years, presented in figure 8-3, shows that cycles of economic activity directly affect consumption levels. At the beginning of the 1980s per capita consumption returned to its 1970 level after having fallen during the severe re-

Figure 8-3. *Index of Consumption per Capita, Chile, 1974–89*
1970 = 100

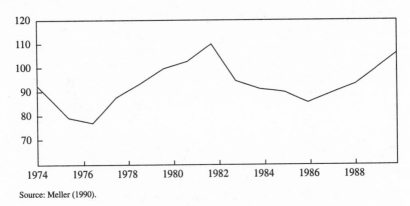

Source: Meller (1990).

cession of 1975–76. Consumption then deteriorated due to the 1981 crisis, and in 1989 the index remained 4 points below the decade's peak in 1981.

The drop in aggregate consumption coincided with a relative deterioration in the distribution of expenditures across income groups. Table 8-6 presents figures on the distribution of household expenditures in greater Santiago in 1969, 1978, and 1988. The figures reveal the progressive deterioration in income distribution, which hurt both low- and medium-income sectors (the poorest 60 percent of the population). This deterioration was progressive and occurred in both absolute and relative terms. The poorest 20 percent of the population thus saw its relative share of total expenditure fall from 7.6 percent in 1969 to 5.2 percent in 1978 and then to 4.4 percent in 1988. This trend accompanied an absolute drop in household spending, which for the lowest quintile implied a reduction of nearly 50 percent in the level of spending between 1969 and 1988.

A final indicator, and perhaps the most conclusive one, of the deterioration in the population's standard of living was the high incidence of poverty in the 1980s despite progress in other areas of the economy. Table 8-7 shows the percentage of households in conditions of poverty or indigence.

The comparison of poverty indexes based on studies by different authors naturally presents difficulties, although most authors use a similar criterion, defining poverty and indigence based on nutritional requirements. One of the biggest differences is that the CEPAL studies adjust income for underreporting, which explains why its poverty estimates are lower (and probably more realistic) than those of studies that use direct income data.

Table 8-6. *Household Expenditures, by Income Quintiles, Greater Santiago, 1969, 1978, 1988*
Thousands of June 1988 pesos unless otherwise specified

Quintiles	1969		1978		1988	
	Pesos	Percent	Pesos	Percent	Pesos	Percent
1 (lowest)	28,617	7.6	19,767	5.2	16,656	4.4
2	44,532	11.8	35,431	9.3	31,255	8.2
3	58,893	15.6	51,832	13.6	48,182	12.7
4	77,636	20.6	79,904	21.0	76,638	20.1
5 (highest)	168,003	44.5	194,372	51.0	207,749	54.6
Average	75,536	...	76,262	...	76,094	...

Sources: INE, *Encuesta de Presupuestos Familiares* (1969, 1978, 1988); and French-Davis and Raczynski (1990, p. 35).

These studies indicate a noteworthy increase in poverty between 1970 and 1990, which is consistent with previous studies of expenditure distribution by income quintile. Moreover, while the economy expanded at a high rate—6.3 percent a year from 1987 to 1990—the reduction in poverty was quite small, from 38 percent to 34 percent.

These negative trends in the evolution of poverty stand in contrast to changes in standard of living based on unsatisfied housing needs. In Chile "extreme poverty" has been measured by a combination of four indicators: housing, crowding, sewage disposal, and possession of durable goods. According to this index, extreme poverty diminished from 21 percent of the population in 1970 to 14 percent in 1980, 13 percent in 1987, and 12 percent in 1990. The data show that four-fifths of the reduction in extreme poverty between 1970 and 1982 was the result of increases in the possession of durable goods, mainly television sets.[19] Various factors may explain this apparent paradox: change in relative prices of durable consumer goods; strong incentives toward the consumption of durable goods such as televisions, radios, and household appliances; and the fact that many of these goods are considered basic needs by families not able to satisfy other basic needs.

This discussion highlights the heterogeneity of poverty in Chile.[20] The characteristics of poverty significantly influence which policies are appropriate to combat it. First, analysis of the population's various needs (income, housing, and education) indicates that poverty is not uniform. Households that are poor

19. For a discussion see Raczynski (1986). The remaining one-fifth is mainly due to the way Chilean households cope with their income and shelter needs: joint housing arrangements with another family, known as *allegados*.
20. For further discussion see Raczynski (1992b); and León (1991).

Table 8-7. *Poor and Indigent Poor Households, Chile and Greater Santiago, Selected Years, 1969–90*[a]

Percent

Year	Indigent poor	Poor	Source
Chile			
1970	6.0	17.0	Altimir (1979, p. 63)
1983	30.3	n.a.	Rodríguez Grossi (1985, p. 38)
1985	25.0	45.0	Torche Lazo (1987, p. 175)
1987	13.5	38.2	CEPAL (1991, p. 15)
1990	11.6	34.5	CEPAL (1991, p. 15)
Greater Santiago			
1969	8.4	28.5	PREALC (1990)
1980	14.4	40.3	PREALC (1990)
1987	22.6	48.6	PREALC (1990)
1990 (metropolitan region)	8.8	29.9	CEPAL (1991, p. 15)

n.a. Not available.
a. Income includes monetary income of the family, including income transfers (monetary subsidies). In rural areas an estimate of self-production and consumption is also included.
   Indigent poor: Household income equal to or less than the cost of one minimum food consumption basket (a basket that meets the caloric and protein requirements). Poor: Household income is equal or less than the cost of two minimum food consumption baskets.

in income are not necessarily poor in education or housing. Households that are poor on all three dimensions are a minority, with 5 percent in urban areas and 15 percent in rural areas. Moreover, the urban poor tend to lack income alone, while the rural poor more frequently lack housing or education in addition to income, which is the definition of chronic poverty.[21] It is also possible to identify an important group of "vulnerable" households that are located near the poverty line and that are seriously affected by specific alterations in the labor market.[22]

Poverty is heterogenous not only at the level of needs, but also in terms of its geographical distribution. Although there are interregional differences in poverty, the biggest differences are intraregional; poverty is concentrated in certain urban communities within each region. This concentration of poverty and the high degree of spatial segregation of most cities, and especially Santiago, makes it possible to identify "pockets of poverty."[23]

In summary, the recession and macroeconomic conditions of the 1980s had high social costs in terms of increased unemployment, decreased real wages, deteriorating per capita household expenditures, and increased income inequality. One analyst has thus argued that the "Chilean structural adjustment

21. See Raczynski (1992b, p. 44).
22. Because the income distribution of households has a modal value very near the poverty line, marginal modifications in the value of the line generate significant changes in the count of poor. See León (1991, p. 47).
23. See León (1991, p. 23).

of the 1980s was implemented primarily through the labor market."[24] The next section examines the nature and results of Chile's social policies in the 1980s, with a focus on how they affected the welfare of the middle-income and poor population strata.

Social Policy Reforms and Expenditures

Starting in the 1920s Chile developed a system of social policies wherein the state gradually assumed direct responsibility not only for the formulation and financing of social policy but also for its execution. The philosophy behind the system was similar to that of a "welfare state" in which the whole population supposedly has access to services that are free or highly subsidized by the state.

The neoliberal economic model that dominated the country in the mid-1970s not only introduced radical changes in the economy but also transformed Chile's system of social policies. Like the structural economic reforms, social policy reforms were to make the state's role subsidiary; to broaden the market's role in the allocation of resources and provision of social services; and to decentralize the public sector by encouraging local or private participation in the management, administration, and delivery of health care, education, social security, housing, and other benefits.

In accordance with these aims, the government instituted major reforms of policies, institutions, and financing mechanisms in the social sectors. In addition, it reduced public social expenditures, designed well-targeted transfers as part of a social safety net for the poorest strata of the population, and tried to reallocate fiscal social expenditures to those groups. The government also defined small children as the priority group for its health, nutrition, and education programs. The following sections address in turn the evolution of public social spending, the nature of institutional and financial reforms in the social sector, and the distributive impact of these changes.[25]

Public Social Expenditures

Under the military government in the 1970s five decades of almost continuous expansion of public and social spending came to an end.[26] This policy

24. Meller (1992, p. 79).
25. This section draws heavily on Arellano (1985); and Raczynski (1992a).
26. Public social expenditures increased from 8 percent of GDP in 1945 to 25 percent in 1971–72. See Arellano (1985, p. 33).

reversal was a deliberate decision based on two strong beliefs: first, that the role of the state should be subsidiary and that social policies should do no more than support the poorest sectors of the population and correct the negative outcomes of the market system operations; and second, that balancing the fiscal budget and controlling inflation took priority over redistributive or social goals. Equity objectives were of secondary importance, and no income policy was considered.

There are two ways to restore and maintain fiscal balance: by decreasing expenditures, or by increasing revenues. In the 1970s the government did both. It implemented a tax reform, waged a successful campaign against tax evasion, and at the same time drastically reduced spending. In the 1980s its fiscal decisions were different. After the crisis of 1982-83, the government reduced social spending, which never significantly recovered. At the same time, it made no efforts to increase tax revenues. On the contrary, in the 1980s it made modifications that actually reduced the tax base.[27]

In keeping with the concept of a subsidiary state and fiscal constraints, public social spending (PSS) decreased in both absolute and per capita terms and as a percentage of GDP (tables 8-8 and 8-9). In every year from 1974 to 1989 except 1982 per capita PSS was below its 1970 level. In 1989 PSS represented 14 percent of GDP, which was lower than its 1970 and 1980 levels. Nevertheless, in accordance with the dictum that public policy should primarily benefit the poorer sectors of society, PSS decreased less than total public spending.[28]

The setback in PSS was particularly strong in housing, education, and health. In these three sectors per capita PSS declined considerably in the mid-1970s, increased between 1977 and 1982 (without reaching its 1970 level), and fell again in the 1980s.[29]

Two sectors of PSS followed a different course, actually surpassing the 1970 level for several years during the 1974–89 period. One is the residual sector, "other," which is very small and includes components of the social net-

27. See Marfán (1988); and Yáñez (1992).

28. The evolution of social expenditure under the military government has caused controversy and debate within the country. When estimating its social spending, the military government almost always cited figures on fiscal expenditures. As a result of accounting modifications in some programs, which were in part a product of the government's institutional reforms, fiscal spending effectively increased while public social expenditures decreased. Figures on public social expenditures in health and social security, however, are not strictly comparable over time after the privatization reforms of the 1980s.

29. Figures on PSS in health in the 1980s exaggerate the drop in health expenditures because they do not factor in the creation of the private health insurance system of ISAPRES. With their creation part of the mandatory social security health contributions were privatized.

Table 8-8. *Public per Capita Social Expenditures, Chile, Selected Years, 1970–93*

1992 pesos unless otherwise indicated

Year	Education	Health	Social Security	Housing	Other	Total	Percent of total expenditures[a]	Percent of GDP
1970	39,503	21,601	81,735	16,578	910	160,328	57.1	21.7
1974	31,545	18,712	48,684	21,527	1,159	121,626	48.8	17.6
1975	24,967	14,498	49,543	12,288	357	101,653	55.3	18.3
1976	26,693	13,543	48,992	9,084	926	99,238	57.0	15.9
1977	31,171	14,650	56,029	10,181	1,830	113,861	60.6	17.4
1978	32,797	16,202	67,008	9,517	1,562	127,086	56.7	16.0
1979	35,886	15,952	74,852	11,881	1,903	140,474	58.4	15.6
1980	35,033	17,789	77,898	11,809	1,924	144,453	59.8	17.0
1981	36,384	16,152	90,509	11,684	1,588	156,318	60.7	18.5
1982	36,753	16,941	104,281	8,193	1,232	167,401	59.0	22.4
1983	31,125	13,479	96,735	6,785	1,872	149,996	64.2	21.1
1984	30,088	14,241	96,398	7,925	1,640	150,292	63.5	21.3
1985	29,858	13,745	88,243	10,876	1,573	144,296	61.6	19.8
1986	28,087	13,428	85,196	10,186	1,649	138,546	60.0	18.4
1987	27,601	18,213	60,811	8,493	16,260	131,378	64.1	16.7
1988	26,956	20,849	61,346	11,120	13,383	133,653	61.3	15.2
1989	26,275	20,614	61,983	10,418	10,747	130,037	63.1	14.0
1990	24,717	19,361	62,095	10,237	10,391	126,802	66.7	14.0
1991	27,220	22,440	63,532	11,971	11,268	136,430	66.7	14.5
1992	31,602	26,535	68,181	13,310	13,010	152,638	65.4	14.7
1993[b]	31,774	29,149	73,114	14,186	15,087	163,310	n.a.	15.3

Sources: For 1970–86, Cabezas (1988); and Marshall (1981). For 1987–93, Crispi and Marcel (1993). Percent of total expenditures and percent of GDP for 1970–86 are from authors' calculations based on sources cited and data from Ministry of Finance. It is not possible to reconcile the two data series.

n.a. Not available.

a. Excludes interest payments on the public debt.

b. Preliminary.

Table 8-9. *Public Social Expenditures as Share of GDP, by Sector, Chile, Selected Years, 1970–92*
Percent

Year	Education	Health	Social security	Housing	Other	Total
1970	5.3	2.9	11.1	2.2	0.1	21.7
1974	4.6	2.7	7.0	3.1	0.2	17.6
1975	4.5	2.6	8.9	2.2	0.1	18.3
1976	4.3	2.2	7.9	1.5	0.1	15.9
1977	4.8	2.2	8.6	1.6	0.3	17.4
1978	4.1	2.0	8.4	1.2	0.2	16.0
1979	4.0	1.8	8.3	1.3	0.2	15.6
1980	4.1	2.1	9.2	1.4	0.2	17.0
1981	4.3	1.9	10.7	1.4	0.2	18.5
1982	4.9	2.3	13.9	1.1	0.2	22.4
1983	4.4	1.9	13.6	1.0	0.2	21.1
1984	4.3	2.0	13.7	1.1	0.2	21.3
1985	4.1	1.9	12.1	1.5	0.2	19.8
1986	3.7	1.8	11.3	1.3	0.2	18.4
1987	3.5	2.3	7.7	1.1	2.1	16.7
1988	3.1	2.4	7.0	1.3	1.5	15.2
1989	2.8	2.2	6.7	1.1	1.2	14.0
1990	2.7	2.1	6.9	1.1	1.1	14.0
1991	2.9	2.4	6.7	1.3	1.2	14.5
1992	3.0	2.6	6.6	1.3	1.3	14.7

Sources: See table 8-8.

work not included in education, health, or housing. Its most significant component is the public emergency employment programs. The second sector whose spending increased was social security. Per capita expenditure in this sector decreased 40 percent in 1974–76 and recovered vigorously afterward. In 1981–82 social security expenditures were 19 percent higher than in 1970. Factors behind this increase, however, include the aging population and, most important, the 1980 social security reform. Between 1983 and 1989 social security spending decreased somewhat compared to 1981–82.

The sectoral distribution of social expenditures shows that social security has the greatest share. The second most important sector is education, followed by health and housing (table 8-10).

Information on the composition of expenditures in each sector reveals that spending on investment and wages decreased greatly. For example, capital investment in health fell from 9–10 percent of total public health expenditures

Table 8-10. *Distribution of Public Social Expenditures, by Sector, Chile,
Selected Years, 1970–92*
Percent

Year	Education	Health	Social security	Housing	Other
1970	24.6	13.5	51.0	10.3	0.6
1974	25.9	15.4	40.0	17.7	1.0
1975	24.6	14.3	48.7	12.1	0.3
1976	26.9	13.7	49.4	9.2	0.9
1977	27.4	12.9	49.2	8.9	1.6
1978	25.8	12.8	52.7	7.5	1.2
1979	25.6	11.4	53.3	8.5	1.3
1980	24.3	12.3	53.9	8.2	1.3
1981	23.3	10.3	57.9	7.5	1.0
1982	22.0	10.1	62.3	4.9	0.7
1983	20.8	9.0	64.5	4.5	1.2
1984	20.0	9.5	64.1	5.3	1.1
1985	20.7	9.5	61.2	7.5	1.1
1986	20.3	9.7	61.5	7.3	1.2
1987	21.0	13.9	46.3	6.5	12.4
1988	20.2	15.6	45.9	8.3	10.0
1989	20.2	15.8	47.7	8.0	8.3
1990	19.5	15.3	49.0	8.1	8.2
1991	19.9	16.4	46.6	8.8	8.3
1992	20.7	17.4	44.7	8.7	8.5

Sources: See table 8-8.

around 1970 to 2–4 percent during 1974–88.[30] Investments that should have
been made in view of the increase in population and deterioration in existing
infrastructure were only made to a minimal degree. This situation led to a crisis in the health sector in 1984–85, when several regional medical associations
publicly denounced the deterioration in the infrastructure and technology of
hospitals as well as the shortage of medicine, personnel, and supplies. In addition, the health sector experienced cuts in personnel and wages.[31]

In education the level of wages, which has been low throughout the country's history, deteriorated even further. In 1990 teachers' minimum salaries
were more than 50 percent lower than in 1980.[32] In other words, part of the reduction in spending meant lower pay and unemployment for workers in edu-

30. Marshall (1981); and Marcel (1984).
31. See Jiménez (1985); and Romero (1985).
32. Espínola (1991, p. 17).

cation and health; another part meant postponing investments in infrastructure and equipment.

Institutional Reform in the Social Sectors

It is impossible to detail and analyze all aspects of social reforms during the 1980s within this chapter. Generally, the reforms broadened the market's role in allocating resources and restructured the institutions responsible for delivering social services and programs. We focus on the reforms that constrained the fiscal budget, directly affected the poorer social strata, or generated new channels for the delivery of social services. The five policy areas we examine in turn are social security, health, housing, the delegation of responsibility to municipal governments, and the selection of targeting strategies.

SOCIAL SECURITY. Historically, Chile had a pay-as-you-go social security system.[33] It began to evolve in the 1920s, gradually incorporating new segments of the population over time. By 1970 the system covered a large proportion of the labor force (70 to 75 percent), but there were enormous internal inequities in benefits and contributions. The system included more than thirty different social security agencies, or *cajas*, that were either public or semipublic. Each one was responsible for a specific category of wage earners.

Participation in the system was mandatory for wage earners. It was financed by payroll contributions from employers and workers and also by fiscal subsidies. Over time the system accumulated many defects: inefficiency, financial deficits, unjustified inequalities, inflated labor costs, and pensions much lower than salaries. One problem that had to be faced in the short term was the financial impasse the system would reach when the ratio of active to inactive participants decreased as a consequence of the aging population.

During the 1970s the military government introduced changes in the existing system designed to correct the most evident inequalities.[34] In 1981 the old pay-as-you-go system was replaced with an individual capitalization system administered by the private sector. In the new system pensions are determined by the contributions workers make throughout their working life. Administra-

---

33. This section draws from Arellano (1985, chapters 2 and 3).

34. These measures included making the family allowance and the minimum pension the same for different categories of workers; defining a uniform system to adjust pensions; eliminating retirement by seniority and fixing uniform retirement ages for all categories of workers (sixty-five for men and sixty for women); and partially standardizing contribution rates and decreasing the rate paid by employers.

tion of contributions was transferred to the private sector, and specifically to pension fund administration companies (AFPs), which are corporations dedicated exclusively to administering their affiliates' funds in the financial market. The state regulates and supervises the system's operation. For example, it defines the kind of capital market instruments funds can be invested in; guarantees a minimum return to affiliates; and provides a minimum pension to workers who, despite twenty years of payments during their working life, are not able to finance a pension above the legally established minimum.[35]

A worker's affiliation with an AFP is an individual choice made freely at all times. As of May 1981 wage earners participating in the social security system for the first time were obliged to pay into an AFP. Workers who had participated in the old system were allowed to choose whether to stay in that system or to transfer to the new one. In the latter case, the government issued a "recognition bond" for payments already made.

There was a voluntary, rapid, and massive transfer of wage earners to the new system. Two factors encouraged this move. First, there was general discontent with the old system, which was compounded by the decline in benefits (pension and family allowance) that took place during the years before the reform (see table 8-11). Second, when a worker changed systems he or she automatically received an increase in his or her net wage. Those who changed to an AFP only had to contribute 16.5 percent of their salary, while those that remained in the old system had to pay 25.6 percent. The decrease in the payment rate was possible due to previous modifications: the elimination of retirement by seniority and the definition of minimum retirement ages for men (65 years) and women (60 years). These modifications made it possible to reduce the contribution rate in both the old and the new system. The law, however, restricted the decrease to affiliates of the new system, imposing a penalty on those who stayed in the old one.

By 1990 fourteen AFPs were operating, and each had accumulated sizable funds. In 1984 the funds accumulated by all AFPs totaled almost 9 percent of GDP, while in 1990 the total was 26 percent of GDP.[36] This figure, however, will decrease as the system matures and the AFPs begin to pay pensions on a massive scale.

The accumulation of social security savings has had important consequences for Chile's financial and capital markets and also for the distribution of property and control of capital. Most affiliates belong to one of four AFPs

35. Arellano (1985, p. 160).
36. See Iglesias and others (1991, pp. 39, 81).

Table 8-11. *Pensions and Family Allowance, Chile, 1970–91*[a]
1990 pesos

	Pensions				Family allowance		Safety net family allowance
		Average monthly value		Social safety net pensions	Monthly average		Monthly average number paid[c]
Year	Total number paid	Civilian[b]	Minimum pension	Number	Average monthly value	number paid	Unit value	
1970	614.2	31354	17150	...	...	...	2429[d]	...
1974	750.3	16184	14518	...	...	...	2547	...
1975	810.2	15812	13916	27.8	5772	...	2448	...
1976	862.0	16475	14684	39.0	7000	...	2274	...
1977	915.6	17964	16046	66.0	6989	...	2118	...
1978	975.5	19580	18954	91.8	6726	...	2061	...
1979	1022.8	22734	18360	113.1	6465	...	1993	...
1980	1071.6	23417	18749	131.7	8807	...	1997	...
1981	1126.4	24582	19117	156.2	9819	3962	1987	...
1982	1189.9	26327	18958	183.9	10474	3871	1944	...
1983	1263.7	26229	18344	229.4	9901	3929	1564	527
1984	1314.8	28264	19139	279.1	10455	3990	1537	699
1985	1375.5	25475	17296	321.5	9202	4026	1337	1041
1986	1382.2	26072	17408	324.7	9059	4024	1119	1086
1987	1366.4	25568	16823	319.3	7398	4015	933	1002
1988	1325.4	26585	17228	291.6	8359	3817	814	914
1989	1322.9	27724	17092	292.9	7840	3777	696	896
1990	1321.2	28040	18428	293.8	8333	3976	826[e]	892
1991	1313.0	30065	20556	289.1	9430	4021	903	879

Sources: Arellano (1989); and Superintendencia de Seguridad Social, *Estadística de Seguridad Social* (various issues).
a. Pension paid by the old social security system. In 1990 the new system paid 146,000 pensions, while the old one, excluding the social assistance pension, paid 1,028,000. Because the new system has been in operation for less than ten years, the monthly value of the pension paid in the new system is primarily defined by the "bono de reconocimiento."
b. Excludes social assistance pensions and pensions of police and armed forces.
c. To children and pregnant women.
d. Blue-collar family allowance.
e. In July 1990 the monthly family allowance had three values depending on the level of income of the worker. The value registered corresponds to the family allowance received by the lowest income workers.

that were owned by the most important economic groups in the country before the 1982-83 crisis. In the middle of that crisis, when forced to intervene in the financial sector, the government also took over the administration of these AFPs. It later reprivatized them, and the new owners are international consortia.[37]

The flip side of the pension system's accumulation of funds was an increase in the public sector's social security deficit. The deficit that historically

37. See Marcel and Arenas (1991).

had fluctuated between 1 and 3 percent of GDP in 1982 reached 8 percent and in 1988 was 5 percent. It has been projected that after thirty to thirty-five years in the new system the deficit would fall to about 2 percent of GDP.[38] The deficit resulted from the transfer of active workers to the new system, from the retention of passive beneficiaries in the old system, and from the state's commitments to pay "seniority bonds" and to guarantee a minimum pension.

In brief, the new system separates access to social security from workers' specific occupational situations. All wage earners are subject to a uniform system that grants them the same benefits regardless of their specific activity, work category, or economic sector. The contributions and requirements to claim benefits are uniform except for a lower age requirement for women's retirement.[39] The new system eliminates the demographic impasse that pay-as-you-go systems inevitably face as the population ages. It also has invigorated the national financial market. Pension values are now tied to fluctuations in the market, introducing a strong link between social security funds and the macroeconomic variables of savings and investment. Nevertheless, the reform implies a long transition period during which there will be heavy pressure on the fiscal budget.

THE HEALTH SECTOR. Chile's health system was closely interrelated with the social security system during its development. Around 1970 the public health sector had two main subsystems: the National Health Service (SNS), created in 1952, which provided free care to about 65 percent of the population, primarily indigent and blue-collar workers and their dependents; and the National Medical Service for Employees (SERMENA), created in the mid-1960s, which provided vouchers and copayments to approximately 20 percent of the population, mostly white-collar workers. With vouchers white-collar workers could receive medical care from public services or from private physicians, clinics, and laboratories that joined the SERMENA system. In addition, 5 percent of the population had access to the publicly financed health services of the armed forces. The remaining 10 percent of population, predominantly higher-income families, relied on private, independent providers.

The SNS was the most important health care program in terms of infrastructure and the proportion of the population covered. It had far-reaching power over policy and financial decisions and the provision of services. It was in charge of designing the country's preventive and curative health programs. It administered 90 percent of the country's hospital capacity. It also played an

38. Marcel and Arenas (1991, pp. 33–39).
39. Armed forces and police personnel kept their old social security agencies and benefits.

important role as the locus of practical training for medical students and the starting point for medical careers.

The reforms in the health sector illustrate all the salient themes of social sector reform in the late 1970s and 1980s: the redefinition of the central government's role with extensive decentralization and transfer of responsibilities to municipal governments and private providers; the creation of a financing mechanism that supports demand rather than supply; the promotion of the private sector; and the reallocation and targeting of public resources to poor areas, mothers, and children.

In the late 1970s, after clashes with the principal medical association, the government introduced significant changes in the organization of public health.[40] It established an institutional separation between policy and standard formulation, financing, and health service provision. Policy and standard setting remained in the Ministry of Health. A National Health Fund (FONASA) was created to control finance. To provide health care the National Health Service was divided into twenty-six autonomous health services, each covering a specific geographic area of the country.[41] Beginning in the 1980s each health service was authorized to transfer its responsibilities for primary health care to municipal governments and the private sector.

FONASA is in charge of allocating health resources, which come from the federal budget and mandatory social security health contributions. Its resource allocation policy has favored demand-driven mechanisms, such as the allocation of funds according to health activities actually delivered. In addition, cost recovery policies have been implemented. Among other reforms, a 1984 law limited free curative health care at public facilities to low-income persons, defining copayment percentages that increased according to income level.[42] Preventive mother-child care continued to be free.

The most radical reform in the health sector took place after the 1980 social security reform. This reform authorized the formation of Health Insurance Institutes (ISAPRES), private profit-making organizations that operate like prepaid health insurance plans. As of 1981 social security affiliates were able to

40. Raczynski (1983).
41. There is an additional health service responsible for environmental problems in the Santiago area.
42. Interviews at the local level reveal that there were problems in implementing this law. It was difficult to certify users' income levels, and the demand for credentials for free service far outstripped initial estimates. There has been no serious evaluation of the law's impact. Cost recovery at local health clinics seems to have been insignificant, and certification of the right to free service—a municipal responsibility—overloaded municipal workers, causing ill will and discontent among users. See Raczynski and Serrano (1987, 1988, and 1990).

place their obligatory health payment, which otherwise went to FONASA, in an ISAPRE. Every ISAPRE offers medical care plans and must also assume responsibility for its members' disability subsidies. Every affiliate signs a private annual contract with an ISAPRE that specifies the monthly amount to be paid and the health care to be provided, as well as reference fees and discounts. If the cost of the health plan is higher than the obligatory contribution, the affiliate must either make an additional payment, find another ISAPRE or plan with fewer benefits, or stay in the state system with FONASA. If the cost of the health plan is less than the obligatory payment, the ISAPRE keeps the balance.

The ISAPRE system grew rapidly beginning in 1985-86 as a result of a series of privileges. The government increased the mandatory health contribution from 4 percent of taxable wages in 1981 to 6 percent in 1983 and 7 percent in 1985. It also eliminated the obligation of ISAPRES to pay the maternity leave subsidy of working mothers, assuming this responsibility itself. Finally, the government allowed employers to increase their payment to ISAPRES by 2 percent for workers who earned close to the minimum salary and to deduct that amount from company taxes.

In 1990 there were thirty-four ISAPRES covering 16 percent of the population. The new system gave this social segment, which primarily included the higher-income strata and the young with fewer health risks, greater freedom of choice regarding medical care and lower copayment (out-of-pocket) costs.[43]

The ISAPRE legislation was an important stimulus to the creation of infrastructure and private health services in higher-income areas. Its counterpart was a decrease in resources for FONASA, the public sector services. In 1988 the ISAPRE system, which then cared for 11 percent of the population, collected more than 50 percent of obligatory health contributions.[44] In other words, an increasing share of the resources collected by the state system were channeled toward the private sector. Some reports suggest there was also a migration of human resources from the public sector to the private sector.[45] FONASA thus received a significantly lower percentage of total social security health resources but continued to care for more than 70 percent of the population. As table 8-12 indicates, the result was that per capita rates for medical

43. Whereas almost half the workers affiliated with an AFP declare income lower than 50,000 pesos a month, among the ISAPRE affiliates no more than 11 percent are in this situation. While nationally 8 percent of the population is over sixty years of age, for ISAPRE beneficiaries this percentage is barely 4 percent. See ISAPRE Superintendency (1990). The incentives behind the operation of the ISAPRE system tend to increase costs. See Covarrubias (1991).

44. See Miranda (1990, tables 11 and 12).

45. See Covarrubias (1991).

Table 8-12. *Health Care Beneficiaries, Payroll Deductions, Expenditures,
and Services Delivered, by Public (FONASA) and Private (ISAPRES)
Sectors, Chile, Selected Years, 1982–88*

	FONASA		ISAPRES		
Item	*Thousands*	*Percent of population*	*Thousands*	*Percent of population*	*Both[a] (percent of population)*
Beneficiaries[b]					
1986	9,439.6	76.6	921.3	7.5	84.1
1987	9,335.7	74.5	1,205.0	9.6	84.1
1988	9,211.9	72.3	1,450.2	11.4	83.7
Payroll deductions[c]	*percent*		*percent*		
1986		59.8		40.2	
1987		52.7		47.3	
1988		48.0		52.0	
Health expenditures[d]	*percent*		*percent*		
1982		96.7		3.3	
1984		84.2		15.8	
1986		72.9		27.2	
1988		62.3		37.8	
Services delivered per capita average 1986–88					
Medical consultations		2.6		3.5	
Laboratory exams[e]		2.5		2.8	
Surgeries		0.115		0.191	

Sources: Ramírez (1990, pp. 44–46); and Miranda (1990, pp. 55–57).
a. The rest of the population is affiliated with the health system that serves the armed forces and police (approximately 5 percent of the population) or is not affiliated with any system.
b. Affiliates and their dependents.
c. Legal deductions. ISAPRES also includes additional payments.
d. Excludes expenditures on labor accidents and medicines and other inputs not covered by each system or plan. FONASA free choice and ISAPRES include copayment.
e. Includes "imagenología" and pathological analysis.

consultations, laboratory exams, and surgery are significantly lower in the public system than in the ISAPRE system.

THE HOUSING SECTOR. In the housing sector the government implemented a central component of its neoliberal model early and thorough, supporting subsidies to demand rather than supply. It transferred many traditional duties of the state to the private sector, including the acquisition of land, urbanization, construction, and financial intermediation. The state's responsibility was restricted to selecting beneficiaries and distributing subsidies.

In the mid-1970s the government decided that housing programs should include a single direct, fixed-amount subsidy for families not able to acquire minimum housing despite having made an effort to save. Initially, these programs favored medium- and high-income strata.[46] Later, around 1980, it initi-

46. Arellano (1985, chapter 4); and Necochea (1984).

ated basic housing and variable housing subsidy programs, which were directed specifically at poor sectors and lower-middle-income strata. In these programs it made the savings requirement more flexible, established strict criteria for selecting beneficiaries, and lowered the maximum value of the housing that could be financed with this subsidy. At the same time the state assumed a more active role, creating favorable conditions for low-income beneficiaries to use their subsidies. For example, it encouraged the development of an adequate supply of minimal housing and facilitated beneficiaries' access to complementary lines of credit.[47] In addition, with support from the Interamerican Development Bank, between 1979 and 1985 it upgraded programs to regularize deeds of ownership and to improve sanitary infrastructure in poor areas. In brief, the government had to complement its initial demand-driven subsidies with policies that improved the supply of housing and infrastructure in poor areas.

MUNICIPAL GOVERNMENT. Municipal governments have had to assume important new functions over the past fifteen years. Before the municipal reform of 1980, local governments played almost no active role in the social sector. Health, education, housing, and poverty alleviation programs were handled directly by the national ministries. Under the military government, local authorities became the agencies that implemented social policy. Their new legal responsibilities required municipalities to administer and manage education and health establishments; to apply a centrally defined poverty screening test; to assign subsidies and benefits from centrally defined programs; to define priorities for action; and to design social programs to supplement those prepared centrally. In housing, the role of the municipalities was limited to certifying the "poverty" status of the beneficiaries of basic housing programs.

In 1980 the central government provided incentives for the transfer of public education and primary health care to the municipalities. Initially, the process was voluntary in the sense that the municipalities had to request the transfer, receiving an economic reward for their initiative. When the economic crisis struck in 1982–83, the government froze all transfers, then reinitiated the process in 1986. In 1988 municipalities managed almost 100 percent of educational establishments and urban and rural health clinics.

The transfers included real estate, equipment, and all personnel. After the transfer, the personnel ceased to be state employees and lost the labor rights and benefits associated with a state career. They also suffered, after 1983, a

47. Vergara (1990, chapter 6).

significant decrease in their wage level, which generated serious opposition to the "municipalization" process.

The transfer took place as the government introduced a new system of resource allocation that sought to tie financing to the level of activity in different health and education establishments. The philosophy behind the new financing mechanisms was that the system would stimulate competition to maintain and attract students or users and that this competition would in turn generate improvements in the efficiency and quality of services. Yet, in general, the new resource allocation mechanisms responded to inputs used (such as health examinations given or students in attendance), not to results obtained. As a result, incentives to improve the quality of services were lacking.[48]

In education the traditional system allocated resources to schools according to their budgets, which were presented annually to the Ministry of Education and based primarily on student registration each March. Under the new system schools receive resources according to the average level of student attendance in the previous month. The value of the monthly per student subsidy varies according to the level of education. To enhance competition among schools, the government offered incentives for the creation of private, state-subsidized schools with free tuition. Registration in these schools increased from 14 percent of students in 1980 to 30 percent in 1986 and remained at this level in subsequent years.[49] Initially, the value of educational subsidies was sufficient to meet the operating costs (personnel, goods and services, maintenance) of providing a minimum standard of education and health care, as the vigorous expansion of the subsidized private schools suggests. Yet, after the 1982–83 crisis, the reimbursement values for education were not adjusted for inflation, which imposed heavy burdens on municipal budgets and the subsidized private schools. The average education subsidy dropped from an index of 100 in 1982 to 83 in 1986 and to 81 in 1989. As a result of this resource squeeze, teachers' wages fell. They then dedicated significant portions of their teaching time trying to attract students, since their salaries depended on the size of school enrollment. The importance of student performance in the educational system lapsed.[50]

The new system for assigning health resources translated the range of dif-

---

48. In both education and health it was necessary to create a detailed monthly record of student attendance and services delivered. On the one hand, this requirement increased administrative duties. On the other hand, it opened the door to an "inflation" of statistics on student and health services rendered—which, in turn, made it necessary to intensify supervisory procedures.

49. See Espínola (1991, p. 17).

50. See Espínola (1991, p. 26, chapters 4 and 5; and 1990).

ferent services into the basis for reimbursement fees. Health establishments received part of their resources (approximately 25 percent) according to the number and type of services they provided during the previous month. The real value of health subsidies deteriorated after the 1982-83 crisis. At the same time, health establishments realized that the reimbursement fee for some activities was lower and for others higher than real service costs. Thus, if possible, establishments tended to inflate those activities where the reimbursement fee surpassed actual service costs.[51]

The government hoped that the transfer of education and health responsibilities would encourage the municipalities to contribute their own resources to these tasks, thus increasing social expenditures. To some extent this increase did occur. For example, between 1980 and 1989 municipalities contributed on average between 2 and 7 percent of total education expenditures. In 1990 the municipal share represented a full 12 percent of current health and education expenditures.[52] Nevertheless, these resources were no great boon; they only partially compensated for the decrease in education and health care spending. Furthermore, the ability of different municipalities to support education and health care expenditures varied significantly according to their per capita revenues.

Chile has more than 330 municipalities. A few have high per capita resources and sufficient budgetary resources for education and health. Most are at the other extreme; they are rather poor and have concentrated populations with tremendous needs. Legislation on municipal revenue created an agency, the Common Municipal Fund, responsible for the redistribution of resources from rich to poor municipalities. This fund effectively redistributes resources, but it still does not overcome the enormous inequalities.[53] It is unclear whether the municipal reform has implied more or less equity in health and educational expenditures.

The problems facing the municipalities, however, are not only monetary. The government imposed new duties on them without offering them any preparation. Local authorities and employees were unaware of the work they were assigned to undertake. Decentralization was to bring government closer to the people, where local management would respond better to the needs and demands of the population. Studies of municipal performance, however, have shown that local governments were overwhelmed. They poured their energy into the direct provision of social welfare on a vast scale, confronting innu-

51. Miranda (1990).
52. Espínola (1991, p. 32); and Stewart and Ranis (1992, table 5).
53. Raczynski and Cabezas (1988).

merable administrative tasks. The social projects of the municipalities themselves were few, discontinuous, curative, and palliative rather than preventive. Municipal work teams were weak and they did not have the necessary tools for local development activities. In addition, municipalities were victims of poorly coordinated decisions by the central government and the ministries. Among the significant problems still pending for the municipalities in 1990 were the designation of mayors and issues of accountability and social participation.[54]

TARGETING. Until the mid-1970s access to social programs and services was nominally universal. The military government decided to break with this norm of universality, beneath which were profound inequalities, and to ensure that state action would benefit only the extremely poor, those persons and households unable to meet their most urgent needs on their own. The new government believed state action should be selective and targeted.

The attempt to target social programs took a different path. On one hand, there was a reallocation of public expenditures toward basic services. For example, free university education was eliminated, and resources were transferred to preprimary and primary education. On the other hand, special programs were developed for pregnant women and children to receive care in certain public establishments, including out-patient facilities, health clinics, and municipal schools. Finally, welfare programs were expanded or created for those found to be below a minimum standard according to a national screening instrument: the social stratification card. Every household receives points according to its relative status regarding employment, housing, income, education, household equipment, and number of persons in the household. Access to welfare programs is limited to those households whose point count on the card falls below the established minimum.

The application process for the card, administered by the municipalities, has faced many technical and practical problems. It also has absorbed a great deal of staff energy. Municipal employees in charge of the card and citizens in search of benefits have both expressed their discontent with the process, noting distortions in the delivery and recording of information.[55]

The distribution of social expenditures in Chile in 1987 was progressive. It is not clear if this progressivity was the result of the card (which was used in

54. For an analysis of municipal organizations and social planning, see Raczynski and Serrano (1987 and 1988).

55. Regarding the social stratification card, see Vergara (1990, chapters 1 and 8); and Raczynski (1991b).

very few programs), the reallocation of resources toward certain social programs, or the operation of self-selection mechanisms. The extent of targeting in any program, of course, also depends on the nature, amount, and quality of the benefits it offers.

Targeting is often considered equivalent to increased efficiency in social expenditure, but they are not necessarily identical. The Chilean case is enlightening regarding the undesirable effects of excessively targeted programs.[56] For example, state-supported day nurseries, originally designed to prepare children of poor families for school, were targeted toward undernourished children and children of extremely poor families. The program concentrated its activities and resources on feeding, giving educational objectives secondary status. Strict targeting encouraged access for undernourished or high-risk children but hindered the attendance of children with working mothers whose income disqualified them from attending. In this way the program tended to discourage women from trying to supplement the family income.[57] The National Supplementary Feeding Program (PNAC), traditionally a preventive program, targeted its resources on new curative programs. Social programs generally were targeted at children under six years of age. The probability that investments at this age would mature was low because school-age children were relatively unprotected.[58]

The Chilean experience suggests that in a situation of diminished public resources and heightened needs, strict targeting tends to transform programs that invest in human capital into purely welfare programs. The most beneficial result of the targeting policy was probably that it improved the technical capacity of social policy administration. Targeting elevated the importance of tasks such as diagnosing poverty situations, defining specific target groups, monitoring progress, and evaluating program impact.[59]

Social Programs and Welfare

This section summarizes the main social programs in social security, health, education, and housing and their welfare impact, especially for the poorer strata. The challenge is to explain how broad measures of well-being—such as mortality, life expectancy, school enrollment, and illiteracy—im-

---

56. See Vergara (1990, chapter 8); Sojo (1990); and Raczynski (1991a).
57. Raczynski, Serrano, and Bousquet (1990).
58. This idea is elaborated in Vergara (1990, chapter 8).
59. In these areas the World Bank gave support. For example, it financed two national surveys (1985 and 1987) to evaluate the distributive impact of fiscal expenditures.

Table 8-13. *Social Security Coverage, Chile, 1974–90*[a]
Thousands of actively paying affiliates unless otherwise specified

Year	Old system	New system (AFP)	Both	Percent in labor force	Percent in employed labor force
1974	1,863	...	1,863	60.8	71.3
1975	1,792	...	1,792	57.5	67.6
1976	1,727	...	1,727	54.3	62.1
1977	1,699	...	1,699	53.1	60.2
1978	1,670	...	1,670	48.0	56.0
1979	1,653	...	1,653	47.5	55.0
1980	1,679	...	1,679	46.2	51.6
1981	732	882[b]	1,614	43.9	49.2
1982	489	907	1,396	38.1	47.4
1983	478	1,055	1,533	41.1	49.4
1984	459	1,139	1,598	42.6	50.4
1985	454	1,322	1,776	45.8	52.7
1986	442	1,494	1,936	45.8	51.4
1987	435	1,676	2,111	49.0	54.1
1988	428[c]	1,772	2,200	49.3	53.8
1989	421[c]	1,918	2,339	50.9	54.3
1990	414[c]	1,962	2,376	50.9	54.1

Sources: For old system, Arellano (1989, p. 67). For new system, Iglesias and others (1991, p. 43). Percentages in labor force and employed are based on data from INE.
a. As of December each year.
b. Information on actively paying affiliates is not available. Data are estimated under the assumption that they represent the same proportion in the total number of affiliates (actively paying or not) as in 1982.
c. Estimated under the assumption that each year the number of affiliates fell in the same proportion as it did between 1986 and 1987.

proved markedly despite the drop in household income and consumption, the increase in absolute poverty, and lower levels of public expenditure.

SOCIAL SECURITY. The coverage of Chile's social security system historically has been high. Affiliates actually paying for social security represented about 60 percent of the labor force in 1974 (table 8-13). In the 1980s this percentage had fallen 15 points. Coverage dropped partly as a result of high, persistent unemployment and an increase in informal sector jobs. Nevertheless, the deterioration in coverage was not due simply to labor market conditions, because coverage fell among the employed as well. Another contributing factor may have been labor law reforms that weakened labor unions, increased worker flexibility, and lessened union control over labor contracts.

The 1981 reform, therefore, did not increase the coverage of the social security system or change the characteristics of the population that is not covered. The nonaffiliated work force, as in the past, is concentrated among self-employed workers and in low-income households, the agricultural sector, the personal service sector, and small companies.[60]

Two items, pensions and family allowances, account for almost all social security expenditures. Other expenses, such as illness, work accidents, and unemployment subsidies, absorb small amounts of total spending. Total pension expenditures rose significantly as a result of the aging population, not of any improvement in the real value of pensions. As shown in table 8-11, the number of pensions paid increased while the monthly per capita real value of pensions stayed below the 1970 level in each year between 1974 and 1989. The real value of the minimum pension established by law developed more favorably. In 1978 it rose above its 1970 level and has remained there since. Nevertheless, its actual coverage fell (table 8-13).

Because most of the pensions paid thus far have been in the old system, the average value of pensions does not directly reflect the impact of the reforms. In the future the value of pensions in the old system will depend on the availability of fiscal resources for extraordinary adjustments by the central government. In the new system the return on funds accumulated in each individual's account is determined by the capital market. Between 1987 and 1990 the situation in this market was very favorable.[61]

With regard to the social security family allowance, the government instituted a positive reform in 1974, standardizing the allowance for dependents of blue-collar and white-collar workers.[62] Nevertheless, the real value of this benefit deteriorated to such an extent that by 1989 the family allowance was 74 percent lower than the amount blue-collar workers received in 1974 (table 8-11).

In summary, throughout the 1974–89 period the coverage and level of social security benefits deteriorated. The 1981 social security reform did not produce increased coverage. At the same time its enduring fiscal costs, coupled with fiscal constraints derived from the 1982-83 crisis, led to a fall in the value of both pensions and family allowances.

During the deep recessions of 1975 and 1982, the government designed two compensatory programs that targeted the poorest sectors: a welfare pension and a welfare family subsidy. In 1975 it reformulated and extended the

60. See Mesa-Lago (1978); Arellano (1989); and Haindl and others (1989, pp. 196–98).

61. The average value of pensions paid increased 20 percent in those three years. See Iglesias and others (1991, p. 175). Nevertheless, the new system paid very few pensions: 46,000 in 1987 compared with 1,366,000 paid under the old system (table 8-11).

62. Around 1970 the family allowance for a white-collar dependent was twice that for a blue-collar dependent.

welfare pension program (PASIS). The program provides temporary benefits
to elderly people over age sixty-five and invalids over age eighteen who qualify as poor and have not been able to obtain benefits from the social security
system. The amount of this pension was legally established to be one-third of
the minimum pension. The program expanded rapidly. In 1986 the number of
PASIS payments reached a peak of 324,000, which signified a 23 percent increase in the number of regular pensions paid (table 8-11).

During the 1981 crisis, when the unemployed lost their social security coverage, they also lost their family allowance. To offset this loss the government
designed a welfare family subsidy program.[63] The amount of the subsidy
equaled that of the social security family allowance. This program restored
one social benefit—the family allowance for pregnant women and children—
to households that had lost social security coverage. At the same time, it extended this benefit to poor households that had never been covered by social
security. In 1988 the number of subsidies paid increased the total number of
family allowances by 24 percent.

HEALTH. As noted, Chile has a long history of social medicine.[64] Around 1970
the public health sector had wide geographic and social coverage. Its programs favored low-income households, especially pregnant women and children, and included integrated programs of health care and supplementary
feeding. Causes of death among the population at that time suggested that the
country was graduating from the first stage of the epidemiological transition.
Patterns of morbidity pointed to a decrease in infectious, parasitic, and nutritional diseases and to an increase in modern diseases: accidents, cardiovascular problems, and cancer, among others. Infant survival and life expectancy
rates were both increasing (tables 8-14 and 8-15).

Public health activities in the 1970s and 1980s, following a tradition initiated in the 1930s, concentrated on providing care for women and children
(table 8-16). From 1975 onward the government expanded, improved, and targeted at the most vulnerable groups a range of existing programs, including
periodic prenatal and postnatal care; checkups for well babies; pathological

63. In August 1981 it instituted a family subsidy for poor children under eight years of age
who did not have access to social security. Children under six had to attend public health clinics
for regular checkups, and those ages six to eight had to enroll in school. The benefit was extended
to pregnant women in July 1982 and to children ages eight to fourteen who attended school in
April 1985.
64. This subsection is based on Raczynski and Oyarzo (1981); and Raczynski (1988,
pp. 57–92).

Table 8-14. Population and Welfare Status Indicators, Chile, Selected Years, 1920–90

Year	Population Total	Population Percent urban[a]	Mortality General (per 1,000 inhabitants)	Mortality Infant (per 1,000 live births)	Life expectancy at birth Men	Life expectancy at birth Women	Birth rate (per 1,000 inhabitants)	Fertility rate[b]	Illiteracy rate[a] (percent in population over age 15)	Drinking water coverage (percent)	Sewerage coverage (percent)
1920	3,730	n.a.	30.5	250	n.a.	n.a.	41.2	n.a.	36.7	n.a.	n.a.
1930	4,287	n.a.	24.1	200	n.a.	n.a.	42.1	5.5	25.3	n.a.	n.a.
1940	5,023	52	21.3	170	n.a.	n.a.	37.2	4.8	27.1	n.a.	n.a.
1950	6,082	n.a.	n.a.	n.a.	n.a.	n.a.	35.1	4.5	19.8	n.a.	n.a.
1952	6,341	60	13.0	129	51.9	55.7	32.7	5.1	19.8	n.a.	n.a.
1954	6,625	n.a.	12.8	118	n.a.	n.a.	35.4	n.a.	n.a.	n.a.	n.a.
1956	6,932	n.a.	12.1	107	n.a.	n.a.	37.0	n.a.	n.a.	n.a.	n.a.
1958	7,263	n.a.	12.2	117	53.8	58.7	37.4	5.3	n.a.	n.a.	n.a.
1960	7,614	68	12.5	120	n.a.	n.a.	37.5	n.a.	16.4	n.a.	n.a.
1962	7,993	n.a.	11.9	109	55.3	61.0	37.9	5.3	n.a.	n.a.	n.a.
1964	8,387	n.a.	11.2	104	n.a.	n.a.	36.2	n.a.	n.a.	49.2	23.4
1966	8,768	n.a.	10.4	98	n.a.	n.a.	33.6	n.a.	n.a.	56.3	26.0
1968	9,142	n.a.	9.2	87	57.6	63.8	28.7	4.4	n.a.	61.7	27.8
1970	9,504	75	8.7	82	n.a.	n.a.	26.4	n.a.	11.0	66.5	31.1
1972	9,851	n.a.	8.9	73	60.0	66.5	27.4	3.6	n.a.	67.9	34.8
1974	10,186	n.a.	7.7	65	n.a.	n.a.	25.9	n.a.	n.a.	69.2	38.2
1976	10,510	n.a.	7.7	57	n.a.	n.a.	23.0	n.a.	n.a.	78.2	51.5
1978	10,816	n.a.	6.7	40	63.9	70.6	21.3	2.9	n.a.	86.0	56.3
1980	11,145	n.a.	6.6	33	n.a.	n.a.	22.2	n.a.	n.a.	91.4	67.4
1982	11,519	82	6.1	24	67.8	74.6	23.8	n.a.	8.9	92.1	70.0
1984	11,919	n.a.	6.3	20	n.a.	n.a.	22.2	2.8	n.a.	94.3	72.9
1986	12,327	n.a.	5.9	19	n.a.	n.a.	22.1	n.a.	n.a.	97.0	77.2
1988	12,748	n.a.	5.8	19	68.0	75.0	23.3	2.7	n.a.	98.0	80.8
1990	13,173	n.a.	6.0	16	n.a.	n.a.	23.3	n.a.	n.a.	n.a.	n.a.

Sources: Banco Central de Chile (1989); Arellano (1985, p. 24); INE, (1989); and INE (1987)
n.a. Not available.
a. According to the census of population figures.
b. Average of five-year periods: 50–55, 55–60, and so forth.
c. Population served or covered.

Table 8-15. *Causes of Death, Chile, 1965, 1975, 1980, 1988*

	1965		1975		1980		1988	
Cause	Percent	Rank	Percent	Rank	Percent	Rank	Percent	Rank
Cardiovascular system	10.6	4	21.1	1	26.6	1	27.9	1
Malignant tumors	9.5	5	14.1	2	15.4	2	18.0	2
Trauma and poisoning	8.3	6	10.2	4	11.9	3	12.1	3
Respiratory diseases	18.3	1	12.1	3	9.5	4	12.0	4
Gastrointestinal tract	11.1	3	6.9	6	8.1	5	6.5	5
Infectious and parasitic diseases[a]	7.2	7	8.5	5	4.8	6	3.5	6
Perinatal diseases	14.5	2	6.0	7	4.3	7	2.5	7
Pregnancy, delivery, and puerperal complications	0.9	8	0.4	8	0.2	8	0.2	8
Other causes	19.6	...	20.7	...	19.2	...	17.3	...
Number of deaths	(91,491)	...	(74,182)	...	(73,710)	...	(74,435)	...

Source: Miranda (1990, table 4).
a. Includes influenza and diarrhea.

Table 8-16. *Hospital Beds and Health Services Delivered, Public Sector, Chile, Selected Years, 1970–89*

Per 1,000 population unless otherwise specified

	Hospital beds		Medical Consultations[a]			Birth assistance		
Year	Total	Obstetric[b]	Adult[c]	Obstetric	Pediatric[d]	Professional	Mid-wife[b]	Emergency consultations
1970	3.5	15	0.87	2.36	0.96	81	4.7	0.21
1974	3.3	16	0.75	2.60	1.02	86	8.4	0.29
1975	3.3	17	0.72	2.72	0.96	87	10.1	0.26
1976	3.2	18	0.77	2.99	1.02	87	11.5	0.29
1977	3.1	19	0.79	3.42	1.04	89	12.7	0.30
1978	3.1	19	0.80	3.57	1.04	89	13.3	0.32
1979	3.1	21	0.84	3.72	1.10	90	13.8	0.35
1980	3.0	20	0.86	3.76	1.12	91	13.5	0.38
1981	3.0	19	0.86	3.70	1.18	92	13.1	0.42
1982	2.9	20	0.92	4.11	1.36	94	13.8	0.44
1983	2.9	20	0.95	4.61	1.46	95	14.6	0.49
1984	2.8	21	0.96	3.43	1.56	97	14.6	0.50
1985	2.8	20	0.95	4.72	1.71	97	15.4	0.50
1986	2.7	18	0.85	4.43	1.56	97	16.7	0.47
1987	2.6	18	0.82	4.11	1.45	98	16.1	0.45
1988	2.6	17	0.83	3.87	1.50	98	16.3	0.47
1989	2.5	17	0.83	3.72	1.48	99	16.4	0.48

Sources: INE Ministerio de Salud, *Anuarios de Atenciones y Recursos* (various issues); INE, *Demografía* (various issues); and INE-CELADE (1987).
a. Excludes consultations at emergency stations.
b. Per 1,000 live births.
c. Per inhabitant fifteen years of age or older.
d. Per child younger than fifteen years of age.

Table 8-17. *Maternal and Child Health Indicators, Chile, 1975–90*
Percent unless otherwise specified

	Mortality rates[a]				Undernourished	Under age 6 population
Year	Maternal	Neonatal	Post-neonatal	Low weight births[b]	children under age 6[c]	in health care program[d]
1975	1.22	25.4	32.2	11.6	15.5	72
1976	1.05	24.1	32.5	11.4	15.9	74
1977	0.94	21.4	28.7	10.9	14.9	75
1978	0.74	18.7	21.4	9.8	13.0	72
1979	0.66	18.7	19.2	8.8	12.0	69
1980	0.55	16.7	16.3	8.2	11.5	70
1981	0.44	13.1	13.9	7.6	9.9	70
1982	0.52	11.8	11.8	6.8	8.8	75
1983	0.41	10.8	11.2	6.0	9.8	76
1984	0.35	9.2	10.4	6.0	8.4	77
1985	0.50	9.9	9.6	6.4	8.7	78
1986	0.47	9.7	9.4	5.6	9.1	77
1987	0.48	9.6	8.9	6.5	8.8	74
1988	0.41	9.5	9.4	6.6	8.6	73
1989	0.43	9.1	8.0	6.4	8.3	72
1990	0.40	8.5	7.5	5.8	7.4	72

Sources: INE, Demografía; and INE-Ministerio de Salud (various years).
a. Rate per 1,000 live births. Neonatal: death during the first four weeks of life (28 days). Postneonatal: death after the first four weeks and before one year of age.
b. Less than 2.5 kg. Excludes births that do not declare weight—2 to 4 percent each year.
c. Percentage of undernourished children (low, moderate, and advanced) as measured by Sempé weight-for-age criterion. Most of the children suffer low-level malnutrition: 76 percent in 1976 and 90 percent in 1990.
d. Percentage of children younger than age six participating in child health care programs at primary care facilities.

diagnosis; prevention, vaccination, and immunization of the population; health and nutritional education for mothers; the promotion of breast-feeding; campaigns for responsible fatherhood and birth control; and, most important, a diversity of nutritional intervention programs.

A set of closely interrelated programs successfully improved maternal health, birth weight, nutrition in children under six, and infant and child mortality despite overall economic instability and a deterioration in income and consumption among lower-income households (table 8-17). In public health clinics the government instituted a system to identify and treat pregnant women and children under six who showed signs of nutritional deficiencies. Three national programs that began in the 1930s and 1940s and covered almost all the eligible poor served as the point of entry into the system: prenatal care, checkups for well babies, and the National Supplementary Feeding Pro-

Table 8-18. *National Supplementary Feeding Program (PNAC), Chile,*
1975–90

Year	Percent of public health expenditures	Milk and milk substitutes distributed (tons) Basic PNAC	Targeted PNAC
1975	13.4	23,504	...
1976	13.2	24,480	...
1977	12.7	28,651	...
1978	9.0	27,180	2,646
1979	9.1	25,707	3,012
1980	6.6	25,195	4,020
1981	7.3	24,636	5,146
1982	7.2	24,762	5,525
1983	6.7	17,053	4,993
1984	8.5	11,718	16,132
1985	7.6	12,641	17,630
1986	6.6	12,854	19,257
1987	9.7	12,841	17,135
1988	6.8	13,052	15,557
1989	9.2	13,249	15,072

Sources: INE, *Anuario de Atenciones y Recursos* (annual); and information from the Ministerio de Salud.

gram (PNAC).[65] The government complemented these broad, preventive, and universal programs with specific programs for children and pregnant women at high risk. It designed a targeted PNAC that provided supplementary food to pregnant women and children suffering from, or at high risk of, malnutrition. State-supported day nurseries and open childcare centers primarily for children certified as undernourished at local public health clinics were created. In 1987 more than 10 percent of children under six years of age attended these centers.[66] Finally, for children under two and in a state of severe malnutrition the government created a network of nutrition rehabilitation centers that provide complete inpatient care until recovery.

The effectiveness of this interconnected system has been widely noted.[67] Indicators of nutrition and infant and child mortality improved significantly until 1982. During the 1982–83 crisis, however, they stagnated (table 8-17).

65. In poor rural and urban areas these programs reach more than 90 percent of the population.
66. Vergara (1990, chapter 4) provides a complete description of these systems.
67. Among others, see González and others (1980a and 1980b); and Monckeberg and others (1984).

As the economic crisis intensified, nutritional programs were reduced rather than expanded. The amount of milk distributed by PNAC was 31 percent lower in 1983 than in 1982, and the amount of food distributed to high-risk children fell by 10 percent (table 8-18). In 1984 the distribution of food to high-risk beneficiaries again intensified, and infant and child mortality and nutritional indexes again improved. This pattern suggests that in Chile the nutritional status of children from poor households depends heavily on public programs. It also shows that targeting, in a context of diminished resources, tends to transform its preventive programs into curative ones.

The success of health and nutritional programs in Chile came largely from the existing coverage and structure of the health sector. Chilean mothers had experience with primary health care, a relatively high level of education, and a belief in their entitlement to well-baby checkups and supplementary feeding, all of which contributed to program success. The drop in birth rates and the concentration of births in low-risk sociodemographic segments also helped, as did the increased availability of drinking water and sewerage.[68] Obviously, medical innovations and the availability of low-technology child survival techniques were important as well.

What happened to the health of the population over five years of age? Empirical evidence is scarce, in part because only certain infectious diseases must be registered with the authorities. Government reports indicate a strong increase during the 1970s and 1980s in diseases linked to the sanitary quality of food and the presence of vectors transmitted through the digestive system, particularly typhoid fever and hepatitis. The increased frequency of these cases since 1975 occurred in the big cities and was associated largely with inadequate waste disposal systems. Other information suggests an increase in diseases that are not life threatening. For example, malnutrition among school-age children, skin infections, alcoholism, drug addiction, mental health problems, and work-related illnesses all appeared to increase.[69]

Regarding the relationship of the population to health services, access became more difficult for all except mothers and small children. Symptoms of this trend included a noticeable increase in the number of emergency health consultations (table 8-16); a one- to two-year waiting list for public hospital beds; and longer stays—for those able to get a bed—in public than in private hospitals due to a shortage of necessary equipment.[70] Furthermore, while per

68. On the role of sociodemographic factors see Raczynski and Oyarzo (1981); and Taucher (1989). Castañeda (1984) analyzes the impact of health and housing-infrastructure variables.
69. Chateau (1981); Foxley and Raczynski (1983); and Echeverría (1984).
70. Rodríguez and Jiménez (1985).

Table 8-19. *Distribution of Expenditures in Education, by Level, Chile, Selected Years, 1970–89*
Percent

Year	Preschool	Primary	Secondary	University	Other	Total
Public expenditures[a]						
1970	n.a.	33.7	13.6	30.8	21.9	100.0
1975	1.1	35.7	12.3	42.0	8.9	100.0
1977	1.8	35.6	11.5	41.1	9.9	100.0
1979	2.6	37.9	15.1	32.6	11.8	100.0
Fiscal expenditures[b]						
1981	1.0	51.6	18.6	27.8	1.0	100.0
1983	4.6	51.6	18.0	25.2	0.6	100.0
1985	5.9	53.1	19.9	20.4	0.7	100.0
1987	7.1	51.9	18.1	21.6	1.3	100.0
1989	7.7	49.8	20.0	21.8	0.7	100.0

Sources: Marshall (1981); and Espínola (1991, p. 97).
n.a. Not available.
a. Total cost of loans effected by centralized and decentralized public organisms and by private sources that receive fiscal subsidies.
b. Effective contribution made by the government for the financing of social programs with freely disposable funds during the year.

capita medical visits per year for those under age fifteen increased from 2.0 in 1968 to 3.4 in 1987, the number of visits by the older population decreased from 2.1 to 1.8. In other words, the visit rate for those under age fifteen improved (especially for those under six), while it deteriorated for the older population.[71]

Chile's health policy during the 1970s and 1980s almost exclusively emphasized primary care for mothers and small children. Although successful in that sector of the population, such a policy is not sufficient in Chile, where the main causes of death are circulatory disease, tumors, cancers, accidents, and poisoning (table 8-15). Any country with this cause-of-death structure must also provide the adult population with preventive and curative programs. It also must not neglect programs for maintaining infrastructure and investment as Chile did, causing the hospital crisis of the 1980s.

EDUCATION. The Chilean government decreased the level of resources allocated to education in the 1974-89 period. At the same time, it made important changes in the way funds were spent, transferring expenditures from the university level to preschool, primary, and secondary levels (table 8-19).

Along with preschool expenditures, the coverage of the preschool system

71. These estimates are based on surveys. The information for 1968 is from the Ministry of Health (n.d., p. 81), and the 1987 information is from Haindl and others (1989, p. 134).

Table 8-20. *Educational Enrollment, by Level, Chile, Selected Years, 1970–92*
Thousands unless otherwise specified

Year	Preschool[a] Number	Preschool[a] Percent population under 6 years	Primary Number	Primary Percent population 6–14 years	Secondary[b] Science and humanities	Secondary[b] Technical and professional	Secondary[b] Percent population 15–19 years	Postsecondary education[c] Number	Postsecondary education[c] Percent population 20–24 years
1970	59.0	3.8	2,200.2	101.8	202.5	99.6	30.9	77.0	7.8
1974	109.6	7.2	2,322.7	101.8	282.7	163.1	40.7	144.5	15.6
1975	117.0	7.7	2,299.0	100.2	285.8	163.1	40.0	147.0	15.3
1976	131.6	8.8	2,203.3	95.8	307.8	158.0	40.4	131.7	13.3
1977	148.2	10.0	2,348.1	102.3	384.1	202.2	46.6	130.7	12.9
1978	157.9	10.8	2,233.6	97.7	388.1	221.4	50.0	130.2	12.5
1979	163.0	11.2	2,332.6	102.6	422.9	211.1	51.0	131.0	12.2
1980	173.3	11.9	2,264.6	97.8	430.4	198.4	49.8	119.0	10.8
1981	175.5	11.9	2,207.3	98.0	453.7	186.9	49.5	118.7	10.5
1982	184.5	12.3	2,146.0	96.0	475.0	168.4	50.5	119.5	10.3
1983	146.4	12.5	2,139.2	96.4	541.7	143.7	54.0	126.2	10.5
1984	176.2	11.2	2,092.1	94.8	581.2	129.8	56.3	186.2	15.2
1985	202.3	12.5	2,099.4	95.3	588.1	143.8	58.3	197.4	15.9
1986	210.0	12.8	2,083.1	94.5	602.3	142.1	59.5	208.0	16.6
1987	228.1	13.5	2,034.1	92.0	606.9	146.1	60.3	217.4	17.4
1988	217.1	12.7	2,027.6	91.2	635.5	152.8	63.4	233.2	18.7
1989	213.2	12.3	2,005.9	89.4	578.6	216.6	64.1	229.5	18.5
1990	220.4	12.5	2,008.1	88.4	492.6	266.4	61.5	245.4	19.9
1991	205.3	11.5	2,020.1	87.4	466.7	272.3	60.4	246.9	20.0
1992	241.8	13.5	2,052.5	86.8	439.2	272.5	58.9	285.4	23.2

Sources: INE (various years); and INE-CELADE. *Provecciones de Población.*
a. State-supported establishments that depend on the Ministry of Education or the Junta Nacional de Jardines Infantiles.
b. Includes adult enrollment, defined as enrollment of population older than eighteen years of age.
c. Includes state-supported and private universities, professional institutes, and postsecondary technical information centers. In 1988 they had 74,000 enrolled students.

grew from 4 percent of the population in 1970 to 12 percent in 1989 (table 8-20). At the same time, alternative care systems developed in the "open centers" run by municipalities, churches, and other nongovernmental organizations. The day nurseries and open centers were an essential component of the social network. They primarily admitted children referred by public health clinics because of malnutrition problems and children whose social stratification cards qualified them as poor.

Statistics on primary school registration for children ages six to fourteen showed a decline. The index, which was 102 in 1974, reached a level of 89 in 1989. This trend was largely the result of improved student progress: the average time it took a student to complete eight years of elementary education fell from 12.2 to 10.6 years between 1985 and 1989.[72] However, national tests that measure the achievement of minimal educational goals in the fourth and eighth grades reveal low, stable performance that fluctuated between 50 and 60 percent over time. The main factor explaining differences in test performance was the socioeconomic level of students.[73]

Within the primary system a School Nutrition Program (PAE) had provided breakfast and lunch in public schools since the mid-1960s. The original aim of this program was to reduce absentee and dropout rates and to improve children's powers of concentration at school. During the 1970s the government targeted this program to the neediest children in public schools. It also increased the protein and calorie content of the food and subcontracted its preparation and distribution with the private sector. However, the number of meals distributed each day declined (table 8-21).

In relation to secondary and higher education, there was a steady increase in secondary school enrollment. Between 1970 and 1989 the gross registration rate rose from 38 to 75 percent of youths ages fifteen to eighteen.[74]

Young people not in school either try to join the labor force or remain idle. Studies of the 1970s and 1980s show that the labor force participation rate of those fifteen to nineteen years old fluctuated around 18 percent, which is low by comparative standards. Unemployment among these youths surpassed the national average by more than 3 times.[75] At the same time, more young men and women than adults worked in retail sales (mainly sidewalk vendors), per-

72. Espínola (1991, p. 53).
73. Espínola (1991, pp. 70–76).
74. The proportion of the population that attends secondary school is higher in urban than in rural areas, and it increases according to family income. In 1987 for the urban areas this proportion was 97 percent in the highest income quintile, 95 percent in the next two, and 80 percent in the lowest two. See Haindl and others (1989, p. 90).
75. Foxley and Raczynski (1983); Marcel (1990); and Haindl and others (1989, p. 188).

Table 8-21. *School Feeding Program Meals Distributed, Chile, 1970–90*
Daily average in thousands unless otherwise specified

Year	Breakfasts and snacks	Coverage[a] (percent)	Lunches and dinners	Coverage[a] (percent)
1970	1,301	63.7	619	30.3
1971	1,408	64.0	654	29.7
1972	1,537	67.9	716	31.6
1973	1,446	62.3	674	29.1
1974	1,339	57.4	663	28.4
1975	746	31.0	594	24.7
1976	770	32.2	361	15.1
1977	1,055	43.7	296	12.3
1978	1,055	43.8	308	12.8
1979	759	31.4	295	12.2
1980	760	32.6	295	12.9
1981	759	33.2	295	12.9
1982	690	30.6	333	14.8
1983	673	30.1	333	14.9
1984	675	30.0	425	18.9
1985	691	30.1	544	23.7
1986	662	29.0	547	23.9
1987	478	21.1	463	20.4
1988	491	21.8	498	22.1
1989	486	21.8	484	21.7
1990	597	26.6	536	23.9

Source: JUNAEB (1991).
a. Percentage of total students enrolled receiving meals. Total school enrollment is higher than in table 8-20 because it includes differential education and preschool enrollment associated with Ministry of Education and Municipal establishments.

sonal services, and until 1988 the Minimum Employment Program. When educated youths obtained a job, it was often incompatible with their educational background and aspirations.[76]

Young high school graduates have also had problems entering the university. Chile's secondary schools are primarily oriented toward the university, and throughout the 1970s and 1980s this tendency became even more pronounced. There was no significant expansion of technical education at the secondary school level (table 8-20).[77]

76. Marcel (1990); and Martínez and León (1984).
77. The higher education system was modified substantially in the 1970s and 1980s. On the one hand, it was diversified: there was a significant expansion of private universities, and many professional institutes and technical training centers were created. On the other hand, education was no longer free, and the state reduced its contribution and modified its system of financing the programs.

Table 8-22. *Housing Units Built and Housing Deficit, Chile, Selected Years, 1970–90*

Year	Units built[a]	Units built per 1,000 inhabitants	Estimated housing deficit (thousands of units)	Estimated new families that did not obtain a house (percent)[b]
1970	36,612[c]	3.5[c]	508	8.9[d]
1974	23,753	2.3	572	59.3
1975	19,369	1.8	615	67.6
1976	37,394	3.6	665	61.7
1977	25,043	2.3	712	73.2
1978	23,226	2.1	766	71.4
1979	37,615	3.4	820	44.6
1980	46,284	4.2	858	33.6
1981	54,550	4.8	888	24.1
1982	27,336	2.4	912	63.0
1983	37,724	3.2	965	50.5
1984	46,769	3.9	1,009	40.4
1985	61,233	5.0	1,068	24.3
1986	52,082	4.2	1,095	37.4
1987	60,316	4.8	1,131	29.7
1988	75,501	5.9	n.a.	14.0
1989	83,891	6.5	n.a.	7.8
1990	78,904	6.0	n.a.	15.8

Sources: Banco Central de Chile (1989); INE, *Compendio Estadístico* (1991); INE-CELADE (1987); Meller (1990); and Scherman Filer (1990, p. 15).

n.a. Not available.

a. Between 1960 and 1974 houses built annually by the public and private sectors in a sample of sixty administration units and between 1975 and 1985 in a sample of eighty units. Since 1985, all administrative units.

b. Units built annually x 100 ÷ estimated number of new families being formed each year.

c. Annual 1960–70 average.

d. 1965–70.

HOUSING. Public expenditures on housing suffered an abrupt cutback under the military government. The average number of houses built annually with and without public funding per thousand inhabitants, which was 3.5 in the 1960s, fell from 4.9 in 1970–73 to only 3.1 in 1974–81. During the 1982–83 recession the index dropped to 2.8, but it then recovered significantly and surpassed the 1960–70 level from 1985 onward. However, the total number of units built in 1974–89 covered only 60 percent of the annual number of new households, increasing the housing deficit (table 8-22).

Restrictions in the housing sector did not affect all levels of society the same, and government programs benefited them differently over time. The programs of the 1970s favored middle-income households, while those of the 1980s targeted poor households. For example, the government eradicated almost all the "shantytowns" and temporary settlements in Santiago either by providing them with electricity, drinking water, and sewer systems or by transferring the population to new areas equipped with basic housing. This program benefited about 60,000 families, or 10 percent of Santiago's poor population.[78]

Despite the expansion and targeting of housing programs in the 1980s, a new social phenomenon—the "allegados"—emerged. They are sons and daughters who start their own families in "shacks" they install on their parent's land. Others live in their parent's house. In 1990 at the national level, about 26 percent of households lived in this situation. The phenomenon affected both lower- and middle-income families.[79]

Subsectors of housing that progressed significantly during the 1970s and 1980s included drinking water, sewage, and electricity. In urban areas 98 percent of households presently have access to drinking water; in rural areas the proportion is 30 percent. In urban areas 72 percent of households have access to sewage; the figure is 53 percent in the lowest income quintile. Electricity covers 98 percent of households in urban areas and 62 percent in rural areas.[80] During the worst of the 1982 recession, the poor had problems paying for utilities, and some had their service suspended. After some delay, the government officially acknowledged this situation and created a legal body that helped pay the public utility debts of poor neighborhoods.

SOCIAL PROGRAMS AND POVERTY. The Chilean government reduced public social expenditures in housing, education, and health. The cutback, however, was not uniform. There was an explicit effort to care for the poorest households. During the most severe moments of the crisis the government developed a package of ad hoc subsidies to offset the effects of the recession. Some of these subsidy programs were new; other existing programs were reformulated and targeted to the poorest segments of the population.[81]

Almost all the programs and subsidies in the social network have already been discussed: emergency employment programs; welfare pensions; welfare family allowances; state-supported open centers and nurseries; nutritional pro-

78. See Molina (1985); and Morales and Rojas (1986).
79. Mercado (1992). See also Ogrodnik (1984).
80. Rodríguez (1985); and Haindl and others (1989, pp. 159–62).
81. Among the new programs were emergency employment, welfare pension, welfare family allowance, and state-supported open centers. The previously existing programs included nutritional programs for children (Programa de Alimentación Escolar, Programa Nacional de Alimentación Complementaria), social security family allowance, and minimum pension.

grams for children; school lunch programs; the eradication of "shantytowns"; basic housing programs; and mechanisms to pay public utility debts.

The various programs in this network tended to benefit the same households. Beneficiaries were chosen on the basis of the same instrument, the social stratification card, and access to one program facilitated access to others. Joining the emergency employment programs, for example, made it easier to obtain the welfare family allowance, free health care, a place in the nursery school, school lunches, and a welfare pension for the elderly person in the household. The health care system worked in coordination with nursery school programs and the welfare family subsidy required regular health checkups and school registration.

Although the value of individual subsidies was rather low, the social network thus played an important role in the survival of the poorest households. In 1985 more than 60 percent of the monetary income of the poorest quintile of households was from cash subsidies obtained from the social network; for the next quintile this percentage was 13 percent. In 1987, after an improvement in employment, the percentages fell to 27 and 7 percent, respectively.[82] Table 8-23 verifies that in every area of Chile's social policy except higher education and the social security family allowance the poorest quintile of families received a relatively high percentage of expenditures.

The social network effectively compensated in part for the drop in the population's standard of living. In the context of high unemployment, decreased salaries, and social spending cuts, this highly targeted social policy helped prevent further impoverishment of extremely poor households.

Challenges for the 1990s

The 1990s began in Chile with a change in government. In March 1990 President Patricio Aylwin took office, having been democratically elected to head a four-year "transition to democracy" government with the support of a broad coalition of socialist and Christian Democrat parties. The previous two decades offer the Aylwin government a wealth of experience regarding links between social and economic policy and social welfare. The Chilean experience in the 1970s and 1980s confirms the strong link between economic poli-

---

82. Haindl and others (1989, p. 59). Raczynski and Serrano (1985) and Haindl and Weber (n.d.) convey qualitative evidence on this topic.

Table 8-23. *Share of Social Programs Reaching the Poorest 20, 30, and 40 Percent of Households, by Program, Chile, 1987*[a]

Program	Target households		
	20 percent	*30 percent*	*40 percent*
Emergency employment	54.8	66.4	74.4
Unemployment subsidies	63.4	78.0	84.1
Assistant pensions (PASIS)	50.3	62.4	73.6
Poor household family allowance (SUF)	57.4	72.2	82.4
Family allowance	19.2	30.2	41.2
Preschool education	36.3	49.1	59.0
Primary education	36.0	49.1	59.8
Secondary education	24.5	36.3	48.7
University education	4.5	8.1	12.1
School feeding program	52.5	68.0	78.5
Public sector health	39.9	55.3	66.6
National supplementary feeding program	40.7	57.0	69.2
Housing subsidies	23.3	35.2	47.2
Sanitary units	38.7	58.1	67.7
All direct subsidies	33.2	44.8	54.7

Source: Haindl, (1989, p. 45).
a. Figures include only those expenditures that directly reach the population. They exclude administrative costs.

cies and the extent of poverty. It also confirms that social policies and public social expenditures have a significant role to play in any antipoverty program. Selective cuts in social spending and the design of targeted programs should aim to protect the most vulnerable strata of society. In the context of increasing absolute poverty and the impoverishment of middle-income households due to changes in the labor market, however, selective and targeted social policies are insufficient to overcome poverty or to diminish social inequality.

The Chilean experience suggests that high economic instability, with pronounced cycles of recession and high growth, is worse for middle-income and poor households than moderate, stable growth rates.[83] The relationship among economic growth, employment, and poverty is not symmetrical across boom and bust periods. Long and profound recessions, like those Chile faced in 1975 and 1982, involve a drastic deterioration in income and a rise in poverty. Economic recovery and growth does not automatically ensure the opposite process. Workers who lose their jobs do not easily find new ones; their chances of success depend heavily on their age, skill, and social standing, as well as on the extent to which they lost any specific human capital. To improve the population's standard of living it is essential to sustain stable growth and to create productive job opportunities for the lower-income strata.

83. See French-Davis (1991).

The social costs of recessions multiply when the economy undergoes structural reforms as in Chile. The level and duration of unemployment are generally higher under a sectoral shock (trade reform, for example) than an aggregate one (debt crisis). In Chile aggregate and sectoral shocks tended to coincide. Under these conditions, sustainable growth and job opportunities are not enough to improve the population's standard of living. It is also necessary to have continuous training and retraining programs for the labor force and policies of sectoral restructuring. Both are essential because economic shocks, economic growth, and technological innovation all imply a mismatch between the population's skills and the demands of the economy.

Chile's experience before 1973 also suggests that state social action should respect macroeconomic balances ensuring adequate financing of social expenditures. Otherwise, only very short-term progress is made, inflationary processes are fueled, and initial improvements are eventually reversed. Budgetary balance is achieved in one of two ways: increasing revenues or decreasing spending. To evaluate the latitude for social action it is important to look at both alternatives. At the same time, a prerequisite for adequate financing is a simple, efficient, and legitimate tax system. A prerequisite for efficient social spending is an institutional capability to implement social programs.

Countries achieve social services that both have broad coverage and reach the poorest population only after a long period of time. The cumulative efforts of successive governments are indispensable in this process. In a country with broad education and health services targeted at the rural and urban poor, it is possible to sustain improvement in welfare indicators despite deteriorating income distribution and increases in absolute poverty. In the Chilean case existing services and longstanding national programs with social legitimacy facilitated the implementation of programs that targeted the very poor.

Nevertheless, targeting during crises has limits. Given a significant reduction of resources, political leaders cut the salaries of employees who work in targeted social programs and sacrifice investment in infrastructure and equipment. In the medium term these decisions lead to a deterioration in the quality of care provided.

Social policies in education and health need to be implemented in phases. First, the services must be created and demand for them must be stimulated, which Chile did between 1920 and 1970. In a second phase, when supply exists but "pockets" of the population remain neglected, it is important to target the programs, which Chile did in the 1970s and 1980s. By 1990 Chile had solved the coverage issue in primary education and mother-child health care and entered a third phase with new challenges. In education the task is to improve quality, to promote technical-vocational education, and to create forms of continuous training for the labor force. In health the challenge is to continue the mother-child programs and at the same time to respond to the problems that result from the population's changing epidemiological profile. These challenges require varied, flexible policy answers.

It is at this point—where the challenge is one of quality rather than quantity—that decentralization is of particular importance. Chile, historically a highly centralized country, initiated policies of decentralization in the 1980s. These policies, however, were partial and incomplete. Many problems remain to be solved, including shortages, distribution inequalities, and the perverse effects of skewed allocation criteria. The teams assigned to administrate social programs at the regional and local levels are often weak. There is both tension and a lack of coordination between centralized policymakers and the decentralized institutions that implement policy. Issues of accountability and social participation remain controversial, while inadequate information systems make it difficult to diagnose needs, to monitor change, and to evaluate the social impact of specific programs.

The state has an essential role in social policy, but it is not necessarily the agent that should execute programs or directly provide services. The private commercial sector, nongovernmental organizations, community organizations, and academic institutions all have an important role in the fight against poverty. That state, regional, and local governments should promote cooperation with these sectors is a consensus view. Nevertheless, how best to arrange this cooperation remains unclear. Also unclear is what the limit of state action should be, which duties it should carry out and which it should not assume under any circumstances.

The democratic government that took office in 1990 has followed some of the lessons learned during the previous decade. From the beginning its economic policy emphasis was stable growth. It sought to reach rates consistent with both macroeconomic balance and the country's productive capacity, avoiding episodes of "overheating" in the economy. During its first year, the government applied an adjustment policy to reduce inflation, which at the beginning of 1990 was 30 percent annually. During that year the economy grew only weakly (less than 1 percent per capita), but the government managed to control inflation (the annual rate fell from 27.3 percent in 1990 to 18.7 percent in 1991 and 12.7 percent in 1992) and to maintain a path of increasing growth (GDP per capita grew 4.3 percent in 1991 and 9.1 percent in 1992).

In view of the need to expand social programs and to reduce poverty, the government promoted and won congressional support for two projects: a tax

Table 8-24. *Fiscal Social Expenditures, by Sector, Chile, 1987–92*
Billions of 1990 pesos

Sector	1987	1988	1989	1990	1991	1992[a]
Education	242.3	242.1	233.5	228.6	249.8	269.6
Health	64.8	73.3	63.1	67.5	84.2	101.3
Housing	50.4	76.3	50.3	59.8	71.4	80.0
Social Security	425.4	466.3	415.6	478.0	516.5	534.3
Subsidies & other	146.4	100.5	79.1	76.9	94.6	102.1
Total	929.3	958.8	841.6	910.8	1,016.5	1,087.2
Percent of total fiscal expenditures[b]	65.5	62.0	60.1	65.2	61.8	63.8

Source: MIDEPLAN (1992a, p. 123).
a. Budget estimation.
b. The figures in this table differ from those in table 8-8 because these refer to total fiscal budget estimation and table 8-8 refers to actual public per capita expenditure.

reform designed to raise additional funds for social expenditures, and labor law reforms designed to correct the imbalance in bargaining power between labor and capital inherited from the military regime. The former made it possible to increase fiscal support for social programs in 1990 by 17 percent compared to the military government's budget, with additional increases in 1991 and 1992 (table 8-24). The labor law reforms restored some balance between worker and employer interests and addressed the issues of labor contracts, union organization, collective bargaining, and the right to strike. In addition, worker organizations, business associations, and the government signed a framework agreement, unprecedented in the country's history, in which they agreed to try to find joint solutions and overcome old confrontational patterns. From this basic consensus followed agreements on public sector wage adjustment, minimum salaries, and pensions.

In its social programs the new government has sought to restore infrastructure, curb the deterioration of wages in social sectors, and address new problems.[84] In addition, it has improved benefits in social safety net programs. In health its priority has been to invest in infrastructure and equipment, while it has also improved administrative access, augmented problem-solving capacity at the primary level, and restored free care at public health clinics. In housing it has sought to freeze the housing deficit and to facilitate access to homeownership for families without savings. It expanded welfare programs to address other housing problems and to help those unable to pay for water service.

In education and health the new government passed legislation regarding

84. For example, see Ministerio de Planificación y Coordinación (MIDEPLAN) (1991 and 1992a).

municipal personnel that standardized labor conditions and set a minimum wage. The new laws began to improve the labor situation in these sectors, but most of the professionals' demands have yet to be satisfied. In education the government initiated programs to improve the equity and quality of primary education. At the same time it began to review the educational curricula of primary and secondary schools and to reinforce technical-vocational high schools. It also expanded the feeding program for poor school children.

The government opened new areas of social policy to support "productive social investment." A training and employment program with on-the-job training in firms will benefit 100,000 unemployed young people between 1991 and 1994. Productive programs for low-income groups such as peasants, poor independent miners or *pirquineros*, nonindustrial fishermen, and small urban businessmen facilitate their access to loans, technical and management assistance, and training, all of which improve their integration into the market.[85]

Table 8.25 compares the social budget by type of expenditure of the military government for 1990 with that of the Aylwin government for 1993.[86] In real terms social spending increased 50 percent overall. The item that grew most was social investment, which is mainly social infrastructure and equipment, labor force training, and small producer support. Its share of total social spending rose from 6.4 to 11.1 percent. The efforts of the new government thus imply a move from welfare to social investment programs. Nevertheless, most of the social budget—more than 70 percent—goes to social security, education, health, and housing.

Another innovation was the creation of a new social policy instrument: the Solidarity and Social Investment Fund (FOSIS).[87] This fund complements sectoral social policy instead of substituting for it like the Social Fund of Bolivia. The resources it manages are less than 1 percent of the social budget. FOSIS operates as an intermediary, financing projects for the very poor that originate at the local level or incorporate the target group in finding ways to solve its own problems. Securing the participation and cooperation of different local agents is important. FOSIS finances projects in three main areas: microproductive enterprises; social development, through support to community organizations, training, and empowerment; and sectoral programs, through collaboration with national ministries in providing resources, access, and support to the poorer strata.

85. Both initiatives are supported by the Interamerican Development Bank. See MIDEPLAN (1992a and 1992b).

86. The classification of type of budget has been elaborated on an ex-post basis by the Ministry of Finance.

87. For a description of the characteristics and objectives of FOSIS see Flaño (1991).

Table 8-25. *Social Budget, by Type of Expenditure, Chile, 1990, 1993*

Percent

Type of expenditure	1990	1993	Real growth 1990–93
Welfare[a]	8.2	7.6	38.8
Social security[b]	43.7	39.2	34.8
Social services[c]	33.8	33.4	48.4
Education	16.7	13.8	24.3
Health	11.4	12.3	62.1
Housing	5.7	7.3	91.2
Social investment[d]	6.4	11.1	159.8
Administrative[e]	7.9	8.7	66.0
Average growth[f]	...	...	50.2

Source: Crispi and Marcel (1993, table 6).
a. Includes SUF, PASIS, unemployment subsidy, family allowance, social emergency programs.
b. Includes pensions and seniority bonds.
c. Excludes investment expenditures.
d. Includes infrastructure, equipment, support to small producers, labor force training.
e. Central government administrative costs.
f. Excludes unclassifiable expenditures: 4.9 percent in 1990 and 2.9 percent in 1993.

In the first two areas FOSIS sponsors contests that specify areas of intervention or define localities or population groups that should be served. Contests, depending on their content, are directed toward local community organizations, municipalities, nongovernmental organizations, and even financial institutions (for loans to microenterprises). In the third area its sectoral programs originate and take shape through negotiations between FOSIS and specific ministries. Another contribution of FOSIS is its dissemination of information to potential beneficiaries. FOSIS provides information on the characteristics of government social programs and on where and how to apply. It has also given a voice to the poorer strata of the population.

The implementation of FOSIS has not been an easy job. It had to justify its role to the ministries, overcome legal and bureaucratic obstacles, design work methodologies, and provide training to those applying these methodologies. By the end of 1992 FOSIS was financing more than 2,000 projects. It is an innovative and promising program whose results and potential should be carefully evaluated. FOSIS has the flexibility to support innovation in productive and social welfare activities. It does not have to provide basic health, education, and other social services for the poor, because they are already available. Finally, it can rely on and take advantage of the strong base of existing nongovernmental organizations.[88]

Some recent policy initiatives have slightly altered the institutional reforms that took place during the 1980s in the social sectors. These initiatives do not

88. Graham (1991, p. 24).

constitute a significant reversal in the trends toward decentralization, privatization, and targeting. Their purpose is merely to incorporate considerations of equity, social participation, and accountability and to reinforce the regulatory role of the state in the social sectors.

There is a broad consensus on the need to maintain the new social security system. The challenges in this area will be to increase coverage; to look for mechanisms that encourage the participation of self-employed individuals, temporary or seasonal workers, and salaried workers in small firms; and to improve the state's regulatory control of the sizable funds accumulated in individual capitalization accounts, which is important for both future retirees and macroeconomic management.

The least consolidated reforms are probably those in the health sector. Financial and management problems plague the public sector. There has been no thorough evaluation of the advantages and disadvantages of "municipalization." There is tension between the private, profit-seeking ISAPRES and the equity criterion emphasized by the government in both social and intergenerational terms. In addition, the incentives of the ISAPRE system encourage cost inflation and curative care, while the organization and incentives of the public system encourage other administrative and medical inefficiencies. So far the government has taken only minor regulatory measures.

The Aylwin government has sought to strengthen the process of decentralization begun in the 1980s. Among its initiatives were municipal elections in June 1992, the first in Chile in twenty years; legislation on regional government, approved at the end of 1992; the regionalization of increasing portions of sectoral ministry budgets; and programs to provide technical support to local and regional governments. Nevertheless, urgent challenges remain, including the search for policies that might break the inverse relationship between social needs and the availability of resources; the search for resource allocation rules that encourage the achievement of results; and the complex problem of making social participation a reality.

References

Altimir, Oscar. 1979. "La dimensión de la pobreza en América Latina." *Cuadernos de la CEPAL* 27. Santiago: CEPAL.
Arellano, José Pablo. 1985. *Políticas Sociales y Desarrollo: Chile, 1924–1984*. Santiago: CIEPLAN.
_____. 1989. "La seguridad social en Chile en los años 90." *Colección Estudios CIEPLAN* 27 (December). Santiago: CIEPLAN.

Banco Central de Chile. 1989. *Indicadores Económicos y Sociales, 1960–1988.* Santiago.

Butelmann, Andrea. 1992. "Deuda Externa y negociaciones financieras." In *Chile: Evolución Macroeconómica. Financiación Externa y Cambio Político en la década de los 80.* España: CEDEAL.

Cabezas, Mabel. 1988. "Revisión metodológica y estadística del gasto social en Chile." *Notas Técnicas* 144 (May). Santiago: CIEPLAN.

Castañeda, Tarsicio. 1984. "Contexto socioeconómico del descenso en la mortalidad infantil en Chile." *Estudios Públicos* 16 (Spring). Santiago: Centro de Estudios Públicos.

Comisión Económica para América Latina (CEPAL). 1991. *La pobreza en Chile en 1990.* Santiago.

Chateau, Jorge. 1981. "Algunos antecedentes sobre la situación de los pobladores en el gran Santiago." *Documento de Trabajo* 115 (June). Santiago: FLACSO.

Corbo, Vittorio. 1985. "Reforms and Macroeconomic Adjustments in Chile during 1974–84." *World Development* 13.

Cortázar, René, and Jorge Marshall. 1980. "Indice de precios al consumidor en Chile: 1970–1978." *Colección Estudios CIEPLAN* 4. Santiago: CIEPLAN.

Covarrubias, Alvaro. 1991. "El sistema de salud en Chile: Una visión crítica y una solución." *Documento de Trabajo* 28/91 (July). Santiago.

Crispi, Jaime A., and Mario Marcel. 1993. "Aspectos cuantitativos de la política social en Chile, 1987–93."

Dahse, Fernando. 1979. *Mapa de la extrema riqueza: Los grupos económicos y el proceso de concentración de capitales.* Santiago: Editorial Aconcagua.

de la Cuadra, Sergio, and Dominique Hachette. 1988. 'The Timing and Sequencing of a Trade Liberalization Policy: The Case of Chile." *Documento de Trabajo* 113. Universidad Católica de Chile.

Echeverría, Magdalena. 1984. *Enfermedades de los trabjadores y crisis económica.* Santiago: Programa de Economía del Trabajo.

Edwards, Sebastián, and Alejandra Edwards. 1987. *Monetarism and Liberalization: The Chilean Exiperiment.* Cambridge: Ballinger.

Espínola, Viola. 1990. "Evaluación de la estrategia de mercado para mejorar la calidad de la enseñanza básica subvencionada." *Documento de Discusión* 5. Santiago: Centro de Investigación y Desarrollo de la Educación.

_____. 1991. *Descentralización del sistema escolar en Chile.* Santiago: Centro de Investigación y Desarrollo de la Educación.

Flaño, Nicolás. 1991. "El fondo de solidaridad e inversión social: ¿En qué estamos pensando?" *Colección Estudios CIEPLAN* 31 (March).

Foxley, Alejandro. 1982. *Latin American Experiments in Neoconservative Economics.* University of California Press.

Foxley, Alejandro, and Dagmar Raczynski. 1983. "Vulnerable Groups in Recessionary Situations: The Case of Children and the Young in Chile." *World Development* 12(3).

French-Davis, Ricardo. 1982. "El experimento monetarists en Chile: Una síntesis crítica." *Colección Estudios CIEPLAN* 9. Santiago: CIEPLAN.

_____. 1991. "Desarrollo económico y equidad en Chile: Herencias y desafíos en el retorno a la democracia." *Colección Estudios CIEPLAN* 31. Santiago: CIEPLAN.

French-Davis, Ricardo, and Dagmar Raczynski. 1990. 'The Impact of Global Recession and National Policies on Living Standards: Chile, 1973–89." *Notas Técnicas 97. Santiago: CIEPLAN.*

Gatica, Jaime, and Molly Pollack. 1986. "Fuentes de cambio en la estructura del sector industrial chileno: 1967–1982." *Estudios de Economía* 13(2). Santiago: Universidad de Chile.

González, Nicolás, and others. 1980a. "Análisis del impacto de la atención primaria de salud sobre los indicadores de salud y nutrición: Chile, 1969–78." *Revista de Pediatría* 23 (April–December). Chile: Hospital Roberto del Rio.

_____. 1980b. "Programas de alimentación complementaria del sector salud en Chile." *Boletín de la Oficina Sanitaria Panamericana*. Washington, D.C.: OPS.

Graham, Carol. 1991. "From Emergency Employment to Social Investment." *Brookings Occasional Papers*. Washington, D.C.: Brookings Institution.

Haindl, Eric, and others. 1989. *Gasto social efectivo: Un instrumento que asegura la superación definitive de la pobreza crítica*. Chile: Oficina de Planificación Social and Universidad de Chile.

Held, Gunther. 1990. "Regulación y supervisión de la banca en la experiencia de liberalización financiera en Chile (1974–88)." In *Sistema financiero y asignación de recursos: Experiencias latinoamericanas y del Caribe*, edited by C. Massad and G.Held. Santiago: CEPALPNUD, Grupo Editor Latinoamericano.

Iglesias, Augusto, and others. 1991. *Diez años de historia del sistema AFP: Antecedentes estadísticos 1981–1991*. Santiago: AFP Habitat.

Instituto Nacional Estadfstica (INE). Various years. *Anuario de Demografía*. Santiago.

_____. Various years. *Compendio Estadistico*. Santiago.

_____. Various years. *Encuesta de Presupuestos Familiares*. Santiago.

INE-CELADE. 1987. *Chile: Prgyecciones de población por sexo y edad, Total Pais 19502025*. (April) Santiago.

INE-Ministerio de Salud. Various years. *Anuarios de Recursos y Atenciones*. Santiago.

ISAPRE Superintendancy. 1990. *Boletín Estadístico*. Santiago.

Jiménez, Jorge. 1985. "Atención médica en Chile, datos y reflexiones." In *Políticas y sistema de salud: Análisis preliminar de la década 1974–83*, edited by Jorge Jiménez. Santiago: Corporación de Promoción Universitaria.

Junta Nacional de Auxilio Escolar y Becas (JUNAEB). 1991. *Anuario Estadístico*. Santiago.

León, Arturo. 1991. "Pobreza urbana en Chile." (November) Santiago: CIEPLAN.

Marcel, Mario. 1990. "El desempleo juvenil en Chile y los desafíos del gobierno democráitico." In *Los jóvenes en Chile hoy*. Santiago: CIDE-CIEPLAN-SUR.

Marcel, Mario, and Alberto Arenas. 1991. "Reforma a la seguridad social en Chile." *Serie de Monografías* 5. Washington, D.C.: Banco Interamericano de Desarrollo.

Marfán, Manuel. 1988. "Una evaluación de la nueva reforma tributaria." *Colección Estudios CIEPLAN* 13 (June). Santiago: CIEPLAN.

Marshall, Jorge. 1981. "El gasto público en Chile, 1969–79." *Colección Estudios CIEPLAN* 5 (June). Santiago: CIEPLAN.

Martínez, Javier, and Arturo León. 1984. "La involución del proceso de desarrollo y la estructura social." *Materiales para* discusión 53 (November). Santiago: Centro de Estudios del Desaffollo.

Meller, Patricio, ed. 1990. "Resultados Económicos de Cuatro Gobiernos Chilenos." *Apuntes* 89 (October). Santiago: CIEPLAN.

_____. 1992. "Adjustment and Equity in Chile." In *Adjustment and Equity in Developing Countries*, edited by Christian Morrisson. Paris: OECD Development Centre.

_____. n.d. "Chile: Policy Experiments." In *Latin American Adjustment: How Much Has Happened?*. edited by John Williamson. Washington, D.C.: Institute for International Economics.

Meller, Patricio, and Pilar Romaguera. 1992. "Crisis, ajuste con éxito y costo social." In *Chile: Evolución Macroeconómica, Financiación Externa y Cambio Políco en la década de los 80*. España: CEDEAL.

Mercado, Olga. 1992. "La situación habitacional: Habitabilidad y allegamiento." In *Población, educación, vivienda, salud, empleo y pobreza. CASEN 1990*. Chile: Ministerio de Planificación y Cooperación.

Mesa-Lago, Carmelo. 1978. *Social Secuity in Latin America: Pressure Groups, Stratification and Inequality*. University of Pittsburgh Press.

Ministerio de Planificación y Coordinación (MIDEPLAN). 1991. *Un proceso de integración al desarrollo: Informe social 1990–91*. (August) Santiago: República de Chile.

_____. 1992a. *Avanzando en equidad: Un proceso de integración al desarrollo 1990–92*. (April) Santiago: República de Chile.

_____. 1992b. *Fomento de la pequeña producción*. (July) Santiago: Repúiblica de Chile. Ministerio de Salud. n.d. *Indicadores Financieros Sector Público* de Salud. Santiago.

Ministry of Health. *n.d. Recursos humanos de salud en Chile*. Santiago.

Miranda, Ernesto. 1990. "Descentralización y privatización del sistema de salud chileno." *Estudios Públicos* 39 (Winter). Santiago: Centro de Estudios Públicos.

Mizala, Alejandra, and Pilar Romaguera. 1991. "¿Es el sector público un sector líder en la determinación de los salarios? Evidencia para la economía chilena." In *Colección Estudios CIEPLAN* 33. Santiago: CIEPLAN.

Molina, Irene. 1985. "El programa de erradicación de campamentos en la región metropolitana (1979–84): Implicancias socioeconómicas y espaciales." Thesis, Pontificia Universidad Católica de Chile, Department of Geography.

Monckeberg Fernando, and others. 1984. "Evolución de la desnutrición infantil y mortalidad infanfil en Chile en los últimos años." *Creces* 10. Chile: Corporación de Nutrición Infantil.

Morales, Eduardo, and Sergio Rojas. 1986. "Relocalización socioespacial de la pobreza: Política estatal y presión popular, 1979–85." *Documento de Trabajo* 280 (January). Chile: FLACSO.

Necochea, Andrés. 1984. "Estructura de subsidios en la política habitacional: Región metropolitana, 1983." *Documento de Trabgjo* 137 (July). Santiago: Instituto de Estudios Urbanos, Universidad Católica de Chile.

Ogrodnik, Esteban. 1984. "Encuesta a los allegados en el Gran Santiago." *Revista de Economía* 22 (April). Santiago: Universidad de Chile.

332 RACZYNSKI AND ROMAGUERA

PREALC. 1990. "Pobreza y empleo: Un análisis del período 1969–87 en el Gran Santiago." *Documento de Trabajo* 348. Santiago.

Raczynski, Dagmar. 1983. "Reformas al sector salud: Diálogos y debates." *Colección Estudios CIEPLAN* 10 (June). Santiago: CIEPLAN.

_____. 1986. "¿Disminuyó la extrema pobreza entre 1979 y 1982?" Notas *Técnicas* 90 (December). Santiago: CIEPLAN.

_____. 1988. "Social Policy, Poverty and Vulnerable Groups: Children in Chile." In *Adjustment with a Human Face: Ten Country Case Studies*, vol. II, edited by Giovanni Andrea Cornia, Richard Jolly, and Frances Stewart. Oxford: Clarendon Press.

_____. 1991a. "Descentrahzación y políticas sociales: Lecciones de la experiencia chilena y tareas pendientes." *Colección Estudios CIEPLAN* 31 (March). Santiago: CIEPLAN.

_____. 1991b. "La ficha CAS y la focalización de programas sociales." *Notas Técnicas* 141 (August). Santiago: CIEPLAN.

_____. 1992a. "Políticas sociales en Chile: Origen, transformaciones y perspectives." Paper prepared for comparative project, "Social Policies for the Urban Poor in the Southern Cone of Latin America: Welfare Reform in a Democratic Context." University of Notre Dame, Helen Kellogg Institute of International Relations (January).

_____. 1992b. "Tipos de pobreza, Chile 1987: Resultados de un ejercicio empírico." *Notas Técnicas* 146 (March). Santiago: CIEPLAN.

Raczynski, Dagmar, and Mabel Cabezas. 1988. "Ingresos y gastos municipales: Chile (1977–87) and Gran Santiago (1985–86)." *Notas Técnicas* 121 (October). Santiago: CIEPLAN.

Raczynski, Dagmar, and César Oyarzo. 1981. "¿Por qué cae la tasa de mortalidad infantil en Chile?" *Colección Estudios CIEPLAN* 6 (June). Santiago: CIEPLAN.

Raczynski, Dagmar, and Claudia Serrano. 1985. *Vivir la pobreza: Testimonio de mujeres*. Santiago: CIEPLAN-PISPAL.

_____. 1987. "Administración y gestión local." *Colección Estudios CIEPLAN* 22 (December). Santiago: CIEPLAN.

_____. 1988. "Planificación para el desarrollo local." *Colección Estudios CIEPLAN* 24 (June). Santiago: CIEPLAN.

_____. 1990. "La comunidad frente a los programas y servicios del Estado: La salud pública en Peñalolén Alto." *Apuntes CIEPLAN* 96 (December). Santiago: CIEPLAN.

Raczynski, Dagmar, Claudia Serrano, and Edgardo Bousquet. 1990. "La comunidad frente a los programas y servicios del Estado: Los jardines infantiles en Peñalolén Alto." *Apuntes CIEPLAN* 95 (November). Santiago: CIEPLAN.

Ramírez, Rolando A. 1990. "Prestaciones de salud." *Revista Administración en Salud* 9.

Rodríguez, Jorge. 1985. La *distribución del ingieso y el gasto social en Chile —1983*. Santiago: ILADES-Editorial Salesiana.

Rodríguez, Jorge, and Jorge Jiménez. 1985. "Comparative Analysis of Productivity in Public and Private Chilean Hospitals." Paper presented at the Annual Conference of Economists 1985 (August). Santiago.

Romaguera, Pilar. 1989. "Diagnóstico del desempleo en Chile y orientaciones de política." *Documento de Trabajo* 66. Santiago: Programa de Economía del Trabajo.

Romero, María I. 1985. "Recursos humanos en salud en Chile: Análisis de una década." In *Políticas y sistema de salud: Análisis preliminar de la década 1974–83*, edited by Jorge Jiménez. Santiago: Corporación de Promoción Universitaria.

Sanfuentes, Andrés. 1988. "Hipótesis acerca de las causas del crecimiento del empleo." *Serie de Investigación* 1-1. Santiago: ILADES.

Scherman, Jorge. 1990. *Techo y Abrigo*. Santiago: PET, Colección Experiencias Populares.

Schmidt-Hebbel, Klaus, and Pablo Marshall. 1981. "Revisión del IPC para el período 1970–1980: Una nota." *Documento* 176. Santiago: Departamento Estudios BHC.

Sojo, Ana. 1990. "Naturaleza y selectividad de la politica social." *Revista de la CEPAL* 41 (August).

Stewart, Frances, and Gustav Ranis. 1992. "Decentralization in Chile." Yale University, Department of Economics.

Superintendencia de Seguridad Social. Various issues. *Estadísticas de Seguridad Social*. Santiago.

Taucher, Erika. 1989. "Effects of Decreasing Fertility on Infant Mortality Levels." *Infant Mortality and Health Studies* 57e. Canada: International Development Research Centre.

Torche, Aristides. 1987. "Distribuir el ingreso para satisfacer las necesidas básicas." In *Desarrollo Económico en Democracia*, edited by Felipe Larraín. Santiago: Ediciones Universidad Católca.

Velázquez, Mario. 1988. "Evolución del empleo público en Chile: 1974–85." *Documento de Trabajo* 59. Santiago: PET.

Vergara, Pilar. 1990. *Políticas hacia la extrema pgbreza en Chile 1973 / 1988*. Santiago: Facultad Latinoamericana de Ciencias Sociales.

Yañez, José. 1992. "Reformas Tributarias." In *Reformas Económicas en Chile*, edited by Oscar Muñoz. Banco Interamericano de Desarrollo Serie Monografías 7.

CHAPTER NINE

Mexico: Social Spending and Food Subsidies during Adjustment in the 1980s

Santiago Friedmann, Nora Lustig, and
Arianna Legovini

IN 1982, Mexico faced a balance-of-payments crisis with far-reaching consequences. During the late 1970s, when the price of oil peaked, oil exports became the major source of both internal and external revenues.[1] The new availability of funds led the government to engage in an expansionary fiscal policy financed not only by oil revenues but by the accumulation of foreign debt. While the situation was sustainable in the favorable environment of the late 1970s, events that began in mid-1981 dramatically reversed this state of affairs. Between 1981 and 1982 the average price of oil fell from U.S. $33.2 a barrel to U.S. $28.7 a barrel, causing a fall in export and government revenues. The interest rate on the external debt rose, doubling the debt service from U.S. $6.1 billion in 1980 to U.S. $12.2 billion in 1982.[2] At the same time, foreign lending became increasingly difficult to obtain. With no alterna-

The authors are grateful to Hans Binswanger and Per Pinstrup-Andersen for their useful comments.

1. By 1981 oil exports represented 72.5 percent of total export revenues; see Lustig (1992, table 2.2). They also represented 27 percent of government revenues; see Salinas (1991, p. 147).
2. See Lustig (1992, table 2.2).

tive source of financing, Mexico was out of reserves and faced a balance-of-payments crisis in 1982. The crisis highlighted the need to rationalize the size and functions of the government and to liberalize domestic and international markets. The size of the fiscal adjustment between late 1982 and 1990 reveals the extent of the effort undertaken by the government.

Such an adjustment, coupled with price liberalization and the lifting of general subsidies, affected all spheres of the economy. The fiscal adjustment decreased the funds available for social expenditures, and the tax increase reduced disposable income. The currency devaluation caused a drop in real income, and price increases on formerly subsidized products further decreased purchasing power. Furthermore, the rise in debt servicing increased the flow of national income going abroad, while at the same time the debt crisis halted the flow of foreign investment and access to new credit except from official sources. The rigidity inherent in a private sector accustomed to protection exacerbated the economic impact of these developments.[3]

This paper focuses on how changes in social spending and the reform of food subsidies affected living standards during adjustment. We assess the Mexican government's response to the crisis and its ability to target social spending and food subsidies. Proper targeting can compensate significantly for the decline in earned income experienced by the poor. Specifically, we address the size of social spending cuts and the nature of food subsidy reform, as well as the government's efforts to mitigate their impact on the poor; the extent to which spending cuts limited human and physical resources in institutions providing public education and health care; and the deterioration in social indicators.

One important question is not addressed. We do not attempt to impute the value of social spending and the change in subsidy schemes to real incomes at the household level. Rather we look at trends in social spending in programs we know are geared to the poorer segments of the population. In particular, we analyze spending and resource availability in primary education, the Secretariat of Health, and the Solidarity and regional development programs. We also examine the process of replacing general food subsidies with targeted ones. First we present an overview of trends in real income, employment, poverty, and income distribution.

---

3. See Lustig (1992, chapter 2).

Earned Real Income

Because Mexico's national accounts do not include a section on personal income, it is difficult to disentangle the effects of adjustment on real family incomes after taxes. Some of the observed variables reflect combinations of the different components of adjustment.[4] Table 9-1 traces the evolution of disposable income and several indicators of real wages. Disposable income implicitly incorporates the impact of higher taxes, and real wages incorporate the elimination of consumer subsidies. Disposable income per capita fell by an average of 5.1 percent a year between 1983 and 1988, which is less than wages, whose annual decline in the same period was between 10.5 and 7.7 percent, depending on the sector and the occupation. The difference between disposable income and wages is significant, but can be explained by the fact that most households receive income from both wage and nonwage sources, and nonwage per capita income declined by considerably less than wage income.

We analyze broad trends in earned real income, which we disaggregate into wage income, nonwage income, and agricultural income. It was not possible to measure the evolution of pure factor (that is, labor and capital) returns, because nonwage income in the national accounts includes imputed wages of the self-employed.

Wage Income

The adjustment process produced a sharp fall in real wages.[5] Table 9-1 indicates the fall in real wages per worker was between 7.7 and 10.5 percent a year (depending on the category) in the period 1983–88, with the sharpest declines occurring during the two years of deepest economic contraction, 1983 and 1986. The total wage bill fell by a similar amount.[6] The behavior of wage income is the combined result of changes in the real wage and in employment. The available indicators show that the decline in wage income is a result of contracting real wages, not reduced employment. According to the national accounts, employment rose an average of 0.4 percent a year between 1983 and 1988.[7]

4. This section comes from Lustig (1992, chapter 3).
5. There was no decline in nominal wages. Real wages declined as nominal wages rose more slowly than the general price level.
6. See Lustig (1992, table 3-2).
7. See Lustig (1992, table 3-3). The definition of employment in the National Accounts measures the number of workposts, that is, the number of laborers needed to produce a certain level of output given some labor-to-output coefficients. It is an indirect estimate of employment.

Table 9-1. Income, Consumption, Wages, and Employment, Mexico, 1981–90[a]
Percentage growth rates unless otherwise specified

| | | | | | | | | | | | Geometric average | |
Indicator	1981	1982	1983	1984	1985	1986	1987	1988	1989	1990	1983–88	1989–90
Disposable income per capita	3.4	-5.4	-14.2	-1.0	1.9	-15.3	5.0	-5.4	7.9	6.3	-5.1	7.1
Private consumption per capita	4.9	-4.8	-7.4	1.1	1.5	-4.6	-2.2	0.3	4.5	4.0	-1.9	4.2
Wage income per worker	4.8	-5.1	-22.9	-5.0	-0.2	-9.4	-3.0	-9.1	4.6	1.9	-8.6	3.2
Wages quoted by industrial survey	5.0	0.1	-24.1	-6.8	1.1	-6.9	-6.5	-0.5	8.9	n.a.	-7.7	4.3
Minimum wage	1.0	-0.1	-21.9	-9.0	-1.2	-10.5	-6.3	-12.7	-6.6	-9.1	-10.5	-7.9
Wages to government employees per worker	5.4	-2.6	-28.0	-5.8	0.3	-14.0	0.6	-8.4	7.1	n.a.	-9.8	n.a.
Urban open unemployment level	4.2	4.2	6.3	5.7	4.3	4.3	3.9	3.5	3.0	2.8	4.7	2.9
Share of nonwage income in total income	60.0	61.8	68.6	69.2	68.4	69.1	70.5	71.5	71.9	72.7	69.5	72.3

a. Real figures are calculated using the CPI from the Banco de Mexico (1990a). The 1991 index was calculated using the average annual change in consumer prices as reported by Banco de Mexico.
b. Preliminary (1990b, table 28). All price indexes are converted to base 1980 = 100.
See note b in table 4-2.
Sources: Population figures: yearly levels calculated using growth rates from Ordorica (1990, pp. 4–6). Ordorica provides yearly growth rates for 1980–90 and cites the eleventh population census preliminary figure for total population in 1990, estimated to be 81.1 million.
Real disposable income per capita: Nominal figures for 1980 to 1984 are from (1988, table 2). Nominal figure for 1985 is from INEGI (1990, table 2). Nominal figures for 1986 to 1987 are from INEGI (1991). Real figures are derived using the consumer price index (1980 = 100) from the Banco de Mexico (1990b, table 28). Figures for 1988 to 1990 are from Eugenia Gomez Luna, director, Direccion de Contabilidad Nacional y Estadistica Economicas, INEGI.
Private consumption per capita: for 1980–84 figures, INEGI (1988, tables 66–69). Figure for 1985 is from INEGI (1990, table 60). The 1986 to 1987 figures are from INEGI (1991, tables 60–63). The 1988–91 figures are from Macro Asesoria Economica, S.C. (July–September 1992, table V.1).
Total wage income per workplace: figures for 1980–86 are from Comision Nacional de los Salarios Minimos (December 1989, table 2.6). Figures for 1987–90 are from INEGI, unpublished document (received from Maria Eugenia Gomez Luna, director of National Accounts, INEGI).
Wages quoted by industrial survey: Comision Nacional de los Salarios Minimos (December 1989, pp. 157–60); and (September 1991). Figures for 1989 are preliminary.
Minimum wage: figures for 1980–86 are from the Comision Nacional de los Salarios Minimos (1986, table 5A). Figures for 1987–90 are respectively from Banco de Mexico, *Informe Anual*, (1987, p. 119; 1988, p. 136; 1989, p. 138; 1990, p. 139).
For 1983–88 average: Macro Asesoria Economica (1990, table 15). For 1989 and 1990, *GEA Economico* (March 12, 1992), p. 5.
Wages to government employees per worker: de Gortari (1991, p. 145).
For 1983–88 average: Macro Asesoria Economica (1990, table 15). For 1989 and 1990, *GEA Economico* (March 12, 1992), p. 5.
For 1980–84 average: Instituto Nacional de Estadistica Geografia e Informatica (1988, table 43). For 1985–86, INEGI (1991, table 37). Figures from 1987–90 are from INEGI, unpublished document (received from Maria Eugenia Gomez Luna, director of National Accounts, INEGI).
n.a. Not available.

At first it seems puzzling that it was possible to inflict such wage cuts without provoking widespread political or social unrest and countless strikes.[8] One possible explanation is that although wages fell sharply, the decline in household income was not as dramatic because many households received income from sources other than wages, which fell substantially less. Data on real per capita consumption support this interpretation. Private consumption per capita declined cumulatively by 11.1 percent between 1983 and 1988, while real wage income fell 41.5 percent during the same period.[9] The difference suggests that Mexican households received nonwage income or used their savings. The lack of resistance to wage cuts can also be explained by the government's long-standing control of the labor movement, exercised through a remarkable combination of coercion and cooptation ever since the 1930s.

Nonwage Income

In contrast to wage income, which declined on average 8.2 percent a year from 1983 to 1988, nonwage income declined only 1.2 percent a year.[10] This produced a sharp increase in the share of nonwage income in total income (wage plus nonwage), which rose from 60 percent in 1981 to 71.5 percent in 1988. The behavior of nonwage income—in contrast to wage income—may reflect the fact that prices of goods and services, excluding those produced by the public sector or subject to price controls, were probably more "freely" set than wages.

The performance of nonwage income is in part explained by rising profits in the modern sector of the economy. Though there are no estimates of profit rates, the profit margin (as a proportion of total sales) rose in most manufacturing sectors during 1982–87.[11] It would be a mistake to believe, however, that all nonwage income is profits, rents, or interest income that accrues only to the wealthy. The nonwage category includes the income of the poor peasant or small shop owner in addition to that of the wealthy modern businessman. Nonwage income is an important share of the total income of the poor as well as the wealthy. To a lesser degree, it also accounts for part of the income of the

8. The number of strikes did rise compared to previous years, but the increase seems modest when compared with the size of wage cuts. In 1982 the number of strikes rose more than sixfold to 675. However, that figure fell in 1983 to 230, even though real wages declined by 25 percent. There was an upsurge with the 1986 oil shock, when the number of strikes reached 312. Thereafter it fell to precrisis levels. (Salinas 1990, p. 334)

9. See Lustig (1992, table 3-2).

10. See Lustig (1992, table 3-4).

11. Ize (1990, table 1, p. 6).

middle sectors. The bottom 10 percent of Mexican households derive one-third of their income from wages, with the other two-thirds more or less equally distributed between nonmonetary income (such as home-consumed crops and imputed housing costs) and nonwage monetary income.[12] Thus part of the drastic fall in wage income must have been compensated by the relatively better performance of nonwage income for all income groups. This may in part explain why consumption per capita fell much less than wages, and why no widespread social protests erupted.

Agricultural Income

Because most of the very poor in Mexico work in agriculture it is important to analyze the evolution of wage and nonwage income in agriculture as well as of the output and price of corn—the basic peasant crop—during the adjustment period.[13] Agriculture seems to have a life of its own in terms of output performance; it does not follow the general pattern. For example, during the severe economywide contraction in 1983, agricultural output grew. Conversely, while the rest of the economy was on a recovery path in 1988–89, agriculture experienced a severe setback.

During the first stabilization program, from 1983 to 1985, agricultural output and employment fared better than the overall economy. Real wages in agriculture fell less than aggregate real wages. Nonwage income in agriculture rose, while nonwage income in the nonagricultural sector contracted. Better prices for agricultural goods and unusually favorable weather conditions may explain this performance. Real devaluations and attempts to align agricultural prices with world prices contributed to an improvement in agricultural prices, and the on-farm price of corn was no exception. Because most poor peasants are corn growers and most of the corn is grown by poor peasants, poor rural households may have suffered less during this crunch than their urban counterparts.[14]

This result has been confirmed by another author who conducted interviews in mid-1985 concerning employment conditions in rural areas.[15] In all but one of Mexico's midsection states, farmers complained of labor shortages.

12. See Lustig (1992, table 3-5).
13. According to the 1984 Household Survey, about 60 percent of the households in the bottom 20 percent of the income distribution list agriculture as their main activity. See Lustig (1992, table 3-1). For agricultural data, see Lustig (1992, tables 3-6 and 3-4).
14. See CEPAL (1982, table 17, p. 152); and (1991, pp. 69–70).
15. Gregory (1987, p. 57).

In several areas wages offered to rural workers were well above the minimum wage. Labor shortages were apparently the result of migration to the United States. In addition, the author found a virtual absence of return migration from urban areas, despite cuts in urban wages.

This favorable pattern reversed itself in 1986, when agricultural output contracted. After 1987, and especially in 1988 and 1989, agriculture's performance was worse than that of the economy as a whole. Bad weather conditions and a deterioration in agricultural prices might explain this downturn. A reduction in agricultural subsidies and credit, as well as the absence of new investment, further explains the decline. During 1988 and 1989 agricultural prices may have lagged as a result of the Economic Solidarity Pact, which clamped down on some prices—including agricultural prices—more than others.[16]

The evolution of corn output and prices, as well as of wage and nonwage agricultural income, indicates that economic hardship in agriculture must have been severe in 1988 and 1989. This finding suggests that during the pact, when the outlook for the rest of the economy appeared promising, the poorest population suffered a deterioration in living standards. The data show an improvement in agricultural output and prices in 1990, so the incomes of the rural poor may have also recovered. The absence of data at the household level prevents further analysis.

Unemployment and Employment

The sharp initial decline in aggregate output growth in 1983 was accompanied by an approximately 50 percent increase in the open urban unemployment rate.[17] However, despite lagging economic performance and continuous additions to the economically active population that were estimated at nearly 1 million a year,[18] the unemployment rate during the 1980s soon descended to levels below those during the oil boom.

This at first surprising result might be explained by the downward flexibility of Mexican real wages. The large decline in real wages on the one hand allowed firms to keep labor costs in check while facing declining demand without having to reduce employment; on the other, it allowed the government to reduce total expenditures without resorting to widespread layoffs. Moreover,

16. Appendini (1991, pp. 64–66, 75–76, 84–85).
17. See table 9-1 and Lustig (1992, tables 3-3 and 1-5).
18. Comisión Nacional de los Salarios Mínimos (1989, p. 27).

those who did not remain employed as wage earners in the formal sector were likely to be willing to work in the informal sector for lower pay or as nonremunerated family labor.[19] In a country like Mexico with no unemployment insurance benefits, it is not surprising that people prefer lower-quality jobs to unemployment. To be unemployed is a luxury that most Mexicans cannot afford.

The urban open unemployment rates seem too low when compared with the aggregate "implicit" unemployment rate, measured by the ratio between total employment and the economically active population. Implicit unemployment was 11.4 percent in 1980 and 20.3 percent in 1985.[20] This discrepancy arises because the two statistics measure different things. To obtain the implicit unemployment levels the national accounts measure the labor posts required to produce a certain amount of output with a given technology. The urban open unemployment statistics are calculated as the difference between the economically active population and those who were employed for at least one hour during the week of reference, including those who worked for no remuneration (among whom are family members who work for no explicit payment). The definition of employment embedded in the urban unemployment statistics thus includes all cases of "precarious" employment, unlike the definition in the national accounts. In practice, for example, one labor post can be occupied by more than one person. The difference between the two indicators can perhaps be interpreted as a rough estimate of underemployment.[21]

The structure of employment, disaggregated according to occupational category, shows the following pattern of change. The proportion of wage earners in the urban labor force fell from 83.4 percent in 1982 to 76.2 percent in 1985, while the proportion of self-employed increased from 12.1 to 15 percent, and the share of unpaid family workers jumped from 2.1 to 4.6 percent.[22] There-

19. There is evidence that formal sector employment declined; see Gregory (1987, p. 56). The percentage of wage earners in total employment fell between 1982 and 1989. The percentage of family workers without remuneration in three major urban centers increased between 1982 and 1985, then held steady afterward. Of the three urban centers, only in Mexico City was there an increase in the percentage of self-employed workers between 1982 and 1985. Between 1985 and 1989, the average percentage of self-employed workers in sixteen urban areas rose. See Lustig (1992, table 9, p. 56); and *Comisión Nacional de los Salarios Mínimos* (1989, pp. 99–100).

20. Figures for total employment are from *Comisión Nacional de los Salarios Mínimos* (1989, table 1.1, p. 27). The figure for the economically active population is a linear extrapolation from the 1980 and 1985 figures in the same source (table 2.6, p. 67).

21. The concept of underemployment is always difficult to define. It usually refers to the fact that people are employed in activities with very low productivity and very low pay.

22. Gregory (1987, p. 55).

after the proportion of wage earners continued to decline, though at the much slower rate of about 1 percentage point a year until 1989.[23] Between 1980 and 1988, employment in services (characteristic of informal employment) as a proportion of total employment increased slightly, whereas employment in agriculture hardly changed and in industry declined, especially in construction. The changes have been 1 percentage point or less in one direction or the other.[24] The rise in the proportion of the self-employed and of those employed in services is consistent with the idea that during adjustment informal employment rose. Income from informal employment probably compensated in part for the dramatic decline in wage income from formal employment.[25]

Poverty and Income Distribution

Unfortunately, Mexico does not have household surveys from immediately before and after the period of crisis and adjustment. Surveys are instead available for 1977, 1984, and 1989. The 1977 survey was taken during the economic slowdown that followed the 1976 crisis.[26] Because of both its timing and differences in sampling techniques and definitions, it is not strictly comparable with the 1984 and 1989 surveys. The 1984 survey, in principle, is comparable to that of 1989. However, one must bear in mind that in 1984 the country had already experienced the severe contraction of 1983 that followed the 1982 balance-of-payments crisis (table 9-1). Because the crisis had already begun to take its toll on household income, 1984 is far from the ideal benchmark.

Official estimates show that extreme poverty rose from 2.5 percent to 7.3 percent between 1984 and 1989, and moderate poverty rose from 16.6 percent to 22.6 percent.[27]

23. *Comisión Nacional de los Salarios Mínimos* (1989, pp. 99–100).

24. *Comisión Nacional de los Salarios Mínimos* (1989, p. 67).

25. An indirect indicator is that real private consumption per capita declined by substantially less than real wages; see Lustig (1992, table 3-2).

26. Lustig (1992, chapter 1).

27. To assess how poverty changed between 1984 and 1989 is less simple than one might think. Data directly from the surveys suggest that poverty in that period actually falls for a range of poverty lines that covers the entire set of estimates most commonly used for Mexico. However, this result is intuitively paradoxical, as all indicators lead one to expect the opposite. For example, agricultural and nonagricultural wages, corn prices and output, and private consumption per capita fell between 1984 and 1989. One possible explanation is that the degree of income underreporting was higher in 1984 than in 1989, which a straightforward comparison with figures from

The distribution of income between clearly worsened between 1984 and 1989: the share of the top 10 percent rose from 32.8 percent to 37.9 percent.[28] Interestingly the "middle" 50 percent of households proportionately lost more than the poorest 40 percent.[29]

Social Spending

The key component in Mexico's stabilization and adjustment program was the cut in the fiscal deficit. One year after the first stabilization program began in December 1982, the fiscal deficit, measured by the public sector borrowing requirement (PSBR), was halved from 16.9 percent of GDP in 1982 to 8.6 percent in 1983 (table 9-2).[30] Because the PSBR is determined in part by factors beyond the government's control, such as interest payments on internal and external debt, a preferable measure of its commitment to fiscal discipline is the so-called primary government surplus, which excludes those factors. Using the primary surplus as an indicator, Mexico's effort appears remarkable and sustained. From a deficit of close to 8 percent a year in 1981–82, the primary accounts rose to an average surplus of 4.1 percent a year between 1983 and 1988 (table 9-2).

The increase in the primary surplus was the result of a combination of measures that affected both the revenue and expenditure sides of the fiscal accounts. The new tax law (which increased the value-added tax, enlarged the tax base, and lowered the top marginal rates) and, more important in its immediate effect, the new pricing of public sector goods and services (especially gasoline and other oil derivatives) enhanced fiscal and nonfiscal revenues, re-

the national accounts supports. When the 1984 income data are corrected for underreporting to match the national accounts, the result is reversed: poverty increases across the entire range of poverty lines between 1984 and 1989. In particular, using the extreme poverty line, the proportion of households below the poverty line rises from 2.8 to 4 percent; based on the highest available poverty line, the proportion increases from 51.5 to 55.2 percent. These results should be taken with extreme reservations, because they are sensitive to the assumptions made in the matching process; see Lustig and Mitchell (1994). These figures were calculated using total household expenditures per capita.

28. See Lustig (1992, table 3-12).

29. The PSBR, however, would again rise to two-digit levels after the second large drop in oil prices in 1986. The magnitude of the PSBR then was not the result of fiscal expansion, but of high inflation and its impact on domestic interest rates, which rose from 48.6 percent in 1984 (1.2 percent in real terms) to 86.7 percent in 1986 (12.3 percent in real terms). See Lustig (1992, pp. 40–41, table 2-4).

30. See Lustig (1992, chapters 2 and 4).

Table 9-2. *Adjustment and Stabilization Efforts, Mexico, 1980–91*
Percent

Year	Primary government surplus[a]	Public sector borrowing requirement	Year	Primary government surplus[a]	Public sector borrowing requirement
1980	-3.0	7.5	1988	6.0	12.3
1981	-8.0	14.1	1989	7.6	5.5
1982	-7.3	16.9	1990[b]	6.9	4.0
1983	4.2	8.6	1991[b]	5.5	1.5
1984	4.8	8.5	Geometric average		
1985	3.4	9.6	1983–88	4.1	11.8
1986	1.6	15.9	1989–90	7.3	4.8
1987	4.7	16.0			

Sources: Figure for 1980 is from Macro Asesoria Economica (1991, table 20.1). Figures for 1981 to 1989 are from the Banco de Mexico as cited in Macro Asesoria Economica, *Macro Perspectivas-2 Trimestre, 1991* (1991, table viii.1). Figure for 1990 is from *Macro Data* (April 1992), table 9. Figures exclude receipts from privatization of public enterprises. Figure for 1991 is from Banco de Mexico, *Informe Anual* (1991), p. 8.
a. The primary surplus excludes interest payments (on internal and external debt).
b. Preliminary.

spectively.[31] The government reduced spending through drastic cuts in subsidies and noninterest expenditures in all sectors. As total expenditures, which include payments on domestic and foreign debt, declined between 1982 and 1988 from 45.4 to 40.6 percent of GDP, primary expenditures fell from 30.7 to 22.2 percent of GDP in the same time period (table 9-3). The reduction in primary expenditures were the result of a huge reduction in public investment, a drastic cut in government wages, and the elimination of most consumer and producer subsidies.[32] Public investment fell from 10.8 percent of GDP in 1982 to 4.9 percent by 1988. Total public sector wage payments fell from 12.8 percent of GDP to 9.7 percent in the same period. The contraction in the public sector wage bill was not achieved by resizing government employment, which actually increased during the period of adjustment, but by cutting the real wage per government worker at an average rate of 9.8 percent a year, in real terms, between 1983 and 1988 (see table 9-1).[33] Expenditures on general food subsidies fell from 1.25 percent of GDP in 1983 to 0.37 percent in 1988.

In particular, expenditures for social development, the major component of social spending, contracted by 6.2 percent a year between 1983 and 1988 (table 9-4). To assess the magnitude of this contraction relative to cuts in other government expenditures, programmable government expenditures (which

31. For a description of changes in food subsidies, see Martín del Campo and Calderón Tinoco (1990).
32. For these government statistics, see Salinas (1991, pp. 145, 165). Total public employment was 3.7 million in 1982 and 4.4 million in 1988.
33. World Bank (1991, table 21, p. 29).

Table 9-3. *Government Expenditures as Share of GDP, Mexico, 1970–90*

Percent

Year	Total expenditures as share of GDP	Primary expenditures as share of GDP[a]	Total programmable expenditures as share of GDP[b]	Year	Total expenditures as share of GDP	Primary expenditures as share of GDP[a]	Total programmable expenditures as share of GDP[b]
1970	19.29	17.60	16.30	1983	43.32	28.19	24.77
1971	19.57	18.04	16.82	1984	40.01	28.05	24.84
1972	21.64	19.94	18.72	1985	39.01	26.29	23.28
1973	24.39	22.78	20.99	1986	42.45	24.78	22.11
1974	25.74	23.85	21.74	1987	43.81	23.05	20.34
1975	30.56	28.54	26.37	1988	40.55	22.19	19.07
1976	28.96	26.40	24.49	1989	34.38	20.43	17.53
1977	27.60	24.83	23.26	1990	30.57	20.37	17.25
1978	28.64	25.76	24.19	1971–75	24.38	22.63	20.93
1979	30.10	27.04	25.02	1976–77	28.28	25.62	23.87
1980	33.04	29.63	27.12	1978–81	32.62	29.04	26.76
1981	38.72	33.73	30.70	1983–88	41.36	25.42	22.40
1982	45.36	30.74	28.07	1989–90	32.48	20.40	17.39

Source: Salinas de Gortari (1991, p. 153). For 1970–86 GDP see Banco de Mexico, *Indicadores Economico* (1987, p. 11-2; 1988, p. 11-24). For 1987–90 see Banco de Mexico, *Informe Anual* (1991, p. 267).

a. Primary expenditures are total expenditures minus interest payments and debt servicing costs.

b. Programmable expenditures exclude interest payments, commissions, and other expenditures associated with domestic and foreign debt, revenue sharing with states, municipalities and others, and fiscal incentives.

Table 9-4. *Public Sector Programmable Expenditures, by Type, Mexico, 1971–90[a]*

Annual percent change

Type	1971	1972	1973	1974	1975	1976	1977	1978	1979	1980	1981	1982	1983
Total	7.47	20.75	21.61	9.87	28.16	-3.23	-1.75	12.57	12.91	17.41	22.20	-9.03	-16.44
Legislative power	-5.57	-5.87	32.98	8.60	-13.59	46.35	-23.33	10.13	1.66	34.20	7.54	-9.30	12.25
Executive power	7.51	20.82	21.68	9.86	28.18	-3.30	-1.70	12.58	12.93	17.40	22.21	-9.03	-16.48
Social	16.47	32.14	13.16	11.56	24.40	9.16	-3.40	9.83	16.56	17.30	18.69	-5.91	-27.34
Rural development	22.98	49.60	30.49	11.30	51.58	-4.65	-16.05	12.09	20.47	45.98	7.98	-19.18	-15.01
Social development	15.17	28.40	8.82	11.65	16.27	14.55	0.70	9.22	15.48	8.99	22.85	-1.39	-30.79
Economic	12.42	13.20	31.04	10.66	33.55	-12.79	-0.58	17.98	13.89	16.46	28.39	-11.44	-6.96
Fishing	...	...	...	-14.67	29.62	6.43	0.40	9.01	5.75	15.24	44.08	15.65	-7.15
Transports and communications	11.38	-3.82	24.49	-14.23	25.58	13.02	-12.94	0.02	20.63	18.10	15.82	-4.06	-0.60
Commerce	-1.47	0.02	33.85	77.71	14.70	-32.50	20.54	21.06	-14.95	29.94	54.65	-14.61	19.63
Tourism	88.86	135.33	-11.35	-2.26	87.22	-3.51	-7.99	-0.07	18.82	13.96	14.31	-13.70	-38.63
Energy	11.15	9.82	14.60	7.80	39.38	-12.25	-2.02	27.11	18.85	10.16	27.03	-14.90	-19.02
Industry	340.67	229.47	99.02	8.11	43.82	-20.50	2.56	3.39	18.86	31.34	22.11	-6.51	4.73
Administrative and defense	-23.42	12.41	17.48	0.94	16.36	-3.46	1.33	-0.72	-10.77	24.98	1.69	-9.92	-16.81
Administration	-30.12	10.67	20.24	-1.98	18.66	-7.80	6.27	-1.70	-19.01	38.83	-11.37	-8.72	-22.68
Justice and security	1.42	16.86	10.82	8.60	10.89	7.52	-9.39	1.76	9.51	-0.23	34.77	-11.92	-6.69

Type	1984	1985	1986	1987	1988	1989	1990	Geometric average				
								1971–75	1976–77	1978–81	1983–88	1989–90
Total	3.98	-4.04	-8.24	-0.60	-5.14	-5.13	2.80	17.3	-2.5	16.2	-5.3	-1.2
Legislative power	34.20	8.51	-4.21	28.58	11.47	5.64	15.01	2.1	5.9	12.7	14.4	10.2
Executive power	3.92	-4.07	-8.25	-0.69	-5.21	-5.18	2.74	17.4	-2.5	16.2	-5.3	-1.3
Social	-0.24	4.24	-9.11	-5.46	-4.11	4.13	8.98	19.3	2.7	15.5	-7.6	6.5
Rural development	-8.39	-8.16	-7.10	-22.76	-19.76	-3.00	8.77	32.3	-10.5	20.8	-13.8	2.7
Social development	2.56	8.03	-9.63	-0.83	-0.85	5.33	9.01	15.9	7.4	14.0	-6.2	7.2
Economic	5.66	-10.15	-7.19	3.26	-7.18	-13.41	-0.34	19.8	-6.9	19.1	-3.9	-7.1
Fishing	-12.60	-11.55	10.21	1.84	-62.29	-76.98	-1.37	2.0	3.4	17.6	-18.0	-52.4
Transports and communications	5.14	1.32	-10.82	3.58	-25.15	-20.83	-3.58	7.5	-0.8	13.3	-5.1	-12.6
Commerce	-3.37	-30.90	-15.76	3.42	4.10	9.05	4.85	21.9	-9.8	19.9	-5.2	6.9
Tourism	-0.49	-16.78	-28.25	14.47	-8.46	-36.98	70.29	48.5	-5.8	11.5	-14.8	3.6
Energy	-1.44	-6.92	-2.73	2.15	-0.55	-6.27	1.58	16.0	-7.3	20.6	-5.0	-2.4
Industry	37.00	-8.53	-10.61	5.45	-6.10	-33.28	-8.62	114.0	-9.7	18.5	2.5	-21.9
Administrative and defense	14.10	3.51	-10.98	-5.17	5.78	10.03	-10.42	3.5	-1.1	3.0	-2.2	-0.7
Administration	5.02	-0.10	-7.78	-10.14	9.70	15.08	-29.65	1.6	-1.0	-0.5	-4.9	-10.0
Justice and security	27.08	7.78	-14.49	0.70	1.64	4.28	13.71	9.6	-1.3	10.6	1.9	8.9

Source: Salinas de Gortari (1991, p. 157).
a. Programmable expenditures exclude revenue sharing with states, municipalities, and others, fiscal incentives and interest payments, and commissions and other expenditures associated with domestic and foreign debt.

excludes debt servicing)—rather than total government expenditures—should be used as the frame of reference.[34] Spending for social development fell more sharply in relative terms than "nonsocial" expenditures. Its average share fell from 32 percent during the 1978–81 oil-boom years to 30 percent in the 1983–88 period (table 9-5). The decline occurred primarily in 1983 and 1984.

Expenditures for social development include primarily spending on education, health and social security, the Solidarity program and urban and regional development,[35] and a number of agencies and trusts that perform activities related to education, health, and other social sectors.

Between 1983 and 1988, cuts in education and health were smaller than in the rest of the components of social spending (tables 9-6 and 9-7). Education and health expenditures constitute about 65 percent of social outlays (excluding the agencies and trusts). Both contracted from 1983 to 1988: spending on education fell 29.6 percent, and spending on health fell 23.3 percent. Education and health expenditures fell less than total social spending, leaving the sharpest cuts in other social programs. Whether this change in the composition of social spending was desirable is unclear. More detailed research is needed to determine the social impact of the reallocation of social expenditures. Some cuts, such as those affecting the programs implemented by COPLAMAR, probably hurt the very poor.[36]

In the case of federal education expenditures, the proportion allocated to basic education (primary school and junior high) was subject to a larger cut than spending on other levels, but suffered a smaller cut than spending on administration (tables 9-8 and 9-9). The share of federal education expenditures allocated to basic education fell from an average of 52.4 percent a year in 1978-81 to 45.3 percent in 1983–88, with most of the reduction absorbed by primary education. This reallocation is in principle undesirable, because spending on basic education tends to benefit the poor relatively more than spending on higher levels of education.

---

34. This is because the largest component of nonprogrammable expenditures is interest payments on domestic and foreign debt, which cannot be affected by direct policy decisions in the same way as the rest of government outlays. During adjustment the government had to allocate a larger proportion of total expenditures to nonprogrammable expenditures which increased from close to 20 percent a year during 1978–81 to 45 percent a year during 1983–88 (table 9-5). As a result, programmable expenditures declined 5.3 percent a year on average between 1983 and 1988 (table 9-4).

35. Regional Development, as a spending category, began in 1982. Since 1990 it has included spending on the Solidarity program, PRONASOL (*Programa Nacional de Solidaridad*). See Salinas (1991, p. 159).

36. See La Forgia (1993).

In the 1983–88 period, health and social security expenditures were cut at an annual rate of 4.8 percent, well below the annual rate of cuts in social development expenditures and somewhat below that for total programmable expenditures (table 9-6). The budget of the Secretariat of Health was cut by even less: 4.1 percent a year during 1983–88. Because services provided by the Secretariat of Health primarily benefit poorer sectors of the population that are not covered by social insurance, this comparison may indicate a progressive reallocation of public health expenditures during the adjustment. However, it is impossible to give a definite answer, because there are no reliable figures on the size of the uninsured population covered by the Secretariat of Health.[37] The decline in expenditures (per legal participant) on the two social insurance schemes, IMSS and ISSSTE, was notable (table 9-10).

The pattern of spending cuts in regional development (table 9-6) and rural development (table 9-4) indicate that programs targeted to the poor were subject to sharp cuts. Examples of such programs include PIDER (Programa de Inversiones para el Desarrollo Rural), which was launched in the mid-1970s to channel investment to rural areas, and COPLAMAR, launched at the end of 1976 to improve human capital and infrastructure in marginal rural and urban areas.[38]

This discussion is subject to one important caveat. To convert expenditures into real constant pesos, expenditure categories were divided by the implicit GDP deflator, rather than a sector-specific deflator, which is not available. But the decline in government social spending may well reflect lower wage outlays in those sectors rather than a reduction in the "output" of government services.[39] To compensate in part for this bias, the next section measures resource availability—physical and human—in health and education.

Human and Physical Resources

Human and physical resources per capita in education and health continued to rise during adjustment, or did not fall by as much as education and health expenditures. This apparently paradoxical result can be explained by two fac-

37. One author reports that the Secretariat of Health claims to cover one-fourth of the population, but others suggest coverage is about half that amount. See La Forgia (1993, p. 90).

38. See La Forgia (1993).

39. This means that actual changes in government services may differ from those the numbers in the text suggest and that, strictly speaking, trends among the various expenditure categories cannot be compared. In particular, sector-specific deflators for programmable and nonprogrammable expenditures are probably different.

Table 9-5. *Public Sector Programmable Expenditures, by Type, as Share of Total Programmable Expenditures, Mexico, 1970–90[a]*

Percent

Type	1970	1971	1972	1973	1974	1975	1976	1977	1978	1979	1980	1981	1982
Total programmable expenditures as share of GDP	16.30	16.82	18.72	20.99	21.74	26.37	24.49	23.26	24.19	25.02	27.12	30.70	28.07
Total programmable expenditures as share of total expenditures	84.48	85.92	86.50	86.05	84.46	86.29	84.56	84.29	84.45	83.13	82.09	79.28	61.89
Legislative power	0.28	0.24	0.19	0.21	0.20	0.14	0.21	0.16	0.16	0.14	0.16	0.14	0.14
Executive power	99.59	99.76	99.81	99.86	99.85	99.86	99.79	99.84	99.84	99.86	99.84	99.86	99.86
Social	35.50	38.47	42.10	39.17	39.78	38.61	43.55	42.82	41.78	43.13	43.09	41.85	43.28
Rural development	5.94	6.80	8.42	9.03	9.15	10.82	10.66	9.11	9.07	9.68	12.04	10.64	9.45
Social development	29.56	31.67	33.68	30.14	30.62	27.78	32.89	33.71	32.70	33.45	31.05	31.21	33.83
Economic	46.55	48.54	45.51	49.03	49.39	51.47	46.38	46.93	49.19	49.62	49.22	51.71	50.34
Fishing	...	...	...	1.45	1.12	1.14	1.25	1.28	1.24	1.16	1.14	1.34	1.71
Transports and communications	10.77	11.17	8.89	9.10	7.11	6.96	8.13	7.21	6.40	6.84	6.88	6.52	6.88
Commerce	6.35	5.83	4.82	5.31	8.59	7.69	5.36	6.58	7.07	5.33	5.90	7.46	7.01
Tourism	0.14	0.24	0.47	0.34	0.31	0.45	0.45	0.42	0.37	0.39	0.38	0.35	0.34
Energy	28.87	29.85	27.15	25.59	25.10	27.30	24.75	24.69	27.87	29.34	27.53	28.62	26.77
Industry	0.41	1.70	4.64	7.59	7.46	8.38	6.88	7.18	6.60	6.94	7.77	7.76	7.98
Administrative and defense	17.54	12.50	11.64	11.24	10.33	9.38	9.35	9.65	8.51	6.72	7.16	5.96	5.90
Administration	13.81	8.98	8.23	8.14	7.26	6.72	6.40	6.93	6.05	4.34	5.13	3.72	3.73
Justice and security	3.73	3.52	3.41	3.10	3.07	2.65	2.95	2.72	2.46	2.38	2.03	2.23	2.16

	1983	1984	1985	1986	1987	1988	1989	1990	Geometric average				
									1971–75	1976–77	1979–81	1983–88	1989–90
Total programmable expenditures as share of GDP	24.77	24.84	23.28	22.11	20.34	19.07	17.53	17.25	20.9	23.9	26.8	22.4	17.4
Total programmable expenditures as share of total expenditures	58.53	62.08	59.67	52.09	46.44	47.02	50.98	56.43	85.8	84.4	82.2	54.3	53.7
Legislative power	0.19	0.25	0.28	0.29	0.38	0.45	0.50	0.56	0.2	0.2	0.2	0.3	0.5
Executive power	99.81	99.75	99.72	99.71	99.62	99.55	99.50	99.44	99.8	99.8	99.8	99.7	99.5
Social	37.64	36.11	39.23	38.86	36.96	37.36	41.01	43.47	39.6	43.2	42.5	37.7	42.2
Rural development	9.61	8.47	8.10	8.21	6.38	5.39	5.51	5.83	8.8	9.9	10.4	7.7	5.7
Social development	28.03	27.64	31.12	30.65	30.58	31.97	35.49	37.64	30.8	33.3	32.1	30.0	36.6
Economic development	56.05	56.96	53.34	53.95	56.04	54.84	50.05	48.52	48.9	45.7	49.9	55.2	49.7
Fishing	1.90	1.59	1.47	1.76	1.81	0.72	0.17	0.17	0.7	1.3	1.2	1.5	0.2
Transports and communications	8.18	8.27	8.74	8.49	8.85	6.98	5.83	5.46	8.6	7.7	6.7	8.3	5.6
Commerce	10.03	9.32	6.71	6.16	6.41	7.04	8.09	8.25	6.4	6.0	6.4	7.6	8.2
Tourism	0.25	0.24	0.21	0.16	0.18	0.18	0.12	0.20	0.4	0.4	0.4	0.2	0.2
Energy	25.95	24.59	23.86	25.29	25.99	27.25	26.93	26.61	27.0	24.7	28.3	25.5	26.8
Industry	10.00	13.18	12.56	12.24	12.98	12.85	9.04	8.03	6.0	7.0	7.3	12.3	8.5
Administrative and defense	5.87	6.44	6.95	6.74	6.43	7.17	8.32	7.25	11.0	9.5	7.1	6.6	7.8
Administration	3.45	3.49	3.63	3.65	3.30	3.82	4.63	3.17	7.9	6.7	4.8	3.6	3.9
Justice and security	2.42	2.95	3.32	3.09	3.13	3.36	3.69	4.08	3.2	2.8	2.3	3.0	3.9

Sources: Salinas de Gortari (1991, pp. 153, 157).
GDP for 1970–86; *Indicadores Economicos* (August 1987, p. II-2); and (March 1988, p. II-24). For 1987–90, Banco de Mexico, *Informe Anual* (1991, p. 267).
a. Programmable expenditures exclude revenue sharing with states, municipalities, and others, fiscal incentives and interest payments, commissions and other expenditures associated with domestic and foreign debt.

Table 9-6. *Social Development Expenditures, by Type, Mexico, 1971–90*

Annual percent change

Type	1971	1972	1973	1974	1975	1976	1977	1978	1979	1980	1981	1982	1983
Total	15.17	28.40	8.82	11.65	16.27	14.55	0.70	9.22	15.48	8.99	22.85	-1.39	-30.79
Education	3.34	15.23	8.63	8.60	27.38	24.22	12.89	7.87	9.49	3.76	32.31	4.48	-33.84
Health and social security	41.64	6.68	12.12	21.99	9.22	6.85	-5.78	6.30	5.62	14.35	7.22	6.62	-21.86
Health ministry	13.31	9.82	26.65	-2.26	8.01	28.23	6.67	7.07	6.05	5.12	136.91	13.38	-30.73
ISSSTE	49.98	29.00	31.78	33.28	1.77	13.61	9.68	1.87	-9.01	29.88	-1.59	-2.65	-25.16
IMSS	41.64	1.37	5.54	19.46	12.33	3.22	-12.90	8.51	12.65	8.98	2.04	9.65	-19.03
Other	-5.57	68.45	38.19	-17.01	-5.59	2.05	-27.59	34.78	33.71	28.74	17.47	75.40	-60.81
Urban development and ecology ministry	-5.57	72.58	39.69	-16.98	-8.70	3.04	-28.88	33.83	33.92	31.26	5.46	-26.38	-77.89
Solidarity and regional development	...	...	...	...	...	...	...	...	...	...	...	...	-50.27
Ministry of labor	-5.57	-5.87	-11.35	-18.55	159.23	-16.37	2.23	49.89	30.71	-8.18	268.76	-31.84	-61.18
Agencies and trusts	-24.00	85.41	6.38	8.60	37.10	29.24	10.35	10.39	33.65	1.31	38.62	-32.26	-23.93

	1984	1985	1986	1987	1988	1989	1990	Geometric average				
								1971–75	1976–77	1978–81	1983–88	1989–90
Total	2.56	8.03	-9.63	-0.83	-0.85	5.33	9.01	15.9	7.4	14.0	-6.2	7.2
Education	9.98	3.31	-12.63	6.95	-0.93	5.99	2.74	12.3	18.4	12.8	-5.9	4.4
Health and social security	-7.29	3.92	0.03	-2.83	1.44	9.45	10.82	17.7	0.3	8.3	-4.8	10.1
Health ministry	6.30	6.76	-8.20	5.38	2.52	-1.63	-2.21	10.7	17.0	29.7	-4.1	-1.9
ISSSTE	-18.20	9.24	-11.15	13.04	-6.27	1.40	13.18	28.2	11.6	4.3	-7.4	7.1
IMSS	-5.27	1.76	5.26	-8.63	3.99	13.94	12.07	15.3	-5.2	8.0	-4.0	13.0
Other	26.37	-26.34	4.66	-36.50	-12.83	21.14	67.13	11.5	-14.0	28.5	-22.8	42.3
Urban development and ecology ministry	24.99	-8.35	3.28	-19.49	-6.31	-27.50	5.40	11.5	-14.4	25.5	-23.7	-12.6
Solidarity and regional development	28.06	-33.47	7.66	-45.41	-19.04	55.23	91.86	...	...	...	-23.4	72.6
Ministry of labor	8.81	10.48	-19.14	0.54	6.62	-4.06	4.65	10.7	-7.5	60.5	-14.0	0.2
Agencies and trusts	5.30	33.50	-22.49	5.27	-2.16	-4.33	1.22	17.4	19.4	20.0	-2.6	-1.6

Source: Salinas de Gortari (1991, p. 159).

Table 9-7. *Social Development Expenditures, by Type, as Share of Total Social Development Expenditures, Mexico, 1970–90*

Percent

Type	1970	1971	1972	1973	1974	1975	1976	1977	1978	1979	1980	1981	1982
Expenditures for social development as share of total programmable expenditures	29.56	31.67	33.68	30.14	30.62	27.78	32.89	33.71	32.70	33.45	31.05	31.21	33.83
Education	24.77	22.22	19.94	19.91	19.37	21.22	23.01	25.79	25.47	24.15	22.99	24.76	26.24
Health and social security	46.73	57.47	47.75	49.20	53.76	50.50	47.10	44.07	42.89	39.23	41.16	35.92	38.84
Health ministry[a]	5.00	4.00	4.12	4.65	3.73	3.69	4.42	5.01	5.04	5.06	4.66	10.29	10.94
ISSSTE[a]	17.00	18.00	21.76	25.58	27.95	26.04	27.69	32.24	30.90	26.61	30.23	27.74	25.33
IMSS[a]	78.00	78.00	74.12	69.77	68.32	70.27	67.88	62.75	64.06	68.32	65.11	61.97	63.73
Other	8.88	7.28	9.55	12.13	9.02	7.32	6.52	4.69	5.79	6.70	7.91	7.57	13.46
Urban development and ecology ministry[b]	94.74	94.74	97.06	98.11	98.15	94.92	95.83	94.12	93.46	93.60	95.44	85.68	35.96
Solidarity and regional development[b]	…	…	…	…	…	…	…	…	…	…	…	…	58.47
Ministry of labor[b]	5.26	5.26	2.94	1.89	1.85	5.08	4.17	5.88	6.54	6.40	4.56	14.32	5.56
Agencies and trusts	19.16	12.64	18.26	17.85	17.36	20.47	23.10	25.31	25.58	29.61	27.52	31.05	21.33

| | 1983 | 1984 | 1985 | 1986 | 1987 | 1988 | 1989 | 1990 | Geometric average | | | | |
									1971–75	1976–77	1978–81	1983–88	1989–90
Expenditures for social development as share of total programmable expenditures	28.03	27.64	31.12	30.65	30.58	31.97	35.49	37.64	30.8	33.3	32.1	30.0	36.6
Education	25.08	26.90	25.72	24.87	26.82	26.80	26.97	25.42	20.5	24.4	24.3	26.0	26.2
Health and social security	43.85	39.64	38.13	42.20	41.35	42.30	43.96	44.69	51.7	45.6	39.8	41.2	44.3
Health ministry[a]	9.70	11.12	11.42	10.48	11.37	11.49	10.33	9.11	4.0	4.7	6.3	10.9	9.7
ISSSTE[a]	24.26	21.41	22.50	19.99	23.25	21.48	19.90	20.33	23.9	30.0	28.9	22.1	20.1
IMSS[a]	66.04	67.48	66.08	69.53	65.38	67.03	69.77	70.56	72.1	65.3	64.9	66.9	70.2
Other	7.62	9.39	6.40	7.42	4.75	4.17	4.80	7.36	9.1	5.6	7.0	6.6	6.1
Urban development and ecology ministry[b]	20.29	20.06	24.96	24.64	31.23	33.57	20.09	12.67	96.6	95.0	92.0	25.8	16.4
Solidarity and regional development[b]	74.20	75.19	67.92	69.86	60.06	55.78	71.48	82.05	...	...	...	67.2	76.8
Ministry of labor[b]	5.51	4.75	7.12	5.50	8.71	10.65	8.44	5.28	3.4	5.0	8.0	7.0	6.9
Agencies and trusts	23.45	24.07	29.75	25.51	27.08	26.72	24.27	22.54	17.3	24.2	28.4	26.1	23.4

Sources: Salinas de Gortari (1991, pp. 157, 159).
a. As percent of health and social security.
b. As percent of other.

Table 9-8. *Federal Expenditures on Education, Mexico, 1978–90*
Annual percentage change in real expenditures

	Federal	*Basic education*[b]					
	expenditures		*Primary*	*Intermediate*	*Higher*		
Year	*on education*[a]	*Total*	*only*	*education*[c]	*education*	*Administration*	*Other*[d]
1978	7.55	–0.89	2.47	22.55	5.42	68.45	14.71
1979	9.97	13.57	7.94	3.75	1.08	0.09	23.10
1980	6.02	–1.09	–7.68	3.15	34.08	–12.45	12.00
1981	23.50	31.06	35.59	25.54	5.13	55.21	7.08
1982	3.98	–0.89	–0.19	18.57	10.75	7.23	–1.22
1983	–31.04	–38.13	–43.34	–26.73	–22.87	–17.49	–26.24
1984	4.61	–3.27	–5.97	–16.98	–18.80	91.75	43.50
1985	4.43	8.82	2.51	25.84	5.35	–18.83	0.57
1986	–10.52	–10.11	–7.92	15.31	–0.62	–43.12	–18.85
1987	3.64	13.41	10.34	–17.99	10.02	–24.89	6.70
1988	0.97	–1.24	–3.71	9.01	–0.88	5.91	1.56
1989	3.46	–1.15	–6.58	5.95	–17.41	82.00	13.03
1990	4.25	9.43	15.17	–8.63	8.32	–10.30	7.64
Geometric average							
1978–81	11.7	10.7	9.6	13.7	11.4	27.8	14.2
1983–88	–4.7	–5.1	–8.0	–1.9	–4.6	–1.1	–1.2
1989–90	3.9	4.1	4.3	–1.3	–4.5	35.4	10.3

Source: Salinas de Gortari (1991, pp. 157, 360).
a. The discrepancy between these figures and the figures in table 9-6 is due to the different original sources reported in Salinas de Gortari. The figures in table 9-6 are from Cuenta de la Hacienda Publica Federal; the figures in this table are from Secretaria de Educacion Publica. Although yearly figures differ, averages do not do so substantially.
b. Includes preschool, primary, special, and junior high school.
c. Includes high school and technical schools.
d. Includes initial, graduate, and adult education, education for natives, and culture and recreation.

tors. First, the price deflator (the implicit GDP deflator) used to measure "real" expenditures in health and education is not appropriate in the sense that it may not be the best way to translate nominal outlays into real output. The contraction in real social spending reflects the reduction in real government wages more than any deterioration in the capacity of those sectors to provide social services. Second, given the reduction in births experienced since the mid-1970s, the demand for some social services, such as primary education and pre- and postnatal care, was declining.

There are, however, two caveats. First, the indicators of human and physical resources used here exclude other important quantitative indicators (such as the availability of complementary materials and the distribution of benefits) and qualitative indicators (such as the physical condition of schools and health facilities and the motivation and skills of teachers and health practitioners,

Table 9-9. *Share of Federal Expenditures on Education, Mexico, 1977–90*

Year	Federal expenditures on education as percent of programmable expenditures[a]	Basic education[b]		Intermediate education[c]	Higher education	Administration	Other[d]
		Total	Primary only				
1977	14.37	56.63	35.44	10.52	18.93	4.85	9.06
1978	13.72	52.19	33.76	11.98	18.56	7.60	9.66
1979	13.37	53.90	33.14	11.31	17.06	6.92	10.82
1980	12.07	50.29	28.86	11.00	21.57	5.71	11.43
1981	12.20	53.36	31.68	11.18	18.36	7.18	9.91
1982	13.94	50.87	30.41	12.75	19.56	7.41	9.41
1983	11.51	45.64	24.99	13.55	21.88	8.86	10.07
1984	11.58	42.20	22.46	10.75	16.98	16.25	13.81
1985	12.60	43.98	22.05	12.96	17.13	12.63	13.30
1986	12.29	44.18	22.69	16.70	19.03	8.03	12.07
1987	12.81	48.35	24.16	13.21	20.20	5.82	12.42
1988	13.63	47.29	23.04	14.27	19.83	6.10	12.49
1989	14.87	45.18	20.80	14.61	15.83	10.74	13.65
1990	15.08	47.42	22.98	12.81	16.45	9.24	14.09
Geometric average							
1978–81	12.8	52.4	31.9	11.4	18.9	6.9	10.5
1983–88	12.4	45.3	23.2	13.6	19.2	9.6	12.4
1989–90	15.0	46.3	21.9	13.7	16.1	10.0	13.9

Source: Salinas de Gortari (1991, pp. 157, 360).

a. The discrepancy between these figures and the figures in table 9-7 is due to the different original sources reported in Salinas de Gortari. The figures in table 9-7 are from Cuenta de la Hacienda Publica Federal; the figures in this table are from Secretaria de Educacion Publica. Although yearly figures differ, averages do not do so substantially.

b. Includes preschool, primary, special, and junior high school.

c. Includes high school and technical schools.

d. Includes initial, graduate, and adult education, education for natives, and culture and recreation.

whose real earnings were contracting). Second, the 11.9 percent average annual decrease in social development investment is almost twice as large as the annual cut in social development spending as a whole (table 9-11). The relatively larger cuts in investment which enabled quick deficit reduction cannot be sustained and will require larger outlays in the future to avoid a shortfall in physical infrastructure. The extent to which consumption smoothing by the government is feasible will depend on the rate of the Mexican economy's recovery.

Table 9-10. *Federal Health Expenditures, by Provider, Mexico, Selected Years, 1970–90*

Thousands of 1991 pesos unless otherwise specified

Year	GNP deflator	Population (thousands)	Uninsured population (thousands)[a]	Public sector insured population (thousands)	Uninsured as percent of total population	Federal health expenditures by provider per legal participant[b]		Index of federal health expenditures by provider per legal participant (1980=100)	
						IMSS	ISSSTE	IMSS	ISSSTE
1970	19	52,771	37,762	12,370	0.72	472	548	143	163
1975	35	61,918	37,938	20,884	0.61	413	330	125	98
1977	55	65,187	38,545	23,382	0.59	437	336	132	100
1979	78	68,628	37,675	27,521	0.55	380	313	115	93
1980	100	70,416	36,122	30,773	0.51	330	337	100	100
1981	126	72,200	35,255	33,335	0.49	347	378	105	112
1982	203	73,900	36,652	33,553	0.50	353	417	107	124
1983	386	75,500	37,837	33,888	0.50	307	282	93	84
1984	615	77,000	36,282	36,869	0.47	278	254	84	75
1985	963	78,500	35,077	39,498	0.45	258	281	78	83
1986	1,680	79,900	36,306	39,599	0.45	238	248	72	74
1987	4,019	81,200	33,787	43,353	0.42	214	231	65	68
1988	8,033	82,500	34,154	44,221	0.41	260	228	79	68
1989	10,148	83,800	32,733	46,877	0.39	226	214	69	64
1990	12,770	85,000	32,465	48,285	0.38	272	216	82	64
Average									
1979–81	101	70,415	36,351	30,543	0.52	352	343	107	102
1983–88	2,616	79,100	35,574	39,571	0.45	259	254	78	75
1989–90	11,459	84,400	32,599	47,581	0.39	249	215	75	64

Source: Calculated with data from Salinas de Gortari (1991, pp. 159, 369, 388, 390, 392).

a. The uninsured population has been estimated by subtracting from the total population the population insured by the public social security institutes and by private health insurance systems (the latter has been estimated as 5 percent of total population). The population has been estimated using data in the 1970, 1980, and 1990 censuses; and Ordarica (1990). There are no per capita figures for the Secretariat of Health because data on the uninsured population covered by public health are not available.

b. A U.S. dollar equaled 2,981 pesos in 1991, average of the market exchange rate during 1991.

Table 9-11. *Annual Growth of Federal Public Investment, by Sector, Mexico,*
1983–90
Percent

| | | | | | | | | | Average | |
| | | | | | | | | | 1983– | 1989– |
Sector	1983	1984	1985	1986	1987	1988	1989	1990	88	90
Federal public investment	−30.08	2.44	−13.19	−9.35	−3.44	−11.38	−7.50	18.90	−11.44	4.87
Social development[a]	−37.77	29.83	−29.44	4.84	−9.93	−13.01	−3.90	34.54	−11.87	13.71
Health and labor[a]	−49.29	14.38	−7.54	35.25	−4.79	−5.75	−8.64	37.47	−6.91	12.07
Education[a]	−19.71	5.51	−5.32	−24.09	2.59	−2.47	−1.56	32.11	−7.93	14.04
Solidarity and regional development[a]	8.73	28.06	−33.47	20.91	3.65	−57.29	37.99	91.86	−11.03	62.71
Urban development[a]	−54.92	−33.53	−41.57	−47.05	−61.36	−39.18	−26.90	−34.42	−47.15	−30.76

Source: Salinas de Gortari (1991), pp. 167–68.
a. Percent of total federal public investment.

Education

The student-per-teacher and student-per-school ratios both declined, the
former from an average of 29.4 in the period 1978–81 to 24.7 in the period
1983–88, and the latter from 214.4 to 178.3 (table 9-12). This decline was
partly due to a sharp slowdown in the rate of increase in matriculations, particularly at the primary level, resulting from the decline in population growth
and dropout rates.[40] However, the drop in first-grade matriculations might
have been larger than the population drop for that age cohort (five to eight
years), indicating that some children were not entering primary school. As
Pinstrup-Andersen has noted, it is hard to believe that the drop in the growth
rate of matriculated primary school students from 7.2 percent a year during
1978–80 to 1.2 percent during 1983–88 is entirely due to the drop in population growth and repetition rates.[41] Families may be postponing their children's
entrance to primary school because of the complementary costs of attendance,
such as transportation and school materials.

Nonetheless, even if the improvement in educational indicators is due in

40. See table 9-8 for population figures and table 15 for dropout rates. The number of elementary schools declined temporarily between 1983–84 and 1984–85 for reasons that remain unclear.
See Salinas (1991, p. 349).
41. Pinstrup-Andersen, (1992).

Table 9-12. *Educational Resources, Total and Primary School, Mexico, 1977–78 to 1991–92*
Percent unless otherwise specified

Year	Rate of change of matriculated students, total	Students per teacher, total	Students per school, total	Rate of change of matriculated students, primary school	Students per teacher, primary school	Students per school, primary school	Free textbooks per student, primary school
1977–78	6.0	30.3	225.7	5.0	42.5	209.6	5.7
1978–79	8.3	30.3	220.5	7.2	42.4	201.2	5.7
1979–80	6.7	29.3	216.7	4.4	40.7	202.8	6.0
1980–81	6.6	28.5	206.1	3.8	39.1	192.9	4.8
1981–82	5.6	27.7	201.5	2.1	37.5	196.4	4.9
1982–83	4.5	27.1	194.9	1.6	36.6	195.4	5.2
1983–84	3.3	26.6	190.2	1.0	35.9	194.9	5.4
1984–85	1.2	25.6	188.5	-1.0	34.8	199.8	5.4
1985–86	2.0	24.8	183.0	-0.6	33.6	197.2	5.4
1986–87	0.7	24.2	172.0	-0.9	32.8	187.3	4.9
1987–88	0.0	23.9	170.5	-1.5	31.9	185.3	5.0
1988–89	0.0	23.3	165.3	-0.8	31.3	180.2	4.8
1989–90	-0.9	22.9	163.7	-1.1	31.1	179.7	5.0
1990–91	-0.5	22.5	156.9	-0.6	30.5	175.0	5.1
1991–92[a]	2.5	22.8	155.1	1.3	30.6	173.8	5.1
Average							
1978/79–1981/82	7.2	29.4	214.4	5.1	40.7	198.9	5.5
1983/84–1988/89	1.2	24.7	178.3	-0.6	33.4	190.8	5.2
1989/90–1990/91	-0.7	22.7	160.2	-0.9	30.8	177.4	5.1

Source: Salinas de Gortari (1991, pp. 345, 346, 349).
a. Estimated.

part to low enrollment, per capita human and physical resources, in contrast to expenditure, rose throughout the crisis. The reduction in education spending, then, primarily reflects the drop in real wages and in investment in the sector. But it might also reflect a cut in the availability of school materials and in the maintenance of existing facilities. Regrettably, we cannot yet assess the impact of such cuts on the quality of education. Over time the teaching profession may absorb less qualified and less motivated people, which would surely affect the quality of education.

Health Services for the Insured

In contrast to education, health service indicators show a cut in the availability of doctors and physical infrastructure per beneficiary (table 9-13). However, the resource cuts do not parallel those in expenditures which again reflect the decline in investment and wages.

Per capita medical units, hospital beds and doctors available in the "formal" health sector declined between 1983 and 1988 (table 9-13). The quality of health care services provided by agencies that cover only those who contribute through the social security system thus probably worsened during adjustment. For example, medical units, hospital beds, and doctors per covered member of the Mexican Institute of Social Insurance (IMSS) on average declined 4.1 percent, and 3.6 percent, respectively, after 1983 (table 9-13). The Health and Social Security Institute for State Employees (ISSSTE), a separate health organization that covers only government employees, faced declines of 3 percent in medical units, 3.1 percent in hospital beds, and 0.3 percent in doctors per legal beneficiary. The two institutions covered, respectively, 41.8 percent and 8.8 percent of the total Mexican population on average between 1982 and 1989 (table 9-13).

The deterioration of per-member IMSS and ISSSTE physical and human resources may have resulted from sudden increases in the number of people who joined the social security health care system in 1984, 1985, and 1987 (table 9-13). This is particularly true in the case of IMSS, which covers private sector employees. A possible explanation of this phenomenon is that more people who previously used private doctors and hospitals sought medical service through social insurance schemes because of their declining incomes.

Table 9-13. *Human and Physical Resources in the Health Sector,*
Mexico, 1980–91
Annual percent change except shares (in percent)

Item	1980	1981	1982	1983	1984	1985	1986
				IMSS[b]			
Population covered							
Thousands	24,125.0	26,916.0	26,885.0	26,977.0	29,388.0	31,529.0	31,062.0
Rate of change	14.9	11.6	–0.1	0.3	8.9	7.3	–1.5
As a ratio of							
total population[c]	36.4	39.6	38.6	37.9	40.4	42.5	41.1
Medical units							
Per thousand	0.050	0.054	0.056	0.057	0.049	0.046	0.047
Rate of change	...	8.5	3.9	0.8	–13.4	–7.5	4.1
Beds							
Per thousand	1.142	1.041	1.095	1.095	1.007	0.851	0.865
Rate of change	...	–8.8	5.1	0.0	–8.1	–15.5	1.6
Doctors							
Per thousand	0.975	0.955	0.931	1.007	0.758	0.760	0.769
Rate of change	...	–2.0	–2.5	8.1	–24.7	0.2	1.2
Nurses							
Per thousand	1.71	1.66	1.68	1.81	1.72	1.74	1.77
Rate of change	...	–2.9	1.7	7.2	–4.5	1.0	1.5
Ratio of nurses							
to doctors	1.8	1.7	1.8	1.8	2.3	2.3	2.3
				ISSSTE[b]			
Population covered							
Thousands	4,985.0	5,319.3	5,467.8	5,611.0	6,080.4	6,447.9	6,957.3
Rate of change	2.2	6.7	2.8	2.6	8.4	6.0	7.9
As ratio of							
total population[c]	7.5	7.8	7.8	7.9	8.4	8.7	9.2
Medical units							
Per thousand	0.2	0.2	0.2	0.2	0.2	0.2	0.2
Rate of change	...	–3.8	0.3	–2.1	–3.4	–4.0	–5.8
Beds							
Per thousand	1.066	0.988	1.002	1.001	1.009	0.951	0.884
Rate of change	...	–7.3	1.4	–0.1	0.8	–5.7	–7.1
Doctors							
Per thousand	1.510	1.515	1.666	1.623	1.674	1.619	1.616
Rate of change	...	0.4	10.0	–2.6	3.1	–3.3	–0.2
Nurses							
Per thousand	1.6	1.7	2.0	2.0	2.2	2.1	1.8
Rate of change	...	4.3	17.9	–1.4	11.6	–3.5	–13.0
Ratio of nurses							
to doctors	1.1	1.1	1.2	1.2	1.3	1.3	1.1

Source: Salinas de Gortari (1991, pp. 370–71, 376–79, 381, 386, 390).
a. Estimated figures.
b. IMSS: Instituto Mexicano del Seguro Social; ISSTE: Instituto de Salud y Seguridad Social de Trabajadores del Estado. Doctors are those in direct contact with patients. Beds are the number of registered beds (censables).

Table 9-13. *(continued)*

					Average		
1987	*1988*	*1989*	*1990*	*1991ᵃ*	*1983–88*	*1983–85*	*1986–87*

IMSS

34,336.0	35,066.0	37,213.0	38,575.0	38,117.0	31,393.0	29,298.0	32,699.0
10.5	2.1	6.1	3.7	−1.2	4.5	5.5	4.4
44.6	44.8	46.7	47.6	43.9	41.9	40.3	42.8
0.043	0.044	0.042	0.042	0.043	0.048	0.051	0.045
−8.3	0.9	−4.2	−1.1	2.5	−4.1	−6.9	−2.3
0.776	0.747	0.715	0.711	0.721	0.89	0.98	0.82
−10.2	−3.8	−4.2	−0.5	1.4	−6.2	−8.1	−4.5
0.725	0.750	0.714	0.719	0.786	0.79	0.84	0.75
−5.7	3.3	−4.7	0.6	9.3	−3.6	−6.6	−2.3
1.66	1.70	1.74	1.70	1.81	1.73	1.76	1.71
−5.9	2.2	2.5	−2.5	6.4	0.2	1.1	−2.3
2.3	2.3	2.4	2.4	2.3	2.20	2.10	2.30

ISSSTE

7,356.6	7,415.1	7,844.5	8,302.4	8,509.7	6,644.7	6,046.4	7,157.0
5.7	0.8	5.8	5.8	2.5	5.2	5.6	6.8
9.6	9.5	9.8	10.2	n.a.	8.9	8.3	9.4
0.1	0.2	0.1	0.1	0.1	0.2	0.2	0.2
−5.4	3.1	−4.9	−3.9	−1.6	−3.0	−3.2	−5.6
0.837	0.830	0.781	0.770	0.755	0.9	1.0	0.9
−5.3	−0.8	−5.8	−1.4	−2.0	−3.1	−1.7	−6.2
1.507	1.640	1.521	1.503	1.580	1.6	1.6	1.6
−6.7	8.8	−7.3	−1.2	5.1	−0.3	−1.0	−3.5
1.9	2.1	2.0	2.0	2.0	2.0	2.1	1.9
2.8	9.3	−3.2	−0.9	3.9	0.6	2.0	−5.4
1.2	1.3	1.3	1.3	1.3	1.2	1.3	1.2

c. Yearly population levels are calculated using growth rates from Ordorica (1991). Ordorica provides yearly growth rates for 1980–89 and cites the eleventh population census preliminary figure for total population in 1990, estimated to be 81.1 million.

Health Services for the Uninsured

Most of the uninsured are poor and had to rely on services provided by the Secretariat of Health, the IMSS-COPLAMAR (later transformed into IMSS-SOLIDARIDAD), and the DIF (Desarrollo Itegral de la famila, or Integrated Development of the Family). Given the difficulty of estimating the population served by each agency and the fact that some insured people use facilities intended for the uninsured, it is very difficult to estimate trends in the physical and human resources of the Secretariat of Health.

If the number of immunizations by the Secretariat of Health is a good indicator, the government seems to have stressed preventive medicine as a means of cost control. As a proportion of visits, the number of immunizations increased from about 50 percent in 1983 to 103 percent in 1988. In another sign of improvement, intestinal infection as a cause of hospitalizations fell from about 6 percent in 1983 to around 3 percent in 1988. Nutritional deficiencies, representing less than one percent of hospitalizations in 1983, was not listed as a major cause of hospitalization after 1989.[42] The data indirectly support the hypothesis that health services to the poor might have continued to improve during adjustment.

The health program of COPLAMAR, launched in collaboration with IMSS in 1979, underwent important changes.[43] This program was designed to deliver health services to the poorest rural communities, and several analyses have acknowledged its success. In December 1982, having recently taken office, President de la Madrid dissolved COPLAMAR. In 1983 he reintroduced it, but under the full authority of IMSS. In 1985 the Secretariat of Health began a process of decentralization, shifting the health services of the Secretariat itself and of IMSS-COPLAMAR to state-run health departments. Between 1985 and 1987 it transferred personnel and infrastructure to fourteen of thirty-two states. However, the decentralization process came to a halt in 1987, in part because of complaints from clients and staff about the deteriorating quality of services under the administration of state governments.

The growth of infrastructure in the IMSS-COPLAMAR program fell sharply between 1981 and 1985 and equaled zero between 1985 and 1988, even including infrastructure decentralized to the states. For example, the number of clinics rose eightfold between 1978 and 1981 and by a multiple of 1.3 between 1981 and 1985, but remained the same between 1985 and 1988. The number of beneficiaries, estimated at about 14 million in 1985, thus stag-

42. Sistema Nacional de Salud, (1991, pp. 84, 105, 109).
43. La Forgia (1993).

nated, even though these free health services had not reached some 45 percent of the rural poor.

Food Subsidies

Because a substantial portion of general food subsidies "leaked" to the nonpoor,[44] the government redefined its food and nutrition policies in the Programa Nacional de Alimentación (PRONAL).[45] The program was to reduce general subsidies; to enhance the purchasing power of poor families through targeted subsidies on tortillas, milk, and corn flour; to provide food assistance to families with pregnant women or young children; and to enhance people's ability to attend to their nutritional needs through monitoring, education, community kitchens, and food production.

CONASUPO's expenditures on general grain and oilseed subsidies were reduced by almost 20 percent in 1984 and by more than 50 percent in both 1985 and 1986. By 1987 expenditures on general food subsidies were lower than those on targeted programs. This trend reversed itself in 1988 and 1989, when general food price subsidies again increased temporarily to support the anti-inflation policies of the December 1987 Pacto de Solidaridad Económica. As a result, CONASUPO's general subsidy expenditures in 1989 were approximately U.S.$ 1 billion, almost double its expenditures on targeted programs.[46]

Expenditures on targeted programs rapidly expanded during the adjustment. CONASUPO extended the coverage of its targeted milk subsidy program and in 1984 introduced a targeted subsidy for corn tortillas.[47] Subsidies to these programs more than quadrupled between 1986 and 1989, lifting total public expenditures on targeted food programs to about U.S.$ 0.5 billion by 1989.[48]

44. Data from the 1984 National Household Income and Expenditure Survey show that monetary food expenditures by households in the lower 40 percent of the income distribution equaled 19.8 percent of national monetary food expenditures; the corresponding percentages for subsidized items ranged from 16.3 for milk to 36.1 for sugar. See Instituto Nacional de Estadística, Geografía e Informática (1984, p. 86). If these firgures are correct, the poorest 40 percent of the population received only a fraction of the food subsidies.

45. Poder Executivo Federal (1983).

46. World Bank (1991, p. 29, table 21).

47. In June 1984 packaged tortillas at subsidized prices were introduced in CONASUPO stores. This program was replaced in April 1986 by the *tortibono* program which allows families with income below twice the minimum wage to buy two kilograms of fresh tortillas at a subsidized price. See Comisión Nacional de Alimentación (1989a, p. 12).

48. World Bank (1991, p. 29, table 21). For a more detailed description of targeted programs during adjustment, see World Bank (1990).

The Comisión Nacional de Alimentación (CONAL) conducted a study of PRONAL's targeted food consumption programs in 1989.[49] It documented their growth during the adjustment and stressed their potential impact, but also showed how far they remained from reaching the most needy. As Binswanger noted in comments on this paper, "the major deficiencies in food subsidies and nutrition programs in Mexico in the first half of the 1980s were the urban bias of the programs and the lack of targeting to the poor and nutritionally deprived." The replacement of general food subsidies with targeted maize and milk programs has not corrected this urban bias, despite the fact that the bulk of poverty and malnutrition is found in rural areas. The CONASUPO's rural stores, which sell goods at below-market prices to prevent private monopolists from extracting quasi-rents, transfer very little to the poor, and the subsidized corn flour subsidy, in Binswanger's words, "barely compensates buyers of maize for the highly protected producer price of maize."[50]

Social Indicators

In terms of education, indicators of performance during the period of adjustment are mixed: some are encouraging, but others are worrisome. For example, the proportion of children between the ages of six and fourteen who attended primary school continued to rise, and the primary school dropout rate fell (table 9-14). However, after 1982 the proportion of each level of graduates who entered the subsequent educational level declined— that is, a larger proportion of children were either dropping out of school or postponing their entry into the next level, probably to enter the workforce (table 9-14).[51] In addition, the dropout rate of high school students rose significantly. These last two trends explain why the average length of schooling of the population during the 1980s improved by one year, while the improvement between 1970 and 1980 equaled two years (table 9-14). This trend may also imply a relative delay in the development of higher skills in the Mexican work force. The decline in high school and higher education enrollment rates may be the result of more young people being forced to join the work force to compensate for the

49. The results of the study are in Comisión Nacional de Alimentación (1989a through 1989j).

50. Binswanger (1993).

51. These trends in the "coverage for demand" statistics should be taken with caution. Some oscillations in the yearly figures are difficult to explain and may be the result of measurement error.

Table 9-14. *Social Indicators in Education, Selected School Years, Mexico, 1970–71 to 1991–92*

Percent unless otherwise specified

Year	Average years of schooling of population 15 years or older	Average schooling of population 15 years or older	Coverage for demand for schooling, total[a]	Coverage for demand for primary school[b]	Coverage for demand for junior high school[c]	Coverage for demand for high school[d]	Coverage for demand for higher levels or university[e]	Dropout rates[f]		
								Primary school	Junior high school	High school
1970–71	3.4	n.a.	51.7	78.4	62.2	69.7	n.a.	n.a.	n.a.	n.a.
1978–79	5.15	3.2	62.7	87.9	77.7	72.1	n.a.	6.6	11.2	10.5
1979–80	5.29	2.7	56.6	89.6	81.3	68.3	90.3	7.6	7.8	14.3
1980–81	5.4	2.1	58.7	91.4	82.0	68.8	88.6	7.2	10.5	12.4
1981–82	5.6	3.7	60.6	92.5	86.8	69.6	82.1	6.9	9.6	15.5
1982–83	5.7	1.8	62.0	93.5	86.2	66.5	84.6	6.0	10.3	15.7
1983–84	5.8	1.8	62.9	95.4	85.4	65.6	78.5	5.7	8.9	16.2
1984–85	5.9	1.7	62.7	98.0	82.9	66.5	70.0	6.4	9.8	16.3
1985–86	6.0	1.7	62.9	98.0	84.4	64.0	77.4	5.4	7.9	16.3
1986–87	6.1	1.7	62.5	98.0	83.7	59.2	63.7	5.3	9.3	18.4
1987–88	6.2	1.6	61.8	98.0	83.0	59.4	63.8	5.9	9.1	15.1
1988–89	6.3	1.6	61.2	98.0	83.2	59.8	57.7	5.3	9.1	16.3
1989–90	6.3	0.0	60.1	98.0	82.4	60.2	62.0	5.7	10.0	18.5
1990–91	6.4	1.6	59.4	98.0	82.3	61.0	64.4	5.3	9.5	16.4
1991–92[g]	6.4	0.0	59.1	98.0	82.4	61.6	66.0	5.0	9.1	16.0
Average										
1978/79–1980/81	5.3	2.7	59.3	89.6	80.3	69.7	89.5[h]	7.1	9.8	12.4
1983/84–1988/89	6.1	1.7	62.3	97.6	83.9	62.7	69.5	5.7	9.3	16.6
1989/90–1990/91	6.4	0.8	59.8	98.0	82.4	60.6	63.2	5.5	9.8	17.5

Source: Salinas de Gortari (1991, pp. 354, 357).

n.a. Not available.

a. Ratio of total population in school at any level to the population between 4 and 24 years of age.

b. Ratio of the population between 6 and 14 years of age in elementary school plus the population between 12 and 14 years who have completed elementary school to the total population between 6 and 14 years.

c. Ratio of population in the first year of junior high to the total population that graduated from elementary school in the previous year.

d. Ratio of population in the first year of high school to the total population that graduated from junior high school in the previous term.

e. Ratio of population in the first year of university to the total population that graduated from high school in the previous term.

f. The dropout rate includes those students who had registered for a year of school and had not finished that same year, or who had not registered for the next course.

g. Estimated.

h. Average is for 1979/80–1980/81.

Table 9-15. *Nutritional Status of Children in Latin American*
Middle-Income Economies, by Country, Selected Years, 1982–87

Country	GNP per capita (1987 U.S. dollars)	Children with low weight for age (percent)[a]	Low birth weight babies (percent)[b]
Argentina	2,390	n.a.	6
Brazil	2,020	12.7 (1986)[c]	8
Chile	1,310	2.3 (1985)	7
Columbia	1,240	11.9 (1986)	15
Costa Rica	1,610	6.0 (1982)	9
Mexico	1,830	13.9 (1988)	15
Panama	2,240	15.8 (1980)	8
Peru	1,470	13.4 (1984)	9
Uruguay	2,190	7.4 (1987)	8
Venezuela	3,230	5.9 (1987)	9

Source: World Bank (1990, table 1).
n.a. Not available
a. More than 2 standard deviations below the standard for weight for age according to the National Center for Health Statistics. Data from national survey taken the year shown in parenthesis.
b. Less than 2.5 kg (5.5 pounds).
c. Northeast only.

drop in family income which reduced the capacity of households to cover the complementary costs of education, such as transportation and books.

In terms of health and nutrition, malnutrition in Mexico is abnormally high. As table 9-15 indicates, the proportions of children with low weight for their age (13.9 percent) and of babies with low birth weight (15 percent) are well above those in most Latin American countries with similar per capita incomes.

Some indicators suggest that while the majority of the poor continued to improve their nutritional status during adjustment, a minority suffering from extreme deprivation may have experienced a further deterioration. For example, the national rural surveys conducted in 1978 and 1989 by the Mexican National Nutrition Institute (INN) reveal that estimated average consumption of calories per capita remained almost unchanged, while that of proteins increased by a little less than 14 percent.[52] The IMSS-COPLAMAR program, which provides basic health care to uninsured families in deprived areas, reported that among some 1 million children under age five the proportion of malnourished fell from 31 percent in 1986 to 21 percent in 1990 and 16.2 percent in the first semester of 1991. The corresponding figures for severely mal-

---

52. Calorie consumption was 1,913 kilocalories in 1979 and 1,880 in 1989; protein consumption increased from 52.0 to 59.2 grams. See Comisión Nacional de Alimentación (1992, p. 98). For more information on nutritional indicators see Mexican National Nutrition Institute (1990, figures 6 and 23).

Table 9-16. *Infant Mortality Rates and Deaths Caused by Nutritional Deficiencies, Mexico, 1980–89*

Year	Infant mortality per 1,000 births	Percent of infant mortality caused by nutritional deficiencies	Percent of total preschool mortality caused by nutritional deficiencies
1980	53.1	1.0	1.5
1981	51.3	1.1	1.6
1982	49.6	1.5	1.8
1983	48.0	1.5	2.4
1984	46.4	1.7	2.7
1985	44.8	2.0	2.9
1986	43.4	2.1	3.0
1987	42.0	2.9	9.1
1988	40.6	5.2	9.1
1989	39.3	n.a.	n.a.
Average 1983–88	44.2	2.6	4.2

Sources: For infant mortality rate, Consejo Nacional de Poblacion (1989). For deaths from nutritional deficiencies, Salinas de Gortari (1991, pp. 367–68).
n.a. Not available.

nourished children were 1.4 percent in 1986, 1.8 percent in 1990 and 1.2 percent in 1991.

The worsening of nutrition in the 1980s for some sectors seems to be confirmed by data on nutrition-related mortality and morbidity. The countrywide infant mortality rate continued to decline between 1982 and 1989 (table 9-16).[53] However, infant and preschool mortality caused by nutritional deficiencies increased after the early 1980s following years of steady decline (table 9-16).[54] One could argue that the infant mortality rate would have improved more rapidly had economic conditions not deteriorated, since nutritional deficiencies are likely to be more sensitive to income levels than other causes of infant mortality whose performance is determined by previous investments in health technology and sanitary facilities.[55]

53. Scholars have observed that the impact of an economic crisis is usually not reflected in average indicators; its effect on health becomes obvious only over the long run. See, for example, Perrott and Collins, (1934), a classic study on the health effects of the Great Depression.

54. Salinas de Gortari (1991, pp. 367–68).

55. To establish this would require more careful analysis. An increase in the death rate due to nutritional deficiencies may be the result of a decrease in a substitute cause such as intestinal diseases. Nonetheless, data show that deaths associated with both causes declined steadily through the 1970s. However, in the 1980s deaths caused by intestinal diseases fell, while those caused by nutritional deficiencies rose in both absolute and relative terms. See Salinas de Gortari (1991, pp. 367–68). Nonetheless, the statistics on causes of death may be subject to large measurement errors, and one should review the trends in table 9-12 with caution.

Other indicators confirm that conditions extreme malnutrition worsened. The ISSSTE recorded an increase in the number of infants, from birth to age one, suffering from slow fetal growth and malnutrition both in absolute terms and in proportion to total diseases. Children suffering from these ailments represented 5.7 percent of the total number of diseased children in 1981. That percentage increased to 7.8 percent in 1982, 7.9 percent in 1983, and 12.4 percent in 1984. The absolute number of infants served by ISSSTE who died of a nutritional deficiency also increased after 1982.[56]

Conclusion

At a general level, perhaps the most important policy mitigating the impact of adjustment was the decision to protect public employment.[57] The drastic cut in public spending at the inception of the crisis in 1982 reduced investment, general subsidies, and real wages, but avoided massive layoffs. Public employment actually increased which dampened the impact of the reduction in public spending on family incomes, and on the level of health and education services by keeping personnel in place.[58] Some might argue that protecting public employment does not really help the poor. However, in a country without unemployment insurance, massive layoffs could have produced a large number of *nouveaux pauvres* and perhaps further real wage cuts in the private sector. Also, maintaining the level of employment in health and education helped sustain the level of social services delivered to the population.

The introduction of targeted food subsidies to replace general subsidies on a number of food items represented a move toward a more progressive use of scarce public funds, since an important portion of general subsidies "leaked" to the nonpoor. Nevertheless, the amount allocated to targeted subsidies may not have been enough to compensate for the elimination of general subsidies as the significant rise in the cost of a basic diet suggests.[59]

The restructuring of public spending did not always focus on the needs of

56. Lustig, (1990, p. 41).

57. Salinas de Gortari (1991, p. 145).

58. The protection of public employment and the fact that a substantial share of income in poor households comes from nonwage sources (that share grew from 62 to 72 percent during the adjustment) help explain the pattern in table 9-1: per capita consumption fell less than disposable income and disposable income fell less than wage income per worker.

59. Estimates of the impact of changes in the subsidy is rudimentary, for it does not incorporate changes in the composition of the diet as a result of changes in relative prices. See Lustig (1990).

the poor. The government cut spending on basic education disproportionately and also slashed spending on rural and regional development. These cuts indicate that programs targeted to the poor at the community level were dismantled or seriously scaled down as the story of COPLAMAR in particular attests.

Perhaps the sharpest public policy difference between the administrations of de la Madrid and Salinas lies in the fact that while de la Madrid did not protect targeted programs, Salinas made social spending and targeted antipoverty programs a centerpiece of his agenda, starting in December 1988. Social spending rose sharply in 1989, and Salinas immediately launched the antipoverty program known as Solidarity.[60] The initial steps to decentralize the health and education sectors began under de la Madrid whose administration also prepared social projects targeted to the poor and provided the proper institutional framework for some programs implemented at the beginning of the Salinas administration.[61]

Moreover, the difference in the expenditure patterns of the two administrations may reflect different macroeconomic and fiscal constraints more than different priorities.[62]

As Mexico successfully absorbed the initial shock of the debt crisis and through macroeconomic adjustment achieved a degree of economic stability, its leaders recognized the need to redirect public spending to the social sectors to improve its equity, efficiency, and effectiveness. They also recognized that new investments were needed to extend coverage to the most needy. Toward those ends they designed health, education, housing and regional development projects that as of 1993 are being implemented with funding assistance from the World Bank, the Inter-American Development Bank, and the Solidarity program.

60. Precursors of this program include the social solidarity program launched by President Echeverra in 1973 and COPLAMAR which was launched by Lopez-Portillo in 1976. See La Forgia (1993). For a description of Solidaridad see, for example, Lustig (1994).

61. For example, the project to correct gaps in health services in the poorest states was prepared during de la Madrid's administration.

62. Also, among the cuts made by the de la Madrid administration at the onset of the crisis were costly programs whose effectiveness and distributional impact were questionable such as generalized food subsidies.

References

Appendini, Kirsten. 1991. "De la milpa a los tortibonos: La reestucturación de la política alimentaria en México." Instituto de Investigaciones de las Naciones Unidas par el Desarrollo Social (June).

Banco de Mexico. Annual. *Informe Anual.* Mexico City.

Banco de Mexico. 1990a. *Indicadores Económicos.* Mexico City.

Banco de Mexico. 1990b. "The Mexican Economy 1991: Economic and Financial Developments in 1990: Policies for 1991." Mexico City.

Binswanger, Hans P. 1992. "Comment." on paper by Nora Lustig, Santiago Friedmann and Arianna Legovini, presented at the conference "Confronting the Challenge of Poverty and Inequality in Latin America." Brookings Institution, Washington, 16–17 July 1992.

CEPAL. 1982. *Economía campesina y agricultura empresarial: Tipología de productores del agro mexicano.* Mexico City: Siglo Veintiuno.

Comisión Nacional de Alimentación. 1989a. "Documento Síntesis: Evaluación de Programas para Mejorar la Situación Alimentaria y Nutricional de la Población de Bajos Ingresos." (June). Mexico City.

———. 1989b. "Evaluación del Programa de Orientación Alimentaria." (March). Mexico City.

———. 1989c. "LICONSA: Programa de Abasto Social de Leche." (March). Mexico City.

———. 1989d. "Marco General de la Situación Alimentaria y Nutricional." (April). Mexico City.

———. 1989e. "Programa de Distribución CONASUPO Rural." (April). Mexico City.

———. 1989f. "Programa Integrado de Apoyo a la Nutrición." (April). Mexico City.

———. 1989g. "Programa Maiz Tortilla: Sistema de Distribución de Formas Valoradas." (March). Mexico City.

———. 1989h. "Programa Nacional de Solidaridad Social para Cooperación Comunitaria IMSS-COPLAMAR." Mexico City.

———. 1989i. "Programa Nutrición y Salud. Descripción Evolutiva, Julio 1987–Diciembre 1988." (March). Mexico City.

———. 1989j. "Propuesta para Establecer el Sistema Nacional de Vigilancia Alimentaria y Nutricional." (April). Mexico City.

———. 1992. "MEXICO: Diagnóstico de la Situación Alimentaria y Nutricional." (February). Mexico City.

Comision Nacional de los Salarios Minimos. 1989. *Compendio de Indicadores de Empleo y Salarios.* Mexico City. December.

———. 1991. *Compendio de Indicadores de Empleo y Salarios.* Mexico City. September.

Gregory, Peter. 1987. "The Mexican Labor Market in the Economic Crisis and Lessons of the Past." In *Mexico's Economic Policy: Past, Present and Future,* edited by William E. Cole. Socioeconomic Research Series. Knoxville, Tenn.: Center For Business and Economic Research (November).

INEGI (Instituto Nacional de Estadística, Geografía e Informática). 1984. *Encuesta Nacional de Ingreso y Gasto de los Hogares, 1er. Trimestre de 1984.* Mexico City.

————. 1988. "Sistema de Cuentas Nacionales de Mexico, 1980–1986: Tomo I, Resumen General." Mexico.

————. 1990a. "Sistema de Cuentas Nacionales de Mexico, 1986–1989: Tomo I, Resumen General." Mexico City.

————. 1990b. "Sistema de Cuentas Nacionales de Mexico, 1985–1988: Tomo I, Resumen General." Mexico City.

————. 1991. "Sistema de Cuentas Nacionales de Mexico, 1986–1989: Tomo I, Resumen General." Mexico City.

Ize, Alain. 1990. "Trade Liberalization, Stabilization, and Growth: some Notes on the Mexican Experience." Working Paper 90/15 (March). Washington: International Monetary Fund.

La Forgia, Gerard M. 1993. "Rural Social Security in Mexico: IMSS-COPLAMAR." In *Health Insurance Practice in Developing Countries: Vol. II*, edited by Gerard M. La Forgia and Charles C. Griffin. Washington: Urban Institute.

Lustig, Nora. 1990. "Economic Crisis and Living Standards in Mexico, 1982–85." *World Development* Vol. 18, No. 10, pp. 1325–42.

————. 1992. *Mexico: The Remaking of an Economy*. Brookings.

————. 1994. "Solidarity as a Strategy of Poverty Alleviation." In *Transforming State-Society Relations in Mexico: The National Solidarity Strategy*, edited by Wayne A. Cornelius, Ann L. Craig and Jonathan Fox. San Diego: Center for US-Mexican Studies, University of California, San Diego.

Lustig, Nora, and Ann Mitchell. 1994. "Poverty in Mexico During the 1980's: 'The Answer My Friend . . . '"

Macro Asesoria Economica. 1990. *Realidad Economica de Mexico: 1991*. Mexico City.

————. 1991. *Macro Perspectivas: 2 Trimestre, 1991*. Mexico City.

————. 1992. "Macro Perspectivas: Diagnostico y Perspectivas de la Economia Mexicana. July-September.

Maldonado Venegas, Luis. 1991. "Situación actual: Esfuerzos de México para familias de bajos ingresos." In *Reunión del grupo de trabajo sobre metodologías para identificar y seleccionar poblaciones afectadas por el ajuste estructural*. Rio de Janeiro.

Martín del Campo, Antonio, and Rosendo Calderón Tinoco. 1990. "Restructuración de los subsidios a productos básicos y modernización de CONASUPO." Mexico City: AMC.

Mexican National Nutrition Institute. 1990. "Encuesta Nacional de Alimentación en el Medio Rural, 1989." INNSZL-86. Mexico City: Community Nutrition Division.

Ordorica, Manuel. 1990. "Las Cifras Preliminares del Censo," in "Demos: Carta Demografica Sobre Mexico." Mexico City: UNAM.

Perrott, G. St. J., and Selwyn D. Collins. 1934. "Sickness among the Depression Poor." *American Journal of Public Health* 24 (February).

Pinstrup-Andersen, Per. 1992. "Comment." on the paper by Lustig, Friedmann and Legovinni presented at the conference "Confronting the Challenge of Poverty and Inequality in Latin America." Brookings Institution, Washington, D.C., 16–17 July 1992.

Poder Ejecutivo Federal. 1983. *Programa Nacional de Alimentación, 1983–1988*. Mexico City.

Salinas de Gortari, Carlos. 1990. *Segundo Informe de Gobierno: Anexo*. Mexico City.
————. 1991. *Tercer Informe de Gobierno, 1991: Anexo*. Mexico City.
Sistema Nacional de Salud. 1991. *Brevario Estadístico Sectorial 1980–1990*. Mexico City: Subsecretaría de Coordinación, Dirección General de Estadística, Informática y Evaluación.
World Bank. 1990. "The Nutrition Sector Memorandum." Report 8929-ME (July). Washington.
————. 1991. "Mexico—Malnutrition and Nutrition Programs: An Overview." LA2HR (August).

CHAPTER TEN

Peru: Social Policies and Economic Adjustment in the 1980s

Adolfo Figueroa

THIS CHAPTER has three central aims. The first is to assess the extent of poverty and inequality in Peru during the crisis and adjustment of the 1980s and early 1990s. The second is to examine how social policies influenced the distributive impact of the crisis. Finally, the third is to identify and discuss policies that can help improve equity and growth.

The empirical parts of the chapter show a profound increase in absolute and relative poverty in Peru. They also report trends in social program expenditures and social indicators during the 1980s. Subsequent sections examine the qualitative changes in Peruvian society that quantitative changes in equity have produced. The section on policy issues explores potential trade-offs between macroeconomic stability and social spending. The conclusion then draws broader lessons about equity and adjustment from the Peruvian case.

I want to thank Iliich Ascarza and Oscar Rodriquez for their very helpful research assistance. My colleagues Oscar Dancourt, Carmen Montero, Maria Remenyi, and Oscar Rodriguez offered very useful comments. In the United States, I gratefully acknowledge comments from Jorge Daly, Nora Lustig, Philip Musgrove, and Paul Winters.

Income Levels and Distribution

In terms of total GDP, Peru achieved substantial growth between 1950 and 1981. However, growth rates have declined over time. The average annual GDP growth rate fell from 6.0 percent during 1950–66 to 4.5 percent during 1967–74 and 2.9 percent during 1975–81. Since 1982 the economy has generally been in recession, except for 1986–87 when annual growth rates were very high (9 percent).[1] As a result, real GDP in 1991 represented only 79 percent of its 1987 value, which was the peak value for the entire period, as table 10-1 shows.

The population growth rate has also experienced important changes. The annual rate of population growth increased from 2.5 percent at the beginning of the 1950s to 2.9 percent by the middle of the 1960s. The rate has since declined continuously, reaching 2.1 percent in 1991.

Peru's economic performance in terms of GDP per capita, therefore, indicates rapid growth only until 1974. Between 1950 and 1966 the annual growth rate in GDP per capita was 3.2 percent, and between 1967 and 1974 it was 1.6 percent. Thereafter, Peru experienced a severe economic crisis: a significant decline in real GDP per capita. As indicated in table 10-1, the 1991 value of real GDP per capita was only 70 percent of its 1981 value and very similar to its 1960 value. In Latin America overall, the present economic crisis has meant a loss of fourteen years in income per capita, as GDP per capita in 1991 nearly equals its level in 1977.[2] In the case of Peru, almost thirty years have been lost.

Private investment has also fallen (table 10-1). Gross investment increased during the 1970s, reached a peak in 1981, and thereafter followed a downward trend. As a result, total investment in 1990 was only 60 percent of the level reached in 1981. In per capita terms, the 1990 figure was barely 49 percent of the 1981 level.

Poverty, in both absolute and relative terms, increased during the crisis, as the labor income data in table 10-2 suggest. Real wages have fallen almost continuously since the mid-1970s. For example, in the private sector in Lima the mean real wage in 1990–91 was less than 25 percent of the mean in 1973–74. Because GDP per capita fell relatively less than real wages, wage earners clearly lost heavily during the crisis.

1. The growth rates for GDP, per capita GDP, and population are taken from Instituto Nacional de Estadística e Informática (1992, table 9.2, p. 32).
2. CEPAL (1992, pp. 29, 41).

Table 10-1. *Real GDP and Private Investment, Peru, Selected Years, 1950–91*

1970 = 100 in 1979 prices

	GDP[a]		Gross private investment[b]	
Year	Total	Per capita	Total	Per capita
1950	34.4	59.4	n.a.	n.a.
1955	46.4	70.6	n.a.	n.a.
1960	59.7	79.4	n.a.	n.a.
1965	80.6	92.8	n.a.	n.a.
1970	100.0	100.0	100.0	100.0
1971	104.2	101.3	118.0	114.7
1972	107.2	101.3	116.0	109.7
1973	112.9	103.8	164.1	150.8
1974	123.4	110.3	175.2	156.7
1975	127.6	111.0	198.4	172.7
1976	130.1	110.2	176.7	149.6
1977	130.6	107.7	170.0	140.1
1978	131.0	105.1	163.5	131.3
1979	138.6	108.4	170.1	133.1
1980	144.8	110.4	203.4	155.1
1981	151.2	112.6	240.5	179.0
1982	151.5	110.2	221.0	160.7
1983	132.4	94.1	143.1	101.7
1984	138.8	96.4	139.2	96.7
1985	141.9	96.4	128.8	87.5
1986	155.0	103.1	159.3	105.9
1987	168.1	109.5	188.1	122.5
1988	154.1	98.3	179.3	114.4
1989[c]	136.1	85.1	132.4	82.7
1990[c]	129.2	79.1	144.4	88.4
1991[d]	132.3	79.3	n.a.	n.a.

Source: Instituto Nacional de Estadística e Informática (1992a, pp. 32, 74–75).
n.a. Not available.
a. Figures do not include cocaine-related activities, which began in the late 1970s.
b. Private investment figures are available as a consistent series only since 1970.
c. Preliminary.
d. Estimate.

For nonwage laborers, table 10-2 presents two real income indexes. An index of the terms of trade for self-employed rural laborers (the peasants) between 1973 and 1989 fell sharply beginning in 1980, recovered in 1986–87, but fell precipitously thereafter. As a result, its level in 1989 was barely 23 percent of its 1980 value. The monthly poverty index, which is based on the incomes of self-employed workers (rural and urban) and those earning the

Table 10-2. *Labor Income Indicators, Peru, 1970–91*
1985 = 100

Year	Real wages			Peasantry's terms of trade	Poverty index
	Private	Public	Minimum		
1970	178.2	n.a.	219.4	n.a.	n.a.
1971	192.7	n.a.	218.7	n.a.	n.a.
1972	207.7	n.a.	231.0	n.a.	n.a.
1973	218.0	n.a.	225.8	167.4	n.a.
1974	212.4	n.a.	230.0	152.6	n.a.
1975	201.6	n.a.	213.6	171.3	n.a.
1976	185.6	n.a.	196.1	153.1	n.a.
1977	160.2	n.a.	173.2	165.4	n.a.
1978	139.4	n.a.	132.0	152.9	n.a.
1979	133.7	n.a.	147.7	145.1	n.a.
1980	141.8	n.a.	182.8	183.4	n.a.
1981	141.4	215.6	155.5	155.9	n.a.
1982	148.3	197.8	143.3	139.5	n.a.
1983	125.2	143.0	145.8	130.5	n.a.
1984	111.5	125.6	116.2	126.9	n.a.
1985	100.0	100.0	100.0	100.0	100.0
1986	128.6	104.1	102.9	150.7	84.7
1987	136.9	117.8	114.2	156.3	73.4
1988	90.7	101.0	84.0	68.0	83.7
1989	60.0	61.6	44.6	42.7	120.5
1990	42.4	34.8	39.5	n.a.	151.2
1991	49.5	16.8	27.5	n.a.	173.3

Sources: For private real wages: Instituto Nacional de Estadística e Informática, *Compendio* (n.d., p. 161); (1991, vol. 1, pp. 430–31); (1992, vol. 1, pp. 602–03). Data are for Lima city only. *Private wages* is an aggregation of *sueldos* and *salarios* in the original data, with weights of 0.4 and 0.6, which were the approximate shares of white-collar and blue-collar workers in the labor force in 1985. As a result of a change in the method for collecting information on private wages introduced in 1986, the figures for 1970–79 were adjusted so as to obtain a consistent series. Because the data estimated with the old and the new methods overlap for 1980–86, the numbers for *salarios* and *sueldos* for 1970–79 were increased by 10 percent and 18 percent, respectively. The increase sets them equal to the average percentage difference in the two sets of data for 1980–86.
   For real public wages and minimum wages: Instituto Nacional de Estadística e Informática, *Compendio* (1992, vol. 1, pp. 584, 636). For peasantry's terms of trade: Figueroa (1992, pp. 35–47). For poverty index: Webb and Baca de Valdez (1992, table 13.18). This index increases as average incomes of the self-employed (urban and rural) and of those earning minimum wages or less decrease.
   n.a. Not available.

minimum wage, also suggests a rise in poverty during the 1980s. This index shows a decline in poverty during 1986–88, but a significant increase thereafter.

   The concept of real income used to measure poverty in this section refers to the ability of the working class to buy goods in the marketplace. This income-based measure of poverty shows a significant expansion of poverty in Peru since the mid-1970s. The next two sections address what happened to poverty in terms of access to public goods.

Table 10-3. *Government Social Spending, Peru, 1970–90*

Year	Index of real social spending[a]		Real social spending as percent of	
	Total	Per capita	GDP	Government spending
1970	100	100	4.5	26.4
1971	105	102	4.5	24.6
1972	114	108	4.8	25.3
1973	127	116	4.9	24.3
1974	127	113	4.5	23.9
1975	133	115	4.6	23.2
1976	137	116	4.7	23.8
1977	120	99	4.3	19.0
1978	113	90	4.0	15.7
1979	121	95	3.9	19.0
1980	154	118	4.6	20.1
1981	153	114	4.6	21.1
1982	136	98	4.0	18.9
1983	119	84	4.1	16.9
1984	125	86	4.1	16.8
1985	123	82	4.0	16.7
1986	155	103	4.6	21.6
1987	119	76	3.2	18.0
1988	92	57	3.2	20.7
1989[b]	66	40	2.6	21.6
1990[b]	43	25	1.6	15.9

Source: Real social spending: Banco Central de Reserva del Perú (1989, p. 217); and *Banco Central* (forthcoming) for the 1988–90 data. Nominal values were converted into constant values using the consumer price index for Lima, as published in Instituto Nacional de Estadística y Censos (1991). Per capita social spending: real social spending divided by population, as it appears in Instituto Nacional de Estadística e Informática, *Compendio* (1991, table 9.2), and converted into index numbers. Real social spending as percent of GDP and government spending: Banco Central de Reserva del Perú (1989, p. 2.18); and Banco Central (forthcoming).
a. 1970 = 100.
b. Preliminary.

Government Social Spending

Table 10-3 presents data on government social spending from 1970 to 1990, incorporating four categories of expenditure: education, health, housing, and employment programs.[3] Total social spending increased, with some fluctuations, until 1980 but fell continuously thereafter (except in 1986). As a

3. Food subsidy programs are not included for three reasons. First, data on these programs are not included in the official data on social spending and they are not available under any other single item. Second, these programs usually include implicit subsidies, such as differential exchange rates for food imports. Third, in a country like Peru, where food is also produced by the rural poor (the peasantry), the distributive impact of these programs is difficult to establish.

Table 10-4. *Structure of Social Spending, Peru, Selected Periods,*
1970–90
Percent

Sector	1970–75	1976–80	1981–85	1986–90
Education	74.3	66.6	70.9	74.2
Health	19.6	24.0	24.9	23.1
Housing	5.2	8.6	3.5	2.0
Employment	0.9	0.8	0.7	0.7
Total	100.0	100.0	100.0	100.0

Source: Banco Central de Reserva del Perú (1989, p. 217); Banco Central (forthcoming) for the 1988–90 data.

result, the 1990 value of public social spending was only 28 percent of its 1980 value. In per capita terms, the fall has been even more dramatic, with the 1990 proportion only 21 percent of the 1980 level.

As a proportion of GDP, social spending started to decline earlier. It reached a peak of nearly 5 percent of GDP in 1972–73, fluctuated until 1986, and then fell sharply. In 1990 social spending was only 1.6 percent of GDP. As a proportion of total government expenditure, including foreign debt service payments, social spending has also declined. At the beginning of the 1970s, almost 25 percent of the government budget was allocated to social expenditures. In 1990 this share fell to 16 percent. Although this relative decline was less severe than the drop in its share of GDP, these figures clearly reveal that the government gave low priority to social spending during the crisis.

The structure of social spending has varied only slightly since the early 1970s (table 10-4). Education has received the highest share with around 75 percent, followed by health with about 23 percent. Housing and employment receive the rest. The most important reallocation was in housing, whose share fell from about 5 percent in the early 1970s to 2 percent in the late 1980s.

The significant drop in government social expenditures during the 1980s must have reduced both the quantity and quality of services provided by the state. Public services in education and health have been supplied with poorly maintained capital goods and buildings, declining supplies of material inputs, and nearly constant supplies of labor. The share of current consumption in the four social sectors spent on wages rose from 88 to 90 percent in the late 1970s to almost 95 percent during 1987–89.[4] Because labor is not a perfect substitute for the other factors of production, this change in factor proportions has probably meant a fall in the quantity and quality of public services supplied.

4. Banco Central de Reserva del Perú (1989, pp. 2.20–2.36; and forthcoming).

The fall in real wages in Peru's public sector has been severe. As table 10-2 shows, real public sector wages in 1991 were less than 10 percent of their level in 1981. One direct effect of lower wages has been lengthy strikes during the crisis years. In 1991, for instance, a majority of Ministry of Health workers were on strike for four months in the midst of a cholera epidemic; public school teachers were also on strike for four months. The decline in real wages may have also reduced worker productivity. As the efficiency wage theory of labor markets suggests, worker productivity depends on the real wage. Therefore, as real wages fell, many of the best-trained professionals probably left the public sector, and the productivity of the remaining workers likely deteriorated.[5]

Distribution of Social Spending

Pure public goods, by definition, have the property that any member of society can consume without depriving any other member of society of the good. All consumers therefore consume the same amount of each public good, since they are supplied at zero market prices. But public expenditures on health, education, and other social services differ from pure public goods in two key ways. First, these services are supplied both by the state (at zero market price) and by the market. Second, families willing to consume the services supplied by the state (even at zero price) also need to purchase complementary private goods. The consumption of public social services still depends on family economic decisions and varies across households. The question of who benefits from public social expenditures is thus an empirical issue that I examine for each category.

Education

A recent study, based on a nationwide household survey conducted in 1985–86, suggests that the benefits of public education expenditure are progressive. Table 10-5 presents the number of students enrolled in public schools and the distribution of budgeted expenditures by income quintile. Approximately 46 percent of students enrolled in public schools are in the bottom

5. To reduce the fiscal deficit, public sector workers received economic incentives to retire voluntarily on several occasions, though with greater force in 1990 and 1991. Those who decided to retire under this program probably included the most capable professionals and workers in the social services.

Table 10-5. *Distribution of Benefits from Education Spending, Peru, 1985–86*

Percent

Quintile	Students	Budget	Ratio of students in public schools to total
1 (lowest)	19.4	17.1	95.9
2	26.2	25.5	97.1
3	23.7	23.4	91.4
4	18.0	18.5	81.2
5	12.7	15.5	62.6
Total	100.0	100.0	85.6

Source: Rodríguez (1992, pp. 13–15).

two quintiles of the distribution, whereas only 30 percent are in the top two quintiles. The fact that the cost per student is higher for higher levels of education, and that the share of students from upper-income quintiles is greater at higher levels of education, does not change the result using the monetary transfer criterion.[6]

How can we explain this progressivity in education spending? Consider the following identity:

$$(10\text{-}1) \qquad X_j/Q_j = X_j/V_j \cdot V_j/W_j \cdot W_j/Q_j,$$

where X_j/Q_j is the number of people enrolled in public schools as a proportion of the number of families in quintile j; X_j/V_j is the number of students attending public schools as a proportion of the total number of students in quintile j (the absorption rate); V_j/W_j is the ratio of the number of students to the number of people of school age (the schooling rate); and W_j/Q_j is the ratio of the number of people of school age to the total population in the quintile j.

Assuming that the ratio W_j/Q_j is constant across quintiles, the only factors that can explain the empirical differences found in X_j/Q_j are the absorption rate and the schooling rate. The lower enrollment rate in the first quintile relative to the second may be due to a lower schooling rate in the first quintile. These families are so poor that they cannot even send their children to a public school. The system becomes progressive in the following four quintiles because the rate of absorption falls. Families with higher incomes send their children, in a higher proportion, to private schools. For Peruvian society as a whole, public schools seem to be an inferior good.

6. It should be clear that the budget distribution in table 10-5 *implies* a progressive system. Even if the budget were equally distributed by quintiles, the system would be progressive, as this distribution would not be proportional to incomes.

An important statistic in table 10-5 is that 86 percent of students in Peru (at all levels, including university) are enrolled in public institutions. Those students who are not attending public schools tend to belong to wealthier families and obviously do not benefit from public education expenditures. In fact, it seems clear that in Peru the rich (the top 1 percent in terms of income) and probably the upper and middle classes (the top 5 percent) are excluded from the benefits of public education. Unfortunately, this study, based on a distribution by income quintiles, does not allow us to test this proposition.

In conclusion, in Peru a decline in the supply of public education (holding the distribution constant) would hurt the poor most. Given a deterioration in the quality of public education, the options for the poor are either to attend a public school and obtain lower-quality education or to drop out, because moving to a private school is not an option. Using Hirschman's terms, one could say that, in this case, the poor have only "voice"; they cannot "exit."[7]

Health

It is often argued that government spending on health primarily benefits the middle class, not the poor, because only a small share of the health budget is allocated to primary health care, with the majority spent on hospitals and doctors. But in the case of Peru, a large proportion of the poor use public health services.

Table 10-6 presents the sources of health care (source location and provider) for poor and nonpoor patients obtained from the 1991 nutritional survey of living standards carried out by the Instituto Cuánto. These data show that the poor make relatively greater use of both health centers and health posts, but relatively less use of hospitals, than the rest of the population. Yet overall the sources of health care do not vary greatly between the poor and the nonpoor.

Furthermore, with the increase in poverty, the demand for these public services must have increased. Like public schools, they are probably inferior goods. Given the fall in health spending, the quality of the service must have declined.

If the quality of health services declines greatly, or the services are not available (due to strikes), the poor seek health care from the private sector. In general, they do not go to a formal hospital, clinic, or professional physician, but rather to paramedics, pharmacists, and traditional healers, which provide

7. Hirschman (1970).

Table 10-6. *Locations and Providers of Health Care for Extremely Poor and Nonpoor Patients, Peru, 1991*

Percent

Source	Extremely poor	Nonpoor
Location		
Hospital	30.1	34.8
Health center	23.4	11.6
Health post	8.1	5.2
Clinic	11.1	33.7
Pharmacy	14.2	9.0
Home of patient	6.9	2.4
Other	6.1	3.3
Total	100.0	100.0
Provider		
Doctor, dentist, nurse	77.0	87.2
Paramedic	4.9	3.1
Pharmacist	14.2	8.9
Traditional healer	3.4	0.5
Other	0.5	0.3
Total	100.0	100.0

Source: Instituto Cuánto and UNICEF (1993, tables 6.4, 6.6).

much lower-quality service. In this case, the poor seem to take the option of exit, instead of voice.

Sanitary Services and the Cholera Epidemic

A cholera epidemic broke out in Peru in January 1991. By December of that year, the number of reported cases had reached nearly 320,000, and almost 3,000 people had died.[8] These figures are very large compared to international experience.[9]

The origin of the cholera epidemic in Peru is unknown. But it certainly resulted from some accidental, exogenous change. The more relevant question is which factors determined the magnitude of the epidemic. The propagation mechanism for the *vibrio cholerae* is the intake of fecal residues. Hence the less access one has to sewerage, potable water, and garbage collection systems, the higher the probability of contracting the disease. Therefore, the mag-

8. Petrera (1992, table 1).

9. According to a press release from the World Health Organization, 388,000 cases, with 5,187 deaths, were reported in the world in 1992; Peru occupied first place, with 192,000 cases and 690 deaths. "El Peru sigue siendo el mas afectado por el colera en el mundo," *El Comercio*, January 16, 1993, p. B2.

nitude of the epidemic depended mainly on the access of the population to sanitary services.

According to the 1985–86 national household survey, 49 percent of Peruvian households had no access to a sewerage system, and 33 percent had no access to potable water.[10] In view of the drastic decline in social spending on those services (included under housing in table 10-3), these shortages must have been even higher in 1991. The magnitude of the cholera epidemic, therefore, was a consequence of the decline in public spending on sanitary systems.[11]

A study of Lima and Chimbote showed that, in fact, the families that contracted the disease had more limited access to sanitary services than those that did not.[12] Because these families also tended to have relatively lower incomes, they were unable to buy the expensive kerosene needed to boil the water.[13]

The poor were the ones terribly hit by the cholera epidemic in Peru. Certainly, no cases were reported from the residential areas of Lima or other big cities. There is some truth in the saying that cholera is a disease of poverty.[14]

Employment Programs

The *Programa de Apoyo al Ingreso Temporal* (PAIT), executed from 1985 to 1987, offered employment in public works for three months at the minimum wage. One study of this program found that close to 80 percent of the people it employed were adult women, mostly household heads or spouses. In terms of previous occupational status, 28 percent of the people it employed came from open unemployment, 27 percent from other occupations, 32 percent from outside the labor force (people that were inactive), and 2 percent from other categories.[15]

Given the similarity in the occupational histories of participants in the pro-

10. Webb and Fernández Baca (1992, table 13.10, p. 455).

11. A well-known Peruvian physician and ex-minister of health said in a public interview that control of the cholera epidemic was more the responsibility of the Ministry of Finance than of the Ministry of Health.

12. Petrera (1992, table 33).

13. The government had increased tremendously the relative price of kerosene in August 1990, as part of the stabilization program. The relative price increased from 19 in July 1990 to 100 in August 1990 and has declined from then on. In December 1991 the index was 58, still a very high increase. Banco Central, *Nota Semanal* no. 8 (February 28, 1994), cuadro 67, p. 67.

14. The economic losses resulting from the cholera epidemic have been significant. For instance, export revenue losses amounted to $175 million (6 percent of total annual exports). Income from tourism declined by $147 million (50 percent of total income in the previous year). See Petrera (1992, table 37).

15. Bernedo (1989, p. 62).

gram and the poor, it is likely that the employment program reached the poor, and primarily the poor. Households in which the head is a woman are usually among the poorest in Peru. Also, individuals that are unemployed generally belong to the poorest segments. The same is true of those described as inactive, who are not looking for a job either because it is too costly, or because the chance of obtaining one is too low.[16]

Compensatory Social Programs

Peru has implemented nearly forty economic stabilization packages since 1976.[17] As in many other Latin American countries, these packages have usually been accompanied by compensatory social programs, with differing coverage and duration.

On August 8, 1990, the new Fujimori administration initiated a drastic package of reforms. State-controlled prices were increased by a factor of thirty overnight. Due to the expected impact of this shock therapy on the poor, the new government designed a large compensatory social program. The minister of finance, on the evening before the reforms took effect, publicly promised $400 million in spending over a period of five months in order to protect the incomes of the 7 million people classified as living in extreme poverty. According to the minister, the shock would eliminate Peru's hyperinflation, which had reached 30 percent a month, by the end of that period.

As a result of the shock therapy, the monthly rate of inflation in August 1990 reached almost 400 percent. Thereafter the inflation rate declined significantly. Annual inflation fell to 139 percent in 1991, compared to 1,722 percent in 1988, 2,775 percent in 1989, and 7,650 percent in 1990.[18]

As table 10-7 indicates, actual government expenditures on compensatory social programs fell far short of the promised amount. Total transfers were only $88 million in the last five months of 1990 and $102 million in 1991. Most of the transfers were in the form of food aid (nearly 80 percent), employment programs (15 percent), and health programs (2 percent).

16. Empirical evidence supporting these results for Lima is in Dancourt and others (1990, pp. 30–33).

17. Figueroa (1990, annex A, pp. 64–68). If one defines as a stabilization package a change in at least two of the nominal prices of goods and services under government control—mainly minimum legal wage, exchange rate, interest rate, public utilities, and gasoline and kerosene—then annex A implies close to forty packages.

18. Different interpretations of the Peruvian inflation can be found in Dancourt and Yong (1989); and Paredes and Sachs (1991).

Table 10-7. *Public Expenditures on Compensatory Social Programs,*
Peru, 1990–91

Percent unless otherwise specified

| Type of program | Social Emergency Program | | FONCODES |
	1990[a]	1991[b]	1991[c]
Food	72.5	84.2	73.1
Health	4.6	0	23.2
Employment	14.3	15.8	3.7
Other	8.6	0	0
Total	100.0	100.0	100.0
Expenditure (millions of U.S. dollars)	88.1	97.5	4.2

Source: Data on Social Emergency Program (Programa de Emergencia de Social) were obtained from Dirección de Asuntos Sociales, Ministerio de Economía y Finanzas, unpublished materials. Data on FONCODES are from Fondo Nacional de Compensación y Desarrollo Social (1991). FONCODES initiated its operations in September 1991, and in January 1992 absorbed the Social Emergency Program.

a. August–December.
b. January–December.
c. September–December.

Three additional actions by the government further diminished the impact of the social fund, which already was low relative to the needs that the shock therapy had created. First, it cut conventional social expenditures financed through the general budget. Average monthly public social expenditures between August and December of 1990 were only 58 percent of the average during the previous seven months. As a share of GDP, these expenditures fell from 2.5 to 1.8 percent.[19] Second, the government did not completely spend the amount it budgeted, as the minister of finance revealed in a public interview. Third, it did not target social fund expenditures toward areas with the greatest levels of poverty. A team of consultants from the United Nations Development Program (UNDP) proposed the use of infant mortality rates to determine the allocation of funds among provinces. With this criterion, Puno (one of the poorest departments in Peru) should have received 11 percent of the funds and Lima 17 percent. In fact, Puno received 1 percent and Lima (where 30 percent of Peru's total population live) received 60 percent.[20]

For several years, nongovernmental organizations have directed a number of social programs in Peru, including food, health, and employment programs of variable coverage and duration. These programs became even more important after the shock treatment. At the end of 1991, there were about fifteen food programs, five employment programs, and several health programs. The

19. Figueroa and Ascarza (1991, tables 6A and 6B).
20. Abugattas (1991, p. 7).

funds for these programs have come from official international sources and from donations. Program funds and services have been distributed to the population through private institutions, such as CARITAS, CARE, OFASA, and PRISMA, among others. The most important recipients have been the Club of Mothers, Popular Kitchens, public schools, hospitals, and municipal governments.[21]

Although data on the amount of money distributed through these programs and agencies are incomplete, the figures for the most important donors or distribution units suggest that their resources have been relatively modest.[22] Most private social programs have operated almost entirely independent of the government, as the lack of official statistical records on them suggests. The limited size and scope of the private programs demonstrate that the most important income transfer has come from the government emergency social funds.

Government action, or lack of action, reveals that poverty has not been a top priority of the Fujimori government. Its compensatory social programs played mostly a political role, making shock therapy politically viable.

Impact on Social Indicators

The drastic fall in real incomes during the crisis, together with an equally acute decline in public social services and the meager effect of compensatory social programs, should have led to a deterioration in living standards. These changes, in turn, should have produced a corresponding deterioration in social indicators. What does the empirical evidence show?

In education a common social indicator is the illiteracy rate. No survey data are available on this rate for the 1980s. However, official estimates based on extrapolations from the 1981 census indicate that the illiteracy rate has continued to fall. The census data show a decline in the illiteracy rate from 58 percent in 1940 to 39 percent in 1961, 27 percent in 1972, 18 percent in 1981, and, extrapolating from 1981, the National Institute of Statistics estimated the rate to be 12 percent for 1989.[23]

This evidence indicates that the illiteracy rate, in the short run, is very inelastic in response to reductions in real income and social spending. The rea-

21. Lists of current social programs in Peru, including their coverage and funding sources, are in the special appendixes of Webb and Fernández Baca (1992, pp. 308–10, 462–80, 516–19).

22. See the appendix on social programs in Webb and Fernández Baca (1992, pp. 308–10, 462–80, 516–19).

23. Webb and Fernández Baca (1990, table 3.10, p.136).

son is that a quantitative change in the flow of illiterates, in the short run, is very small compared to the accumulated stock. Primary education rates may behave similarly.

School enrollment rates followed their historical trend during the 1980s, but a significant change occurred in the early 1990s. Official estimates show that total enrollment in 1991 was 18 percent below its projected level. However, a private institution has estimated that the dropout rate reached 28 percent, representing almost 2 million students. With respect to 1990 enrollment, this magnitude represents 30 percent of all students.[24] Because school directors tend to underreport the cases of dropouts (for the fear of losing vacancies, teachers, and budget), the private estimates seem more reliable. Because of the very low rate of enrollment at the beginning of the 1992 school year, the Ministry of Education has extended the enrollment period, imposing no definite time limits.

The fall in the rate of school enrollment observed in 1991–92 may be explained by the long economic crisis. Families initially adapted to the reduction in government spending on education by accepting some decline in the quality of education or by paying for the service themselves. Parents contributed both their labor and their money to schools at increasing rates during the crisis.

In 1991 and 1992, however, the quality of education declined too dramatically, and the meager real incomes of the poor declined even further. The private cost of attending a public school is now too high relative to the quality of education and the present real income of the poor, causing dropout rates to rise.[25]

Infant mortality rates, estimated by extrapolation, continued to decline during the crisis period, falling from 102 per thousand in 1980 to 93 in 1985 and 82 in 1990. Official estimates of life expectancy also improved, rising from 58 years in 1980 to 60 in 1985 and 63 in 1990.[26] But, again, these figures do not measure the actual rates; they are merely extrapolations.

What has prevented the infant mortality rate from deteriorating during the crisis? One explanation of why infant mortality did not rise with poverty is that immunization programs were not abandoned. Official statistics show that the proportion of protected infants did not decline in the 1980s. The number of child vaccination doses given (for polio, tuberculosis, DPT, and smallpox) rose from 3.5 million in 1983 to 4.5 million in 1984 and 8.9 million in 1985 and averaged 6.2 million a year with little variation during 1986–

24. See Instituto de Forrento de una Educación de Calidad (1991).
25. For a description of the public schools in 1990–91, see Burgos (1991).
26. Instituto Nacional de Estadística e Informática y Centro Latinoamericano de Demografía (1992, p. 63).

91.[27] Because these programs are relatively low-cost and have broad international support, they were maintained despite the crisis, thereby preventing a rise in infant mortality rates, which nevertheless remain very high.

Changes in the economic behavior of the poor may also provide an explanation. Poor families may reallocate their resources to protect infants. The demand for child-related goods and services tends to be inelastic to changes in prices and income. Unfortunately, no empirical evidence is available to support this argument. Of course, this reallocation would imply sacrifices of other components of the family's living standard.

The morbidity rate is directly measured each year based on reports collected by the Ministry of Health. Although there may be differences in the quality of data between years, it is one of the few social indicators that can be used to measure, however imperfectly, the actual effect of a fall in social spending. Table 10-8 shows a significant increase in morbidity rates from the most common preventable diseases, such as gastric and intestinal diseases, malaria, and tuberculosis, between 1980 and 1989. Morbidity rates increased for all the diseases presented in table 10-8 between the late 1970s and the first half of the 1980s. The largest increases in morbidity rates were in gastric-intestinal diseases, as the average annual number of cases per 100,000 persons during 1985–89 was four times the average during 1977–80.

When evaluating changes in living standards of the poor, not all conventional social indicators provide the same information. There should be a distinction between indicators that change in the short run and those that change only in the long run. Also, some indicators may reflect either changes in technology (vaccinations) or changes in the poor's survival strategies (protecting the infant and child more than the adult). In the case of Peru, for instance, it would be a mistake to cite declining infant mortality rates or illiteracy rates as evidence that the poor have not suffered much during the economic crisis.

The empirical part of this chapter can be summarized in two broad points. First, the severe economic crisis in Peru, which in terms of GDP per capita started around 1976, meant a decline in both real incomes and access to social services for the majority of the population. GDP per capita in 1991 was only 72 percent of its value in 1976, whereas the weighted average of wages in 1991 was only 19 percent of the 1976 figure.[28] Nonwage labor incomes fol-

27. Webb and Fernández Baca (1992, table 8.17, p. 284).

28. Using the wage categories in table 10-2, the weights applied to make this calculation are 0.4 for private-sector wage earners (in firms with five or more employees), 0.2 for public-sector wages earners, and 0.4 for those earning minimum wages. These figures roughly correspond to the proportion of each category in total wage labor; they are gross estimates made by the author on the basis of the 1981 population census.

Table 10-8. *Morbidity Rates, by Disease, Peru, Selected Periods,*
1977–89

Per 100,000 persons

Disease	1977–80	1981–85	1986–89
Gastric-intestinal	320	873	1,214
Helmintiasis	201	247	235
Malaria	129	142	178
Tuberculosis	98	122	148
Typhoid	74	111	88.4

Source: Ministerio de Salud (1991, figure 1.2).

lowed a similar pattern (table 10-2). Per capita social spending in 1990 was only 22 percent of its 1976 value. Compensatory social programs had only a marginal effect on poverty, which increased tremendously in both absolute and relative terms.

Second, not all social indicators reflect the recent increase in absolute poverty in Peru. This is because some indicators capture short-run trends in poverty, while others capture long-run trends. In health, for example, changes in morbidity rates clearly reflect increasing poverty. The rise in preventable diseases, including the cholera epidemic, is a clear indication of the falling living standards of the poor. Infant mortality rates, on the other hand, have not deteriorated due to the maintenance of immunization programs and campaigns, and possibly due to family strategies to protect infants. In education, all indicators seem to reflect long-run trends. The fact that dropout rates started to rise in 1991–92, after so many years of crisis, seems to indicate the beginning of a long-run cumulative effect.

An Interpretation of the Facts

Have these significant quantitative changes in poverty (absolute and relative) produced any qualitative changes in Peruvian society? I contend that changes in equity in Peru have led to a distributive crisis, which occurs when income inequality surpasses a threshold of social tolerance. In this situation, workers no longer accept the rules of production and distribution that prevail in the economic system. Noncontractual incomes expand; property rights are challenged; the social contract breaks down; and social violence and instability prevail.

The impact of a distributive crisis on economic growth depends on what happens to private investment, the engine of growth in a capitalist economy. Private investment refers to expenditures on plants and equipment, research and development, and human capital—that is, on those factors that are the basic sources of economic growth. These expenditures depend on long-term decisions by investors who are sensitive to the level of uncertainty. Since a distributive crisis implies social instability and a higher degree of uncertainty, private investment is likely to contract.

In a dynamic economy, decisions on investment today have consequences for income levels and distribution tomorrow. A fall in investment today increases poverty tomorrow, in both absolute and relative terms. Increased poverty leads to a further fall in investment, and so on. Hence, as a consequence of a distributive crisis, the economy may get trapped in a vicious circle, characterized by declining investment and rising poverty.

Empirical data on Peru's current crisis seem consistent with this hypothesis. First, the drastic fall in real wages since the mid-1970s has been followed by a decline in private investment since the beginning of the 1980s. What may seem a paradox—that in spite of drastic reductions in real wages investment has fallen—can be explained by the existence of a distributive crisis.[29]

Second, social violence has increased since the beginning of the 1980s. Three types of violence can be distinguished in Peru: political, economic, and redistributive. The origins of subversive political groups may be exogenous, but the magnitude of the movement is the result of endogenous factors. Increased poverty and the lack of prospects for economic growth have induced many people, and particularly the young, to join these groups. Economic violence is related to the cocaine industry. Again, the origin of the industry may lie in an exogenous factor, such as a rise in external demand. But the size of the industry is endogenous. Thousands of campesinos have left impoverished rural communities in the Andes to work in coca cultivation. Redistributive violence is related to the daily struggle of the masses for survival. Because the government has abandoned redistributive policies, the poor are claiming a larger share directly. Stealing, kidnapping, and bribing can all be viewed as rational behavior for anyone trying to survive. In this sense, income redistribution has been privatized. As a result, the security and protection industry in Peru is booming in the midst of the recession.

Peru's social violence, particularly the political violence, is usually inter-

29. Dornbusch has argued similarly that "if government went far enough to create the incentives that would motivate a return of capital and the resumption of investment on an exclusive economic calculation, the implied size of real wage cuts might be so extreme that . . . asset holders might consider the country too perilous for investment." Dornbusch (1991, p. 45).

preted as a cause of the nation's present economic problems. According to my hypothesis, however, social violence is not a cause but a consequence of the difficult situation in Peru. In a dynamic process, it is an endogenous outcome.

What has caused Peru to fall into a distributive crisis? My hypothesis is that macroeconomic policies—both of the orthodox and the heterodox types—intended to control the initial debt crisis were the basic cause. They are the exogenous variables. The foreign debt problem guided the government's choice of macroeconomic stabilization and adjustment policies.

Peruvian governments have used orthodox stabilization policies since 1976, with the sole exception of the first two years (1985–87) of President Garcia's administration, which implemented heterodox policies. Webb has argued that at the end of 1988 Garcia applied an orthodox stabilization policy, setting all the targets prescribed in the so-called "Washington Consensus." He has written:

> We can ask ourselves whether all this amounts to adjustment. True, we [in Peru] met all the targets. And the targets we set are probably a lot more ambitious than any program that the [International Monetary] Fund have set for Peru or anyone else. Even so, we would not want to say that this is adjustment. The main reason is that inflation in late 1989 is still ranging at 25 percent to 30 percent a month. . . . At the same time the fiscal deficit has not been eliminated . . . and the official exchange rate is clearly overvalued. Above all, the debt is still not paid. It is this criterion, of course, that looms largest in any Washington Consensus definition of adjustment.[30]

An efficient adjustment policy is supposed to stabilize the economy and create the conditions for a resumption of growth in the shortest possible time period. Advocates of orthodox stabilization have repeatedly argued that orthodox policies are painful, but that they will work. In the case of Peru, however, these policies have not worked. Instead, they have led to a distributive crisis. Even the severe adjustment policies begun by the Fujimori administration have not worked. Although the inflation rate has declined significantly (to around 3 to 4 percent a month in mid-1992), private investment has not recovered.

Neoclassical economists admit that orthodox structural adjustment policies, including stabilization programs, increase poverty during the period of adjustment. But at the same time they argue that the benefits of the post-adjustment period, when growth is expected to resume, will more than compensate for these social costs. This argument assumes that the transitional rise

30. Webb (1990, pp. 103–04).

in poverty has no additional social consequences, that society will accept the new higher level of income inequality, as if social tolerance to inequality were unlimited. But the case of Peru has proven this assumption wrong.

As noted, the Fujimori administration's adjustment policies further increased poverty in both absolute and relative terms, reducing income and access to public goods. In a society already trapped in a distributive crisis, the effect of this additional impoverishment was fatal. It raised not only social but also political instability, as the country became ungovernable under democratic rules. The new dictatorship established in April 1992 by the Fujimori regime, under this interpretation, is a result of this process, an endogenous outcome.

Since the restoration of democracy in 1980 after twelve years of military dictatorship, Peru's democratic political system has been unable to halt the deterioration in social equity. As a result, citizens became disaffected with the democratic system. By blaming this system for Peru's failure to stabilize and to resume growth, President Fujimori even received popular support, at least initially, for changing the political regime.

Macroeconomic Stability and Social Spending

To resume economic growth, Peru must solve its distributive crisis. The efficient path to economic growth, therefore, must include a reconstruction of the social equilibrium. From this perspective, redistribution is an essential component of an effective adjustment policy. When an economy is in a distributive trap, improving equity is a necessary condition for resuming growth.

The Peruvian experience has shown that in a distributive crisis any increase in the income of the rich, created by the incentive system of orthodox economic policy, does not go toward domestic investment. It is either sent abroad in capital flight or put into speculative domestic investments. In a distributive crisis, investors, domestic and foreign alike, simply gamble. This behavior is clearly not conducive to growth.

In a distributive crisis everyone loses, even the rich. Hence if equity is improved, everyone should gain, including the rich. Once a society is in a distributive trap, there is no conflict between growth and equity. This does not mean that a redistributive policy is socially and politically viable in Peru today. Were this policy so good, why would it not have already been taken? One possible answer is the myopic view of the ruling class. There is probably some truth to this argument, but I would like to propose another. Although everyone would benefit from social stability (a public good), no social actor is willing to pay the price of maintaining or reestablishing it. Peru thus faces a typical situation of the prisoner's dilemma, with its noncooperative solution. Although both would benefit from a socially stable equilibrium, neither the rich nor the poor have the incentive to cooperate to achieve it.

The rich are uncertain about future gains from financing a redistributive program through taxes. They fear that tax revenues may be used to pay the foreign debt or be given to the middle class or the bureaucracy, but not to the poor. Even if the funds reached the poor, it is not clear whether the poor would cooperate to reestablish social stability. The poor, in turn, are uncertain about whether the government is capable and willing to improve equity, and whether the rich will respond to higher growth by increasing investment and expanding jobs. A new social contract, therefore, is needed to escape the distributive trap. This contract, in turn, requires coordination.

In a distributive crisis, who is able to coordinate the new social contract? In the case of Peru, the new social contract is being coordinated through a dictatorship. The new Congress, to be elected democratically, will have the task of writing a new constitution that in part expresses the social contract. The 1993 constitution may specify, in addition to new rules of production and distribution, a new platform of rights designed to resolve the present distributive crisis. If legislators fail to produce the terms of a new social contract, the crisis will continue.

What should be the content of a new social contract? This question leads to the nature of democracy in a capitalist economy. Okun said that a capitalist democracy is a social system that operates with a double standard: the political system preaches equality, but the market system generates inequality.[31] This implies that the rights of society should be determined not by the market system, but by the political one. These rights include not only political rights (freedom of expression, voting), but also economic rights to public goods, such as education, health, and unemployment insurance. These rights set limits on absolute poverty, and on inequality as well.

A capitalist democracy is able to resolve this double standard by allocating some scarce resources to the production of public goods. A capitalist democracy operates with market and political institutions, with commodities and rights, and with private and public goods. On these principles capitalist democracy is able to operate. The market may then operate with ruthless competition, once the equity problem (absolute and relative poverty) has been resolved. These are the terms of the social contract.

31. Okun (1975, p. 1).

It follows that a social contract can be viewed as an implicit agreement among the members of a society to tolerate inequality, but only up to a certain limit. This definition is consistent with Rawls's proposition that "justice [as fairness] is the first virtue of institutions."[32] When income distribution becomes unfair, the social contract breaks down. In this situation, the poor invoke the *clausula rebus sic stantibus* and exercise their right to cancel the contract. This is not only a legal principle; it seems to be a social principle as well. The social violence observed in Peru, throughout Latin America, and in other parts of the world where equity has deteriorated significantly is evidence of the breakdown of the social contract.

What is the role of social policies in a capitalist democracy? In recent literature, social policy is viewed as part of society's social security system. Jean Dreze and Amartya Sen, for example, have said that social policy is intended to protect and promote living standards of the poor. It works by increasing the capability of individuals to nourish and clothe themselves, and to avoid escapable morbidity and preventable mortality. Social policy is needed when economic growth alone cannot improve equity. Growth is inadequate when the poor's income increases very little due to the higher income concentration; when the income of the poor varies significantly over time; and when higher real incomes do not improve the capabilities of the poor. Social policy is also needed when economic recession occurs, primarily to protect the poor.[33]

In my view, economic rights in a capitalist democracy are secured mostly through social policies, which play a fundamental role in the social contract and, for that matter, in the functioning of society. Social policies help establish an economic platform or floor in society, so that competition and rivalry can govern the market system. Social policies set limits on poverty, in absolute and relative terms, minimizing the risk of crossing the threshold of inequality that leads to social instability. Social policy, in sum, is an instrument for achieving and maintaining the social contract.

How can Peru escape the distributive trap? In this interpretation, social expenditure is an exogenous variable; by increasing it the government can reach a new equilibrium with higher investment and lower poverty. Social policies should establish targets for both income security (employment programs) and access to basic social services (health and education).

The financing of social policies, of course, is a critical problem. In Peru there is no room for increasing social spending through reallocation of current

32. Rawls (1971, p. 3).
33. Dreze and Sen (1991).

government expenditures, which are already too low. The remaining options are to raise taxes; to reduce government expenditure on foreign debt service; to obtain more international donations; or to increase efficiency in the production and delivery of public goods. Some combination of these options is also possible. But, as noted, the redistributive policy I propose will be viable only under a new social contract.

Conclusion

The empirical evidence in this chapter seems consistent with the hypothesis that Peru is trapped in a distributive crisis. A distributive crisis occurs when real wages, and living standards in general, fall below a threshold that is socially tolerable. In such a crisis, the fall in private investment, increase in social violence, and further impoverishment of the masses are all endogenous variables, outcomes of the same dynamic process. Even the political change from democracy to dictatorship is endogenous. Among the exogenous factors that led to the crisis, the most important seems to be the orthodox and heterodox stabilization and adjustment policies designed to resolve the foreign debt problem.

In the Latin American context, Peru is usually considered an exceptional case due to its political violence. In my view, Peru is only an extreme case of the general problem in the region: the continuous rise in inequality. If some exogenous factor made the political violence disappear overnight, there would still be violence in Peru. The distributive violence may even expand, because the activities of popular organizations, such as labor unions, peasant organizations, and mothers' clubs in shantytowns, have been restrained by the political violence. Peru would then resemble many other Latin American countries that are operating on the verge of a distributive crisis.

A lesson that emerges from the Peruvian experience is that too much inequality can lead to economic inefficiency. Although there are possibilities for mutually beneficial exchanges, they are not exploited because the society is trapped in a distributive crisis. Dynamic efficiency is lost as private investment falls despite the existence of profits, trapping the economy in a vicious circle.

When a society experiences instability as the result of a distributive crisis, there is an economic argument for income redistribution policies; that is, equity must be improved not only for ethical, but also for economic reasons. Social policies, understood as measures that set limits on the degree of inequality, are appropriate instruments for improving equity. These measures should guarantee access to basic social services and to a minimum money income.

When a society is in a distributive trap, income redistribution is necessary for the resumption of growth. "Redistribute first to grow later" is a policy that will be financed with growth itself. In this context, the orthodox argument "grow first and redistribute later" does not hold, because orthodox economic adjustment only makes the situation worse.

However, given the prisoner's dilemma nature of the problems, redistribution may not be socially viable. Although everyone gains from social policies that produce social stability and growth, no individual has the incentive to cooperate to implement such policies. The redistributive policy, therefore, requires a new social contract.

In sum, income distribution is not only an ethical question. Equity plays a fundamental role in the social viability of capitalist democracy, particularly in developing countries, where income inequality is pronounced. A distributive crisis is thus the result of failures in both the market and the state. Capitalist democracies are subject to this type of crisis, and they will need more than just liberalization policies to escape it.

References

Abugattas, Javier. 1991. "Interview." *Mujer Urbana* (April).

Banco Central de Reserva del Perú. 1989. *Peru: compendio estadístico del sector público no financiero*. Lima.

———. Forthcoming. *Memoria 1991*. Lima.

Bernedo, Jorge. 1989. *El Programa PAIT*. Lima: Fundación F. Ebert.

Burgos, Hernando. 1991. "Adiós a la escuela." *Quehacer* 73:37–50.

CEPAL. 1992. *Balance preliminar de la economía de América Latina y el Caribe* (December). Santiago.

Dancourt, Oscar. 1990. *Pobreza Urbana*. Lima: Pontificia Universidad Católica del Peru.

Dancourt, Oscar, and Ivory Yong. 1989. "Sobre la hiperinflación peruana." *Economía* 12(23):13–44.

Dornbusch, Rudiger. 1991. "Policies to Move from Stabilization to Growth." *Proceedings of the World Bank Annual Conference on Development Economics 1990*. Washington: World Bank.

Dreze, Jean, and Amartya Sen. 1991. "Public Actions for Social Security: Foundations and Strategy." In *Social Security in Developing Countries*, edited by Ahmand Etishan and others. Oxford University Press.

Figueroa, Adolfo. 1990. "De la distribución de la crisis a la crisis de la distribución." Serie Documentos de Trabajo 90. Economics Department, Catholic University of Peru.

————. 1992. "La agricultura peruana y el ajuste." *Debate agrario* 13: 35–47.

Figueroa, Adolfo, and Iliich Ascarza. 1991. "El efecto distributivo de la política fiscal: Peru, 1970–90." Serie Documentos de Trabajo 96. Economics Department, Catholic University of Peru.

Fondo Nacional de Compensación y Desarrollo Social. 1991. *Objetivos y Metas.* Lima.

Hirschman, Albert. 1970. *Exit, Voice, and Loyalty: Responses to Decline in Firms, Organizations, and States.* Harvard University Press.

Instituto Cuánto, and UNICEF. 1993. *Nivelas de vida, Perú: Subidas y Caídas, 1991.* Lima.

Instituto de Forrento de una Educación de Calidad. 1991. "Político social en la estrategía de desarollo." In *Quehacer* 73:53.

Instituto Nacional de Estadística e Informática. Annual. *Peru: compendio estadístico.* Lima.

Instituto Nacional de Estadística e Informática y Centro Latinoamericano de Demografía. 1992. "Peru: Estimaciones y proyecciones de la poblacion urbana y rural, 1980–2010." *Boletín de Análisis Demográfico* 33 (March).

Ministerio de Salud. 1991. *Estadística de Salud y Población, 1988–89* (August). Lima.

Okun, Arthur. 1975. *Equality and Efficiency: The Big Tradeoff.* Brookings.

Paredes, Carlos, and Jeffrey Sachs. 1991. *Peru's Path to Recovery.* Brookings.

Petrera, Margarita. 1992. "Impacto económico de la epidemia del cólera: Perú 1991." Lima: Organización Panamericana de la Salud y Organización Mundial de la Salud.

Rawls, John. 1971. *A Theory of Justice.* Harvard University Press.

Rodriguez, José. 1992. "La enseñanza pública gratuita como mecanismo redistributivo." *Boletín de Opinión, Consorcio de Investigación Económica* 4 (April).

Webb, Richard. 1990. "Comments." In *Latin American Adjustment: How Much Has Happened?*, edited by John Williamson. Washington, D.C.: Institute for International Economics.

Webb, Richard, and Graciela Fernández Baca. 1990. *Perú en números, 1990.* Lima: Cuánto.

————. 1992. *Perú en números, 1992.* Lima: Cuánto.

CHAPTER ELEVEN

Venezuela: Poverty and Social Policies in the 1980s

Gustavo Marquez

THIS IS A STORY of "riches to rags." It is about how a natural resource–rich country, which was blessed by good fortune during the 1970s, managed as a result of bad judgment to find itself 15 years later with over a third of its population in poverty. It is true that bad fortune, in the form of adverse external shocks, contributed to this evolution. But misguided economic policy and the repeated postponement of adjustment are at least equally responsible for the dismal results.

In the 1980s, successive Venezuelan governments were prisoners of the same dilemma: the desire to sustain the expansion of the public enterprise sector, while at the same time providing sufficient resources to traditional social sectors. The competing interests of groups supporting deficit-ridden public enterprises and social service institutions that were under increasingly tight fiscal constraints, generated an unsustainable increase in the external debt, then rising inflation, and finally economic collapse in 1989.

As social sector budgets began to stabilize and then fall, bureaucrats with vested interests in these institutions attempted to cushion the blow by defending their personnel and budgets at the cost of reducing the availability of com-

The author would like to thank Harold Alerman and Moises Naim for their helpful comments.

plementary inputs. This dynamic caused a reduction in the quantity and quality of services available to the population.

In 1989 the government, facing growing social unrest as a result of a drastic stabilization program, implemented a policy of direct transfers narrowly targeted to the poorer segments of the population. The rationale was that the new programs would compensate these groups for the elimination of a widespread and quite inefficient system of indirect subsidies. However, the programs have not in any reasonable measure compensated the poor for the loss they suffered from the decline in real wages and the relative increase in food prices.

The main problem was not the size of the transfers but the government's contention that they constituted a new social policy. In reality, the government failed to reform the social service system and to change the distribution of budgetary allocations to traditional social programs. On the contrary, it accelerated past trends after 1989.

Poverty clearly increased in Venezuela; it now affects more than one-third of the total population. This increase has been the result of a protracted decline in real wages. Compared with a decade ago, the poor are both a more heterogeneous group and more like the rest of the population. Poverty in 1991 was mainly an urban phenomenon that affected two-parent families with at least one or two family members working. The income shortfall they suffered is not covered by the new direct transfers, although some specific programs—such as *Hogares de Cuidado Diario,* a subsidized day-care system—do help the poor. Life for poor families is complicated by the low availability of, and poor access to, social services.

Venezuela needs a policy shift from poverty alleviation to human resource development. Poverty alleviation is by no means unimportant: the immense loss that poverty represents in terms of forgone development and production is obvious. But an exclusive emphasis on poverty alleviation is inadequate. Social policies also need to increase the level of human capital necessary for integrating the poor as consumers and producers into a growing economy.

Therefore, far-reaching reforms in the production, financing, and provision of social services are needed. The crucial elements of such a reform include the incorporation of market discipline into social service production; the transfer of responsibilities and authority from central to local governments; and the introduction of greater experimentation and diversity in the technology of social service production, financing, and access.

Improved availability and access to high-quality social services (particularly education and health) will make an escape from poverty possible. For countries like Venezuela today, social service programs are necessary for sustainable democracy. What is not yet clear is whether the Venezuelan political leadership is willing and able to deal with the conflicts the required reforms will necessarily provoke.

Economic Crisis and Policy Response

Between the 1950s and the end of the 1970s the Venezuelan economy was a model of high growth and price stability. In the 1950s GDP per capita grew 4 percent annually, while the average inflation rate was 0.9 percent. In the 1960s per capita GDP growth slowed to 2.4 percent annually, and inflation rose to 2.4 percent. During the 1970s, even when inflation was 3.5 times what it was in the 1960s (averaging 8.6 percent annually), per capita GDP continued to grow at an annual pace of 1 percent.[1] Even by Latin American standards at that time, Venezuela was exceptional. By 1970 only Argentina, Chile, and Costa Rica had poverty head-count ratios lower than Venezuela.[2]

This enviable performance ended in the 1980s, when annual inflation rose to an average of 23.3 percent, and per capita GDP contracted by 1.8 percent. To explain what went wrong is not simple. Exogenous factors such as the debt crisis and the collapse of oil prices no doubt played an important role. Nevertheless, bad fortune, if countered with good policies, does not necessarily lead to economic collapse, as the reaction of Southeast Asian countries to the same events has shown. Bad judgment is an important factor in the explanation of Venezuela's economic decline during the 1980s.

The Political Economy of the Crisis

The political alliance that took power in Venezuela in 1958 was essentially composed of urban workers and entrepreneurs in incipient import-substitution industries. The political strength of this alliance was an important factor in ex-

1. All figures are on an annual basis, calculated from first year of the decade to first year of the next decade. Author's calculations based on Banco Central de Venezuela, *La economía venezolana en los últimos 35 años*; *Anuario de Cuentas Nacionales*, various years; *Agregados maccroeconómciso a precios corrientes y constantes de 1984: Resumen de la Serie Estadistica 1983/86*; *Anuario de Estadísticas—Precios y mercado laboral 1984*.

2. Altimir (1982, p. 82).

plaining why Venezuela adopted domestic market protection as a basic principle of economic policy.[3]

Economic policy in Venezuela at that time was a simple matter. The government obtained most of its revenues from the oil sector, which was controlled by foreign companies. These revenues were spent on infrastructure and on the expansion of the educational and health systems. Fiscal deficits, constitutionally forbidden, were easy to avoid even when oil revenues were unstable, given the short-term nature of budgetary commitments related to infrastructure and social services.

Entrepreneurs enjoyed a high effective rate of protection that made it possible to obtain high profit margins in an environment that was basically tax free. Workers and the population at large benefited from increased employment opportunities and from improved conditions for human capital accumulation. This Keynesian paradise is not uncommon at the beginning of the import-substitution process, especially in countries that enjoy a large natural resource base that is not affected by import-substitution regulations.

On the macroeconomic side, this arrangement implied that fiscal and balance-of-payments equilibria were synonymous: the government financed its expenditure through taxes on oil companies, which obtained their income from the world market. With rising oil prices, the export income of the oil companies increased, and so did tax revenues, which the government could use to expand the budget or to increase foreign exchange reserves. To the extent that the windfall gain was spent, the fiscal budget increased, the Keynesian multiplier accelerated domestic economic activity, imports grew, and the balance-of-payments surplus decreased. If oil prices were to fall the following year, the government would soften the adjustment with foreign reserves and budget cuts. However, this strategy works only when fiscal commitments are short term, allowing for an effective, and politically painless, fiscal contraction.

On the political side, the new democratic parties created their own support base through the unionization of public sector workers.[4] Powerful unions appeared in the water distribution, port, electricity distribution, phone service, and social service (the Education and Health Ministries) sectors, among others. These unions were able, through their privileged position in the political system, to defend real wages in economic downturns. This privileged position also made unions the partners of government and business, which kept wage demands in line with the requirements of price stability and continuous

3. See Hausmann (1981).
4. For an excellent account of the role of unionization and unions, see McCoy (1989).

growth. The result was the political stability that Venezuela enjoyed for almost thirty years.

In 1973 the oil boom prompted the government to develop a large public enterprise sector concentrated mainly in basic industrial activities such as steel and aluminum. These budget commitments were completely different from previous public sector involvement in social services and infrastructure development, and they involved a growing portion of the budget. In addition, once they were made, future reductions would mean large financial and economic losses. This created fiscal rigidity, which translated world oil price fluctuations into macroeconomic instability. The irony is that the same mechanisms that had created remarkable macroeconomic stability were also responsible for the subsequent low growth and high inflation.[5] The sobering lesson is that it was the change in the nature of fiscal commitments made (bad judgment), and not the increasing instability of the world economy at the end of the 1970s (bad fortune), that was responsible for Venezuela's economic instability.

The government's attempt to satisfy the demands of both the powerful group supporting its traditional activities and the new, increasingly powerful group supporting the public enterprise sector caused the external debt to rise rapidly. While current receipts financed traditional government activities, foreign debt financed the expansion of the public enterprise sector. Large deposits encouraged international banks to lend money carelessly to firms in clearly declining sectors such as steel, which were seriously mismanaged by overeager and inexperienced public managers.

The debt crisis in 1982 put an end to this marriage of sorts between traditional government activities and the expanding public enterprise sector. Capital flight, which had begun in 1979, became widespread in 1982, signaling the end of the public's faith in the stability of the Venezuelan bolívar. By the beginning of 1983 the depletion in foreign reserves forced the government to introduce a nominal devaluation, but it did so with a frenzy of price controls. The government put in place a system of foreign exchange; import, price, and interest rate controls; and reduced fiscal expenditures. Growth stopped, unemployment grew, and real wages fell.[6] Perhaps as a result of these events, the incumbent Social Christian party lost the 1983 presidential election to the Social Democratic party.

The policy did succeed as a short-term stabilization program: inflation fell, and the fiscal deficit was nearly eliminated in 1983 and transformed into a surplus in 1984 and 1985. However, because price and import controls hindered

5. See Hausmann and Márquez (1983).
6. See Márquez (1991).

the allocation of resources, the real devaluation did not push resources into the tradable goods sector. Tradable goods production grew modestly as a proportion of nonoil GNP between 1983 and 1985, aided by the introduction of import controls, but it then stagnated. Unemployment remained well above 10 percent, real wages continued to fall, and per capita GDP growth was negative in real terms (tables 11A-2 and 11A-3).

The fall in oil prices in 1986 deepened the crisis. The government, perhaps viewing the 1983 vote as a signal that good economic sense does not win elections and facing new elections in 1988, decided simply to ignore the collapse in the terms of trade. Fiscal deficits reappeared, the current account of the balance of payments became increasingly negative, and inflation almost tripled. In the labor market, unemployment fell but real wages continued to decline (tables 11A-2 and 11A-3). Nevertheless, the Social Democratic party won the 1988 election.

The new government took office at the beginning of 1989 in the midst of an economic hangover. Operational foreign exchange reserves were $300 million, and overdue short-term commercial debt reached more than $1 billion.[7] The price system had collapsed, and shortages were widespread, particularly in heavily controlled foodstuffs.

Making a virtue out of necessity, the government announced a radical economic program with the support of the international financial institutions. The program consisted of a classic economic stabilization policy (to be enacted immediately) and an economic restructuring program (to be enacted gradually according to agreements signed with the IMF and the World Bank). In exchange for these announcements, the government received immediate financial support for its ensuing debt-refinancing efforts.[8]

The stabilization program included exchange rate unification, the elimination of import controls, the lifting of price and interest rate controls, and increases in the prices of public sector goods (such as gasoline) to reduce the fiscal deficit.[9] The economic restructuring program included trade and foreign investment liberalization, the privatization of public enterprises, and a general restructuring of the public sector.

The short-term effects of the stabilization program were mixed: after the drastic real devaluation, inflation moved 84 percent and GDP per capita dropped sharply, but fiscal and balance-of-payments equilibria were restored at once (tables 11A-2 and 11A-3). The government, faced with growing social

7. Hausman (1990).
8. CORDIPLAN (1990).
9. Hausmann (1990).

unrest expressed forcefully in the urban riots of February, announced an ambitious package of social policy measures, including direct transfers.

Trade liberalization was a resounding success, as was the refinancing of the external debt. Good fortune, in the disguise of the Iraqi invasion of Kuwait, pushed oil prices up in 1990, allowing Venezuela to produce more oil and to sell it at higher prices. Growth resumed, accompanied by strong current account balances. In 1991 an ambitious expansion program in the oil industry generated strong growth that continued in 1992 (tables 11-1 and 11A-2). Venezuela was becoming the darling of international financial organizations and the showcase of successful adjustment under a democratic government. However, two factors overshadowed this success.

The first problem is related to public sector reform. On the one hand, the government had made little progress in the privatization of public enterprises. By the end of 1991, the port authority system had been decentralized (with its administration passed to the regional governments), and the national airline, the telephone company, and some hotels and sugar plants had been privatized. The worst losers in the public enterprise sector (steel, aluminum, water and electricity distribution), however, had not been privatized.[10] On the other hand, the delivery of public services (education, health, urban security, water) was visibly worsening, and reform of the organizations responsible for these services was blocked by strong union and political opposition.

The second problem is related to the composition of GDP between the tradable and nontradable sectors. As an oil economy, Venezuela has long suffered the busts and enjoyed the booms of the world oil market. Economic adjustment and the achievement of greater macroeconomic and fiscal stability required economic diversification, in particular a shift of resources to the nonoil tradables sector.

But as table 11-1 shows, the production of nonoil tradables was not growing as a proportion of nonoil GDP. Overall growth was dominated by a strong expansion in oil and nontradable activities. By the end of 1991, while oil GDP was 25 percent higher and nontradable GDP 4.5 percent higher than in 1988, nonoil tradable GDP was at about the same level as it had been the year before the adjustment. These numbers imply that, after the adjustment, growth was stimulated by the same force whose influence adjustment was trying to reduce.

There was increasing social unrest throughout 1991. People believed that they had survived the adjustment period and were anxious to claim a share of its benefits. When at the beginning of February 1992 an army faction at-

10. See "Cinco grupos extranjeros generacon 69 porciento de ingresos por privatización," *El Universal*, March 30, 1993, p. 2-1.

Table 11-1. *Growth Rates, by Sector, Venezuela, 1989–91*
Percent

Sector	1989	1990	1991	Growth 1988–91
Total	−8.6	6.5	10.4	7.5
Tradables	−6.9	9.2	9.4	1.2
Oil	−0.4	13.9	10.3	5.1
Nonoil	−12.1	5.0	8.5	0.1
Nontradables	−8.3	4.4	9.1	4.5
Share of nonoil tradables in nonoil GDP	28.7	28.5	27.6	...

Source: Banco Central de Venezuela, *Informe Económico* (1991, p. 35).

tempted a coup, the political forces that were dividing Venezuelan society and paralyzing adjustment became evident. The reform process immediately stopped.

The government currently faces three principal sources of opposition. First, for adjustment to be successful in the current world oil market, the fiscal deficit must be reduced through privatization of the big losers (steel, electricity distribution, perhaps aluminum) in the public enterprise sector. To do this the government must confront powerful forces in the party that are connected to the public enterprises. Second, to develop the human resources necessary for successful integration into the world economy, the government must also restructure the social service system, overcoming the opposition of bureaucrats affiliated with the party. Finally, the government faces opposition from the citizenry, which strongly opposes paying new taxes to close the fiscal gap, having already suffered falling real wages and standards of living.

Persistent student demonstrations aggravate the situation by creating a feeling of acute social unrest. Improving the population's living conditions, as the government did with direct transfer programs after the February 1989 riots, requires resources that are now being monopolized by public enterprises and the social service bureaucracy.

The Evolution of Social Spending

In addition to real wages and growth rates, social spending is one of the primary factors explaining changes in income distribution and poverty. Most of the population in a highly urbanized and underdeveloped country such as Venezuela have only their labor and their human capital as assets. Growth tends to increase the demand for labor and thus raise real wages. However, because wages are in fact the return on human capital, the gains that result from increasing wages are as unequally distributed as human capital.

Public social spending contributes to growth in the stock of human capital, and if social spending is directed to progressive activities (primary schooling, preventive and basic health care) that tend to benefit primarily the poor, its effect is to decrease the inequality of human capital distribution. Therefore, long-term increases in social spending in these areas are likely to improve income distribution and reduce poverty.

Venezuela's experience in the 1950s and 1960s is a good case in point. An increase in social expenditure was the basis for improvements in the standard of living of the poor. The government increased funding for health and education, dedicating growing shares of the budget to the Ministries of Education and Health (table 11-2). As a result, literacy rates increased rapidly, and primary and secondary school enrollment grew much faster than the population.

In the subsequent two decades, however, the shares of the Education and Health Ministries in the total budget stagnated as the government moved toward a less aggressive social policy. The rate of improvement in social indicators also slowed, which, paradoxically, was partly a consequence of previous progress. Reducing infant mortality from 86 per thousand to 60 per thousand, as Venezuela did in the 1950s and 1960s, is much easier than reducing it further to 26 per thousand, which Venezuela did in 1990. The reasons are many and are related to the complexity of services and the scope of coverage required to reach very low levels of infant mortality.

A more detailed examination of the long-term trends in total social expenditure (including direct transfers) in Venezuela appears in figures 11-1 and 11-2. As figure 11-1 indicates, the share of social spending in total government spending increased from 1962 until the early 1970s. It then fell sharply in 1974, gradually rose again, and oscillated around 30 percent through 1990.

Despite the decline in the relative share of social spending, real per capita social expenditures, shown in figure 11-2, did not contract until 1980, because the oil boom enabled total government expenditures to rise. The reduction in per capita social spending since the early 1980s was similar to that of other items in the budget.

These figures suggest that expenditures on social services did not suffer disproportionately large cuts during the long adjustment of the 1980s. Clearly, the weight of fiscal adjustment has not fallen disproportionately on the social sector. However, it should be noted that this relative stability belies the pre-1974 trend, when social expenditure rose from 22 percent of the primary budget in 1962 to 35 percent in 1973.

Table 11-2. *Social Indicators, Venezuela, Selected Years, 1950–90*

Indicator	1950	1961	1971	1981	1990
Literacy rates (percent)					
Total	51.0	64.5	75.9	88.1	90.7
Age 15–19	57.3	74.1	86.7	96.0	95.8
Population[a]		4.58	4.01	3.42	2.48
Primary school enrollment[a]		9.48	4.04	3.44	2.48
Secondary school enrollment[a]		7.21	10.87	5.77	2.49
Infant mortality per					
1,000 live births	85.6	52.6	49.8	35.2	25.5
Physicians per					
10,000 inhabitants	5.43[b]	6.93	9.62	12.00	18.01
Share of central government					
budget (percent)					
Education Ministry	6.0	7.8	14.8	14.4	12.0
Health Ministry	6.3	6.6	7.4	5.7	6.7

Sources: Banco Central de Venezuela (1978): literacy rates, table I-8; population growth, table I-4; enrollment, table V-14; physicians, table V-15; budget shares, table XI-8. Also República de Venezuela (1986); OCEI, *Anuario Estadístico de Venezuela*; 1991 (1991); OCEI (1992), OCEPRE (1988), and Ministerio de Hacienda (1991).
a. Average annual interperiod growth rates.
b. 1953.

During a medium-term economic downturn, social expenditure may suffer from a combination of three developments: reductions in the spending effort, as measured by the share of social expenditure in total government spending; reductions in the absolute level of social spending, as measured by per capita social spending; and changes in the composition of social sector budgets.

Analysis of these trends is complicated by changes in the nature and definition of social spending. Before 1989 social spending covered the traditional social services, mainly public education and health production and delivery. Since 1989, however, the definition of social spending has grown to include direct transfer programs. The growth in social expenditures in 1990 was thus the result of an expansion in new poverty-oriented direct transfer programs.

It is important to analyze the evolution of traditional social services apart from direct transfer programs because they fulfill different roles in human capital accumulation and preservation. Traditional social services contribute directly to human capital accumulation by delivering educational services and keeping the population healthy. Direct transfers to the poor are transitory instruments that defend vulnerable groups from the deleterious effects of a drop in real income. By themselves, they do not increase human capital, though it can be argued that they raise the long-term rate of human capital growth by

Figure 11-1. *Central Government Social Spending, Venezuela,*
1962–90ᵃ

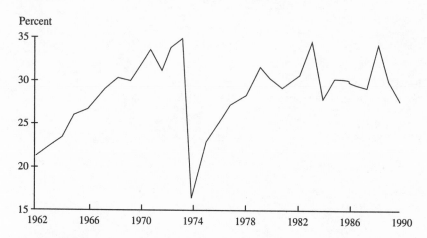

Source: Ministerio de Hacienda, *Ley de Presupuesto* (various years).
Data were elaborated by Roberto Palacios, IESA, 1991.
a. Social expenditure includes housing, education, health, social security, and direct social transfers (since 1989)
following IMF methodology. Shares are calculated on total primary central government budget, excluding debt service
from total budget.

preventing permanent damage to the more vulnerable groups of the population, such as children and pregnant women.

Even direct subsidies designed to keep children at school may contribute
little to human capital when schools have inadequate buildings and poorly
motivated teachers who operate without the necessary materials. Direct transfers do prevent the malnourishment of children at these schools, but to the extent that there are no improvements in physical infrastructure, teacher morale,
and resource availability, these children do not learn the skills needed to earn a
decent salary as adults. As a result, even though children are kept well fed and
in school, there is very little improvement in the long-run rate of human capital accumulation.

Furthermore, analysts may seriously overstate the net contribution of direct
transfer programs when they do not take into account the reduction in traditional social service expenditures. Table 11-3 shows that during 1989 and
1990 expenditures on direct social programs were too small to offset budget
cuts in the traditional social service activities of the Ministries of Health and
Education. Throughout this period children were well fed, but studying within
a deteriorating school system. In 1991, thanks to the 1990 oil bonanza caused
by the Persian Gulf War, expenditures on both social services and direct transfers increased, along with the rest of the budget.

Figure 11-2. *Central Government per Capita Social Spending,*
Venezuela, 1962–90[a]

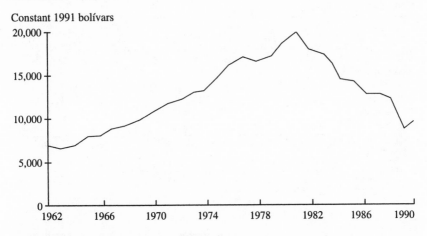

Constant 1991 bolívars

Source: Ministerio de Hacienda, *Ley de Presupuesto* (various years).
Data were elaborated by Roberto Palacios, IESA, 1991.
a. See note a, figure 11-1.

The pattern of traditional social service expenditures clearly shows that the 1989 fiscal adjustment did not exclude social sectors. Table 11-4 presents the composition of budget allocations to traditional services in the Ministries of Education and Health, excluding the budget assignments to direct transfer programs. It shows that social expenditures fell sharply in 1989 and 1990, but expanded in 1991. However, over the whole 1988–91 period, education expenditures fell 4.5 percent annually, while the health expenditures expanded 0.7 percent annually.

The composition of these budgets since 1980 suggests a budgetary process that reduces efficiency and quality. In both ministries there was an increase in the share of expenditures allocated to support, planning, and administration (and in the associated personnel costs) and a reduction in the share of operational programs and inputs (table 11-4).

This shift in the composition of expenditures is the result of a budgeting process in which personnel expenses and related outstanding liabilities have priority, followed by the pet programs of high-level authorities; the remainder goes to equipment and operational inputs.[11] Union, pressure groups, and vocal university and medical lobbies ensure that personnel, university, and high-

11. For a description of the budgetary process, see Márquez (1990).

Table 11-3. *Direct Transfer and Traditional Social Services*
Expenditures, Venezuela, 1988–91
Billions of 1991 bolívars[a]

Item	1988	1989	Change 1988–89	1990	Change 1990–91	1991	Change 1991–92
Direct transfer programs	0	9.3	9.3	29.1	19.8	54.0	24.9
Traditional social services[b]	153.6	131.4	−22.1	108.3	−23.1	140.2	31.8
Education Ministry	109.6	93.7	−16.0	74.5	−19.2	95.4	20.9
Health Ministry	43.9	37.8	−6.1	33.9	−3.9	44.8	10.9
Net change (total)			−12.9		−3.2		56.8

Source: Ministerio de Hacienda, *Ley de Presupuesto* (various years). All figures are updated expenditure data deflated by CPI.

a. Data on direct transfers inclue all the programs in Plan de Enfrentamiento de la Pobreza; see table 11-6.

b. Ministry budgets for traditional social services exclude budget lines assigned to direct transfer programs as follows: Education Ministry, 1991: B28,603.1 million, Beca Alimentaria and Uniformes y Utiles Escolares; B5,242.3 million, Beca Lactea; B5,155.8 million, Bono de Cereales.

level medical facility claims on the budget are fulfilled. Users, and particularly poor users, are ignored because they do not have a strong voice or political organizations to back their claims. Medical treatment and primary education thus receive a decreasing share of the budget.

Obviously, this budgeting process has dire consequences in terms of resource allocation when the budget is being reduced in real terms. The first consequence is that real wages in the social service sector decrease, making these jobs highly unattractive and inducing the self-selection of low-quality personnel. Second, operational material and other complementary inputs, whose prices rise with the general level of prices, suffer a more than proportionate reduction in supply, as less money is allocated to these increasingly expensive items. Finally, the supply of equipment is reduced to a minimum to make room for the competing claims of personnel and operational inputs in the reduced budget. The resulting structure favors those activities that are bureaucracy-intensive and deliver very little to the users: central planning, hospitals at the expense of primary health care, universities at the expense of basic education, and so on.

Is there any other way to reduce budget allocation while maintaining a proper level of social services? Many analysts argue that wage reductions are less disruptive to both social service personnel and users than staff cuts. Yet any attempt to rationalize budget allocations to the social sector is bound to meet powerful opposition from unions and professional organizations, often producing strikes that seriously obstruct social service operations.

Reformers should expect resistance to change, but not use it as an excuse

Table 11-4. *Budget for Traditional Social Services, by Program and Budget Function, Venezuela, Selected Years and Periods, 1980–91*[a]

Percent

Program and Function	Average annual rate of growth						Share of total budget					
	1980–85	1985–88	1988–89	1989–90	1990–91	1988–91	1980	1985	1988	1989	1990	1991
Ministry of Education												
Program												
Support, planning, and administration	-3.71	10.10	20.27	-55.45	110.24	4.05	29.6	24.2	33.2	46.7	26.2	43.0
Preschool and basic education	9.42	-7.68	-39.87	15.09	-18.42	-17.35	19.9	30.8	24.9	17.5	25.4	16.2
Secondary education	1.38	-10.11	-10.44	12.33	-18.32	-18.24	8.0	8.7	6.4	4.4	6.4	4.1
Universities and superior	-2.74	-1.79	-24.64	6.95	11.75	-3.43	42.4	36.4	35.4	31.3	42.1	36.7
Function												
Personnel	3.32	-0.13	-10.94	-25.32	30.13	-4.70	43.3	50.2	51.5	53.7	50.4	51.2
Operations	-5.66	-14.02	-54.09	-1.48	-39.52	-35.08	6.3	4.7	3.0	1.6	2.0	1.0
Transfers	-1.78	-0.69	-21.15	-9.90	28.69	-2.94	50.0	45.0	45.4	44.7	47.5	47.7
Total	0.31	-0.95	-14.59	-20.48	28.06	-4.54	100.0	100.0	100.0	100.0	100.0	100.0
Ministry of Health												
Program												
Support, planning, and administration	2.67	5.68	-12.97	-12.30	26.67	1.93	57.8	65.3	70.9	71.7	70.1	73.4
Medical attention	-3.25	-3.26	-25.04	8.60	13.46	-2.61	36.5	30.6	25.5	22.2	26.9	23.1
Disease control and prevention	-5.58	2.82	60.85	-52.51	52.50	5.22	3.8	2.8	2.8	5.2	2.8	3.2
Function												
Personnel	5.74	-3.37	-1.36	-22.33	57.33	6.43	44.6	58.3	48.4	55.5	48.0	57.1
Operations	-17.89	3.42	24.71	-33.21	-21.09	-11.28	36.3	13.4	13.6	19.8	14.7	9.3
Transfers	9.80	13.33	-44.10	35.30	4.14	-3.15	17.7	28.0	37.5	24.4	36.7	33.4
Total	0.21	2.85	-13.99	-10.29	32.28	0.68	100.0	100.0	100.0	100.0	100.0	100.0

Source: Ministerio de Educación, *Memoria y Cuenta* (various years); and Ministerio de Sanidad y Asistencia Social, *Memoria y Cuenta* (various years).
a. Data are aggregated according to the methodology developed by Márquez (1990). Data exclude budget assignments for direct transfer programs included in the approved budget as described in note b, table 11-3. Capital expenditure is included in other ministry budgets.

for maintenance of the status quo. Social service reform requires a new government-led covenant that unifies users and the general public behind a feasible agenda that at a minimum includes a reallocation of personnel and reduction in employment where needed; an increase in the share of expenditures allocated to operations at the expense of planning and administration; and a shift in resources from high-level services to primary education and preventive health care. What is lacking in Venezuela is precisely this agenda for reform.

What were the consequences of this process on social indicators in Venezuela? Navarro and Piñango, Reimers, and Jaen, among others, contend that shifts in resource allocation and organizational problems have resulted in widespread inefficiency and deteriorating quality.[12] This contention unifies the research community and politicians, whose criticisms fill the newspaper pages. However, hard indicators are hard to find. Data presented by Schiefelben suggests that indicators of educational efficiency in Venezuela did not deviate too much from the Latin American average.[13]

Health and education indicators, presented in tables 11A-6 and 11A-7, do not suggest that there was long-term deterioration in Venezuela. Even though infant mortality rates have risen since 1989, the drastic impoverishment of low-income families may have played a more important role than resource constraints or inefficiencies in the public health system.

Still, the question remains. How consistent are social indicators with the overall resources available in the economy and the level of social service spending? Table 11-5 makes such a comparison, matching economic and social indicators for Venezuela, Latin American and Caribbean (LAC) countries, and OECD countries. Venezuela spent 8.1 percent of GDP on education and health services in 1988, which compares quite favorably with the LAC average of 5.4 percent. Approximately the same ratios appear in social service shares of central government spending.

In terms of the total resources made available to social services, Venezuela thus made an important effort that is not fully reflected in the social indicators.

The data presented in table 11-5 do not clearly indicate failure or success. However, it should be noted that the distance between Venezuela and the LAC average in social indicators is less than what Venezuela's economic advantage suggests it should be. Venezuela in 1988 had a GDP per capita 77 percent higher than the LAC average, while secondary school enrollment was 13 percent higher, higher education enrollment 59 percent higher, and infant mortal-

---

12. Navarro and Piñango (1991); Reimers (1991); and Jaen (1990).
13. Schiefelbein (1991).

Table 11-5. *Social Indicators, Venezuela and Selected World Areas, Selected Years, 1980–88*
Percent unless otherwise specified

Indicator	Venezuela	Latin America and Caribbean	OECD countries
Economic conditions			
GDP per capita (1988 U.S. dollars)	3,250	1,840	17,470
GDP per capita growth (average 1965–88)	–0.9	1.9	2.3
CPI inflation (average 1980–88)	13.0	117.4	4.7
Population			
Urban population as percent of total (1988)	83	71	77
Population growth (1980–88)	2.8	2.2	0.6
Birth rate (per 1,000 1988)	30	28	13
Mortality rate (per 1,000 1988)	5	7	9
Education			
Adult illiteracy (male, 1985)	13	17	2
School enrollment as percent of age group			
Primary (1988)	106	107	103
Secondary (1988)	54	48	95
Higher (1988)	27	17	41
Education spending as percent GDP (1988)	5.4	3.9	5.7
Education spending as percent central government spending (1988)	19.6	11.0	4.7
Health			
Life expectancy years at birth (1988)	70	67	76
Infant mortality per 1,000 live births (1988)	35	53	8
Health spending as percent GDP (1988)	2.7	1.6	4.7
Health spending as percent central government spending (1988)	10	5	12.6
Nutrition			
Low weight at birth (1985)	9	12	7
Daily availability calories per capita (1986)	2,494	2,700	3,390
Women in development			
Adult illiteracy (1985)	15	17	—
School enrollment			
Primary (1987)	107.0	110.0	103.0
Secondary (female, 1987)	59.0	53.0	97.0
Maternal mortality per 100,000 live births (1988)	59.0	106.0	10.0

Source: World Bank (1990, 1991). Data on maternal mortality and share of education expenditure on GDP are from *Economist* (1990).

ity 34 percent lower than the LAC average. Moreover, Venezuela dedicated much larger shares of both GDP and central government resources to social services than the average LAC country.

Targeted Transfers: A New Social Policy?

In designing its agenda for "mitigating the social cost of adjustment," the government chose to circumvent the resistance of vested interests in traditional social services by creating a whole new apparatus for delivering highly effective and tightly focused services to the poorer segments of the population. In fact, this new government emphasis on direct transfer programs marked the beginning of a war of attrition against powerful vested interests in the social service organizations. It also presented an important learning opportunity for reformers seeking to develop the most efficient and tightly focused services.

After the urban riots of February 1989, the government enacted a number of measures to counteract the effect of the stabilization program on the low-income population. Table 11-6 describes these social measures. They encompassed a broad spectrum of actions, including direct cash transfers to families with children in the school system, medical attention and food delivery for pregnant and breast-feeding women, and a new unemployment insurance system.

A subset of these policies, officially grouped under the name *Plan de Enfrentamiento de la Pobreza*, was the first to receive special budget allocations. The programs listed in table 11-7 received special budgetary assignments between 1989 and 1991, and the amounts listed were registered in the budget law as having been disbursed. At the end of 1989 Congress allocated an additional B15 billion under the heading *Plan de Empleo e Inversión Social*, but these funds were dedicated to infrastructure development and repair and equipment provision. They are not included under the *Plan de Enfrentamiento de la Pobreza* budget because they were used to offset in part the budget cuts suffered by the ministries that control infrastructure development. The amounts listed thus represent government efforts to support the poor during the adjustment process.

These programs represent the most important initiative ever made by a government in Venezuela to support low-income groups in a time of economic crisis. Resource transfers to the poor through these programs were much smaller than the income losses caused by the increase in relative food prices and the fall in real wages, among other factors. Even if more resources had been available, the magnitude of the loss imposed on the low-income population by the elimination of direct and indirect (through the multiple exchange rate system) subsidies made any real compensation effort infeasible.

A thorough assessment of the relative loss of different income groups during adjustment would require the development of a computable general equilibrium model and would involve endless debate over the appropriate counterfactual for comparison. Nevertheless, some idea of the losses involved can be determined through more easily available information. Between December 1988 and December 1989 foodstuff inflation reached 103 percent, while the increase in the consumer price index (CPI) was 81 percent.[14] Given the relatively larger share of foodstuffs in the consumption basket of the poor, the data suggest that the poor experienced a larger loss in purchasing power than the rest of the population. Both the increase in unemployment and the fall in real wages (table 11A-3) suggest that the relative income loss of the poor was large, especially when compared to changes in per capita GDP; the minimum wage fell 16.9 percent in real terms in 1989, while real per capita GDP fell only 11.4 percent.

A switch from indirect to direct subsidization represents a large efficiency gain in terms of the impact of a given amount of resources transferred. However, this efficiency gain will be overstated if one does not take into account changes in the total amount of resources transferred. Targeting is intended to eliminate spillover to nonpoor income groups. If the transfer is reduced by 50 percent, the poor do not experience the full 50 percent loss; but they are still worse off than before.

A quick calculation illustrates this point. In 1988 Venezuela imported $1.48 billion of foodstuffs and associated products. Under the multiple exchange rate system, the subsidy on imported foodstuffs was equal to the difference between the food imports exchange rate (14.5 bolívars per dollar) and the free exchange rate used by commercial banks (33.95 bolívars per dollar), resulting in a 57.3 percent unit subsidy.[15] The total cost of the subsidy on imported foodstuffs was thus $848.5 billion. If one assumes that 70 percent of these resources were appropriated by nonpoor groups, the amount received by the poor in 1988 was $255 billion. Therefore, even if 100 percent of the resources in direct transfer programs in 1989 ($146.4 billion) were received by the poor (a fictional world of zero administrative costs and perfect targeting), they were still worse off than in 1988 under the indirect subsidy system. Furthermore, this estimate does not take into account the indirect effect of the subsidization of inputs or other imports.

14. Banco Central de Venezuela (December 1990, p. 78).
15. Banco Central de Venezuela (1990, tables II-5 and III-3).

Table 11-6. *Social Policy Measures Enacted in Venezuela, 1989*

Policy description	Target group	Responsible institution
Increasing income and consumption transfers		
Beca Alimentaria		
B500 per child, (up to 3 children), delivered to mothers through the banking system	Families with children in preschool and elementary school located in urban slums and rural areas. Planned coverage in 1990: 1.8 million	Ministerio de Educación Banking system
Subsidio a la leche popular (milk consumption subsidy)		
Distribution of milk at subsidized prices through nongovermental organizations and neighborhood organizations. Phased out in September 1990 and replaced by Beca Lactea distribution of milk coupons to the same mothers targeted by the Beca Alimentaria program	Low-income neighborhoods Families with children in preschool and elementary school located in urban slums and rural areas	Instituto Nacional de Nutrición (dependent from MSAS) Ministerio de Educación Banking system
Dotación de útiles y uniformes escolares		
Free distribution of school clothing and supplies	Children in preschool and elementary school located in urban slums and rural areas. Planned coverage in 1990: 1.8 million	Ministerio de Educación
Pasaje Estudiantil		
Indirect subsidization of student transportation. Students pay half fare; the balance is paid to transport operators by government. Phased out in January 1991 and replaced by a direct subsidy paid through the educational system	Student users of transport system (including university students)	Ministerio del Transporte Ministerio de Educación
Control de precios de la cesta básica / Cestas CASA		
Price controls on eighteen products, including basic foodstuffs and medicines	Nontargeted	Ministerio de Fomento

Table 11-6. (*continued*)

Policy description	Target group	Responsible institution
Subsidio a la Cesta Básica / Cestas CASA		
Indirect subsidy for a limited number of mass consumption products consumed by the poor.	Nontargeted	Ministerio de Hacienda
Distribution of subsidized products through neighborhood organizations and employee savings plans (cajas de ahorro)	Low-income families Public and private employees	Corporacion de Abastecimiento y Servicios Agricolas (CASA)
		Ministerio de Agricultura
Increasing returns on assets held by the poor		
Minmum wage increase		
Urban from B2,010 to B4,000 monthly, and rural from B1,500 to B2,500 monthly (March 1989).	Public and private employees.	Ministerio del Trabajo
Wage increase by decree		
Across-the-board wage increase of B2,000 monthly (March 1989) Across-the-board wage increase on a progressive sliding scale between 10 and 30 percent (March 1989). Repeated in January 1990	Public and private employees with monthly wages below B20,000	Ministerio del Trabajo
Transport and food compensation bonuses		
Increase in maximum monthly wage of recipients to B6,500 Increase in bonuses to B300 monthly (March 1989), and B500 monthly (effective June 1990)	Public and private employees	Ministerio del Trabajo
Increase in employer's and employee's contribution to social security		
Maximum monthly salary accountable to contributions increased to B15,000 (from B3,000). Increase in employer's contribution from 7, 8, and 9 percent to 9, 10, and 11 percent of payroll	Public and private employees under social security	Instituto Venezolano de los Seguros Sociales

Table 11-6. (*continued*)

Policy description	Target group	Responsible institution
Seguro de Paro Forzoso		
Unemployment insurance covering 50 percent of last salary for a thirteen-week period for laid-off workers. Insurance financed by employer and employee contributions (0.85 percent of payroll and 0.25 percent of salary respectively), and a one-time public sector contribution of B3 billion effective November 1, 1989	Laid-off workers that contributed to social security for a minimum of thirteen weeks (temporary regime). Definitive implementation will require fifty-two weeks	Instituto Venezolano de los Seguros Sociales Ministerio del Trabajo

Increasing the access of the poor to productive assets

Programa de Apoyo a la Economía Popular		
Credit, technical assistance, and training program for microenterprises; 1990 budget allocation B750 million	3,000 informal sector enterprises in 1990	Ministerio de la Familia

Maintaining human capital through social expenditures and transfers

Programa Ampliado Matero-Infantil (PAMI)		
Preventive and curative health program, plus nutritional assistance and detection of high-risk population	Pregnant and breast-feeding mothers and their children in 10 poor states	Ministerio de Sanidad
Hogares de Cuidado Diario		
Day care and nutritional program for children of low-income families in slum areas. House repairs and provision of inputs for "madres cuidadoras"	Children up to 6 years old. Programmed 1990: 90,000 children	Ministerio de la Familia Fundación del Niño
Increase of preschool coverage		
Investment program oriented to extension of preschool coverage (including private sector)	Children of preschool age	Ministerio de Educación
Plan de Inversión en Infraestructura Social		
Investment in basic services, housing and connected services, and human resource development	Low-income population	Various agencies
Compensación socio-pedagógica		
Remedial and recreational assistance to elementary and high school students, supporting nonformal education	Students belonging to low-income families	Ministerio de la Familia

Institutional strengthening

Reorganization of the Instituto Nacional de Capacitación Educativa (INCE)		
A commission for restructuring was created in March 1989, and its first report presented in August		Comisión Presidencial Directorio del INCE

Table 11-6. (*continued*)

Policy description	Target group	Responsible institution
Reorganization of the Instituto Venezolano de los Seguros Sociales (IVSS) A commission for restructuring was designated in March 1989, and its first report presented in August. A degree of reorganization was issued in August, encompassing reform of contribution rules, separation of medical assistance and social security funds, creation of unemployment insurance, and administrative measures to improve collection		Comisión Presidencial Comisión de Seguimiento (presided over by Ministro del Trabajo)
Reorganization of the Ministerio del Trabajo, changing its name to Ministerio del Trabajo y la Segoridad Social Intended to improve the effectiveness of control and enforcement of Ministerio del Trabajo		Ministerio del Trabajo
Creation of the Comisión Nacional para el Enfrentamiento de la Pobreza Unit intended to coordinate and develop a plan for confronting poverty at national and local level		Ministerio de la Familia Other social agencies
Creation of the Escuela de Gerencia Social Teaching unit for training social program managers		Ministerio de la Familia
Reorganization of the Ministerio de la Familia, changing its name to Ministerio de Desarrollo Social Ministry will have a coordination and supervisory role in all social policy areas		Ministerio de la Familia
Creation of the Fondo Venezolano de Inversión Social (FONVIS) Parastatal foundation created to speed the transfer of resources from donor agencies		Ministerio de la Familia
Creation of the Fundación PAMI Parastatal foundation created to speed the process of contracting and controlling food distribution to PAMI beneficiaries		Ministerio de Sanidad

Source: Cartaya and Márquez (1990).

422

Table 11-7. *Plan to Confront Poverty, Venezuela, 1989–91*
Millions of current dollars

Program	1989	1990	1991
Direct transfers			
Beca Alimentaria[a]	102.91	191.23	n.a.
Beca Alimentaria and Dotación útiles y uniformes[b]	35.47	n.a.	n.a.
Beca Láctea[c]	...	26.55	90.78
Bono de Cereales[c]	...		89.29
Uniformes y Utiles escolares[a]		73.78	
Pasaje Estudiantil[a]	...	14.76	32.90
Programa niños no escolarizados	...	...	n.a.
Cestas CASA	n.a.	n.a.	n.a.
Nutritional			
Vaso de Leche[d]	...	36.00	29.57
Merienda Escolar[d]	...	4.22	3.46
Comedores Escolares[d]	...	...	11.19
Lactovisoy al escolar	n.a.	n.a.	n.a.
Programa Ampliado Materno Infantil (PAMI)[d]	...	6.58	90.56
Human capital accumulation and protection			
Hogares Cuidado Diario (HCD)[e]	7.99	24.25	48.32
Compensación Sociopedagógica[e]	...	3.46	3.55
Ampliación pre-escolar	n.a.	n.a.	n.a.
Employment and social security			
Seguro de Paro Forzoso[f]	...	74.89	37.73
Apoyo a la economía popular[e]	...	0.84	0.94
Plan de Empleo e Inversión Social[g]	...	0.07	n.a.
Fondo de Inversión Social (FONVIS)[c]	...	0.42	1.83
Fundación Fondo Cooperación y Financiamiento de Ampresas Asociatives	...	...	n.a.
(FONCOFIN)[e]	0.17	13.40	11.11
Total	146.38	457.03	935.47
As percent of GDP	0.32	0.95	1.78

Sources: a. Ministerio de Hacienda, *Ley de Presupuesto* (1991). On Beca Alimentaria, data for 1989 were obtained from Ministerio del Trabajo, *Ley de Presupuesto* (1991). On Pasaje Estudiantil, data for 1991 were obtained from Ministerio de Transporte y Comunicaciones, *Ley de Presupuesto* (1992). The programa niños no escolarizados was implemented in the third quarter of 1991.
   b. Ministeri. de Educación, *Ley de Presupuesto* (1992).
   c. Ministerio de Educación, Dirección de Asuntos Socioeducativos (n.d.).
   d. Ministerio de Sanidad y Asistencia Social, *Ley de Presupuesto* (1991, 1992). PAMI was created in December 1989. Vaso de Leche was created in 1990.
   e. Ministerio de la Familia, *Ley de Presupuesto* (1992). Apoyo a la Economía Popular and FONVIS were created in 1990.
   f. Ministerio del Trabajo, *Memoria y Cuenta* (1990); 1991 figure is from January to August and was obtained from Dirección General del Seguro de Paro Forzoso-IVSS.
   g. Ministerio de Desarrollo Urbano, *Ley de Presupuesto* (1992).
   n.a. Not available.

The mechanisms used for the delivery of direct subsidies represented a real effort to target resources to the needy, in contrast to indirect subsidies, which involve considerable spillover to higher income groups. In less than a year, Venezuela set up organizational channels untainted by corruption that allowed swift and effective delivery of substantial resources to narrowly targeted groups. This "miracle" should not be discounted, for it provided an invaluable example for future reform, proving that innovative action in the area of social policy is possible.

Although these targeted programs were efficient and effective, their success did not reduce the need for comprehensive reform of the social service system, particularly in the Ministries of Health and Education. In some cases the failure to introduce reforms in the coordinating ministries, on which the programs depended for administrative support, hindered the effectiveness of the programs, especially when they were expanded to the national level. An example is the experience of the Programa Alimentario Materno-Infantil (PAMI). This program provided a series of medical examinations for pregnant women and follow-up visits for breast-feeding women. At the time of the examination, the mother and child received immunization shots, medicines if necessary, and a can of milk powder. All of the services were delivered at primary health care facilities in poor areas that were built or repaired and equipped with PAMI funds, all of which were managed by a private institution created to circumvent the budgetary nightmare of the Ministry of Health. The program was implemented in the state of Trujillo, one of the poorest in the country, and was evaluated as a success in terms of both efficiency and community involvement.

While the PAMI effort remained at the local level, with important support from World Bank experts, there was no need to interact with bureaucrats from the Ministry of Health. But as soon as the government attempted to extend the program nationally, the lack of reform at the Ministry of Health stalled the project. The expansion of PAMI to the national level required the ministry to revamp the primary health care system and to shift resources over the opposition of public sector unions. The attempt to decentralize administrative control, transferring authority to regional governments, has been fought by unions from the Health and Education Ministries, which have threatened the government with a national strike.[16]

Successful program implementation requires administrative reform. But in the face of such strong resistance, reform requires support from the highest

16. See "La huelga nacional dedocentes so indetenible," *El Universal*, April 13, 1993, pp. 1–14.

levels of government. Three years after the implementation of the new programs, the government had done nothing to break the resistance of unions and the bureaucracy, which makes it impossible to improve the efficiency and quality of traditional social service activities.

The fact that the new programs are more efficient (per unit of expenditure they produce more and better services for poor users) does not imply that they represent sufficient reform of the social service sector. The all-encompassing reforms that are needed must recognize the political nature of the conflict as they introduce market discipline in the production and delivery of social services. Otherwise, instead of creating a new social policy, reforms will only divert energy and resources away from the crucial problems, which involve the budgetary procedures of the core ministries.

As long as historical entitlements—rather than the quantity and quality of services delivered—are the basis for budgetary allocations, unions and powerful bureaucratic groups will continue to manipulate the allocation of resources. Market discipline, in the form of increased reliance on user fees to finance some services, the reallocation of employment away from administrative duties, and employment reduction where necessary, could lead to improved efficiency and services. Budgetary allocations made on the basis of services produced would encourage bureaucrats to improve efficiency and quality, as their share of the budget would depend on their performance. This reform is not a simple matter, nor is it one that can be solved immediately by decree. It requires experimentation that can emerge only after a diffusion of authority to operational and local levels.

Such a reform agenda requires more than direct transfers and targeting. It requires a new vision of social services, in which local autonomy replaces centralized decisionmaking, community involvement replaces bureaucratic controls, and experimentation replaces uniformity. The greatest obstacles to reform are not technical but political, as vested bureaucratic interests provoke intense conflicts.

To summarize, policy reform in the social services requires the government to incorporate market discipline with a budgeting system defined not in terms of entitlements but in terms of measurable results; to transfer authority to local governments to increase accountability to the public; and to introduce experimentation and diversity in social service production, financing, and access.

Data and Methodology

The database used for poverty estimations in this chapter is the Venezuelan *Encuesta de Hogares por Muestreo*, a household survey collected twice a year by the *Oficina Central de Estadística e Informática* (OCEI). The survey contains information on the personal characteristics of all household members, plus information on employment and wages for individuals in the labor force. The survey is based on a sample of 35,000 households, selected randomly from both urban and rural areas.

From the second semester sample for each year I selected households that reported some income and provided complete information for all members. I then took a small random sample of 3,500 households, keeping the weights in the original OCEI sample for each individual observation.

The elimination of households with zero reported income may bias my poverty estimates compared to studies based on CEPAL's database, which does not exclude such observations. However, the proportion of households eliminated for this reason never exceeded 5 percent of the total sample, so the bias is not likely to be very large.

The use of the household survey database implies that the estimates of total income are limited to labor income and do not reflect national income as reported in the national accounts. The figure in the national accounts that corresponds to my estimates is the line reporting wages and labor income. Because property income is more unequally distributed than labor income, this chapter systematically underestimates the degree of inequality in the distribution of income.[17]

Underreporting of income is a pervasive problem in poverty estimations based on household survey data.[18] Poverty estimates based on uncorrected data tend to overestimate the extent of poverty, and if underreporting is not constant over time, the evolution of poverty can be seriously misstated.

To estimate the degree of underreporting I compared average wages from the national accounts with those from the household survey. The procedure differs from correction procedures that use per capita GNP to correct income figures obtained from household surveys.

Wage figures in the national accounts are the quotient of the wages and labor income line and the total number of wage employees from the household

17. See Altimir (1987).
18. I want to thank Samuel Morley for his help in devising the correction method described in this section.

survey. Because the wages and labor income line includes payroll taxes and other contributions, I corrected it to obtain a figure closer to take-home payments.[19] More formally,

$$w_{NA} = \frac{wage \ and \ labor \ income_{NA} \ (0.8084)}{Number \ of \ wage \ employees_{Hs}},$$

where the subscripts *NA* and *HS* identify the national accounts and the household survey, respectively. The figure for average monthly wages from the household survey corresponds to the average income of wage employees. The correction factor was then obtained as the multiplier needed to equalize wage figures from the national accounts and household survey.

Table 11-8 shows the result of these calculations and the resulting correction factor. Data for 1991 is missing because the national accounts for that year have not yet been published. In my 1991 estimations I used the 1989 correction factor. I then multiplied the reported income figures in the household survey by the correction factor. Note that the correction implicitly assumes that the self-employed underestimate their income by the same percentage as wage employees. The resulting family income figures equal the national accounts wage income figures and are thus consistent with Venezuelan macroeconomic data.

The household survey data used here do not account for some types of income, particularly nonmonetary income. Poverty estimates may be more accurate when based on household expenditure data, but unfortunately this type of data is not available for Venezuela. My estimates thus overstate poverty by an unknown (but probably small) amount, given that the direct impact of government transfers and individual and community consumption-smoothing mechanisms are not taken into account.

The next step is an assessment of the poverty line. The most widely used method is to use the cost of a fixed food-consumption basket, multiplied by some factor to allow for complementary consumption. Using Atkinson's notation,[20] the poverty line at time $t = 0$ is estimated as the cost of buying a vector of goods x^* at prices p_0:

$$(1 + h)\, p_0 \cdot x^*,$$

19. The wages and labor income figures in the national accounts result from the application of an estimated cost structure to the estimated gross production value of each sector. This cost structure includes as labor costs all payroll taxes and contributions. Total payroll taxes and contributions amount to 23.7 percent of take-home payments.

20. Atkinson (1991).

Table 11-8. *Estimation of Correction Factors for Underreporting of Income, Venezuela, Selected Years, 1981–89*
Bolivars

Year	Average monthly wages		Correction factor
	National accounts	Household survey	
1981	2,533.57	2,200.67	1.1513
1983	2,558.29	2,312.77	1.1062
1985	3,270.60	2,621.61	1.2476
1987	4,173.70	3,250.33	1.2841
1989	8,221.63	5,526.59	1.4876

Source: National accounts data are from Banco Central de Venezuela, *Anuario de Cuentas Nacionales* (various years). Household survey data correspond to author's tabulations of the database described above.

where h is an allowance for the consumption of goods other than food. Subsequently, the poverty line is updated every year by making $p_t = p_0$ (CPI inflation rate). This generates a nominal poverty line that, when deflated by the CPI, is constant over time. Problems with this updating method arise when relative food prices change drastically during the period under analysis, as in Venezuela.

This study defines the poverty line as the actual cost of a fixed food-consumption basket. The cost of the consumption basket for a family of five is estimated once a year by the *Instituto Nacional de Nutrición* based on food prices at the main wholesale market in the Caracas metropolitan area.[21] The per capita cost was determined by dividing by five. For rural areas, the cost of the per capita food-consumption basket was estimated to be 80 percent of the cost of the food basket.

Setting $h = 0$, I obtain the cost of the food-consumption basket that defines the extreme poverty line. Setting $h = 1$, I define the critical poverty line as a subsistence standard equal to double the cost of the food basket. Table 11-9 presents the total cost of the food basket in nominal and real terms (deflated by the CPI) and in table 11-10 its per capita cost in urban and rural areas.

Note that the CPI-deflated cost of the food basket varied substantially over time, increasing when the relative price of food increased, such as in 1989 when the government adopted a drastic stabilization program. This method is therefore an improvement over studies based on CEPAL data that use a poverty line indexed by the overall CPI and fail to account for changes in the relative price of food.

A final question concerns the robustness of poverty estimates that depend

21. See Instituto Nacional de Nutrición (1992).

Table 11-9. *Nominal and Real Values of the Poverty Line,*
Venezuela, 1991

Years	Nominal bolivars	Current U.S. dollars	Real 1991 bolivars
December 1980	697.5	162.5	7,599.1
May 1981	840.0	195.7	7,877.8
May 1982	943.5	219.8	8,083.6
May 1983	1,080.0	126.4	8,694.4
November 1984	1,144.5	90.4	8,214.6
November 1985	1,404.0	102.0	9,046.5
November 1986	1,677.0	85.0	9,687.3
November 1987	2,338.0	82.7	10,540.2
January 1988	2,373.0	68.4	8,263.0
November 1989	5,428.5	139.9	10,246.5
August 1990	6,796.5	143.3	9,120.6
May 1991	7,873.5	136.3	7,873.0

Source: Instituto Nacional de Nutrición (1992, table 1).
Current U.S. dollar values for the period 1983–88 were obtained by conversion through the noncontrolled exchange rate. Real 1991 values are deflated by the overall CPI. Data on income from the Household Survey use September as the reference month.

on the position of the poverty line relative to the central tendency of the per capita income distribution. If the poverty line is close to the mode of per capita income, it is likely that minor variations in the poverty line will produce large changes in head-count ratios and other poverty indicators.

In this regard, the data in table 11-11 allow for moderate optimism about the robustness of the poverty estimates. The poverty line is always below the central tendency measures of the per capita income distribution and is never close to the mode.

Table 11-10 *Cutoff Points for Extreme and Critical Poverty, Venezuela,*
1981–91[a]

Current bolivars

Year	Extreme poverty line		Critical poverty line	
	Rural	Urban	Rural	Urban
September 1981	139.7	174.6	279.4	349.3
September 1985	217.1	271.4	434.2	542.8
September 1987	322.7	403.3	645.3	806.7
September 1989	847.1	1,058.9	1,694.3	2,117.8
September 1991	1,356.3	1,695.4	2,712.7	3,390.8

Source: See table 11-9.
a. The values of the food basket reported as cutoff points are updated to the reference month of the Household Survey by interpolation.

Table 11-11. *Poverty Line and per Capita Income Distribution,*
Venezuela, Selected Years, 1981–91
Current bolívars

| Year | Poverty line | Per capita income | | |
		Mean	Median	Mode
1981	349.3	1,006.9	690.8	1,151.3
1985	542.8	1,310.8	831.7	1,247.6
1987	806.7	1,599.0	1,131.6	1,248.1
1989	2,117.8	3,520.1	2,380.2	1,487.6
1991	3,390.8	6,314.4	4,562.0	4,462.8

Source: Table 11-8 and author's tabulation of household survey data.
Per capita income data are corrected for underreporting.

The Evolution of Poverty

The resulting poverty estimates for Venezuela from 1981 to 1991 appear in table 11-12. Poverty clearly increased during the 1980s, as measured by all of the usual indicators. More robust criteria, such as the "first-order dominance" of Foster and Shorrocks,[22] also indicate a rise in poverty, although space prevents me from presenting the results here.

The incidence of poverty and the poor's income shortfall measured by P_1 doubled in the decade between 1981 and 1991. P_2 more than tripled between 1981 and 1989, indicating an intensification of acute poverty. P_2 fell in 1991 but still remained at 2.7 times its 1981 value (table 11-12).

Between 1981 and 1991 the proportion of the poor located in urban areas increased from 63 to 72 percent, while the share of the urban population in the total population rose from 75 to 85 percent. Families headed by females, which in 1981 represented 18 percent of all households and 22 percent of the poor ones, in 1991 accounted for 20 percent of the total and 25 percent of the poor.

These findings are consistent with the work of Morley and Alvarez, who found that during the 1981–89 period 93 percent of the increase in poverty occurred in urban areas and that female-headed households contributed to total poverty only slightly more than their share in the total population. They document two other surprising findings: the increase in poverty among households

22. See Foster and Shorrocks (1988). By the "first-order dominance" criterion, if the frequency distribution of per capita income in year $t+j$ ($j > 0$) lies entirely above that of year t, then, independent of the poverty line or degree of poverty aversion, poverty rose between years t and $t+j$.

Table 11-12. *Household Poverty Indicators, Venezuela, Selected Years, 1981–91*

Percent

Indicator	1981	1985	1987	1989	1991
Headcount ratio					
Extreme poverty	3.67	7.64	8.64	14.09	11.18
Critical poverty	14.06	20.74	23.14	27.25	23.46
Total	17.73	28.38	31.78	41.34	34.64
Income gap ratio	33.99	39.82	38.05	42.96	41.75
Foster-Greer-Thorbecke					
P_1	6.03	11.30	12.09	17.76	14.46
P_2	2.89	5.90	6.27	9.99	7.77

Source: Author's calculations based on a subsample of OCEI, *Encuesta de Hogares por Muestreo.* Data correspond to the second semester of each year, with September as the reference month. For a description of data and methodology see the appendix. All indicators are presented on a percentage basis. They refer to households, not individuals.

headed by well-educated persons and the increase in poverty-affected households headed by both modern and informal sector employees.[23]

The deep changes experienced in Venezuelan society during the 1980s complicate the analysis. During that period, the urban share of the total population increased, families became smaller, and overall labor participation rates rose (mainly because of a higher participation rate among women). Changes in the demographic and economic characteristics of poor households must be compared with changes in nonpoor households to understand their influence on poverty.

Potential explanations for the rise in poverty include an increase in household size that reduced per capita income, a decrease in participation rates that reduced the number of income earners per household, a rise in unemployment rates with the same consequence, and a decrease in income per employee that reduced total family income.

The first two factors are associated with behavioral patterns, in the sense that they involve decisions about the number of children a couple decides to have and the effort adult members of the household are willing to make to sustain their livelihood. The latter two are beyond the scope of household decisions. Both unemployment rates and the evolution of wages are the product of a complex chain of events involving public policy and private sector investment decisions.

If the increase in poverty was associated with behavior, one should observe an increase in family size and in the number of children, a reduction in partic-

23. Morley and Alvarez (1992, pp. 13–15).

Table 11-13. *Family Poverty Indicators, Venezuela, 1981, 1991*

	1981			1991		
Indicator	Poor	Nonpoor	Total	Poor	Nonpoor	Total
Female-headed families						
(percent)	22.1	17.0	17.9	24.9	18.0	20.4
Demographic characteristics						
Total members	7.1	5.1	5.4	6.1	4.5	5.1
Number of children	3.9	1.8	2.2	2.9	1.4	1.9
Child-adult ratio	1.2	0.6	0.7	0.9	0.4	0.6
Working-age members	3.3	3.2	3.3	3.2	3.1	3.2
Members in the labor force	1.6	2.0	1.9	1.8	2.1	2.0
Members employed	1.4	1.9	1.8	1.6	2.0	1.9
Members unemployed	0.2	0.1	0.1	0.2	0.1	0.1
Economic characteristics (percent)						
Participation rates	49.1	60.0	58.1	56.1	67.6	63.7
Unemployment rates	13.0	4.1	5.7	10.7	4.7	6.8
Dependency ratios	4.4	2.6	2.9	3.4	2.1	2.6
Structure of income (current bolívars)						
Total family income	1,624.8	5,005.2	4,405.9	11,972.0	34,785.4	26,882.8
Per capita income	230.5	1,174.2	1,006.9	1,975.4	8,614.1	6,314.5
Income per employed	1,164.5	2,676.6	2,408.5	7,305.1	17,220.5	13,785.8
Percent of income from informal sector	60.1	48.9	50.9	45.1	31.2	36.0
Percent of total family income earned by household head	71.5	60.7	62.6	59.6	55.0	56.6

Source: Author's calculations based on a subsample of OCEI, *Encuesta de Hogares por Muestreo*, second semester 1981 and 1991. Income data are corrected according to the methodology presented in the appendix.

ipation rates, and an increase in dependency ratios (the number of persons each working member of the household supports).

Between 1981 and 1991 the average size of nonpoor families decreased 11.7 percent, while the size of poor families fell 14.1 percent, from 7.1 members to 6.1 (table 11-13). As a result, poor families in 1991 had 36 percent more members than nonpoor families, down from a 39 percent difference in 1981. Similarly, the average number of children per adult in poor families fell from 1.2 in 1981 to 0.9 in 1991, a 25 percent reduction that is relatively less than the 33 percent reduction in nonpoor families.

Members of poor households were working as hard in 1991 as in 1981, and they were suffering less from unemployment, both in absolute and relative terms. In 1981 poor families had on average 1.4 labor force participants, while in 1991 the number was 1.6, even though the average size of poor households had fallen. Between 1981 and 1991 participation rates for poor households increased by 14.3 percent, while nonpoor participation rates increased by only 12.7 percent. Therefore, more working-age members of poor families were either working or looking for a job in 1991 than in 1981.

As a result of these changes in participation and unemployment rates, the dependency ratio fell by 22.7 percent for the poor (from 4.4 members per labor force participant to 3.4), but fell only 19.2 percent for the nonpoor. In 1991 the dependency ratio of poor families was 1.31 times that of the average family, a decrease from a multiple of 1.52 in 1981.

Because none of these demographic and family-controlled factors explain the increase in poverty, two other explanations remain: rising unemployment and falling wages. Surprisingly, unemployment rates for the poor fell 17.7 percent between 1981 and 1991, while they increased 14.6 percent for the nonpoor (table 11-13). In 1981 the unemployment rate for members of poor households was 13 percent, 2.3 times the 5.7 percent average. In 1991 this ratio was only 1.6, with unemployment at 10.7 percent for poor households versus 6.8 percent overall.

Poor families did not rely on the earning power of only a few members of the household. In fact, poor families were more successful at diversifying their incomes away from the head of the household than the average family: in 1981 the proportion of total family income in poor families contributed by the head of household was 1.18 times the proportion in nonpoor families, and the ratio fell to 1.08 in 1991. The share of income earned by household heads in total family income decreased 16.5 percent for poor families (from 72 percent in 1981 to 60 percent in 1991), while it fell only 9.4 percent for nonpoor households (table 11-13).

Income earned in the informal sector became less important for poor households: its share of total family income fell from 60 percent to 45 percent. However, this share fell only 25 percent for poor families in the period, while it fell 36.2 percent for nonpoor households, leaving poor families relatively more vulnerable to the fluctuating fortunes of the informal sector.

The increase in nominal income per employed household member was smaller in poor than in nonpoor households: 527 percent versus 543 percent. As a consequence, income per employee in poor families was 44 percent of the level among nonpoor families in 1981 and only 42 percent in 1991.

Between 1981 and 1991 the poverty line increased by 871 percent in nominal terms (table 11-10). Therefore, despite the efforts of poor families to work

Table 11-14. *Wages and Poverty, Venezuela, Selected Years, 1981–91*
Constant 1991 bolívars

Indicator	1981	1985	1987	1989	1991
Minimum hourly wage[a]	49.07	56.19	52.68	43.90	34.88
Mean hourly wage	137.39	123.26	108.11	96.37	88.11
"Poverty" hourly wage[a]	103.41	106.96	110.15	119.24	99.95
Full-time workers needed for a family of average size to reach the poverty line					
Each worker earns minimum wage	2.11	1.90	2.09	2.72	2.87
Each worker earns mean wage	0.75	0.87	1.02	1.24	1.13
Variance of log (income)	0.5017	0.6213	0.4728	0.5418	0.5519

Source: Author's tabulations of subsample of OCEI, *Encuesta de Hogares por Muestreo* (various years).
a. Minimum hourly wage is the monthly urban minimum wage divided by (40 hours a week × 4.3 weeks a month) (monthly hours worked by a full-time worker). "Poverty" hourly wage is the per capita poverty lines times the average number of family members divided by 40 × 4.3.

more, the failure of nominal wages to keep pace with inflation implied that an increasing number of households were pushed below the poverty line. At the same time, the income distribution, which had improved after 1985, worsened again in 1989, as the variance of the log of income indicates. Assuming decreasing marginal utility of income, the loss suffered by the poor vastly surpassed the loss suffered by nonpoor households.

The reasons for this phenomenal failure of poor families may be better understood by looking at the evolution of wages and the poverty line. Table 11-14 presents the evolution of the average hourly wage, the minimum hourly wage, and the hourly wage needed for the worker of an average-sized family to reach the poverty line (the "poverty" wage). Between 1981 and 1989 the minimum hourly wage fell 10.5 percent in real terms, while the average hourly wage fell 29.9 percent. In the same period, the poverty wage rose by 15.3 percent. Between 1981 and 1991, even though the poverty wage fell 3.3 percent in real terms, the minimum wage and the average wage fell by 28.9 percent and 35.9 percent, respectively. In these conditions, it should not be surprising that the incidence of poverty increased so dramatically.

From another perspective, in 1981 a worker earning the average wage could earn enough to keep an average-sized family (5.4 persons) above the poverty line. But in 1991, although family size had fallen to 5.1 persons, workers earning the average wage could not keep their families above the poverty line. Between 1981 and 1991 the number of average-wage workers needed by an average-sized family to reach the poverty line increased by 51 percent; the number of minimum-wage workers required increased 36 percent (table 11-11).

These developments in the labor market produced changes in the characteristics of the poor. Whereas in 1981 poverty was associated mainly with the failure of poorly educated parents to support large families, in 1991 the poor also included educated parents and smaller families victimized by the adverse economic conditions of the 1980s.

Who Are the Poor Now?

Poverty is a multifaceted phenomenon that affects all dimensions of household life. To devise adequate policies to help the poor cope with the situation, it is necessary to understand who the poor are, why they are poor, and what risks poverty imposes on them.

Single-parent households are more vulnerable to poverty than two-parent households, if for no other reason than because the number of available adults is presumably diminished by the absence of an adult partner. Usually, this vulnerability is augmented by the fact that part of the available labor has to be used in taking care of young children, further reducing the family's earning power.

In terms of the risks imposed by poverty, the poor should be divided into two very different groups. The first group, the ultrapoor, faces immediate nutritional risks. The second group, the critical poor, manages to fill nutritional requirements but falls short in other complementary consumption items. The ultrapoor require immediate intervention to protect the more vulnerable among them (women in reproductive age and children) from permanent damage in their learning and earning abilities.

In 1991 poverty was definitely an urban phenomenon affecting mostly two-parent families. Even if rural and female-headed[24] households are more likely to be poor, with their smaller population weights they are dominated by their urban and two-parent counterparts (table 11-15).

Children are also particularly affected by poverty: 19 and 34 percent of all children younger than fourteen live in extreme and critical poverty, respec-

24. The use of "female-headed" as equivalent to "single-parent" follows the household survey, which practically requires that no adult male be present if a woman is determined as household head.

Table 11-15. *Distribution of Poverty, Venezuela, 1991*
Percent

Item	Extreme poverty	Critical poverty	Nonpoor	Total population
Poverty-level distribution				
Rural	20.6	32.5	46.9	100.0
Urban	9.5	21.8	68.7	100.0
Two-parent families	9.7	23.0	67.3	100.0
Female-headed families	16.9	25.2	57.9	100.0
Poverty-level share				
Rural	28.1	21.2	11.0	15.3
Urban	71.9	78.8	89.0	84.7
Two-parent families	69.3	78.1	82.0	79.7
Female-headed families	30.7	21.9	18.0	20.3

Source: Author's calculations based on a subsample of OCEI, *Encuesta de Hogares por Muestreo,* second semester 1991.

tively.[25] In other words, more than half of Venezuela's children grow up in a disadvantaged environment, with a large fraction having serious nutritional problems that may impair their learning abilities.

Most household heads in ultrapoor, two-parent families are not young (more than one-third are older than fifty, and only 11 percent are younger than thirty) and barely know how to read and write. Those who work, which 84 percent of extremely poor household heads do, are working hard (87 percent work full time) in an informal or private sector job. Because of their education, they earn an hourly wage less than one-third of that earned by nonpoor counterparts. Wives in poor households are somewhat younger and slightly more educated than their husbands. They are less likely to work (only one-fifth of spouses participate in the labor force), and if they work it is most likely in a part-time informal sector job (though 39 percent work full time), earning a wage less than one-fourth of that earned by nonpoor counterparts.

The typical poor couple shares living quarters with two children younger than six, one younger than ten, and another younger than fourteen. There is another adult in the house, usually an older sibling, for a grand total of seven persons. The two youngest children usually remain at home, cared for by their mother. Most of the other children go to school, though school enrollment rates for this group are low: 12 percent of the children between six and ten and 16 percent of those between ten and fourteen do not go to school. Those that go to school receive instruction in the public school in the neighborhood dur-

25. All figures in this section are from tables 11A-4 and 11A-5.

ing half the day and hang around the house the other half. The school is run-down, led by demoralized teachers without educational materials to distribute. However, the students have notebooks and some textbooks, which were handed out at the beginning of the school year by the government. They remain in school to obtain the *Beca Alimentaria* and other direct transfers from the government.

Their access to public services is low in the best of cases, and usually nonexistent. Water supply and general sanitation services do not reach the upper areas of the barrios where they live, producing an unhealthy environment that, combined with nutritional deficiencies, makes family members prone to diverse forms of enteritis and diarrhea. When they fall sick, they often have to go directly to a crowded hospital emergency room, because there is no primary health care facility in the neighborhood—or, if there is one, the doctor or nurse is not there. They receive attention in the hospital on an emergency basis: the sicker the patient, the higher on the waiting list. As a result, what could have been solved yesterday by oral rehydration has to be solved today by intravenous rehydration that uses the scarce qualified personnel available in the emergency room. Under these conditions, morbidity easily gets translated into mortality, as the increase of infant mortality rates since 1989 indicates.

Even if the household head works full time, his income is less than two-thirds of total family income. The rest has to be provided either by the wife in a part-time informal sector job or by the older sibling. Each of the working adults in this house has to support four family members; quite naturally, they fail to do so. The cost of just feeding the people at home is $175 a month, and all they manage to earn is $113.[26] Because they are to some extent removed from the mainstream, it is not certain that the government's direct transfers reach them. But even if they receive all the direct transfers, the total is an additional $30 a month per family, which leaves them $32 short of their feeding needs.

As time passes, members of the extremely poor household may begin to feel bad about themselves, their family, and society at large. The man is likely to move out. By himself he is making $70 a month, and it is very unlikely that his wife will sue him for alimony payments or that she will collect any payment if she does. His wife will remain with the kids and become the head of an ultrapoor single-parent family. If she can hold the family together, she will do her best to keep the children in school. She is not so young now; a full 46 per-

26. All magnitudes in bolívars are translated to U.S. dollars at an exchange rate of 67 bolívars per dollar.

cent of ultrapoor female household heads are older than forty, and almost two-thirds are older than thirty. However, she will begin to look for a job: almost 60 percent of female household heads work, two-thirds of them full time. The informal sector is the choice for 58 percent of them, but more than 25 percent work in the private sector and 15 percent in the public sector (table 11A-5). The older sibling will also go to work, but still they cannot make ends meet. The family's total monthly income will fall to $100, and they still need $144 to feed the family. Counting the additional income from direct transfers, they will remain $14 short.

This is not the typical profile of poverty; it describes the 11.2 percent of households that are extremely poor (table 11-12). They are suffering intensely, and they need immediate support if permanent damage to their children's learning abilities is to be avoided. Even worse, if they remain in poverty too long, the mainstream rules of behavior will begin to make little sense to them. If you are working as hard as you can and still cannot feed your family, you and some members of your family are likely to develop antisocial behavior (robbery, drinking problems, domestic violence), and that conduct will begin to appear legitimate to younger members of your household.

The bulk of poverty is less dramatic, but hurts a larger fraction of the population: almost a quarter of the total population can feed themselves, but do not have access to complementary consumption goods that define subsistence. They live in critical, not extreme, poverty. The typical head of a two-parent critically poor household is older than twenty (they are evenly spread over the whole age distribution). He probably has some education: just over one-fourth of these household heads have some secondary education, but still one-third barely know how to read and write. He is as likely to be working and to have a full-time job as his nonpoor neighbor, but his wage is one dollar per hour, half that of his nonpoor counterpart. He is equally likely to be holding a job in the informal or private sectors, and 16 percent hold a public sector job. His wife is definitely younger than he is, with roughly the same educational level. Again, despite her education, she is very unlikely to be working: the participation rate of critically poor wives is 22 percent, not too different from that of ultrapoor wives.

Critically poor households have fewer children and smaller families. Their children are mostly youngsters less than six years old, but one to two are between seven and fourteen years old, and the other is an adult who helps sustain the family. They send all their children to the same public school in the neighborhood, and they try to keep them in school, noticing that their less educated neighbors are going through rougher times than they are and that the difference is in their education. The quality of the education the children receive, however, is not as high as when the parents went to school ten years ago. This decline may be attributed in part to the drop in family income that made for less well-fed students, but it is mostly the result of budget cuts that reduce the quality of teachers and the availability of educational materials.

The household head is an important source of family support: a full two-thirds of family income comes from his job. He is making $145 a month, and total family income is $211. Even so, the family remains $93 short of subsistence.[27] They are working hard, but they still fall short of the income needed to live a decent life. Because they are closer to the mainstream of society, they are more likely to get government assistance, but the additional $30 still leaves them in poverty by a hefty margin.

If they get sick they face problems similar to those of the ultrapoor. Because they live in areas close to main city roads, they probably have access to a private primary health care facility, and they use part of their income for treatment there. For routine health problems the primary care facility is sufficient, but more serious illnesses force them to turn to crowded public hospital emergency rooms. Those who work in the private sector and live in a major city are lucky, because they can visit a social security hospital and obtain somewhat better attention there. In recent years, however, financial problems in the social security system have caused services in those hospitals to deteriorate.

If the household head loses his job, the family will slide into extreme poverty. In a sense, they are lucky to hold their jobs, even if their effort leaves them short of subsistence. They cannot escape poverty by working any harder, unless they manage to liberate women to enter the labor market. Even if prejudice plays a role in keeping women at home (and it clearly does), they have to find day-care facilities or preschools to leave their children in while the mother is working. In that respect the government is helping through the Hogares de Cuidado Diario and the development of a publicly subsidized preschool system.

Female heads of critically poor households are older (more than three-fourths are more than forty years old) and less educated than their male counterparts. Their families are not much smaller than two-parent families even if they have fewer children, which suggests that some children grow up and stay in the house with their mother. Their total income is slightly higher than that of critically poor two-parent households, and they have diversified their in-

27. For income figures see table 11A-4; for subsistence see the poverty line in table 11-9. All magnitudes in bolívars are translated to U.S. dollars at an exchange rate of 67 bolívars per dollar.

come sources away from the household head, whose share of total income is less than 40 percent. The household head is still most likely to work in the informal sector, but private and public sector jobs each account for close to 25 percent. Total family income is $215, $79 short of the subsistence income for a family of this size. Again, if they receive direct transfers from the government, they get an additional $30, but remain almost $50 below subsistence (tables 11-4 and 11-10).

Is it possible for the poor to escape poverty? If so, how? The answer is not obvious, but one can pinpoint some elements in a possible answer. First observe that for the critically poor to reach the subsistence standard, wages would have to increase 40 percent in real terms.[28] Such an increase sounds impossible, but then it also seemed impossible at the beginning of the 1980s that real wages would fall more than 36 percent during the decade (table 11A-3).

There is very little we can do for the ultrapoor, beyond helping them barely nourish themselves and helping their children to grow up in a more or less protected environment by keeping them first at the *Hogar de Cuidado Diario*, then at preschool, and finally at elementary school. Achieving this goal requires a sweeping reform of the educational system that vested interests within the system have effectively resisted.

All of these goals depend on the maintenance of a healthy growth rate with low inflation and require an immense effort in public sector reform, particularly in public sector finances, including both new taxes and the privatization of unprofitable public enterprises.

With all these conditions, the only hope for the poor is that the adjustment process begun in 1989 ends successfully with the announced public sector reform. If fiscal deficits fade away and deep organizational reforms occur in the social services, the poor have some hope of obtaining improved education for new and higher-paying jobs that can be created in a growing, low-inflation economy. There is no question of which agenda has priority between economic and social policies. Each must move in pace with the other to achieve sustainable economic growth based on the development of human resources.

---

28. A two-parent critically poor family with six members, with 1.63 members employed and each one earning 8,677.69 bolívars a month in 1991 had a total family income of 14,144.64 bolívars monthly. To put this family at the poverty line (3,390.8 bolívars times 6 members = 20,344.8 bolívars), wages must increase by 43.8 percent to 12,481.77 bolívars, so total family income equals 20,344.8 bolívars monthly (12,481.4 x 1.63). All figures are from table 11A-4, except the poverty line from table 11-11.

From Targeted Programs to Human Resource Development

During the last ten years Venezuela has tried to correct its misguided policy of public enterprise development and to adjust to the sharp deterioration in its terms of trade. The adjustment failed in part because the government did not implement comprehensive reforms in the public sector. As powerful bureaucratic interests resisted reform, the public sector's recurrent financial disequilibria generated macroeconomic instability. Inflation eroded real incomes, and particularly wages. The pervasive effects of inflation and fiscal and external account disequilibria soon made the adoption of a stabilization program unavoidable, which further impoverished the population.

These events have harmed the Venezuelan population enormously. Poverty now affects more than one-third of the total population, and these poor face daunting risks if the situation continues. The deterioration in the public education and health systems further limits growth in the stock of human capital held by the poor, consigning future generations to poverty.

The debate in Venezuela has centered on how to ease the social costs of adjustment. The government's solution has been to replace a massive and quite inefficient system of indirect subsidies with well-targeted direct transfer programs. This shift from indirect to direct and narrowly targeted subsidies is a welcome development. Although the amount of resources transferred through these programs was small compared to the loss imposed on the poor by declining real wages and rising food prices, the government's effort was sizable; it allocated about 7 percent of the budget to these programs in 1991.

Furthermore, these programs have generally been both effective and efficient. Programs such as the Hogares de Cuidado Diario, PAMI, the Beca Alimentaria, and associated direct transfers have improved the living conditions of the poor. Other social programs, such as the development of preschools and unemployment insurance, have also helped the poor.

However, these programs do not provide a long-term solution, because they do not enable the poor to escape poverty through human capital accumulation. Direct transfer programs can effectively provide transitional relief from poverty and they can prevent further deterioration in social indicators. They cannot, however, by themselves build new human capital, because they do not address organizational and financial problems in the social services. Without fundamental changes, social programs will ameliorate the conditions of the poor, but will not provide the tools needed to increase their skills and improve their opportunities in the labor market.

Two related problems threaten to undermine the government's current policies. First, the long-term sustainability of its programs is uncertain. With climbing fiscal deficits and with the population actively resisting new taxes, budget allocations for these programs are likely to fall in real terms through direct government action or rising inflation. Second, the government has unwisely emphasized economic reform over social service reform, arguing that growth depends on macroeconomic stability, which in turn requires sound economic policy. The discussion of whether economic reforms should precede social policy reforms, or vice versa, is senseless. Both are essential, and urgent, ingredients in any modernization process. Although the effects of educational reforms may take more time to be felt, such reforms are just as critical as realignment of the exchange rate or increases in public sector prices.

Appendix

For comparative purposes table 11A-1, adapted from Morley and Alvarez, presents the results of various studies of poverty in Venezuela.[29] This study tends to show a lower incidence of poverty than other studies for all years in the sample. The primary reason is my correction procedure for underreporting, though a minor difference may be caused by my exclusion of households with zero income from the sample.

My estimates of the headcount ratio in 1981 are well below those of the other studies, but the difference tends to be smaller in later years. For instance, the difference between my 1981 headcount ratio and the World Bank's 1982 estimate is 83 percent, while the difference in 1989 is 29 percent. The differences between this study and the Inter-American Development Bank study are 33 percent and 17 percent in 1981 and 1989, respectively. Because I use a poverty line indexed to the price of food, and the relative price of food increased in 1989, the narrowing variance between headcount ratios is consistent with methodological differences in each study.

The profile of changes in poverty over time, however, is not very different. Between 1982 and 1989, the World Bank study estimates a 61 percent increase in the headcount ratio. Between 1981 and 1989, the IDB study estimates an increase of 100 percent; the IESA study, 150 percent; while this study shows an increase of 128 percent. Given the complexity of the calculations in each study, the magnitude of these differences is quite encouraging with respect to the robustness of results regarding changes in poverty in Venezuela.

29. Morley and Alvarez (1992).

Table 11A-1. *Households below the Poverty Line in Five Studies, Venezuela, Selected Years, 1981–89*
Percent

	World Bank			CEPAL			IESA	IDB	This study		
Year	Urban	Rural	Total	Urban	Rural	Total	total	total[a]	Urban	Rural	Total
1981	n.a.	n.a.	n.a.	22	43	25	24	24	15	26	18
1982	25	58	33	n.a.	n.a.	n.a.	n.a.	n.a.	n.a.	n.a.	n.a.
1985	n.a.	n.a.	n.a.	n.a.	n.a.	n.a.	n.a.	n.a.	23	47	25
1986	n.a.	n.a.	n.a.	33	42	32	n.a.	29	n.a.	n.a.	n.a.
1987	38	71	44	n.a.	n.a.	n.a.	45	n.a.	28	49	32
1989	49	74	53	n.a.	n.a.	n.a.	60	48	38	60	41
1991	n.a.	n.a.	n.a.	n.a.	n.a.	n.a.	n.a.	n.a.	31	53	35

Sources: World Bank (1991); CEPAL (1990); (IESA) Márquez (1993, p. 17); and (IDB) Morley and Alvarez (1992).
a. Individuals below the poverty line.
n.a. Not available.

Table 11A-2. *Macroeconomic Indicators, Venezuela, 1981–91*

Year	GDP per capita (index)	Real exchange rate (index)	Terms of trade (index)	Current account balance of payments (U.S. $ millions)	Tradables/ nonoil GDP (percent)	CPI inflation (percent anually)	Fiscal balance (percent of GNP)
1981	100.0	100.0	100.0	4,000.0	21.9	16.2	2.2
1982	97.6	1358.4	102.0	–4,246.0	22.5	9.5	–2.1
1983	89.4	76.9	105.1	4,427.0	23.6	6.4	–0.6
1984	87.4	1776.5	117.2	4,651.0	26.9	12.2	2.7
1985	85.5	115.4	112.1	3,327.0	28.0	11.4	2.0
1986	88.5	152.3	54.5	–2,245.0	28.4	11.5	–0.4
1987	89.2	227.3	66.7	–1,390.0	28.3	28.1	–1.6
1988	91.8	248.4	54.5	–5,809.0	28.4	29.5	–7.4
1989	81.3	538.3	62.6	2,496.0	28.7	84.5	–1.0
1990	82.3	761.5	72.7	7,960.0	28.5	40.7	–2.0
1991[a]	87.3	926.9	n.a.	n.a.	27.6	34.2	2.6

Sources: IDB (1991, pp. 184, 285, 289–90, 298, 310). For CPI inflation and real exchange rate, author's calculations based on data from Banco Central de Venezuela. Inflation is average annual rate of change of the CPI. Real exchange rate refers to the imports exchange rate between 1983 and 1988. Tradables/non-oil GDP is the quotient of agriculture and manufacturing value added.
n.a. Not available.
a. Preliminary figures.

Table 11A-3. *Labor Market Indicators, Venezuela, 1981–91*

Year	Unemployment rate	Informal/ total employment	Real wages[a] (1981=100) Average	Formal	Informal	Minimum urban
1981	6.1	38.7	100.0	100.0	100.0	100.0
1982	7.1	39.3	87.0	91.5	80.0	91.4
1983	10.3	41.8	84.5	90.0	77.3	85.8
1984	13.4	42.4	88.3	96.0	78.2	76.5
1985	12.1	43.8	86.1	97.8	71.1	114.5
1986	10.3	42.0	83.6	93.4	69.7	137.6
1987	8.5	39.7	82.3	88.8	71.5	107.4
1988	6.9	38.4	80.3	85.7	70.8	107.7
1989	9.6	40.2	67.0	71.2	60.8	89.5
1990	9.9	41.8	60.5	65.6	53.5	63.6
1991	8.5	38.0	62.8	66.5	56.8	71.1

Source: OCEI, *Encuesta de Hogares por Muestreo* (various years); and Banco Central de Venezuela, *Anuario de Cuentas Nacionales* (various years).

a. Real wages are calculated from special tabulations from OCEI, *Encuesta de Hogares por Muestreo,* and are deflated by the annual average of the CPI.

Table 11A-4. *Economic and Demographic Characteristics of Two-Parent Households, Venezuela, 1991*
Percent unless otherwise specified

Household Characteristics	Extreme poverty	Critical poverty	Nonpoor
Demographic			
Total members	6.9	6.0	4.6
Children	3.5	2.8	1.5
Less than 6 years	1.6	1.4	0.7
6–10	0.9	0.7	0.4
10–14	1.0	0.7	0.3
Child/adult ratio	1.0	0.9	0.5
School assistance rates (percent of age group)			
Less than 6 years old	30.4	25.9	33.4
6–10	88.1	94.8	97.3
10–14	84.4	95.2	93.4
Working-age members	3.4	3.2	3.1
Members in the labor force	1.7	1.8	2.1
Members employed	1.5	1.6	2.0
Members unemployed	0.3	0.2	0.1
Economic			
Labor participation rates	51.0	56.5	67.8
Unemployment rates	14.5	9.4	5.2
Dependency ratios	4.0	3.3	2.2
Total income (bolivars)	7,545.9	14,144.6	35,623.5
Per capita income	1,087.7	2,358.1	8,673.8
Income per employed	5,133.3	8,677.7	17,723.1
Percent income from informal sector	52.8	42.5	31.8
Percent total income from household head	61.9	67.9	58.8
Head of household			
Age			
less than 20	n.a.	0.3	0.3
20–30	10.9	20.6	16.3
30–40	27.4	28.0	30.7
40–50	24.3	23.7	23.4
50 or older	37.5	27.4	29.3
Schooling			
Less than 3d grade	51.7	32.1	15.4
3d to primary complete	27.3	39.4	31.1
High school	16.7	26.6	36.7
College	4.3	1.8	16.9
Labor participation rate	84.2	91.3	93.8
Unemployment rate	10.2	3.0	1.3

Table 11A-4. (*continued*)

Household Characteristics	Extreme poverty	Critical poverty	Nonpoor
Hours worked			
Less than 20	4.2	1.6	0.7
Part time	8.8	5.0	4.8
Full time	87.0	93.4	94.5
Hourly wage	38.6	64.0	131.0
Employment sector			
Modern private	33.9	40.1	41.9
Public	9.0	15.8	20.9
Informal	57.1	44.1	37.2
Spouse			
Age			
Less than 20	1.5	5.2	3.1
20–30	19.3	27.9	23.2
30–40	33.5	33.0	31.3
40–50	22.3	19.7	25.3
50 or older	23.4	14.3	17.1
Schooling			
Less than 3d grade	46.1	31.9	16.5
Between 3d and primary complete	34.5	38.6	26.6
High school	14.7	27.5	43.2
College	4.8	1.9	13.7
Labor participation rate	21.1	21.6	47.5
Unemployment rate	3.5	2.7	2.1
Hours worked			
Less than 20	25.5	9.8	4.1
Part time	35.8	20.8	25.2
Full time	38.8	69.4	70.7
Hourly wage	26.6	39.3	112.9
Employment sector			
Modern private	14.9	13.7	21.1
Public	10.6	17.3	44.2
Informal	74.4	69.0	34.7

Source: Author's calculations based on a subsample of OCEI, *Encuesta de Hogares por Muestreo,* second semester 1991. Income data corrected according to methodology in text.
n.a. Not available.

Table 11A-5. *Economic and Demographic Characteristics of Female-Headed Households, Venezuela, 1991*
Percent unless otherwise specified

Household Characteristics	Extreme poverty	Critical poverty	Nonpoor
Demographic			
Total members	5.7	5.8	4.1
Children	2.7	2.4	1.0
Less than 6 years	1.0	1.2	0.5
6–10	0.8	0.6	0.2
10–14	0.9	0.6	0.3
Child/adult ratio	0.9	0.7	0.3
School assistance rates			
(percent of age group)			
Less than 6 years	22.7	32.0	33.8
6–10	84.7	91.8	89.7
10–14	90.7	93.2	88.4
Working-age members	3.0	3.4	3.1
Members in the labor force	1.8	2.1	2.2
Members employed	1.5	1.9	2.1
Members unemployed	0.2	0.2	0.1
Economic			
Labor participation rates	58.6	61.0	68.7
Unemployment rates	13.0	8.3	4.6
Dependency ratios	3.2	2.8	1.9
Total income (bolívars)	6,753.4	14,385.5	30,975.1
Per capita income	1,138.1	2,509.1	8,342.9
Income per employed	4,385.3	7,692.8	15,036.5
Percent income from informal sector	46.7	41.5	27.6
Percent total income from			
household head	41.3	38.2	35.1
Head of household			
Age			
Less than 20	1.2	0.1	1.0
20–30	7.0	5.5	2.7
30–40	32.1	19.0	23.0
40–50	18.0	28.4	26.2
50 or older	41.7	46.9	47.1
Schooling			
Less than 3d grade	53.2	41.6	32.1
3d to primary complete	35.1	34.1	25.4
High school	10.5	22.5	32.0
College	1.3	1.8	10.5
Labor participation rate	58.9	61.5	62.5
Unemployment rate	4.8	0.1	

Table 11A-5. (*continued*)

Household Characteristics	Extreme poverty	Critical poverty	Nonpoor
Hours worked			
Less than 20	9.3	4.4	4.1
Part time	26.1	29.1	12.0
Full time	64.6	66.5	83.9
Hourly wage	35.7	62.2	113.2
Employment sector			
Modern private	26.8	25.8	27.3
Public	14.9	21.6	37.6
Informal	58.3	52.6	35.1

Source: See table 11A-4.

Table 11A-6. *Education Indicators, Venezuela, Selected Years, 1975–90*
Percent unless otherwise specified

Indicator	1975	1980	1984	1987	1989[a]	1990[a]
Literacy rates		87.7	89.6	90.2	91.8	92.2
10–14 years		95.1	97	96.4	97.2	97.5
15–24 years		95.2	96.3	96.5	97.2	97.4
25 and older		81.1	83.8	85.3	85.6	85.7
School attendance rates[b]						
Preschool		26.4	28.5	27.9	27.1	n.a.
Elementary		110.0	108.0	110.0	107.6	n.a.
High school		43.5	44.7	45.4	45.4	n.a.
Higher education		17.9	19.3	21.2	23.1	n.a.
Preschool and elementary education						
Students per teacher						
Preschool	36.0	20.9	26.0	27.4	23.0	16.6
Elementary	27.8	27.3	26.0	26.6	22.7	22.6
Students per class						
Preschool	35.8	33.0	30.8	27.5	27.2	27.4
Elementary	27.5	33.4	32.8	26.0	32.8	32.7
Repetition rates	9.3	9.8	9.7	9.6	10.4	11.0
Desertion rates	8.2	7.1	6.7	7.0	5.3	2.9
Continuation rates	82.5	83.1	83.6	83.4	84.3	86.1
High school						
Students per teacher	16.8	17.3	17.4	17.5	9.0	8.7
Students per class	43.1	33.5	35.1	32.8	29.0	28.6
Repetition rates	10.8	12.1	11.2	12.2	12.9	13.0
Desertion rates	15.3	16.0	15.2	16.7	19.3	18.9
Continuation rates						
(to last year)	37.0	39.0	37.0	37.0	n.a.	n.a.
Continuation rates						
(to 9th grade)	65	65	62	65	n.a.	n.a.
Higher education						
Students per teacher	13.7	10.9	13.1	15.5	13.7	13.2
Universities	14.4	11.4	13.7	15.0	14.8	13.3
Colleges	11.0	9.6	11.6	17.0	11.9	13.1
Graduates	9,562	15,819	26,625	28,406	31,398	41,887
Universities	7,986	10,896	17,289	18,933	19,015	28,511
Colleges	1,576	4,923	9,336	9,473	12,383	13,376

Table 11A-6. (*continued*)

Indicator	1975	1980	1984	1987	1989[a]	1990[a]
Graduate distribution by areas of knowledge						
Basic sciences	n.a.	2.9	n.a.	0.1	0.8	n.a.
Engineering	n.a.	24.4	n.a.	24.3	21.7	n.a.
Agriculture and sea sciences	n.a.	5.3	n.a.	5.7	6.0	n.a.
Health sciences	n.a.	11.8	n.a.	12.3	11.1	n.a.
Education	n.a.	20.3	n.a.	18.2	16.9	n.a.
Social sciences	n.a.	33.4	n.a.	38.4	42.7	n.a.
Humanities	n.a.	1.9	n.a.	1.0	0.9	n.a.

Sources: Ministerio de Educación, *Memoría y Cuenta* (various years); OCEI, *Anuario Estadístico de Venezuela* (various years); and CORDIPLAN, Diasper Informe Social 3.

n.a. Not available.

a. Elementary and high school data for 1989 and 1990 are not comparable to previous years.

b. Data are for 1982, 1984, 1987, 1989.

Table 11A-7. *Health Indicators, Selected Years, Venezuela, 1975–90*

Indicator	1975	1980	1984	1987	1988	1989	1990
Infant mortality (rates per 1,000 live births)							
Less than 1 year old	43.8	31.7	28.5	24.3	22.8	24.9	25.9
Neonatal	21.7	16.7	15.7	14.5	13.8	14.6	15.2
Postnatal	22.1	15.0	12.8	10.3	9.0	10.3	10.7
General mortality (rates per 100,000 persons)							
Total	621.8	552.2	467.6	443.3	441.7	460.5	439.5
Heart diseases	79.5	88.6	74.4	73.5	79.2	76.6	75.3
Accidents	55.7	65.6	47.0	44.9	41.9	38.7	38.1
Cancer	54.0	53.0	49.6	51.6	52.5	50.2	49.3
Afflictions originating at birth	46.7	40.8	33.1	31.6	30.0	31.8	32.4
Cerebrovascular diseases	30.5	33.2	26.5	28.4	28.7	28.3	27.8
Pneumonias	38.9	21.0	15.7	18.1	16.3	15.3	15.1
Enteritis and other diarrheic	35.5	21.0	15.9	12.6	10.2	12.0	11.2
Suicides and homicides	12.8	14.7	15.3	11.8	13.2	16.6	16.3
Human resources (per 1,000 inhabitants)							
Physicians	1.13	1.17	n.a.	1.58	1.66	1.73	n.a.
Graduate nurses	0.68	0.79	n.a.	0.80	0.78	0.80	n.a.
Auxiliary nurses	1.94	2.36	n.a.	2.23	2.17	2.13	n.a.
Odonthologists	0.31	0.35	n.a.	n.a.	0.39	0.42	n.a.
Other	0.23	n.a.	n.a.	n.a.	0.29	0.30	n.a.
Infrastructure and equipment							
Hospitals (per 100,000 inhabitants)	3.17	3.29	3.04	3.03	2.95	2.88	3.14
Public	1.55	1.22	1.26	1.30	1.26	1.23	1.36
Private	1.62	2.07	1.77	1.73	1.69	1.65	1.78
Hospital beds (per 1,000 inhabitants)	2.99	2.97	2.72	2.65	2.59	2.52	2.69
Public	2.49	2.28	2.09	2.04	1.99	1.94	2.06
Private	0.50	0.70	0.64	0.61	0.60	0.58	0.63
By specialty							
Obstetrics	0.49	0.50	n.a.	0.38	0.37	0.36	0.32
Surgery	0.66	0.59	n.a.	0.44	0.42	0.41	0.31
Pediatrics	0.50	0.55	n.a.	0.46	0.45	0.44	0.38
General medicine	0.50	0.50	n.a.	0.47	0.46	0.45	0.52
Others	0.84	0.84	n.a.	0.91	0.88	0.86	1.16
Immunizations (per child under 4 years)							
Polio	1.42	1.38	0.81	0.66	2.23	2.04	2.08
Triple	0.44	0.31	0.26	0.27	0.39	0.35	0.73
Measles	0.21	0.27	0.19	0.25	0.28	0.24	0.39
Antimalaria (per 1,000 inhabitants)	0.05	0.03	0.03	0.05	0.03	0.05	0.04
BCG	0.26	0.24	0.31	0.28	0.24	0.27	0.22

Source: OECI, *Anuario Estadístico de Venezuela* (various years), tables 451-01 to 451-10. Population basis for per capita indicators, tables 211-01 and 211-04.
n.a. Not available.

References

Altimir, Oscar. 1982. "The Extent of Poverty in Latin America." Working Paper 522. Washington, D.C.: World Bank.

———. "Income Distribution Statistics in Latin America and Their Reliability," *Review of Income and Wealth,* June 1987, series 33, no. 2: 111–55.

Atkinson, Anthony B. 1991. "Comparing Poverty Rates Internationally: Lessons from Recent Studies in Developed Countries." *World Bank Economic Review* 5 (1): 3–21.

Banco Central de Venezuela. 1984. *Agregados macroeconómciso a precios corrientes y constantes de 1984.* Caracas.

———. *Anuario de Cuentas Nacionales.* Caracas.

———. *Anuario de Estadísticas—Precios y mercado laboral 1984.* Caracas.

———. *Anuario de Balanza de Pagos serie estadística 1984–1989.* Caracas.

———. 1990. *Boletin Mensul.* Caracas, December.

———. 1978. *La economía venezolana en los últimos treinta y cinco años.* Caracas.

———. 1991. *Informe Economico, 1991.* Caracas.

CORDIPLAN. 1990. "El Gran Viaje—Lineamientos generales del VIII Plan de la Nación." Caracas (January).

Foster, James, and Anthony F. Shorrocks. 1988. "Poverty Orderings." *Econometrica* 56 (January): 173–77.

Hausmann, Ricardo. 1981. "State Landed Property, Oil Rent, and Accumulation in Venezuela." Ph.D. dissertation, Cornell University.

———. 1990. "The Big-Bang Approach to Macro Balance in Venezuela: Can the Effects Be Predicted? Can the Pains Be Avoided?" Paper presented at World Bank Economic Development Institute senior policy seminar (July). Caracas.

Hausmann, Ricardo, and Gustavo Márquez. 1983. "La crisis económica venezolana: origen, mecanismos y encadenamientos." *Investigación Económica* 42 (July–September): 117–54.

Instituto Nacional de Nutrición. 1992. *Costo de la canasta normativa concertada y básica de alimentos: Venezuela, 1980–1982.* Caracas.

Jean, María Elena. 1990. "Impacto de la crisis socio-económica sobre la población." *Señales de Alerta.* Caracas: Fundación CAVENDES (August).

Marquez, Gustavo. 1990. "The Recent Evolution of Public Expenditure in Education, Health, and Housing in Venezuela." Caracas: World Bank.

———. 1991. "La inflación en Venezuela." In *Inflación: economía, empresa y sociedad,* edited by Antonio Francés and Lorenzo Davalos. Caracas: Ediciones IESA.

McCoy, Jennifer. 1989. "Labor and the State in a Party-Mediated Democracy: Institutional Change in Venezuela." *Latin American Research Review* 24 (2): 35–67.

Morley, Samuel, and Carola Alvarez. 1992. "Poverty and Adjustment in Venezuela." Washington, D.C.: Inter-American Development Bank.

Navarro, Juan Carlos, and Ramón Piñango. 1991. "La formación de los recursos humanos en Venezuela: Realizaciones de la democracia y los costos de la ausencia de debate." Paper presented at the Retos y Opciones de la Formación de Recursos Humanos en Venezuela seminar (June). Caracas.

Reimers, Fernando. 1991. *Educación para todos en América Latina en el siglo XXI: los desafíos de la estabilización y el ajuste para la planificación educativa.* Caracas: Centro Interamericano de Estudios e Investigaciones para el Planeamiento de la Educación.

Schiefelben, Ernesto. 1991. "Problemas y opciones en las políticas de formación de recursos humanos en América Latina." Paper presented at the Retos y Opciones de la Formación de Recursos Humanos en Venezuela seminar (June). Caracas.

Discussants and Panelists

Harold Alderman
World Bank

Oscar Altimir
CEPAL

Luis Beccaria
CEPAL

Jere Behrman
University of Pennsylvania

Mario Blejer
World Bank

Hans Binswanger
World Bank

Ricardo Carciofi
CEPAL

Eliana Cardoso
Tufts University

William Cline
Institute of International Economics

Jorge Daly
George Washington University

Alain de Janvry
University of California, Berkeley

Jaime de Melo
World Bank

Richard Feinberg
Inter-American Dialogue

Gary Fields
Cornell University

Adolfo Figueroa
Universidad Católica del Peru

Ariel Fiszbein
World Bank

Nicolás Flaño
World Bank

Santiago Friedmann
World Bank

Carol Graham
Brookings Institution

Margaret Grosh
World Bank

Arianna Legovini
University of Maryland

Gustavo Marquez
IESA

Index

ACCION, 168

Adjustment policies. *See* Stabilization and adjustment policies

Argentina:

    economic indicators, 60–63, 188–93; GDP, 18, 19, 189, 190, 192; income inequality, 44, 73–75, 79–81, 90, 93; income per capita, 75; macroeconomic indicators, 188–93; public finances by sector, 189; public sector debt, 189, 190; tax reforms, 191, 193

    education, 28, 59, 84, 203–11; educational attainment, 13, 204, 207; illiteracy rates, 13, 56; public expenditures, 209, 210; school attendance, 204; school enrollment, 14, 204, 205

    employment and labor market, 193–95; unemployment, 29, 194, 195; wages and real earnings, 59, 193, 194, 195; working population, 29, 78

    income surveys, 88

    poverty data: in Greater Buenos Aires, 196; by group, 57; head-count ratios, 7, 57; households below poverty line, 19, 52; methodology, 231–33; national level, 4; urban areas, 5

    social policy: adjustment process and, 55–60; in *1980s*, 187–236; programs, 18–20; reforms, 226–28

    social welfare indicators: infant mortality, 11; life expectancy, 11

    social welfare programs: education, 203–11; food subsidy, 19, 152, 219; health, 212–16; housing, 216–19; Obras Sociales, 212–16; pension system, 221–26; public social spending, 19–20, 197–203

    urban riots of *1993,* 3

BMI. *See* Bono Maternal-Infantil program (Honduras)

BMJF. *See* Bono Madre Jefe de Familia (Honduras)

Bolivia:

    Emergency Social Fund (ESF), 147, 148, 152, 164–67

    ethnic discrimination, 28, 84

    income inequality, 44

    poverty data: head-count ratios, 8; urban areas, 5, 10

    poverty reduction programs, 169, 170–74

    Social Investment Fund (SIF), 164

Bono Madre Jefe de Familia (*BMJF*), 57, 197

Bono Materno-Infantil (BMI) Program, 157, 158, 159, 161, 179

Brazil:

    economic indicators: GDP per capita, 20; inflation rate, 237–38; macroeconomic indicators, 237–38; macroeconomic variables, 29

    education, 84; educational attainment, 13, 255–60; illiteracy rates, 256; school attendance, 256–58; school enrollment rates, 14

    employment and labor market, 238–44; economically active population, 241, 242; labor relations, 243–44; minimum wage, 64, 252, 266; unemployment insur-